`D1565974`

A VICTORIAN ART OF FICTION

*Essays on the Novel
in British Periodicals
1870 – 1900*

GARLAND REFERENCE LIBRARY
OF THE HUMANITIES
(VOLUME 166)

A VICTORIAN ART OF FICTION

*Essays on the Novel
in British Periodicals
1870 – 1900*

John Charles Olmsted

GARLAND PUBLISHING, INC.
NEW YORK & LONDON
1979

Library of Congress Cataloging in Publication Data

Main entry under title:

A Victorian art of fiction.

(Garland reference library of the humanities ;
v. 100, 165, 166)
CONTENTS: [1] 1830–1850.—[2] 1851–1869.—
[3] 1870–1900.
1. English fiction—19th century—History
and criticism—Addresses, essays, lectures.
2. European fiction—19th century—History
and criticism—Addresses, essays, lectures.
I. Olmsted, John Charles.
PR454.V5   823'.03   77-83397
ISBN 0-8240-9772-6 (v. 3)

Printed on acid-free, 250-year-life paper
Manufactured in the United States of America

For Lou and Doug

Contents

Preface

This collection of theoretical writings on the novel reprints thirty-nine essays drawn from seventeen periodicals published in Great Britain from 1870 to 1900. Although the essays were chosen to reflect the central issues which concerned journal critics of the time, it should be remembered that writings on fiction in the last third of the century exist within what Kenneth Graham rightly calls "a complex system of interdependence and contradiction that can never be reproduced."* Among the essays reprinted here are important statements by Leslie Stephen, G.H. Lewes, Anthony Trollope, R.L. Stevenson, Henry James, Matthew Arnold, George Saintsbury and George Moore, but essays of real interest by lesser-known writers are also included.

Identification of anonymous articles in this collection is based on the information contained in the three published volumes of *The Wellesley Index to Victorian Periodicals*. For access to their collections I am grateful to the University of Michigan Graduate Library, the Oberlin College Library and the libraries of the University of California, Berkeley. For their advice and support I am grateful to Jeffrey Welch, Larry Buell and Robert Longsworth.

*English Criticism of the Novel 1865–1900 (Oxford: Clarendon Press, 1965), p. vii.

Introduction

In a satire published in the *Contemporary Review* in the early summer of 1890 (pp. 481–91), J.M. Barrie imagined an encounter between the novelists of the present and their ancestors. Gathered in a Piccadilly club room are four novelists of the day, each representing a type of fiction: the Realist, who argues for a rigid kind of mimesis; the Romancist, exponent of a fiction of the "ideal"; the "Elsmerian," convinced that only novels with a purpose can be ethically justified; and the Stylist, who proudly affirms that "I am such a stylist that I dare not write anything" (p. 486). Later an American who sounds suspiciously like W.D. Howells or Henry James joins the group. Summoned to meet these eminences of the day are Scott, Fielding, Smollett, Dickens and Thackeray. To the bewilderment of these worthies, the Elsmerian triumphantly announces that "fiction has become an art." The Romancist informs a wistful Sir Walter that novelists of the modern day no longer merely scribble stories. "Now that fiction is an art," he intones, "the work of its followers consists less in writing mere stories (to repeat a word that you will understand more readily than we) than in classifying ourselves and (when we have time for it) classifying you" (p. 485). The novelists from the past listen politely enough, but before they make a grateful return to Elysium, the shade of Thackeray offers some advice: "perhaps if you thought and wrote less about your styles and methods and the aim of fiction, and, in short, forgot yourselves now and again in your stories, you might get on better with your work. Think it over." The novelists of the day are left "looking at each other self-consciously" (p. 491).

The self-consciousness of novelists and critics which Barrie is so amusingly pillorying here had by the last two decades of the century become obvious. Journals and newspapers were filled with debates about the stature of fiction and the importance of "construction" and "technique" in the novel. The period from roughly 1880 to 1900 saw more writing directly concerned with the art of fiction than had appeared in the previous half-century.

There was little evidence in the published reviews of the 1870s of this coming burst of interest in the novel. Rather, the decade was one of restatement and synthesis. A writer for *Tinsleys' Magazine*, while warning that fiction does not need to be "a grand moral engine" (p. 3), went on to restate the mid-Victorian moral aesthetic. The great value of novels, the writer argued, is

> to give us wider and better conceptions of life and its possibilities; to keep before us an ideal which must have some beneficial effect on actual conduct; to prevent our forming false and narrow notions of human nature from the limited sphere in which we move [pp. 5–6].

Despite the emphasis on the techniques of fiction which had characterized many reviews published in the 1860s, Edith Simcox could affirm in 1871 that "there are no general principles of criticism recognised at once in the production and the appreciation of works of fiction" (p. 12). G.H. Lewes, who had argued so forcefully in the 1850s and 1860s for taking the art of fiction seriously, warned that overemphasis on matters of form might even be harmful. Critics must be wary, Lewes wrote, of "the bias of technical estimate," the tendency by critics to value the pleasures of form over the more essential pleasures of the experience of art (p. 27).

This turning away from an interest in the techniques of fiction can be traced in the many essays of reevaluation which appeared in the 1870s. Leslie Stephen, in a series of articles which appeared in his *Cornhill Magazine*, tended to judge a book by Sterne, Fielding, Scott, Hawthorne or Charlotte Bronte "pretty much in proportion as it makes me love the author" (42 [July 1880], 86). We turn again to Sir Walter Scott not for the pleasures of form, for Scott's readers could not appreciate anything other than daubs; instead, we value in his novels "that healthy open-air life" they celebrate (24 [September 1871], 290, 293). Fielding we similarly value for his "element of masculine observation" (35 [February 1877], 157). Stephen praises Hawthorne because he leads us "away from the commonplace region of newspapers and railways to regions where the imagination can have fair play" (26 [December 1872], 719). Despite his claim to be a "scientific" critic (36 [December 1877], 723), Stephen often substitutes impressionism for more rigorous forms of critical response. For Stephen,

Charlotte Bronte's work is "morbid and unsatisfactory"; her sister's *Wuthering Heights* is "a kind of baseless nightmare, which we read with wonder and with distressing curiosity, but with far more pain than pleasure or profit" (36 [December 1877], 739, 738). George Barnett Smith is like Stephen in being unconcerned with matters of technique in the novel. Thackeray is vaguely praised for his "elevated form of fidelity" to human experience (*Edinburgh Review* 137 [January 1873], 118); Fielding is praised on similar grounds as "the great observer and interpreter of human nature" (p. 83). Questions of form are for Smith largely irrelevant in dealing with any work of fiction: "The novel will never be able to assume a position of equal importance with the drama, because of its comparative defectiveness of construction" (p. 83).

However unsure critics might be about the value of analysis of the techniques of fiction, most believed the novel to have reached a remarkable summit of achievement. Robert Laing, in his review of *Middlemarch* (pp. 45–80), asserted that English imaginative literature "has become the most objective, the most trustworthy and the most historically instructive, of modern times." The excellence of the novel seemed to Laing to suggest that "the finest creative fancy" would now turn to other forms of intellectual inquiry, to the study of ancient law, primitive society and natural history (p. 70). The excellence of the fiction produced by his contemporaries makes Leslie Stephen treat a novelist of an earlier generation such as Bulwer Lytton with some contempt. Despite Lytton's earnestness and skill, his novels are, according to modern standards, superficial and unconvincing: "he cannot send through his creations that electric current which makes them start into reality, or give to his reflections that force which can be drawn only from the deepest emotions of a powerful nature" (p. 44).

In 1879 two essays appeared which neatly suggest the coming change in the direction of novel criticism. Anthony Trollope's "Novel-Reading" (pp. 109–30) represents a synthesis of the moral aesthetic that was implicit in the work of novelists and critics alike at mid-century. Suspicious of theorizing, careless in the use of critical terminology, Trollope argues that the novelist's sympathy with his characters is the final touchstone of success in the novel (p. 130). In her review-essay on the novels of George Meredith (pp. 131–47), Arabella Shaw brings more exacting standards to bear. Meredith is praised for his "imaginative realism," for the

complex unity of his narratives and for the intellectual significance of his subject matter.

For many critics in the early 1880s, the "new fiction," characterized by a concern with ideas and by rigorous new standards of
form, was a largely American import. The fiction and theoretical
writings of the most well-known Americans, William Dean Howells
and Henry James, were analyzed with scant sympathy by Arthur
Tilley in 1883. The new school can best be defined, Tilley wrote,
by comparing James's *Portrait of a Lady* with Howells' *A Modern
Instance*. These works, whose popularity will be necessarily confined "to a small and select circle of admirers," resemble each
other

> in the elaborate analysis of character, in the absence of plot, in the
> sparing use of incident, in the studied realism, in the conscientious
> subordination of the artist to his art, in the acute powers of observa-
> tion, and in the humour, which, never forced or obtrusive, seems to
> exist, not because the writer's own gifts lie specially in that direction,
> but because, as a healthy and impartial observer of human life, he
> cannot fail to take note of its humorous side [p. 255].

Most critics were even less sympathetic than Tilley in their analysis
of the new school. W.B. Rands found most such theorizing about
fiction "self-conscious talk to fill up time" (p. 151) and longed for a
"return to the healthy simplicity of Scott and his school." For
Rands the "studied realism" Tilley had identified as characteristic
of the new fiction too often represented an unwholesome fascination with "the skeleton in the cupboard of daily life" (p. 160).
Writing in the *Quarterly Review*, L.J. Jennings hinted darkly that
the new fiction was little more than a conspiracy to puff one
another's books by the "Boston Mutual Admiration Society"
(p. 251). Novelists such as Howells and James have founded a new
school of criticism "based upon the principle that the best novelist
is he who has no story to tell" (p. 225). Their fiction is no more
satisfactory than their theorizing; *The Portrait of a Lady*, Jennings
laments, has "not a single interesting incident in it from beginning
to end" (p. 235).

Writing in the *Westminster Review* in 1884, John M. Robertson
proved more sympathetic to the aims of the new school. Published
in the month following James's own brilliant apologia for the new
fiction (pp. 285–306), Robertson's essay justifies the seeming

"plotlessness" of much modern fiction: "a good fictionist is not simply to concoct for us a story with an agreeable ending, but is to impress us with a sense of his faithfulness to an actual life which is full of broken threads and pathetic failures" (p. 312). Howells is condemned by another writer not for adherence to the new aesthetic but for his swerving from it in pursuit of a more general popularity. This new insistence on artistry and the demand for significant subject matter had devastating effects on the reputation of classic English novelists. By 1882, critics were united in deploring Dickens' "want of proportion, of the artistic sense of limitation and restraint" (pp. 208–09).

By the mid-1880s, the "new fiction" seemed to have won so many adherents that many observers sought to redress the balance by calling for a return to a fiction of adventure and pure entertainment. Robert Louis Stevenson wrote eloquently in *Longman's*:

> Conduct is three parts of life, but it is not all the four. There is a vast deal in life and letters both which is not immoral, but simply a-moral; which either does not regard the human will at all, or deals with it in obvious and healthy relations; where the interest turns, not upon what a man shall choose to do, but on how he manages to do it; not on the passionate slips and hesitations of the conscience, but on the problems of the body and of the practical intelligence, in clean, open-air adventure, the shock of arms, or the diplomacy of life [p. 190].

H. Rider Haggard's plea for the romance, for the "calm retreats of pure imagination" (p. 387), and Hall Caine's prediction that the romance will triumph (pp. 469–80) are implied concessions to the importance of the revolution in novel criticism that James and Howells had helped to bring about. William Watson wished a plague on both the houses of fiction in his 1888 essay ominously entitled "The Fall of Fiction" (pp. 447–61). The movement in taste from the novels of the American school to the romances of Rider Haggard is a swing between unacceptable alternatives: "From elegant listlessness fiction has suddenly leapt into paroxysmal life. From coma it has passed into convulsions" (p. 449). George Saintsbury, despite a concern for craftsmanship evident in his *Academy* reviews, chose to ridicule the "American" insistence on greater artistry in fiction. Dismissing Howells' "comic little critical excursions" (p. 393), he expresses a preference for the romance and tales of adventure. The sober probings of the new fiction have become stale and pretentious:

> The average man and woman in England of the middle and late nineteenth century, has been drawn and quartered, analysed and "introspected," till there is nothing new to be done with him or her either as an *écorché*, or with the skin on, or with clothes on the skin [p. 398].

But the important claims of the "new" fiction and the criticism that supported and defined it were not to be so easily dismissed. Oscar Wilde's assertion that "Lying, the telling of beautiful untrue things, is the proper aim of Art" (*Nineteenth Century* 25 [January 1889], 35–56) was unconvincing, as he knew all too well it would be, to the intellectuals who regarded the novel as an important vehicle of thought for that saving remnant who wanted more than empty pleasure from their reading. Increasingly critics turned to the European novel for evidence of that high seriousness and technical skill lacking in English fiction. Despite his belief that the sprawling canvas of *Anna Karenina* cannot really be considered as a work of art, Matthew Arnold admired it for the insight it provides into the intellectual and emotional life of mature people (pp. 399–417). George Moore preferred French novels for a similar reason: "the object of the English novel has ever been to divert young people rather than to help men and women to understand life" (p. 597). Arthur Symons admires in Balzac that "shock of life" which is the mark of a mature fiction (p. 631), while J.A. Symonds easily disposes of the charge that Zola is an undiscriminating realist by arguing that his narrative is "ideally" unified. "The unity of subject, movement, composition, interest" in *La Bête Humaine* distinguishes it from "the haphazard incompleteness of reality" (p. 495).

The candor and seriousness of European fiction were held up by many writers in the 1890s as goals for the English novel. Edmund Gosse, writing in 1892, deplored the conventionality of subject matter in much English fiction. That love interest that Trollope had held to be essential to any popular novel was for Gosse far too limiting a subject. Novelists might better turn their attention to an accurate rendering of "the life of a sailor, of a game-keeper, of a railway-porter, of a civil engineer" (p. 532). Hardy was greeted by some critics, among them Janetta Newton-Robinson (pp. 505–18), as a novelist capable of mingling poetry and realism in the depiction of ordinary human experience. Hardy's *Jude the Obscure* was praised by Havelock Ellis (pp. 577–93) for its devastating portrayal of "the reality of marriage."

Increasingly reviewers concerned themselves with technical analyses of the novels presented for review. Vernon Lee, despite her occasional suspicions that the novel "has ample resources for fascinating our attention without the help of the very special quality called beauty" (p. 637), devoted many of her reviews to discussions of the art of the novel.

By the mid-nineties, however, no great consensus about the aesthetics of the novel had emerged. Alfred C. Lyall could still theorize about the origins of the novel in a way that would not have surprised such late eighteenth-century writers as Clara Reeve (*Quarterly Review* 179 [October 1894], 530–52). Past masters of the novel such as Scott and Dickens were in partial eclipse, but the *Quarterly Review* could still rouse itself to defend the Waverley Novels, although the grounds for its praise were more political than aesthetic (180 [April 1895], 431–60). Finally, despite the serious discussion of novel-writing that had appeared in periodicals throughout the century, a critic writing for the *Yellow Book* in 1894 admitted that the general public still remained indifferent to those who would announce like the Elsmerian in Barrie's satire that "fiction has become an art":

> the popular mind, while willingly acknowledging that there are technical difficulties to be surmounted in the creation of the sonata, the landscape, the statue, the building, in the case of the short story, or of the longer novel, declines to believe even in their existence, persuaded that in order to produce good fiction, an ingenious idea, or "plot," as it is termed, is the one thing needed. The rest is a mere matter of handwriting [p. 544].

"The Uses of Fiction"

Tinsley's Magazine 6 (March 1870), 180–85

THE USES OF FICTION.

WE hope that the title of this paper will mislead no one as to its purport. We are not going to make any apology for fiction on the ground that it answers some grand moral or educational end. It may do both; but fiction which does neither may amply fulfil an excellent purpose if it only amuses. We are too much given in this utilitarian age to demand that everything which engages our attention shall leave behind it some definite product; forgetting that the more utilitarian and practical and hard-working an age is, the more does it require to be enlivened and amused by means which need only last the passing hour. Some excellent people have lately been given to judging of the position and prospects of the drama by calculating what educational results it can possibly at present produce; and doubtless these people would have fiction to be what they would have the drama to be, a grand moral engine. If either can be made so, good and well; but it must be remembered that this is not their chief aim and end. That is amusement. If we can combine instruction of any kind with this amusement, so much the better; but the quantity of instruction conveyed must not be allowed to be the criterion of the excellence of a novel or play.

Nevertheless novels have very definite uses apart from that of beguiling an hour or two in the course of one's graver duties. The first incentive to reading fiction, we are convinced, is curiosity to know how other people live, how they regard life, how they act under certain circumstances, and what are their prevailing sentiments and characteristics. The world which any one man or woman inhabits is remarkably small. The shortness of life, to say nothing of other circumstances, prevents our becoming intimately acquainted with more than a few people; and these soon become so familiar, that we forget to remark their characteristics. So small is this world, that events and accidents which happen every day to thousands become singular and peculiar when they happen to ourselves; for we are not aware that other people are so situated. Did ever any girl believe that any other girl ever fell in love as she did? Does she not consider this new experience as a strange and wonderful thing, similar to nothing that ever happened upon earth? Yet she is aware that other people have been placed in somewhat similar situations; and she is curious to know how they felt, how they acted, what they thought. This curiosity she finds amply gratified in novels. There every possible situation is described with a minuteness that is extremely interesting; for every now and again the writer hits upon some little bit of his reader's experience, and she is charmed by such tiny revelations. She reads how Evelina, or Edith, or Alice fluttered with a secret joy the first time that Alfred, or Alexander, or Henry timidly presented a rose; and with what profound and solemn anxiety she watched the burning of two chestnuts on a certain Hallowe'en. All the little sensations and incidents and hopes of love-making are a matter of exceeding curiosity to her; and here she finds in what measure other people have felt what she now feels, and how far they have acted as she has done.

This desire to know what other people say and do and think is universal. Every man and woman must necessarily have some sort of theory of the little world in which they move; and they cannot help wishing to know if other people see with the same eyes, and meet with the same facts. Every man knows that, outside of his own circle of acquaintances, there exists a great abstract thing which he calls the world, that has its opinions and habits, which are not the opinions and habits of any particular person he knows. He will do such and such an act in defiance of the opinions of Tom, or Jack, or Harry, whom he knows, and whose scruples he can combat or laugh over; but he will not do it in defiance of the world's opinion, which he fears. Now no single man knows this great outside world. Every man knows his own section of it; and the only way in which you can arrive at some notion of the world and humanity in general is, by taking these several reports and comparing them. You listen to men of experience, and judge of their theories of life, accepting that which is most probable. You find that some great traveller has certain odd notions about the feminine character in general; or that some great author has very decided opinions about the selfishness of humanity; or that some great philanthropist has a no less decided opinion about its being unselfish and honest at the core; and all these various estimates modify each other, until you come to the conclusion that the logical deduction from them all would be an utter blank. The anxious inquirer falls back, as an alternative, upon the notion that every man's picture of the world is more or less a picture of himself; and that not the least interesting part of these life-pictures is the glimpse you get of the artist, who stands modestly in the corner. As a very great novelist himself said, 'The world is a looking-glass, which shows to each man the reflection of his own face.'

However ineffectual, therefore, may be the attempt of any single person to portray the world by painting the portraits of his acquaintances, that limited circle is still of immense interest to us. We meet with types of character and examples of conduct which we should not have met with in our own spheres; and are able to compare them, and select that which is most beautiful. One of the first uses of fiction is, that it keeps awake a good ideal of life. In their own narrow spheres, men have a tendency to run in narrow grooves, and become the victims of petty desires and mean theories. Without that constant communion with other natures which enlarges the sympathies and widens the understanding, men are apt to settle down into a sordid selfishness. Fiction steps in and shows the beauty of a healthier, more active and beneficial life. It kindles new desires, awakens a little heroism to purify the tainted moral air, and lets a man see what, after all, ought to be the chief pleasures and the real aim of living. A man who loves fiction cannot be altogether a sneak. The multitude of honourable people he meets would shame him into better conduct. A man is known by the company he seeks; and your churlish, contemptible, avaricious, and mean-spirited man is not likely to court the society of these fictitious ladies and gentlemen, who would be constantly rebuking him by their unselfishness, their generosity, and kindly demeanour. The novelist may be said to be always on the side of the virtues. He does not—or, at least, ought not to—make his virtuous people invariably triumphant in the end; for, in real life, they are not so; but the mere fact that he exhibits certain lines of conduct as being praiseworthy and commendable, and certain others as being contemptible and bad, makes him, in spite of himself, a moralist. Farther: however realistic may be his treatment of ordinary life, it must catch a glow of richness and colour from his imagination. He must so far idealise his scenes as to give them dramatic vigour, howsoever faithful in detail they may be; and hence we find that in fiction life is always presented to us as something a little richer, and finer, and more noble than most of us discover it to be in reality. This is the ideal life which is presented to every one who reads fiction. It shows us what real life might be; and thus puts before us a high standard by which to measure every-day conduct and speech. We not only find in novels the world as it appears to another man's eyes; but we also find, in general, that world rendered a trifle better than we know it, so that we have always something to aim at.

Nothing can be more natural than this tendency to construct imaginary scenes, with imaginary people in them. Novel-building is the involuntary action of the mind in sleep. When a man loses control of his imagination, it revels in all manner of fancy combinations of life, weaving-up his impressions of men and women, and his recollections of scenery, into kaleidoscopic stories of every possible form. And these have always the advantage of being more picturesque than ordinary life; for the simple reason that all the commonplace detail, which alternates with the rapid and brilliant actions of life, is omitted. We have all the strong points of a man's nature presented to us; and we have the movements of years compressed into a few seconds, with all the dull intervals left out. In a drama we leave out five or seven years, as the case may be, between the acts, and step on to the striking *dénouement.* A drama or a story has all the salient points of a life's-history picked out; and it must therefore be more striking and impressive than ordinary life, even were no other idealisation permitted to the author. They resemble a plum-pudding that is all plums and no flour; or a collection of a man's witty sayings, with none of the commonplace that he must have talked between-whiles. To this is added the choice of convenient and picturesque conditions. Did ever any one notice how lovely, as a rule, is the climate of novels? We never have the weather interfering with a merry party, or destroying the effect of an unexpected meeting. Was there ever a novelist who had the courage to send his heroine, at the end of the third volume, off upon her marriage-tour in a shower of rain? Indeed, we never find rain in novels, unless when some outcast is to be made particularly wet and weary, or when some dreadful deed of villany is to be perpetrated, and then thunder and lightning are invariably added. In novels it almost never rains but it pours; and when there is no necessity for terror—when the lovers want to go a-walking, or the hero goes out for his morning stroll—all Nature rejoices, and shows her utmost complaisance. This choice of conditions has a great effect in a novel; for without calm twilights and romantic moonlights the love-business could scarcely be carried on.

This, then, is one great use of novels—to give us wider and better conceptions of life and its possibilities; to keep before us an ideal which must have some beneficial effect on actual conduct; to prevent our forming false and narrow notions of human nature from the limited sphere in which we move. Another direction in which novels are eminently useful is in giving us the best results of other people's experiences. In anything approaching to good fiction, an author must test the probability of the things he narrates by the possibility of their happening to himself. He must throw himself into such and such a position, and consider, from past experience of himself, how he would act under the circumstances. Or he may boldly make use of his own direct personal experiences, and show how human nature exhibits itself in the face of certain conditions. Besides this, he brings to his work all the fund of knowledge and observation which he has acquired. He may allow his imagination to colour and improve, but there must be a basis of fact; otherwise his work is forced and unnatural; and the reader, without clearly perceiving the cause, feels himself repelled by the unreality of the scenes presented to him. There is something very curious in the manner in which uneducated persons may, by this appeal to their own common sense (which is the fruit of experience), judge of a literary work. Molière made a looking-glass of his housekeeper's face, in which he could see the really human and humorous bits of his plays faithfully reflected, while the artificial and unnatural passages produced nothing but a blank dulness. The young person, of whom we have already spoken, who has just passed through the successive phases of a flirtation, a term of love-making, and an engagement, becomes in these matters an expert critic. Her newly-awakened sensitiveness may constitute her a better judge of the naturalness of the love-scenes in a novel, than the reviewer who has grown gray-haired in dissecting books, and who looks upon such scenes merely as a more or less artistic product. She immediately appeals to her own experiences, and the notions to which they naturally give rise, to say whether at such and such a moment Arthur would be likely to become rhetorical. She says to herself, 'No! If he was so much in love as this, he would sit still and trembling, perhaps seeking to touch her hand, and waiting for the answer of her eyes. He would not begin to rave, any more than to argue her into accepting him by telling her how much he had a-year.'

It may seem rather hard that a novel is to be judged by the individual experiences of a girl of nineteen; but these experiences, as we say, have rendered her sensitive and appreciative on this one point, so that she can make allowances for difference of situation, and judge the result fairly enough. She does not ask that all the heroes and heroines of her favourite stories shall make love as she and her particular lover did; but the experience she has gained during those solemn and tender interviews so far qualifies her to say whether such and such a course of conduct on the part of the imaginary lovers is probable.

Besides, she has acquired a good deal of experience from other novels. Long before she entered upon these experiences herself, she had read accounts of how other people had encountered them. These accounts must, in many cases, have been absurd; and much has been said of the false views of life and conduct which novel-reading must give to a young girl. It must be remembered, however, that, even if she reads novels on no principle of selection—supposing she takes them as they are published, good, bad, and indifferent—they will, in a good measure, modify each other. What is extravagant and false will be tempered by what is true and natural; and as there must be in every readable novel a certain truth—a certain faithfulness to some phase or impression of life — promiscuous novel-reading, even if not qualified by personal experience, will produce less erroneous conceptions of the world and its inhabitants than many people would suppose. We consider it to be less likely that a girl should be taught false views of life by reading many novels than by reading one or two. Let us take the case of the girl who is just entering upon the idyllic period of courtship. If it has been her peculiar misfortune to have read only one or two of the Rosa-Matilda novels, she may very probably have a notion that the proper thing for her lover to do, in proposing to her, is to go down on his knees, place his hand on his heart, and swear ridiculous vows. Unless her own good sense teaches her that, under no circumstances, could a man look other than ridiculous in going through this programme, it is just possible that she may be anticipating some such pantomime, and be rather vexed when it does not come off. Or perhaps she may only have read one or two of the novels written by the Brontë family, and have come to the conclusion that the proper mood for a heroic lover is one of savage and churlish rudeness—Orson finding himself in love, and sneering at himself for being such an ass, yet not the less inclined to dare heaven and earth in order to gratify his sulky passion. But if the girl has read plenty of novels—if she has found that Thackeray's lovers treat their sweethearts with a courtesy and deference that is at once

simple and stately; that Dickens's lovers make love with a homeliness and tenderness that yet admits of some glimpses of the humorous; that Mr. Trollope's girls, even in their love-affairs, talk with a commonplace matter-of-fact dulness, which leaves no doubt about their portraits having been painted from the life—she gets to consider that, after all, there is no typical or normal behaviour which a lover ought to assume, and that she had better meet her own personal experiences in her own personal way, and be merely natural. But all this novel-reading must, at least, have produced the one effect of teaching her the possibility of making the world around her a little better, and more picturesque, and more enjoyable, by the exercise of these virtues of unselfishness, and kindliness, and courtesy, which the novelist inculcates.

There are many women, and some men, who would never have any proper notion of the world around them but for novels. It is not permitted to the young country curate, whose experiences of life are limited to quiet tea-meetings and an occasional meeting with a hardened sinner in the shape of a surly poacher, to visit the *coulisses* of a music-hall in the company of two half-tipsy guardsmen, and listen to the theories of life propounded by them and the young ladies they meet there. Even the ordinary conversation of a club smoking-room is modified before 'the cloth;' and there is much more than naughty words that is left out when a clergyman is present. Yet it is of importance to a clergyman who would properly know and understand what his fellow-men are in the habit of thinking and doing, that he should not limit his acquaintance to a few ignorant labourers and the lamb-like young ladies of the rectory. A 'guardsman's novel' would do him good; but we would warn him to dip into this kind of reading for the first time under the escort of a male author. A 'guardsman's novel' written by a lady would probably revolt his feelings too much at the outset.

It is of the greatest importance, therefore, that novels should be as nearly as possible true in their descriptions of life; for they convey information, if not instruction, into the most unexpected quarters. Necessarily they cannot be actually true, any more than a drama can; for, as we pointed out, both seize the more striking features of a character, or scene, or story, and omit all the characterless detail which is familiar to us in nature. And we are of opinion that novels do fulfil this end of yielding information in a very marked way. The experienced novel-reader soon becomes able to distinguish that which is merely melo-dramatic and 'sensational' in a book from that which is the reflection of the author's personal experience. Some personal experience must always lie in every book; for the days of miracles are over, and we no longer make something out of nothing. Not only, as we say, are these descriptions of life useful in showing us how some other man sees the world, and what section of it he sees, but they also contain the results of this observation on his own mind. There is no vehicle so useful as the novel for conveying odds and ends of knowledge. Some happy notion, or point of observation, that could in no wise form the subject of an elaborate essay, may be put into a novel in the form of a single sentence. Some experience of foreign travel, that could not be published

as a pretentious volume, may fill up a chapter in a story, or become an admirable background for the principal personages in the drama. Indeed, there is nothing a man knows that he cannot put into a novel; and if this is done with skill and grace, these chance embellishments greatly increase the pleasure one finds in reading the book. In the works of George Eliot, for example, we meet with simple phrases or sentences that are as suggestive, and frequently more satisfactory than a ponderous volume. They are the results of a long course of thinking; and we get the product without the process. But everything depends on the manner in which the novelist introduces these glimpses of thought, or erudition, or wit. They must not be obtruded, or the illusion of the story is destroyed. Mrs. Poyser must find a fitting opportunity for her sarcasms; or we look upon her as a mere puppet, and think of the hand that is pulling the cords. If a man uses a story for the purpose of stringing together maxims or reflections, then let him say so; and we accept as a graceful sort of foil—as in the case of *Sartor Resartus*, or *Companions of my Solitude*, or *Henry Holbeach*—the connecting link of narrative. The first and chief business of the novel, however, is to give us authentic descriptions of this or that section of the world; and we cannot have the face of the picture disfigured by prominent aphorisms. That is not the use of the novel; yet the novel has its uses, as we have endeavoured to show; and we are not of those who would deprecate the prevalence of fiction, merely because it does not announce a creed or inculcate a doctrine.

"H. Lawrenny"
(Edith Simcox)

"Recent Novels"

Academy 2 (December 15, 1871), 552–54

RECENT NOVELS.

THERE have not been any great or startling events in the world of fiction during the past year. No new writer of striking merit has appeared, and the existing schools seem to muster recruits in about the same proportions as before ; so that the time is favourable for an appeal to the leading novelists not to let the next change of fashion—change of some kind being inevitable every two or three years—be for the worse. It would be invidious to decide who *are* the leading novelists, and a perfectly fair opinion on the subject could not be formed without, as Pascal says, reading a great many very bad books ; but it is not difficult to see which schools compete most successfully for popular favour. There is a safe and steady sale for domestic twaddle tempered by religion, and a still larger sale for domestic twaddle tempered by crime, but the followers of Miss Yonge and Mrs. Henry Wood do not presumably read the *Academy*, nor, should we imagine, do readers of the *Academy* seek recreation in the works of those authoresses ; so it is unnecessary to analyze their claims to attention—

"Non ragioniam di lor, ma guarda e passa."

The novels which it is still possible for rational beings to read generally belong to one of three varieties, which we may call, for convenience, the sensational, the literary, and the didactic ; though the former class can be subdivided, and the last is very small, consisting in fact as a rule of stray works by writers of acknowledged merit, who have taken up a crotchet and earned the right of submitting it to the public for digestion. Such is an unfortunate tract about deceased wives' sisters, by the author of *John Halifax*, which has been published in *St. Paul's ;* such is the serial story in *Good Words*, by M. B. Edwards, though here the moral, which has something to do with socialism, is not so obvious as to explain why the author gave the probabilities their *congé* to clear the ground for preaching. This is only half a defect, for of course nothing is so fatal to a novel as the appearance of a foregone conclusion to which incidents and characters are made to conform. As an example of a fixed purpose, masked and extenuated with all the skill possible under the circumstances, we should mention *The Member for Paris,* a tale of the Second Empire, which has (it must be owned at less frequent intervals) most of the merits possessed by the French sketches which appear from time to time in *Cornhill.* The plot is compact and symmetrical, though perhaps too simple for expansion into three volumes ; and the author expends much cleverness and local knowledge in giving an appearance of impartiality and necessity to his account of the young radical duke's gradual fall into temptation and discredit. The catastrophe, however, is a little too abrupt ; Horace Gérold should have survived the loss of position and popularity for at least two or three years, and then he might, with more truth to life and nature, have died by suicide instead of apoplexy.

By literary novels, the most tantalizing and disappointing of their class, we mean works by men of education and a kind of genius, who have something to say and endeavour to say it with some degree of literary propriety ; who know a work of art when they see it, who aspire after ideal truth and beauty, who are, it may be, too conscientious to write poetry without a vocation, and who certainly ought to be able to write imaginative prose. If they cannot do this to the satisfaction of a high critical standard—and it would be plainly unfair to try, let us say, *The Adventures of Harry Richmond* and *A Daughter of Heth* by a low one—there must be something rotten in the state of the literary republic. As a matter of fact there are no general principles of criticism recognised at once in the production and the appreciation of works of fiction. Writers of more than common originality and semi-poetical instincts, instead of approaching proportionately nearer to a common type of excellence, wear out their own individuality by making it serve to supply not only the materials and the form of their work, but also, too often, the only standard which they will admit as adequate. If this were all, we might be deluged with prose Alastors, Werthers, and Frankensteins, but eccentric genius would be free, and once in a generation or two a great anomalous work might take the world by surprise. But the only semblance of a principle which presided at the birth of the British novel was the principle of realistic probability. Fielding and Miss Austen painted their contemporaries as truly as Gainsborough and Hogarth did theirs, and the scores of painstaking scribblers, who fancy they too are sketching life as it is, are sufficiently influential, thanks to this tradition of what was once an idea, to compel a half-hearted compliance with their usages on the part of the more able idealists. The result of the fusion is naturally a mongrel kind of production ; two good things either simply spoilt, or blended together into an extravaganza at once lamentable and absurd. If Lessing had been alive to expound the laws of romance and to assign their proper share of representation and respect to the eternal nature of humanity, to the accidental usage of society, and to the variations of individual character, Mr. George Meredith would perhaps have taken the trouble to write a readable novel, at least his imagination would not have skipped in such an unaccountable manner from studies of high life as Thackeray might have seen it to studies of low life as only Mr. Henry Kingsley does see it, from clear dramatic invention to muddled psychological insight, from the virtues of a clever story-teller to the tricks of a conjuror or a medium. As it is, *Harry Richmond* is as dull as it is perverse, and the reader's patience breaks down long before the author is tired of inventing new characters, performing fresh feats for incomprehensible motives in a world which is not only unreal but inconsistent. *A Daughter of Heth* is not so flagrant an instance of misapplied power, and yet it is nearly as far from being a satisfactory work of art. Mr. Meredith has the raw materials for a good novel, Mr. Black at most for a pretty idyll or pastoral ; one wants judgment and self-denial, the other invention and vigour. Yet the popularity of *A Daughter of Heth* is on the whole a consolatory symptom, for it can only be accounted for by its purely literary merits, and as these are not of a kind to be discovered by the general public, they must have been taken on faith from the ordained leaders of opinion in the press, so that criticism cannot be quite impotent yet. As a study of character in good English and diversified by refined and appreciative descriptions of scenery, the book obtained a *succès d'estime* amongst reviewers, who naturally suffer more than ordinary readers from the blank stupidity of ordinary novels, and on their recommendation it was largely ordered from the libraries and read without conscious disappointment, though the plot is weak, the serious characters rather unreal, and the comic ones very conventional. Worse writers than Mr. Black are often more amusing and more life-like, and he is not quite good enough to dispense with those everyday merits. He has poetical feeling and enough literary power to give pleasure for a moment to a cultivated taste, but he is not *interesting*—to borrow a favourite word from the vocabulary of novel readers ; and we therefore doubt whether the success of his present work will outlast that of less deserving ones which catch the public taste at once without help from the critics and often in defiance of their protests.

The sensationalists come next in order, for, though the novel of character was at one time a popular and esteemed variety, its day seems over for the present. Even Mr. Trollope deserts the men and women of the world, and, a prey to the creations of his own fertile pen, can see nothing else, but draws Lady Glencora Palliser after herself in one volume after another on a diminishing scale, like the image in two opposite mirrors, or multiplies by ten and by twenty the maiden we all know so well, from whom the story of her love, or perhaps, for a change, her indifference, has to be wrung in a dozen pages of diplomatic dialogue, in which the longest sentence does not exceed two lines and a half. The founders of the sensation novel, the masters of honest burglary and bigamy, murder and madness, poison and police, have, like Mr. Trollope, seen their best days. Mr. Charles Reade and Mr. Wilkie Collins pile up horrors and hairbreadth escapes with nearly all their old circumstantial vividness, and the former at least still retains a touching faith in the potency of capitals, italics, and notes of exclamation. But their public is a hardened public ; no mere story of adventure suffices to stir its sluggish pulses ; it demands to "put itself in the place" of the murderer or the maniac, to know what it feels like to commit forgery or bigamy. The school of subjective sensationalism which arose in obedience to so natural and consequent a desire is generally supposed to look on Miss Braddon as its founder, though the author of *Guy Livingstone* did something towards popularising what we may call the æsthetics of crime. But Miss Braddon's reputation, like most which are made in a season, is being steadily written away ; besides which she really occupied a transitional position between the melodrama of incident and of sentiment. Those of her followers, like "Ouida" and Florence Marryatt (Mrs. Ross Church), who are content to treat a criminal situation altogether from within, can, while such a proceeding has the charm of novelty, extract much stronger sensations out of it than is possible by any other means. It is true, to do these writers and English society justice, that their pictures of vice always have rather the appearance of being constructed *à priori* or else in servile imitation of the traditional French novel. The virtuous indignation of reviewers may succeed for a moment in advertising a stupid book, but it seems probable, though only the statistics of "Mudie" could make it certain, that fiction of this class would soon go out of fashion if treated to a little wholesome neglect on the part of the critics. The breach of no one of the Ten Commandments is intrinsically more interesting than that of the other nine, and *toujours perdrix* is tiresome even when the Divorce Court supplies the game.

Sensational novelists who depend upon one motive only for their sensational effects write themselves out fast, but not faster than young authors spring up to take their place. *Temple Bar*—a magazine which would not be ill-conducted if "padding" were done away with and the standard of its shorter stories raised—generally contains two serial novels by the best representatives of the latest development of whatever passes for sensational. To judge from *Ought we to visit her?* and *Good-*

bye, Sweetheart! the authoresses who are most popular for the moment are those who hover just on the verge of immorality or indecorum (like children trying to summon up courage to say " a bad word "), but, instead of passing the Rubicon, trade upon the common delusion that, if they only went just a little farther, they would come to something very exciting indeed. The lady who is known by her romantic and elliptical titles delights chiefly in representing a beautiful and unconventional young woman in the act of throwing herself at the head or, more literally, into the arms of a peculiarly ugly and unresponsive hero. The author of *Archie Lovell* prefers situations in which the same unconventional young lady is on the verge of being " compromised " more or less innocently, so that some skill is required to extricate and marry her. There is not much to be said for either of these views of the elements ·of romance, but both writers, and especially the one last mentioned, show a capacity for better things, which makes us regret the vulgarisation of their powers nearly as much as Mr. Meredith's vagaries. They can write readable dialogue, and they can conceive a group of characters who are either natural or at least sufficiently life-like to keep up the illusion of reality on which the interest of an ordinary novel depends ; they have no need to resort to dishonest or unlawful artifices to amuse and interest their readers. *Ought we to visit her?* would really be a pretty story, but for the recurrence of false alarms to the effect that some one is going to run away with the wife of some one else ; and as the threatened impropriety is not committed after all, we cannot see why the authoress should so unnecessarily distract attention from her central and quite unexceptionable position, that when a virtuous ballet-girl marries into Chalkshire society, Chalkshire society ought to call on her. If this writer would study human nature as it is, not as it lends itself to a conventional type of intrigue, and if she would write in accordance with some reasonable conception of what novels *ought* to be liked, instead of being guided by a vague and very possibly mistaken impression of what *is* liked, she might look forward to occupying a respectable place in the second rank of her profession. The prospects of Miss Broughton are not quite so easily determined ; her range of subjects is even narrower, and the furious way in which her heroines make love soon palls upon the mental palate ; but she has some technical skill, and if she would only write one novel a year, and study the principal dramatists, she might learn to vary her theme and not meddle with the outside of stronger passions than she can either interpret or represent.

In so cursory a review of the fiction of the year some few books with a degree of modest merit must naturally be overlooked. Mr. George Macdonald, who has written *inter alia* a story in *St. Paul's*, should perhaps be mentioned as the nearest heir and representative of the once thriving school of muscular Christians, though in *Wilfred Cumbermede* both the muscles and the Christianity seem a good deal attenuated. In the other magazines there is nothing which calls for notice except the belief which seems to be gaining ground amongst editors, that any novel by a known writer will do to cut up and publish in serial parts, though the ordeal which was dangerous even to *Romola* is fatal to many harmless little romances. On the whole we have not much to congratulate ourselves upon in the works we have been noticing, except that none of them have achieved the extravagant success which sometimes falls to the lot of a bad book. Our hopes for the future depend upon two improbable events, namely, that some clever lady sensationalists will take the trouble to educate themselves, or some clever men of letters acquire the mechanical rudiments of the art of story-telling. Pending either contingency, there would be an opening for literary partnerships of the Erckmann-Chatrian type, in which one writer should supply the ideas and the other the execution. At present both leave room for improvement.

H. LAWRENNY.

G.H. Lewes

"Dickens in Relation to Criticism"

Fortnightly Review 17 (February 1872), 141–54

DICKENS IN RELATION TO CRITICISM.

THE old feud between authors and critics, a feud old as literature, has not arisen on the ground of chariness in praise, but rather on the ground of deficient sympathy, and the tendency to interpret an author's work according to some standard which is not his. Instead of placing themselves at his point of view, and seeing what he has attempted, how far he has achieved the aim, and whether the aim itself were worthy of achievement, critics have thrust between his work and the public some vague conception of what they required, and measured it by an academic or conventional standard derived from other works. Fond as an author necessarily is of praise, and pained as he must always be by blame, he is far more touched by a sympathetic recognition of his efforts, and far more hurt by a misrepresentation of them. No hyperbole of laudation gives a tithe of the delight which is given by sympathetic insight. Unhappily for the author, this can but sparingly be given by critics, who trust less to their emotions than to their standards of judgment; for the greater the originality of the writer, and the less inclination he has for familiar processes and already-trodden tracks, the greater must be the resistance he will meet with from minds accustomed to move in those tracks, and to consider excellence confined within them. It is in the nature of the critical mind to judge according to precedent; and few minds have flexibility enough to adopt at once a novelty which is destined in its turn to become a precedent.

There is another source of pain. Besides the very great difficulties of independent judgment, of adjusting the mental focus to new objects under new perspectives, and the various personal considerations which trammel even open minds—considerations of friendship, station, renown, rivalry, &c.—there is the immense difficulty which all men find in giving anything like an adequate expression to their judgments. It is easy for us to say that a book has stirred, or instructed us; but it is by no means easy to specify the grounds of our pleasure, or profit, except in a very general way; and when we attempt to do so we are apt to make ludicrous mistakes. Thus it is that the criticism which begins with a general expression of gratitude to the author, will often deeply pain him by misplaced praise, or blame misdirected.

Longinus declares that criticism is the last result of abundant experience; he might have added that even the amplest experience is no safeguard against utter failure. For it is true in Art as in the commonest details of life, that our perceptions are mainly determined by our pre-perceptions, our conceptions by our preconceptions. Hence I have long maintained the desirability of preserving as far as possible the individual character of criticism. The artist in his work gives expression to his individual feelings and conceptions, telling us how Life and Nature are mirrored in his mind ; we may fairly state how this affects us, whether it accords with our experience, whether it moves or instructs us ; but we should be very chary of absolute judgments, and be quite sure of our ground before venturing to assume that the public will feel, or ought to feel, as we feel. Now it is the tendency of criticism to pronouce absolute verdicts, to speak for all ; and the exasperation of the artist at finding individual impressions given forth as final judgments is the main cause of the outcry against criticism. The writer who would feel little irritation on hearing that A. and B. were unmoved by his pathos, dead to his humour, unenlightened by his philosophy, may be excused if he writhe under the authoritative announcement that his pathos is maudlin, his humour flat, his philosophy shallow. He may be convicted of bad grammar, bad drawing, bad logic ; and if the critic advances reasons for particular objections, these reasons may be weighed, and perhaps accepted with resignation if not without pain ; but no verdict which does not distinctly carry its evidence can be accepted as more than an individual judgment ; and in matters of Art there is always a great difficulty, sometimes a sheer impossibility, in passing from the individual to the universal. It is impossible to resist feeling. If an author makes me laugh, he is humorous ; if he makes me cry, he is pathetic. In vain will any one tell me that such a picture is not laughable, not pathetic ; or that I am wrong in being moved.

While from these and other causes, especially from the tendency to exaggerate what is painful, authors have deeply resented "the malevolence" of critics—a malevolence which has been mostly incompetence, or inconsiderateness—it is not less true that there has been much heartfelt gratitude given by authors to critics who have sympathised with and encouraged them ; and many lasting friendships have been thus cemented. It was thus that the lifelong friendship of Dickens and his biographer began, and was sustained. Nor is it just to object to Mr. Forster's enthusiasm on the ground of his friendship, since he may fairly answer, " Dickens was my friend because I so greatly admired him." One thing is certain : his admiration was expressed long before all the world had acknowledged Dickens's genius, and was continued through the long years when the majority of writers had ceased to express much fervour of admiration, preferring rather to dwell on his shortcomings and exaggerations.

And this brings me to the noticeable fact that there probably never was a writer of so vast a popularity whose genius was so little *appreciated* by the critics. The very splendour of his successes so deepened the shadow of his failures that to many eyes the shadows supplanted the splendour. Fastidious readers were loath to admit that a writer could be justly called great whose defects were so glaring. They admitted, because it was indisputable, that Dickens delighted thousands, that his admirers were found in all classes, and in all countries; that he stirred the sympathy of masses not easily reached through Literature, and always stirred healthy, generous emotions; that he impressed a new direction on popular writing, and modified the Literature of his age, in its spirit no less than in its form; but they nevertheless insisted on his defects as if these outweighed all positive qualities; and spoke of him either with condescending patronage, or with sneering irritation. Surely this is a fact worthy of investigation? Were the critics wrong, and if so, in what consisted their error? How are we to reconcile this immense popularity with this critical contempt? The private readers and the public critics who were eager to take up each successive number of his works as it appeared, whose very talk was seasoned with quotations from and allusions to these works, who, to my knowledge, were wont to lay aside books of which they could only speak in terms of eulogy, in order to bury themselves in the "new number" when the well-known green cover made its appearance—were nevertheless at this very time niggard in their praise, and lavish in their scorn of the popular humorist. It is not long since I heard a very distinguished man express measureless contempt for Dickens, and a few minutes afterwards, in reply to some representations on the other side, admit that Dickens had "entered into his life."

Dickens has proved his power by a popularity almost unexampled, embracing all classes. Surely it is a task for criticism to exhibit the sources of that power? If everything that has ever been alleged against the works be admitted, there still remains an immense success to be accounted for. It was not by their defects that these works were carried over Europe and America. It was not their defects which made them the delight of grey heads on the bench, and the study of youngsters in the counting-house and school-room. Other writers have been exaggerated, untrue, fantastic, and melodramatic; but they have gained so little notice that no one thinks of pointing out their defects. It is clear, therefore, that Dickens had powers which enabled him to triumph in spite of the weaknesses which clogged them; and it is worth inquiring what those powers were, and their relation to his undeniable defects.

I am not about to attempt such an inquiry, but simply to indicate two or three general points of view. It will be enough merely to mention in passing the primary cause of his success, his overflowing fun, because even uncompromising opponents admit it. They may be ashamed of their laughter, but they laugh. A revulsion of feeling at the preposterousness or extravagance of the image may follow the burst of laughter, but the laughter is irresistible, whether rational or not, and there is no arguing away such a fact.

Great as Dickens is in fun, so great that Fielding and Smollett are small in comparison, he would have been only a passing amusement for the world had he not been gifted with an imagination of marvellous vividness, and an emotional, sympathetic nature capable of furnishing that imagination with elements of universal power. Of him it may be said with less exaggeration than of most poets, that he was of "imagination all compact;" if the other higher faculties were singularly deficient in him, this faculty was imperial. He was a seer of visions; and his visions were of objects at once familiar and potent. Psychologists will understand both the extent and the limitation of the remark, when I say that in no other perfectly sane mind (Blake, I believe, was not perfectly sane) have I observed vividness of imagination approaching so closely to hallucination. Many who are not psychologists may have had some experience in themselves, or in others, of that abnormal condition in which a man hears voices, and sees objects, with the distinctness of direct perception, although silence and darkness are without him; these revived impressions, revived by an internal cause, have precisely the same force and clearness which the impressions originally had when produced by an external cause. In the same degree of vividness are the images *constructed* by his mind in explanation of the voices heard or objects seen: when he imagines that the voice proceeds from a personal friend, or from Satan tempting him, the friend or Satan stands before him with the distinctness of objective reality; when he imagines that he himself has been transformed into a bear, his hands are seen by him as paws. In vain you represent to him that the voices he hears have no external existence; he will answer, as a patient pertinently answered Lélut: "You believe that I am speaking to you because you hear me, is it not so? Very well, I believe that voices are speaking to me because I hear them." There is no power of effacing such conviction by argument. You may get the patient to assent to any premises you please, he will not swerve from his conclusions. I once argued with a patient who believed he had been transformed into a bear; he was quite willing to admit that the idea of such a transformation was utterly at variance with all experience; but he always returned to his position that God being omnipotent there was no reason to doubt his power of transforming men into bears: what remained fixed in his mind was the image of himself under a bear's form.

The characteristic point in the hallucinations of the insane, that which distinguishes them from hallucinations equally vivid in the sane, is the coercion of the image in *suppressing comparison* and all control of experience. Belief always accompanies a vivid image, for a time; but in the sane this belief will not persist against rational control. If I see a stick partly under water, it is impossible for me not to have the same feeling which would be produced by a bent stick out of the water—if I see two plane images in the stereoscope, it is impossible not to have the feeling of seeing one solid object. But these beliefs are rapidly displaced by reference to experience. I know the stick is not bent, and that it will not appear bent when removed from the water. I know the seeming solid is not an object in relief, but two plane pictures. It is by similar focal adjustment of the mind that sane people know that their hallucinations are unreal. The images may have the vividness of real objects, but they have not the properties of real objects, they do not preserve consistent relations with other facts, they appear in contradiction to other beliefs. Thus if I see a black cat on the chair opposite, yet on my approaching the chair feel no soft object, and if my terrier on the hearthrug looking in the direction of the chair shows none of the well-known agitation which the sight of a cat produces, I conclude, in spite of its distinctness, that the image is an hallucination.

Returning from this digression, let me say that I am very far indeed from wishing to imply any agreement in the common notion that " great wits to madness nearly are allied ;" on the contrary, my studies have led to the 'conviction that nothing is less like genius than insanity, although some men of genius have had occasional attacks ; and further, that I have never observed any trace of the insane temperament in Dickens's works, or life, they being indeed singularly free even from the eccentricities which often accompany exceptional powers ; nevertheless, with all due limitations, it is true that there is considerable light shed upon his works by the action of the imagination in hallucination. To him also *revived* images have the vividness of sensations ; to him also *created* images have the coercive force of realities, excluding all control, all contradiction. What seems preposterous, impossible to us, seemed to him simple fact of observation. When he imagined a street, a house, a room, a figure, he saw it not in the vague schematic way of ordinary imagination, but in the sharp definition of actual perception, all the salient details obtruding themselves on his attention. He, seeing it thus vividly, made us also see it ; and believing in its reality however fantastic, he communicated something of his belief to us. He presented it in such relief that we ceased to think of it as a picture. So definite and insistent was the image, that even while knowing it was false we could not help, for a moment, being affected, as it were, by his hallucination.

This glorious energy of imagination is that which Dickens had in common with all great writers. It was this which made him a creator, and made his creations universally intelligible, no matter how fantastic and unreal. His types established themselves in the public mind like personal experiences. Their falsity was unnoticed in the blaze of their illumination. Every humbug seemed a Pecksniff, every nurse a Gamp, every jovial improvident a Micawber, every stinted serving-wench a Marchioness. Universal experiences became individualised in these types; an image and a name were given, and the image was so suggestive that it seemed to *express* all that it was found to *recall*, and Dickens was held to have depicted what his readers supplied. Against such power criticism was almost idle. In vain critical reflection showed these figures to be merely masks,—not characters, but personified characteristics, caricatures and distortions of human nature,—the vividness of their presentation triumphed over reflection: their creator managed to communicate to the public his own unhesitating belief. Unreal and impossible as these types were, speaking a language never heard in life, moving like pieces of simple mechanism always in one way (instead of moving with the infinite fluctuations of organisms, incalculable yet intelligible, surprising yet familiar), these unreal figures affected the uncritical reader with the force of reality; and they did so in virtue of their embodiment of some real characteristic vividly presented. The imagination of the author laid hold of some well-marked physical trait, some peculiarity of aspect, speech, or manner which every one recognised at once; and the force with which this was presented made it occupy the mind to the exclusion of all critical doubts : only reflection could detect the incongruity. Think of what this implies! Think how little the mass of men are given to reflect on their impressions, and how their minds are for the most part occupied with sensations rather than ideas, and you will see why Dickens held an undisputed sway. Give a child a wooden horse, with hair for mane and tail, and wafer-spots for colouring, he will never be disturbed by the fact that this horse does not move its legs, but runs on wheels— the general suggestion suffices for his belief; and this wooden horse, which he can handle and draw, is believed in more than a pictured horse by a Wouvermanns or an Ansdell. It may be said of Dickens's human figures that they too are wooden, and run on wheels; but these are details which scarcely disturb the belief of admirers. Just as the wooden horse is brought within the range of the child's emotions, and dramatizing tendencies, when he can handle and draw it, so Dickens's figures are brought within the range of the reader's interests, and receive from these interests a sudden illumination, when they are the puppets of a drama every incident of which appeals to the sympathies. With a fine felicity of instinct he seized upon situations having an irresistible hold over the domestic affections and ordinary sympathies. He spoke in the mother-tongue of the heart, and was always sure of ready listeners. He painted the life he knew, the life every one knew ; for if the scenes and manners were unlike those we were familiar with, the feelings and motives, the joys and griefs, the mistakes and efforts of the actors were universal, and therefore universally intelligible ; so that even critical spectators who complained that these broadly painted pictures were artistic daubs, could not wholly resist their effective suggestiveness. He set in motion the secret springs of sympathy by touching the domestic affections. He painted nothing ideal, heroic ; but all the resources of the bourgeois epic were in his grasp. The world of thought and passion lay beyond his horizon. But the joys and pains of childhood, the petty tyrannies of ignoble natures, the genial pleasantries of happy natures, the life of the poor, the struggles of the street and back parlour, the insolence of office, the sharp social contrasts, east-wind and Christmas jollity, hunger, misery, and hot punch—these he could deal with, so that we laughed and cried, were startled at the revelation of familiar facts hitherto unnoted, and felt our pulses quicken as we were hurried along with him in his fanciful flight.

Such were the sources of his power. To understand how it is that critics quite competent to recognise such power, and even so far amenable to it as to be moved and interested by the works in spite of all their drawbacks, should have forgotten this undenied power, and written or spoken of Dickens with mingled irritation and contempt, we must take into account two natural tendencies—the bias of opposition, and the bias of technical estimate.

The bias of opposition may be illustrated in a parallel case. Let us suppose a scientific book to be attracting the attention of Europe by the boldness, suggestiveness, and theoretic plausibility of its hypo-theses ; this work falls into the hands of a critic sufficiently grounded in the science treated to be aware that its writer, although gifted with great theoretic power and occasional insight into unexplored relations, is nevertheless pitiably ignorant of the elementary facts and principles of the science ; the critic noticing the power, and the talent of lucid exposition, is yet perplexed and irritated at ignorance which is inexcusable, and a reckless twisting of known facts into impossible relations, which seems wilful ; will he not pass from marvelling at this inextricable web of sense and nonsense, suggestive insight and mischievous error, so jumbled together that the combination of this sagacity with this glaring inefficiency is a paradox, and be driven by the anger of opposition into an emphatic assertion that the belauded philosopher is a charlatan and an igno-ramus ? A chorus of admirers proclaims the author to be a great teacher, before whom all contemporaries must bow ; and the critic observes this teacher on one page throwing out a striking hypothesis of some geometric relations in the planetary movements, and on another assuming that the hypothenuse is equal to its perpendicular and base, because the square of the hypothenuse is equal to the squares of its sides—in one chapter ridiculing the atomic theory, and in another arguing that carbonic acid is obtained from carbon and nitrogen—can this critic be expected to join in the chorus of admirers ? and will he not rather be exasperated into an opposition which will lead him to undervalue the undeniable qualities in his insistance on the undeniable defects ?

Something like this is the feeling produced by Dickens's works in many cultivated and critical readers. They see there human character and ordinary events pourtrayed with a mingled verisimilitude and falsity altogether unexampled. The drawing is so vivid yet so incorrect, or else is so blurred and formless, with such excess of *effort* (as of a showman beating on the drum) that the doubt arises how an observer so remarkably keen could make observations so remarkably false, and miss such very obvious facts ; how the rapid glance which could swoop down on a peculiarity with hawk-like precision, could overlook all that accompanied and was organically related to that peculiarity ; how the eye for characteristics could be so blind to character, and the ear for dramatic idiom be so deaf to dramatic language ; finally, how the writer's exquisite susceptibility to the grotesque could be insensible to the occasional grotesqueness of his own attitude. Michael Angelo is intelligible, and Giotto is intelligible ; but a critic is nonplussed at finding the invention of Angelo with the drawing of Giotto. It is indeed surprising that Dickens should have observed man, and not been impressed with the fact that man is, in the words of Montaigne, *un être ondoyant et diverse.* And the critic is distressed to observe the substitution of mechanisms for minds, puppets for characters. It is needless to dwell on such monstrous failures as Mantalini, Rosa Dartle, Lady Dedlock, Esther Summerson, Mr. Dick, Arthur Gride, Edith Dombey, Mr. Carker—needless, because if one studies the successful figures one finds even in them only touches of verisimilitude. When one thinks of Micawber always presenting himself in the same situation, moved with the same springs, and uttering the same sounds, always confident on something turning up, always crushed and rebounding, always making punch—and his wife always declaring she will never part from him, always referring to his talents and her family—when one thinks of the " catchwords " personified as characters, one is reminded of the frogs whose brains have been taken out for physiological purposes, and whose actions henceforth want the distinctive peculiarity of organic action, that of fluctuating spontaneity. Place one of these brainless frogs on his back and he will at once recover the sitting posture; draw a leg from under him, and he will draw it back again; tickle or prick him and he will push away the object, or take *one* hop out of the way; stroke his back, and he will utter *one* croak. All these things resemble the actions of the unmutilated frog, but they differ in being *isolated* actions, and *always the same :* they are as uniform and calculable as the movements of a machine. The uninjured frog may or may not croak, may or may not hop away; the result is never calculable, and is rarely a single croak or a single hop. It is this complexity of the organism which Dickens wholly fails to conceive; his characters have nothing fluctuating and incalculable in them, even when they embody true observations; and very often they are creations so fantastic that one is at a loss to understand how he could, without hallucination, believe them to be like reality. There are dialogues bearing the traces of straining effort at effect, which in their incongruity painfully resemble the absurd and eager expositions which insane patients pour into the listener's ear when detailing their wrongs, or their schemes. Dickens once declared to me that every word said by his characters was distinctly *heard* by him; I was at first not a little puzzled to account for the fact that he could hear language so utterly unlike the language of real feeling, and not be aware of its preposterousness; but the surprise vanished when I thought of the phenomena of hallucination. And here it may be needful to remark in passing that it is not because the characters are badly drawn and their language unreal, that they are to be classed among the excesses of imagination; otherwise all the bad novelists and dramatists would be credited with that which they especially want—powerful imagination. His peculiarity is not the incorrectness of the drawing, but the vividness of the imagination which while rendering that incorrectness insensible to him, also renders it potent with multitudes of his fellowmen. For although his weakness comes from excess in one direction, the force which is in excess must not be overlooked; and it is overlooked or undervalued by critics who, with what I have called the bias of opposition, insist only on the weakness.

This leads me to the second point, the bias of technical estimate. The main purpose of Art is delight. Whatever influences may radiate from that centre,—and however it may elevate or modify,— the one primary condition of influence is stirred emotion. No Art can teach which does not move; no Art can move without teaching. Criticism has to consider Art under two aspects, that of emotional pleasure, and that of technical pleasure. We all—public and critics —are susceptible of the former, are capable of being moved, and are delighted with what stirs the emotions, filling the mind with images having emotional influence; but only the critics are much affected by technical skill, and the pleasure it creates. *What* is done, what is suggested, constitutes the first aspect; *how* it is done the second. We all delight in imitation, and in the skill which represents one object in another medium; but the refinements of skill can only be appreciated by study. To a savage there is so little suggestion of a human face and form in a painted portrait that it is not even recognised as the representation of a man; whereas the same savage would delight in a waxwork figure, or a wooden Scotchman at the door of a tobacconist. The educated eye sees exquisite skill in the portrait, a skill which gives exquisite delight; but this eye which traces and estimates the subtle effects of colour and distribution of light and shade in the portrait, turns with disgust from the wax figure, or the wooden Highlander. In the course of time the pleasure derived from the perception of difficulty overcome, leads to such a preponderance of the technical estimate, that the sweep of the brush, or the composition of lines, becomes of supreme importance, and the connoisseur no longer asks, What is painted? but How is it painted? The *what* may be a patch of meadow, the bend of a river, or a street boy munching bread and cheese, and yet give greater delight by its *how*, than another picture which represented the Andes, Niagara, or a Madonna and Child. When the critic observes technical skill in a picture, he pronounces the painter to be admirable, and is quite unmoved by any great subject badly painted. In like manner a great poet is estimated by the greatness of his execution of great conceptions, not by the greatness of his intention.

How easily the critic falls into the mistake of overvaluing technical skill, and not allowing for the primary condition, how easily he misjudges works by applying to them technical rules derived from the works of others, need not here be dwelt on. What I wish to indicate is the bias of technical estimate which, acting with that bias of opposition just noted, has caused the critics to overlook in Dickens the great artistic powers which are proved by his immense success; and to dwell only on those great artistic deficiencies which exclude him from the class of exquisite writers. He worked in delf, not in porcelain. But his prodigal imagination created in delf forms which delighted thousands. He only touched common life, but he touched it to "fine issues;" and since we are all susceptible of being moved by pictures of children in droll and pathetic situations, and by pictures of common suffering and common joy, any writer who can paint such pictures with sufficient skill to awaken these emotions is powerful in proportion to the emotion stirred. That Dickens had this skill is undisputed; and if critical reflection shows that the means he employs are not such as will satisfy the technical estimate, and consequently that the pictures will not move the cultivated mind, nor give it the deep content which perfect Art continues to create, making the work a "joy for ever," we must still remember that in the present state of Literature, with hundreds daily exerting their utmost efforts to paint such pictures, it requires prodigious force and rare skill to impress images that will stir the universal heart. Murders are perpetrated without stint, but the murder of Nancy is unforgettable. Children figure in numberless plays and novels, but the deaths of little Nell and little Paul were national griefs. Seduction is one of the commonest of tragedies, but the scene in Peggoty's boat-house burns itself into the memory. Captain Cuttle and Richard Swiveller, the Marchioness and Tilly Slowboy, Pecksniff and Micawber, Tiny Tim and Mrs. Gamp, may be imperfect presentations of human character, but they are types which no one can forget. Dr. Johnson explained the popularity of some writer by saying, " Sir, *his* nonsense suited *their* nonsense ;" let us add, " and his sense suited their sense," and it will explain the popularity of Dickens. Readers to whom all the refinements of Art and Literature are as meaningless hieroglyphs, were at once laid hold of by the reproduction of their own feelings, their own experiences, their own prejudices, in the irradiating splendour of his imagination ; while readers whose cultivated sensibilities were alive to the most delicate and evanescent touches were, by virtue of their common nature, ready to be moved and delighted at his pictures and suggestions. The cultivated and uncultivated were affected by his admirable *mise en scène*, his fertile invention, his striking selection of incident, his intense vision of physical details. Only the cultivated who are made fastidious by cultivation paused to consider the pervading commonness of the works, and remarked that they are wholly without glimpses of a nobler life; and that the writer presents an almost unique example of a mind of singular force in which, so to speak, sensations never passed into ideas. Dickens sees and feels, but the logic of feeling seems the only logic he can manage. Thought is strangely absent from his works. I do not suppose a single thoughtful remark on life or character could be found throughout the twenty volumes. Not only is there a marked absence of the reflective tendency, but one sees no indication of the past life of humanity having ever occupied him; keenly as he observes the objects before him, he never connects his observations into a general expression, never seems interested in general relations of things. Compared with that of Fielding or Thackeray, his was merely an *animal* intelligence, *i.e.*, restricted to perceptions. On this ground his early education was more fruitful and less injurious than it would have been to a nature constructed on a more reflective and intellectual type. It furnished him with rare and valuable experience, early developed his sympathies with the lowly and struggling, and did not starve any intellectual ambition. He never was and never would have been a student.

My acquaintance with him began soon after the completion of

"Pickwick." Something I had written on that book pleased him, and caused him to ask me to call on him. (It is pleasant for me to remember that I made Thackeray's acquaintance in a similar way.) He was then living in Doughty Street; and those who remember him at that period will understand the somewhat disturbing effect produced on my enthusiasm for the new author by the sight of his bookshelves, on which were ranged nothing but three-volume novels and books of travel, all obviously the presentation copies from authors and publishers, with none of the treasures of the bookstall, each of which has its history, and all giving the collection its individual physiognomy. A man's library expresses much of his hidden life. I did not expect to find a bookworm, nor even a student, in the marvellous " Boz ; " but nevertheless this collection of books was a shock. He shortly came in, and his sunny presence quickly dispelled all misgivings. He was then, as to the last, a delightful companion, full of sagacity as well as animal spirits ; but I came away more impressed with the fulness of life and energy than with any sense of distinction. I believe I only saw him once more before I went to Germany, and two years had elapsed when next we met. While waiting in his library (in Devonshire Terrace) I of course glanced at the books. The well-known paper boards of the three-volume novel no longer vulgarised the place ; a goodly array of standard works, well-bound, showed a more respectable and conventional ambition ; but there was no physiognomy in the collection. A greater change was visible in Dickens himself. In these two years he had remarkably developed. His conversation turned on graver subjects than theatres and actors, periodicals and London life. His interest in public affairs, especially in social questions, was keener. He still remained completely outside philosophy, science, and the higher literature, and was too unaffected a man to pretend to feel any interest in them. But the vivacity and sagacity which gave a charm to intercourse with him had become weighted with a seriousness which from that time forward became more and more prominent in his conversation and his writings. He had already learned to look upon the world as a scene where it was the duty of each man in his own way to make the lot of the miserable Many a little less miserable ; and, having learned that his genius gave him great power, he was bent on using that power effectively. He was sometimes laughed at for the importance he seemed to attach to everything relating to himself, and the solemnity with which he spoke of his aims and affairs ; but this belonged to his quality. *Il se prenait au sérieux*, and was admirable because he did so. Whatever faults he may have committed there were none attributable to carelessness. He gave us his best. If the effort were sometimes too strained, and the desire for effect too obtrusive, there was no lazy indulgence, no trading on a great renown, no " scumbling " in his work. " What-

ever I have tried to do in life," he said, speaking through Copperfield, " I have tried with all my heart to do well. Never to put one
hand to anything on which I could throw my whole self, and never
to affect depreciation of my work, whatever it was, I now find to
have been my golden rules."

Since I have been led in the course of argument to touch upon
my personal acquaintance with Dickens, I may take advantage of
the opening to introduce a point not mentioned in Mr. Forster's
memoir, though he most probably is familiar with it. Mr. Forster
has narrated Dickens's intense grief at the death of his sister-in-law,
Mary—a grief which for two months interrupted the writing of
" Pickwick," and which five years afterwards thus moves him in a
letter to Mr. Forster on the death of her grandmother. The
passage itself is in every way interesting, displaying a depth and
delicacy of feeling, combined with a tenderness towards the sacredness due to the wishes of the dead, which is very noticeable :—

" It is a great trial to me to give up Mary's grave; greater than I can
possibly express. I thought of moving her to the catacomb, and saying
nothing about it; but then I remembered that the poor old lady is buried next
her at her own desire, and could not find it in my heart directly she is laid in
the earth to take her grandchild away. The desire to be buried next her is as
strong upon me now as it was five years ago; and I *know* (for I don't think
there ever was love like that I bear her) that it will never diminish. I cannot
bear the thought of being excluded from her dust; and yet I feel that her
brothers and sisters and her mother have a better right than I to be placed
beside her. It is but an idea. I neither hope nor think (God forbid) that
our spirits would ever mingle *there.* I ought to get the better of it, but it is
very hard. I never contemplated this; and coming so suddenly, and after
being ill, it disturbs me more than it ought. It seems like losing her a second
time."

Again, when writing from America and describing his delight at
the Niagara Falls, he says :—

" What would I give if you and Mac were here to share the sensations of
this time! I was going to add, what would I give if the dear girl whose
ashes lie in Kensal Green had lived to come so far along with us; but she has
been here many times, I doubt not, since her sweet face faded from my earthly
sight."

Several years afterwards, in the course of a quiet chat over a cigar,
we got on a subject which always interested him, and on which he
had stored many striking anecdotes—dreams. He then narrated,
in his quietest and most impressive manner, that after Mary's death
her image not only haunted him by day, but for twelve months
visited his dreams every night. At first he had refrained from
mentioning it to his wife; and after deferring this some time, felt
unable to mention it to her. He had occasion to go to Liverpool,
and as he went to bed that night, there was a strong hope that the
change of bed might break the spell of his dreams. It was not so
however. That night as usual the old dream was dreamt. He
resolved to unburthen his mind to his wife, and wrote that very

morning a full account of his strange experience. From that time he ceased to dream of her. I forget whether he said he had never dreamt of her since; but I am certain of the fact that the spell had been broken then and there.

Here is another contribution to the subject of dreams, which I had from him shortly before his death. One night after one of his public readings, he dreamt that he was in a room where every one was dressed in scarlet. (The probable origin of this was the mass of scarlet opera-cloaks worn by the ladies among the audience, having left a sort of *afterglow* on his retina.) He stumbled against a lady standing with her back towards him. As he apologised she turned her head and said, quite unprovoked, "My name is Napier." The face was one perfectly unknown to him, nor did he know any one named Napier. Two days after he had another reading in the same town, and before it began, a lady friend came into the waiting-room accompanied by an unknown lady in a scarlet opera cloak, "who," said his friend, "is very desirous of being introduced." "Not Miss Napier?" he jokingly inquired. "Yes; Miss Napier." Although the face of his dream-lady was not the face of this Miss Napier, the coincidence of the scarlet cloak and the name was striking.

In bringing these detached observations to a close, let me resume their drift by saying that while on the one hand the critics seem to me to have been fully justified in denying him the possession of many technical excellencies, they have been thrown into unwise antagonism which has made them overlook or undervalue the great qualities which distinguished him; and that even on technical grounds their criticism has been so far defective that it failed to recognise the supreme powers which ensured his triumph in spite of all defects. For the reader of cultivated taste there is little in his works beyond the stirring of their emotions—but what a large exception! We do not turn over the pages in search of thought, delicate psychological observation, grace of style, charm of composition; but we enjoy them like children at a play, laughing and crying at the images which pass before us. And this illustration suggests the explanation of how learned and thoughtful men can have been almost as much delighted with the works as ignorant and juvenile readers; how Lord Jeffrey could have been so affected by the presentation of Little Nell, which most critical readers pronounce maudlin and unreal. Persons unfamiliar with theatrical representations, consequently unable to criticise the acting, are stirred by the suggestions of the scenes presented; and hence a great philosopher, poet, or man of science, may be found applauding an actor whom every play-going apprentice despises as stagey and inartistic.

GEORGE HENRY LEWES.

Leslie Stephen

"The Late Lord Lytton
as a Novelist"

Cornhill Magazine 27 (March 1873), 345–54

The late Lord Lytton as a Novelist.

THE eulogies which are very rightly pronounced over the graves of distinguished men have this inconvenience—that they are apt to make an impartial estimate of the dead sound like a protest. To speak generously and tenderly of those whom we have recently lost is only becoming; and it follows that we should touch lightly upon their faults, and linger with some emphasis upon their merits; but it does not follow that we should invent imaginary merits. If there were no other reason, it would be sufficient to say that such overcharged panegyric is in fact the bitterest of satires. Can you not praise the dead man sufficiently, unless you tell lies about him? Do you not then implicitly assert that the plain truth is not complimentary? Some illustrations of these obvious remarks—more pertinent than that which we are about to produce—might be drawn, were it desirable, from some recent events. They have, however, been immediately suggested by the case of Lord Lytton. Of the many articles devoted to his memory, some were judicious, and some generous, and some at once generous and judicious; but many were in that modern style of highly-spiced writing which has added a new terror to death. A poor human creature cannot now retire to his grave, humbly hoping that he has done rather more good than harm in the world —a frame of mind which is surely confident enough for most, even of those whom we call eminent men—without a discharge of fulsome rhetoric, which would have disgusted him in his lifetime, and sounds terribly hollow in the solemn presence of death. The memory of Lord Lytton was honoured or insulted by some estimates of his literary eminence, limited only by the writer's command of epithets. Yet, as a poet, he was not equal to Milton; nor as an orator, to Burke; nor as a dramatist, to Sheridan; nor as an essayist, to Addison. Such parallels are foolish; and, in fact, we need not hesitate to admit at once that Lord Lytton's real claims to posthumous reputation must rest upon his novels. A most versatile, laborious, and cultivated intellect enabled him to play his part very creditably, and with a certain air of scholar-like polish, in many capacities for which he had no special aptitude. His poetry, for example, is not of the inspired, but of the skilfully manufactured variety; his facility in versemaking was a graceful accomplishment, not a heaven-born instinct—and a critic, whilst receiving such poetry with all due courtesy, should not do it the complimentary injustice of comparing it to really great works of art.

Let us attempt, then, to make a fair estimate of the value of his novels. That they deserve to stand far above the great mass of fictitious literature of the day, needs no demonstration. Lord Lytton deserved—as every critic has admitted—one praise which has a value in proportion to its rarity. He was a thoroughly good workman. Whatever faults may be imputed to him, are not the faults of a man who despises his art, or is slovenly in his execution. He resisted, that is, temptations which have been not a little injurious to some greater writers and have ruined many smaller ones. The temptation to turn popularity to account by writing as much as possible, and to win it on the easiest terms, by writing down to the level of an audience which only asks for amusement, has been too often found irresistible. Lord Lytton, during a career of some forty-five years, never sought for easy successes whilst relaxing his exertions. And, doubtless it is for this reason that he is one of the few men who have written so much, without writing themselves out. The success with which he opened an entirely new vein in *The Caxtons*, at an age when the style of most men has long been definitely fixed; and the success which he so recently gained in the *Coming Race*, whilst declining to use the prestige of his name, are remarkable proofs of his continued vigour. Beyond all cavil, he was a man of remarkable powers; and, indeed, to deny him praise of a very high kind, would be to run in the teeth of that general verdict of public opinion which, if not infallible, possesses an authority superior to that of any individual. But a further question still remains open. Great success may be won, and deservedly won, by writers who are essentially in the second rank. There are two races of men—the mortals and the immortals. Swift's *Strulbrugs* bore upon them from their birth the signs of the awful destiny which divided them from their kind; but that is by no means the case with the heirs of literary immortality. Their prerogative often fails to make itself recognised until it is actually asserted. Not till we see that their vitality persists, whilst others, who once seemed to be their equals, are dropping off around them, do we recognise their surpassing value. Gradually it turns out that the work of some few men in a century has something about it which defies corruption. Perhaps it may be some trifling fragment of prose or poetry, which lives upon men's lips, when other works, to all appearance of equal merit, have sunk into eternal silence; and even whilst we admit the fact, we are unable to analyse the cause, of its survival. Only when we find such a fragment, we know that another immortal has been amongst us, not recognised, and it may be, taken for a fool in his lifetime. To discover the indefinable essence which constitutes genius, before it has revealed itself to the world at large, should be the highest triumph of criticism; but such discoveries are generally made by the multitudinous judgment of public opinion before the professional critic has awaked to them. Whether the possession of genius, even in an imperfect form, places a man at once in a class above his fellows—whether, for example, the author of a song which lives for centuries should be by that fact alone ranked above the writer of an epic which secures the applause of a generation, and then sinks into darkness, is a question probably insoluble, and certainly not to be solved here. Would one rather have written Southey's respectable, but unmistakably mortal poems, or the stanzas on the burial of Sir John Moore, which alone preserve the memory of their author? Perhaps an ingenious person might suggest some reasons on behalf of the wider, though less enduring reputation. It is, however, plain that to entitle any man to be placed in the first class of writers, even into the lowest rank of that class, he must come of the strain of the immortals. Even to admit that such a question is an open one, in regard to almost any author, is to pay him a high compliment; and we venture to ask it in regard to Lord Lytton. Was he in any true sense a man of genius, or only a man of very great talent? Is he one of the originators, or only one of the transmitters of the great contemporary impulses—a creative artist, or a skilful manipulator of the materials given by others?

Some memories would lead one to answer in favour of the loftier claim. There is a certain force and freshness about some of his writings, *Pelham* for instance, which has a close resemblance to genius. There is one at least of his novels upon which we are unable to express a distinct opinion, for a reason which will probably be appreciated by many readers. It happens that his *Last Days of Pompeii* is sanctified for us by school-day associations. Glaucus exposed to the lions stands in our memory beside Charles O'Malley in his Peninsular adventures, and Ivanhoe in the castle of Frontdebœuf and Robinson Crusoe discovering the footprint in the sand. We can no more reason about the merits of the story than we can seriously entertain the question whether the captain of the boats in those days was the biggest, strongest, and most active of men since the days of Achilles. Its excellence is with us an article of faith, not of reason. And we therefore decline, even in the discharge of a critical duty, ever again to consult its pages. The eruption of Vesuvius may have been very sublime, and the fights in the circus very spirited, and the Egyptian magician very imposing; but it is impossible that they should ever again be so imposing and so spirited as they appeared to us at the time. There is a kind of irreverence in returning in the colder spirit of mature life to the haunts of one's boyhood, to discover that our mountains have shrunk to hills and our palaces to commonplace houses. We should preserve soundly those early illusions which, once dispelled, can never be restored. Why should an elderly person ever return to a pantomime to discover that the actresses are painted women instead of *bona fide* fairies? Let there be still a sanctuary to which we can retire by the help of memory, where the toys of childhood retain the ancient glow of the imagination and are not pulled to pieces by the colder reasoning faculty. As to the enduring value of the great bulk, however, of Lord Lytton's novels we can judge more dispassionately. Most of them belong to that class of literature which presupposes a certain amount of experience in the writer. They are, even ostentatiously, the productions of a man of the world, who has taken his part in serious business and is familiar with all the wheels of the great machinery of life. The peculiarity, indeed, is only too prominent. The most palpable defect of his novels is their extreme self-consciousness. The writer is evidently determined that we shall not overlook his claims to be a teacher of mankind. He is always philosophising in good set terms, which is a very different thing from writing philosophically. His moral is not embodied in his work, but exhibited with all the emphasis of sententious aphorisms. He aims at the Ideal, and very rightly, but the Ideal and the True and the Beautiful need not always be presenting themselves with the pomp of capital letters. And though we honour him for not despising his art, we should be glad if he could occasionally forget his art in his instincts. As it is, we are always asking whether he is not rather artificial than truly artistic. Extreme cleverness is the word which suggests itself much oftener than genius; we exclaim how ingenious! rather than how true! and are more impressed by the judicious balancing of his scenes than by their genuine beauty. In short, Lord Lytton is wanting in that spontaneity and vigour which is the surest mark of genius. We do not meet, in his pages, with those sudden electric flashes which thrill us as we study the really great men; and we have an uncomfortable sensation that there is something stagey and unreal about the whole performance.

In some of his earlier novels, these faults are the most painfully conspicuous. The thoroughness of his work shows itself in the careful construction of his plots; but that very carefulness is indicative of a certain weakness. Far be it from us to say that a plot should not be well put together! Undoubtedly that is one of the demands which a reader is fairly entitled to make of his author; for it contributes infinitely to the satisfaction of reading a story. But ingenuity in constructing complicated series of events, fitting into each other as neatly as the parts of a Chinese puzzle, is a very dangerous talent. Lord Lytton did not sink to the level of merely appealing to his reader's curiosity, and making a novel a conundrum to be guessed at the last page, and then to lose all interest. He always has some central idea to present, and the story is designed to illustrate some moral or psychological or artistic theory. And yet, the mechanical perfection of his devices is apt to interfere with their higher meaning. Let us take for example, though it is not a favourable specimen of his style, the novel of *Eugene Aram*. He speaks with considerable complacency of the merits of his story. None of his books, he says, have been so much attacked, and none so completely triumphed over attack. The attacks, indeed, were chiefly directed against its morality; and we may fully admit that no homicidal mania was produced, or was likely to be produced, by the history of this remarkable murder. But the merits which he claims of excellence in style and in construction are more doubtful. The problem to be considered was worthy of his powers. Eugene Aram, as at once an inoffensive student, a man of singular kindness to animals, and a murderer, is certainly an interesting subject for speculation. The subject might be treated artistically in various ways. As a study of character, or of the tendencies of certain social or religious theories, or of the terrible passions which preceded and followed the crime, there is abundant room for a pathetic or speculative writer. A very similar subject has been treated in the singularly impressive novel of *Caleb Williams*, to which Lord Lytton refers. In spite of some obvious faults, *Caleb Williams* has the distinct mark of genius; and the difference in the mode of treatment is characteristic. Godwin's hero, Falkland, like Eugene Aram, has committed a murder, although a man of highly cultivated mind and an excessively delicate sense of honour. Caleb Williams, being a dependent of Falkland's, discovers his patron's crime; and Falkland persecutes the possessor of the secret, succeeds in fixing a false imputation of theft upon him, and then makes his life a burden to him; Falkland at last breaks down under the tortures of his own conscience, and dies after confessing his guilt. Godwin's purpose was, of course, to illustrate his own eccentric social theories; but the picture which he draws is interesting for its own sake. The proud man, conscious of hideous guilt—for he has allowed two other men to be hanged in his place, and yet resolved to wade through any amount of crime rather than part with his honour—is opposed to the miserable victim of his tyranny, innocent of any crime and yet shunned by all honest men, and entangled in a net woven with diabolical ingenuity. Those two figures, with a few subsidiary actors, are constantly before us, and though the plot is awkward and even absurd in details, the force of the conception is unmistakable. Lord Lytton's mode of dealing with Aram is curiously different. We can see how the story was put together. Aram must fall in love with a beautiful young lady, to make his fate more disagreeable. The young lady is contrasted with a sister, after the conventional fashion of Minna and Brenda or the inevitable pair of young women in *Femme Cooper;* and is provided with an admirer to act as rival and counterpoise to Aram. Having got thus far, the plot is worked with infinite dexterity. Aram's rival is also, as it ultimately turns out, the son of the man whom Aram murdered. And thus, in hunting up the traces of his father's death, he is at the same time unmasking the villain who has supplanted him with his mistress. Nothing can be more ingenious than the gradual development of events; Aram is kept judiciously balancing between the altar and the gallows; the mystery is unveiled by carefully measured degrees; we change imperceptibly from curiosity as to the lonely scholar to dark suspicions of his character, and finally to conviction of his guilt. All the persons concerned come together in the most natural way for an affecting tableau at the conclusion; and there is abundant opportunity for heartrending displays of sentiment.

Lord Lytton's complacency is entirely justified; for no French dramatist could have worked out the problem more neatly; and the contrast with Godwin's clumsy devices for convicting Falkland and torturing his victim is triumphant. And yet *Eugene Aram* has become barely readable by anyone who seeks for more than clever manipulation of complicated threads of intrigue. The reason is simple. In the first place, all this ingenious byeplay distracts our attention from the murderer. A number of irrelevant characters have to be introduced ; such as a comic servant, of the Andrew Fairservice variety, but as wooden as that excellent Scotchman is full of life ; a conventional crone who rejoices in funerals ; and two or three elderly gentlemen, who are butts for rather commonplace satire. The humour is, of course, poor ; but the worst is, that so much pains is bestowed on showing how the murder was found out that our attention is distracted from the murder itself. All the rules of art have been observed ; the light and shade is most carefully distributed, and the composition elaborately balanced ; and when it is done, the central figure has become merely one in a crowd instead of absorbing our whole attention. For, besides this, poor Eugene Aram himself is one of Lord Lytton's most palpable failures. Our wonder is, not that such a good man should have had the heart but that such a prig should have had the courage to commit a murder. The extraordinary delight with which he pours out his pinchbeck philosophy upon his father-in-law, and his mistress, and his accomplice, may be venial in a man who has long led a solitary life ; but one cannot be seriously annoyed at his execution. Hanging is too good for a man who could address the lady to whom he has just become engaged after this fashion : " Oh, Madeline ! methinks there is nothing under heaven like the feeling which puts us apart from all that agitates and fevers and degrades the herd of men : which grants us to control the tenor of our future life, because it annihilates our dependence upon others ; and while the rest of earth are hurried on, blind, and unconscious, by the hand of fate, leaves us the sole lords of our destiny ; and able, from the past, which we have governed, to become the prophets of our future ! " If society were arranged on ideal principles, a human being capable of such a monstrosity would be sentenced to solitary confinement for life. The character of Eugene Aram corresponds to a favourite type of Lord Lytton's. In almost all his novels there are one or more gentlemen with a morbid propensity for apostrophising the heavenly bodies, and talking sham philosophy about the true and the beautiful. Often, however, they are subsidiary personages, and are something more than mere talking machines. The misfortune is that in *Eugene Aram*, the central figure— the character whose passions and sufferings should be the moving power of the story—is a mere windbag, and a windbag of the most pretentious kind. The problem is, given a man of intellect and amiable temper, to account for his committing a murder. Lord Lytton's answer would suggest, not that he was driven to desperation by poverty or jealousy or sense of unrequited merit, but that his mind had run to seed owing to an unfortunate habit of talking twaddle, till he had lost all sense of reality and fancied that a few fine words would convert a murder into a noble action. And yet the creator of this mere wooden dummy in philosophical robes takes him for a living human being.

In *Eugene Aram* we see proofs of remarkable technical skill ; but we also see the very weakest side of his art. No writer could afford to be judged by his failures, and we turn gladly to a story which, to many readers, appears to be his best. *The Caxtons* is, beyond all doubt, an admirable novel. Whatever its defects, it carries one along with it. The characters are skilfully contrived, if not vividly conceived; they harmonise with the scenery; and, except an irrelevant pamphlet on colonization intruded in the disguise of fiction, the whole story is worked out with great force and abundant dexterity. If not a work of real genius, it resembles a work of genius so closely that only a rigid examination will detect the difference. To decide whether it belongs to one or the other category, we may examine the principles on which it was constructed. Lord Lytton had resolved to strike out a new line. The interest of his story was to turn upon domestic life, and an element of the humorous was to be introduced. There is something curiously characteristic in this preconceived determination to appeal to new motives of interest. In nine cases out of ten such a purpose would be fatal to an author's success, because it would imply a total absence of that spontaneity to which all genuine art owes its charm. Lord Lytton, however, succeeded beyond expectation, though his success had very definite limits. To write a domestic novel was comparatively easy; but how could any man, and especially a man of forty-five, with no previous success of the kind to give him confidence, say, I will be humorous? Humour is the last quality to be acquired of *malice prepense* or at a time of life when the animal spirits have grown weak. Lord Lytton, however, set about his task systematically. He went to one of the best masters in that department of literature, and engaged at one blow a whole dramatic company. Sterne's Tristram Shandy became Pisistratus Caxton: the pedantic father and the chivalrous uncle appeared with little change as the two elder Caxtons; and the wife, the doctor, and the corporal, accepted their old parts. There could be, of course, no plagiarism in adopting children whose paternity was so notorious; and, although the first idea is palpably taken from Sterne, the subsequent development of character is characteristically different. The Shandy family have changed in the course of their transmigration. They have become far more decent and perhaps more coherent; but to say the truth, they have pretty well lost their humour. The essence of humorous writing of any high order is the power of thoroughly fusing into a harmonious whole the ludicrous and the pathetic elements of character. Sterne, with all his faults—and they are many—has effectually performed that feat. The foibles of the Shandies are absolutely inseparable from their virtues; you cannot think of the one without the other. But the foibles of the Caxtons appear only in the first chapter. Caxton *père* begins as a pedant, so absorbed in his books as to forget that a child is being born in his house; and when the child has forced itself upon his attention, he evolves the ingenious theory of the influence of names upon character which was his characteristic opinion in his previous avatar. But Mr. Caxton, unlike Mr. Shandy, forgets his foibles after he has once introduced himself to the reader, and becomes a respectable old scholar, with a full share of that worldly wisdom which is so predominant in all Lord Lytton's heroes. In the same way Roland Caxton begins with a set of crotchets worthy of uncle Toby ; but he develops almost at once into the old Peninsular officer, with a rather Quixotic sense of honour, but still able to pass muster in good society without any taint of decided eccentricity. In fact, it must be said that both of these excellent old men, though amiable and excellent in their way, descend with great alacrity into the regions of commonplace. The purely humorous element, if it does not exactly disappear, is so softened as to be scarcely perceptible, and adds at most a slight provincial flavour like the faint suspicion of a Scotch accent in the mouth of a pretty woman. They are still most serviceable characters in a novel ; we like and even admire them ; but the change which has passed over them is not the less a change destructive of their perfect originality. The difference may be expressed in scientific language by saying that the combination of the odd and the loveable is with Sterne a stable combination, whereas with Lord Lytton it is unstable in the highest degree. The intensity of the truly imaginative writer forms a new and delightful compound ; where the skilful literary artist is able at most to give a slight tinge of oddity to his performers, but not to make it an essential element in their character. Mr. Caxton, in fact, and Uncle Roland, very soon begin to use the same dialect which we have noticed in the case of the distinguished Eugene Aram. It is materially altered and improved. Mr. Caxton's declamations are ornamented by classical quotations instead of references to abstract qualities. We have quotations from Horace or Strabo instead of platitudes about the True and the Beautiful. The doctrine has been skilfully adapted to the tastes of the British public. Nothing flatters that respectable body so much as to hear a man of the world testifying that, after familiarity with the most refined cookery at the Clubs and the tables of the aristocracy, he has come to the conclusion that nothing is so good as plain bread and butter. Such teaching satisfies the two strongest impulses of our nature, the snobbish and the self-satisfied—the tendency to worship our nobility and to worship ourselves. Lord Lytton was a profound believer in the existence of what is called knowledge of the world, or knowledge of human nature. He held that there was a body of sound maxims familiar to men who combine literary and philosophical tastes with an intimate acquaintance with the worlds of literature and politics. We by no means deny that such persons acquire a shrewd practical instinct which has its value, and the lessons of which may be judiciously compressed into pithy aphorisms. We are inclined, indeed, to doubt whether they are really much wiser than their neighbours ; but it was at least natural that Lord Lytton should believe in the surpassing value of a body of doctrine which he was admirably qualified, both by temperament and by circumstances, for acquiring. And when he gives us frankly and unaffectedly the results of his observations, he utters much shrewd sense of which we should be very sorry to underrate the value. Unluckily, it is seldom that he is quite unaffected. His characters are generally too self-conscious, and are apt to think that a very obvious platitude can be made philosophical by giving it a sententious turn, and sprinkling it with a few adjectives beginning with capital letters. To this tendency we owe those portentous statesmen, who appear in *The Caxtons* and *My Novel*, and who are intended to represent the essence of worldly wisdom. To people who are not quite imposed upon by their dogmatic airs, they appear more frequently to be the very incarnation of red tape. We cannot conceive two greater bores than Mr. Trevanion and Audley Egerton. They might be taken as model specimens of Mr. Carlyle's " miserable creatures having-the-honour-to-be." We altogether decline to fall down and worship them, as their creator expects us to do. They may be strangely familiar with bluebooks, full of parliamentary experience, and crammed with " knowledge of human nature; " but to us they are intolerable prigs, and remain so to the end of the chapter. A characteristic peculiarity of a prig is a profound belief in the omnipotence of good advice ; and this is one of the most marked peculiarities of Lord Lytton's great men. We all remember, for example, the lecture delivered by Parson Dale and Riccabocca to Leonard Fairfield, on the aphorism " Knowledge is power," attributed to Bacon. It is not a bad sermon, but it is terribly commonplace ; and, at the end of it, we are just as much convinced as before that knowledge, after all, is power ; though it is quite true, as those worthy gentlemen take infinite pains to prove, that other things are also power, and that knowledge by itself is not everything. Nobody ever asserted that it was. But few things are more characteristic of would-be originality than delight in pulling to pieces an aphorism —as if it was not the essence of aphorism to be a partial truth. One of the most characteristic passages in *The Caxtons*, is that where the amiable old pedant converts the youthful scapegrace by a little good advice, by telling him stories of his virtuous cousin. The same excellent adviser—whose advice on paper is so admirable—converts a young infidel by making him read Tucker's *Light of Nature*, some scraps of Scotch metaphysics, and a little German transcendentalism. It is all very well ; but is it not marvellously unreal ? Are scapegraces and infidels converted on such easy terms in real life ? Are they not much more likely to be bored than edified by the infliction of a few commonplaces by an elderly gentleman given to preach sermons composed of pedantic quotations and secondhand metaphysics ? We might wish, perhaps, that the real world were more like the world of fiction ; and that vice and rash speculation could be eradicated so summarily by a few sententious aphorisms. Unluckily it is not so ; and to represent things as carried on in this fashion is to show a want of that penetrative imagination which goes down to the roots of character, and appreciates at their true value the forces of human passions.

This element of portentous platitude—we know not what else to call it—very much interferes with our enjoyment of the Caxtons. A little genuine vigour of mind would dissipate this atmosphere of sham philosophy. Old Mr. Caxton, in fact, is a bore ; and his brother—though there is much that is affecting about him—is a sentimentalist ; and young Caxton is a prig ; and Mr. Trevanion is unconscionably fond of red tape. A writer with a firmer grasp of real life, that is to say, of more imaginative intensity, would have detected this feeble side of his character, and would have made him more interesting because presenting him with less parade of profound wisdom. And yet, in spite of these obvious defects, we repeat that *The Caxtons* is an admirable novel. It is a book which we can read for a second and even for a third time with increased pleasure. There is abundant vigour about it; though not many symptoms of high imaginative power. And, in short, it is as clever as a book can be of which we nevertheless come to be perfectly clear that cleverness is the highest epithet that can be fairly applied to it. Compared with the ordinary run of novels, it is to be placed in a class by itself; compared with the few novels of which we can say that they bear unmistakable marks of genius, it is as distinctly in the second rank. There is not in it one really living and moving character; but there are a large number of characters, who live and move as much as most of the persons who pass themselves off for real human beings in the course of our daily lives.

We have spoken at much length of one of Lord Lytton's worst and of one of his best performances. If we were to examine his others, the historical novels, such as *Rienzi, The Last of the Barons,* and *Harold;* or of the sentimental novels, such as *Ernest Maltravers;* or of the wilder romances, such as *Zanoni* and *A Strange Story,* we should exceed our limits, and perhaps we should not find any material additions to our means of forming an opinion of his merits. It would be instructive, indeed, to compare such a novel as *Zanoni* with the writings of a man of genuine genius such as Hawthorne. We should see how the man of second-rate ability takes refuge in a mere accumulation of wonder, where the more imaginative artist is able to cause a deeper thrill by a far slighter tinge of the mysterious. But we do not wish to attempt anything like an exhaustive account of Lord Lytton's versatile performances. The same characteristics, in fact, meet us everywhere. So far as industrious labour can take a man of great ability and of studiously cultivated literary skill, Lord Lytton is an admirable model. Nobody could combine his materials more judiciously, or turn to better account the results of much laborious thought guided by excellent taste. But we always feel the want of that vivifying power which is possessed in its perfection only by a few men in the course of ages, and in an inferior degree by a large number of writers whose works show greater faults but are also by fits more impressive than any of Lord Lytton's. He can put together all the elements of a story or a character according to the most approved rules of art; he can discourse to us with abundant felicity and fertility of illustration upon philosophy and morality; but then he cannot send through his creations that electric current which makes them start into reality, or give to his reflections that force which can be drawn only from the deepest emotions of a powerful nature. He is not a creator of new types, but is so ingenious in restoring the old that to a careless observer they are almost as good as the originals. And, therefore, whilst we willingly concede to him a very high place amongst the mortals, we cannot admit his claims to a loftier place.

Robert Laing

"Middlemarch,
a Study of Provincial Life"

Quarterly Review 134 (April 1873), 336–69

ART. II.—*Middlemarch, a Study of Provincial Life.* By George Eliot. 4 vols. Edinburgh and London. 1872.

WHEN the history of literature during the times in which we live comes to be written, it will perhaps contain a chapter on the English Positivists. It is not necessary to suppose that such a chapter will be a very long one or have more to do than to describe the passing attitude of a small number of persons of talent. But it is sufficiently probable that English Positivism will require literary notice; and, in our opinion, it will even be found to have possessed a rhetorical grace and a brilliant air, which are lacking in French Positivism, from which it is, after all, an offshoot. The figures in this movement are a little academic band of men. The leader, in youth a master at Rugby in the best days of the famous school, then, as a college tutor, collected about him a few disciples to a new creed from the very centres of Oxford Evangelicalism; finally he turned to London and its suburbs, on week-days labouring as a physician among the poor, on the seventh day addressing a tiny congregation, at which it was noticed by a chance visitor that (sad augury for the permanence of the work) among the audience but one child was to be seen. Round this leader have to be grouped some fifteen or twenty personal friends, chiefly University men, many of them of the same University generation, London barristers, London professors, London doctors, sharply and fiercely criticizing English political and religious life from the point of view of a narrow Continental philosophical sect, founded by Auguste Comte, a strangely isolated Parisian student, who, after the collapse of the French Revolution and the First Empire, strove once again to contrive a complete system of human faith, morals, government, and discipline. The most remarkable characteristics of these writers—so free from prejudice, from scruple, from embarrassment, as, at first glance, they appear to think and write—are, on closer examination, seen to be their intensely and exclusively French sentiment, the thoroughness with which they have acclimatised and assimilated a French doctrine and a French style, their corresponding ignorance of and contempt for Teutonic literature and German ideas, and their desire to discard the historical traditions and to overthrow the existing framework of English society.

But the writer, for whose sake the little circle will hereafter arrest attention, will, it may without hazard be predicted, be the novelist and poetess known under the name of George Eliot. It might, we hold, be questioned, whether with any sweeping meaning, and especially in regard to final social and religious maxims, George Eliot should be numbered with the followers of Comte in this country, and yet the signs are everywhere and unmistakable in her method and tone of a very close intellectual relationship to them. There are, however, two particulars, in which certainly she stands in strong contrast to their school. So far as width of training, of sympathy, of insight, is concerned, George Eliot has none of its faults ; she has a full and broad knowledge, not merely of modern French, but of general European culture, and she is entirely English in spirit and speech. One has, indeed, only to consider her in relation to the great contemporary French novelist, whose example may have suggested to her the adoption in literature of a masculine title, one has only to compare George Eliot with Georges Sand, in order to appreciate the distance which still extends between French and English rules and results in thought and composition.

The continued theoretical revolt, the profound political despair of French society, tinges, through and through, the language and the scenery of French imaginative literature. And these features of the national literature belong, in eminent distinction, to the writings (we are thinking mainly of her earlier and more permanently important works) of Georges Sand. Her heroes and heroines are rebels; they combat with or detach themselves violently from the regulated life around them; they break down the various barriers which may interpose between themselves and the objects of their desires and ambitions; they feel themselves (and their creator means them to be felt) to be embodiments of central ideas and omnipotent passions, which must and shall prevail; the rocks and walls, against which they shatter themselves, cannot stand for long, but are the last grotesque relics of a departed age.

It was only for a short time that this inspiration, born of the French Revolution, seemed to become that of English literature. Byron and Shelley are its representatives among us—Byron so thoroughly, that, not only in English but in European literature, he stands acknowledged its chief and most eloquent mouthpiece. And if, in our own times, the sentiment of Continental revolutions has shown itself again in the verses of a few of our younger writers, this sentiment has hitherto not been able at their hands to take an English dress, and the poems, in which it wraps itself, challenge inquiry and discussion rather as exotic curiosities than as native products of the English mind. For even in Byron's day the measured and placid stateliness of English poetic genius soon reasserted itself. Wordsworth, in his love of Nature and her simplicity, and his belief in the simplicity of Art, owed much, as we know from the story of his life, to the French Revolution; but he owed more to the English skies and the English lakes—to the contented solitude and steady survey of a quiet rural life, in which, like so many of our great poets, he found the retreat most congenial to his Muse.

What a close connection there is between history and literature! How often has our literature returned upon our history, gathered from the traditions of the past new strength and hope! At a time, when the world rings with the strife and sorrows of overgrown and distracted cities; when the most insoluble political problems perplex civilisation; when the Latin and Teutonic races stand, almost as one man, under arms; when at Rome Pope and King are face to face in implacable antagonism, at Paris the palaces and the names of royalty and imperialism are defaced and dishonoured, at Cologne there is a new Catholic church, at Berlin a new German empire; and while England, too, tingles and quivers, in her degree, under the shocks which convulse the Continent—it is not a little noteworthy how a writer like George Eliot, with all her refinement and enlightenment and large range of outlook, true to the genius of our history, seeks employment and instruction in minute and tranquil studies of a past stage of English life, marks once more for us islanders the continuity and gradual evolution of our national spiritual and social character. She stands thus, with regard to the second half of the nineteenth century, in the position which Walter Scott occupies in relation to the first half. 'The age of Chivalry,' Burke had cried, 'is gone.' In the neighbouring kingdom, at that moment the stage of Europe, the Middle Ages, so people at least deemed, were past; life and letters yearned towards the future; Church and monarchy, the old institutions and the old enthusiasms, all the tokens and insignia of rank and office, had vanished; a new era of universal happiness was to break, and former days were to be no more remembered. Voltaire and Rousseau had done their work, and French novels, from the date of Voltaire and Rousseau to the present, in their inevitable investigations into education and morals, still keep in the old groove.

In England the charm and glamour of the age of chivalry remained; the old glories of English history were renewed. Under the directing sway of the mighty master of romantic narrative, his delighted readers watched once more the conflict of Christian and Muhammedan, of Norman and Englishman; royal Tudor and royal Stuart had their own again, ruined monastery and battered castle stood restored by the magician's wand, and a great flush of national pride and poetry was thrown over the whole English-speaking race from the distant border and dim Highland hills, where Saxon speech and blood were yet arrayed in conflict, but in a conflict, in which they could afford to be generous, with the old Keltic enemy.

After Chaucer and Shakespeare, no writer can be named who has done so much to nourish British patriotism and that sense of inheritance, which their literature in view of their historic name gives to Englishmen, as Walter Scott.

And George Eliot follows, though dwarfed and darkened by the long shadow of her predecessor, in the wake of Walter Scott, and has the same happy fortune with him to be able readily to link the present to the past. Possibly the life of England is changing, perhaps has already changed, far more than we realise. The growth of enormous cities, the ease of travelling and the taste for travelling, the largeness and organisation of commercial and industrial energy, the disappearance of those local attachments and local peculiarities, which used to hold us so strongly because they had bound our fathers and grandfathers before us—these imply, it may be, a more rapid transition from one state of national development to another than can be made clear to those in whose unconscious presence the process has accomplished itself. But somewhere, half in memory and half in fact, there lies for each of us the little country town, a Milby, a St. Ogg's, a Middlemarch: such spots surely, though no longer the representative and typical seats of English life, retain still immense general influence and importance; they are the haunts of our earliest and dearest reminiscences, and even now, for a month or two, they sometimes beguile us away into their restorative retirement. And the foreign traveller, who visits our country, finds nothing to explain so well our national position and our special qualities as our provincial manners: old sites, like those of Abingdon, or Salisbury, or Truro, or Stratford, are those at which he can best carry on his researches; to these his thoughts will frequently recur; there he discloses and disentangles the roots of our character.

But, on the other hand, what a mental interval there is between two such authors as Walter Scott and George Eliot! From how many points of view are they entirely dissimilar in the intention and effect, with which they write! In particular, what complexity of design appears in the more recent writer! Much more has to be taken into account, beside her love for what is at once homely and picturesque, in the endeavour to explain her passage into the regions which her gifts of fancy and description have painted for us so faithfully. It is to be remembered that she does not strictly confine herself (no more, by the way, does Scott) to English soil, though, of her prose works, one alone has its scenery laid entirely away from England.

Her three published poems * have, all of them, foreign surroundings. Two of these deal very subtly and gracefully with the meaning and value of Art to its votaries, exemplified in connexion with that art which is best understood and most needed in modern times, Music; in one she relates the legend of ‘ Jubal,’ in the other, in ‘ Armgart,’ she sketches a situation or two from the professional experience of the prima donna of some little German ‘Residenz.’ In the third and most elaborate of her poetical works, she sets herself to depict the struggle between two pure races, two absolutely opposing faiths, two types, sundered for ever, of art and life and customs: the ‘Spanish Gipsy.’

Her poems are her least successful productions, though in these the peculiar religious and philosophical ideas of the

---

* We might have said four instead of three, but the little poem of German village life, called ‘Agatha,’ is scarcely known to the public, and it is much slighter in plan and construction than the others.

school of thinkers, with which she is associated, are most easily traced.

Of the novels, the most didactic and philosophical—until the appearance of 'Middlemarch,' in which last work a further advance in definiteness of view and determination of purpose may be marked—was 'Romola.'

'Romola' is a marvellously able story of the revival of Hellenic and Latin thought and spirit in Florence, at the end of the fifteenth century, the revival of the taste and beauty and freedom of Hellenic manners and letters, under Lorenzo de' Medici and the scholars of his court, side by side with the revival of Roman virtue, and more than the ancient Roman austerity and piety, under the great Dominican, Savonarola. The contacts of Heathenism with Christianity, of Greece and France with Italy, of scepticism with credulity, of knowledge with despair,—contacts now of man with man, now of cravings and doubts within an individual soul,—present an opportunity for representing on a large canvas a noble picture of humanity in trial and in triumph. The period of history is one which, of all others, may well have engrossing interest for George Eliot. Treasures of learning and discipline, amassed for mankind ages before, for ages stored and hidden away, see again the sun, are recognised and put to use. What use will they be put to, with what new and fruitful effects on the State and the citizen, with what momentary and with what lasting consequences, this she strives to discover ; this she follows through the public history of Italy, during the invasion of Charles VIII. and the events which succeeded his invasion, and through the private fortunes of her admirably chosen group of characters, some of them drawn from life, all of them true to nature.

The motive and plot of 'Romola,' it may be worth while to observe, had been previously handled by George Eliot, on a much smaller scale and with very different background and setting, in one of her very striking shorter tales of English middle-class society named 'Janet's Repentance.'

George Eliot's first more ambitious work (the 'Scenes of Clerical Life' had already been published in a periodical) was 'Adam Bede.' This novel, 'The Mill on the Floss,' and 'Silas Marner' appeared before 'Romola ;' since 'Romola,' have come the poems already referred to and two more novels of English manners, 'Felix Holt' and the recently concluded 'Middlemarch.'

In 'Adam Bede,' all the peculiar strength and delicacy of George Eliot were shown, and her reputation instantly made. Is it not because of the recollection in the minds of her admirers of their original impression, derived from this book, of the ability of the new author, that 'Adam Bede' is still by so many persons reckoned her masterpiece? Otherwise it might be difficult to account for the preference accorded to this rather than to any other of her more elaborate novels, with the exception, it may be, of 'Felix Holt.' For, on re-reading 'Adam Bede,' now that the mystery which at first so much perplexed people, as to whether it was the product of a man's or of a woman's pen, has been cleared away, there may be detected a slight flaw, which, it is possible, should be attributed to the desire on the part of the writer to maintain her *incognito*. ' George Eliot,' wonderful as her skill in delineating character is, has never quite so sure and perfect a command of male as of feminine character. In her minor personages, this inequality of power eludes exposure; she indicates character always with an exquisite facility; she suggests, so as nearly to finish; but in painting her heroes at length and in detail, she is sometimes not quite so felicitous. In her later books she seems to have been conscious of this failing, and she has accordingly put her heroines into the foreground. And if she had given the book under discussion another title—had she, for instance, called it 'The Hall Farm'—the defect noticed would be less perceptible. As it is, Adam Bede himself is felt to be far less exhaustively and completely portrayed, though far more pains and space have been allotted to him, than Dinah or Hetty; and both Arthur Donnithorne and Adam's brother, Seth, are somewhat too indistinct and insufficient. It was the love of this stamp of man which misled George Eliot: the character of Adam Bede is very dear to her; it re-appears often, last of all in the fine and tender features of Caleb Garth.

The novel which followed on 'Adam Bede' is, in its way, not likely to be excelled. The rough substance may be more malleable, and the workmanship less intricate, but there is not less vigour and truthfulness in 'The Mill on the Floss' than in 'Middlemarch' itself.

There is a simplicity about 'The Mill on the Floss,' which reminds one of the classic tragedy. The vast power of Nature over the career and fate of a family, figured forth in the river, beside which the child Maggie played, filling her mother's heart with gloomy and not unveracious presentiments, down which she passed with Stephen in her hour of temptation, with Tom in her last moments; the whole strength of association and of the ties and instincts of blood breaking in, at every critical point in the story, like the voice of a Greek chorus, full of traditionary warning and stern common sense, but speaking in the dialect of English rusticity, and by the mouths of Mr. Tulliver and his wife's relations.

And amongst all George Eliot's English landscapes, most distinct and most memorable, lie the town of St. Ogg's, Dorlcote, the Red Deeps.

The 'old, old town of St. Ogg's,' with its legends of 'the long-haired sea-kings, who came up the river and looked with fierce eagerness at the fatness of the land,' its patron saint, a localised St. Christopher, Ogg, the son of Beorl, St. Ogg's, with the deceitful ocean in the distance, to which hastens the smooth, but untameable, river. And the people of St. Ogg's, coarse, money-getting, prosaic, yet with strange currents in their veins, due to the influence of ancestors, who had been governed through long bygone ages by the unwritten law of the family and the tribe, and whose household chronicles had been full of recitals concerning the avenger of blood. Many of these inhabitants, as contemporaries with the story, introduce themselves in its course, none of them to be forgotten, chief among them that—Baxter's 'Saint's Rest' notwithstanding—strictly heathen Englishwoman, Mrs. Glegg.

Dorlcote Mill, with its more recent and fatal visions of the river and the flood, and with, hard by, Dorlcote churchyard, 'where the brick grave that held a father, whom we know, was found with the stone laid prostrate upon it after the flood,' and where 'near that brick grave there was a tomb erected, very soon after the flood, for two bodies that were found in close embrace.' Father and son and daughter, with all the freight of their lives and deaths carried on 'the dark changing wavelets of the little river.' Had they lived centuries before, doubtless the father and Tom would have pushed out into the open sea and sailed, courageous and wrathful, with the Vikings, and Maggie would have wept by the shore, like Gudrun.

All the fire of the pure Danish* breed glimmers in Mr. Tulliver. He has the old sense of a warfare, single-handed, against the world, and he has the old nature-worship of his forefathers:—

'There's a story as when the mill changes hands, the river's angry —I've heard my father say it many a time. There's no telling whether there mayn't be summat in the story, for this is a puzzling world, and Old Harry's got a finger in it—it's been too many for me, I know.'

He is far more certain of the activity of the Powers of Evil than of those of Good:—

---

* Norman or Danish. The name seems playfully derived from the great Taillefer himself.

'The morning light was growing clearer for them, and they could
see the heaviness gathering in his face, and the dulness in his eyes.
But at last he looked towards Tom and said—

'"I had my turn—I beat him. That was nothing but fair. I
never wanted anything but what was fair."

'"But, father, dear father," said Maggie, an unspeakable anxiety
predominating over her grief, "you forgive him—you forgive every
one now?"

'He did not move his eyes to look at her, but he said—

'"No, my wench, I don't forgive him . . . . What's forgiving to
do? I can't love a raskill" . . . .

'His voice had become thicker; but he wanted to say more, and
moved his lips again and again, struggling in vain to speak. At
length the words forced their way.

'"Does God forgive raskills? . . . . but if He does, He won't be
hard wi' me."

'His hands moved uneasily, as if he wanted them to remove some
obstruction that weighed upon him. Two or three times there fell
from him some broken words—

'"This world's . . . . too many . . . . honest man . . . . puzzling."'

He and his should have lived at another epoch, when rough
and ready measures were allowable with regard to the creations
of Old Harry: 'rats, weevils, and lawyers,' and when language
was in an unfallen state :—

'"Not but what, if the world had been left as God made it, I
could ha' seen my way, and held my own wi' the best of 'em; but
things have got so twisted round and wrapped up i' unreasonable
words, as aren't a bit like 'em."'

He has all the love for his children of the old Norse stock :—

'"Shake hands wi' me, my lad. It's a great thing, when a man
can be proud as he's got a good son. I've had that luck."

'"You must be good to her, my lad. I was good to my sister.
Kiss me, Maggie."'

How strong in him and in his son is the primitive love of
revenge !—

'"Write—write it i' the Bible."

'"O father, what?" said Maggie, sinking down by his knees, pale
and trembling; "it's wicked to curse and bear malice."

'"It isn't wicked, I tell you," said her father fiercely. "It's wicked
as the raskills should prosper—it's the devil's doing. Do as I tell you,
Tom. Write."

'"What am I to write, father?" said Tom, with gloomy submission.

'"Write as your father, Edward Tulliver, took service under John
Wakem, the man as had helped to ruin him, because I'd promised my

wife to make her what amends I could for her trouble, and because I wanted to die in th' old place where I was born and my father was born. Put that i' the right words—you know how—and then write, as I don't forgive Wakem, for all that; and for all I'll serve him honest, I wish evil may befall him. Write that."

'There was a dead silence as Tom's pen moved along the paper. Mrs. Tulliver looked scared, and Maggie trembled like a leaf.

'"Now let me hear what you've wrote," said Mr. Tulliver. Tom read aloud, slowly.

'"Now write—write as you'll remember what Wakem's done to your father, and you'll make him and his feel it, if ever the day comes. And sign your name Thomas Tulliver."

'"O no, father, dear father!" said Maggie, almost choked with fear. "You shouldn't make Tom write that."

'"Be quiet, Maggie!" said Tom. "I *shall* write it."'

The Red Deeps, steeped in the glory of June sunsets, and blushing with the bloom of June roses, or trembling in the changes of April lights and April meetings, vocal with 'the hum of insects like tiniest bells on the garment of Silence,' here the great leaning ash, there the russet bark of the Scotch firs, the enchanted ground of Maggie's babyhood and of her maidenhood, where, in the final sentences of the book, we leave Philip,—always solitary, except for hovering spiritual companionships, words from 'The Pirate' and 'Corinne,' songs of the King's Lorton drawing-room, hither he had brought one evening the miniature of a little girl in a pink frock, hence he had taken away another inspiration: 'You will look like a tall Hamadryad, dark and strong and noble, just issued from one of the fir-trees, when the stems are casting their afternoon shadows on the grass,'—Philip, on whose weak and crippled shoulders the sins of the Wakems and the superstitions of the Tullivers weighed so cruelly, and who was, nevertheless, in the end so fain to bear the weight.

And this soil, this air, and the echoes within her of the soul of her race are too strong for passionate and wistful Maggie. All her life long tempted to break through the chain, to flee from the restraints of her narrow environment and to escape the repulses of her masterful affections, as a girl of nine rushing away to the attic and the Fetish, then to the gipsies, and then in her later years alienated altogether in feeling and principle from her household, she nevertheless cannot tear herself away. At their meeting in the Red Deeps she said to Philip, 'The first thing I ever remember in my life is standing with Tom by the side of the Floss, while he held my hand: everything before that is dark to me.' She had seen unconsciously her own doom in the beloved allegory of her infancy. 'Maggie, when she read about

Christiana passing " the river over 'which there is no bridge," always saw the Floss between the green pastures by the Great Ash.'

How many actual scenes does a man take note of himself with his open eyes, which leave on him such a spell, as these, with which the novelist enchants his inner vision!

With more stringency of analysis, and with more moral firmness than before, and with final and fully-matured convictions, George Eliot returns in ' Middlemarch ' to the same problems as were discussed in ' The Mill on the Floss.' It was impossible to take up the first volume and read the opening pages without being made aware of the renewed strength and determination with which the work had been undertaken. This book must have been a sore plague to the rapid eyes of the ordinary novel-reading world. A reader must often pause and think, and fill in for himself, where the writer has condensed a long meditation into a sentence, and pages of preparatory writing into a few lines of print. Her style was never so careful as here; it has received its last delicate elaboration. Let us take the first chapters. How boldly and clearly are the features of the chief personages drawn! The whole material, which coming events are to test and shape, is brought into the light, the play of inbred propensities, the leadings of education, the bent of personal longing and hope; it is as if the authoress had felt impelled, at the commencement, to fix forcibly upon herself the laws of her work as much as, and more than, to enlist the interest of her public in her creations.

In all her novels the women without distinct family history, without pre-occupying and enthralling home instincts and attachments, are short-lived and broken-spirited. They contribute to the startling accidents, but not to the sustained action, of life, leave behind them no permanent and substantial traces, 'are as if they had never been born, and their children after them,' though, like Hetty or Caterina, they may impress a mark or colour, out of general sight, on the memory and mind of, here and there, a survivor, whose more significant course of existence their fleeting shadow crossed and touched. The vital stream informs generation after generation, it has no promise of the future, if it have not treasures of the past, it is strongest in the most conspicuous individual of a race or family; but the pleasures and glories it bears on its flood are not for that individual to exhaust, though it makes the charm and trouble of his life to try and catch for himself what is meant to be distributed over a long line of descendants. The stream flows on with its wealth to distant posterities. On the other hand, a creature like Hetty has no early history; her parents have to her as blank a life as her child, which was never more to her than an accusing voice; there were for her no familiar and cherished recollections to dull and eclipse the splendours of those dangerous and hazy delights, lying out of her proper world, by which she was ensnared and destroyed.

Dorothea Brooke has inherited a strong family character. She belongs to a more modern, more enlivened, more inquisitive, time than Maggie Tulliver. Her life has not so far-reaching a background. Maggie came of centuries of quiet agricultural ancestors; she became, on a sudden, conscious in the conflict of modern opinion and social order of the old stubborn spirit and wild fire of forefathers forgotten and overlaid in the interval of commonplace existence in farm and mill. Dorothea comes of the country gentry. 'There was an ancestor discernible as a Puritan gentleman, who served under Cromwell, but afterwards conformed, and managed to come out of all political troubles as the proprietor of a respectable family estate,' and in Dorothea ' the hereditary strain glowed alike through faults and virtues.' We recognise at once in her the lineaments of some white-kerchiefed Dorothy Brooke of the days of the Great Rebellion. Even in her bachelor uncle, though he has not much of the energy of his house, in his crotchets, unconventionalities, political queerness, ramblings in talk and thought, the stamp of former revolutionary times is not effaced. ' There's such an odd mixture of obstinacy and changeableness in Brooke,' says Mr. Cadwallader once of him.

The history of Dorothea is like the most accurate of biographies, and it will, for example, not do to forget that her taste and piety, naturally unaffected and pure, have already, when we make her acquaintance, been brought into communion with some contrasts and divergencies of social and religious opinion, and that she had been partly educated in a Swiss family at Lausanne.

Her spiritual and physical being are in complete unison. She is described as a shortsighted girl, disliking lapdogs, but fond of a horse, with beautiful profile, beautiful bearing, and particularly beautiful and frequently ungloved hands—' they were not thin hands, or small hands; but powerful, feminine, maternal hands '—with perfect sincerity of thought, and as perfect straightforwardness and transparency of expression, though she yet cannot always make others understand her.

She dislikes ' to have any small fears or contrivances about her actions.' ' To ask her to be less simple and direct, would be like breathing on the crystal that you want to see the light through.' ' Nothing could have seemed more irrelevant to

Dorothea than insistence on her youth and sex, when she was moved to show her human fellowship.' She is without suspicion, but, when in a false position by the fault of others, feels it soon. ' You speak to me as if I were something you had to contend against,' are the words which rise to her lips, when her husband is becoming utterly unworthy of her, and they exactly describe the state of the facts. And, when her fears are kindled, insight and promptitude do not fail her.

The reader soon has for himself, thanks to George Eliot's care and tact, no doubts about Dorothea. The easy but consummate skill, with which the heroine is put in the right light, can hardly .be overpraised. Two scenes are foremost in our mind : that in which the sisters divide their mother's jewels, and that in which the newly-married wife consults the doctor, Lydgate, about Mr. Casaubon s health. We may besides refer to the passages describing Dorothea's behaviour and sentiments on the day of old Featherstone's funeral, and the whole thirty-seventh chapter, quite true throughout to its motto from Spenser, as further instances of that skill. Indeed that division of the work, to which these last two references are made, the fourth book, is throughout written at George Eliot's best. In addition to the chapter already mentioned, the fortieth and forty-second chapters are exemplary exhibitions of the disciplined power of her genius.

The fortieth chapter describes domestic relations at Caleb Garth's house, when the owner unexpectedly has his engagement renewed as estate-agent of the Tipton and Freshitt property. ' It's a fine bit of work, Susan ! ' he says ; ' a man without a family would be glad to do it for nothing.' Everything here— morning at the breakfast-table, and, afterwards, evening with Mary Garth and Mr. Farebrother in the apple-garden—brims with health, sense, agility, intelligence ; the chapter ends with an unusual piece of sententiousness from the father of the house :—

' " What reason could the miserable creature have for hating a man whom he had nothing to do with ?" said Mrs. Garth.

' " Pooh! where's the use of asking for such fellows' reasons ? The soul of man," said Caleb, with the deep tone and grave shake of the head which always came when he used this phrase, " the soul of man when it gets fairly rotten, will bear you all sorts of poisonous toad-stools, and no eye can see whence came the seed thereof."

' It was one of Caleb's quaintnesses, that in his difficulty of finding speech for his thought, he caught, as it were, snatches of diction which he associated with various points of view or states of mind ; and whenever he had a feeling of awe, he was haunted by a sense of Biblical phraseology though he could hardly have given a strict quotation.'

The forty-second chapter carries us into the secrets of another home. Mr. Casaubon's disease, mental and corporal, is wearing him out. All the enviousness and bitterness of his morbid and solitary nature is stirred, he broods over the fatigues of his studies, the tedium of his marriage; he cannot hide away in silence his suspicions and his fears; it is with him as with us, ' when we hear with the more keenness what we wish others not to hear.' The doctor meets him, by appointment, in the Yew Tree Walk at Lowick. Lydgate, as he approaches, notices the lovely afternoon, the dropping of the lime-leaves past the sombre, firmset evergreens, the dirge-like cawing of the rooks, and pities the victim whom he sees pacing the desolate avenue, and to whom he can give but little hope or comfort. Casaubon, after hearing the doctor's warning, hurriedly dismisses him. In his anguish he shrinks from sympathy, from company, even from Dorothea, who, knowing the medical interview to be over, has stepped into the garden, at the moment willing and ready, with a resolution which would have overturned every physical and moral obstacle, to offer herself a modern Alcestis, and to sacrifice her life to her husband's plans. But his glance is chill, and he will not let her put her arm in his. They turn to the house, to turn on its threshold from each other in a severance beyond disguise and irremediable. It is a terrible picture : the gaunt old manor-house—death menacing the wretched invalid, who sits in selfish hopelessness amid the worthless lumber of his wasted life, among ' the dark bookshelves in the long library '—while upstairs, in the ancient boudoir, the afternoon sun falls on the faded, slender furniture, the delicate miniatures, the prim volumes of polite literature, the blue-green tapestry with the pale stag in it; and on the strong, hot, wild grief of a young, noble-hearted woman, who, for all her dreams of hero-worship and high communings with a grand ambition, has nothing but the murky presence of a shadow of unfructifying erudition, ghostly and bloodless, without spark of natural fire or public benevolence, with one threadbare passion—jealousy—and that 'hardly a passion, but a blight bred in the cloudy, damp despondency of uneasy egoism.'

We have so far in our treatment of ' Middlemarch ' been trying to indicate the power manifested by its author in imagining and describing men and women to the life, and in gathering individuals, families, and wider societies into suggestive grouping. To go much further, to trace out at length the incidents of the plot or even the growth of character in any of the leading personages in the novel, would be inconsistent with our limits, and, indeed, beside our purpose.

But let such of our readers, as desire to realise the consistent patience and infinite pains with which our authoress works, follow carefully through the various volumes, noting the trueness of the first draft of character and the harmoniousness and distinctness of each subsequent word and deed, any even of quite the minor actors in the tale—Sir James Chettam, or Mr. Cadwallader, or Celia, or Mr. Farebrother, or Mrs. Garth, or Mrs. Vincy. To rest for a moment the eye on one of the first three mentioned,—who might be classed together as much alike in position and aim, all three good specimens of the pure-blooded, well-bred, fastidious human animal; acting almost always on a true instinct, though almost always on unjustifiable principles ; the senses, like those of a racehorse or greyhound of the best strain, sharpened and pointed so as to take the place of any conscious exercise of intellect or any permitted encounter of passions ; doing, with wrong reasons and for wrong objects, the right thing ; and giving, if called to account for doing it, the wrong explanation. To take Sir James Chettam : one or two short sentences about him may serve as samples of the perfection of George Eliot's art :—

' As to the excessive religiousness alleged against Miss Brooke, he had a very indefinite notion of what it consisted in, and *thought that it would die out with marriage*' (i. 27).

'He did not usually find it easy to give his reasons: *it seemed to him strange that people should not know them without being told*, since he only felt what was reasonable' (i. 116).

'His disregarded love had not turned to bitterness; its death had made sweet odours—floating memories that clung with a consecrating effect to Dorothea. He would remain her brotherly friend, *interpreting* her actions *with generous trustfulness*" (iii. 111).

' "I do wish people would behave like gentlemen," said the good baronet, *feeling that this was a simple and comprehensive programme* for social well-being' (iv. 290).

' "Agitator," said Sir James (he uses the word after Mr. Brooke, who used it as suitably conveying the prospective political importance of Ladislaw), with bitter emphasis, *feeling that the syllables of this word properly repeated were a sufficient exposure* of its hatefulness' (v. 105).

Sir James's ' Oh why ? ' is as characteristic as Mr. Brooke's ' You know ! '

Again, such remarks as the following might be collected to indicate the grasp which the author secures, from the first moment of their appearance on the horizon of her imagination, over her creations.

Of Lydgate (ii. 272) :—

' Strange, that some of us, with quick, alternate vision, see beyond our infatuations; and even while we rave on the heights, behold the wide plain where our persistent self pauses and awaits us.'

Of Ladislaw (ii. 372): how completely is here the charm of an artistic nature rendered, and the way in which such a nature either entirely attracts or repels!—

'Will Ladislaw's smile was delightful, *unless you were angry with him beforehand:* it was a gush of inward light illuminating the transparent skin as well as the eyes, and playing about every curve and line.'

Of Bulstrode (iv. 226): showing the possible extent in modern society of self-concealment, and the shortsightedness which may accompany close, if prejudiced, observation:—

'Mrs. Bulstrode believed that her husband was one of those men whose memoirs should be written when they died.'

Or, again, let the juxtapositions and oppositions of character be considered. Take the slight sketch of Mr. and Mrs. Cadwallader, the fine social salad of the best circles of their neighbourhood, he the oil, she the vinegar, the dish mixed and adjusted to the nicest palate, all natural flavours masked and transfused with the biting fire of high-priced and long-kept condiments; or take, on a larger scale, the surroundings of Ladislaw and Lydgate: Ladislaw, the poetical nature, fated always to be indebted to those in whom he detects the worst faults possible according to his view of life, finding, except in Dorothea, everywhere self-deceivers: in Casaubon, in Bulstrode, in Brooke, in Rosamond (let us hope that in after life Ladislaw and Farebrother saw more of one another), yet whose seeming dependence never saps his real independence; and Lydgate, the man of science, so instinctively scrupulous as to the duty of keeping clear of pecuniary entanglement, despising the needy vicar, who is reported to win at cards, and then gradually brought to seek the very help he thought he would have scorned, and that from one benefactor after another, Lydgate, whose independence is never regained, when he has made the first step towards dependence.

Or let the work be studied in its structural symmetry: the first volume leading up to the scenes at Rome, where Dorothea arrives on her wedding journey—

    'A child forsaken, waking suddenly,
    Whose gaze afeard on all things round doth rove
    And seeth only that it cannot see
    The meeting eyes of love;'—*Motto to* chap. xx.

the second volume ending at Lowick with the incident, which

best expresses the gracious tenderness with which, throughout Mr. Casaubon's life, his wife avoids the least departure from loyalty and obedience ; the third volume, containing the record proper of provincial life, and terminating with Ladislaw's farewell to Middlemarch.

The conclusion of the fourth volume—the eighth and last book—will detain us for a few moments. Such studies of human motive and action have rarely been attempted, even by great dramatists, as are compressed into the last two hundred pages of "Middlemarch." The labour is almost too minute and severe. Taken by themselves, the mottoes to these final chapters might serve as texts for an exhaustive series of essays on the problems of modern society. One might fancy a German professor giving his life to an exposition and commentary of this little green volume from the title 'Sunset and Sunrise' to the reflection, with which the authoress looks up from her long task : 'Every limit is a beginning as well as an ending.'

The utmost strain is put here upon all the central personages. The occasion for all the subsequent great collisions and tests of character is no very strange or special one, is a common incident in the career of any medical practitioner, and very likely to happen in the case of a doctor who is the pioneer of a new science and method. Lydgate, while under obligations to the banker Bulstrode, attends professionally a guest who is dangerously ill. The patient dies, Lydgate suspecting that his instructions have been disregarded. Rumour obtains scent of, exaggerates, and makes public his situation. Then follow illustrations, only too real, of the sense of general and personal insecurity, of the doubt as to one's own motives and the honesty of the honest-seeming world, of the staring though silent fear of precipice and pitfall along the highways of a society, where every rough place is assumed and asserted to be smooth, of all the turbid and repressed emotions which continue to bring horror and tragedy into ordinary lives.

Lydgate's best friends cannot feel sure about him. The new vicar of Lowick, Mr. Farebrother, a man of large brain and heart, who has fought with temptation and knows his own weakness, what can he say?—except, with regard to current reports : 'There is the terrible Nemesis, following on some errors, that it is always possible for those that like it to interpret them as a crime ;' and, with regard to the heretofore unspotted reputation, which is aspersed : 'Character is not cut in marble —it is not something solid and unalterable. It is something living and changing, and may become diseased as our bodies do!' Lydgate cannot feel sure about himself. He is conscious that, somehow or other, the whole moral atmosphere about him has deteriorated. ' Only those who know the supremacy of the intellectual life—the life which has a seed of ennobling thought and purpose within it—can understand the grief of one who falls from that serene activity into the absorbing soul-wasting struggle with worldly annoyances.' He examines and re-examines himself without being able to get at that clear self-assurance of perfectly right action after which he strives : ' Is there a medical man of them all in Middlemarch who would question himself as I do ? ' The world, well aware of the exist-ence of many offences, and ever glad to identify an unexpected delinquent, passes sentence and suggests punishment summa-rily and effectively : ' The doctor says,' remarks Mrs. Sprague, quoting her husband, a rival physician, ' that he should recom-mend the Lydgates to go and live abroad somewhere. He says Lydgate ought to have kept among the French.' ' That would suit her well enough, I dare say,' said Mrs. Plymdale, ' there is that kind of lightness about her.' Lydgate's own father-in-law has no relief to offer. ' I don't pretend to say what is the truth —as far as the world goes a man might often as well be guilty as not.' And by Rosamond, Lydgate's shallow, vain, heartless wife, ' shame is felt to be the worst part of crime,' and what she acquires out of her husband's trouble is ' a sense of justified repugnance ' towards him.

Side by side with the trials of Lydgate go those of Dorothea. Man after man, in concert with whom Dorothea strives to realise some of her plans, fails her. Her uncle was too de-sultory, Sir James Chettam too mechanical, Mr. Casaubon has been found utterly irresponsive and is dead, and Lydgate and Ladislaw—men awake, the one to the practical needs of his fellows, the other to the beautiful influences of art and imagi-nation over the conduct of life, the best men she has met, about the best she will have a chance of meeting—are to appear, at their lowest, before her. The day and night of Dorothea's sorest distress make up the central scene in the volume and form the most impressive portion of the novel. The sweet young widow, starting happy and hopeful on an unselfish mission, delighting in the scents, the colours, the freshness of the early spring, full of a desire to talk to Rosamond about Lydgate's pride in his calling and his wife, and to take a comfort into a friend's home she herself had never been permitted to know, discovers the woman she had expected to find in downcast and unsupported affliction, flirting with her, Dorothea's, sole separate hero. ' She had drunk a great draught of scorn. She felt power to work and walk for a day without meat and drink.' She rushes from one

occupation to another in excited unrest. Then close in the dark
hours of misery, when it seems to her that she must blot out the
one figure from her mind, to which, with no desire but to
idolise it in thought and memory, she had hoped to be able
always to turn. 'Why had he not stayed among the crowd of
whom she asked nothing—but only prayed that they might be
less contemptible?' Until, with another morning, comes back
unkilled, enhanced, the desire to be industrious and helpful.

'She opened her curtains, and looked out towards the bit of road
that lay in view, with fields beyond, outside the entrance gates. On
the road there was a man with a bundle on his back, and a woman
carrying her baby. In the field she could see figures moving, perhaps
the shepherd with his dog. Far off in the bending sky was the
pearly light, and she felt the largeness of the world and the manifold
wakings of men to labour and endurance. She was a part of that
involuntary, palpitating life, and could neither look out on it from
her luxurious shelter as a mere spectator, nor hide her eyes in selfish
complaining' (viii. 282-3).

She goes back a second time, for Lydgate's sake, to Rosamond. They meet, the woman, who is uplifted and inspired
by suffering, with the woman whose heart and soul are bleached
and impoverished by it. The first advantage is with the cold,
reserved, thin nature, with Rosamond, whose eye is quick for
faces, whose presence suggests all mildness and innocence, she
is on her guard, she cannot make out the visit, its real purpose
could never have spontaneously suggested itself to her. The
other is conscious of nothing but her message, the utterance,
which hours of inarticulate sorrow and struggle have been preparing, which she delivers from the depths of her shaken existence that can right itself only in view of the wants of others and
for their benefit, now that the last hidden treasure it had stored
for itself lies crushed by daylight in the mire. And Rosamond
cannot defend herself against the infectious enthusiasm of Dorothea's desperate disinterestedness. She feels, in physical contact
with a lofty spirit and by a communicated impulse, for once
in her life an heroic thrill, and by her confession she restores
Ladislaw to his old place in Dorothea's fancy; 'all their vision,
all their thought of each other had been as in a world apart,
where the sunshine fell on tall white lilies, where no evil lurked,
and no other soul entered.'

But Ladislaw still felt that he had himself to clear. He
waited in the churchyard while Miss Noble begged Dorothea
to see him. 'The sky was heavy and the trees had begun to
shiver as at a coming storm.' She would receive him. She
would be doing something daringly defiant for his sake, and he

had been badly treated. They stood apart, but gradually the friendship between them was restored. The room darkened and rustled with the wind and the tossing of the trees outside. The parting words had to be said. They were spoken, and the love each had fostered for the other, hitherto unconfessed, found also its voice. And now, it seemed to Dorothea, all would be over between them, when the tempest should cease; he would go from the door, and she had steeled herself for the last look.

But, when the rain was quiet, Ladislaw, in the irritable irresoluteness which was a large part of him, would still keep dwelling insistently on the hopelessness of their union : to him it was, after all, not enough to reign only the dear, but always absent, lover of her dreams.

' " Your life need not be maimed," said Dorothea gently.

' " Yes it must," said Will angrily. " It is cruel of you to speak in that way—as if there were any comfort. You may see beyond the misery of it, but I don't. It is unkind—it is throwing back my love for you as if it were a trifle, to speak in that way in the face of the fact. We can never be married."

' " Some time—we might," said Dorothea, in a trembling voice.

' " When ? " said Will bitterly. " What is the use in counting on any success of mine ? It is a mere toss-up whether I shall ever do more than keep myself decently, unless I choose to sell myself as a mere pen and a mouthpiece. I can see that clearly enough. I could not offer myself to any woman, even if she had no luxuries to renounce."

' There was silence. Dorothea's heart was full of something that she wanted to say, and yet the words were too difficult. She was wholly possessed by them : at that moment debate was mute within her. And it was very hard that she could not say what she wanted to say. Will was looking out of the window angrily. If he would have looked at her, and not gone away from her side, she thought everything would have been easier. At last he turned, still resting against the chair, and stretching his hand automatically towards his hat, said with a sort of exasperation, " Good-bye."

' "Oh, I cannot bear it—my heart will break," said Dorothea, starting from her seat, the flood of her young passion bearing down all the obstructions which had kept her silent—the great tears rising and falling in an instant : " I don't mind about poverty—I hate my wealth."

' In an instant Will was close to her and had his arms round her, but she drew her head back and held his away gently that she might go on speaking, her large tear-filled eyes looking at his very simply, while she said, in a sobbing child-like way, " We could live quite well on my own fortune—it is too much—seven hundred a-year—I want so little—no new clothes—and I will learn what everything costs " ' (viii. 324, 5).

Now that we have caught a glimpse from this rapid review of George Eliot's literary achievements, and these few extracts from two of her principal works of the position from which she contemplates, and the paths into which she follows modern society, let us once more resume the train of general reflection from which we diverged. The two qualities which mark George Eliot as a prominent representative of English lite-rature are her Realism and her Dignity. For may it not be asserted that these are the distinctive qualities which, in a comparative view of modern literature throughout the civilised world, would be assigned to the literature of our own country and language : Realism based on the provincial limitations and contractions of English society, Dignity derived from the sense of personal co-operation on the part of the individual in the most far-reaching and the most substantial of existing Political systems ? All studies, as was hinted above, though in another connection, all studies of English history and literature are, on one side of them, studies of provincial life. English rules of government, English rules of thought and speech, lie beyond the scope and power of the great European sources and systems— Latin, Imperial, Catholic, Democratic alike. It has been frequently observed, how thus the common use of the words, England and English, has a noteworthy force and significance. We may sometimes employ, though such employment has only recently become general, such expressions as the British empire or Anglo-Saxon literature, but, both amongst ourselves and in the eyes of the other members of the family of nations, we bear pre-eminently the character, which belongs to, in the narrowest sense, England and the English, it is the English government, the English language, English literature, which have decisive importance. A more stimulating and inspiring scenery, a more keen and daring spirit might seem to belong to the extensive districts, which form a wide fringe round the English counties and their population, to Wales, to Scotland, and to Ireland, or it might have been supposed that the adventurous national life, bursting from the insular privacy in which it had been nursed, would, in the course of time, and of a long series of political and military advances, have found some new and more appropriate centre for a world-wide territorial and maritime dominion. It has not been so. Neither Rouen nor Bordeaux in the Middle Ages, though for long the points of departure of the military and dynastic ambition of our sovereigns, nor in later days any of the wealthy and magnificent cities, conquered or founded by Englishmen in America, Asia, and Australia, have wrested, or even tried to wrest, from the old dwelling-places of the race on-

Thames and Severn the gifts of intellectual and administrative supremacy, the glory of the English presence, of the English speech, of the English sceptre.

Also it was remarked before, that our finest poets in every age, such as Chaucer and Shakespeare, are alike in this respect, that they feel genius and patriotism kindle in unison as they dwell on this salient aspect of the history of their countrymen, it is to them the dearest and the worthiest of themes to have to examine and to record, carefully and accurately, the principles and the prejudices of English home life.

Not only our poets. There came a time in our history when our political life began to lie in fruition as much as in expectation, in the labours of national maturity more than in the dreams of national youth, when our religious and intellectual maxims, as well as those of domestic and colonial Government, had become fixed, and when the boundaries of the geographical area, over which these maxims were to prevail, could be at least roughly designated. After the heroic period of English history, the period of her confessors and martyrs in Church and State, and of the most illustrious of those who formed and reformed her institutions in every department of national activity, after the period marked by such names—names linked together, yet each recalling such different associations—as Cecil, Somerset, Cranmer, More, Raleigh, Sidney, Drake, Strafford, Cromwell, Hobbes, Locke, Newton, after this period surviving still for us fitly in immortal verse never in our mother-tongue to be surpassed, in the grandeur and sweetness of Shakespeare, Spenser, and Milton; there came another period, more historical for us inasmuch as we still make part of it, and less full of matter for epic or tragedy, in which, indeed, the foundations and the edifice of national greatness remain the same and as imposing as ever, but where the principles they represent require not to be proclaimed as new, but maintained as proved and established.

This period in our history is usually and most conveniently dated from the accession of William of Orange. Its commencement coincides—and this gives it its immediate interest for us—with the beginning of a new movement in English literature, with the appearance of the English novel. Chaucer and 'The Canterbury Tales' usher in the literary era, which culminates in Shakespeare and Spenser; Addison and 'The Spectator' introduce the era, some of the finest examples of which have been produced within recent recollection: the novels of Thackeray were still full of the first flavour; Colonel Newcome and Major

Pendennis are reverently placed in our memories very close to·
Sir Roger de Coverley and Will Honeycomb.

Addison is the type of those who follow. How tender, how
sympathetic, how solicitous to catch every little detail in the
familiar atmosphere of the fatherland and the peculiar habits of
his fellow-citizens; yet, at the same moment, how conscious of
the magnitude of the political transactions of England and of the
place of honour due to English statesmanship! He himself is
in the midst of the political struggle, so are his literary brethren
and partners in the new venture. Steele is at once editor of the
official newspaper, 'The Gazette,' and of 'The Tatler.' Defoe
is as versed in political controversy as in *belles-lettres*. Let us
only notice the titles and remember the intentions of his most
famous works—of his great political poem, 'The True-born
Englishman,' then of 'The Family Instructor,' with its complete
regulations for the management and training of a household, then
of his undying story, 'The Life and Surprising Adventures of
Robinson Crusoe.' How romantic yet how domestic is the charm
of this last book, the earliest and in its way still unrivalled
masterpiece among all the prose fictions of the modern languages
of Europe! How domestic yet how full of political allusion, of
social instinct! It is the narrative of the origin and growth of a
little polity, the history of English discovery and colonisation
freely projected into and idealised in the fields of imagination.

It is the stupendous political mission of England which gives,
then, to our literature its dignity; it is the seclusion, the remote-
ness, the insulation, the homeliness of England, which gives to
our literature its realistic character. No famous literature ever
existed which was primarily meant for so small, so rugged, so
unenlightened, so self-satisfied, so exclusive an audience. Except,
and that with much modification of circumstance, in ancient
Greece and Rome, there is no parallel to the peculiar conditions
under which English literature flourishes. The great authors of
Continental literature have written for France, Italy, Germany,
civilisation at large, with a cosmopolitan purpose, striving to
touch the general sense of humanity, to cast off all special accent
and emphasis, to publish general ideas, to speak a language suited
to every race and country. Our foremost writers have thought
of a most restricted public—the English parsonage, the English
country-house, the mechanics' institute, at most the common-
rooms of our universities and the clubs of the metropolis; before
them has been ever the little English land, the cradle and hearth-
stone of their nation, whence it draws its physical strength and
its moral energy. Therefore it was that, in the later Stuart period,

the sparkling and seductive comedies, reproductions from French models, which obtained favour with the Court, could, though rich in gracefulness and wit, gain no permanent place, but had to make room for the fresh and native pictures of the early English novel, quaint, well-beloved figures, sketched with the irony, fun, pathos, which belong to fireside love, in their rude health, clean blood, and tough temper, full of faults and whims, angular and awkward, but sound at the core and with unshaken and untiring vigour of brain and body.

Thus English imaginative literature has become the most objective, the most trustworthy and the most historically instructive, of modern times. But there is about books, such as those of George Eliot, much to make one ponder whether the course of the English novel may not be well-nigh run. And, if we look beyond at the literature of other countries, such an impression finds much confirmation. It appears as if, in Europe, we had reached the highest point of excellence in the development of a prose imaginative literature. Already the finest creative fancy begins to turn into other ways. How much suppressed imagination, which, a while ago, would have sought expression in works of fiction, is traceable in the investigations, which gain moreover an ever-increasing popularity, into the problems of ancient law, of primitive society, and of natural history ; * how much has not the study of manners of late yielded to the study of scenery and of art! Modern society everywhere has been exhaustively explored by the novelist. As was said at the outset, in origin and in purpose, the French novel differs altogether from the English, the English novelist being essentially an historian, the French essentially a philosopher. The English novelist sketches living and self-determining persons ; the French novelist either creates an ideal being or dissects some shuddering human specimen, whom he holds, soul and body, at the mercy of his sharp and torturing pen. The French novel is, however, at the present moment in the same position as the English ; it has become as elaborate as possible—it has, in the nature of things, become so even more rapidly than the English. In this respect there is as great a distance between a writer like the late Charles de Bernard, or like Victor Cherbuliez, and Voltaire, as there is between George Eliot and Defoe. If we look, too, at Germany, quite inferior in

---

* To us indeed it seems, that future criticism, dealing with our greatest living naturalist, his current doctrines, and his so vast and unanimous following, will find nothing in the whole literature of our day so amazing as the way in which, by common consent, 'imagination' was re-christened ' science,' and the at once most ingeniously fanciful and most singularly subjective arrangement of personal notes and experiments taken to be the enumeration of the very *facts*, the syllabus of the very *system* of *Nature*.

regard to this branch of literature to England and France, we perceive the same symptoms. In Germany the most successful attempts in this department have been short tales or stories—to use the German name for them—'Novellen.' The master of the German 'Novelle' is Paul Heyse. His handiwork has just the same stamp upon it as that of Cherbuliez or Eliot. It is almost impossible that any successor should be able to equal it in involution, precision, polish. And here fewer years have wrought greater change. Let any one, wishing to verify our argument, compare—the two stories are selected because of some similarity in plan and construction—Grillparzer's tale, 'Der arme Spielmann,' published in 1848, and Heyse's 'Lottka,' written in 1869. Dr. Strauss has repeated in his last book a favourite observation of his, that nothing could have delighted Goethe more than to have had in his lifetime an opportunity of listening to the exposition of Mr. Darwin's views. We must, for our part, take leave to doubt whether, if the chronological position of great poet and great naturalist could have been reversed, the illustrious author of the 'Wahlverwandtschaften' would have held so high a place among novelists. George Eliot is clearly very susceptible to the leadings of philosophical and physical speculations; and she, under the promptings of her scientific interests, once did very nearly lose her artistic perception and her whole capacity for unbiassed observation and statement. 'Felix Holt' was a failure. Its perusal led many to fear that its author had passed the zenith of her fame. One could scarcely avoid overlooking its frequent beauties to remember particularly its faults.

As sedulously as we can, we are, throughout this review, confining ourselves to a literary criticism of George Eliot, and we trust that we shall be thought not to be lacking in the impartiality and consideration due, from strictly literary criticism, to a writer of such rare excellence; but there is no point of view from which we could pass judgment on 'Felix Holt,' without using language of most distinct disapproval and condemnation. There was, in the book, a quality of—shall we say ?—coarseness, reminding one of, and in some respects reproducing in distortion, the more objectionable features of Charlotte Brontë's characters: there was an ill-controlled tendency to theorize concerning the animal basis of all the social and moral virtues, a sort of doubt, whether recent theories about the transmutations of the human body would not, in effect, call back in a modernised shape a vain and ancient superstition concerning the transmigrations of the human soul. People were offended, and with reason, at the too searching and all but medical enquiry into the influence of the dispositions of the respective father over Durfey and Harold

Transome, at the possibly to a zoologist ingenious but in a novel decidedly unpleasant relations between Jermyn and his son—at the quasi-allegorical portrait of Mr. Transome in his dotage falling back into the company of his dogs, insects, and minerals. And there was, even in the treatment of political life, a far too strongly marked leaning to put forward types rather than individuals. It was after all not a little forced to transplant, in order to give a kind of smack of foreign revolutions, a dainty little French demoiselle into English provincial Radical surroundings, and to associate with her as stepfather an old Independent minister to represent in a kind of patriarchal garb British political and religious Dissent. The author of ' Felix Holt' gave way to a temptation, which is of necessity always very close to her, so close, that it is a matter of marvel, not that she should in an exceptional instance have yielded to it, but that she should have withstood it so long and so firmly. She allowed her philosophy to draw her away from her art. The story was used, too palpably and inconsistently, as a vehicle for certain opinions. The novel slid into a treatise. The conclusion was unavoidably left with an opponent of views not obscurely suggested, that scenes and actors were introduced to suit a programme, to elucidate a scientific dogma, that one more missionary had passed into the service of a particular propaganda.

'Middlemarch' rehabilitates George Eliot. 'L'esprit,' it was happily said, ' a sa pudeur comme la beauté,' and our author has quickly discerned and repaired her error. Not that there is in 'Middlemarch' any repudiation of principles, which, we need not say, we should have been very glad to see her shake off altogether, but there is no unfair or inartistic prominence given to them ; she has her accustomed and conscientious moderation, if, indeed, there does not appear now and again something like the implied acknowledgment that, after all, the system remains for her undiscovered which can furnish any useful key to the riddles of the universe. Nevertheless, we may look upon 'Middlemarch' as the most remarkable work of the ablest of living novelists, and, considered as a study of character, as unique, without being blind to the existence in it of evident and even glaring defects.

First among these defects, and more conspicuous, we think, in 'Middlemarch' than in any of her previous novels, is a certain want of enthusiasm in the writer, which tells very seriously upon the reader, on behalf of the narrative she has to relate. She does not write, like the great names among her predecessors, for the sake of the story, she feels none of the zest with which, in some degree Dickens and Thackeray, in greater degree Fielding and

Goldsmith, above all, Scott, lose themselves in the current on which toss the chances of their heroes, and into which the strained attention of their readers is absorbed. George Eliot comes to novel-writing from strange schooling for a writer of novels. It is always the motive of action which interests her more than the effect, it is only her love for her characters which induces her to follow them through the weariness of their lives.

She wants altogether Scott's elasticity, expansiveness, and exuberance. He is going to fascinate, to transport his reader; it shall be a tale of real life, which shall at the same time cast an ideal and brightening ray upon the lives of those who read it; the exact costume of the period, the exact copy of the landscape shall be caught, but so shall the airy legendary charm which first lured the novelist to the theme; there shall be some freak of fortune, there shall be some fear of fate; he is happy in the prospects, he revels in the progress of the plot, his impatience equals that of the most impulsive among his audience to arrive at and to enjoy the last chapter. And those old-fashioned and simple novels were more perfect and complete as works of art. They gratified and invigorated; one went from them as from the contemplation of some classic example of Greek statuary, or of some well-preserved painting by a serene Venetian master with a delightful sensation of improved taste and satisfied fancy. But George Eliot has none of Walter Scott's passion for, to use his own phrase, his 'occupation as a romancer.' 'Middlemarch' will leave all of us, in greater or less measure, restless and distressed. There has been no hero, there has been no romance, there has been no last chapter; the 'finale' repeats the sad note of the 'prelude.'

Again, the authoress is much too eager, in and out of season, to point her moral and to enforce upon her readers certain particular views concerning the great problems of life. Archbishop Whately observed, in one of the earlier numbers of this 'Review,' 'Any direct attempt at moral teaching, and any attempt whatever to give scientific information will, we fear, unless managed with the utmost discretion, interfere with what, after all, is the immediate and peculiar object of the novelist, as of the poet, *to please*.'* The inclinations he well and wisely censured are far too apparent in 'Middlemarch.' We could have accepted Lydgate's scientific education and professional aims on trust. The long explanations of his desire to follow out the discoveries of M. Bichat, and to ascertain 'what was the primitive tissue,' and the disquisitions and meditations upon true and false methods

* See 'Quarterly Review,' vol. xxiv. p. 358.

of medical treatment, are tedious in the extreme. It is in a scientific essay, not in a novel, that such a passage as the following should have been placed :—

'That great Frenchman (Bichat) first carried out the conception that living bodies, fundamentally considered, are not associations of organs which can be understood by studying them first apart, and then, as it were, federally; but must be regarded as consisting of certain primary webs or tissues, out of which the various organs—brain, heart, lungs, and so on—are compacted, as the various accommodations of a house are built up in various proportions of wood, iron, stone, brick, zinc, and the rest, each material having its peculiar composition and proportions. No man, one sees, can understand and estimate the entire structure or its parts—what are its frailties and what its repairs, without knowing the nature of the materials. And the conception wrought out by Bichat, with his detailed study of the different tissues, acted necessarily on medical questions as the turning of gas-light would on a dim oil-lit street, showing new connections and hitherto hidden facts of structure which must be taken into account in considering the symptoms of maladies and the actions of medicaments.'—ii. pp. 263, 264.

Here is a sentence, which could scarcely be more obscure ; we have vainly sought its veiled meaning :—

'These kinds of inspiration Lydgate regarded as rather vulgar and vinous compared with the imagination that reveals subtle actions inaccessible by any sort of lens, but tracked in that outer darkness through long pathways of necessary sequence by the inward light which is the last refinement of energy, capable of bathing even the ethereal atoms in its ideally illuminated space.'—ii. p. 295.

And the ordinary narrative, in its struggle after conciseness, gets sometimes to look like an inexplicable verbal puzzle :—

'What could two men, so different from each other, see in this "brown patch," as Mary called herself? It was certainly not her plainness that attracted them (and let all plain young ladies be warned against the dangerous encouragement given them by society to confide in their want of beauty). A human being, in this aged nation of ours is a very wonderful whole, the slow creation of long interchanging influences ; and charm is the result of two such wholes, the one loving and the one loved.'—iv. p. 341.

Also we must mention a far more serious blemish, the repetitions of which, if we were to cite them, would fill and, we regret to have to add, would sully many a page. There is an acerbity about her satire with a studied flippancy about her diction, when she chooses to misrepresent amiable weakness and even religious faith, which will have startled and shocked many gentle and candid souls, and which is altogether indefensible in a writer of fiction, who makes personages in order to malign them, and has the whole domain of thought and language to ransack for characters and for expressions.

Further, the humour of 'Middlemarch' strikes us as both less independent and less natural than was the case in the earlier books. Not only in the general management of her humorous personages in this work, but even in the verbal construction and in the cadence of continuous bits of description, there is noticeable a resemblance to what we may, we hope without irreverence, term the tricks and mannerisms of the greatest of our recent humourists.

'In the large wainscoted parlour, too, there were constantly pairs of eyes on the watch and own relatives eager to be "sitters up." Many came, lunched and departed, but Brother Solomon, and the lady who had been Jane Featherstone for twenty-five years before she was Mrs. Waule, found it good to be there every day for hours, without other calculable occupation than that of observing the cunning Mary Garth (who was so deep that she could be found out in nothing) and giving occasional dry wrinkly indications of crying —as if capable of torrents in a wetter season—at the thought that they were not allowed to go into Mr. Featherstone's room.'—iii. 150, 1.

This, for instance, is a passage, admirable in its way, but clearly, as it seems to us, in the manner of Charles Dickens. And throughout 'Middlemarch' George Eliot's wit shows itself rather in the quaint working out of detail than in those spicy, epigrammatic sayings, which gave so much pungency and spirit to her former writings. Thus Mr. Brooke, who at first promised so well, degenerates sadly. He might have been rendered equal to one of Thackeray's charming old gentlemen, but he sinks into a vexatious and infelicitous bore, drawn from Dickens's models, and not first-rate after his kind, for we doubt if even Dickens would have made him reiterate himself so often and labour so hard to become, through the simple absence of originality, an original. We had been informed, quite at the beginning of the first volume (i. p. 58), that Mr. Brooke speaks not 'with any intention;' but 'from his usual tendency to say what he had said before;' we have been much surprised, that the authoress should have thought it necessary to publish, as we vaguely surmise, the bulk of his conversations during several years. We are sorry— and Mr. Brooke shall help us to a phrase—'that she couldn't put the thing better, couldn't put it better, *beforehand, you know.*' (i. p. 63.)

We have already praised the structure of the book, and, as a framework to character, we could not well overpraise it, and yet we confess to a suspicion that there has been a change of plot in the course of composition; that the story, as originally conceived, was to have concluded with more startling and exciting incidents (cf. i. 164), but that the author found a less painful narrative sufficient for the analysis of the moral and intellectual characteristics of Lydgate and Dorothea, and dispensed, accordingly, with the more terrible trial, involving more visible and widespread disaster, which had been designed for them.

That inconsequence and incompleteness in 'Middlemarch' and its personages, to which we have already made reference, baffles and, we might say, defies criticism. What is the lesson of this book, what its conclusion, not that verbal one on the last page, but the logical inference, when reading is done, and judgment would settle itself? Why must Dorothea marry Casaubon, endow Farebrother, restore Lydgate, on her way to provide and embellish a home for—Ladislaw? Why should Lydgate and Dorothea be no wiser and better, why should author and reader be no wiser and better, at the end of the story than at the beginning? And can we have more hope for Lydgate's (and Rosamund's) sons than for him—for Dorothea's (and Ladislaw's) daughters than for her? Are we soberly and seriously told to see the whole rich round of private and public life through the spectacles of the malicious gossip, who points to the ill-assorted marriage-column as index, compendium, and supplement of all the rest? There is a pent-up outcry against society throughout the book, which should, anyhow, have made itself articulate. What is George Eliot's new Providence, what her ideal training for scientific men and emotional women? Towards what in earth and heaven does she beckon us on?

We must sum up. Assuredly, unless we have misread this book altogether, it, at all events, is not written as by a person with a mission, who desires converts, plans a Utopia, preaches new dogmas. About none of her other writings was there such a profound despondency. Truly it would be the most melancholy and forlorn historical situation (if actual and historical it were), that in which a reflective reader, rising from a study of George Eliot, might be inclined to place modern society, though, all the while, he would hardly be able to make out to himself how far his hopeless mood had grown directly out of the words of his author or out of his own musings.

We repeat, and lay all possible stress upon, our protest. It is not the moral nor is it the artistic purpose of a work of fiction, (or indeed of sound literature at all) to produce this state of mind and to invite such afterthoughts.

It is the darkest of prospects which is conjured up. Great

and distinctive careers—for so, very readily, the temptation might run to shape such afterthoughts—for individuals have then passed away entirely with the sympathetic belief on the part of the multitude, and with the sincere conviction on the part of isolated personages, in direct and special Divine inspiration and warrant. Humanity as such makes progress. In new countries tribes, recently savage, in Europe classes, heretofore below and outside the influences of culture, aspire after, and attain to, intellectual and moral eminence, but there are no vacant spaces left, where once there was room for Savonarola, where there was justification for Zarca, where there was hope even for Macchiavelli, and a sure heaven for Thomas à Kempis. Like the surface of the globe, which in civilised countries has for the most part rendered itself captive to civilisation—earthquakes, deluges, volcanoes being for us things of the past or of the distance—the stream of human life has adapted itself to general needs, it obeys uniform laws, it has renounced all fury and eccentricity, it has hollowed and mastered its channel, it flows deeply and persistently without storm or spray, ' moving altogether if it move at all.' Enthusiasms and ambitions, inherited from ancestors, who may have been prophets and apostles, or awakened by a spirit in literature, which is a survival from the times of preparation, may still break out to disturb and vex here and there, and transiently young men and maidens; but both the great occasions and the great benefits of self-immolation and of new messages from God have for ever gone by, and, in their later years, the would-be saints and preachers are marked only by a more compassionate and humane charity among their fellows, and by a strengthened sentiment, that personal opinion has rightfully but a very limited range, and is not easily to be kept distinct from conceit or prejudice; they are content to fall in with and be merged in the general movement.

It is because of our author's silence, rather than of her speech, of what she implies rather than of what she asserts, of her constant search after sunshine and her manifest continuance in twilight, that a view of life in these gloomy hues is not unlikely to pass before her readers with its mournful and complaining argument. Doubtless much of the philosophy, which shone too transparently through the flesh and blood of the personages in ' Felix Holt,' is still to be discovered in ' Middlemarch.' In ' Middlemarch,' and, we might add, in ' The Spanish Gipsy,' there is an attempt to draw out into action some of the views of Comte, there is a trust—rather, perhaps, a faint hope—that the fervour of mediæval Catholicism, the life of a consecrated order or tribe, may at some future time revive in and warm the Worship of Humanity, and that it may some day be possible, especially for the sake of high-souled women, who shun a mean and empty existence, to find, outside of marriage, some organisation through which they may again, as of old, minister as spiritual mothers and sisters to the friendless and afflicted. But the author of ' Middlemarch ' is less sanguine now than ever. Such conclusions as she has arrived at (and some of them must be quite settled conclusions) seem neither altogether to explain the past nor at all to transfigure the future. In her scrupulous honesty she admits as much. In the ' prelude ' and ' finale ' of ' Middlemarch ' she attributes, indeed, Dorothea's failures to her defective education and her sex ; but Lydgate and Ladislaw are men, and men as full of accomplishments as they are free from superstitions, and yet is not Dorothea more successful in securing fitting companionship than Lydgate, and in living a fine life than Ladislaw ? Our author has come under the shadow of much advanced philosophy, of much extreme theology. Before she published any of her own writings she had translated Strauss's ' Life of Christ ' and Feuerbach's ' Essence of Christianity.' And to us one of the most remarkable points in her thought and tone has been the way in which these convey reminiscences of Feuerbach ; we have sometimes fancied that, among English landscapes and with English traditions, Feuerbach might have written 'Silas Marner,' or George Eliot, reared in German academic society, 'das Wesen der Religion.'

The harmony, if accidental, is the more startling between leading ideas of the novelist and fundamental doctrines of the philosopher. For instance, in Feuerbach's terrible system —and all his straightforwardness of thought, depth of feeling, lucidity of language, only make its negations more terrible —there is no topic, on which he dwells so often and with such pained endeavours to soften its irresistible horrors, as that of death. He wrote monograph after monograph on death, he discussed death from the standpoint of ethics, psychology, metaphysics, natural science, he became a poet, and all his verses were upon death. George Eliot's critics have sometimes remarked that the death scenes in her works occur too frequently, and that the issues and effects given to them betray some poverty of invention. Zarca's death established his design, Maggie's death was the great event in the lives of Philip and Stephen, Savonarola's death graved its final expression into Romola's character, Edgar Tryan's death saved Janet Dempster ; and we are, in the pages of these books, always meeting with otherwise insignificant persons, for whose lives no good reason is forthcoming were it not for the results of the supreme moment on others. Such, by way of example, are old Featherstone, Godfrey Cass's wife, Edgar Tryan's lost sweetheart. All this is like the burden of some of Feuerbach's most touching thoughts and most eloquent passages. ' Wenn kein Tod wäre, so wäre auch keine Religion.' . . . 'Nur das Grab der Menschen ist die Geburtstätte der Götter' . . .

> ' Die lieben, bessern, andern Wesen,
> Die sind, weil du zuvor gewesen ;
> Der lieben Kindlein Engelgeister,
> Der itz'gen Meister künft'ge Meister,
> Die rufen dich vom Leben ab
> Und säuseln Ruhe dir ins Grab,
> Die schläfern sanft zum Tod dich ein
> Und weben in das Nichts dein Sein.
> Dein eignes Kind, dein eignes Blut
> Entziehet dir des Lebens Gluth.
> So lange nicht dein Ich zerbricht
> Den Kleinen du noch trübst das Licht.'

George Eliot has learned many lessons from many masters, but it would be impossible to designate her with certainty and without reservation as the disciple of any of her teachers. Her scrutiny of literature has been close, her sympathy with science is intense, she has brought to her literary and scientific studies a most powerful intellect and unimpeachable integrity of aim. We have, however, great doubt whether she would be willing to formulate at all a comprehensive theory of life, though we have, unfortunately, little doubt that, were she to formulate such a theory, it would be one we should be compelled to contravene and to combat at every step. But it has been her wont to study men even more than books, and we are glad to acknowledge the value of the practical lessons she has striven with all her skill as artist, and weight as moralist, to enforce. It shall not be to what is dubious and dreary—as we hold needlessly dubious and dreary—in her view of human affairs, that, as we take leave of her, we will look back, but to that calm, strong, constant sense of duty, of the necessity of self-control, of the law of benevolence, which she has somehow rescued for herself, by which she is manifestly animated, and which she desires to fortify in others. She condemns alike licence and lassitude. She counsels resignation when she cannot impart peace, she rejoices in sight of the field of labour, though she sees not the place of rest.

Our last reference, as we conclude, shall be to one of her most beautiful stories, the most poetical of them all, the tale of ' Silas

Marner,' who deems himself deserted and rejected utterly of God and man, and to whom, in his deepest misery, in place of lost gold, a little foundling girl is sent. This tale is the most hopeful of all her books. The contemplation of the renewal of enterprise and energy, which comes with little children, and of the promise with which each new generation gilds the crown of honour for its sires, is pleasant and grateful to her. She writes upon the title-page the lines of Wordsworth :—

> ' A child, more than all other gifts
> That earth can offer to declining man,
> Brings hope with it and forwardlooking thoughts.'

' The Weaver of Raveloe ' and ' Eppie ' are creations after Wordsworth's own heart, and, throughout her narrative, our novelist never strays far from the auspicious guidance, under which she set out, of Wordsworth's moderating and elevating spirit.

George Barnett Smith

"Our First Great Novelist"

Macmillan's Magazine 30 (May 1874), 1–18

OUR FIRST GREAT NOVELIST.

HENRY FIELDING, for he it is upon whom we place the distinction of being England's first great novelist, has for a century past been the constant subject of criticism. His surpassing merits have compelled even his most pronounced foes to assign him a lofty place in the art which he adorned. Attempts to depreciate his genius, because the moral backbone was lacking in some of his characters, have been repeatedly made, but with no permanent effect upon his renown. For ourselves, we affirm at the outset that we consider him the Shakespeare of novelists. By this, of course, it will be understood, we do not imply that the sum of his genius was in any way comparable to that of the illustrious dramatist; but that he achieved his results in the same way. He was the great artist in fiction because he was the great observer and interpreter of human nature. The novel will never be able to assume a position of equal importance with the drama, because of its comparative defectiveness of construction. But to such perfection as it is capable of being brought, Fielding almost attained. It is, then, for the reason of the similarity of his method to that of Shakespeare that we have ventured to award him the highest title of eminence. It will be our endeavour, while not hiding his defects, to set forth the grounds of justification for the position we have assumed.

With that perversity which only men of the same class or profession can exhibit towards each other, it was the fashion with literary men of Fielding's time—and indeed for many years subsequently—to compare him unfavourably with his rival, Richardson. It is singular how frequently individuals of professed literary acumen are willing to accept the *dicta* of others in matters of criticism. We are only just now losing the effects of this empiricism. Some unfortunate epigram, or some warped and fantastic judgment, has frequently been passed upon an author by those who were supposed to be competent judges, and the depreciatory observations have had the same effect upon the public mind as that of the pebble cast into the pool. The waters have been agitated and disturbed by ever-widening circles of discontent, even to their utmost limits. Much laborious effort has been required to exorcise the prejudice thus established; and it is just this power which a wrong judgment possesses over the minds of men in an equivalent degree with a right one, which makes criticism dangerous. In the hands of an incapable person it is an engine of incalculable mischief. And the fact that now and then this engine destroys its foolish owner is no satisfaction for the wrong done to men of undoubted genius. The self-righting power of criticism certainly moves slowly. We are somewhat diffident, for example, when we find it necessary to differ strongly from such authorities as Dr. Johnson; or at any rate should unquestionably have been so had we been amongst his contemporaries. Now that we are out of reach of his terrible voice and his overbearing demeanour, and regarding him thus from a safe distance, we do not find it so difficult to designate his capacity for judging in literary matters as often shallow and pretentious. Most people admit that his view of Milton is far from a just and worthy one of that sublime poet. He lacked the balance of mind, the intellectual equipoise, which is the foundation of the critical faculty. Consequently, with the lapse of time, his reputation in this respect will crumble away. Even the obsequious Boswell has ventured to insinuate that at times Johnson was so swayed by his feelings that, when making comparisons between writers, he very often contradicted his intellect by his affection; and, while saying the utmost he could of the inferior qualities of his personal favourite, ignored those which were superior in the person with whom he was ranged in comparison. Some such treatment as this was meted out to Fielding when he placed him in juxtaposition with Richardson. Let us reproduce his criticism. "Sir," said he, in that pompous manner in which we can fancy the burly old Doctor was wont to settle the affairs of men and mundane concerns generally, "there is all the difference in the world between characters of nature and characters of manners; and *there* is the difference between the characters of Fielding and those of Richardson. Characters of manners are very entertaining; but they are to be understood by a more superficial observer than characters of nature, where a man must dive into the recesses of the human heart." There is very little in this beyond saying that there is a great deal of difference between things which differ. Yet it is the kind of criticism which bears a deceptive sound with it, and acquires a reputation far in excess of its value, as being an expression of great apparent profundity. We

shall hope to show that in his attribution of the one method to Fielding and the other to Richardson, Dr. Johnson came to an erroneous conclusion. For the present his observations lend some force to what has gone before, and it is an undoubted fact that the weakness of Fielding's moral character had much to do with Johnson's estimate of him. The formidable lexicographer was of that class of men who are almost prepared to find fault with the sun because of the spots upon his surface.

Horace Walpole was another of the critics who appear to have been either blinded by envy or unable to detect the effects of true genius, for we find that he was amongst the earliest detractors of Fielding — a prominent member of the school of depreciators which endeavoured to humble him in the eyes of his contemporaries. It is pleasant, however, to think that some who bear great names have expressed the most unqualified admiration for the novels of our author, and the opinion of one really master mind outweighs that of a hundred Walpoles. Byron gave it as his belief that "Fielding was the prose Homer of human nature;" the far-seeing Goethe was delighted with his art; and Gibbon demonstrated his literary sagacity by the following eloquent eulogium : — "Our immortal Fielding was of the younger branch of the Earls of Denbigh, who drew their origin from the Counts of Hapsburgh, the lineal descendants of Eltrico, in the seventh century Dukes of Alsace. Far different have been the fortunes of the English and German divisions of the family of Hapsburgh ; the former, the knights and sheriffs of Leicestershire, have slowly risen to the dignity of a peerage ; the latter, the Emperors of Germany and Kings of Spain, have threatened the liberties of the Old, and invaded the treasures of the New World. The successors of Charles V. may disdain their brethren of England ; but the romance of 'Tom Jones,' that exquisite picture of human manners, will outlive the palace of the Escurial, and the Imperial Eagle of Austria." Ornate as is Gibbon's language it yet contains a judgment upon Fielding which has been in gradual process of verification since the words were written. Most of those who have dispassionately considered Fielding's works, and compared them with the works of his contemporaries and successors, will arrive at a conclusion much nearer that expressed by Gibbon than that of the detractor, Horace Walpole. Of course, an argument which we have previously used for another purpose, may possibly be inverted and turned against ourselves. It may be replied that after all criticism is only the opinion of one man, though it is often acted upon by the multitude : and that judgments upon literary works attain an inordinate influence when delivered by individuals of acknowledged reputation. Supposing this were to some extent true, every single reader has the opportunity of righting the matter so far as he is personally concerned. But what we do find valuable about the art of criticism, notwithstanding its numerous and manifest imperfections, is this, that it not unfrequently results in the deposition of much that is unworthy, and in the exaltation of some works which have been threatened with an undeserved obscurity. The critic is really nothing more than a leader of men ; he is supposed to have the capacity of leading in the right way, and when it is found that there is no light in him, and he is incapable of perceiving eternal Truth, we should withdraw ourselves from his guidance. We say, then, that while it is necessary for a man's self-culture and intellectual independence that he should not accept off hand the opinions of any critic, however eminent, in the bulk and without scrutiny, yet when judgments come to us stamped with the names of those who have devoted themselves to the art of criticism, they should at any rate receive candid, if searching, investigation. The destruction of the empiricism of the critic need not involve the destruction of the eclecticism of the art. It must come to us as a friendly guide, and

not as a tyrant. Our own opinion of Fielding stands very little short of the most eulogistic which has been expressed concerning him ; but we trust we have arrived at it out of no slavish regard for other minds.

A glance at the novelist's life is almost a necessity, for it elucidates many points in connection with his works which would otherwise be obscure. There has probably been no instance where the impress of the author's character has been more perceptible upon his writings than that of Fielding. Some of his novels confessedly contain passages from his own life, with very little variation of detail. It will have been perceived by the quotation from Gibbon that Fielding was of illustrious descent, but the wealth of the family must have flowed into another channel, for he got none or little of it. He was born on the 22nd of April, 1707, at Sharpham Park, near Glastonbury. His father was a distinguished soldier, having served with Marlborough at Blenheim, and at length obtained the rank of Lieutenant-general. Besides being grandson of an Earl of Denbigh, this warrior was related to other noble families. The mother of Fielding was a daughter of Judge Gold, one of whose immediate descendants was also a baron of the Exchequer. Posterity may thus rest satisfied with the novelist's birth. Fielding, however, was not the only one of his family who appears to have been talented in literature. One of his sisters wrote a romance entitled "David Simple," and was also the author of numerous letters, which, with the story, earned the encomiums of her brother. We cannot, of course, now say to what extent she may have been indebted to him in regard to these compositions. There is every reason to believe that he was most accessible to advice and sympathy, whilst his affection for his relatives was deep and sincere. This —in addition to a warm affection for children—is one of the redeeming traits in a character that was subsequently marred by many imperfections. Having received the earlier part of his education at home, from the Rev. Mr. Oliver, his private tutor—who is supposed to have been laid under contribution as the original of Parson Trulliber—Fielding was sent to Eton, where he became intimate with Fox, Lord Lyttelton, Pitt, and others, who afterwards acquired celebrity with himself, and at various crises in his history sustained towards him the part of real friendship. Unlike many literary men, whose scholastic career has been rather a *fiasco* than otherwise, Fielding was most successful in his acquisition of knowledge, and when only sixteen years of age was acknowledged by his masters to possess a very sound acquaintance with all the leading Greek and Latin writers. Traces of this linguistic proficiency are again and again beheld in his novels. From Eton he went to the University of Leyden, where he immediately entered upon still wider and more liberal studies ; but at the threshold of his life the demon of misfortune which seems to have dogged his footsteps all through his career found him out. His university career closed prematurely, for his father, General Fielding, had married again, and having now two large families to keep out of a small income, discovered that his original intention with regard to his son must be abandoned. This could not have been a pleasant intimation to a youth of twenty, who had just begun to feel the expansion of his faculties, and doubtless to be conscious that his future "might copy his fair past" as regards the accumulation of the stores of knowledge. Whatever laxity of mind overtook him in after life, the earlier years of Fielding show him to have been enamoured of learning, and in no wise averse to its routine. His spirit was keen and eager, and though at twenty years of age he was somewhat given to pleasure, he at the same time was always desirous to excel, and never allowed his recreations and amusements to bar his intellectual progress.

Undismayed, however, by this rebuff of fortune, Fielding returned to London with comparatively little depression of spirits, and even this entirely cleared off as soon as he began to mingle in the society of the metropolis. It was here, as we shall presently see, that greater dangers afterwards attended him, which he was less able to withstand than the assaults of adversity. Fielding was especially distinguished for all those gifts which make a man the darling of the circle in which he moves : and accordingly we learn that in a very few months after his settlement in London he was an established favourite of its great literary and dramatic lions, Lyttelton and Garrick amongst the number. Under the auspices of the latter he speedily commenced writing for the stage, and at the age of twenty, as Mr. Roscoe tells us in his excellent life of the novelist, produced his first comedy of " Love in several Masques." We shall postpone what comments we have to make upon this and Fielding's other works till the close of our remarks on his personal history. Necessity compelled him to turn to the writing of comedies, for though he was supposed to be enjoying an allowance of some 200*l.* per annum, he made a joke about this income to the effect that it was a sum which really anybody might pay who would. At this juncture some of our most brilliant wits were writing for the stage, so that the young author might be pardoned for the degree of nervousness he felt on entering upon the same career. Indeed, although his genius was not naturally that of the dramatist, the probability is that what aptitude he really possessed for it was somewhat cramped by the circumstances in which he was placed, and the diffidence with which he undertook a profession that at the time enjoyed two of its keenest and wittiest ornaments. It appears, nevertheless, that the comedy already mentioned, and his second one of " The Temple Beau," were well received, though his success was by no means proportioned to his increasing embarrassments. That his efforts at comedy were well appreciated is testified to by Lord Lyttelton's assertion, when some one was alluding to the wits of the age, that

" Harry Fielding had more wit and humour than all the persons they had been speaking of put together." This language seems to have been concurred in by others who were continually looking out for some new thing in that age of wit and humour. Fielding must have worked with great rapidity, for during the nine seasons in which he wrote for the stage, and before he attained his thirtieth year, he had written no fewer than eighteen pieces, reckoning both plays and farces.

It was in the midst of his unsatisfactory career in connection with the stage —unsatisfactory because of its restlessness and its recklessness—that an event occurred which promised to change the whole tenor of his life for ever ; and had Fielding been as strong in his will as he was in the perception of what is right, we should now probably have been able to write him in different characters. In his twenty-seventh year he fell in love with a young lady named Cradock, residing at Salisbury. She was possessed of both beauty and accomplishments, but her fortune was small. Fielding, however, never hesitated in the pursuit of an object wherein his heart was deeply enlisted, and accordingly he married Miss Cradock with her small fortune of fifteen hundred pounds. The old, old passion had thus again its good old way. Shortly after his marriage his mother died, and Fielding became possessed of a little estate in Dorsetshire, worth some two hundred a year. Hither he bore his bride, and made many resolves to lead the life of a model country gentleman. But with all his affection for his wife—and it was genuine and sincere—he was led by the example of others into great extravagance. Setting up his coach, and living as though he could make one pound do duty for a hundred, it can evoke no surprise that at the end of three years he discovered all his patrimony to be gone, and found himself faced by the terrible spectre of absolute poverty which he himself had raised. It is held by many that genius should never be tried by the ordinary standpoints of thrift and virtue. This is

a position to which we can give no kind of countenance ; but what we may look at with regard to Fielding, as some mitigation for his conduct at this period, are those social qualities for which he was so famous. Though they ultimately proved his pecuniary ruin, they were marked by a generosity which cannot but breed in us a pity for the man himself. The delights of society were more than he could bear ; he entered into them with a zest which completely overmastered his *aplomb*, and for the time being made him their slave. So far this was unquestionably bad ; but his case must not be confounded with that of the essentially vicious, with the man who never had Fielding's lofty appreciation for the good, and never even felt the most spasmodic striving after an ideal. To the one we can extend our unfeigned sympathy, to the other only our unmitigated abhorrence. As the sequel to the difficulties which overtook Fielding, he was compelled to resume the study of the law, which he had at one time hoped to abandon for ever. Entering himself at the age of thirty as a student of the Inner Temple, he at once began to work with a will, in order to recover himself from his embarrassments. His devotion to his studies was most praiseworthy, and, as he had great natural shrewdness, there is every reason to believe that in the legal profession he would have been most successful. But one cause or another continually interrupted him, and whatever he undertook through life seems to have met with a premature ending. For his failure, however, ultimately to earn distinction at the bar, he was himself in the first instance responsible. He was not only called, but assiduously went the Western circuit for two or three years, though briefs appear to have been very scanty with him. Suddenly, and in consequence of an intimation that he proposed issuing a work upon law, his practice increased immensely, but only, we are told, to decline again as rapidly. Meanwhile physical retribution began to overtake him for the convivial years he had spent in London society ; he was seized with gout, in addition to which, his constitution was much weakened and enfeebled; though in justice it must be said that late hours of study, with literary work executed under great pressure, acted as additional causes in the general break-up of his system. The upshot of it all was that after ceasing the active exercise of his profession, and writing two large volumes (a " Digest of the Statutes at Large"), which remained for many years unpublished, he finally quitted the bar, and returned to literary pursuits. As might be expected from the nature of his talents, he contributed for a time most successfully to periodical literature. But a period of great distress quickly came upon him. With failing health, which interfered somewhat with the operations of his brilliant intellect, his mind was still further racked with the consciousness that his wife and family were entirely dependent upon his exertions. Heroic he undoubtedly was under difficulties, but there are some odds against which men cannot possibly contend. Note, nevertheless, how the true spirit of the man shone through all the darkness which surrounded him at this trying moment. His biographers, one and all, bear testimony to the native strength of his mind. We are assured that " when under the most discouraging circumstances—the loss of comparative fortune, of health, of the fruits of years of successful toil; his body lacerated by the acutest pains, and with a family looking up to him for immediate support—he was still capable, with a degree of fortitude almost unexampled, to produce, as it were, *extempore*, a play, a farce, a pamphlet, or a newspaper. Nay, like Cervantes, whom he most resembled both in wit and genius, he could jest upon his misfortunes, and make his own sufferings a source of entertainment to the rest of the world." He did, in fact, at this precise period, and in the darkest hour of his misery, indite a rhyming letter to Sir Robert Walpole, with himself and his position for its subject; which is full of the most humorous allusions. One cannot help thinking, while reading this incident, of the much later humourist of our own time, Hood, whose experience was almost its counterpart, with the exception of the difference in the cause of Hood's suffering, a naturally frail constitution being the sole reason of his bodily decay. Fielding was now writing because, as he expressed it, "he had no choice but to be a hackney writer or a hackney coachman." This was the man who had been the pride of London fashionables, who had doubtless kept a hundred tables in a roar, and whose very enjoyment of life for its own sake was so keen as to cause Lady Mary Wortley Montagu (his second cousin) to say in comparing him with Steele, that "he ought to go on living for ever." When writing for the stage, Fielding was frequently obliged to pass off work which did not satisfy his critical judgment. For this he was now and then remonstrated with by Garrick, and he once replied that the public were too stupid to find out where he failed. The consensus of the pit, however, is tolerably keen, and when the audience began on this occasion to hiss the weak part of the comedy Fielding was astonished, exclaiming, "They have found it out, have they?" An anecdote characteristic both of the man and his times is told of the novelist which affords a clue to some of his pecuniary difficulties, though it is a credit to his generosity. It appears that some parochial taxes had long remained unpaid by Fielding, a fact which need not greatly surprise us. At length the collector—as tax-collectors always will—became rather threatening in his aspect, and Fielding went off to Dr. Johnson, that friend-in-need of the impecunious, to obtain the necessary sum of money by a literary mortgage. He was returning when he met with an old college friend who was in even greater difficulties than himself. He took him to dinner at a neighbouring tavern, and emptied the contents of his pockets into his hands. Being informed on returning home that the collector had twice called on him for the amount, Fielding replied, "Friendship has called for the money, and had it; let the collector call again." Other anecdotes could be cited illustrating the *bonhomie* and natural benevolence of the novelist's character.

It was during the period in which Fielding was most busily employed upon his literary ventures that he married a second time (having lost a few years before the lady to whom it has been seen he was devotedly attached); and we now find him bending to his work with redoubled energy. But all his assiduity was in vain, and he was compelled to announce with regret that he could no longer continue the publication of "The Covent Garden Journal"—a paper he was then editing. The mental and physical strain had been too severe, and there were now added to his other ailments the alarming symptoms of dropsy. The only hope held out by his physician for the prolongation of his life was that he should go abroad; and this, upon the earnest solicitations of his friends, Fielding consented to do. Portugal having been recommended, he tore himself from his wife and children, and set sail for Lisbon on the 26th of June, 1754.

At this juncture, noting that Fielding makes his references to the matter in the introduction to his "Voyage," we may allude to him in another capacity, one in which the literary man has seldom an opportunity of exhibiting himself. In 1748 he had been appointed Justice of the Peace for Westminster and Middlesex, an office which, as we learn, was then paid by fees, and was very laborious, without being particularly reputable. As affording some idea of the nature of the work which fell to the accomplished Justice, we may recapitulate certain facts narrated by himself. While preparing for a journey to Bath, which it was hoped would result in his restoration to health, there was placed upon his shoulders no enviable piece of work. When nigh fatigued to death by reason of several long examinations relating to five different murders committed by gangs of street robbers, he received a message from the Duke of Newcastle to wait upon him the next morning upon business of great importance. Though in the utmost distress he attended, and found that what was desired of him was a statement of the best plan he could devise for the suppression of robberies and murders in the streets, offences which had become alarmingly common. Fielding submitted a plan that was highly approved of by the Duke, who promised to lay it before the Privy Council. All the terms of the proposal were complied with, one of the principal being the depositing of 600*l.* in its author's hands. At this small pecuniary charge he undertook to demolish the gangs complained of, and also to put civil order in such a state of security that it should be thenceforth impossible for these gangs to enrol themselves in bodies and pursue their nefarious occupations. It is interesting to note, as demonstrating Fielding's executive ability in his new post, that in a few weeks the whole gang of cut-throats was entirely dispersed. But the occupation of Justice was anything save a pleasant one, whilst its remuneration was paltry in the extreme. Fielding himself says that by refusing to make the most of his position, by composing instead of inflaming the quarrels of porters and beggars, by not plundering the public or the poor, and by refusing to take a shilling from a man who would most undoubtedly not have had another left, he had reduced "an income of about 500*l.* a year of the dirtiest money upon earth to little more than 300*l.*," a considerable portion of which remained with his clerk. It was acknowledged on all hands that Fielding made an excellent justice, and it is moreover affirmed that his charge to the grand jury, delivered at Westminster on the 29th of June, 1749, is to be regarded, for that time, as a very able and valuable state paper. It was most lucid and searching, as were certain legal investigations which he subsequently made. Furthermore, it may be noted that in a "Proposal for the Maintenance of the Poor," of which he was the author, Fielding was the first to make the recommendation of a county work-house, in which the different objects of industry and reformation might be united. The paper also contained numerous suggestions creditable to Fielding's magisterial sagacity, some of which have since been carried into effect. Altogether he appears to have justified the high eulogium passed upon him in the capacity of Justice of the Peace.

The journey to Lisbon was of no avail for the novelist; his poor, shattered constitution had already failed beyond hope of recovery; in fact, it is stated that he was a dying man when he reached the port. He lingered, however, for two months after his arrival, in great suffering, and at length died in the Portuguese capital on the 8th of October, 1754, being then only in his forty-eighth year. It is not too much to say that in that brief span of life Fielding had exhausted both the mental and physical energy of the seventy years allotted to humanity; and when we consider the wearing and excited existence he led in the metropolis, it is almost marvellous that he should have been able to accomplish so much intellectual labour. There is something touching in the fate which compels a man whose genius was so native to the soil of England, to die in a foreign land, away not only from those he loved, but from the scene of his literary triumphs. The last tribute of respect paid to the novelist emanated from the Chevalier de Meyrionnet, French Consul at Lisbon, who not only undertook his interment, but followed his remains to the grave, and celebrated the talents of the deceased in an epitaph. The people of the English Factory in the city also erected a monument to him. In Fielding's absence from England, he was not forgotten by his friend Mr. Allen, who, after his death, educated his children, and bestowed pensions both upon them and their widowed mother. This Mr. Allen was the original of one of Fielding's best and most satisfactory characters.

The title of honour which we have accorded to our author at the outset may seem to need some justification when it is remembered that Defoe and Richardson were writers at and before the same period, and had produced novels anterior to those of Fielding. Defoe, however, can scarcely be treated as the ordinary novelist, or put into competition with the race of writers of fiction : he was rather the fierce polemic and satiric author. In the fictitious element he was, of course, remarkably strong ; his art was undoubtedly good, but it was the art of the inventor, and not the narrator. Crusoe was a real creation, but not in the same sense as Tom Jones. He was a greater effort of the imagination, and excites the faculty of wonder in us accordingly to a greater degree ; but while Tom Jones was not a being of such strange singularity as Crusoe, he became so realizable to the rest of humanity that his conception must be deemed more admirable from the novelist's point of view. Then, again, Defoe seems to let it be understood, from the general drift of his writings, that he meant them to have a personal interest, that they were to be saturated by his own individuality, that his scorn, his anger, his sorrow, were to shine through them. His energy, his irrepressibility, his misery, all combined to make him one of the strongest writers of his age ; but he must yield the palm to Fielding in the art of novel writing. The latter had individuality too, but it was individuality of a higher stamp than Defoe's. It selected human beings not from the imagination, but from the species itself, and the types are as unmistakeably real, and more true, though not so astounding in conception to the general consciousness.

With regard to Richardson, though, as we have said, it was the fashion at one time to extol him as the superior of Fielding, this is a position which has now been abandoned by the best critics. The man in possession has necessarily always the advantage of the man who is desirous to succeed him, and Fielding, having written one novel in imitation of his predecessor, had to struggle for some time against that fact, which was continually hurled against him. Richardson was evidently a man of high moral principle; indeed, he always strikes us as a perfect compendium of innocence and the virtues. We are willing not to see in him what others have seen, merely the priggish moralist, but he comes terribly near earning that character. Yet let us not be unjust to him. His "Pamela" is a very original work, and its author deserves no small meed of praise for daring to make it a pure one in an age so strikingly celebrated for vice. But the fact that Richardson commenced to write at fifty years of age, precludes the idea of his having possessed lofty creative genius : talent may slumber, as in his case, but genius never. In some respects, "Clarissa" is a stronger novel than the one which preceded it, but here again it is difficult to avoid the idea that we are in church, listening to the homilies of the clergyman. The spiritual psychologist is at work again ; he is flinging his code of morals at us on every page. We could admire the strength of his virtuous characters without the endless panegyrics upon morals to which we are treated, but we implore in vain. The strings of conscience were what Richardson desired to lay hold upon, and to do this he thought it necessary to follow both virtue and vice from their very inception, and to write as it were their autobiography. How powerfully he has done this let his characters of Clarissa and Lovelace testify. But the permanent impression remaining is that, in spite of his acknowledged power and Puritanical tendencies, he is not one who loves his fellow-men so much as one who would wish to see them made better by the rigid exercise of those virtues to the exposition of which he has devoted his talents. Courage, talent, purity, all these Richardson exhibits, but little genius.

How greatly dissimilar to him was Fielding! Inheriting the frailties of humanity, and feeling himself bound up with its joys and sorrows, he was gifted with a mind incredibly rich in resource. Richardson had some of the weaker elements of woman's nature mingled with his own, but Fielding had its real tenderness, its compassion. Tripped up repeatedly by his follies, his nature never hardened ; he was the same genial spirit as ever. Betwixt the chariot of excess and the stool of repentance a great portion of his time seems to have been passed. He had the voice of mirth for those who wished to rejoice, and the tears of sympathy for those who were called upon to suffer. He flung no sermons at the head of men and women overtaken in their sins, though he never wrote one book wherein he failed to let it be gathered that he honoured virtue and scourged vice. He was not the kind of man to be the favourite of Richardson. More magnanimous than the latter, though not so severe in his morality, his knowledge of humanity was at once wider and deeper, and he could gauge it to its greatest depths. His invention and his naturalness were far superior to those of Richardson. His mind was more plastic, his wit keener, his intellect altogether of a superior order. He had, in one word, what Richardson lacked, genius. In his boyhood the marvellous gift began to develop itself, and in after years it achieved its greatest results with the apparent ease by which the operations of genius are often attended. In Richardson there burned the lambent flame which neither surprises nor destroys ; in Fielding there was the veritable lightning of soul. These, then, are some of the reasons why we have assigned to Fielding the right to be considered our first great novelist : but others will be apparent as we proceed.

It is fair to assume that, to a very large extent, those works which attain the widest celebrity must be national in their character—that is, must bear an unmistakeable impress of the national genius upon them. See how that is borne out. Shakspeare, Bunyan, and Fielding in England, Goethe in Germany, Voltaire in France, have each produced individual works in their various languages which have acquired world-wide celebrity. And are not all those works imbued with national characteristics? Do we not find the strength, and at the same time the singular mobility and elasticity of the English mind developed in the writings of the three authors whom we have named? Are not the speculative thought and transcendentalism of Germany adequately embodied in Goethe? Does not Voltaire sum up in himself the force, the point, the fickleness, and the scepticism, which lie at the core of the French character? An English Voltaire, or a French Goethe, is a sheer impossibility. We feel it to be so in the very nature of things. And with respect to Fielding, he has taken root in foreign soil because of his distinctly national character, and yet, at the same time, cosmopolitan genius, as genius in its highest form must always be. We have no writer to whom we can point who excels Fielding in the art of setting out his characters by means of strong, broad lights and shadows. The drawing is masterly and accurate. And nothing deters him from telling the whole truth. He is full of a sublime candour. His narrative is no mere record of events, but personal history of the most effective description. Whoever comes in the way of his pencil must submit to the most rigorous and unflinching representation. However great, rich, or powerful, he will be drawn exactly as he is—himself, the veritable man, or, as Cromwell wished to be limned, with the warts on his face. We are getting, through these observations, to the secret of the success of "Tom Jones." It is marked by the characteristics to which we have been referring, and all the world has acknowledged the truthfulness of the work. Where is the novel in existence which has reached so many corners of society?

As it is considered, and with reason, its author's masterpiece, we may well devote some space to its examination. Notwithstanding its vast popularity, it is regarded in two lights by opposing classes of readers. The first, those who are overcome by its wonderful power, have no eye for blemishes; the second, those who are afraid of seeing plain truths

stated in a plain way, and men and women represented with their masks off, have nothing for it but terms of reproach, on the ground of what they call its indecency. With the exception of certain phrases which are redolent of the period at which Fielding wrote, it is one of the purest books in our literature. Pure, we affirm, in its general tendency; and surely that is the way in which any work should be regarded. If we adopt the objectionable principle of selecting words and phrases which are obnoxious to the sensitive ear, and from them forming an adverse opinion, what will become of some of the finest effusions of Chaucer and Shakspeare, whom these same purists doubtless cherish most closely? We are inclined to agree with the distinguished critic who asserted that the man who read "Tom Jones" and declared it an essentially evil book, must be already corrupt. Of course, to the evil there is a ministry of evil, which can find sustenance everywhere, turning even good so that it may become food for their debased natures. But to a really healthy nature we can conceive no ill accruing from an acquaintance with this novel. It is but fair, however, in a matter upon which there is some difference of opinion, to hear the author himself speak before delivering judgment. In dedicating "Tom Jones" to Lord Lyttelton, Fielding trusts that he will find in it nothing whatever that is prejudicial to religion and virtue; nothing inconsistent with the strictest rules of decency, or which could offend the chastest eye. It was obvious that the author had little fear that he would be charged with indecency, and he goes on to declare that goodness and innocence had been his sincere endeavour in writing the history. Further, besides painting virtue in the best colours at his command, he was anxious to convince men that their true interests lay in the pursuit of her. What more exalted end could an author have in his work than this? and we are bound to affirm that, read in the right spirit, the novel has fulfilled its writer's original intentions. He has no scruple in laugh-

ing men out of their follies and meannesses, for he is a satirist as well as a
romancist. , But throughout the work
he has done nothing contrary to the
rules which a great artist is bound to
follow. The book is indeed full of
overwhelming excellences in this respect
of art. Look how each character is
painted in! There is no scamping with
the humblest individual honoured by
reproduction on the canvas. The same
truthfulness to life which we find in the
portraits of Mr. Allworthy and Sophia
Western we find in the depiction of a
maid or a man-servant at an inn. With
the enthusiasm which is as necessary to
art as is the air we breathe to humanity,
he labours at the minutest details till
he brings all to perfection. Then the
story appears rounded and complete,
with no patchwork to mar its artistic
effect. Dr. Warburton gave expression
to our novelist's merits in this regard
excellently when he said : " Monsieur
de Marivaux, in France, and Mr. Fielding in England, stand the foremost
among those who have given a faithful
and chaste copy of life and manners ;
and by enriching their romance with
the best part of the comic art, may be
said to have brought it to perfection." •
M. Taine, whose criticism may too
often be described as the sound of "a
rushing mighty wind," never exhibited
his faults and his excellences more
strikingly than he does in his observations upon Fielding. Nearly always
vigorous, and endowed with a jerky,
but oftentimes an admirably epigrammatic, force, the French critic is now
and then erratic in his judgments. His
eye travels faster than his mind. He
perceives, and writes what he perceives
before he has given full time for reflection. For instance, he says in describing
Fielding : " You are only aware of the
impetuosity of the senses, the upwelling
of the blood, the effusion of tenderness,
but not of the nervous exaltation and
poetic rapture. Man, such as you conceive him, is a good buffalo ; and perhaps he is the hero required by a people
which is itself called John Bull." This
is a smart use of a synonym, but one

incorrect both as regards what the individual novelist supplies, and what the
nation demands. The whole gist of M.
Taine's complaint against Fielding is
that he wants refinement. " In this
abundant harvest with which you fill
your arms, you have forgotten the
flowers." But Fielding is quite as refined as Cervantes, to whom the critic
awards the possession of that excellence. Let anyone who wishes to be
convinced that Fielding possesses refinement read the chapter in " Tom Jones "
which gives a description of Sophia.
There will be found both the poetry
and the grace which M. Taine desires.
But the critic has misrepresented Fielding in other respects. Not only has
he declared the author to be without
natural refinement, but he has denied it
to all his characters. After the lapse of
more than a hundred years, the character of Sophia Western stands forth
one of the purest, sweetest, and most
attractive in literature. We seem to
see the very bloom of health upon her
cheek, a bloom only equalled by the perfections of her mind—not so much intellectual perfections simply as those other
virtues and charms which make woman
the idol of man. Compare this character
with those which crowd too many of the
novels of the present day. How absurd
are the latter as living representations,
and stiff as wooden puppets in the
hands of their literary parents ! Tinged
with false sentiments, lacking in real
femininity, they form as great a contrast
as could be imagined to the true woman
we find depicted in Sophia Western :—

"Her pure and eloquent blood
Spoke in her cheeks, and so distinctly wrought,
That one might almost say her body thought."

This dainty conceit of Dr. Donne's exactly expresses the most perfect heroine
drawn by Fielding. In Jones himself, too, we may discover some traces
of that refinement which lifts a man
out of the merely animal category.
The namby-pamby element was entirely
absent from him, and he was in the
habit of calling a spade a spade—a
habit much in vogue at the time in

which his life was fixed. We should join in the verdict delivered by Mr. Allworthy, after he had carefully studied Jones's character—viz., "in balancing his faults with his perfections, the latter seemed rather to preponderate." It must not be forgotten that Fielding never intended to depict a perfect hero; he would have shuddered at the thought. Whilst he "would nothing extenuate, or set down aught in malice," he at the same time never failed to place in full relief—with not a shadow less or more than they deserved—all the characters which he took upon himself to delineate. Remembering this, we feel at once how admirably he fulfilled his task in the picture of Western, the jolly, rollicking squire. Had he softened in any degree the violence, prejudice, passion, and boisterousness attaching to this man, its value as a faithful picture of a Somersetshire squire would have been utterly destroyed. He is no worse than Falstaff, and why should we yield to the one conception the merit we deny to the other? But the world has within its keeping all characters which have been truly realized, and will not let them die. There is much of the bull in Western's constitution; and it is meant that there should be, for he is typical. Fielding's power has lain principally in supplying types. Other portraits are drawn in "Tom Jones" (besides those we have named) with remarkable skill. There is Mr. Allworthy, upon whom the author has laboured with affectionate zeal, and who appears as one of the most finished specimens of his class of humanity. He has the generous heart which prompts to benevolent deeds, and the ready hand to carry out what that heart dictates. He is himself a strong protest against the assertion that Fielding takes no thought of virtue as regards its inculcation upon others, for one instinctively feels that he is purposed by the author to be represented as a being worthy of imitation. Precisely the opposite lesson is intended to be taught by the portrait of Blifil. The villainy of this character is singularly striking, and when the book is closed, the reader will admit that he has followed the fortunes of but few beings who have been rendered more despicable in his eyes. This unredeemed scoundrel, whose meanness is matched only by his cowardice, is flayed alive according to his deserts. And yet the novelist has exercised no prejudice in the matter; he has simply turned the heart inside out, and made its fetid character apparent to the world. There is no artistic bungling, because there has been no attempt to tamper with the character. Fielding has allowed knavery to show itself, just as on the same page he keeps open the way for innocence and virtue.

The genius of Fielding was not strongly developed until the appearance of "Joseph Andrews," which, as is well known, preceded the publication of "Tom Jones." Before the production of his first novel, the talents of this great wit and humourist seem to have been devoted to the hurried writing of brilliant dramatic and other pieces, which had in them but little positive assurance of a lasting fame. One can well understand, however, what a flutter the launching of "Joseph Andrews" must have caused in London society. The author's leading idea was to write a story in imitation of the style and manners of Cervantes; and it was his intention therein to set forth the folly of affectation, which he regarded as the only true source of the ridiculous. Great vices, he considered, were the proper objects of detestation, and smaller faults of pity; but affectation held its own place aloof from both. Referring to the scope of his work, he has the following remarks: "Perhaps it may be objected to me that I have, against my own rules, introduced vices, and of a very black kind, into this work. To which I shall answer: first, that it is very difficult to pursue a series of human actions, and keep clear from them. Secondly, that the vices to be found here are rather the accidental consequences of some human frailty or foible, than causes habitually existing in the mind. Thirdly, that they are never set forth as the objects of ridicule, but detestation. Fourthly, that they are never the principal figure at that time on the scene; and, lastly, they never produce the intended evil." All which is very sound and true, but it availed him nothing; for did not the leading characters of his novel immediately strike people as strong and pronounced caricatures of those in the novel by Richardson which had just been all the rage? It was in vain for him to assert that he meant to vilify or asperse no one, or to copy characters hitherto conceived, with the addition of considerable burlesque colouring. Richardson himself, on reading through the work, felt what he described as its covert satire keenly, and, it is said, never forgave Fielding for this novel. The closing portion of it was held to put the question of satiric aim beyond doubt, when Fielding makes the lady conduct herself in such a manner that, as one critic observes, "she enacts the beggar on horseback in a very superior manner." Yet, making allowance for whatever element of parody there may be in it, "Joseph Andrews" is a remarkable book for the individuality of its characters. We might search in vain for a more worthy or more vividly-drawn personage than Parson Adams. His natural goodness and simplicity of heart endear him to us beyond measure, and must mitigate our condemnation of his share in certain scenes which are scarcely seemly to the cloth. This character was evidently a favourite of Fielding's, and in his plea on Adams's behalf to his brother clergymen, for whom, "when they are worthy of their sacred order, no man can possibly have a greater respect," the author says: "They will excuse me, notwithstanding the low adventures in which he is engaged, that I have made him a clergyman; since no office could have given him so many opportunities of displaying his worthy inclinations." Of the originality of Parson Adams there is little to say, for criticism is disarmed; he is perfect in that respect. Many commentators on Fielding have been unable to dis-

cover a resemblance of even the faintest character between "Joseph Andrews" and the immortal work of Cervantes. But making allowance for the variation in scenes and incidents, we consider that Fielding's novel displays a great deal of the breadth of treatment pertaining to the Spanish master. It is somewhat similar in conception also, being a mock-heroic narrative, and in it the romance and the apologue are blended in happy proportions. The spirit of Cervantes has been caught, while the author has avoided a professed imitation, and several of the ludicrous catastrophes which occur in the course of the story, give full weight to the assertion that Fielding had in his mind's eye the author of "Don Quixote" when he wrote. The humour of Fielding's history is rich and yet inoffensive; it possesses not the slightest tinge of bitterness, and is distinguished by a remarkable mellowness. Whatever else the work demonstrated, or failed to demonstrate, one thing was clear—it predicted the rising of a humourist of the highest order, and had its authorship been unknown on its first publication, there was but one man to whom the finger of society could point as its literary father. Of "Tom Jones" the second novel written by Fielding (taking them in the order of their appearance) we have already spoken at length.

The third novel from this master-mind of fiction is one to which a peculiar interest attaches. Whilst it is considered to be, in point of talent, inferior to the others, it is noteworthy as being a transcript of a portion of Fielding's family history. We refer to the story of "Amelia." Its fault, as a novel, seems to us to lie in the absence of any supreme interest in the several characters individually. They are not boldly drawn; and the fact that the gold was not of so rich a quality as that previously dug from the same soil, immediately induced the detractors of Fielding to rejoice over the supposed decay of his powers. They forgot, in their spite, that Shakspeare only produced one "Hamlet," and that if Fielding had written no other work but his crowning novel, that alone had ensured him his place amongst the gods. But, in truth, while " Amelia " is not by any means equal to its predecessors, it exhibits many graces of style, and its pathos is deep and true. The style is not so strong nor the humour so ceaseless, so abundant ; but there are frequent genuine touches of passion in it, and some scenes of truthful domestic painting. Captain Booth is a strange mixture of weakness and fidelity ; his character is supposed, and truly, to bear some resemblance to Fielding's own ; there was the same readiness in both to fall a victim to their own passions, and the same deep tenderness when they had recovered themselves. Booth is trustful and devoted, and worships the woman of his love. " If I had the world," he says, " I was ready to lay it at my Amelia's feet ; and so, Heaven knows, I would ten thousand worlds." He is not the man to inspire admiration so much as to provoke an affectionate interest. Herein is one of the failures of the novel : the hero is not strong enough to occupy the centre. We expect to do something more with a hero than condole, laugh, or shed with him an occasional tear. He must appeal to wider sympathies. He must be greater than ourselves in some way, no matter what ; but never beneath or even on a level with us. The same trait of devotion is very conspicuous in Booth's wife Amelia, who is supposed to be the representation of Fielding's first wife. We can partially agree with M. Taine in his criticism of this character when he says that Amelia is " a perfect English wife, an excellent cook," so devoted as to pardon her husband for his numerous failings, and "always looking forward to the accoucheur." This may be accepted as true with regard to a great number of the English wives of that period, though there were many of a superior *calibre*, such as we could imagine Sophia Western might make. Amelia is happy because she is typical—typical of a portion of English wives, but not by any means a universal type. The novel in which these two

amiable beings appear may be beautiful, but it lacks the pith which stronger characters would have given to it. We have to travel away from these to a subordinate individual in the story to discover a genuine point of interest— which is a great transgression of one of the cardinal principles of novel writing. Fielding, nevertheless, did not prove by this story that he had written himself out. It is neither so brilliant nor so incisive as his other novels, and has no concentration of force or continuity of plot, and for these reasons it cannot be expected to take so worthy a position ; but it is without doubt far above mediocrity.

Incensed by the adulation paid to successful villainy, Fielding wrote the history of "Jonathan Wild, the Great." In his day, more than in our own, perhaps, the world worshipped at the shrine of success—certainly of a lower order of success—nor stayed to inquire too closely into the cause of any rapid rise of fortune, however disreputably acquired. It is our general rule not to measure a man by the inherent qualities of good which he possesses, or by the claim which his genuine acts of benevolence establish upon us, but by the figure he is able to make in Society, even though that gilded exterior be a covering for much that is base and contemptible. An income of ten thousand a year will always cover a multitude of sins. Virtue itself has a terrible struggle to maintain its own against' it. And this insane feeling of adulation of material success was, as we have observed, carried still further and still lower in Fielding's day. It went so far as to shed a halo round the head of the man whose natural place was the felon's cell, provided he were clever enough to evade the grasp of justice, and preserve a bold and brilliant outward appearance. This hollowness in the conditions of society annoyed Fielding deeply ; he was moved to his innermost depths of contempt by it ; and in his apology for treating the subject of the great criminal, Jonathan Wild, he explains the motives which led to the production of this extraordinary piece of satirical writing. "Without considering Newgate," he remarks, "as no other than human nature with its mask off, which some very shameful writers have done—a thought which no price should purchase me to entertain—I think we may be excused for suspecting that the splendid palaces of the great are often no other than Newgate with the mask on. Nor do I know anything which can raise an honest man's indignation higher than that the same morals should be in one place attended with all imaginary misery and infamy, and in the other with the highest luxury and honour. Let any impartial man in his senses be asked for which of these two places a composition of cruelty, dust, avarice, rapine, insolence, hypocrisy, fraud and treachery, was best fitted, surely his answer must be certain and immediate. And yet I am afraid all these ingredients, glossed over with wealth and a title, have been treated with the highest respect and veneration in the one, while one or two of them have been condemned to the gallows in the other." This, of course, is the fault of Society, which rarely estimates a man for his intrinsic worth, whatever groove he moves in. He may be as gigantic a fraud as was ever palmed off upon the human race, but if he only manages to dazzle the eyes of those who are beneath him on the ladder, nothing will be whispered about his peccadilloes. Let him make one slip, however, and lose his hold, and a thousand gazers will rejoice in his fall, declaring that they always knew it would come. It was to help in destroying, therefore, the bombastic greatness of society, that Fielding wrote his "Jonathan Wild." It is marked by a singular perception of motives, and a careful dissection of those unworthy passions which attain so great a sway over men. He invariably keeps one leading point in view, viz., the proper distribution of strict justice amongst his various characters. The hero, who flourishes in apparent security before our eyes through the course of the narrative, cannot escape his just doom at the last. On the gallows he fulfils the proper ends of his being, which was corrupt and unreformable. Fielding's position as magistrate undoubtedly furnished him with many ideas for this history, which he failed not to make the most of, though as a composition, regarded in its entirety, it is somewhat deficient. It was written for a special purpose ; it fulfilled that purpose admirably ; but beyond that fact, and that it contains much of its author's sarcastic genius, the fragment is not in any other aspect very noticeable.

Little has been said at any time of Fielding as a writer of verse, and yet he appears to have penned a considerable amount of rhyme in his day. But his verse is much inferior to his prose, his strength seeming to evaporate under the influence of rhyme. He has not the polish or the strength of Swift in this respect ; but he might have made some figure as a rhymester had he adhered to the Muse. What he has left behind him is necessarily completely dwarfed by his excellence as a writer of fiction. It will not be without interest, notwithstanding, if we glance slightly at his attempts in verse. In a poem on "Liberty" he gives vent to a noble exordium upon the good which she has accomplished for the human race, and for the progress in arts which we owe chiefly to her. Then comes the following apostrophe :—

" Hail, Liberty ! boon worthy of the skies,
Like fabled Venus fair, like Pallas wise.
Through thee the citizen braves war's alarms,
Though neither bred to fight, nor paid for arms ;
Through thee the laurel crowned the victor's brow,
Who served before his country at the plough ;
Through thee (what most must to thy praise appear)
Proud senates scorn'd not to seek Virtue there."

In form and conception the poem reminds us something of Goldsmith, being, however, in parts less pastoral than he, but having more force. The whole concludes with the following lines, which will stir an echoing sentiment probably in the mind of every reader :—

" But thou, great Liberty, keep Britain free,
Nor let men use us as we use the bee ;
Let not base drones upon our honey thrive,
And suffocate the maker in his hive."

Other poetical effusions by Fielding,
while not exhibiting the strength and
width of view which we gain in this
poem, show considerable tenderness of
feeling and delicacy of treatment. He
has a set of verses "To Celia," supposed to be addressed to the lady whom
he afterwards married, and which he
closes thus happily, after descanting
upon the hollowness of the world and
the sickness of heart which the knowledge of it has produced in him :—

" Ask you then, Celia, if there be
The thing I love ? My charmer, thee ;
Thee more than life, than light adore,
Thou dearest, sweetest creature, more
Than wildest raptures can express,
Than I can tell, or thou canst guess.
Then though I bear a gentle mind,
Let not my hatred of mankind
Wonder within my Celia move,
Since she possesses *all* I love."

Other poems could be cited which betray a lively fancy, and as a specimen
in another vein we may reproduce his
lines for Butler's Monument. Fielding
was moved to great indignation at the
treatment of Butler by an ungrateful
court, and his sarcasm took the following
form :—

" What though alive, neglected and undone,
O let thy spirit triumph in this stone !
No greater honour could men pay thy parts,
For when they give a stone they give their
hearts."

In contrast to Fielding's poems in
the didactic and sentimental vein, we
may turn, lastly, to a specimen of the
humourous. When labouring under
pecuniary embarrassments, he addressed
an appeal to Sir Robert Walpole, in
which, under a playful guise, he administered a rebuke to that great
minister for his neglect. In this rhyming
missive the following stanzas occur :—

" Great sir, as on each levée day
I still attend you—still you say—
' I'm busy now, to-morrow come ; '
To-morrow, sir, you're not at home ;
So says your porter, and dare I
Give such a man as him the lie ?

" In imitation, sir, of you
I keep a mighty levée too ;
Where my attendants, to their sorrow,
Are bid to come again to-morrow.
To-morrow they return no doubt,
And then, like you, sir, I'm gone out."

In other verses the poet presses
Walpole to assign him some appointment ; he is not particular what, as will
be gathered from the following cosmopolitan choice which he gives to the
Minister :—

" Suppose a Secretary o' this isle,
Just to be doing with for a while ;
Admiral, gen'ral, judge, or bishop ;
Or I can foreign treaties dish up.
If the good genius of the nation
Should call me to negociation,
Tuscan and French are in my head,
Latin I write, and Greek—I read.
If you should ask, what pleases best ?
To get the most, and do the least.
What fittest for ?—You know, I'm sure,
I'm fittest for—a sine-cure."

Of Fielding as a dramatist, there is,
perhaps, no necessity to say much ; and
what must be said is not of the most
flattering character. His comedies are
not so suggestively indecent as those of
Wycherley, but there is a good deal of
actual impurity in them. The license
of the stage, to a large extent, has been
pandered to, while the literary talent
displayed is not of so high an order as
that which shines through his novels.
One point should be remembered in connection with these comedies and farces
—that they were written under great
pressure, their production having been
a matter of urgency with the author.
A good deal of the wit of Fielding is
encountered, but altogether they are not
equal to his fine intellect. Smart sayings flash from the page now and then, as
in " Don Quixote in England," where he
remarks that " Every woman is a beauty
if you will believe her own glass : and
few if you will believe her neighbours."
Again : " all men cannot do all things ;
one man gets an estate by what gets another man a halter ; " which is a very
acute remark upon the disjointed conditions of English life. In " The Modern
Husband," a comedy whose general scope
must be condemned as being worthy of
the worst period of the Restoration,

the following reflection occurs: "Never fear your reputation while you are rich, for gold in this world covers as many sins as charity in the next : so that, get a great deal and give away a little, and you secure your happiness in both." A remark made by Sir Positive Trap in one of Fielding's comedies seems to have anticipated the conduct of society in the nineteenth century, or if not of the whole of our present society, of more of it than we like to admit, if whispers from its sacred circle are to be believed —" I hope to see the time," said the worthy knight, "when a man may carry his daughter to market with the same lawful authority as any other of his cattle." Of all Fielding's dramatic pieces "Pasquin" seems deserving of the highest praise, and it touches pretty freely upon the political corruptions of the times. Considered in the light of a satire alone it may be pronounced very successful, showing its author as usual at his best in the unsparing use of the lash. It is of course difficult to say where the line should be drawn upon the stage in regard to satire. The power of the press is not so strong as that of personal ridicule, and it is on record that the Great Chancellor Hyde was ruined at Court by the absurd manner in which he was mimicked in farces and comedies, an end which would never have happened to him by mere abstract criticism. Fielding was, upon occasion, exceedingly free in his use of this weapon of ridicule ; and however deficient his comedies may be in those qualities which are admitted to sustain the drama upon the boards, there are many passages in them of unquestioned brilliancy and power. His strong capacity for parodying the great is demonstrated in more than one of the comedies ; and it is but just to add the observation that what is good and virtuous in itself is always exempt from ridicule. He perceived the moral fitness of things so clearly that he never transgressed propriety in this respect. Shocked we may occasionally be when he reproduces too faithfully the follies and vices of his period, but never through the whole of his works do we remember a single sneer at what is good, honest, or noble.

In " A Journey from this World to the Next " Fielding has been the forerunner of a host of works of our own day, of which the reading public has become unconscionably weary. Undoubtedly the best of these modern efforts to describe another world is " Erewhon ; " but it is singular to find Fielding, upwards of a hundred years ago, describing what took place in another sphere, after the death of the supposed writer of the narrative. It shows what little originality there is in the matter of great bold outlines of thought in the world ; and doubtless many things which we consider new and of great merit in our own day have been done in ages past, and in much superior style. We do not mean to imply in any way that the work we have named and other similar works which followed it resemble in detail Fielding's "Journey," but simply desire to point out how early the author of " Tom Jones " was in the field in this very idea of describing another world, for which there appears at present to be an unreasonable mania. His work is both curious and interesting, and excellent occupation for a quiet hour's literary relaxation.

Authors are measured in various ways ; some are fitted for the great mass of ordinary readers alone ; others find their devotees in a few choice intellectual spirits ; but of few can it be said that they are favourites of both. When we are able to affirm that this last is the true position of a writer we have paid him the highest tribute it is in our power to offer. It means that we are speaking of lofty genius ; for that is really great which can satisfy the philosopher and the peasant at the same moment. "Hamlet" is the product of such a mind; so is the "Pilgrim's Progress," and to these books must indubitably be added the masterpiece of Fielding. It possesses that salt of genius which will arrest dissolution. Years roll on and only add to the imperishable character of all such works.

What novelist has delighted a greater number of individuals than Fielding, or satisfied more with his exquisite delineations of human nature ? We know what his influence has been over millions of undistinguished men ; but look for a moment at the estimation in which he is held by the conspicuous descendants of his own craft. Dickens always had the most unfeigned admiration for him, and has described the keen relish with which he devoured his works as a boy. This love grew as he grew, and there was no novelist for whom Dickens cherished such a feeling of respect for his singular power as Fielding. It is said that he took him for his model ; but if so he has failed in catching his spirit, notwithstanding his profound admiration ; for in truth to us the two methods—those of Fielding and Dickens—seem to differ most widely. That is a question, however, which cannot be discussed here, and we pass it by with the observation that Fielding's power over Dickens was unquestionably immense. The same remark applies to Thackeray, whose genius, far more than that of Dickens, resembled Fielding's own. "What," said the author of "Vanity Fair," when speaking of his great predecessor in fiction, "an admirable gift of nature it was by which the author of these tales was endowed, and which enabled him to fix our interest, to waken our sympathy, to seize upon our credulity, so that we believe in his people. What a genius, what a vigour ! What a bright-eyed intelligence and observation ! What a wholesome hatred for meanness and knavery ! What a vast sympathy ; what a cheerfulness ; what a manly relish of life ! What a love of human kind ! What a poet is here, watching, meditating, brooding,

creating ! What multitudes of truths has the man left behind him ! What generations he has taught to laugh wisely and fairly !" And again, speaking of his works as a whole—"Time and shower have very little damaged those. The fashion and ornaments are, perhaps, of the architecture of that age ; but the building remains strong and lofty, and of admirable proportions—masterpieces of genius and monuments of workmanlike skill." Who is there who cannot subscribe to this exalted opinion of our author, first given utterance to in its full boldness and generosity by Gibbon, and perpetuated by Thackeray ? Whether we regard Fielding in the light of an observer of human nature or as a humourist, he has but few rivals. In the matter of the combination of both these excellences in the garb of fiction, we fearlessly reassert that he is entitled to the position we assigned him in the outset. He is at the head of his race. Other novelists may show a particular aptitude, he is the one being who has no aptitudes, for his art is universal. The temple he has reared has no dwarfed or stunted columns ; it is perfect and symmetrical, and of towering and magnificent dimensions. Years have not defaced its beauty or shaken its foundations.

Another tribute to those already paid to this great king of fiction—more ephemeral, perhaps, than some, but as sincere as any—is now laid at his feet. Henry Fielding, we would that thou hadst been a better man, but it is impossible not to love thee, and to recognize shining through thee that glorious light of genius which grows not dim with Time, but whose luminous presence is ever with us to cheer, to reprove, to delight, and to elevate !

GEORGE BARNETT SMITH.

from

"Ouida's Novels"

Westminster Review 105 (April 1876), 360–86

ART. IV.—OUIDA'S NOVELS.

Folle-Farine. Idalia: a Romance. Chandos: a Novel. Under Two Flags. Tricotrin. Cecil Castlemaine's Gage. Held in Bondage. Pascarel: Only a Story. Puck; his Vicissitudes, Adventures, &c. A Dog of Flanders. Strathmore. Two Little Wooden Shoes: a Sketch. Signa.

WHAT is a novel, and what are the laws to which it must conform? It was said long ago, and has since been frequently repeated, that the novel is a prose epic; and most assuredly it is. One might almost go so far as to say that the novel, by the capabilities it offers, affords the greatest scope for the expression of genius. For, a perfect novel should be an epitome of life: in it all human nature should declare itself as a unity; no typical property of the human mind should be omitted either by action, suggestion, or description. But who has yet compassed it? One writer may have possessed within himself the mastery of the passions, another of the affections, a third of the sentiments, and with it the highest imaginative powers. But who has yet been able to combine all these with reason, to set all their earnestness at defiance by exhibiting them equally in their humorous as in their serious light, by bearing them safely through the ordeal of irony, and by lashing them with satire when they fail in their great pretensions; and having placed them in the order of harmony and contrast, conducted them to a conclusion that satisfied the requirements of art? Such a Shakespeare amongst novelists has yet to appear; meanwhile we must rest satisfied with efforts in particular directions.

Novels may, broadly speaking, be classed as realistic and romantic. Both take nature as their starting-point, the only difference being, that the novelist proper studies to represent his little world as the great world is; whereas the romance-writer takes some striking characteristic in human nature, and builds an ideal world therefrom by the very force of his imagination, and that fact alone constitutes him the greater writer. A novel, therefore, in which imagination prédominates, and realism is not wanting, would, by this combination, merit the highest rank. The first broad principle to lay down, without the due observance of which no novel has a right to exist, is that one taught us by a study of the *chef-d'œuvres* of ancient art, and so admirably expressed by Shakespeare, "Hold the mirror up to Nature." This must be the constant endeavour of the true artist; and another equally important one is this, that throughout his work he should prove himself to be influenced by an artistic sense of, and due reverence for, the laws of beauty. With these to guide him, and imbued with the sense of an exalted aim, he must perforce produce work that will be lasting because true, ennobling because refined.

The component parts of a novel are character, scenery, and plot, each of which has its due position and importance.

And first as to character. Regarding the novel as an epic, we may say that no character should be admitted that is not worthy of special study or development from its capacity to throw light on human nature. This rule would not apply to the minor characters, which, like figures in a landscape, may be regarded as part of the scenery.

It is difficult, if not impossible, to find a new character, but one already well known may be placed in new situations, and so lead to novel developments without end. There should always be one or more great and true characters, on which the reader may rely, not only as the touchstone of the moral purpose, but as a means of affording a commentary on the actions of base persons. The physical characteristics, *i.e.*, the forms and features of the characters, should be indicated only by light touches. More than this fails to convey the desired effect. The reader should be allowed to infer the physical qualities from the mental, and from the conduct of the work. Every one, in fact, should form his own conception of the character, as is done by an actor of the drama. The development of wisdom, like that of character, should be almost confined without exception to the dialogue and action. It consists in the development of those virtues which throng around prudence and foresight, but it may show itself in every situation. If well managed, such qualities as humility, kindness, a deference to the opinion of others, may be manifested in the light of wisdom, not only in their effects, but in the noble experience they ensure.

There can be no greatness of character without a suppression, or perfect concealment of selfishness. Nevertheless, what is true to human nature may be in a measure great; and selfishness is unfortunately true to human nature, and in itself a great element of strength. Lastly, a character should be typical of a class, and the art of the writer is shown in exhausting it thoroughly, so that no one else can describe it without imitation.

Scenery, *in itself*, consists in the physical conformation of Nature, and her varying aspects under the influence of climate, season, and other changes; but the mere description of such soon wearies the mind, without creating an adequate image, unless the scenery be made to speak. The feeling that it is capable of bearing must be drawn out either in sympathy or in contrast with the characters and actions, and in illustration of these. A love scene in the midst of a storm would be inappropriate and ludicrous, unless under circumstances of deep tragedy, in which case the human affections must be raised to a pitch of intensity that surpasses the violence of the storm and exceeds it in majesty. Among scenes of grandeur which recall to mind the changeableness of Nature, or among the falling leaves of autumn, while the air is yet balmy but nature is in its decay, a love scene would be the more effective by the contrast, and by the feelings such scenery would arouse. To the sensitive poetic mind a scene which ordinary men would abhor for its monotony and tameness has an exquisite feeling and an eloquence which appeal to him with meaning as deep and solemn as do the peaks of the Alps. He can see beauties and wonders moving over the surface of the sandy plains, of the level heath, or of the far-reaching swamp, which are hidden to other minds. Let us instance a fenny district, covered with swamps and sedges, and extending as far as the eye can reach. In the midst of this scene let us place one who can see true nature in every circumstance and situation. Here he would behold the sun rise and set as on a sea. In the mists that ascended as the luminary rose and set, in the flight of wild birds, shrieking as they descended on the waters, he would be carried back to the times when creation was struggling onwards to higher states of being which it was far from having yet reached. Possessing all the sympathies of humanity, he would shudder all the more as he seemed to look upon an unfinished world where man was absent. As the rays of light sparkled on the deadly waters, and lit up the rank vegetation, he might almost conceive himself to be a guest bearing witness to those secret operations of Nature, which, in fertile and cultivated scenes, might be dreamt of only as a portion of the unknown and forgotten history of the past. Suppose this scene to be rendered more horrible by a rising wind and blackening clouds, which in a moment darken the waters and ruffle their lately smooth surface to the farthest banks. Let the storm bend the tree-tops in its course, whilst they cling with their roots to the swampy ground. Let the rain beat on them, and, as it falls on the waters, rebound in opposing showers. Here the imagination might see Nature despising her own works, and trying to over-throw them, perhaps to make way for a brighter epoch. At the same time it might see patient endurance in the landscape, whilst the trees and herbage resistingly clung to the place of their birth and life. Here and there a tree, torn up by its roots, falls with a strange cry, its prostrate branches quivering in the wind, and seeming to pant in the agony of death, like a huge animal with its antlers levelled to the earth. And in the midst of these studies, if his mind were of a wide cast, he would laugh at his own sorry condition and insignificance in the midst of the storm. By such treatment scenery becomes a living picture, instead of a dry catalogue of details.

Although the plot of a novel is the least important of its three great divisions, it is not without its difficulties. While character and scenery may be said to unfold a mystery, it is the purpose of the plot to create one. It is the most artificial portion of the work, and, therefore, the furthest removed from nature. The characters and scenery must, with due restriction, be made to follow nature; whilst it is the purpose of the plot to so involve them as to conceal from the view every possible means of extri-cating them from the labyrinth in which they are entangled. The creative hand commences its work despotically, and in the due order of fate. It has to bring its elements forward singly and without disorder; to conduct them through the doubts and dangers which must always attend inevitably on the soul that presses itself forward towards the fulfilment of some great end, and which it might reach with facility but for the antagonistic action of other souls equally seeking to achieve their purpose in the game of life. Opposing minds thus earnestly set to work must not only meet, but clash; and the skill of the plot will be manifested in the art with which the one or the other is made to triumph; with which, if justice fails at one time, it succeeds at another; and above all, with which it is made to fail, only to triumph the more at the conclusion ; yet, in conducting these contests of man with man, it is necessary to make the results appear such as must naturally occur in life ; and these results, being only too often lamentable in themselves, afford ample scope for interest, by suspending the hope and exciting the fear of the reader, without destroying the one or giving too great vitality to the other.

A plot, it should be borne in mind, is the conduct of a war, not of interests, but of principles. Interests have no development in nature ; they have no true foundation, no certain career. But principles have a birth, a growth, and an aim. In their struggle through life they lead each other on, and of themselves penetrate the most intricate mazes of our being, combating and defeating vulgar interests in their noble career ; often having to endure the shock of power, but never defeated. This sketch of the great divisions of the novel is necessary to show that, at the same time that character is the all-ruling element, and, while it stands apart, it must yet give its tone to scenery, and be the main instrument of the plot itself.

Anthony Trollope

"Novel-Reading"

Nineteenth Century 5 (January 1879), 24–43

NOVEL-READING.

The Works of Charles Dickens.
The Works of W. Makepeace Thackeray.

In putting at the head of this paper the names of two distinguished English novelists whose tales have been collected and republished since their death,[1] it is my object to review rather the general nature of the work done by English novelists of latter times than the contributions specially made by these two to our literature. Criticism has dealt with them, and public opinion has awarded to each his own position in the world of letters. But it may be worth while to inquire what is and what will be the result of a branch of reading which is at present more extended than any other, and to which they have contributed so much. We used to regard novels as ephemeral; and a quarter of a century since were accustomed to consider those by Scott, with a few others which, from *Robinson Crusoe* downwards, had made permanent names to themselves, as exceptions to this rule. Now we have collected editions of one modern master of fiction after another brought out with all circumstances of editorial luxury and editorial cheapness. The works of Dickens are to be bought in penny numbers; and those of Thackeray are being at the present moment reissued to the public with every glory of paper, print, and illustration, at a proposed cost to the purchaser of 33*l*. 12*s*., for the set. I do not in the least doubt that the enterprising publishers will find themselves justified in their different adventures. The popular British novel is now so popular that it can be neither too cheap nor too dear for the market.

> Æquo pulsat pede pauperum tabernas
> Regumque turres.

I believe it to be a fact that of no English author has the sale of the works been at the same time so large and so profitable for the first half-dozen years after his death as of Dickens ; and I cannot at the moment remember any edition so costly as that which is now being brought out of Thackeray's novels, in proportion to the amount

---

[1] *The Collected Works of Charles Dickens.* In 20 volumes. Chapman & Hall.
The Collected Works of W. M. Thackeray. In 22 volumes. Smith, Elder, & Co.

and nature of the work. I have seen it asserted that the three English authors whose works are most to be found in the far-off homes of our colonists—in Australia, Canada, and South Africa—are Shakespeare, Macaulay, and Dickens. Shakespeare no doubt is there, as he is in the houses of so many of us not so far off, for the sake of national glory. Macaulay and Dickens, perhaps, share between them the thumbs of the family, but the marks of affection bestowed on the novelist will be found to be the darker.

With such evidence before us of the wide-spread and enduring popularity of popular novels, it would become us to make up our minds whether this coveted amusement is of its nature prone to do good or evil. There cannot be a doubt that the characters of those around us are formed very much on the lessons which are thus taught. Our girls become wives, and our wives mothers, and then old women, very much under these inspirations. Our boys grow into manhood, either nobly or ignobly partly as they may teach, and in accordance with such teaching will continue to bear their burdens gallantly or to repudiate them with cowardly sloth.

Sermons have been invented, coming down to us from the Greek Chorus, and probably from times much antecedent to the Greek dramatists, in order that the violence of the active may be controlled by the prudence of the inactive, and the thoughtlessness of the young by the thoughtfulness of the old. And sermons have been very efficacious for these purposes. There are now among us preachers influencing the conduct of many, and probably delighting the intellectual faculties of more. But it is, we think, felt that the sermon which is listened to with more or less of patience once or twice a week does not catch a hold of the imagination as it used to do, so as to enable us to say that those who are growing up among us are formed as to their character by the discourses which they hear from the pulpit. Teaching to be efficacious must be popular. The birch has, no doubt, saved many from the uttermost depth of darkness, but it never yet made a scholar. I am inclined to think that the lessons inculcated by the novelists at present go deeper than most others. To ascertain whether they be good or bad, we should look not only to the teaching but to that which has been taught,—not to the masters only but the scholars. To effect this thoroughly, an essay on the morals of the people would be necessary,—of such at least of the people as read sufficiently for the enjoyment of a novel. We should have to compare the conduct of the present day with that of past years, and our own conduct with that of other people. So much would be beyond our mark. But something may be done to show whether fathers and mothers may consider themselves safe in allowing to their children the latitude in reading which is now the order of the day, and also in giving similar freedom to themselves. It is not the daughter only who now reads her *Lord Aimworth* without thrusting him under the sofa when a strange visitor comes, or feels it necessary to have Fordyce's sermons open on the table. There it is, unconcealed, whether for good or bad, patent to all and established, the recognised amusement of our lighter hours, too often our mainstay in literature, the former of our morals, the code by which we rule ourselves, the mirror in which we dress ourselves, the *index expurgatorius* of things held to be allowable in the ordinary affairs of life. No man actually turns to a novel for a definition of honour, nor a woman for that of modesty; but it is from the pages of many novels that men and women obtain guidance both as to honour and modesty. As the writer of the leading article picks up his ideas of politics among those which he finds floating about the world, thinking out but little for himself and creating but little, so does the novelist find his ideas of conduct, and then create a picture of that excellence which he has appreciated. Nor does he do the reverse with reference to the ignoble or the immodest. He collects the floating ideas of the world around him as to what is right and wrong in conduct, and reproduces them with his own colouring. At different periods in our history, the preacher, the dramatist, the essayist, and the poet have been efficacious over others;—at one time the preacher, and at one the poet. Now it is the novelist. There are reasons why we would wish it were otherwise. The reading of novels can hardly strengthen the intelligence. But we have to deal with the fact as it exists, deprecating the evil as far as it is an evil, but acknowledging the good if there be good.

Fond as most of us are of novels, it has to be confessed that they have had a bad name among us. Sheridan, in the scene from which we have quoted, has put into Lydia's mouth a true picture of the time as it then existed. Young ladies, if they read novels, read them on the sly, and married ladies were not more free in acknowledging their acquaintance with those in English than they are now as to those in French. That freedom was growing then as is the other now. There were those who could read unblushingly; those who read and blushed; and those who sternly would not read at all. At a much later date than Sheridan's it was the ordinary practice in well-conducted families to limit the reading of novels. In many houses such books were not permitted at all. In others Scott was allowed, with those probably of Miss Edgeworth and Miss Austen. And the amusement, though permitted, was not encouraged. It was considered to be idleness and a wasting of time. At the period of which we are speaking,—say forty years ago,—it was hardly recognised by any that much beyond amusement not only might be, but must be, the consequence of such reading. Novels were ephemeral, trivial,—of no great importance except in so far as they might perhaps be injurious. As a girl who is, as a rule, duly industrious, may be allowed now and then to sit idle over the fire, thinking as nearly as possible of nothing,—thus refreshing herself for her daily toils; as a man may, without reproach, devote a small portion of his day to loafing and lounging about his club; so in those perhaps healthier days did a small modicum of novel-reading begin to be permitted. Where now is the reading individual for whom a small modicum suffices?

And very evil things have been said of the writers of novels by their brethren in literature; as though these workers, whose work has gradually become so efficacious for good or evil, had done nothing but harm in the world. It would be useless, or even ungenerous now, to quote essayists, divines, and historians who have written of novelists as though the mere providing of a little fleeting amusement, —generally of pernicious amusement,—had been the only object in their view. But our readers will be aware that if such criticism does not now exist, it has not ceased so long but that they remember its tone. The ordinary old homily against the novel, inveighing against the frivolities, the falsehood, and perhaps the licentiousness, of a fictitious narrative, is still familiar to our ears. Though we may reckon among our dearest literary possessions the pathos of this story, the humour of another, the unerring truth to nature of a third; though we may be aware of the absolute national importance to us of a *Robinson Crusoe* or *Tom Jones*, of an *Ivanhoe* or an *Esmond*; though each of us in his own heart may know all that a good novel has done for him,—still there remains something of the bad character which for years has been attached to the art.

> Quo semel est imbuta recens, servabit odorem
> Testa diu.

Even though it be true that the novels of the present day have in great measure taken the place of sermons, and that they feed the imagination too often in lieu of poetry, still they are admitted to their high functions not without forebodings, not without remonstrances, not without a certain sense that we are giving up our young people into the hands of an Apollyon. Is this teacher an Apollyon; or is he better because stronger, and as moral—as an archbishop?

It is certainly the case that novels deal mainly with one subject, —that, namely, of love; and equally certain that love is a matter in handling which for the instruction or delectation of the young there is much danger. This is what the novelist does daily, and, whatever may be the danger, he is accepted. We quite agree with the young lady in the *Hunchback* who declared that Ovid was a fool. 'To call that thing an art which art is none.'

> No art but taketh time and pains to learn.
> Love comes with neither.

So much the novelist knows as well as Sheridan Knowles's young lady, and therefore sets about his work with descriptive rather than didactic lessons. His pupils would not accept them were he to tell them that he came into the house as a tutor in such an art. But still as a tutor he is accepted. What can be of more importance to us than to know whether we who all of us encourage such tutors in our houses, are subjecting those we love to good teaching or to ill? We do not dare to say openly to those dear ones, but we confess it to ourselves, that the one thing of most importance to them is whether they shall love rightly or wrongly. The sweet, innocent, bashful girl, who never to her dearest bosom friend dares to talk upon the matter, knows that it must be so for herself. Will it be her happy future to be joined to some man who, together with the energy necessary for maintaining her and her children, shall also have a loving heart and a sweet temper?—or shall she, through dire mistake, in this great affair of her life fall into some unutterable abyss of negligence, poverty, and heartless indifference? All this is vague, though still certain, to the girl herself. But to the mother it is in no way vague. Night and morning it must be her dearest prayer that the man who shall take her girl from her shall be worthy of her girl. And the importance to the man, though not so strongly felt, is equal. As it is not his lot to rise and fall in the world as his partner may succeed or the reverse, the image of a wife does not force itself upon his thoughts so vividly as does that of a husband on the female mind; but, as she is dependent on him for all honour, so he is on her for all happiness. It suits us to speak of love as a soft, sweet, flowery pastime, with many roses and some thorns, in which youth is apt to disport itself; but there is no father, no mother, no daughter, and should be no son, blind to the fact that, of all matters concerning life, it is the most important. That Ovid's *Art of Love* was nothing, much worse than nothing, we admit. But nevertheless the art is taught. Before the moment comes in which heart is given to heart, the imagination has been instructed as to what should accompany the gift, and what should be expected in accompaniment; in what way the gift should be made, and after what assurance; for how long a period silence should be held, and then how far speech should be unguarded.

By those who do not habitually read at all, the work is done somewhat roughly,—we will not say thoughtlessly, but with little of those precautions which education demands. With those who do read, all that literature gives them helps them somewhat in the operation of which we are speaking. History tells us much of love's efficacy, and much of the evil that comes from the want of it. Biography is of course full of it. Philosophy deals with it. Poetry is hardly poetry without it. The drama is built on it almost as exclusively as are the novels. But it is from novels that the crowd of expectant and ready pupils obtain that constant flow of easy teaching which fills the mind of all readers with continual thoughts of love. The importance of the teaching is mainly to the young, but the existence of the teaching is almost equally present to the old. Why is it that the judge when he escapes from the bench, the bishop even,—as we are told,—when he comes from his confirmation, the politician as he sits in the library of the House, the Cabinet Minister when he has a half-hour to himself, the old dowager in almost all the hours which she has to herself,—seek for distraction and reaction in the pages of a novel? It is because there is an ever-recurring delight in going back to the very rudiments of those lessons in love.

'My dear,' says the loving but only half-careful mother to her daughter, 'I wish you wouldn't devote so many of your hours to novel-reading. How far have you got with your Gibbon?' Whereupon the young lady reads a page or two of Gibbon, and then goes back to her novels. The mother knows that her girl is good, and does not make herself unhappy. Is she justified in her security by the goodness of the teaching? There is good and bad, no doubt. In speaking of good and bad we are not alluding to virtue and vice themselves, but to the representations made of them. If virtue be made ridiculous, no description of it will be serviceable. If vice be made alluring, the picture will certainly be injurious. Sydney Smith, as far as it went, did an injury to morality at large when he declared in one of his letters that the Prime Minister of the day was 'faithful to Mrs. Percival.' Desiring to make the Prime Minister ridiculous, he endeavoured to throw a stone at that domesticity which the Prime Minister was supposed to cherish, and doing so he taught evil. Gay did injury to morality when he persuaded all the town to sympathise with a thief. The good teaching of a novel may be evinced as much in displaying the base as the noble, if the base be made to look base as the noble is made to look noble.

If we look back to the earlier efforts of English novel writing, the lessons taught were too often bad. Though there was a wide world of British fiction before the time of Charles the Second, it generally took the shape of the drama, and of that, whether good or bad, in its results we have at present nothing to say. The prose romances were few in number, and entertained so limited an audience that they were not efficacious for good or evil. The people would flock to see plays, where plays could be produced for them, as in London,—but did not as yet care to feed their imaginations by reading. Then came the novelists of Charles the Second, who, though they are less profligate and also more stupid than is generally supposed of them, could certainly do no good to the mind of any reader. Of our novelists the first really known is Defoe, who, though he was born almost within the Commonwealth, did not produce his *Robinson Crusoe* till the time of George the First. *Robinson Crusoe* did not deal with love. Defoe's other stories, which are happily forgotten, are bad in their very essence. *Roxana* is an accurate sample of what a bad book may be. It relates the adventures of a woman thoroughly depraved, and yet for the most part successful,—is intended to attract by its licentiousness, and puts off till the end the stale scrap of morality which is brought in as a salve to the conscience of the writer. Putting aside *Robinson Crusoe*, which has been truly described as an accident, Defoe's teaching as a novelist has been altogether bad. Then, mentioning only the names which are well known to us, we come first to Richardson, who has been called the inventor of the modern English novel. It certainly was his object to write of love, so that young women might be profited by what he wrote,—and we may say that he succeeded. It cannot be doubted that he had a strong conscience in his work,—that he did not write only to please, or only for money, or only for reputation, nor for those three causes combined ; but that he might do good to those for whom he was writing. In this respect he certainly was the inventor of the modern English novel. That his works will ever become popular again we doubt. Macaulay expressed an exaggerated praise for *Clarissa*, which brought forth new editions,—even an abridgment of the novel ; but the tone is too melancholy, and is played too exclusively on a single string for the taste of a less patient age. Nor would his teaching, though it was good a hundred and thirty years ago, be good now. Against the horrors to which his heroine was subjected, it is not necessary to warn our girls in this safer age,—or to speak of them.

Of Fielding and Smollett,—whom, however, it is unfair to bracket, —it can hardly be said that their conscience was as clear in the matter of what they wrote as was that of Richardson, though probably each of them felt that the aim he had in view was to satirise vice. Defoe might have said the same. But when the satirist lingers lovingly over the vice which he castigates so as to allure by his descriptions, it may be doubted whether he does much service to morality. Juvenal was perhaps the sternest moral censor whom the world of letters has produced ; but he was, and even in his own age must have been felt to be, a most lascivious writer. Fielding, who in the construction of a story and the development of a character is supreme among novelists, is, we think, open to the same reproach. That Smollett was so the readers of *Roderick Random* and his other stories are well aware ; and in him the fault was more conspicuous than in Fielding,—without the great redeeming gifts. Novelists followed, one after another, whose tales were good enough to remain in our memories, though we cannot say that their work was effective for any special purpose. Among those Goldsmith was the first and the greatest. His *Vicar of Wakefield* has taken a hold on our national literature equalled perhaps by no other novel.

It is not my purpose to give a history of English fiction. Its next conspicuous phase was that of the awe-striking mysterious romances, such as the *Mysteries of Udolpho* and the *Italian,* by which we may say no such lessons were taught as those of which we are speaking, either for good or bad. The perusal of them left little behind beyond a slightly morbid tone of the imagination. They excited no passions, and created no beliefs. There was Godwin, a man whose mind was prone to revel in the injuries which an unfortunate might be subjected to by the injustice of the world; and Mrs. Inchbald, who longed to be passionate, though in the *Simple Story,* by which we know her, she hardly rose to the height of passion; and Miss Burney, who was a Richardson in petticoats, but with a woman's closer appreciation of the little details of life. After them, or together with them, and together also with the names which will follow them, flourished the Rosa Matilda school of fiction, than which the desire to have something to read has produced nothing in literature more vapid or more mean. Up to this time there was probably no recognised attempt on the part of the novelist himself, except by Richardson, and perhaps by Miss Burney, to teach any lesson, to give out any code of morals, to preach as it were a sermon from his pulpit, as the parson preaches his sermon. The business was chance business,—the tendency being good if the tendency of the mind of the worker was good;—or bad if that was bad. Then came Miss Edgeworth and Miss Austen, who, the one in Ireland and the other in England, determined to write tales which should have a wholesome bearing. In this they were thoroughly successful, and were the first to convince the British matron that her darling girl might be amused by light literature without injury to her purity. For there had been about Miss Burney, in spite of her morality, a smell of the torchlights of iniquity which had been offensive to the nose of the ordinary British matron. Miss Edgeworth, indeed, did fall away a little towards the end of her long career; but, as we all know, a well-established character may bear a considerable strain. Miss Austen from first to last was the same,—with no touch of rampant fashion. Her young ladies indeed are very prone to look for husbands; but when this is done with proper reticence, with no flavour of gaslight, the British matron can excuse a little evil in that direction for the sake of the good.

Then Scott arose, who still towers among us as the first of novelists. He himself tells us that he was prompted to write Scotch novels by the success of Miss Edgeworth's Irish tales. 'Without being so presumptuous as to hope to emulate the rich humour, pathetic tenderness, and admirable tact of my accomplished friend, I felt that something might be done for my own country of the same kind with that which Miss Edgeworth achieved for Ireland.' It no doubt was the case that the success of Miss Edgeworth stimulated him to prose fiction; but we cannot but feel that there must have been present to him from first to last, through his long career of unprecedented success, a conviction of his duty as a teacher. In all those pages, in the telling of those incidents between men and women, in all those narratives of love, there is not a passage which a mother would feel herself constrained to keep from the eye of her daughter. It has been said that Scott is passionless in his descriptions of love. He moves us to our heart's core by his Meg Merrilies, his Edie Ochiltree, his Balfour of Burley, and a hundred other such characters; but no one sheds a tear over the sorrows of Flora Mac Ivor, Edith Bellenden, or Julia Mannering. When we weep for Lucy Ashton, it is because she is to be married to one she does not love, not because of her love. But in admitting this we ought to acknowledge at the same time the strain which Scott put upon himself so that he should not be carried away into the seducing language of ill-regulated passion. When he came to tell the story of unfortunate love, to describe the lot in life of a girl who had fallen,—when he created Effie Deans,—then he could be passionate. But together with this he possessed the greater power of so telling even that story, that the lesson from beginning to end should be salutary.

From Scott downwards I will mention no names till we come to those which I have prefixed to this paper. There have been English novelists by the score,—by the hundred we may say. Some of them have been very weak; some utterly inefficacious for good or evil; some undoubtedly mischievous in their tendencies. But there has accompanied their growth a general conviction that it behoves the English novelist to be pure. As on the English stage and with the English periodical press, both scurrility and lasciviousness may now and again snatch a temporary success; so it is with English fiction. We all know the writers who endeavour to be so nearly lascivious that they may find an audience among those whose taste lies in that direction. But such is not the taste of the nation at large; and these attempts at impropriety, these longings to be as bold and wicked as some of our neighbours, do not pay in the long run. While a true story of genuine love, well told, will win the heart of the nation and raise the author to a high position among the worthies of his country, the prurient dabbler in lust hardly becomes known beyond a special class. The number of those who read novels have become millions in England during the last twenty-five years. In our factories, with our artisans, behind our counters, in third-class railway carriages, in our kitchens and stables, novels are now read unceasingly. Much reaches those readers that is poor. Much that is false in sentiment and faulty in art no doubt finds its way with them. But indecency does not thrive with them, and when there comes to them a choice of good or bad, they choose the better. There has grown up a custom of late, especially among tea dealers, to give away a certain number of books among their poorer customers. When so much tea has been consumed, then shall be a book given. It came to my ears the other day that eighteen thousand volumes of Dickens's works had just been ordered for this purpose. The bookseller suggested that a little novelty might be expedient. Would the benevolent tea-dealer like to vary his presents? But no! The tradesman, knowing his business, and being anxious above all things to attract, declared that Dickens was what he wanted. He had found that the tea-consuming world preferred their Dickens.

In wide-spread popularity the novels of Charles Dickens have, I believe, exceeded those of any other British novelist, though they have not yet reached that open market of unrestricted competition which a book reaches only when its copyright has run out. Up to this present time over 800,000 copies of *Pickwick* have been sold in this country, and the book is still copyright property. In saying this I make no invidious comparison between Scott and Dickens. I may, indeed, be in error in supposing the circulation of *Waverley* to have been less. As it is open to any bookseller to issue Scott's novels, it would be difficult to arrive at a correct number. Our object is simply to show what has been the circulation of a popular novel in Great Britain. The circulation outside the home market has been probably as great,—perhaps greater, as American readers are more numerous than the English. Among the millions of those into whose hands these hundreds of thousands of volumes have fallen, there can hardly be one who has not received some lesson from what he has read. It may be that many dissent from the mode of telling which Dickens adopted in his stories, that they are indifferent to the stories themselves, that they question the taste, and fail to interest themselves in the melodramatic incidents and unnatural characters which it was his delight to portray. All that has no bearing on the issue which we now attempt to raise. The teaching of which we are speaking is not instruction as to taste, or art,—is not instruction as to style or literary excellence. By such lessons as Dickens taught will the young man learn to be honest or dishonest, noble or ignoble? Will the girl learn to be modest or brazen-faced? Will greed be engendered and self-indulgence? Will a taste for vicious pleasure be created? Will the young of either sex be taught to think it is a grand thing to throw off the conventional rules which the wisdom of the world has established for its guidance; or will they unconsciously learn from the author's pages to recognise the fact that happiness is to be obtained by obeying, and not by running counter to the principles of morality? Let memory run back for a few moments over those stories, and it will fail to find an immodest girl who has been made alluring to female readers, or an ill-conditioned youth whose career a lad would be tempted to envy. No ridicule is thrown on marriage constancy; no gilding is given to fictitious pleasure; no charm is added to idleness; no alluring colour is lent to debauchery. Pickwick may be softer, and Ralph Nickleby harder than the old men whom we know in the world; but the lessons which they teach are all in favour of a soft heart, all strongly opposed to hardness of heart. 'What an impossible dear old duffer that Pickwick is!' a lady said to me the other day, criticising the character as I thought very correctly. Quite impossible, and certainly a duffer,—if I understand the latter phrase,—but so dear! That an old man, as he grows old, should go on loving everybody around him, loving the more the older he grows, running over with philanthropy, and happy through it all in spite of the susceptibility of Mrs. Bardell and the fallings off of Mr. Winkle! That has been the lesson taught by *Pickwick*; and though probably but few readers have so believed in Pickwick as to think that nature would produce such a man, still they have been unconsciously taught the sweetness of human love.

Such characters as those of Lord Frederick Veresopht and Sir Mulberry Hawk have often been drawn by dramatists and novelists,— too frequently with a dash of attractive fashion,—in a manner qualified to conceal in the mind of the unappreciating reader the vices of the men under the brightness of their trappings. Has any young man been made to wish that he should be such as Lord Frederick Veresopht, or should become such as Sir Mulberry Hawk? Kate Nickleby is not to us an entirely natural young woman. She lacks human life. But the girls who have read her adventures have all learnt to acknowledge the beauty and the value of modesty. It is not your daughter, my reader, who has needed such a lesson;—but think of the eight hundred thousands!

Of all Dickens's novels *Oliver Twist* is perhaps artistically the best, as in it the author adheres most tenaciously to one story, and interests us most thoroughly by his plot. But the characters are less efficacious for the teaching of lessons than in his other tales. Neither can Bill Sikes nor Nancy, nor can even the great Bumble, be credited with having been of much service by deterring readers from vice;— but then neither have they allured readers, as has been done by so many writers of fiction who have ventured to deal with the world's reprobates.

In *Martin Chuzzlewit*, in *David Copperfield*, in *Bleak House*, and *Little Dorrit*, the tendency of which I speak will be found to be the same. It is indeed carried through every work that he wrote. To whom has not kindness of heart been made beautiful by Tom Pinch, and hypocrisy odious by Pecksniff? The peculiar abominations of Pecksniff's daughters are made to be abominable to the least attentive reader. Unconsciously the girl-reader declares to herself that she will not at any rate be like that. This is the mode of teaching which is in truth serviceable. Let the mind be induced to sympathise warmly with that which is good and true, or be moved to hatred against that which is vile, and then an impression will have been made, certainly serviceable, and probably ineradicable. It may be admitted in regard to Dickens's young ladies that they lack nature. Dora, Nelly, Little Dorrit, Florence Dombey, and a host of others crowd upon our memory, not as shadows of people we have really known,—as do Jeanie Deans, for instance, and Jane Eyre;—but they have affected us as personifications of tenderness and gentle feminine gifts. We have felt each character to contain, not a woman, but something which will help to make many women. The Boythorns, Tulkinghorns, Cheerybles and Pickwicks, may be as unlike nature as they will. They are unlike nature. But they nevertheless charm the reader, and leave behind on the palate of his mind a sweet savour of humanity. Our author's heroes, down to Smike, are often outrageous in their virtues. But their virtues are virtues. Truth, gratitude, courage, and manly self-respect are qualities which a young man will be made not only to admire, but to like, by his many hours spent over these novels. And so it will be with young women as to modesty, reticence, and unselfish devotion.

The popularity of Thackeray has been very much less extended than that of Dickens, and the lessons which he has taught have not, therefore, been scattered afield so widely. Dickens, to use a now common phrase, has tapped a stratum lower in education and wealth, and therefore much wider, than that reached by his rival. The genius of Thackeray was of a nature altogether different. Dickens delighted much in depicting with very broad lines very well-known vices under impossible characters, but was, perhaps, still more thoroughly at home in representing equally well-known virtues after the same fashion. His Pinches and Cheerybles were nearer to him than his Ralph Nicklebys and his Pecksniffs. It seems specially to have been the work of Thackeray to cover with scorn the vices which in his hands were displayed in personages who were only too realistic. With him there is no touch of melodrama. From first to last you are as much at home with Barry Lyndon, the most complete rascal, perhaps, that ever was drawn, as with your wife, or your private secretary, if you have one, or the servant who waits upon you daily. And when he turns from the strength of his rascals to the weaker idiosyncrasies of those whom you are to love for their virtues, he is equally efficacious. Barry Lyndon was a man of infinite intellectual capacity, which is more than we can say for Colonel Newcome. But was there ever a gentleman more sweet, more lovable, more thoroughly a gentleman at all points, than the Colonel? How many a young lad has been taught to know how a gentleman should think, and how a gentleman should act and speak, by the thoughts and words and doings of the Colonel! I will not say that Barry Lyndon's career has deterred many from rascaldom, as such a career can only be exceptional; but it has certainly enticed no lad to follow it.

Vanity Fair, though not in my opinion the best, is the best known of Thackeray's works. Readers, though they are delighted, are not satisfied with it, because Amelia Sedley is silly, because Osborne is selfish, because Dobbin is ridiculous, and because Becky Sharp alone is clever and successful,—while at the same time she is as abominable as the genius of a satirist can make her. But let him or her who has read the book think of the lessons which have been left behind by it. Amelia is a true loving woman, who can love her husband even though he be selfish—loving, as a woman should love, with enduring devotion. Whatever is charming in her attracts; what is silly repels. The character of Osborne is necessary to that of Dobbin, who is one of the finest heroes ever drawn. Unselfish, brave, modest, forgiving, affectionate, manly all over,—his is just the character to teach a lesson. Tell a young man that he ought to be modest, that he ought to think more of the heart of the girl he loves than of his own, that even in the pursuit of fame he should sacrifice himself to others, and he will ridicule your advice and you too. But if you can touch his sentiment, get at him in his closet,—or perhaps rather his smoking-room,—without his knowing it, bring a tear to his eye and perhaps a throb to his throat, and then he will have learned something of that which your less impressive lecture was incapable of teaching. As for Becky Sharp, it is not only that she was false, unfeminine, and heartless. Such attributes no doubt are in themselves unattractive. But there is not a turn in the telling of the story which, in spite of her success, does not show the reader how little is gained, how much is lost, by the exercise of that depraved ingenuity.

Pendennis is an unsteady, ambitious, clever but idle young man, with excellent aspirations and purposes, but hardly trustworthy. He is by no means such a one as an anxious father would wish to put before his son as an example. But he is lifelike. Clever young men, ambitious but idle and vacillating, are met every day, whereas the gift of persistency in a young man is uncommon. The Pendennis phase of life is one into which clever young men are apt to run. The character if alluring would be dangerous. If reckless idle conceit had carried everything before it in the story,—if Pendennis had been made to be noble in the midst of his foibles,—the lesson taught would have been bad. But the picture which becomes gradually visible to the eyes of the reader is the reverse of this. Though Pendennis is, as it were, saved at last by the enduring affection of two women, the idleness and the conceit and the vanity, the littleness of the *soi-disant* great young man, are treated with so much disdain as to make the idlest and vainest of male readers altogether for the time out of love with idleness and vanity. And as for Laura, the younger of the two women by whom he is saved, she who becomes his wife,—surely no female character ever drawn was better adapted than hers to teach that mixture of self-negation, modesty and affection which is needed for the composition of the ideal woman whom we love to contemplate.

Of Colonel Newcome we have already spoken. Of all the characters drawn by Thackeray it is the most attractive, and it is so because he is a man *sans peur* and *sans reproche*. He is not a clever old man,—not half so amusing as that worldly old gentleman, Major Pendennis, with whom the reader of the former novel will have become acquainted,—but he is one who cannot lie, who cannot do a mean thing, who can wear his gown as a bedesman in the Grey Friars Hospital,—for to that he comes,—with all the honour that can hang about a judge's ermine.

Esmond is undoubtedly Thackeray's greatest work,—not only because in it his story is told with the directest purpose, with less of vague wandering than in the others,—but by reason also of the force of the characters portrayed. The one to which we will specially call attention is that of Beatrix, the younger heroine of the story. Her mother, Lady Castlewood, is an elder heroine. The term as applied to the personages of a modern novel,—as may be said also of hero, —is not very appropriate ; but it is the word which will best convey the intended meaning to the reader. Nothing sadder than the story of Beatrix can be imagined,—nothing sadder though it falls so infinitely short of tragedy. But we speak specially of it here, because we believe its effect on the minds of girls who read it to be thoroughly salutary. Beatrix is a girl endowed with great gifts. She has birth, rank, fortune, intellect and beauty. She is blessed with that special combination of feminine loveliness and feminine wit which men delight to encounter. The novelist has not merely said that it is so, but has succeeded in bringing the girl before us with such vivid power of portraiture that we know her, what she is, down to her shoe-ties,—know her, first to the loving of her, and then to the hating of her. She becomes as she goes on the object of Esmond's love,—and could she permit her heart to act in this matter, she too would love him. She knows well that he is a man worthy to be loved. She is encouraged to love him by outward circumstances. Indeed, she does love him. But she has decided within her own bosom that the world is her oyster, which has to be opened by her, being a woman, not by her sword but by her beauty. Higher rank than her own, greater fortune, a bigger place in the world's eyes, grander jewels, have to be won. Harry Esmond, oh, how good he is ; how fit to be the lord of any girl,—if only he were a duke, or such like! This is her feeling, and this is her resolve. Then she sets her cap at a duke, a real duke, and almost gets him,—would have got him only her duke is killed in a duel before she has been made a duchess. After that terrible blow she sinks lower still in her low ambition. A scion of banished royalty comes dangling after her, and she, thinking that the scion may be restored to his royal grandeur, would fain become the mistress of a king.

It is a foul career, the reader will say ; and there may be some who would ask whether such is the picture which should be presented to the eyes of a young girl by those who are anxious, not only for the amusement of her leisure hours, but also for her purity and worth. It might be asked, also, whether the Commandments should be read in her ears, lest she should be taught to steal and to murder. Beautiful as Beatrix is, attractive, clever, charming,—prone as the reader is to sympathise with Esmond in his love for this winning creature,—yet by degrees the vileness becomes so vile, the ulcered sores are so revolting, the whited sepulchre is seen to be so foul within, that the girl who reads the book is driven to say, ' Not like that ; not like that ! Whatever fate may have in store for me, let it not be like that.' And this conviction will not come from any outward suffering,—not from poverty, ill-usage, from loss of beauty or youth. No condign punishment of that easy kind is inflicted. But the vice is made to be so ugly, so heartbreaking to the wretched victim who has encouraged it, that it strikes the beholder with horror. Vice is heartbreaking to its victim. The difficulty is to teach the lesson,— to bring the truth home. Sermons too often fail to do it. The little story in which Tom the naughty boy breaks his leg, while Jack the good boy gets apples, does not do it. The broken leg and the apples do not find credence. Beatrix in her misery is believed to be miserable.

I will not appeal to further instances of good teaching among later British novelists, having endeavoured to exemplify my meaning by the novels of two masters who have appeared among us in latter days, whose works are known to all of us, and who have both departed from among us ; but I think that I am entitled to vindicate the character of the British novelist generally from aspersions often thrown upon it by quoting the works of those to whom I have referred. And I am anxious also to vindicate that public taste in literature which has created and nourished the novelist's work. There still exists the judgment,—prejudice, I think I may call it,—which condemns it. It is not operative against the reading of novels, as is proved by their general acceptance. But it exists strongly in reference to the appreciation in which they are professed to be held, and it robs them of much of that high character which they may claim to have earned by their grace, their honesty, and good teaching.

By the consent of all mankind who read, poetry takes the highest place in literature. That nobility of expression, and all but divine grace of words, which she is bound to attain before she can make her footing good, is not compatible with prose. Indeed, it is that which turns prose into poetry. When that has been in truth achieved, the reader knows that the writer has soared above the earth, and can teach his lessons somewhat as a god might teach. He who sits down to write his tale in prose makes no such attempt, nor does he dream that the poet's honour is within his reach. But his teaching is of the same nature, and his lessons tend to the same end. By either, false sentiment may be fostered, false notions of humanity may be engendered, false honour, false love, false worship, may be created; by either, vice instead of virtue may be taught. But by each equally may true honour, true love, true worship, and true humanity be inculcated; and that will be the greatest teacher who will spread such truth the widest. At present, much as novels, as novels, are sought and read, there still exists an idea,—a feeling which is very prevalent,—that novels at their best are but innocent. Young men and women,—and old men and women too,—read more of them than they read of poetry because such reading is easier; but they read them as men eat pastry after dinner,—not without some inward conviction that the taste is vain if not vicious. We think that it is not vicious or vain,—unless indeed the employment be allowed to interfere with the graver duties of life.

A greater proportion of the teaching of the day than any of us have as yet acknowledged comes, no doubt, from the reading of these books. Whether the teaching be good or bad, that is the case. It is from them that girls learn what is expected from them, and what they are to expect when lovers come; and also from them that young men unconsciously learn what are, or should be, or may be, the charms of love. Other lessons also are taught. In these days, when the desire to be honest is pressed so hard on the heel by the ambition to be great, in which riches are the easiest road to greatness; when the temptations to which men are subjected dull their eyes to the perfected iniquities of others; when it is so hard for a man to decide vigorously that the pitch which so many are handling will defile him if it be touched,—men's conduct will be actuated much by that which is from day to day depicted to them as leading to glorious or inglorious results. The woman who is described as having obtained all that the world holds to be precious by lavishing her charms and caresses unworthily and heartlessly, will induce other women to do the same with theirs; as will she who is made interesting by exhibition of bold passion teach others to be spuriously passionate. The young man who in a novel becomes a hero,—perhaps a member of Parliament or almost a Prime Minister,—by trickery, falsehood, and flash cleverness, will have as many followers in his line as Jack Sheppard or Macheath will have in theirs; and will do, if not as wide, a deeper mischief.

To the novelist, thinking of all this, it must surely become a matter of deep conscience how he shall handle those characters by whose words and doings he hopes to interest his readers. It may frequently be the case that he will be tempted to sacrifice something for effect ; to say a word or two here, or to draw a picture there, for which he feels that he has the power, and which, when spoken or drawn, would be alluring. The regions of absolute vice are foul and odious. The savour of them, till custom has hardened the palate and the nose, is disgusting. In these he will hardly tread. But there are outskirts on these regions in which sweet-smelling flowers seem to grow and grass to be green. It is in these border-lands that the danger lies. The novelist may not be dull. If he commit that fault, he can do neither harm nor good. He must please; and the flowers and the soft grass in those neutral territories sometimes seem to give too easy an opportunity of pleasing !

The writer of stories must please, or he will be nothing. And he must teach, whether he wish to teach or not. How shall he teach lessons of virtue, and at the same time make himself a delight to his readers? Sermons in themselves are not thought to be agreeable; nor are disquisitions on moral philosophy supposed to be pleasant reading for our idle hours. But the novelist, if he have a conscience, must preach his sermons with the same purpose as the clergyman, and must have his own system of ethics. If he can do this efficiently, if he can make virtue alluring and vice ugly, while he charms his reader instead of wearying him, then we think that he should not be spoken of generally as being among those workers of iniquity who do evil in their generation. So many have done so, that the English novelist as a class may, we think, boast that such has been the result of their work. Can any one, by search through the works of the fine writers whose names we have specially mentioned,—Miss Edgeworth, Miss Austen, Scott, Dickens, and Thackeray,—find a scene, a passage, or a word that could teach a girl to be immodest or a man to be dishonest? When men in their pages have been described as dishonest, or women as immodest, has not the reader in every instance been deterred by the example and its results? It is not for the novelist to say simply and baldly: ' Because you lied here, or were heartless there ; because you, Lydia Bennet, forgot the lessons of your honest home, or you, Earl Leicester, were false through your ambition, or you, Beatrix, loved too well the glitter of the world, therefore you shall be scourged with scourges either here or hereafter ;' but it is for him to show, as he carries on his tale, that his Lydia, or his Leicester, or his Beatrix, will be dishonoured in the estimation of all by his or her vices. Let a woman be drawn clever, beautiful, attractive, so as to make men love her and women almost envy her ; and let her be made also heartless, unfeminine, ambitious of evil grandeur, as was Beatrix,—what danger is there not in such a character ! To the novelist who shall handle it, what peril of doing harm ! But if at last it has been so handled that every girl who reads of Beatrix shall say : ' Oh, not like that ! let me not be like that !' and that every youth shall say : 'Let me not have such a one as that to press to my bosom,—anything rather than that !' Then will not the novelist have preached his sermon as perhaps no other preacher can preach it ?

Very much of a novelist's work, as we have said above, must appertain to the intercourse between young men and young women. It is admitted that a novel can hardly be made interesting or successful without love. Some few might be named in which the attempt has been made, but even in them it fails. *Pickwick* has been given as an exception to this rule, but even in *Pickwick* there are three or four sets of lovers whose amatory flutterings give a softness to the work. In this frequent allusion to the passion which most strongly stirs the imagination of the young, there must be danger, as the novelist is necessarily aware. Then the question has to be asked, whether the danger may not be so handled that good shall be the result, and to be answered. The subject is necessary to the novelist, because it is interesting to all ; but as it is interesting to all, so will the lessons taught respecting it be widely received. Every one feels it, has felt it, or expects to feel it,—or else regrets it with an eagerness which still perpetuates the interest. If the novelist, therefore, can so treat his subject as to do good by his treatment of it, the good done will be very wide.´ If a writer can teach politicians and statesmen that they can do their work better by truth than by falsehood, he does a great service ; but it is done in the first instance to a limited number of persons. But if he can make young men and women believe that truth in love will make them happy, then, if his writings be popular, he will have a very large class of pupils. No doubt that fear which did exist as to novels came from the idea that this matter of love would be treated in an inflammatory and unwholesome manner. 'Madam,' says Sir Anthony in the play, 'a circulating library in a town is an evergreen tree of diabolical knowledge. It blossoms through the year ; and, depend upon it, Mrs. Malaprop, they who are so fond of handling the leaves, will long for the fruit at last.' Sir Anthony, no doubt, was right. But he takes it for granted that longing for the fruit is an evil. The novelist thinks differently, and believes that the honest love of an honest man is a treasure which a good girl may fairly hope to win, and that, if she can be taught to wish only for that, she will have been taught to entertain only wholesome wishes.

There used to be many who thought, and probably there are some who still think, that a girl should hear nothing of love till the time comes in which she is to be married. That was the opinion of Sir Anthony Absolute and of Mrs. Malaprop. But we doubt whether the old system was more favourable to purity of manners than that which we have adopted of late. Lydia Languish, though she was constrained by fear of her aunt to hide the book, yet had *Peregrine Pickle* in her collection. While human nature talks of love so forcibly, it can hardly serve our turn to be silent on the subject. 'Naturam expelles furca, tamen usque recurret.' There are countries in which it has been in accordance with the manners of the upper classes that the girl should be brought to marry the man almost out of the nursery,—or rather, perhaps, out of the convent,—without having enjoyed any of that freedom of thought which the reading of novels and poetry will certainly produce ; but we do not know that the marriages so made have been thought to be happier than our own.

Among English novels of the present day, and among English novelists, a great division is made. There are sensational novels, and anti-sensational ; sensational novelists, and anti-sensational ; sensational readers, and anti-sensational. The novelists who are considered to be anti-sensational are generally called realistic. The readers who prefer the one are supposed to take delight in the elucidation of character. They who hold by the other are charmed by the construction and gradual development of a plot. All this we think to be a mistake,—which mistake arises from the inability of the inferior artist to be at the same time realistic and sensational. A good novel should be both,—and both in the highest degree. If a novel fail in either, there is a failure in art. Let those readers who fancy that they do not like sensational scenes, think of some of those passages from our great novelists which have charmed them most, —of Rebecca in the castle with Ivanhoe ; of Burley in the cave with Morton ; of the mad lady tearing the veil of the expectant bride in *Jane Eyre* ; of Lady Castlewood as, in her indignation, she explains to the Duke of Hamilton Harry Esmond's right to be present at the marriage of his Grace with Beatrix. Will any one say that the authors of these passages have sinned in being over-sensational ? No doubt a string of horrible incidents, bound together without truth in details, and told as affecting personages without character,—wooden blocks who cannot make themselves known to readers as men and women,—does not instruct, or amuse, or even fill the mind with awe. Horrors heaped upon horrors, which are horrors only in themselves, and not as touching any recognised and known person, are not tragic, and soon cease even to horrify. Such would-be tragic elements of a story may be increased without end and without difficulty. The narrator may tell of a woman murdered, murdered in the same street with you, in the next house ; may say that she was a wife murdered by her husband, a bride not yet a week a wife. He may add to it for ever. He may say that the murderer burnt her alive. There is no end to it. He may declare that a former wife was treated with equal barbarity, and that the murderer when led away to execution declared his sole regret to be that he could not live to treat a third after the same fashion. There is nothing so easy as the creation and cumulation of fearful incidents after this fashion. If such creation and cumulation be the beginning and the end of the novelist's work,—and novels have been written which seem to be without other attraction,—nothing can be more dull and nothing more useless. But not on that account are we averse to tragedy in prose fiction. As in poetry, so in prose, he who can deal adequately with tragic elements is a greater artist, and reaches a higher aim, than the writer whose efforts never carry him above the mild walks of everyday life. The *Bride of Lammermoor* is a tragedy throughout in spite of its comic elements. The life of Lady Castlewood is a tragedy. Rochester's wretched thraldom to his mad wife in *Jane Eyre* is a tragedy. But these stories charm us, not simply because they are tragic, but because we feel that men and women with flesh and blood, creatures with whom we can sympathise, are struggling amidst their woes. It all lies in that. No novel is anything, for purposes either of comedy or tragedy, unless the reader can sympathise with the characters whose names he finds upon the page. Let the author so tell his tale as to touch his reader's heart and draw his reader's tears, and he has so far done his work well. Truth let there be,—truth of description, truth of character, human truth as to men and women. If there be such truth, I do not know that a novel can be too sensational.

Anthony Trollope.

Arabella Shore

"The Novels of
George Meredith"

British Quarterly Review 69 (April 1879), 411–25

ART. VI.—*The Novels of George Meredith.*

THE two principal agencies whereby literature puts itself in relation with human life in general, and the life of the age in especial, are the newspaper and the novel. The former gives us the facts of life as they are objectively and materially; the latter subjectively and spiritually, as they might be. We might say that the novel reproduces the newspaper in another form, subjecting its selected material to the forms of art, though acknowledging, on the whole, the conditions of the world of which the newspaper is the creation and the type.

In speaking of the novel, we use the word in its largest and most comprehensive sense as the successor of the poem, the sense in which that is at once the efflux of the spirit of the age and the interpreter of human nature. In that character poetry for us at present exists no longer. It is recognized still by the imaginative faculty; every mind has a period of life in which that faculty is comparatively active—a period when it dreams and loves; to that brief season the love of poetry is for the most part confined. There are a few minds to which, even when that stage is past, poetry still remains the interpreter of thought and feeling and passion, the teacher of the lessons of life, the mirror of humanity. But for the most part it has resigned that office to its successor, the prose fiction; the drama, in a word (for that was the especial channel through which these functions were once fulfilled), has been transformed into the novel. Human life, social and personal, is now exhibited in its pages. In this point of view even the poorest three volume puppet-show—such as we are now deluged with—has its meaning. The modern drama, as set forth on the stage, does not pretend to mirror nature or real life; it has no mission, no parable; it has quite other purposes to serve. All this is transferred to the novel. And it is not only as a picture of outward life, with its varied action and passion, that it serves us. It gives us also the springs of that action and the elements of that passion; it gives us, more or less truly, the thought of the age as to the meaning of the social and moral phenomena amidst which we live. We have accepted it at once as our exponent and our instructor. Thackeray, Dickens, George Eliot, have taken the place of Shakespeare, Byron, and Wordsworth. No doubt one great cause of this preference is the realism that accompanies writing in prose. The exercise of the abstract imagination, and the submission to the restrictive artistic laws of form in verse, required for the appreciation of poetry emphatically so called, is an effort which the ordinary mind is glad to dispense with.*

But the novel, as the highest minds deal with it, can have some of the noblest attributes of poetry. It does not need that it should enforce truth by logic, that it should teach like a philosophical treatise, still less like a sermon. It may be true to its object of giving us the external aspects of human life, of setting forth those moral and social phenomena we have spoken of; may delight us with characters so painted that fiction becomes reality; and may yet attune our minds to the music of the spheres. The novel can but reflect the mind of him who wrote it; the most set purpose of giving a lesson will be frustrated if it has not been lived in the writer's heart and intellect already. Writing as one who aims always at discerning and being true to the deeper, underlying truth of things, he will show you the meaning of those phenomena; he

---

* To analyze the causes of this present prevailing realism and reluctance to make the effort above-mentioned would require almost an essay in itself, tracing, as we should have to do, the development of our present state of social and intellectual civilization.

will reflect not only the thought of the age, but will prepare our minds for the thought of the future. He will paint human nature as it exhibits itself, the good and bad impartially, the mingling of the lofty and the base, the petty aims and still pettier fulfilment, the frustration and demoralization of the higher, the prejudices, self-interests, and self-delusions of society and individuals. But under all that realism, a noble ideal will be discernible, the more strikingly so from the contrast on the surface.

Such writers and such novels exist among us, however rare in their complete development. Of these, George Eliot stands first. Among those who approximate nearly to this standard, though the most opposed possible to professed moralists and writers with a set purpose, we would place Mr. Meredith.

Before going further, we will quote Mr. Swinburne's memorable words on ' that highest and rarest quality which supplies the hardest and surest proof of a great and absolute genius for the painting and handling of human character, in mutual relation and action.' This and the following statement might have been more tersely put; but the latter, which we are about to quote, is almost Greek in its form of expression, and is besides absolutely just.

> The gift of which I would speak is that of a power to make us feel in every nerve, at every step forward which our imagination is compelled to take under the guidance of another's; that thus, and not otherwise, but in all things even as we are told and shown, it was and it must have been, with the human figures set before us, in their action and their suffering; that thus, and not otherwise, they absolutely must and would have felt and thought and spoken under the proposed conditions.

There can be no question that this test is absolute. Tried by it, many even of the finest and most admired fiction writers of this or other days, are wanting; they are constructors, not creators. There are those who in setting forth ' human character in mutual relation and reaction' obey simply the established laws of representation, with whatever seductive brilliancy of form and colouring; and the heart in us never falls under the domination either of nature or of that individual author's view of it, however near he seems to come to both. There are others who pass the subject through an alembic in their own mind, and give it out again thus worked up; but we see and feel their handling, and, in spite of a redundance of intellectual power therein displayed, we know that this did not come to us from the heart of nature. There is a third class, in which must be placed the great works conceived in the glorious childhood of the races—works of imaginative realism — such as those of the old Hebrew writers, Homer, and him who made the 'Tale of Beowulf.' These treat of human nature, but have no subjectivity in them, nor yet have they any prosaic literalness. With all their objective simplicity, they belong to that class of works which may be named creations. To the authors of the highest of these belongs that true genius which has the gift of assimilating everything to itself, and yet making it appear absolutely real, whether, as in Cervantes, in our own immortal Jane Austen, and (with qualifications) in Thackeray, it takes subjects of pure realism and handles them accordingly, or achieves its loftiest triumph in so moulding all conceivable relations, be they natural or supernatural, fact or dream, into the ideal form of their own all-fusing imagination, that they issue before us at once as though created by that inner fire, yet as wholly true to the essential laws of human life, and recognized by us as nature itself. The feeling born of such work—and this may be taken as a note of its possession of that absolute genius—is an instant and a growing astonishment, under the sense of a quality in which Originality and Reality are one and the same. Such were Dante and Shakespeare, such the author of the perfect tale of 'Undine,' such in spite of extravagance is Victor Hugo,* and such, to come to our especial theme of modern English novelists, are Charlotte Brönte and George Meredith.

We have, in saying this, implied Mr. Meredith's place as at once aloof from and above the crowd of novelists not only of the 'season,' but of what is called the 'day.' From these Mr. Meredith's difference is not of degree but of kind. His place is with those writers whose works have already been stamped with an enduring fame; yet even from these he stands apart in his unique individuality.

We have no fear for Mr. Meredith's future fame; it would not even much surprise us to see him spring to a sudden present popularity. It needs but that some great critic should pronounce that sentence, which sooner or later excelling work must extort from criticism, to place him, even in popular recognition, among the few great writers of the time. In the

---

* While using this word extravagance, we yet remember that in writers who possess the divine gift, whatever seems incongruous with their lofty standard (as the violence and pedantry of Dante or the conceits of Shakespeare) springs from some root of excellence whose efflorescence only has been affected by the conditions of the time they lived in; and this, as the ages go on, is unconsciously so recognized, that all such clouds are absorbed into the clear sun-image of their fame.

meanwhile he remains for the private delight of those who can discover genius for themselves—a choice, if a somewhat isolated, ground, and much such as has been attained in poetry by Mr. Browning, who, though acknowledged as a first-rate poet, and studied by true poetry-lovers, has never become the favourite of those who read for amusement.

If we search for reasons why so brilliant a fiction writer should not command universal success, the most obvious of these is that his stories are weighted with so much subtle and profound thought working its way through such concentrated and sometimes quaint phraseology, that the popular reader is liable to an exertion of which the popular reader is most apt to be impatient—that of pausing to study the meaning. In this and other respects he resembles the German, Jean Paul Richter, whose pages, a flowery, thorny tangle of ideas and characters, a jungle as it were, difficult and delightful alike, cannot certainly be galloped over by the breathless reader as in a steeplechase.

Another reason why he is not always easy to follow, may be that he sometimes indulges in indirect expression of his meaning, and in not so much presenting before us as implying or suggesting the links of his narrative. But this is only occasional, and then the meaning is always worth making out; and the indirect expressions embody so much wit, or sense, or fancy, that we love the work the more for the trouble it has given us.

To analyze Mr. Meredith as a writer a little more closely—he is made up of philosopher, poet, and humourist, these characters being intrinsically, almost perplexingly, mingled in him. As a philosopher, he stands outside his creations and the world he places them in, and notes with tranquil, impartial, never unkindly, sarcasm all the weak points of classes and individuals. He does not in general deal in pathos, though often one sharp touch will betray what he knows of the deepest depths of suffering. But he prefers always the attitude of the calm observer and critic of the various tragic or comic, or, as he mostly makes them, tragi-comic, situations of human life. In favour of this his chosen mood he mostly fixes on incidents which do not involve final despair so much as stages of struggle, perplexity, and distress; although as little is he addicted to giving us a close of perfect satisfaction. Entangled social and personal relations are his *forte*, for he studies the laws which underlie their phenomena and produce their various combinations. As was once said of Mr. Browning, he 'takes little account of the stock passions.' That is, he does not care to exhibit characters and actions merely in their elementary form. He traces their development from various causes, he shows them rooted in exceptional conditions, or in conflict with other motives and circumstances, and finally analyzes the outcome of all this with a great delicacy of insight and touch, while never losing sight of general laws and the resultant phenomena.

We have said that Mr. Meredith is a poet, and it needs not to refer to the glowing and vigorous verse which he has written to satisfy ourselves that the very essence of the poetical inspiration is in him. It breathes through single phrases and through whole passages of beautiful nature-picturing, and in the imagery which accompanies his analyses of mental conditions, and especially the conditions of feeling. But this imagery is not the imagery of what we must call the sentimental (chiefly feminine) novel writing of the present day, limited, that is, to the purely emotional kind, with fancy relations between the immediate atmospheric conditions and the subjective moods of the moment. There is a backbone of strength through all his play of fancy, for it is all strictly in aid of that searching analysis which forms the groundwork of the whole. This combination of poetic perception with philosophic thought, so conspicuous in George Eliot also, is essential to creative intellect of the highest order, though the thinking need not be gone through before the reader's eyes.

To say a word on Mr. Meredith's humour, it may be defined as the Philosophy of the Comic. It is very peculiar, almost unique; in style it is marked by a certain laborious conscientiousness, a painstaking gravity which seems to be carefully searching for the exact words that may fit his meaning, and produces at last a sense of the most appropriate absurdity. The grotesque may sometimes be carried a little too far; but on the whole Mr. Meredith's own phrase of 'thoughtful laughter' will well express the sensations that his pleasantry excites.

Mr. Meredith has published seven complete novels, besides three or four clever, humorous little extravaganzas, these latter most comically realistic or strangely shot through with fantastic idealism. Of the novels, the first and probably best known is the 'Ordeal of Richard Feverel,' of which a republication has recently appeared, a work loaded to excess with thought and youthful imagination, that seems to throw over its pages a shine as of the morning. It has also, perhaps, the most fire of passion and force of pathos of all Mr. Meredith's works, and in one of the personages, Sir

Austen Feverell, the paternal System-monger, the analysis of character is as fine and subtle as anything he has written. Still there is a crudeness of handling, situations too violent, and humour, to our taste at least, unpleasingly broad. The work, in fact, is so clearly youthful, alike in its promise and its faults, that we prefer to pass it over, and single out for detailed criticism two only, 'Emilia in England' and 'Beauchamp's Career,' two of the latest, and, while quite as original in conception and treatment as the others, the most carefully worked and entirely successful, as we consider, of all. In 'Emilia,' as story and treatment, the faults are too obvious to need pointing out, but it is brilliant with genius which promises art: in 'Beauchamp' we gladly recognize a maturity, a mellowing, a beautiful finish, which sets it as a crown upon all his other works. In almost all these others, certain errors of taste, chiefly connected with the comic element, occur to mar our enjoyment: here the fault is, we think, wholly absent.

The object of 'Emilia in England' is to paint a being accidentally evolved and developed, under no conventional constraint, of absolute naturalness, and with the addition of one splendid faculty. There is another object, too, which we trace more confusedly, in the history of the Pole family—a picture of artificial and sentimental refinement, with small root of reality in it, pretensions which prove unequal to any strain, which wreck the one in whom they represented something true, and frankly subside in the others into meanness and vulgarity. Perhaps, next to the heroine, the most distinctive figure is that of the delightfully odious Mr. Pericles, the great millionaire, the Greek merchant, the musical virtuoso, selfish, determined, unscrupulous, and not wholly repellent only because he is so irresistibly humorous. Such characters do not give us the idea that he is designedly creating humorous figures, or casting about for subjects for laughter, but as if he had actually known them, and was reproducing with grave fidelity their strong and quaint traits, so that we know them too. But by far the happiest of his creations is Emilia herself. She is at once vividly real, and singularly difficult to define. We feel only a strong and constant attraction, as if we were always watching some object of curious study, wondering with pleasant perplexity what she will do next. She has at once transparent sincerity, intensity, and childlike objectiveness; she does not theorize about herself; she exerts no command, no deliberate fascination; she seems simply to cling to others, to need them and their love; and is as successful as if she were the most finished coquette in drawing hearts after her. Perhaps with all her truthfulness and devoted passion she is a kind of artless coquette. She has that need which a great French writer has signalized as the woman's ruling characteristic, the need that the men about her should be interested in her, as if she instinctively knew that that personal magnetism is all the power that woman can hope for—and she has it. Poor, obscure, a foreigner, of lowly birth and ignoble surroundings, absolutely devoid of culture, with nothing but her divine voice, her wondrous eyes, and her ardent simplicity, she makes for herself a sphere and a destiny. Her nature has the purity of fire, whose life and movement reject all taint, but it has too the sudden rash impulses hurrying her into perils that might be ruin, were it not for the good star that seems always pledged to protect her. So all at last goes well with the generous, impassioned creature; and the grateful self-devotion which makes her bind herself to three years' subjection in order to pay her benefactor's debts, and the patriotic feeling which gradually takes hold of her heart as the first ill-fated passion is burnt out, give the stamp of nobleness to her character.

That germ of a new element indicated at the close of this story is fully developed in the novel which is meant as its sequel, 'Vittoria.' Here we have her career as a patriotic singer in Italy, devoted to her country's cause, and closely linked with the men who champion it. There is nothing in the undeveloped Emilia which might not mature into the grave and lofty Vittoria: that strenuousness which is one of her vital attributes, though appearing at first fitfully amongst the unorganized conditions of her life, is all concentrated in the double-stranded passion for her country and her lover. Yet it must be owned that Mr. Meredith has drawn with more vivid strokes the little witch of the first story than the stately sibyl of the second.

The main object of 'Beauchamp's Career' is, no doubt, like that of 'Emilia in England,' to paint one marked individuality; but, from the conditions in which he has placed it, 'Beauchamp's Career' may fairly be called a political novel. The young aristocratic Radical, fiercely *aux prises* with all the social and political forces of his class, is for ever throwing himself into the boiling surges of political agitation, and stirring up the problems that lie seething in the deeps around us. These problems Mr. Meredith fearlessly lays hold of, and sets before us as seen and interpreted by various minds, but does not affect to solve them himself. He could not perhaps have done so without committing himself to that objectionable thing, a novel with a purpose. Yet these vital matters are so touched on as to make us feel that he regards them as great realities, not as mere art-properties; that he must have felt them as a man before handling them as an artist; and we here and there find glimpses of opinions which tell us that he has sought at least within himself for their solution.

One reason perhaps why the great principles and causes involved in the controversies of the present time are thus left undecided, and still in conflict, is because such a view of the subject suits best with the career of the hero, which concludes nothing. He is a fine crusading nature, doomed to be one of the noble failures of a world not yet ripe for the root-and-branch changes he would force upon it. He fails also because he can see but one object at a time, and that isolated from all the other objects that modify it, and from all the facts that would suggest the best mode of attaining it. He has will, resolution, self - devotion, sharp perception, passionate eloquence, but he has not insight. He is described by one of the onlookers as the '*ingénu,* or peculiarly heavenly messenger, who pretends that he ought never to have any harm done him, although he carries a lighted match.' It must be owned that he has, too, some moral deficiencies that partly account for his failure in 'winning souls.' He can never accommodate his means or modify his action; and courtesy, consideration, fairness and patience even towards women, disappear when he sees himself obstructed in his course, or when, as must often happen to such uncalculating natures, he finds himself at variance with himself. These defects stand very much in his way in the two love affairs which with sailor-like illogicalness he is pursuing at one and the same time, and which are further damaged by a half-hearted irresolution much less sailor-like; though luckily these faults do not greatly hinder him with the third, which follows immediately on the heels of the two others. One is vexed to find that this seemingly fiery lover has never really made up his mind about any of the 'objects,' and fixes upon the last apparently because she is the only one left him.

The story, then, is the history of Beauchamp's loves and politics: round these are grouped his party friends and enemies, his antagonistic kindred, his female friends, sympathizing, compassionately disapproving, loving. The incident which colours the whole story, producing by a natural series of consequences all the difficulties and leading to the conclusion, springs out of Beauchamp's candidature for Bevisham, and his consequent close alliance with the leading Radical there. An outrageous injury inflicted on the latter estranges his devoted follower from all his own relations and friends, cuts short his love-suit, embitters his nature, and throws into a ferment the society of which he forms a part. All these various results are traced with skill; and many and sometimes entangled as the threads of the story are, we follow them with unflagging interest till the whole skein is reeled off. We cannot pretend to be quite contented with the solutions of the respective love struggles which we have been studying so long. But Mr. Meredith seems more penetrated with the bathos of human life than with its occasions of climax, and is apt to prefer even a fiasco to a triumphant success. The last chapters, full of beauty as they are, are in other respects not quite satisfactory : the conclusion seems to be hurried over, and we suspect that the author had planned a different one, more led up to by the preceding scenes. We think that the story would have been better arranged if the beginning, dwelling on Beauchamp's boyhood, had been abridged in favour of a fuller working out of the end —the more so as this beginning does not promise the interest which is awakened as soon as the hero becomes man and lover.

But it is only when we have closed the book, and the spell is dissolved, that we become conscious of these objections. It is indeed no easy matter to criticize 'Beauchamp's Career' aright. It keeps us *thinking* the whole way, and when we have come to the end we feel that we have learnt so much, or rather had so much suggested to us, we have had to trace so many roots of human action laid bare, and have been dazzled with so much splendour of language, have had to keep hold of so many threads and possess ourselves of so many enigmatically-stated truths, that we feel at once the difficulty and yet the necessity of trying to summarize our impressions and define the charm that has so constrained us. Perhaps one chief element of that charm is in the variety and lifelikeness of the characters which surround Beauchamp, in various relations; and though Mr. Meredith's personages ·a little too much resemble their author in the intellectual subtlety of their ideas and the terse epigrammatic quaintness of their speech, they have yet a rare dramatic truthfulness. Such are his uncle, Lord Romfrey (perhaps the best drawn character in the book), 'the splendid old man,' 'in mind a mediæval baron, in politics a crotchety unintelligible Whig,' 'to whom the game laws are the corner-stone of law and of a man's right to hold his own,' with his interest in birds, and beasts, and herbs, 'what ninnies call nature in books,' who, stormed by his nephew's impetuous indignation, only 'takes a chair, saying, with the utmost placidity, " Windy talk, that ;" ' Rosamond Culling, who interests more than she attracts us, with her 'habit of wringing an unanimous verdict from a jury of temporary impressions ;' Dr. Shrapnell, who is made to lay a strong hold on our affections, as he did on Beauchamp's, who ' stooped from his height to speak, or rather swing the stiff upper half of his body down to his hearer's level and back again, like a ship's mast on a billowy sea ;' the warmhearted, bigoted, testy old Tory gentleman, Colonel Halkett ; and Blackburn Tuckham, 'an exuberant Tory, who was the reverse of the cavalier : ' but we must give the description of him.

Mr. Tuckman had a round head, square flat forehead, and ruddy face. He stood as if his feet claimed the earth under them for his own, with a certain shortness of leg that detracted from the majesty of his resemblance to our Eighth Harry, but increased his air of solidity ; and he was authoritative in speaking. ' Let me set you right, sir,' he said sometimes to Colonel Halkett ; and that was his modesty. ' You are altogether wrong,' Miss Halkett heard herself informed ; which was his courtesy. He examined some of her water-colour drawings before sitting down to dinner, approved of them, but thought it necessary to lay a broad finger on them to show their defects. On the question of politics, ' I venture to state,' he remarked, in anything but the tone of a venture, ' that no educated man of ordinary sense who has visited our colonies will come back a Liberal.'

As for the three fair creatures who are the objects of Beauchamp's polytheistic worship, and who are all subtly and tenderly delineated, we have Renée, with the pathos of her destiny, her French grace, and the ' wild sweetness of her eyes,' the story of whose relations with Beauchamp during that idyllic Venetian episode is like a long lyrical sigh of love and sorrow ; Cecilia, the very flower of high - born, high - bred English girlhood, the lily of maidens, with its golden heart where the possibilities of passion lie enfolded, who ' sees suitors come and go, as from a watch - tower in the skies ;' and Jenny, ' whose eyes Beauchamp had seen weighing and balancing questions more than he quite liked,' the embodiment of delicate feminine intellect, complete at all points, young, gentle, firm, and wise.

We will not further anticipate the course of the story, but must just notice what we think perhaps the raciest and most lifelike picture in the whole, that of the electoral canvass, of which the characters and humours—especially the ' general piety' of Mr. Oggler, and the melancholy fanaticism of that ' young monster of unreason,' Colpendike the shoemaker—are admirably hit off.

We must wind up our notice of this particular work with

a few words on the author's style, shown, as we think, here in its maturity. But it would need almost his own powers to do justice to the splendour and strangeness of it, joined with an exactness of expression, such as can proceed only from clearness of idea and a perfect sense of the value of words—that sense which almost in itself constitutes genius. This style of his is so unique, that it calls for a word or two more, as, though thoroughly native to the writer, it is evidently very carefully wrought. There is a marked absence of the obvious seductive cadences, the easy pathetic tricks which express the receptive and gently emotional, rather than the creative and passionate mind. Not even the wild music of passion does he freely indulge in, and for all the rant that simulates it he has an utter abhorrence. His ordinary style, especially that of his vivid dialogue, is terse, abrupt, full of force, point, and colour, in brief, strong sentences, like the waves of a short chopping sea. But in his most reflective and most touching passages he has that grave sustained tone which seems to dominate the situation, using its restrained pathos, its musical suggestions, and its deep inquiring murmur, according to a law of his own.

We must attempt to give some idea of our author's peculiar style of thought and language, as far as three or four of the briefest and slightest touches can avail.

The state of feeling in England between the time of the first Great Exhibition and the Crimean War.

England was drifting into foreign complications. . . . The governing people, which is looked to for direction, in grave dilemmas, by its representatives and reflectors, shouted that it had been accused of pusillanimity. No one had any desire for war, only we really had (and it was perfectly true) been talking gigantic nonsense of peace and of the everlastingness of the exchange of fruits for money, with angels waving rare groceries of Eden in joy of the commercial picture.

Two candidates at an election, the old Whig and the young Radical.

They had to run as twins, but Beauchamp's conjunct would not run, he would only walk. . . . Beauchamp, with a furious tug of Radicalism, spoken or performed, pulled Cougham on his beam ends. . . . A word saved him—the word 'practical.' 'Are we practical?' he inquired. . . . And that question penetrates the bosom of an English audience, and will surely elicit a response if not plaudits. Practical or not, the good people affectingly wish to be thought so. It has been asked, 'If we are not practical, what are we? Ah!'—Beauchamp talking to Cougham apart, would argue that the daring and the farsighted course was often the most practical. Cougham extended a deprecating hand. 'Yes, I have gone over all that.' Occasionally he was maddening.

The condition of the ' silent stricken, unused to dialectics.'

Of course she could have shot a rejoinder to confute him with all the force of her indignation, save that the words were tumbling about her head like a world in disruption, which made her feel a weakness at the same time that she gloated on her capacity, as though she had an enormous army quite overwhelming if it could but be got to move in advance.

Here are two little pictures of incipient maiden-love.

If there was any warm feeling below the muffled surface of the girl's deliberate eyes while gazing on him, it was that he who had saved her brother must be nearly brother himself, yet was not quite ; yet must be loved ; yet not approached. He was her brother's brother-in-arms, brother-in-heart, not hers, yet hers through her brother.

He had not trifled with her, hardly flattered ; he had done no more than kindle a young girl's imaginative liking. The pale flower of imagination, fed by dews, not by sunshine, was born drooping, and hung secret in her bosom, shy as a bell of the frail wood-sorrel. Yet there was pain for her in the perishing of a thing so poor and lowly.

In this, and in his other novels, as indeed in most novels of any thought, we find frequent suggestions on that most fruitful of subjects—the social relation of the sexes. His allusions are either light playful glances, or suggestive hints, absolutely impartial in their tone, and as little committing him to any fixed view on the subject as do the many-sided lights in which he has set the more general problems of which we have spoken. We shall here touch only on the ideas that may be gathered from this work as to his view of that now much debated question, the position of women in the social system, as fixed by nature or defined by conventional law. Whatever are Mr. Meredith's opinions as to the natural mental tendencies of women, we were hardly prepared to find the woman of high intelligence and culture, lovingly trained in an atmosphere of generous Liberalism, retrograde into what the hero and we imagine the author would regard as the prejudices of more commonplace women. We can hardly suppose that a writer of such fine insight and catholic comprehension gives in his adhesion to that metaphysical theory of some modern philosophers, which asserts a mysterious, invariable, ineradicable instinct of sex and temperament, leading women to one particular type of intellectual, moral, and political ideas.* Perhaps we may take comfort in the argument—whether intended or not—against this theory, supplied by another woman's intellectual growth, her power of taking in new ideas, and candidly

* We are not, be it remembered, speaking of those Conservative tendencies as right or wrong, but only mooting the theory that makes them a characteristic of sex, independent of reason or influence.

admitting their force. Granting that all this development is first wakened by a strong personal interest—a case which, whether in man or woman, is in early youth almost the rule— yet opposed as it is to all the influences of her position and bringing up, to the thousand prejudices of hearth and home and caste and convention, and coupled, even before her ' conversion,' with an independence of judgment which could not always be hoodwinked by father or lover, we may fairly, we think, check the conclusion from the former instance with what may be drawn from this.

The picture of this clear and ripening intellect, framed in so fair a form, suggests the hope that Mr. Meredith is no friend to that ' hard and fast line' which would deny to women, and to women only, all those potentialities of growth and that requisite previous enlargement of traditional limits and removal of obstructions which have in all else become the law.

For Beauchamp himself, it may be observed that, with characteristic inconsistency, he tries to convert Cecilia by force of reasoning, while still finding it ' impossible to believe that women thought.' A false and lowering estimate of half the human race is not uncommon in young men, whose knowledge of women has been gathered mainly from tradition or unwise experience. Such an estimate is apt, in after years, to harden into a contemptuous uncompromising determination to 'keep things just as they are,' or to justify itself by the metaphysical theory above alluded to. In either case society is the worse, and justice missed in legislative decisions which these ideas underlie. No definition of woman's nature can be sound that does not take into account, and is not limited by, the conditions under which social laws have placed her.

We have scarcely done justice in our preceding remarks to the delicate charm, at once a subtly sympathetic insight and a generous truthfulness, with which Mr. Meredith has pourtrayed the best feminine types among those that come to view on the social surface. He has so pourtrayed them that we can believe him to have, kept to himself, an ideal of something rarer still, of what woman might be, perhaps will be, of what possibly some women even now are. Half-faces of this ideal appear in his works, ranging from the exquisite intellectual German princess, Ottilia, in the 'Adventures of Harry Richmond,' to the untrained child of nature, Emilia. The former indeed is but a charming suggestion; but even as she is, placed in this present generation of young men, she would appear to have been found by them

> too wise, too good
> For human nature's daily food.

Yet may we not hope from Mr. Meredith some day a fuller exposition of that 'perfect woman' who we are sure is no stranger to his conceptions?

To conclude. To all those questions that arise out of that great organization of humanity that we call civilized society there is an answer in the eternal moral code, to which we can but approximately attain, but which all who think and write on these matters are bound to study and set forth as well as they can. This work is nobly done by reproducing the noblest examples of those who live to find it. May not we trust that he who has seen so well and thrown with so bold a hand on the canvas the different lights in which the most serious problems present themselves to different minds, may, by some clear illuminating ray cast from his own in some future work, aid in the great task of social regeneration.

"Henry Holbeach"
(W.B. Rands)

"The New Fiction"

Contemporary Review 37 (February 1880), 247–62

THE NEW FICTION.

The Egoist: A Comedy in Narrative. By George Meredith.
Pendennis. By W. M. Thackeray.
David Copperfield. By Charles Dickens.
Villette. By Currer Bell.
Sylvia's Lovers. By Mrs. Gaskell.
Three Brothers. By Mrs. Oliphant.
Madcap Violet. By William Black.
Far from the Madding Crowd. By Thomas Hardy,
Cripps the Carrier. By R. D. Blackmore.
Phineas Finn. By Anthony Trollope.
Daniel Deronda. By George Eliot.
The Heir of Redclyffe. By Miss Yonge.
Alec Forbes of Howglen. By George MacDonald.

I T has been more than once remarked that when history came to be
properly written it would eclipse in attractiveness all the fiction
that could be invented and put into books; and, indeed, there is some
such saying to be found either in the writings or the reported words of
Macaulay. That distinguished man and delightful historian had his own
reasons for knowing that the biography of nations might be found
interesting even by readers outside the class of students proper.
But the day is yet far off when the historian shall jostle the novelist
out of his place. Within the last twenty years the novel proper
has undergone a development which may still be pronounced astonishing
even by those who have been accustomed to consider it, and has taken
rank side by side—at no humiliating distance, though, of course, not
close—with poetry and philosophy, formally so entitled. It is far
otherwise than sarcastically true that "Romola" and "Daniel Deronda"
cannot be called light reading; and, passing away from fiction of that
graver sort, it is abundantly clear that not even yet has criticism done
all the work which the New Fiction has cut out for it in the way of
widening its scope and improving the instruments by which it
endeavours to trace the more subtle affiliations of literature. It may
almost be said that there is now a branch of criticism specially, if not
exclusively, applying to novels; and, perhaps, it may be added that the
critics who cultivate this branch of work do not yet feel themselves
quite up to their work. In fact, the New Fiction is a product for which
the canons were not ready, and some of the best things said about it
and what it foretells are little better than self-conscious talk to fill up
time.

Of course the notion that the historian could ever supersede the
novelist is absurd. However little short of chaotic our present criticism

may be in such matters, there can be no risk in laying it down that the historic faculty and the poetic faculty are two very different things. So much to begin with; and it carries us a long way. Macaulay had poetic faculty, though it was very narrow; but it is certain he would have made a grotesque failure of a novel, if he had attempted one. Lord Brougham did write a novel, but it was rather aborted than produced; and those who have never seen it may be thankful for a mercy not small—there are things one would much rather never have known. What sort of novel would Mr. Grote have written? But novelists have written history, and Mr. Thackeray, who contemplated writing it, would possibly have succeeded. We say possibly; because his Lectures on the Four Georges, and on the Humourists of the Eighteenth Century, do not encourage one to dispense with phrases of conjecture in this matter. That George Eliot could write history is certain, and it would surprise no one if she were to leave some really monumental work of that order behind her. Bulwer-Lytton did write history, and not unsuccessfully. So did the author of " Caleb Williams" and " St. Leon." If Defoe could not have succeeded as an historian, it would only have been because he was such " a matter-of-lie man" (to quote Charles Lamb's phrase), that he could never copy straight on. " Is that all ?" asked the Scotch advocate, when his client had apparently completed his statement of his case—" Is that all ?" And the client replied, " Ou ay, man; that's a' the truth; ye maun put the lees till't yoursel." It is to be feared that Defoe, while he was telling his true historical story, would, by the necessity of his nature, have added " lees till't" in abundance. And as this brings us up to a point, we may as well stop in an enumeration which might easily be carried on to an indefinite length.

Let a man tell what story he will, he is sure to add "lees till't," though unconsciously. Lord Macaulay did it in his historical and biographical writings, and no man has done it more than Mr. Carlyle. The involuntary false touches come out of a writer's idiosyncrasy. But it is not here that we arrive at the essential difference between the genius of the novelist and that of the historian. Even when the writer is fond of taking an historical basis for his work—like Sir Walter Scott, for example—his manner is obviously different. Nor does mere excess of detail or picturesqueness make all the difference. It lies largely in the *filling up* and in the pervading air of *personal intimacy* which belongs to the novel, as distinguished from the history. You are supposed to know how the historian came by his knowledge, and when he makes a fancy picture he tells you so, directly or indirectly. Not so the novelist. The novelist tells you with impossible minuteness the most secret soliloquy of a man's mind; has unrestrained access to a lady's boudoir, and will tell you all she did there at a given time, though the door was locked, and the curtains drawn. From end to end of his story he does not give you his authority, and you are not expected to ask for it. On the contrary, that would destroy the illusion. The whole of his work consists of digested and transformed experience presented to you under arrangements new to himself. It is all true, except as to " the way it is put," and you feel that it is true— that is, if the work be good of the kind ; but you cannot " condescend upon particulars" as to when and where it all happened. Of course, we are now taking only a general view of the matter—there are plenty of books coming under the category of the novel which are more or less historical ; but it is admitted that the task of writing a work of fiction avowedly founded on fact is one of extreme delicacy.

It is upon the point of *filling up* that we easily arrive at perhaps the most obvious difference between novel and history. It is quite certain that Napoleon dined ; and that he had many interestingly painful discussions with Josephine before putting her away. In point of fact, our interest in Napoleon was so great that the driest and least expressive of historians gave us a good deal of personal gossip about him, and in proportion, as we come to feel intimate with a personage, we excuse such writing. But to introduce it into history, if the scale of the writing be large, is a difficult task, and we are sure to be sensible of a sort of jolt or jerk in passing from one passage to another, unless the artist be one of consummate skill. If a novelist had conceived a Napoleon, and had introduced the repudiation of Josephine and the marriage to Marie Louise, he would have told the story by fixing on occasions and scenes unimportant in themselves, and filling up till he interested us ; at the same time telling the story in the most complete manner conceivable. You would have been introduced, perhaps, to the lady and the Little Corporal taking coffee together,—the most insignificant and domestic scene in the world,—and then you would have been told all the conversation : how Napoleon knit his brow at a particular moment ; how Josephine panted with suppressed anger and suppressed affection, but put her hand to her left side and kept the tears down ; how the coffee got cold ; how the bread-and-butter was left untasted ; or how one little slice was eaten as a feint. You would have had as much of the humour and the pathos as the novelist's imagination of what passed (all in the most minute detail) could help you to ; and by the time you got to the end of the chapter you would find you had passed a crisis of the story. Anybody who has never done such a thing before, but will upon this hint examine the structure of a modern novel, will be struck, above all things, with the manner in which the main story is left to be gathered from details in themselves commonplace. " Jane was giddy and Alfred was irritable ; they had a quarrel and parted last June." That would be in the manner of the historian, and it would be sufficient for his purpose ; but, of course, the novelist would fill up that outline, while the historian was off and away to something else with which the quarrel between Jane and Alfred stood, we will suppose, in some large relation. It is a pleasant exercise to analyze a good novel in this way—to take the chapters one by one, and note what they are made of; how little "incident" and how much story. We undertake to affirm that the result of such an analysis will invariably be a surprise to the reader—it should, of course, be made after he has read the novel, and if it is a familiar one, so much the better.

But let us listen to a few sentences from the prelude to Mr. George Meredith's last novel "The Egoist."

"The world is possessed of a certain big book, the biggest book on earth; that might indeed be called the Book of Earth; whose title is the Book of Egoism, and it is a book full of the world's wisdom. So full of it, and of such dimensions is this book, in which the generations have written ever since they took to writing, that to be profitable to us the book needs a powerful compression. . . . . The realistic method of a conscientious transcription of all the visible, and a repetition of all the audible, is mainly accountable for our present branfulness, and that prolongation of the vasty and the noisy, out of which, as from an undrained fen, steams the malady of sameness, our modern malady. . . . . We have the malady, whatever may be the cure, or the cause. We drove in a body to Science the other day for an antidote; which was as if tired pedestrians should mount the engine-box of headlong trains; and Science introduced us to our o'er-hoary ancestry—them in the Oriental posture; whereupon we set up a primæval chattering to rival the Amazon forest nigh nightfall, cured, we fancied. And before daybreak our disease was hanging on to us again, with the extension of a tail. We had it fore and aft. We were the same, and animals into the bargain. That is all we got from Science.

"Art is the specific. . . . . In Comedy is the singular scene of charity issuing out of disdain under the stroke of honourable laughter; and Ariel released by Prospero's wand from the fetters of the damned with Sycorax. And this laughter of reason refreshed is floriferous, like the magical great gale of the shifty spring deciding for summer. You hear it giving the delicate spirit his liberty. Listen, for comparison, to an unleavened society: a low as of the udderful cow past milking hour! O for a titled ecclesiastic to curse, to excommunication, that unholy thing! So far an enthusiast perhaps; but he should have a hearing.

"Concerning pathos, no ship can now set sail without pathos, and we are not totally deficient of pathos."

Mr. George Meredith is an original writer of fiction, who has never quite fallen into the ranks of the order; indeed, he is perhaps more of a poet, specifically, than of a novelist, and above all things capable of being a humourist of the Shandean school. If that novel of his with which, for convenience, we have headed our list, had been written as a series of sketches or "magic lantern slides," to use Coleridge's phrase concerning Goethe's "Faust," it would have been more successful; but he was bound down to the forms of the novel proper, and the need of continuity of narration has strained the genius of the author of "The Shaving of Shagpat"—that very delightful book. But it would not be easy to find a modern writer of fiction better entitled than he is to express opinions like those we have quoted. At all events, that curious passage concerning the Book of Earth, which is "full of the world's wisdom," and the dictum that "the realistic method . . . . is mainly accountable for our present branfulness" and

" the modern malady of sameness," should be considered, though the present paper may be too small in compass to take them in. Deferring that, however, we will glance at the more recent fortunes of the novel, especially with regard to the " religious classes."

Even lately—within a month or two—we have had intelligent men condemning novels as worthless, not to say mischievous reading; and it is surely not more than seven or eight years ago since the Archbishop of York caused some surprise and a little downright wonder by admitting in some public address of his, that there were novels which might be read without harm, and indeed with both pleasure and profit. The word " Evangelical" has, like many other words, been very much clipped as to its ordinary meaning, and we do not know whether Dr. Thomson would claim it as a descriptive adjective or not; but it is more than safe to say that among Evangelical people in the old sense the novel has not yet been naturalized, and never can be without a breach of logical propriety. Nevertheless, novels go everywhere now-a-days, leaving out of consideration a few very " close" circles. The number of Evangelical readers—using the word in its old narrow sense— is larger than ever; but the increase has been chiefly among the uneducated classes. These, we need not say, have multiplied enormously, and among them there is no intentional or conscious relaxation of the old straitlaced notions of what is good for " saints" to read. There is a considerable difference in the practice; but the theory is the same; the formal teaching is the same; and when the law is laid down it is laid down in the old terms—exactly, fully, and without abatement. As it happens, the questions thus arising lie at the root of some that strongly interest us in this discussion; and though we cannot here push them to their limits, we cannot possibly omit them.

It is not more than thirty years—it is not twenty years—since the condemnation of the novel, in what were known as the "religious circles," was absolute and unreserved. How the change in practice and senti- ment (we are careful not to use the word opinion) came about is another matter; one that will fall to be considered by us almost imme- diately. But we might almost say that it was brought about surrepti- tiously—that the New Fiction, so different from the Old, made good its footing in the teeth of reasons which remained the same, and were felt to remain the same. In plain words, the majority of the strictly-so- defined religious public have, in admitting the novel, " sinned against light and knowledge" (as they would say). We have, in truth, one more episode of a very old story. Wrong opinions (we are, of course, assuming that the old religious judgment against novels was wrong) rarely give way, so far as the multitude are concerned, before right reason; they are gradually weakened by the force of circumstance; then a new tone of sentiment grows up by degrees, rises " like an exhala- tion," and influences conduct; but it is long before it consolidates or takes decided shape, so that the new *opinion* may adopt it as a garment or a shell. The subject is so curious, as well to deserve treatment in some detail, however brief.

There is a well-known work for students, written by an American divine, which had an immense circulation in this country a generation ago, and is still largely read. It contains some admirably wise counsel, and not a little really powerful writing. Thirty years ago this work was edited by no less respectable an authority than " the Rev. Thomas Dale, M.A., Canon Residentiary of St. Paul's, and Vicar of St. Pancras," a writer who had, in his day, some repute as a poet among readers who were not exacting in the matter of verse : some of his poems, such as " A Father's Grief," " A Daughter's Grief," are still prized for the purposes of the popular selections in use among mildly serious readers. We mention this for an obvious reason : Mr. Dale was a man of taste; he was supposed, like Mr. Melvill (for example), to have a peculiarly intellectual class of hearers, and his readers were of about the same order and rank as those of Dr. Croly and L. E. L. He might, therefore, have been expected to append a foot-note if he felt that what the American divine said about works of fiction was absurd, or even very wide of the mark. But he does nothing of the kind, and the young English student is left to make the best he can of despicable trash, such as we are now going to abbreviate. The general topic of the author is poetry and fiction :—

" ' What shall be said of such works as those of Byron? Can we not learn things from him which cannot be learned elsewhere ?' I reply, yes, just as you would learn, while treading the burning lava, what could not be learned else-where. . . . . Would you thank a man for fitting up your study, and adorning it with much that is beautiful; and if, at the same time, he filled it with images and ghosts of the most disgusting and awful description, which were to abide there, and be continually dancing around you all your life? Is he a benefactor to his species, who, here and there, throws out a beautiful thought, or a poetic image ; but as you stoop to pick it up, chains upon you a putrid carcase, which you can never throw off ? I believe a single page may be selected from Lord Byron's works, which has done more hurt to the mind and the heart of the young than all his writings have ever done good ; but he will quickly pass from notice, and is doomed to be exiled from the libraries of all virtuous men. It is a blessing to the world that what is putrid must soon pass away. The carcase hung in chains will be gazed at for a short time in horror ; but men will soon turn their eyes away, and remove even the gallows on which it swung."

Now, it must not for one moment be imagined that this verdict concerning Byron is one that would be considered out of date in circles which are the immediate successors, at this moment, of such circles as those which welcomed invective like the above. And the same might be said of the verdict concerning the novel proper (as distinguished from stories in verse like Byron's). Let it be noticed that Scott is inculpated :—

" ' But,' say you, ' has my author ever read Byron and Moore, Hume and Paine, *Scott*, Bulwer, and *Cooper ?*' Yes, he has read them all with too much care. He knows every rock and every quicksand ; and he solemnly declares to you that the only good which he is conscious of ever having received from them, is a deep impression that men who possess talents of such compass and power, and so perverted in their application, must meet the day of judgment under a responsibility which would be cheaply removed by the price of a world. . . . . When you have read and digested all that is really valuable—and that is comprised in what describes the history of man in all circumstances in which he has actually been placed—then betake yourself to works of imagination. 'But can you not, in works of fiction, have the powers of the imagination enlarged, and the mind taught to soar?' Perhaps so—but the Lectures of Chalmers on Astronomy will do this to a degree far beyond all that the pen of fiction can do. 'Will they not give you a command of words and of language, which shall be full, and chaste, and strong?' Perhaps so—but if that is what you wish, read the works of Edmund Burke."

The question raised with regard to the comparative effects of different portions of the work of a mind of the size and splendour of Byron's is almost ludicrous; but we allow it to be thus stated, as it opens in a convenient way a question which lies, otherwise, in our path. The author of the book, however, is conscious that it is over Sir Walter Scott that the main battle will be fought, and he certainly does not flinch from flinging his torch on to the pile at which the *auto-da-fé* is to take place :—

"The question in regard to works of fiction, usually has a definite relation to the writings of Sir Walter Scott. But, because the magician can raise mightier spirits than other magicians, is he, therefore, the less to be feared? No. While I have confessed that I have read him—read him entire—in order to show that I speak from experience, I cannot but say, that it would give me the keenest pain to believe that my example would be quoted, small as is its influence, after I am in the grave, without this solemn protest accompanying it."

Now, it will be remembered that the terms of the "solemn protest" are that it will be found "at the day of judgment that the responsibility under which" a writer like Scott (who is incriminated by name in the very passage in question) labours, for having written novels, "would be cheaply removed by the price of a world."

In writing of this order, which still represents the opinions of large masses of serious people, we come across the proper and natural contrast with the view suggested by the passage quoted from Mr. Meredith's new novel. It will be observed that in the adverse criticism just quoted there is, in the first place, an utter blindness to any kind of literary influence except that of the didactic kind : Byron and Hume wrote things which were very wrong, things adverse to just impressions on the most solemn subjects; therefore their writings must do infinitely more harm than good. Of the value of poetry like Byron's in communicating impulse to the mind, in giving a sense of largeness to life, and in suggesting innumerable by-paths which lead to nothing but what is (on the more recent and liberal hypothesis) good, there is no sense whatever. The same as to Hume. The real truth is that a moderately intelligent use of Hume's admissions and collateral sallies is one of the most valuable of moral tonics. Recall that unhappy *jeu d'esprit* in which he goes out of his way* to emphasize the moral aber-

---

* "A Dialogue" beginning, "My friend Palamedes."

rations of different men and different races, and the different verdicts which have been applied to the same act in different ages,—recall that very disagreeable essay, and do not forget the conclusion. Hume ends with an enumeration of the particulars in which men called good have in all ages agreed, and this candid close undoes the mischief of what goes before. " Behold, thou hast blessed them altogether." So far is pretty clear, and we are sure of having carried moderately intelligent and liberal readers a good part of the way with us.

But this does not touch, except remotely, what most concerns us. It shows, indeed, a startling insensibility to the value of the pictorial or dramatic manner of teaching, as opposed (in literary form) to the didactic. But that is not all. When we come to Sir Walter Scott, we are fairly flung backwards, unless we can, by habit, by instinct, or by reflection, take the unfortunate critic's point of view. One would think, notwithstanding Scott's shortcomings in the matter of the Cove- nanters, it must have required authoritative supernatural illumination to entitle a critic to lay it down that the guilt incurred by the author of " Ivanhoe," " Marmion," " Waverley," would be " cheaply removed by the price of a world." At first sight it would seem absolutely impossible that any human being of ordinary mould could receive one drop of poison from books like Scott's, unless he went very far afield to gather the plant, and then spent a good deal of semi-diabolical labour in dis- tilling the venom. Looking at the matter from the highest secular standpoint, one might be tempted to say that no human being had ever helped others to such a large amount of innocent pleasure as Sir Walter Scott, and that his novels would be cheaply acquired at the price of a world. But the matter cannot quite stop here; for we have at hand a lecture, by an educated English divine, and of later date still, in which the lec- turer uses language about works of fiction quite as bad as any that we have quoted, and goes on to depreciate the character *and brains* of Scott, Fielding, and others. They had " no particular pretension to high mental power." Godwin's intellectual qualities are disposed of by the remark, that he " made but an indifferent Dissenting minister"—a new *crux* for genius. It is a very shocking thing that anybody should have read the story of Jeanie Deans in Scott, and yet be ignorant of the life of——Marlborough! or have read " Tom Jones," and yet be " ignorant of *the real Joneses** (*sic*), the true and lasting ornaments of our country." This reverend critic then assures us that " writers of fiction" are " morally unhealthy," and supports this by reminding us that " Defoe was a bankrupt, and had been twice in Newgate," and that Sir Walter Scott was " placed in painful circumstances." Lastly, lest we should draw any inference in favour of fiction from the innocent ten- derness of the " Vicar of Wakefield," we are told that Goldsmith's " mode of life and thoughts *while writing it* brought him into distress." We are not exaggerating—the words are before us. The argument, of

* Inigo Jones and Sir William Jones.

course, stands thus :—Goldsmith was evidently unable to write the " Vicar of Wakefield " without falling into vice, such is the influence of fiction on its producer, and we are bound to conclude that upon the reader its influence will be similar.

Now, it is not to the purpose to say that all this is antiquated. For to begin with, it is nothing of the kind ; though it is much more shame-faced in its policy than it used to be. When writers such as Charles Kingsley, Miss Yonge, and George MacDonald have written novels, which have been read and relished by millions of good and pure souls within distinctly sectarian enclosures—when such books awaken all but universal shouts of delight and gratitude—when *that* is the case, common love of approbation (which is usually very strong in a certain order of mind) makes certain people hold their tongues. They do not want to be laughed at, that is all,—but their (more or less) secret opinions remain unaltered ; the judgment condemning works of fiction is held as exten-sively as ever among the serious classes now incriminated ; and—here we have prepared a surprise for some—we will do them more justice than they, by their shame-faced reticence, do themselves, and will boldly repeat that if the logic of their creed is the same their condemnation of fiction ought to stand. Robert Hall has left it on record that no writings ever did him so much harm as those of Maria Edgeworth :*

"In point of tendency, I should class Miss Edgeworth's writings among the most irreligious I ever read. Not from any desire she evinces to do mischief, or to unsettle the mind, like some of the insidious infidels of the last century; not so much from any direct attack she makes upon religion, as from a universal and studied omission of the subject. In her writings a very high strain of morality is assumed, she delineates the most virtuous characters, and represents them in the most affecting circumstances of life,—in sickness, in distress, even in the immediate prospect of eternity, and finally sends them off the stage with their virtue unsullied,—and all this without the remotest allusion to Christianity, the only true religion. Thus, she does not attack religion, or inveigh against it, but makes it appear unnecessary, by exhibiting perfect virtue without it. No works ever produced so bad an effect on my own mind as hers. I did not expect any irreligion there; I was off my guard, their moral character beguiled me, I read volume after volume with eagerness, and the evil effect of them I experienced for weeks."

Now, here we have the whole case in little,—the whole case, we mean, as to one of its most serious elements. Robert Hall was bound by his creed (which was, however, liberal) to find fiction objectionable unless it was written with a certain dominating purpose. And so are those who, nowadays, hold a creed resembling his. They may and do dodge the obligation ; they cannot destroy it. The whole " situation " in this particular is thoroughly insincere.

But Robert Hall had not got to the bottom or nearly to the bottom of his own mind in this matter. What he felt,—what he thought was so mischievous (and what, unless he had altered his belief, really was mischievous to him) was not so much the absence of any element of

* "Life and Writings of Robert Hall, M.A." 6 vols., vol. i. p. 174.

positive Christianity, as the diffused, interpenetrating, unconquerable delight of the novelist in life as it is, and the presence of moral elements for which there was no room under shelter of his beliefs—for example, love, as understood among us of the Western nations—a thing of which there is not a germ in the Semitic mind, or a hint in the Old and New Testament. Now, it was the more or less impassioned, but always *direct,* delight in life and this world, without reference to any positive Christian institute or dogma, which was at the bottom of it all, and spoiled Mr. Hall's religious life for weeks : and it is this delight which is the essential condition of all good poetry or fiction. Write fiction on any other plan, and nobody will read it. The literary artist in this kind turns over the pages of what Mr. Meredith calls the " Book of Earth,"—which is also, as he says, the " Book of Egoism,"—and he finds it full, not only of " wisdom," but of delight. And poor Mr. Hall—his tortured organs crammed with sharp-pointed calculi—found that even as little as he got of it in Miss Edgeworth (who is, however, full of animal spirits) took the savour out of his closet and pulpit exercises for " weeks."

Now, here we impinge, end on, upon one of the most interesting questions, and from its character necessarily the foremost of the questions suggested by the relation of the New Fiction to the Moral and Spiritual Culture of the age. It would recur again and again in dealing with novelists like Kingsley, Thackeray, and George Eliot, not to mention others. The startling point in the case is that so much of our fiction has lost the healthy simplicity of Scott and his school, and is as much occupied, though in a *subauditur,* with the skeleton in the cupboard of daily life as even a Robert Hall could be with " the corruption of the human heart," and the " miseries of the perishing creature."

It is the fashion to try to trace things to remote origins, and show more or less plausibly how complex products have been evolved from beginnings held for simple,—we say *held for* simple, because the egg is in reality as complex as the chick ; and, as Dogberry said, " it will go near to be thought so" before long. What, however, if we follow the fashion, may we suppose to have been the beginning of deliberately composed fiction among human beings ? Reserving that point for future consideration, we may pause upon the one which has been already raised, because it is, in the anatomy of the subject, vital. If a man maintains not only that man is imperfect, but that he is corrupt and, without supernatural aid connecting itself with certain beliefs, incapable of good, then he must feel that to him the fountains of art, in poetry, fiction, or otherwise, are sealed. But, whatever else may be said of the essential logic of such an opinion as that, it is plain that poetry and fiction have in all ages set themselves in battle array against it, and that the victory seems more and more to lean to their side. Now, as we have already noticed, the *zeit-geist* does not argue—it is in the air, and it conquers by inconsistencies. However, we cannot now follow up this, or trace the history of story-telling, so far as we know it, from Jotham's parable down to Mr. George Meredith's Book of Egoism.

Most, if not all, of the critics of the old-fashioned school who have condemned novels and romances have been anxious to explain that they do not extend their condemnation to books like the " Pilgrim's Progress,," or stories carefully written in order to inculcate religious truths, or moral truths set in organic relation to religious truths. It is true they have always been very jealous in admitting stories of actual life to any position of even qualified honour, because of the difficulty of introducing what they would call the *sal evangelicum* into such stories, and also because to tell a story of natural human feeling is, from their point of view, slippery work—the " interest" being apt to slide, under the workman's very eye, into paths held to be dangerous. But, of course, it would never do to condemn simple parables, or even complicated parables, or narratives as inartificial and as little discursive as those of Joseph and his brethren, or Job. This would land them in an obvious difficulty. The great *crux* with them is always the passion of love between man and woman. In the first place, paint it as he will, the artist is sure to get too much colour on the canvas— for their taste. In the second place, they are vaguely influenced by the fact already mentioned that love, as understood among the Westerns, is not to be found in the Bible. When the description of love is carried to the height which is necessary to make it interesting in itself, there are, in the eye of these critics, two evils. The first they see clearly and constantly point out—namely, that " the perishing creature" occupies too large a space in the heart. The second they do not see clearly, but they feel it—and they flinch from pictures of life which attribute so much exalting power to an "earthly" passion : the good woman in the Book of Proverbs, or a subordinated figure like the wife sketched by St. Paul, does not show very congruously with woman as the inspirer and regenerator of the man ; a being seen in a seventh heaven of divine lustre, and utterly alien in conception to anything to be found in the Fathers or the Apostles. Governor Winthrop's wife writes to her husband —" I love thee, first, because thou lovest Christ ;" but the good man would have been very much hurt if he had believed her. This, I repeat, is the everlasting difficulty as to the poetic, or thoroughly " human," novel, regarded from what we have (without committing any one) agreed to call the " evangelical" point of view. A novel may contain no vice, or other wrong-doing, or it may treat the wrong-doing with the most orthodox severity, and yet the work may be obnoxious to criticism of the kind now contemplated. Hawthorne's " Scarlet Letter" is a case in point. True, Hawthorne makes it plain here and there that he did not understand Puritanism after all ; but Cotton Mather himself, or a grimmer than he, might be satisfied with the climax—the scene in which the minister dies on the scaffold. Nevertheless, the predominant influence of the story is Naturalistic, and it does not require a *very* subtle intellect to gather doubtful oracles from it. External nature and human nature are both handled with the sympathetic touch of the artist, not with that of the moralist. The Rev. Mr. Wilson would have turned sourly away from the last chapter, in which it is suggested that " a new truth" will some day be " revealed," in order to place certain matters on a more satisfactory footing. " New truth ? new truth ? Why, what new truth can there be in such a case ?" he would have said. " My unlearned and unregenerate brother, you have given your mind too much to ballads and play-books. Learn the lesson of self-abasement, and be not wise above that which is written."

The exact process by which the literature of any given age, or any given branch of literature assumes a new colour is sometimes very obscure, but now and then it is amusingly obvious. Many reasons have been assigned for Queen Elizabeth's remaining unmarried. If one of them were proved to be true (which is not possible), then it would follow that very much of the poetic and romantic literature of her age and Milton's received a peculiar tinge from facts which had no more to do with literature or morals than the shape of Cleopatra's nose. As it happens, we can trace the fact that in our own time the religious classes (with large exceptions) read novels extensively and without scruple to *immediate* causes which lie upon the surface. We are not now taking the larger or deeper view of the matter—we are not going to pause upon the question of the influence of Sir Walter Scott and Miss Austen in breaking fresh ground among that large class of serious readers who take what might be roughly described as the ordinary old-fashioned Church of England view of religion, nor upon the influence in fostering latent naturalistic tendencies which was exercised by the revival of the old ballad literature : the writings of Wordsworth and Coleridge, and the cultivation of German. The last, however, has had more to do with it than would at first sight be supposed. The *childlike* poetic naturalism of German romance and poetry stole upon the mind before there was time to think how Naturalism in art stood related to hard-and-fast literalism of creed— and the waters were out before any one knew it. The direct influence of stories like Fouqué's and ballads like Uhland's was confined, of course, to a few minds. But these were minds that could be swiftly kindled, and that were sure to pass on the torch. However, to pass from such generalities, it may plausibly be said that writers like Miss Yonge, Charles Kingsley, and Dinah Mulock (Mrs. Craik), were the foremost among those who led the way to the new state of things. So far as we know, Mr. Kingsley was the only one who avowedly took up Naturalistic-poetic ground as land lying within the territory of any Biblical creed. He did this with great ardour, and got himself into trouble by it; but he was within his commission as a disciple of Mr. Maurice, whatever may be thought of his policy or his arguments. " It may seem paradoxical, yet is hardly hazardous, to say that the Maurice theology owes its power not less to its indulgence, than to its correction, of the pantheistic tendency of the age. It answers the demand of every ideal philosophy and every poetic soul for an indwelling Divine presence, living and acting in all the beauty of the world and the good of human hearts." These sentences of Dr. Martineau's are aimed at the influence of the Maurice dogma upon the practical religious " benevolence " of the age, but they apply with even more obvious weight to the question of the relation between poetic literature and the old stiff orthodoxy. And here, once more, the minds impregnated by Maurice and his school were themselves propagators, and what one man like Dr. George MacDonald acquired he passed on to thousands. We do not pretend to determine to what extent, if any, Dr. MacDonald was at any time indebted to the elder prophet; but the reader may find in the former's poem of " The Disciple " a fragmentary statement of the case as we have put it, and Dr. MacDonald's solution. Now, Dr. MacDonald, like Kingsley, has written no novel without distinctly Christian assumptions. But to a reader within the Christian precincts there is no great harshness in the transition from, say, " Robert Falconer " to a story by Mrs. Oliphant; from Mrs. Oliphant it is easy to pass to Mr. Trollope; and from him to Mr. Blackmore or Mr. Charles Reade.

In this scale I have left out Mrs. Gaskell, but her influence in making novels acceptable reading in certain circles has been incalculable. It was not on account of any poetic naturalism that her " Ruth " was ever shut out. But Mrs. Gaskell was one of three very notable novelists whose early training lay within Puritan or quasi-Puritan boundaries. The other two are Mrs. Beecher Stowe and George Eliot. Both these writers had the command of a certain dialect (not to say more) which gave them the entry into " Evangelical " circles at once. There are thousands of such circles where " Mr. Gilfil's Love Story," and much more " Adam Bede," would meet a doubtful welcome; but none where " Uncle Tom's Cabin " or " The Minister's Wooing " would not take the readers by storm. It is interesting, by the way, to note the prominence which the question of Poetic Naturalism and Puritanism assumes in Mrs. Stowe's earlier novels. Her own mind was evidently much " exercised " upon it.

The end of it is that, now a days, nearly everybody reads a story of some kind. Nearly all, if not all, the avowedly religious periodicals, in which a story is at all possible, take care to have one running from number to number. True, the " human interest " in these tales is never strong, nor is the humour; and the range of allusions is narrow. In other words, we find the old antagonism still present—when we look closely. But the general reader does not look closely, and the very thinnest of such narratives approximates more closely to the character of the novel proper than, say, Legh Richmond's " Dairyman's Daughter," or Hannah More's " Coelebs in Search of a Wife."

It will probably be said that the extended acceptance of the novel in our own day is largely due to the fact that fiction is no longer the indecent thing it once was. But this, so far as it is true, refers us back to the larger question of Poetic Naturalism as against dogmatic literalism; for the purification of fiction has gone on hand-in-hand with certain wide improvements and greater freedom of construction as to what may be good to read. We might here recall the outcry made in certain circles about " Jane Eyre," and later about " Ruth." But it is undoubtedly true that within the boundaries of literature proper there is little fiction that is offensive. Indeed, too much stress—or at least stress of the wrong kind—has been laid upon the presence in recent literature of what might be called the luxurious-wanton novel. The importance of this product has been overrated, and certainly its real significance has not been shown or hinted at. The exaggeration in the treatment of it is easily accounted for. There is a considerable class of leading-article writers and reviewers who are, naturally enough, on the look out for exciting topics, and fond of exhibiting their parts of speech. It is from these gentlemen that we get those amazingly indignant criticisms of a certain class of novels, which ring so false. The object with which the articles are produced is, in too many cases, worse than that with which the stories are written. The latter are often the work of inexperienced writers, women in particular, who have got into a fume about they know not what, and who really mean no harm. The critics, on the other hand, know very well what they are about; their virtuous indignation is artificial lather; their object is to produce a " spicy" paper, which, under cover of zeal for purity, shall be full of impure suggestion. So much for one class of journalists who make capital out of such novels. But there is another and a still larger class, made up of half-sincere social critics, usually young. These gentlemen (for lady reviewers seldom get into an indecorous passion of decorum) are generally on the right side, so far as intention goes, but they make mountains out of molehills. When you go to the poor abused novel itself you find, probably, that the harm in it is of a kind or a size which would never have struck anybody who was not in want of " a cat to tear—this is Ercles' vein." We have, in fact, but very little fiction which is, in the high and true sense, immoral. There are numerous hints of social heresy, and some nibbling at things which would be better left alone. This seems inevitable in a state of society in which clever young women abound, marriage is difficult, and luxury great. One result of these facts—taken with the vivacity of the modern style of living, and the throwing open of nearly all libraries to all comers—is naturally that men and women, but especially women of imperfect experience, should be imaginatively stretching out their hands towards closed doors of mature experience, and should make a sad muddle of their work. But of wicked intention in such novelists there is small evidence.

The matter, however, goes deeper than what would be generally recognised as immorality, and a wide-spread but quiet and unsuspected conflict is going on, as we have already said, between Poetic Naturalism in general, and the spirit or the belief which would cast it out as a thing unholy or unprofitable. The objection to novels and romances, poems and plays (we use only general phrases), has not been confined strictly to Christian critics of a certain class. It is to be traced in minds of a certain dogmatic order everywhere and in various ages. There is something *like* it, for example, in Plato, and it has its last roots in a philosophy of life which is not necessarily either Christian or anti-Christian. But it is certain that Christian dogmatists of various types have carried the dislike to Poetic Naturalism of all kinds to lengths which leave one in no doubt as to the logic of the dislike. To take a small instance. About twenty-four years ago, Dr. Campbell—a great *malleus hæreticorum* in his day—led a fierce attack upon Mr. Lynch's "Rivulet"—a little book of sacred poems, whose one fault, in the eyes of those who disliked it, was its way of fusing religious faith and the sentiment of natural beauty with the intermediate simply human affections. Dr. Campbell was justly condemned for his virulence, but he knew what he was about when he proclaimed to the like-minded, "Either this book is all wrong, or some of our dogmatic bases must be revised." I do not remember whether Dr. Campbell had an organ at his Tabernacle, but, of course, the question goes to music (nay, to singing) in public worship, to pictures everywhere: and so on, and on. A "spiritual" man of a certain school, who happens to be acutely sensitive to music, will tell you, and tell you truly, that he finds the special emotive agitation caused by music unfavourable to "spirituality." Similarly with novels and romances and poetry. These all arouse more impulse than the dogma or received law of the mind can control, or is, at least in most cases, likely to control. So that the observance of certain rules of conduct is felt to be endangered, and at all events the whole nature is for a time in a tumult.* An outsider may say, "That is your own fault; why do you not put things in their places, subordinate what should be subordinated, and work all the results into your higher life?" Such an appeal, however, comes practically to nothing; for you cannot give eyes to the blind or ears to the deaf.

But this is not the whole of the case. We naturally attach something of sacred force and right divine to all spontaneous emotion of the kind which is said to "carry us out of ourselves." The "spiritually-minded" objector would be the last to deny that spontaneity is of the essence of some kinds of sacredness—and, to put it roughly, he is jealous of competing spontaneities. He finds they surge upward from the sensations caused by music, novels, romances, plays, &c., and he attributes them to—the Devil. They are a sort of dæmonism. He puts them all from him with averted head, attributing them to the great spontaneous source of evil. That phraseology is not so common now as it used to be—we can trace it through the Middle Ages back to the Fathers, and it belonged to the "Manichæanism," against which Kingsley made such incessant war. That that way of meeting the case

* See what is said upon Music at page 743 of "An Inquiry into the Process of Human Experience," by William Cyples.

is wholly candid is not in my brief to affirm.   But, as we have seen, the matter is in course of settlement by the usual non-argumentative methods. Novels go everywhere, more or less.   The recent revivals of the old-fashioned " Evangelicalism" are against them, but the victory will remain with the novelist.   He is largely aided by the usual accommodated phraseology of the pulpit and the religious press.   All this stands connected with the spread of scientific knowledge, the increase of luxury, the far-reaching æsthetic revival, and some other topics, which would at the first glance appear utterly alien.   There are great changes in the air, and in these the novel will play a large and even increasing part.   What will be the probable course of events in this respect is a question which will connect itself with certain typical stories of the last decade, and may, perhaps, be considered in another article.

HENRY HOLBEACH.

Leslie Stephen

"The Moral Element
in Literature"

Cornhill Magazine 43 (January 1881), 34–50

The Moral Element in Literature.*

I WAS reading the other day—if you will permit me to start with a brief personal reference—an article written by the finest of our living critics. Whilst following his remarks with complete sympathy, I was brought to a stand by finding myself cited as an advocate of a theory which the critic pronounced, very rightly, in my judgment, to be absurd. This theory, to put it briefly, was that the literary value of a great poet might be fairly estimated by the scientific value of his ethical teaching. Now it is my opinion that in the forum of literature it is a crime to be misunderstood and a folly to explain. If one's meaning is so badly expressed as to be unintelligible to a candid and acute critic, it must certainly be one's own fault ; and the attempt to put oneself right by a mending and qualifying the original statement is only productive of intricate and wearisome wranglings. It is better to submit in silence to the implied rebuff, and try to speak more plainly the next time. Accordingly I only mention this little incident by way of introducing the remark that an attempt at such plain speaking may not be without interest. The question involved may briefly be stated thus : How far is our estimate of the moral worth of a writer relevant in forming a judgment of his æsthetic value? The principles which I shall attempt to lay down are very simple and commonplace. Happily that is pretty generally the case in regard to ethical problems. I have no ambition to be original in my views of morality; for I hold that the old doctrines as to what is right or wrong are, on the whole, remarkably sound. Still I have had to recognise the fact that one is liable to be misunderstood even in stating very simple theories ; and, moreover, a good deal has been said by various schools of criticism which, to my thinking, tends rather to perplex the whole question. Certain humourists, for example, chose to maintain that there is no relation whatever between art and morality ; which meant, it would seem, if it meant anything, that one might say that a man's writings were those of a beast and a blackguard without committing oneself to any opinion about their literary value. Offences to the moral sense were not to count, though all other instincts were to be respected. In reality, perhaps, it meant that the writer knew that he gave offence to the decent part of mankind, and that he did not care. This might pass for a congenial joke. When, however, the doctrine was seriously taken up by pedantic disciples, and converted into a sham philosophical canon, it gave rise to a good deal of wearisome cant,

---

* A lecture delivered at the London Institution, December 6, 1880.

which may be left to the tender mercies of contemporary satirists; and, on the other hand, some critics, who profess to take a high moral tone, often make tacit assumptions which would condemn every great writer from Æschylus to M. Victor Hugo. They would revive the old bigotry which banished all poets, playwrights, and novelists from the sphere of permitted reading, and sentence all future writers to wear a livery of respectable drab, and confine their energies to the production of tracts and sermons. Nothing, to my thinking—and, I fancy, to that of most people—could be in the long run less conducive to the morality which it was supposed to encourage.

I do not wish to wander into controversy. I would much rather start from opinions in which we can all agree; and I will begin by observing that there is one sense in which we may all agree to put the moralist out of court. We shall agree, that is, that the good old-fashioned practice of regarding a neat little moral as the final cause of every work of art, was, to say the least, unsatisfactory. An old dramatist, who is very fertile in such sentiments, may give us a sufficient example of the practice. "May we," he says, at the end of a tragedy, "make use of this great example, and learn from it that—

> There cannot be a want of power above
> To punish murder and unlawful love! "

This edifying truth is proved by the representation of a sinner brought to repentance by the appearance of his son's ghost, half naked and full of wounds, and leading in the shadow of a lady with a leprous face; after which, he has just time to confess his sin before being struck dead by a flash of lightning. It does not require any great logical acuteness to discover the weakness of the argument. To say nothing of the rarity of ghosts, the method of reasoning is clearly defective. The fact that a particular murder has come out does not prove the universal proposition "All murder will out." If neither murder nor discovery are facts, they cannot possibly prove anything; and, in any case, the moral objection to a crime is not that it will be found out, but that it is intrinsically pernicious. We can only smile at the *naïveté* of our ancestors who used to commend some very questionable works of art by tagging to them these quaint little morals; and we will abandon the practice to the writers of edifying tracts, with the advice that they should not use the expedient too freely. But more refined forms of the same fallacy still find favour with some writers; for what is called "the novel with a purpose" is not yet extinct, though it has been long exposed to a heavy fire of ridicule. We still have books which are outwardly fictions, but inwardly and substantially tracts in favour of a religious dogma, or pamphlets in support of a political theory. We find ourselves somehow tricked into an argumentative and statistical discussion; we resent the unfairness of the method, and are vexed at being baulked of our proposed engagement. I don't know how many people in these days have ever tried to read Miss

Martineau's *Illustrations of Political Economy*, or have suffered the annoyance of finding that a promising story of artisan life in the North is nothing but a covert exposition of the orthodox economical doctrine of the wages funds. That is a typical instance of the worst possible case of an unhallowed alliance between the artistic and scientific methods, which leads to the degradation of both, though we are almost cheated into admiration by the heroic audacity which tried to convert the "dismal science" into the raw material of romance. We may find illustrations of the principle more instructive in some ways, because the error is less palpably absurd, in some of Dickens' fictions. Take, for example, his assault upon the Circumlocution Office, which purports to be the translation into fiction of some of Mr. Carlyle's eloquent denunciations of red tape, and of "the miserable creatures having the honour to be." Let us take for granted that Dickens was perfectly right in his doctrine; let us admit, too, that it is a perfectly legitimate end of fiction to give the most graphic picture possible of varying phases of social life. Dickens was as fully justified in describing the English governing classes as Scott, for example, in giving his inimitable types of Scotch peasantry, or Balzac in portraying the corrupt society which flourished in the Paris of his day. Nobody, we may again admit, could read Scott without understanding better than he would do from many volumes of political philosophy what was the real strength and weakness of Scott's countrymen; nor, again, is it possible to become acquainted with Rastignac or the Père Goriot without learning a great deal as to the sources of political weakness under the old *régime* in France. Both Scott and Balzac, and Dickens himself, when he was discharging his proper function, threw much light upon facts which every statesman should take into account. But when the novelist tries to invade the province of the statesman, and is really writing in order to justify some pet theory, he makes the blunder which deprives this part of Dickens of all serious value. It is thoroughly unsatisfactory artistically, because we feel that the personages whom he holds up to ridicule are caricatures—absurd and impossible beings, who can reveal nothing to us because they never existed. The British official may be as blundering and pedantic as you please; but he is, at any rate, a human being, a creature with intellect and affections like our own : if you prick him, he will bleed; if you tickle him, he will laugh. And the really great artist cannot help remembering this, and therefore making you understand his Shylock even when he is intending to make him thoroughly hateful. That was just the kind of self-restraint of which Dickens was incapable, and which therefore leads him to paint mere monsters as unlike any possible human being as the figures which Gillray and Rowlandson put to represent Napoleon or Pitt. And, of course, the same fault is as injurious in a logical sense; for the real problem is (assuming the accuracy of the facts) how does it come to pass that honourable and intelligent men, such as we know many English officials to be, come to make such a mess of it ? And Dickens, when he once permits himself to describe them as being not men at all, but mere puppets pulled by the satirist's wires, virtually leaves the problem altogether unanswered. He utters a shrill scream of impatience, instead of giving us a fair diagnosis of the social disease ; and therefore you can learn incomparably more from writers who had no thought of any political doctrine at all, but who were simply anxious to paint men as they saw them.

Hence we may, I think, define the objection to such work a little more accurately. It implies a confusion of functions. An astronomical diagram is a very good thing in its place, and so is a picture of the heavenly bodies ; but if you try to put either in the place of the other, or to combine the two in one, you are pretty certain to make a disastrous muddle of the result. The novelist, as Fielding often tells us, is the true historian of the time. He tries to show us, as clearly as his powers allow, the real moving forces in the great tragi-comedy of human life. He has to make the world intelligible to us, and the deeper and truer his insight, the greater his permanent power. So far his attitude is the same as that of the scientific observer or the philosophic reasoner. And this—without going further for the moment—is enough to condemn the disguised pamphlets which are called novels with a purpose. For purpose of this kind is inconsistent with that spontaneity which is the most obvious and essential condition of artistic success. There is, as we are rightly told, only one sufficient excuse for writing poetry—the fact, namely, that you cannot help it. The poet should be under an over-mastering impulse which compels him to seek relief in utterance, and, for the moment at least, he should be under no other impulse. He should speak because his heart burns within him, and because, whilst he keeps silence, it is pain and grief to him. That is the test of genuine inspiration, and his art consists in such a selection and combination of his materials as can present his ideas in the most effective and striking form. But so soon as he is writing with a purpose—to advocate female suffrage or a better observance of the Sabbath, or a change in our administrative system—he is narrowing and lowering his aim. He is forced by the conditions of his art to give us a story of the lives and fortunes of concrete human beings. He should lay bare—as far as he can—the true play of passion, make intelligible the development of character, and invite our tears and smiles by our interest in his typical characters. The main interest of any real study of life can never consist in its bearing upon some particular political problem. And so far as we feel that the writer's interest is really in that minor problem and not in the deeper and more permanent interests involved, we feel also that the true centre of interest is displaced. The author has created his characters, not because he was interested in them, or in his fellows generally, but because he was interested about some pet crotchet of his own. He is really manufacturing evidence for an imaginary blue-book, or trying to insinuate into us a belief in a table of statistical information. The true centre of interest is, in his mind, the least interesting part of the work, and therefore fails to interest us. And, of course, characters manufactured for such a purpose, and in the interests of a collateral theory, tend to become mere caricatures, for that which is incidental is exaggerated at the cost of that which is really essential.

The conclusion, then, is that a poet should not have the same purpose as the politician or the economist, but certainly not that he should have no purpose. To have no purpose is simply not to be a reasoning being. Every man must of necessity have some purpose in his actions. Even the poet—if I may say so—may rightly aim at making a little money by his poetry. If he writes simply with a view to making money, his poetry will probably be worthless; but, like other men, he has to live, to pay his bills, and to support his family; and he ought to consider whether he is justified by those circumstances in yielding to or in cultivating the poetic impulse. And, still more, he may certainly consider whether on the whole his poetry is likely to be at least harmless to the world. When a man has composed his epic poem, the question always arises whether it would not be wise to put it in the fire; and that question, I need hardly say, is generally decided in the wrong way. All that we mean, therefore, by objecting to a purpose is that in the art of composition a man's whole purpose should be to utter his assertions in the most perfect and vigorous way possible, and not the attainment of any special practical aim. And this condition follows from the very nature of the performance; for, in truth, a genuine work of art can be no more limited to any such particular end than a history of real facts. It is as absurd to ask what is the moral of *Faust* or *Hamlet* as to ask what is the moral of the history of Napoleon. That is not because there is no moral, but because there are infinite morals. The politician, the moralist, the physiologist, and so forth, will each find their own moral in the story of Napoleon, according to the special point of view from which they regard it. The historian must give the facts as fully and impartially, and leave it to others to apply the innumerable morals with which the facts are pregnant; and so far as he descends from that level he becomes, like too many historians, a mere party pamphleteer. If he discharges his duty worthily, he is stating facts which may be of the most critical importance in deciding the value of specific theories, but it is not his duty to write from the point of view of any such particular theory. The imaginative writer is so far in the same position, and if he does not deal with the facts of a real history, and therefore does not in the same way supply materials to the scientific reasoner, he has a prerogative of a different kind. He "proves" nothing, you say, and yet in another sense he proves a great deal, and even proves it to demonstration. He proves, and proves beyond a doubt, that certain modes of feeling or types of character are beautiful or hideous. *Paradise Lost*, as the proverbial senior wrangler remarked, proved nothing: that is, it did not prove the truth of Milton's cosmogony or of his peculiar doctrines about predestination. Clearly not, but it did prove beyond cavil the grandeur of certain great moral conceptions, and the strength which a great intellect might draw from certain religious beliefs. And so, to take a lower instance, it is quite true that Addison, for example, did not prove the value of a particular set of political institutions when he drew " Sir Roger de Coverley," but he did show what a charm might be found in the character of a simple-minded and kindly squire under the old *régime*. This would certainly not show that the contemporary system of county franchise was right or wrong, but it revealed certain social truths which any statesman bent upon reform would do well to take into account.

This, it is easy to observe, is rather a strained use of the word " proof." I admit the plausibility of the criticism, and I will not go into metaphysical inquiries to ask whether the use of the word be legitimate. At any rate it may illustrate the legitimate function of the imaginative writer in regard to such truths. He reveals to us certain aspects of the world in which we live and the men who live in it. If these revelations can be called proofs, they must be considered as proofs which do not proceed beyond the truths capable of being proved by direct intuition. He shows us certain facts as they appear to him. If we are so constituted as to be unable to see what he sees, he can go no further. He cannot proceed to argue and analyse, and apply an elaborate logical apparatus. There is the truth, and we must make what we can of it. But, on the other hand, so far as we are in sympathy with him, the proof—if it be a proof—has all the cogency of direct vision. He has couched our dull eyes, drawn back the veil which hid from us the certain aspect of the world, and henceforward our views of life and the world will be more or less changed, because the bare scaffolding of fact which we previously saw will now be seen in the light of keener perceptions than our own.

And now, to come a little nearer to our special problem, we must ask in what sense and how far the value of this artistic revelation may be dependent upon the moral qualities of the seer ? and I shall suggest the answer which I consider to be the most satisfactory by answering a preliminary question. As we have not time for roundabout approaches according to the rules of logical strategy, I shall venture to answer it dogmatically. To me, at least, it seems that literature may be sufficiently regarded as simply one form of personal intercourse. It is a subordinate question whether I know a man through his books, or hear him discourse to me *vivâ voce*, or talk to him in ordinary society ; the only difference is, that in a man's books, if they are good for anything, I expect to have the highest part of the man : the refined essence of his thoughts, and his most confidential communications. In talking to a man at a dinner-party I am distracted by considerations as to the way in which he parts his hair or uses his knife and fork, or am treated to an exposition of his views upon the relative merits of hock and claret. It would be prudish to deny that such topics are often exceedingly interesting. But even at a dinner-party I desire more than this, and in either mode of intercourse, the higher and the lower, I am equally putting myself within the sphere of that indefinable personal influence which acts in a thousand subtle and inexplicable ways, and more by direct sympathy or antipathy than by producing any tangible and calculable effect. To sum up the influence and to analyse its modes of operation, is simply impossible. When I know a man, especially if he attracts my love or reverence, I am influenced, or, in other words, my whole character is more or less modified. I have breathed a new intellectual atmosphere, and my constitution is affected by the materials which I have unconsciously assimilated. I may, of course, treat a man as I treat a book of reference; that is, I may simply acquire from him a certain amount of definite information—true or false; I may, again, treat him as I treat a scientific treatise—that is, I may argue with him till I am more thoroughly persuaded of the truth of my own opinions. The man who affects me in such ways is so far useful or the reverse, and I probably consider him, to use the irreverent phrase, as a mere " book in breeches." The phrase is irreverent, because a book does something more, and that something corresponds to the other kind of personal power, which, generally speaking, is of incomparably greater importance. When we have summed up all the facts and arguments which a teacher has transferred into our minds, we have only accounted for the lowest part of his influence, and it is the part beyond all others which corresponds to the true teaching of a great imaginative intellect. We learn much more even from a philosopher by our sympathy with his modes of thinking and feeling than from the particular formulæ which he inculcates; and in the case of a great poet, this kind of influence is the essential and all-important.

The influence is just the same, I will observe in passing, whether the teacher belongs to what is called the objective or subjective class. It is the man Shakspeare who really influences us in reading *Hamlet* and *Othello*, and not the less because critics generally repeat the assertion that we know very little of a man who retires so carefully behind his characters. We have, it is true, next to nothing of the kind of information about Shakspeare which Boswell gave us about Johnson. But surely we know a good deal about a man if we know only this—that he is capable of sympathising impartially with a vast variety of characters; and, in some very important respects, it seems to me that we know even more of Shakspeare than of Johnson. If we know less of his domestic relations and his taste in cookery, we know what he felt and thought about some of the most profoundly interesting of all the problems of life. But, whether we have or have not framed any theory as to Shakspeare's personality, and have or have not constructed a theory of the man from his books, it is not the less the man who really influences us. For what really impresses us in Shakspeare, or in any great writer, is the extraordinary force and vividness with which he has embodied certain general truths and deep emotions; and his power of achieving that feat clearly depended upon his own emotional and intellectual temperament. The nature of the influence is not the less clear that it acts as from behind a cloud.

The ultimate nature of any personal influence is, I say, beyond our feeble powers of analysis. It must, of course, always depend partly upon our personal idiosyncrasy : we like or hate Dr. Fell without being able to say why. But so far as it is independent of such variable fancies, so far as your great men are able to influence men in all ages and countries, we should say in very general terms that the influence depends upon a man's total power, upon his intellectual and emotional vigour, upon the strength of his passions, the clearness of his reason, the delicacy of his perceptions, the general harmony of faculties so co-ordinated and correlated as to give unity and consistency to his whole life and character. Briefly, the man is greater so far as he corresponds to the highest type of man conceivable, or represents the very utmost that can be got out of human flesh and blood. This is the standard—vague enough, in all conscience—by which we measure the magnitude of the great luminaries of the intellectual heavens. But we cannot take any narrower standard, and indefinite as it is, it is clear enough to suggest some obvious inferences. For we may notice, in the first place, that if by morality you mean spontaneous obedience to a certain code of rules—a dislike to lying, stealing, drunkenness, and so forth, the possession of any such qualities is an utterly inadequate measure of a man's total excellence. Some of the best, nay, some of the most attractive men I have ever known, have been specimens of the great class, dunce. Stupidity does not necessarily imply wickedness. I have known a man to whom the Latin grammar was an impenetrable jungle of insurmountable difficulties, who was yet one of the purest, the kindest, and most loveable of human beings. Considering how many men, according to high authority, fall under the description fool, it is happy that we need not therefore set them down as knaves. And, conversely, I have known some most brilliant and fascinating companions whom I would not trust unreservedly with my spoons, and whom, perhaps, I should introduce with some scruple to the more delicately-minded part of the species. For all this, I prefer to have for a friend—specially for a friend who is to influence my character—a man with two or more ideas in his head, and, if possible, I should like to feel that I might leave him alone in my library or my cellar without having afterwards to count my books or my bottles.

Now, as I have said, I measure the worth of a book by the worth of the friend whom it reveals to me. And, putting aside the personal affinities which may determine us to love one man better than another without affecting our estimate of his intrinsic value, I further say that the worth of the author is in proportion to his whole intellectual force. Physicists compare machines in respect of the amount of energy stored up in them, or, as they say, by the number of foot-pounds of work done. There is no such thing as a spiritual foot-pound. If there were, it might give us a measure. As there is not, I can only say vaguely that the value of a great writer is measured by the amount of energy which he represents and by the vigour of his impact upon the world of thought. That is to say, again, it is proportioned to his strength, remembering that in this sense delicacy is itself a form of strength; for the clumsiness which wastes power is as prejudicial as the weakness which implies absolute defect of power. What, then, has become of the moral test? Simply this, I imagine. Without going into disputed ethical questions, we may adopt the old and profound conception, according to which morality may be regarded as being a kind of health; or, if you will, as being in the sphere of thought and feeling what health is in the material sphere. Morality is not coincident with health in this sense of the word, for there are many defects and shortcomings of the spiritual nature which do not imply immorality. But the converse remains true. To say that a man is immoral is so far to say that he is in some way spiritually diseased; that his mental and material organisation is somehow out of joint; that some of his instincts are defective or perverted, and therefore that the vital functions are not being properly discharged. And therefore, as every disease is so far a source of weakness or deficient vitality, this is pre-eminently true of those diseases of which the external symptom is immorality. Or, taking the opposite case, what we call a fine moral sense is a proof that the whole organisation is working soundly and is in the highest condition of intellectual training.

Thus, to start from this analogy, I admire an athlete primarily and simply for his strength and agility, for the ease with which he can perform any given feat, and for the force which he can apply to achieve a great labour. I may not even ask whether he is or is not healthy, but I admire him for performances of which thorough bodily health is an essential condition. The man may be diseased in some way which does not affect his particular performance; or he may be thoroughly healthy and yet unable to achieve any considerable feat; or, again, his very strength in particular directions may lead to the development of morbid states. Still nobody would deny that a thoroughly healthy state of body is the normal and most essential condition of athletic excellence. And just the same things may be said of what we call spiritual and intellectual health; though the complexity and uncertainty of that irritating compound, known as human nature, often leads to still more anomalous results in the higher sphere. So, for example, a man may, as I have said, be stupid and yet thoroughly healthy in mind. Health is not a sufficient, though it is generally a necessary condition of excellence. Or he may combine the most admirable powers in some directions with debasing and shameful because morbid instincts in other directions. He may be a subtle logician and yet thoroughly heartless. If so, he may write an excellent treatise upon formal logic, though he will probably be a bad poet. In any case, his heartlessness is so far a defect and a source of weakness as well as of immorality. Or, again, it is so common a case that some people regard it as the normal case, that great powers of a certain kind predispose a man to certain intellectual diseases. This I believe to be true and important, in a sense. I can only say at present that, so far as the disease exists, it is always a source of weakness, and that the highest powers of any kind are perfectly compatible with, and indeed can only be fully developed in association with the highest conceivable health. So, to take an obvious case, Cowper's extreme sensibility made him a poet and helped to drive him mad. Still, as far as it drove him mad, it distorted his perceptions and marred his poetry. Some great men have been as sensitive as Cowper, and yet have been thoroughly good men of business as well as men of genius. That genius has its special dangers is a doctrine which I am certainly not inclined to dispute; but until you can prove—what is to my mind the very reverse of the truth—that it essentially implies disease, we may still hold the doctrine which I take to lie at the foundation of all sound doctrine upon this subject, that the highest powers can only reach their fullest development in a thoroughly healthy organism, using health in the widest possible sense, which therefore includes moral health. It may be as well to illustrate the application of this theory to our particular problem by some of the most familiar cases.

In the first place, there is a wide sphere of literary art to which moral doctrines have no direct application. It is sometimes asked, for example, what has morality to do with such poems as Coleridge's *Christabel* and *Kubla Khan*, or Keats's *Hyperion*, or Milton's *Lycidas?* They are admirable because they are the utterances of nobly endowed natures, implying marvellous richness of emotion, delicate perception of all the harmonies of language, command of all the resources of poetic association, and so forth. But it would be as idle to talk of the moral of such poems as to ask for the moral of a magnificent piece of music. To all this I fully agree, and I will add that such work could only be condemned by those who think—as some great men have thought—that in a world where so much evil has to be encountered, all purely æsthetic indulgence should be forbidden. This is virtually to hold that morality is not only good, but the sole good. As to my mind, it is truer to say that morality is ultimately admirable because it is a condition of happiness, than to reverse the order of thought, I certainly do not share this theory. I hold, on the contrary, the commonplace doctrine that everything which makes the world brighter and more beautiful is so far a good thing, and that all innocent enjoyment should be encouraged. And, therefore, the only question which the moralist has to ask is whether the enjoyment is in fact innocent. It is innocent, again, if it does not imply any morbid sentiment. We may, therefore, say that morality has a certain negative relation to such work, in so far as it is true that the great poets in question do not appeal to any degrading emotions. When Coleridge wrote *Kubla Khan*, he was thinking as little of morality, in the ordinary sense of the word, as he was thinking of mathematics and political economy. We can only say that a man of impure mind might possibly have introduced into such a poem something which would have jarred upon the moral sense. But this, in such a question, is a rather far-fetched and remote consideration. It is more relevant in regard to another great class of poetry, which will probably last as long as the world continues. It is applicable to any of the innumerable singers who have " panted forth a flood of rapture," more or less " divine," " in praise of love and wine." A critic must belong to a very ascetic school of morality indeed who would condemn such poetry as immoral ; and, for my part, I sincerely hope that young men and young women will go on falling in love with each other for a considerable time to come, and will be always making the fresh discovery that " love " rhymes to " dove," and making use of it in the composition of a quantity of verses, the vast majority of which, I must also hope, will find a speedy euthanasia. I only say that such poetry is admirable in proportion to the strength, sincerity, and nobility of the passion. That which makes a Burns, for example, incomparably superior as a writer of love-songs to such a sparkling versifier as Tom Moore, is the masculine force of intellect and emotion which they display. But we may add that the poetry is the finer, as it implies a chivalrous and pure-minded passion, and a width of tender sympathy with all human feeling, and that vice manifests itself by narrowing and lowering the range of sentiment as well as by giving a coarser form to the utterance. The æsthetic judgment includes far more than the strictly moral judgment ; but the moral judgment coincides, so far as it goes, with the æsthetic.

Hence, briefly speaking, poetry is great as it is the utterance of the loftiest and most richly endowed natures ; as it is such as no one could have written unless he had been a man of high character and delicate feeling, and can impregnate his work with the magical attraction which is only derivable from contact with such men. The poet, like the man, is lower in rank, so far as he is wanting in sincerity, and therefore puts us off with sham conventional phrases ; or wanting in purity of feeling, and therefore incapable of appreciating the purest essences of character ; or in tenderness of heart and quickness of sympathy, and therefore incapable of exercising that potent and yet lenient sway over our affections in which Johnson rightly found the ultimate secret of Goldsmith's literary excellence. Goldsmith's power, you may retort, was not due to the goodness of his heart, but to the fineness of his workmanship and the perfection of his powers of expression. That, I think, is about as reasonable as to say that a great painter owes his power not to his eye for colour, but to the merit of his technical execution. No doubt, the technical instrument is essential to the artist, but it is useless unless it has something to express. And the fineness of Goldsmith's literary execution was merely one aspect of a delicate organisation which included an emotional as well as an intellectual subtlety. The two powers are but different applications of the same quality. Literary work may be as clever as you please, and unite the highest admiration of the authorised critics of such qualities; but that which gives it charm, and makes it capable of reaching the hearts of mankind, is the underlying tenderness and delicacy of the emotional sentiment.

This could hardly be better illustrated than by the famous controversy in which—as we all remember from Macaulay's brilliant article—the High-Church parson Collier triumphed over all the wits and poets of his day. The arguments used by Collier and his supporters were often crude enough. They naturally provoked a protest from such critics, for example, as Lamb and Hazlitt, who enjoyed Congreve's or Wycherley's wit, and did not like to be called immoral for their taste. Lamb's familiar argument in defence of the dramatists has its value against some such criticisms. The Mirabels, and Witwoulds, and Manlys, he urged, lived in such a fictitious world that it was sheer pedantry to judge of them by moral rules. If they made a mock of marriage, for example, we are always to remember that they did not really exist and were therefore laughing at a law not applicable to imaginary beings. We may agree, for the sake of argument, that the theory might hold water in regard to some imaginary worlds. Mere sylphs and gnomes, even if they choose to masquerade in everyday costumes, are not held to respect our observances. But the argument seems to me at least to fail curiously as applied to these dramatists. My objection to them is precisely that the world which they represent is a great deal too real. Very odd things happen in it, it is true; impossible conglomerations of intrigue combined to bring the characters into collision, and to strike out of them the greatest possible number of witty repartees. But the world is essentially the prosaic world of the selfish, cynical, unprincipled men about town of the day. Its inhabitants are wittier than any real beings; but the substance of their wit is simply the coarse and brutal sentiment which was likely to find favour with the rakes of the coffee-houses. The world is idealised not by omitting the prose, but by leaving out the poetry. Congreve was writing to amuse ladies who had just enough modesty to wear masks at his plays, and fine gentlemen who staggered into the theatre with brains just sufficiently clear to appreciate their own sentiments put into smart language. He was bound to say nothing which would fly over the heads of such an audience or to cause them to blush for the only thing which would make them blush, the accidental blundering into a really generous or romantic sentiment. Of course I do not deny that Congreve shows both wit and sense; I do not think that he could fairly be called a blackguard, a phrase which is certainly applicable to Wycherley; and I will admit that I can find pleasure even in some of Wycherley's blackguardly writings; for, after all, the shrewd sense of a keen man of the world, though it may not be elevating, is not despicable. It is an element in human life with which we have to reckon, and if you pay more attention to the point with which a sentiment is given, than to the value of the sentiment itself, you may admire without reserve. But that which is wanting in all such works is charm, the charm 'of chivalrous feeling, of hearty laughter, of sympathetic good nature, of interest in simple human passion. Where that is absent the connoisseur will never be able to force his creed upon the simple-minded reader, and will vainly try to excuse himself by lamentations over the deficient taste of the poor Philistine for pure literature.

In this matter I hold that the average reader is entirely in the right. He does not care for Congreve, because no brilliance of phrase will atone for intrinsic poverty of thought and meanness of sentiment. But I do not mean to say that your uncritical reader is always right in these matters. We all know for example that the respectable public was shocked by Byron's immorality, and, indeed, is still apt to express itself pretty strongly about such works as *Don Juan.* We are in a position, it is to be hoped, to judge more calmly, and our first remark would probably be, that the offence given by Byron was in part due to an irreverence which is not really what it seems. It is amusing, for example, to compare Byron's *Vision of Judgment* with the poem of the respectable Southey which it burlesqued. Southey set down Byron as Satanic, and undoubtedly Byron deals pretty freely with some of the objects of Southey's reverence. But if you ask which of the two poems is really the more irreverent, there cannot be a doubt that Southey is the real offender. For Southey's quiet identification of the divine element in the universe with poor old George III. and his ministers, his calm assumption that he has a right to speak as the authorised mouthpiece of Providence, and the familiarity which he displays with its counsels, are certainly incomparably more offensive to any reverent mind than Byron's scornful onslaught upon all the respectabilities, and his thorough conviction that many kings and statesmen stripped of their robes and their wigs will appear to be very miserable human beings. Southey, in short, is respectful to the outside shams, whilst Byron's mockery, if it shocks the worshippers of the symbols, is really far more respectful to the realities which the symbols represent. If, however, we should try to generalise this remark, and unreservedly claim moral elevation for Byron, we should be undertaking a rather difficult piece of literary whitewashing. Without trying to sum up a controversy still undecided, I will say what is in my view the true criterion. We admire Byron not primarily as a moralist, nor the reverse, but simply as a man of splendid force of mind and character, as one endowed with a thoroughly masculine intellect, of intense passions and generous sympathies, capable of tearing to pieces the flimsy sophistries and sham conventionalities in which the respectable people of his time had enveloped themselves, and breaking to pieces the fetters which they wished to impose upon human nature. That is the nobler Byron. And, if you ask, what limits our admiration, it is that there was another and baser Byron. His literary eminence has, I should say, two great drawbacks. The first is the insincerity, the affectation, the snobbishness, the hungering and thirsting for the praises of the very men whom he affected to despise, the petty delight in the lower kinds of notoriety which marred his life, and shows itself equally in the utter unreality of much of his poetic declamation. The other great fault is the coarseness of nature which makes him an ignoble figure beside Shelley, to whom, in sheer force of intellect, he was greatly superior, and which gives to his assaults upon cant and hypocrisy the lower tone of the mere sensualist, when we require the tone of the generous advocate of human rights. The Colossus, as every one feels, is of iron mixed with clay, and the earthy part of the man is at times unpleasantly predominant. So far, therefore, from admitting that we can separate our moral judgment of the man from our literary judgment of the author, they seem to me to be identical; though, happily, the poetry is less stained than the life by his baser qualities. I admire Byron both as man and poet, so far as he represents the revolt of a nature of magnificent strength against cant and hypocrisy and sham morality, against loyalty which has become mere servility, and patriotism which implies indifference to the welfare of mankind, or a servile worship of military glory, against a conservatism which represents only the selfish fears and interests of the comfortable, and a religion which has sunk to be mere bigotry and a cowardly dread of intellectual freedom. I cease to respect him in either character when he becomes a mere dandy and lady-killer, as he bids for cheap admiration by insincere cant, or by pandering to the more debasing passions. I can pardon, perhaps, I can enjoy, buffoonery when it is aimed at mere prudery and the pedantry of the self-styled virtuous: I can respect even the cynicism which is the bitterness of a noble nature tortured by disappointment and remorse. But so far as these tendencies show blunted perceptions and incapacity for appreciating the ennobling elements in human life, they are as objectionable in the poet as in the man.

And this may suggest a remark upon one commonplace of modern criticism. The literary equivalent of moral degradation is blunted feeling; the loss of the delicate perception which enables a man to distinguish between exalted passion and brutish appetite, and disqualifies him from dealing with the highest problems of human nature, as a deficient sense of colour would disqualify a man for painting a sunset, or a lovely complexion. This gives the true meaning, I think, of the modern complaints about what is called sensationalism. It is, indeed, a curiosity of criticism that the same people who profess an idolatrous veneration for Shakspeare complain of any modern writer for dealing with the passions which supply the motive of *Othello* or *Hamlet*. We profess to admire the Elizabethan dramatists who sometimes kill so many of their characters that they scarcely leave enough actors standing to carry off the dead bodies, and yet I have seen the morality of Dickens compared with that of Scott by counting the number of murders in two of their novels. Sensationalism is the name of a bad quality, not so far as it indicates that a writer takes into account the crimes and horrors, and evil passions of our time; but so far as it means that he deals with them as the man of blunted feeling deals with them; that is to say, as he makes the sense of raw, undisguised horror supply his own want of sentiment. When poor Edgar Poe, a man undoubtedly of some rare and fine qualities, had to write with exhausted faculties, he had recourse to a very simple expedient. He introduced a decaying dead body, or a whole shipful of bodies. That is, he could not appeal to your sympathies, but he could turn your stomach. Devices of this kind imply not power, but the absence of power. Anybody can be impressive in this way, and the most commonplace newspaper reporter might find, within a mile of this place, materials enough for exciting a deeper sense of horror and disgust than any which could be produced by Shakspeare. The true inference, however, is not that a great writer is never to deal with such materials as excite pity or horror. In a world where good and evil are so intricately blended, where we have so many causes for sorrow and sympathy, the greatest men will be most profoundly sensitive to the sadness of the world, and will often set before us the darker and more terrible phases of human nature. But the real interest, so far as it is truly artistic in nature, is not that aspect of the horrible which is visible to every commonplace observer, but the thoughts and feelings which it excites in the great mind and the noble nature. Even in the most purely dramatic representation, the dramatist is, as I have said, really present, and without obtruding himself, is really teaching us how to look at the dark side of the world. He descends to be a mere sensationalist whenever the interest is derived purely from the objects which he describes and not from the light cast upon them by his intellect. And, therefore, a tendency to deal in the purely disgusting, in representing objects so hideous in themselves that they overpower any attempt at artistic treatment, is generally a proof of the presence of a baser element in the describer.

I will not here try to develop this consideration, or to apply it to certain recent developments of the realistic, or naturalistic school, as it is called. I may just remark that a man may conceivably deal even with the disgusting without being therefore simply immoral; for he may deal with it so as to excite our disgust. But I think that the practice is dangerous, in so far as the disgust is very apt to be reflected upon the writer; and for the stronger reason that such a method panders to the morbid sentiment, which unfortunately exists as a fact, and which induces men to take a degrading pleasure in the hideous for its own sake. The writer appeals to the brute within us, which has not been quite suppressed by the growth of civilisation. But I am anxious to conclude by one other remark.

I have really dealt with only half the subject. I have asked how far a writer's moral qualities affect the value of his work; but the effect depends as much upon the reader as upon the writer. A man may study the art of medicine to learn how to concoct poisons, or how to stupefy himself with unwholesome opiates; and a reader may extract poisonous material from writings which produce a very wholesome effect upon a healthy mind; or, again, he may read very vicious writing and derive from it only a greater hatred of vice. The problem, therefore, as to the intrinsic merit of literary work should be followed by an inquiry as to the right means of using literature. This inquiry is part of the general theory of education, using that word in the widest possible sense. Here I can only suggest a brief hint as to the bearing of the principles stated.

The true service which any great writer renders to his age is not to be summed up by calculating the amount of information, as to facts, or the number of verifiable theories which he has propounded. He is great so far as he has been the mouthpiece through which some new and fruitful idea has been added to the general current of thought. If he be a philosopher, or a man of science, he is great so far as he has revealed new and efficient methods of inquiry, and applied a stimulus to our intellectual activity. If a poet, he is great so far as he has set before us some impressive ideal of life, or found utterance for the deepest emotions of his contemporaries. The stimulus received from a great mind acts in countless indirect ways, and produces an intellectual ferment which may lead to results entirely unforeseen by him, and possibly very different from those which he would have approved. Now, it is undoubtedly a matter of great importance to every one capable of intellectual interests that he should bring himself into frequent and close contact with the great men of all times, and especially with the great men of our own time; for if such men are uttering old truths they are yet bringing out those aspects, and clothing them in those forms, which are most important at the present day. Nobody, I need hardly say, can appreciate the great issues of the time, or sympathise with the great currents of thought, who has not been more or less at home with the writings of such men as Mr. Carlyle, or Cardinal Newman, or J. S. Mill, or Mr. Darwin, or Mr. Tennyson, or Mr. Browning—I will mention no one whose name could excite a controversy. And the service which such men render is not that they impress upon us some specific moral axiom, or that they provide us with additional arguments against stealing, lying, or drunkenness; but that they rouse, excite, and elevate our whole natures—set us thinking, and therefore enable us to escape from the fetters of ancient prejudice and worn-out platitude, or make us perceive beauty in external nature, or set before us new ideals of life, to which we should otherwise have been indifferent. But we have to co-operate in the result, if it is to be of any real value. We are not to be passive buckets to be pumped into, as Mr. Carlyle puts it, mere receptacles for ready-made ideas, but fellow-creatures capable of being roused into independent activity. Now, in this sense, it is difficult to say where a man may not find some valuable matter. An active-minded man should be awake to all the interests of the day, and should find food for thought everywhere; he may learn something even from the flippant leading article in which a youth fresh from college puts all the philosophers and statesmen of the day in their proper places of due subordination to his own theories; he may even learn something as to the ways of thought and feeling of his neighbours from novels of the vapid and sentimental, or purely silly order, or from that kind of literature—if it deserves the name—which is devoted to mere tittle-tattle, or personal scandal; or again, even from some realistic representations of ugly things, which are sometimes called immoral, because they describe those dark places in society, which we have agreed not to mention, but which may incidentally be useful, in so far as they show how hideous such things really are. I am often half inclined to think that the next best thing to a good book is a bad book; for, after all, the one hopeless evil is stagnation of mind. The question, however, what will do a man harm or good depends very much upon his own constitution. And it would be mere pedantry to insist upon any one's confining himself to the higher and severer class of literature— to say that he is never to condescend to amuse himself with mere trifles, or to condescend to take an interest in contemporary gossip; or what would become of half the literary craftsmen of the day? All, then, that is to be said is this: that to get from literature the best that can be got from it, to use books as instruments for developing our whole natures, the true secret is to select our friends judiciously; to become as intimate as possible with some of the greatest thinkers of mankind, and to study the works of some great minds until we have been saturated with their influence, and have assimilated and made part of ourselves the sentiments which they express most vigorously. To study literature is not merely (as has been said) to know what has been best said by the greatest men, but to learn to know those men themselves. In so doing, the particular moral doctrines which they inculcate, or the effect upon our moral nature of their teaching, is only a part of the whole influence. But still it is a part of no small importance; and the condition upon which a man is able to exert such influence is a profound interest in those ideas with which purely ethical teaching is strictly bound up; and, moreover, a capacity for feeling rightly and vigorously upon ethical questions. In that sense, it is impossible ever really to exclude moral considerations from æsthetical judgments; though it is easy to misapply them, or to overlook the importance of other aspects of a man's total influence. To make a poet into a simple moralist—a teacher of a certain definite code of ethics, is to put him into a wrong place, and judge him implicitly by an inappropriate criterion; but it is equally true that he can only be deprived of moral quality if he takes no interest in the profoundest and most comprehensive topics of human thought and faith; and in so far as he has a moral quality, it is desirable that it should be of the loftiest and purest kind obtainable.

R.L. Stevenson

"A Gossip on Romance"

Longman's Magazine 1 (November 1882), 69–79

A Gossip on Romance.

IN anything fit to be called by the name of reading, the process itself should be absorbing and voluptuous; we should gloat over a book, be rapt clean out of ourselves, and rise from the perusal, our mind filled with the busiest, kaleidoscopic dance of images, incapable of sleep or of continuous thought. The words, if the book be eloquent, should run thenceforward in our ears like the noise of breakers, or the story, if it be a story, repeat itself in a thousand coloured pictures to the eye. It was for this last pleasure that we read so closely, and loved our books so dearly, in the bright, troubled period of boyhood. Eloquence and thought, character and conversation, were but obstacles to brush aside as we dug blithely after a certain sort of incident, like a pig for truffles. For my part, I liked a story to begin with an old way-side inn where, 'towards the close of the year 17—,' several gentlemen in three-cocked hats were playing bowls. A friend of mine preferred the Malabar coast in a storm, with a ship beating to windward, and a scowling fellow of Herculean proportions striding along the beach: he, to be sure, was a pirate. This was further afield than my home-keeping fancy loved to travel, and designed altogether for a larger canvas than the tales that I affected. Give me a highwayman and I was full to the brim; a Jacobite would do, but the highwayman was my favourite dish. I can still hear that merry clatter of the hoofs along the moonlit lane; night and the coming of day are still related in my mind with the doings of John Rann or Jerry Abershaw; and the words 'postchaise,' the 'great North road,' 'ostler,' and 'nag' still sound in my ears like poetry. One and all, at least, and each with his particular fancy, we read story-books in childhood, not for eloquence or character or thought, but for some quality of the brute incident. That quality was not mere bloodshed or wonder. Although each of these was welcome in its place, the charm for the sake of which we read depended on something different from either. My elders used to read novels aloud; and I can still remember four different passages which I heard, before I was ten, with the same keen and lasting pleasure. One I discovered long afterwards to be the admirable opening of 'What will he Do with It': it was no wonder I was pleased with that. The other three still remain unidentified. One is a little vague: it was about a dark, tall house at night, and people groping on the stairs by the light that escaped from the open door of a sick-room. In another, a lover left a ball, and went walking in a cool, dewy park, whence he could watch the lighted windows and the figures of the dancers as they moved. This was the most sentimental impression I think I had yet received, for a child is somewhat deaf to the sentimental. In the last, a poet, who had been tragically wrangling with his wife, walked forth on the sea-beach on a tempestuous night and witnessed the horrors of a wreck. Different as they are, all these early favourites have a common note—they have all a touch of the romantic.

Drama is the poetry of conduct, romance the poetry of circumstance. The pleasure that we take in life is of two sorts—the active and the passive. Now we are conscious of a great command over our destiny; anon we are lifted up by circumstance, as by a breaking wave, and dashed we know not how into the future. Now we are pleased by our conduct, anon merely pleased by our surroundings. It would be hard to say which of these modes of satisfaction is the more effective, but the latter is surely the more constant. Conduct is three parts of life, but it is not all the four. There is a vast deal in life and letters both which is not immoral, but simply a-moral; which either does not regard the human will at all, or deals with it in obvious and healthy relations; where the interest turns, not upon what a man shall choose to do, but on how he manages to do it; not on the passionate slips and hesitations of the conscience, but on the problems of the body and of the practical intelligence, in clean, open-air adventure, the shock of arms, or the diplomacy of life. With such material as this it is impossible to build a play, for the serious theatre exists solely on moral grounds, and is a standing proof of the dissemination of the human conscience. But it is possible to build, upon this ground, the most joyous of verses, and the most lively, beautiful, and buoyant tales.

One thing in life calls for another; there is a fitness in events and places. The sight of a pleasant arbour puts it in our mind to sit there. One place suggests work, another idleness, a third early rising and long rambles in the dew. The effect of night, of any flowing water, of lighted cities, of the peep of day, of ships, of the open ocean, calls up in the mind an army of anonymous desires and pleasures. Something, we feel, should happen; we know not what, yet we proceed in quest of it. And many of the happiest hours of life fleet by us in this vain attendance on the genius of the place and moment. It is thus that tracts of young fir, and low rocks that reach into deep soundings, particularly torture and delight me. Something must have happened in such places, and perhaps ages back, to members of my race; and when I was a child I tried in vain to invent appropriate games for them, as I still try, just as vainly, to fit them with the proper story. Some places speak distinctly. Certain dank gardens cry aloud for a murder; certain old houses demand to be haunted; certain coasts are set apart for shipwreck. Other spots again seem to abide their destiny, suggestive and impenetrable, 'miching mallecho.' The inn at Burford Bridge, with its arbours and green garden and silent, eddying river—though it is known already as the place where Keats finished his 'Endymion' and Nelson parted from his Emma—still seems to wait the coming of the appropriate legend. Within these ivied walls, behind these old green shutters, some further business smoulders, waiting for its hour. The old Hawes Inn at the Queen's Ferry is another. There it stands, apart from the town, beside the pier, in a climate of its own, half inland, half marine—in front, the ferry bubbling with the tide and the guardship swinging to her anchor; behind, the old garden with the trees. Americans seek it already for the sake of Lovel and Oldbuck, who dined there at the beginning of the 'Antiquary.' But you need not tell me—that is not all; there is some story, unrecorded or not yet complete, which must express the meaning of that inn more fully. So it is with names and faces; so it is with incidents that are idle and inconclusive in themselves, and yet seem like the beginning of some quaint romance, which the all-careless author leaves untold. How many of these romances have we not seen determine at their birth; how many people have met us with a look of meaning in their eye, and sunk at once into idle acquaintances; to how many places have we not drawn near, with express intimations—'here my destiny awaits me'—and we have but dined there and passed by! I have lived both at the Hawes and Burford in a perpetual flutter, on the heels, as it seemed, of some adventure that should justify the place; but though the feeling had me to bed at night and called me again at morning in one unbroken round of pleasure and suspense, nothing befell me in either worth remark.

The man or the hour had not yet come ; but some day, I think, a boat shall put off from the Queen's Ferry, fraught with a dear cargo, and some frosty night a horseman, on a tragic errand, rattle with his whip upon the green shutters of the inn at Burford.

Now, this is one of the natural appetites with which any lively literature has to count. The desire for knowledge, I had almost added the desire for meat, is not more deeply seated than this demand for fit and striking incident. The dullest of clowns tells, or tries to tell, himself a story, as the feeblest of children uses invention in his play ; and even as the imaginative grown person, joining in the game, at once enriches it with many delightful circumstances, the great creative writer shows us the realisation and the apotheosis of the daydreams of common men. His stories may be nourished with the realities of life, but their true mark is to satisfy the nameless longings of the reader and to obey the ideal laws of the daydream. The right kind of thing should fall out in the right kind of place ; the right kind of thing should follow ; and not only the characters talk aptly and think naturally, but all the circumstances in a tale answer one to another like notes in music. The threads of a story come from time to time together and make a picture in the web; the characters fall from time to time into some attitude to each other or to nature, which stamps the story home like an illustration. Crusoe recoiling from the footprint, Achilles shouting over against the Trojans, Ulysses bending the great bow, Christian running with his fingers in his ears, these are each culminating moments in the legend, and each has been printed on the mind's eye for ever. Other things we may forget; we may forget the words, although they are beautiful; we may forget the author's comment, although perhaps it was ingenious and true ; but these epoch-making scenes, which put the last mark of truth upon a story and fill up, at one blow, our capacity for sympathetic pleasure, we so adopt into the very bosom of our mind that neither time nor tide can efface or weaken the impression. This, then, is the plastic part of literature : to embody character, thought, or emotion in some act or attitude that shall be remarkably striking to the mind's eye. This is the highest and hardest thing to do in words ; the thing which, once accomplished, equally delights the schoolboy and the sage, and makes, in its own right, the quality of epics. Compared with this, all other purposes in literature, except the purely lyrical or the purely philosophic, are bastard in nature, facile of execution, and feeble in result. It is one thing to write about the inn at Burford, or to describe scenery with the word-painters; it is quite another to seize on the heart of the suggestion and make a country famous with a legend. It is one thing to remark and to dissect, with the most cutting logic, the complications of life, and of the human spirit; it is quite another to give them body and blood in the story of Ajax or of Hamlet. The first is literature, but the second is something besides, for it is likewise art.

English people of the present day are apt, I know not why, to look somewhat down on incident, and reserve their admiration for the clink of tea-spoons and the accents of the curate. It is thought clever to write a novel with no story at all, or at least with a very dull one. Reduced even to the lowest terms, a certain interest can be communicated by the art of narrative; a sense of human kinship stirred; and a kind of monotonous fitness, comparable to the words and air of 'Sandy's Mull,' preserved among the infinitesimal occurrences recorded. Some people work, in this manner, with even a strong touch. Mr. Trollope's inimitable clergymen naturally arise to the mind in this connection. But even Mr. Trollope does not confine himself to chronicling small beer. Mr. Crawley's collision with the Bishop's wife, Mr. Melnotte dallying in the deserted banquet-room, are typical incidents, epically conceived, fitly embodying a crisis. If Rawdon Crawley's blow were not delivered, 'Vanity Fair' would cease to be a work of art. That scene is the chief ganglion of the tale; and the discharge of energy from Rawdon's fist is the reward and consolation of the reader. The end of 'Esmond' is a yet wider excursion from the author's customary fields; the scene at Castlewood is pure Dumas; the great and wily English borrower has here borrowed from the great, unblushing French thief; as usual, he has borrowed admirably well, and the breaking of the sword rounds off the best of all his books with a manly, martial note. But perhaps nothing can more strongly illustrate the necessity for marking incident than to compare the living fame of 'Robinson Crusoe' with the discredit of 'Clarissa Harlowe.' 'Clarissa' is a book of a far more startling import, worked out, on a great canvas, with inimitable courage and unflagging art; it contains wit, character, passion, plot, conversations full of spirit and insight, letters sparkling with unstrained humanity; and if the death of the heroine be somewhat frigid and artificial, the last days of the hero strike the only note of what we now call Byronism, between the Elizabethans and Byron himself. And yet a little story of a shipwrecked sailor, with not a tenth part of the style nor a thousandth part of the wisdom, exploring none of the arcana of humanity and deprived of the perennial interest of love, goes on from edition to edition, ever young, while 'Clarissa lies upon the shelves unread. A friend of mine, a Welsh blacksmith, was twenty-five years old, and could neither read nor write, when he heard a chapter of 'Robinson' read aloud in a farm kitchen. Up to that moment he had sat content, huddled in his ignorance; but he left that farm another man. There were daydreams, it appeared, divine daydreams, written and printed and bound, and to be bought for money and enjoyed at pleasure. Down he sat that day, painfully learned to read Welsh, and returned to borrow the book. It had been lost, nor could he find another copy but one that was in English. Down he sat once more, learned English, and at length, and with entire delight, read 'Robinson.' It is like the story of a love-chase. If he had heard a letter from 'Clarissa,' would he have been fired with the same chivalrous ardour? I wonder. Yet 'Clarissa' has every quality that can be shown in prose, one alone excepted: pictorial, or picture-making romance. While 'Robinson' depends, for the most part and with the overwhelming majority of its readers, on the charm of circumstance.

In the highest achievements of the art of words, the dramatic and the pictorial, the moral and romantic interest rise and fall together by a common and organic law. Situation is animated with passion, passion clothed upon with situation. Neither exists for itself, but each inheres indissolubly with the other. This is high art; and not only the highest art possible in words, but the highest art of all, since it combines the greatest mass and diversity of the elements of truth and pleasure. Such are epics, and the few prose tales that have the epic weight. But as from a school of works, aping the creative, incident and romance are ruthlessly discarded, so may character and drama be omitted or subordinated to romance. There is one book, for example, more generally loved than Shakespeare, that captivates in childhood, and still delights in age— I mean the 'Arabian Nights'—where you shall look in vain for moral or for intellectual interest. No human face or voice greets us among that wooden crowd of kings and genies, sorcerers and beggarmen. Adventure, on the most naked terms furnishes forth the entertainment and is found enough. Dumas approaches perhaps nearest of any modern to these Arabian authors in the purely material charm of his romances. The early part of 'Monte

Christo,' down to the finding of the treasure, is a piece of perfect story-telling; the man never breathed who shared these moving incidents without a tremor; and yet Faria is a thing of packthread and Dantès little more than a name. The sequel is one long-drawn error, gloomy, bloody, unnatural and dull; but as for these early chapters, I do not believe there is another volume extant where you can breathe the same unmingled atmosphere of romance. It is very thin and light, to be sure, as on a high mountain; but it is brisk and clear and sunny in proportion. I saw the other day, with envy, an old and a very clever lady setting forth on a second or third voyage into 'Monte Christo.' Here are stories, which powerfully affect the reader, which can be reperused at any age, and where the characters are no more than puppets. The bony fist of the show-man visibly propels them; their springs are an open secret; their faces are of wood, their bellies filled with bran; and yet we thrillingly partake of their adventures. And the point may be illustrated still further. The last interview between Lucy and Richard Feverell is pure drama; more than that, it is the strongest scene, since Shakespeare, in the English tongue. Their first meeting by the river, on the other hand, is pure romance; it has nothing to do with character; it might happen to any other boy and maiden, and be none the less delightful for the change. And yet I think he would be a bold man who should choose between these passages. Thus, in the same book, we may have two scenes, each capital in its order: in the one, human passion, deep calling unto deep, shall utter its genuine voice; in the second, according circumstances, like instruments in tune, shall build up a trivial but desirable incident, such as we love to prefigure for ourselves; and in the end, in spite of the critics, we may hesitate to give the preference to either. The one may ask more genius—I do not say it does; but at least the other dwells as clearly in the memory.

True romantic art, again, makes a romance of all things. It reaches into the highest abstraction of the ideal; it does not refuse the most pedestrian realism. 'Robinson Crusoe' is as realistic as it is romantic; both qualities are pushed to an extreme, and neither suffers. Nor does romance depend upon the material importance of the incidents. To deal with strong and deadly elements, ban-ditti, pirates, war, and murder, is to conjure with great names, and, in the event of failure, to double the disgrace. The arrival of Haydn and Consuelo at the Canon's villa is a very trifling incident; yet we may read a dozen boisterous stories from beginning to end, and not receive so fresh and stirring an impression of adventure. It was the scene of Crusoe at the wreck, if I remember rightly, that so bewitched my blacksmith. Nor is the fact surprising. Every single article the castaway recovers from the hulk is 'a joy for ever' to the man who reads of them. They are the things he ought to find, and the bare enumeration stirs the blood. I found a glimmer of the same interest the other day in a new book, 'The Sailor's Sweetheart,' by Mr. Clark Russell. The whole business of the brig 'Morning Star' is very rightly felt and spiritedly written; but the clothes, the books, and the money satisfy the reader's mind like things to eat. We are dealing here with the old cut-and-dry, legitimate interest of treasure trove. But even treasure trove can be made dull. There are few people who have not groaned under the plethora of goods that fell to the lot of the 'Swiss Family Robinson,' that dreary family. They found article after article, creature after creature, from milk kine to pieces of ordnance, a whole consignment; but no informing taste had presided over the selection, there was no smack or relish in the invoice; and all these riches left the fancy cold. The box of goods in Verne's 'Mysterious Island' is another case in point: there was no gusto and no glamour about that; it might have come from a shop. But the two hundred and seventy-eight Australian sovereigns on board the 'Morning Star' fell upon me like a surprise that I had expected; whole vistas of secondary stories, besides the one in hand, radiated forth from that discovery, as they radiate from a striking particular in life; and I was made for the moment as happy as a reader has the right to be.

To come at all at the nature of this quality of romance, we must bear in mind the peculiarity of our attitude to any art. No art produces illusion; in the theatre, we never forget that we are in the theatre; and while we read a story, we sit wavering between two minds, now merely clapping our hands at the merit of the performance, now condescending to take an active part in fancy with the characters. This last is the triumph of story-telling: when the reader consciously plays at being the hero, the scene is a good scene. Now in character-studies the pleasure that we take is critical; we watch, we approve, we smile at incongruities, we are moved to sudden heats of sympathy with courage, suffering, or virtue. But the characters are still themselves; they are not us; the more clearly they are depicted, the more widely do they stand away from us, the more imperiously do they thrust us back into our place as a spectator. I cannot identify myself with Rawdon Crawley or with Eugene de Rastignac, for I have scarce a hope or fear in common with them. It is not character, but incident, that wooes us out of our reserve. Something happens, as we desire to have it happen to ourselves; some situation, that we have long dallied with in fancy, is realised in the story with enticing and appropriate details. Then we forget the characters; then we push the hero aside; then we plunge into the tale in our own person and bathe in fresh experience; and then, and then only, do we say we have been reading a romance. It is not only pleasurable things that we imagine in our daydreams; there are lights in which we are willing to contemplate even the idea of our own death; ways in which it seems as if it would amuse us to be cheated, wounded, or calumniated. It is thus possible to construct a story, even of tragic import, in which every incident, detail, and trick of circumstance shall be welcome to the reader's thoughts. Fiction is to the grown man what play is to the child. It is there that he changes the atmosphere and tenor of his life. And when the game so chimes with his fancy that he can join in it with all his heart, when it pleases him with every turn, when he loves to recall it and dwells upon its recollection with entire delight, fiction is called romance.

Walter Scott is out and away the king of the romantics. ' The Lady of the Lake ' has no indisputable claim to be a poem beyond the inherent fitness and desirability of the tale. It is just such a story as a man would make up for himself, walking, in the best health and temper, through just such scenes as it is laid in. Hence it is that a charm dwells undefinable among these slovenly verses, as the unseen cuckoo fills the mountains with his note; hence, even after we have flung the book aside, the scenery and adventures remain present to the mind, a new and green possession, not unworthy of that beautiful name, ' The Lady of the Lake,' or that direct, romantic opening—one of the most spirited and poetical in literature—' The stag at eve had drunk his fill.' The same strength and the same weaknesses adorn and disfigure the novels. In that ill-written, ragged book, ' The Pirate,' the figure of Cleveland—cast up by the sea on the resounding foreland of Dunrossness—moving, with the blood on his hands and the Spanish words on his tongue, among the simple islanders—singing a serenade under the window of his Shetland mistress—is conceived in the very highest manner of romantic invention. The words of his song, ' Through groves of palm,' sung in such a scene and by such a lover, clench, as in a nutshell, the emphatic contrast upon which the tale is built. In ' Guy Mannering,' again, every incident is delightful to the imagination; and the scene when Harry Bertram lands at Ellangowan is a model instance of romantic method.

' " I remember the tune well," ' he says, ' " though I cannot guess what should at present so strongly recall it to my memory." He took his flageolet from his pocket and played a simple melody. Apparently the tune awoke the corresponding associations of a damsel. . . . She immediately took up the song :—

> Are these the links of Forth, she said ;
> Or are they the crooks of Dee,
> Or the bonny woods of Warroch Head
> That I so fain would see ?

' " By heaven ! " said Bertram, " it is the very ballad." '

On this quotation two remarks fall to be made. First, as an instance of modern feeling for romance, this famous touch of the flageolet and the old song is selected by Miss Braddon for omission. Miss Braddon's idea of a story, like Mrs. Todgers's idea of a wooden leg, were something strange to have expounded. As a matter of personal experience, Meg's appearance to old Mr. Bertram on the road, the ruins of Derncleugh, the scene of the flageolet, and the Dominie's recognition of Harry, are the four strong notes that continue to ring in the mind after the book is laid aside. The second point is still more curious. The reader will observe a mark of excision in the passage as quoted by me. Well, here is how it runs in the original : ' A damsel, who, close behind a fine spring about half-way down the descent, and which had once supplied the castle with water, was engaged in bleaching linen.' A man who gave in such copy would be discharged from the staff of a daily paper. Scott has forgotten to prepare the reader for the presence of the 'damsel'; he has forgotten to mention the spring and its relation to the ruin ; and now, face to face with his omission, instead of trying back and starting fair, crams all this matter, tail foremost, into a single shambling sentence. It is not merely bad English, or bad style; it is abominably bad narrative besides.

Certainly the contrast is remarkable ; and it is one that throws a strong light upon the subject of this paper. For here we have a man, of the finest creative instinct, touching with perfect certainty and charm the romantic junctures of his story; and we find him utterly careless, almost, it would seem, incapable, in the technical matter of style; and not only frequently weak, but frequently wrong, in points of drama. In character parts, indeed, and particularly in the Scotch, he was delicate, strong, and truthful; but the trite, obliterated features of too many of his heroes have already wearied two generations of readers. At times, his characters will speak with something far beyond propriety, with a true heroic note; but on the next page they will be wading wearily forward with an ungrammatical and undramatic rigmarole of words. The man who could conceive and write the character of Elspeth of the Craigburnfoot, as Scott has conceived and written it, had not only splendid romantic, but splendid tragic, gifts. How comes it, then, that he could so often fob us off with languid, inarticulate twaddle?

It seems to me that the explanation is to be found in the very quality of his surprising merits. As his books are play to the reader, so were they play to him. He conjured up the beautiful with delight, but he had hardly patience to describe it. He was a great daydreamer, a seeër of fit and beautiful and humorous visions; but hardly a great artist; hardly, in the manful sense, an artist at all. He pleased himself, and so he pleases us. Of the pleasures of his art he tasted fully; but of its toils and vigils and distresses never man knew less. A great romantic—an idle child.

R. L. Stevenson.

Mowbray Morris

"Charles Dickens"

Fortnightly Review 38 (December 1882), 762–79

CHARLES DICKENS.

IT is stated, and on the very best authority, that within the twelve years that have passed since Dickens's death no less than 4,239,000 volumes of his works have been sold in England alone! A long way the first on this astonishing list stands *Pickwick*, while *David Copperfield*, the second, is almost equally far in front of *Dombey and Son; 'Little Dorritt* has found nearly as many readers as *Martin Chuzzlewit*, while, with the exception of *Edwin Drood*, *The Tale of Two Cities* and *Great Expectations* take the lowest place. Nor has his popularity been confined to England or to English-speaking people. French, German, and Italian, Russian and Swedish translations of his works appeared during his lifetime; when he was still but a young man the pages of "Boz" were devoured, we have been told, with enthusiasm in Silesian villages; *Pickwick*, it is said, and on no less circumstantial authority, was found equal, when all else failed, to the task of soothing the sleepless nights of Mehemet Ali; Mr. Forster has published a story of a strange half-human recluse who had built his cell amid the eternal snows of the Sierra Nevada, and who found in *Pickwick* and in *Nicholas Nickleby* the only intercourse with humanity that he desired. If it were true, as has been said by one who has certainly managed to refute his own words,[1] if it were true that present popularity is the only safe presage of future glory, what an eternity of glory should await Charles Dickens!

And yet present popularity, a vogue, how brilliant and irresistible soever it may be, or what manner of prologue it may furnish to future glory, is quite another matter from that glory itself, from the real definitive glory, the one thing, as M. Renan tells us, which has the best chance of not being altogether vanity. That posterity will regard Dickens as he was regarded in his lifetime, or even as we now regard him, is of course out of the question. "To the public," said Professor Ward, in a lecture delivered at Manchester in the year of Dickens's death, "to the public his faults were often inseparable from his merits; and when our critical consciences told us that he was astray in one of his favourite directions, the severest censure we had for him was that he was growing 'more like himself' than ever." That the critical conscience of posterity will have far severer censure for Dickens than this one cannot doubt, nor indeed can any one thoughtful for the fame of English literature desire that it should not.

(1) Jeffrey.

"No man," it has been well said, "can trust himself to speak of his own time and of his own contemporaries with the same sureness of judgment and the same proportion as of times and men gone by." Even Goethe could not criticise Byron as he criticised Shakespeare or Molière. Not, indeed, that Dickens rested from criticism during his lifetime. So sudden and universal a popularity as his, so original, so self-contained and self-reliant a genius, could not but attract criticism, or what often passes by the name of criticism among contemporaries, both kindly and otherwise. He found, indeed, plenty of both, but all or almost all the criticism he encountered in his lifetime took a bias of one kind or other, the bias of enthusiasm or the bias of opposition, the one perhaps an irresistible consequence of the other—the enthusiasm seeing all things in him because of his marvellous popularity, the opposition seeing nothing in him but that popularity, which, according to its wont, it made every effort to explain away. Neither bias is, of course, so strong now, and particularly the bias of opposition, which is in most cases the soonest counteracted by death. Nevertheless, to form a just estimate of his work, to weigh its merits and its defects and to strike a balance between them, is still perhaps impossible, must certainly, even for us of a later generation, be very difficult. Brought up, as most of us have been, in the faith of Dickens, whose earliest laughter has been stirred by Sam Weller and Dick Swiveller and Mr. Micawber, whose earliest tears have flowed for the sordid wretchedness of David Copperfield's forlorn childhood, or for Florence Dombey toiling up the "great wide vacant stairs," with her brother in her arms, and singing as she goes—who have stolen trembling after Jonas Chuzzlewit through that awful wood, or stared with face as pale as Pip himself at that grim midnight visitor in the lonely Temple chambers ; to such it must surely seem little short of pro-fanity to consider too curiously the old familiar pages, to stand afar off, contemplating with cold impartial scrutiny the old familiar figures, as though, like Trabb's boy, we did not know them.

And besides such sentimental hindrances, the temporary and, as one may say, local hindrances to all criticism, there are others which must always render more than commonly difficult, if indeed possible at all, an absolute judgment on works of fiction which deal so primarily, if not wholly, with the emotions as do the works of Dickens. "It is impossible to resist feeling," said George Henry Lewes, ten years ago in this very Review, in his paper on Dickens which moved the scandalised Forster almost to vituperation, "it is impossible to resist feeling. If an author makes me laugh, he is humorous; if he makes me cry, he is pathetic. In vain will any one tell me that such a picture is not laughable, is not pathetic ; or that I am wrong in being moved." There are no doubt some passages in imaginative writing which one may fairly say *should* stir the heart of every man. One could hardly, for example, think very nobly of the soul of him who could read how Priam knelt at the feet of Achilles, "and kissed those hands, the terrible, the murderous, which had slain so many of his sons,"[1] without feeling that he was in the presence of a more than common sorrow; or who could not recognise the incomparable pathos that breathes in such verse as

> " do not laugh at me,
> For, as I am a man, I think this lady
> To be my child Cordelia."

Nevertheless, with works of a lower class, with works rather of the fancy than the imagination, we cannot in reason quarrel either with those who indulge in the "luxury of woe" over passages which leave ourselves unmoved, or with those who can read dry-eyed the words which unlock for us "the sacred source of sympathetic tears." And so with Dickens's humour. It is conceivable that human souls exist who do not laugh at Dick Swiveller or Mrs. Gamp. We should not, some of us, perhaps care greatly for travelling in far countries with such, or for passing many hours in commune with them anywhere; but it would be vain to attempt to demonstrate to them that they should laugh, or to insist upon regarding them as lost to all sense of literary or artistic decency because they did not. Wordsworth could find Voltaire dull; and what Carlyle thought of Charles Lamb we all know.

Of course, with the other qualities or characteristics of Dickens's work, as of all work—his powers of description, for example, of observation, his powers of narration and composition, his style and his literary workmanship generally—the case will be different. But these two, the qualities of humour and of pathos, so largely predominate all his work, that it seems to me almost impossible for any judgment to be *absolute*, to use Lewes' phrase; it must, I think, be *individual*. Still, from many individual judgments a deduction may perhaps be made which, though not in itself absolute, nor even tending to the absolute, may yet be of avail in promoting a sounder estimate, in counteracting the bias both of enthusiasm and opposition.

Merely personal considerations, that " soul of good nature and kindness," which Mr. Matthew Arnold has found so irresistible in *David Copperfield*, and which his friends loved so wisely and so well in the man, largely as such influences must always inform contemporary judgment, will not avail with posterity, nor is it right that they should. Despite M. Scherer's high recommendation, the historical method of criticism, the " analysis of the writer's character and the study of his age" will not really insure the " right understanding"

(1) *Iliad*, xxiv. 478-9.

of his work. It may enable us, no doubt, to *account* for much of his work, but not necessarily to understand, and surely still less to judge it. It will help us often to understand how the particular good comes to be so good, and the bad so bad; but to assist us in discriminating the good and bad it must surely be of little worth. Nevertheless, a clear knowledge of Dickens's life and character, of his age and his position with regard to his age—to which knowledge Mr. Forster's very full biography, ardent admirer and affectionate friend as he was, must always largely contribute—will go far to explain and to account for many things in his writings which may puzzle posterity, which would certainly puzzle a posterity which had derived its knowledge only from that other friend of his who has described him as "followed, admired, courted, lionised, almost idolised, by almost all that was wealthy and dignified and beautiful in society." It will go far, for instance, to account for the extraordinary one-sidedness and the consequent ineffectualness of so much of his satire, and especially of his satire on the governing classes and the upper classes of society generally. It will go far to explain whence it happens that, despite his own disclaimer of "placing in opposition those two words, Aristocracy and People," he yet seems so often unable to resist the temptation of the contrast, and always, or nearly always, to the disadvantage of the former; to explain whence it comes, though he has avowed that he "would not on any account deprive either of a single just right belonging to it," that the rights of the one seem to him so much more just, so much more certain than the rights of the other. "I believe," he said, speaking at Boston during his first visit to America, "I believe that virtue dwells rather oftener in alleys and byways than she does in courts and palaces." A judicious use of the historical method will no doubt help to explain the grounds for this belief, to explain the lack of firmness in the step, of keenness in the eye, of sureness in the touch, as he gets farther away from the alleys and byways, and nearer to the courts and palaces; but to say that this method will be necessary to enable the reader to *detect* the faults which arise from the prevalence of these sentiments, and their too aggressive advocacy, is surely to attribute to him an incapacity for judging which no method of criticism hitherto revealed to man could really hope to counteract. Professor Ward has told us in his interesting and sensible little book,[1] that there was "something singular in the admiration that Dickens and Carlyle felt for one another." He has pointed out how many are the proofs in the former's works of his "readiness to accept the teachings of one whom he declared he would go at all times farther to see than any man alive." He has reminded us how Carlyle, after an acquaintance of almost thirty

(1) *English Men of Letters : Dickens.* By A. W. Ward. Macmillan & Co.

years, spoke of Dickens as a "most cordial, sincere, clear-sighted, quietly decisive, just, and loving man ; " and he adds: " There is not one of these epithets but seems well considered and well chosen." " But," he also adds, " neither Carlyle nor Dickens possessed a moral quality omitted in this list, the quality of patience, which abhors either 'quietly' or 'loudly' deciding a question before considering it under all its aspects, and in a spirit of fairness to all sides." One may observe, perhaps, in passing, that a man who did not possess the patience necessary to consider fairly all sides of a question could not well be called *clear-sighted* in the best sense of the word. But to know this, to know how deep the admiration Dickens felt for Carlyle, and his readiness always to accept the latter's teachings, will no doubt help the future student to *account* for much of Dickens's work, but will hardly help him to judge it.

Again, the historical method, to keep it with us a while longer, may undoubtedly avail to enable the reader to account for that note of extravagance which is too rarely absent from Dickens's work, and which, it seems to me, is likely to tell most strongly against it in the future—the want of a capacity of self-judgment and restraint. He tells us, through the mouth of David Copperfield,[1] that his two "golden rules" were, " never to put one hand to anything on which I could throw my whole self ; and never to affect depreciation of my work, whatever it was." Two golden rules, no doubt, but without the power of seeing and judging that work as it really is, no less certainly capable of leading the workman at times a little astray. We can hardly doubt that they sometimes led Dickens astray. Every one who has read Mr. Forster's biography will remember the exuberant delight with which Dickens recounts the increasing sale of each successive work, without any apparent thought of their respective deserts. That his bad work should sell as well as his good suggested nothing to him, because to him there seemed no difference between the two ; the work he was for the moment engaged on was to him the best. " *Little Dorrit*," he writes, " has beaten even *Bleak House* out of the field. It is a most tremendous start, and I am overjoyed at it ;" and " you know," he adds, " that they sold 35,000 of number two on New Year's Day." He can see no reason why this should not be ; he sees no distinction, or he does not care to see any, between perhaps the worst book he ever wrote and one which is certainly among his best. We are told that he was extraordinarily sensitive both to praise or blame. No great writer has ever really despised or ignored either, whatever indifference he may have affected in moments of pique ; but with Dickens it is clear, from many things Mr. Forster tells us, and from much in his own letters, this only meant that he swallowed every sort of praise and rejected

(1) *David Copperfield.* Ch. xlii.

every sort of blame; that, in short, he was rather minded to regard the critics who did not accept all his outpourings unreservedly much as Mr. Micawber regarded his wife's family, as, "in the aggregate, impertinent Snobs; and, in detail, unmitigated Ruffians." We may detect the same note, too, in what Mr. Ward calls his "innocent ecstasies" over the success of his readings, ecstasies which, as Mr. Ward so truly says, would in any other man have furnished him with inexhaustible subjects for parody. And still more clearly do we find it in his feverish descriptions to Forster of the manner in which he flung himself into his characters, and of the reality which their counterfeit emotions aroused in him. I will not instance his well-known letter about little Nell, for with that was interwoven the recollection of a real sorrow which removes it without the pale of criticism. But the death of little Paul affected him in an equal manner, and he seems to have regarded it as an equal masterpiece of pathetic writing. "Paul's death," he writes, "has amazed Paris" (it was written in Paris), "and all sorts of people are open-mouthed with admiration;" and elsewhere he is described as throughout the greater part of the night of the day on which it was written wandering about the streets "desolate and sad." As far as the little girl is concerned, perhaps the balance of opinion leans towards Dickens; but certainly nowadays the majority of readers experience a sense mostly of relief at the premature blighting of the other of these two "opening buds." Jeffrey, to be sure, thought it, as Dickens tells us, "the best thing, past, present, and to come;" and, indeed, he himself has told us how he "cried and sobbed over it," and felt his heart "purified by those tears:" but Jeffrey was then, we must remember, in his seventy-fifth year, and man, when past the three score years and ten, is apt to be a little ἀρτίδακρυς, as Medea says. Again, we find Dickens writing from Genoa, "This book (*The Chimes*) has made my face white in a foreign land. My cheeks, which were beginning to fill out, have sunk again; my eyes have grown immensely large; my hair is very lank; and the head inside the hair is hot and giddy. Read the scene at the end of the third part twice. I wouldn't write it twice for something." Such a diagnosis as this is, perhaps, the most striking instance on record of what Mr. Ruskin has so happily styled the "pathetic fallacy."

All that we know of Dickens forbids us to doubt that he wrote such things in perfect sincerity, and not merely with a view to effect, as so many distinguished men have written to a sympathetic friend in whom they foresaw a future biographer: to doubt that he really was, or—which is practically the same—really believed himself to be, in the mental and bodily condition he has described, whether in sober earnest he was so or not. And with this assurance do we not come at once to the secret of that want of proportion, of the

artistic sense of limitation and restraint, which, now showing itself
in this phase and now in that, is the one capital defect of Dickens's
work? A man who could write about himself as he has so often
written to Forster, and write in perfect honesty, could not, one
feels, have the shaping power, the control of the true artist so
important in all works of the imagination, so vital to an imagination
of such astonishing fertility and vividness working without a basis
of training and education—an imagination which many, by no means
inclined to accept Dickens without reservation, have thought is not
to be surpassed outside the works of Shakspeare. And just as Mr.
Arnold has shown us how we do not conceive, or should not at least
conceive, of Shakspeare as pre-eminently the *great artist* in that
sense, which is the real sense, of the word, the sense of "pure and
flawless workmanship," so, it seems to me, we cannot properly conceive of Dickens, often as the word has been applied to him, often,
no doubt, as it will be. It is not necessary to compare him with
Thackeray in the sense in which such comparisons may be said to be
odious, to affect to decide which is the greater of two so great writers.
Hereafter, of course, such a comparison will have to be made, as it
must inevitably be made in the case of all fellow-workers of importance in any field; but for us now, standing so close to them
as we do, it were better, perhaps, to remember the saying of
Goethe: "For twenty years the public has been disputing which
is the greatest, Schiller or I; and it ought to be glad that it has
got a couple of fellows about whom it *can* dispute." Nevertheless, that unthinking partisanship which we so often meet with
among the admirers of Dickens, and which "stares tremendous with
a threatening eye" at the very name of Thackeray, is surely no less
idle. To compare these two men—friends, contemporaries, each
working in the same field of letters, to examine their different
modes of handling similar, or nearly similar, subjects—to compare
them, in short, in the sense of illustrating the one by the other,
must surely be as inevitable as it should be fruitful. And so, in
thinking of Dickens's position as the *artist,* of the quality of his
workmanship, in considering him, if I may coin the word, *architecton-*
ically, there inevitably rises also in one's thoughts the predominance
of this quality in Thackeray. Profound as is my admiration for
Thackeray, and ever fresh the pleasure with which I go back again
and again to his writings, it seems to me impossible to deny that
Dickens was the more abundantly gifted of the two; he had, I mean,
a larger proportion of the gifts which go to make the writer of
fiction, and those he had in which the other was wanting, or
possessed, at least, in a less degree, are precisely those which commend themselves most immediately and vividly to the majority of
readers, which take soonest hold of the popular imagination and

sympathy, and keep them longest. But the true artist's touch, the sense of limitation, of symmetry, the self-control, the sure perception, in a word, of the exact moment when "the rest *should be* silence," which so powerfully impresses us in Thackeray's best work —in such work as *Vanity Fair*, and *Esmond*, and *Barry Lyndon*— we never, or hardly ever, find in Dickens. And is it not by this quality, in this secret of consummate workmanship, that the novelist has, after all, the best chance of surviving; that the works which show this pre-eminently, or even conspicuously, are likely to keep sweet the longest? The fictions which paint the manners and humours of contemporary life, which deal with portraits rather than with types of humanity, with the individualities of nature rather, and not with her universal and eternal properties, must inevitably lose, for an age which cannot recognise the fidelity of the painting, cannot, perhaps, comprehend the possibility of fidelity, much of that which once constituted its chiefest charm. But the charm of perfect workmanship can never die. *Tom Jones* will outlive the palace of the Escurial, not because it is a picture of humour and manners, but because it is an *exquisite* picture.

It has been the fashion with us to depreciate M. Taine's criticism of Dickens; and there is, undoubtedly, something comical to an English reader in hearing that Dickens had not "the quality of happiness." English wit, M. Taine says, consists in saying light jests in a solemn manner, and so "Dickens remains grave while drawing his caricatures." Undoubtedly, too, it is a little startling to an Englishman to find that "French taste, *always measured*, revolts against affected strokes and sickly prettinesses;" and to find the critic gravely ignoring the one quality in which to most English readers Dickens stands pre-eminent—the quality of humour; though this, to be sure, will be less inexplicable to those who remember how gravely M. Taine has quoted the cant use among young people of the word *governor*, as an instance of the high authority and dignity with which the father is invested in an English household. But M. Taine's criticism is very far indeed from being all as wayward as this; on the contrary it is often remarkably just and acute. On this defect, for example, this want of controlling and shaping power, he seizes at once, and illustrates it very happily. "In a writer of novels," he says, "the imagination is the master faculty; the art of composition, good taste, appreciation of truth, depend upon it; one degree more of vehemence destroys the style which expresses it, changes the character which it produces, breaks the framework in which it is enclosed. Consider that of Dickens, and you will perceive therein the cause of his faults and his merits, his power and his excess." And the effect of this "one degree more of vehemence" he often points out with signal felicity. He shows how the source of those extraordinary minute descriptions of localities, and of phases of nature—a windy day, a storm, and so forth—which impress the reader at first with what seems their marvellous reality, is in very truth the ʻimagination. We often talk of Dickens's astonishing powers of observation, and astonishing indeed they are; but too often they produce no more than a half result, because he had not at the same time perceptiᴏ ᴊ, which is the crucible of observation. His observation kept him constantly supplied with a crude mass of material, on which his imagination worked often with wonderful power and effect, but the capacity for refining this mass, for selecting and shaping it, he had not.

" An imagination," M. Taine says again, " so lucid and energetic cannot but animate inanimate objects without an effort. It provokes in the mind in which it works extraordinary emotions, and the author pours over the objects which he figures to himself something of the ever-willing passions which overflow in him." Mr. Forster has expended a great deal of somewhat clumsy irony in ridiculing this passage, but in truth it is only saying in other words that Dickens had in an eminent degree the temperament which admits the " pathetic fallacy," the temperament, to use Mr. Ruskin's words, " of a mind and body in some sort too weak to deal fully with what is before them ; borne away, or overclouded, or overdazzled by emotion." Mr. Ruskin, it will be remembered, makes use of this phrase, the pathetic fallacy, to point the difference between the ordinary, proper, and true appearance of things to us, and their extraordinary or false appearance when we are under the influence of emotion or contemplative fancy—false appearance, that is to say, as being entirely unconnected with any real power or character in the object, and only imputed to it by us. And this fallacy, he says, is of two kinds—there is the fallacy of wilful fancy, which involves no real expectation that it will be believed ; or else it is a fallacy caused by an excited state of the feelings, making us for the time more or less irrational.

It would be easy to fill a volume with instances of this fallacy from Dickens's works. M. Taine gives one from *The Chimes*,[1] a description of the wind blowing in a church at night, and the famous description of Venice is full of them.[2] But, indeed, Dickens hardly ever describes the aspects or the workings of Nature without having recourse to it, at first unintentionally, as " borne away, or overclouded by emotion ;" latterly because he found it very popular (for, as Mr. Ruskin says, much of our favourite writing, though he is dealing only with poetry, is full of it, and we like it all the more

---

(1) *The Chimes*, first quarter. " For the night wind ʰas a dismal trick of wandering round and round a building of that sort," &c.

(2) *Pictures from Italy ;* an Italian dream.

for being so), and because the vividness of his fancy made it very easy to him. For, powerful as his imagination was, his fancy was yet more powerful. In all great writers the fancy at first overbears the imagination; in Shakspeare's early work, for example, in the *Venus and Adonis* and the *Lucrece*, the fancy is almost supreme; but with the greatest, in time the imagination prevails. In Dickens, on the contrary, as time wore on, the imagination became weaker, and the calls upon the fancy in consequence more frequent and urgent: instead of the death of Nancy we get the death of Miss Haversham, and Mr. Sapsea instead of Mr. Pecksniff.

Scott, when he describes a scene or an incident, does so in a few broad strokes; Dickens with an extraordinary number of minute touches, each one of astonishing accuracy and fineness, such as would have occurred probably to no other man. In reading Scott we are not at the moment struck with the felicity or the power of any particular touch, but the general impression left upon our imagination is singularly precise and luminous. On the other hand, in reading Dickens, we are continually pausing to wonder at the quickness, the accuracy, the range of his vision, but the general impression is often vague and confusing from this very many-sidedness. He seems, as it were, to see too many things, and to see them all too instantaneously, to allow his reader to get a clear recollection of any one. He catalogues rather than describes. Admirable in their way as are the pictures of the French Revolution in *The Tale of Two Cities*, or of the Gordon Riots in *Barnaby Rudge*, the impression of them we keep with us as we lay the book down is hardly so clear and strong as the impression left on us, for example, by the description of the death of Porteus in the opening chapter of *The Heart of Midlothian*. The most profuse and elaborate embellishments of Dickens's fancy cannot vie with the stern and grand straightforwardness of the incomparable scene in Wandering Willie's tale, where Steenie Piper goes down into hell to win the receipt back from his old master.[1] Hazlitt says somewhere of Crabbe's poetry, that he "describes the interior of a cottage like a person sent there to distrain for rent." The illustration is not inapplicable sometimes to the method of Dickens.

And yet at other times how large and free that method can be in painting scene or incident! Here, as elsewhere, Dickens can himself supply the antidote no less surely than the bane. He himself can show us how differently he works when he is describing, as M. Taine says, like Scott, "to give his reader a map, and to lay down the locality of his drama;" and when "struck with a certain spectacle, he is transported, and breaks out into unforeseen figures." If any one will turn to *Great Expectations* and read the description

---

(1) *Redgauntlet*, letter xi.

of that fruitless journey down the river from Mill-Pond Stairs to the Nore,[1] or to almost any of the descriptive passages in *Oliver Twist*,[2] and then turn to *Dombey and Son* and read the description of Carker's return to England,[3] he can make the contrast for himself.

It is only natural that this want of proportion and control, this riot of fancy, should be most conspicuous on the romantic and sentimental side of Dickens's work. But we may trace it with more or less distinctness everywhere. We find it even in his own particular domain, in the scenes where he walks supreme, the mighty master of a humour incomparable and his own. There we are so completely in his power that he has but to wave his wand and we are prostrate. Yet it is impossible not to feel even here that he uses this power too indiscriminately, intemperately sometimes, and unreasonably. It is so rich and so wonderful, that humour of his, that we cannot but welcome it whenever and wherever it greets us. Yet when the " burst of joyful greetings" is over, reflection will sometimes obtrude. There is an instance in *David Copperfield*—in which delightful book, by the way, instances of this or of any other of the writer's defects are few and far between. It is in the scene where that " HEEP of villany " has forced his suspicions on the old Doctor, and has dragged David in as his unwilling witness. David, it will be remembered, concentrating years of distrust and loathing into one moment, has struck the scoundrel in the face, and the singularly calm reception of the insult has not improved his temper. Then he leaves him : "merely telling him that I should expect from him what I always had expected, and had never yet been disappointed in. I opened the door upon him, *as if he had been a great walnut put there to be cracked*, and went out of the house."[4] One cannot but smile at the quaintness of the fancy here, and one cannot but feel how sadly out of place it is in so serious, so pitiful a scene. In *Martin Chuzzlewit* there is a still more painful instance in the description of the poor old clerk's grief for his dead master, where he mixes up recollections of the counting-house with his sorrow in the strangest and most incongruous manner. "Take him from me, and what remains ? "[5] Every one must be conscious what a terribly false note is struck here. It is in such writing as this that Dickens's vulgarity lies. He is not vulgar because he deals with common subjects—subjects which are called vulgar by his genteel depreciators, the Mr. and Mrs. Wititterleys of our day—but because he too often deals with great subjects in a

---

(1) *Great Expectations*, chap. liv.

(2) The journey of Sikes and Oliver to Chertsey, for example, in chap. xxi., or the description of Jacob's Island in chap. l., and, indeed, the whole of that wonderful scene.

(3) *Dombey and Son*, chap. lv.   (4) *David Copperfield*, chap. xlii.

(5) *Martin Chuzzlewit*, chap. xix.

vulgar, an ignoble manner. There is extraordinary humour, and wit too, in the old clerk's wail of despair—"Take him from me, and what remains?" but in the circumstance how cruel it is! how brutal, one feels inclined almost to say! It is, to use Joubert's phrase, a monstrosity of literature. Professor Ward talks of Dickens's characters being as true to nature as the "most elaborated productions of Addison's art." But there is a production of Addison's art in which an old servant bewails his master's death in a very different fashion to this—I mean the letter in the 517th number of the *Spectator.*

But who would speak harshly of Dickens, of that "soul of good-nature and kindness!" There are instances in plenty of this want of perception and proportion, where it exists only, and does not shock; where, too, it not seldom has an effect, though an inharmonious, an isolated effect of its own. Take, for example, that so common trick of his, of pointing, of underlining, as it were, his characters' comical sayings with an explanation of his own—comical, too, in itself often enough—as though he were so delighted with the fun (and who can blame him for it!) that he could not leave it. The immortal Mrs. Gamp supplies an instance of it, in her magnificent apostrophe to the "Ankworks package." "'And I wish it was in Jonadge's belly, I do,' cried Mrs. Gamp, *appearing to confound the prophet with the whale in this miraculous aspiration.*"[1] If this were our first introduction to Mrs. Gamp, possibly some explanation might be due. But already, when we meet her among the steamboats, we know her well, her marvellous phraseology, her quaint illustrations, her irrelevant turns of thought. Nothing could be happier than the explanation, but it is a mistake. "I wish it was in Jonadge's belly, I do;" this ends it. Thackeray, let me say, is singularly free from this fault, which is of course by no means common to Dickens. Thackeray never explains. He will talk often enough in his own person, too often, perhaps, some may think; but while his characters are talking he stands aside and lets them speak for themselves. Take the scene at Rosenbad, where Warrington tells, for Pen's edification, the great mistake of his life.

"By gad, sir," cried the major, in high good-humour, "I intended you to marry Miss Laura here."

"And, by gad, Master Shallow, I owe you a thousand pounds," Warrington said.

"How d'ye mean a thousand? It was only a pony, sir," replied the major simply, at which the other laughed.[2]

Does not one feel here how comical Dickens would have been over the major's simplicity, how comical and how superfluous? And

(1) *Martin Chuzzlewit,* chap. xl.
(2) *Pendennis,* chap. lvii.

cannot one, too, conceive into what an ingenious labyrinth of explanations he would have led us as he followed that astonishing housekeeper over the galleries of Carabbas Castle?[1] But Dickens himself can sometimes be nobly free from this defect, and when free how far more effective he is. In one of Montagu Tigg's speeches there is a capital instance in the speech where he seeks to impress upon Pecksniff his earnestness and good faith, and the necessity for their all banding together in the common cause, the cause being the money-bags of old Martin Chuzzlewit, then lying sick at the Dragon. "I give you my brightest word of honour, sir, that I've been looking through that keyhole, with short intervals of rest, ever since nine o'clock this morning."[2] How admirable is that touch, "I give you my brightest word of honour!" How the rogue stands before us in his unblushing impudence! Volumes could not say more; and, happily, it comes here in the middle of the speech, and Dickens cannot stop to add any words of his own to it. "Underlining," he once wrote to Mr. Wilkie Collins, "is not my way." Alas! is there another writer of equal genius who goes astray by this way more often than he?

How far a regular education would have supplied the one thing wanting to Dickens, or whether it would not rather have tended to restrict and weaken his native gifts without any counterbalancing advantages, has always been, and probably always will be, a disputed point. Mr. Bagehot was root and branch opposed to the notion.[3] Men of regular and symmetrical genius, he allows, may be benefited by it, but Dickens's genius, he says, was irregular and anomalous. It would have been absurd, he argues, "to have shut up his observant youth within the walls of a college. They would have taught him nothing about Mrs. Gamp there; Sam Weller took no degree." A regular education, in the sense in which the phrase is too commonly understood, might have done little to cultivate the peculiar faculties with which Dickens worked, and might possibly have given them a wholly different ply. It is clear that a nice appreciation of the Ethics of Aristotle would have added no touch to Mrs. Gamp; that Sam Weller would have profited nothing by his creator's capacity for turning a page of the *Spectator* into Ciceronian prose. And Dickens, as he is, is so wonderful, so delightful, that it is, perhaps, no more than natural to distrust any proposition which might have tended to make him other than he is.[4] Nevertheless his defects

(1) *Book of Snobs*, chap. xxviii.
(2) *Martin Chuzzlewit*, chap. iv.
(3) *Literary Studies: Charles Dickens*, vol. ii.
(4) "Personne," says M. Edmond Scheres, "personne ne reconnaît plus que moi ce qu'il y a d'injuste, pour ne pas dire d'absurde, à demander d'un auteur autre chose que ce qu'il a voulu donner, ou pire encore, à lui reprocher de ne pas être un autre homme que la Nature ne l'a fait."

exist, and are what they are; and, remembering what they are, it is surely impossible to doubt that some stricter intellectual and æsthetical discipline than fell to his share would not have greatly lessened, if not altogether removed them. This prime defect, the defect from which all his others spring, the want of artistic perception and control, is precisely such as a larger and deeper acquaintance with "the best that has been said and thought in the world" would have been most instrumental in removing. It would have tempered his fancy and strengthened his imagination; it would have fertilised a soil naturally rich and productive, but inevitably weakened by a system which drained without renewing the gifts of nature. When those splendid and untiring spirits which count so eminently in his earlier work died, as in the course of nature they could not but die away, it would have given him in their stead a second harvest, less easy to gather perhaps, and less alluring to the eye, but of larger grain and mellower growth. Reading alone does not, it is true, make a full man. "Reading," wrote Burke to his son, "and much reading, is good; but the power of diversifying the matter infinitely in your own mind, and of applying it to every occasion that arises, is far better." But the power of diversifying the matter is of little avail without the matter. That Dickens's acquaintance with any kind of literature was extremely superficial even Mr. Forster is obliged to confess; and though that thorough-going friend has sought to show that Dickens's judgments on such literature as he had read were sound, he does not really prove much more than that he had read very little. No doubt the influence of his great forerunners, Fielding and Smollett, may be detected in his writings—of Goldsmith, the traces that Professor Ward discovers are hardly so clear—but it seems to me that it was less the way in which they worked that had influenced him than the material with which they worked. "His writings," says Mr. Bagehot, "nowhere indicate that he possesses in any degree the passive taste which decides what is good in the writings of other people, and what is not, and which performs the same critical duty upon a writer's own efforts when the confusing mists of productive imagination have passed away. Nor has he the gentlemanly instinct which in many minds supplies the place of purely critical discernment, and which, by constant association with those who know what is best, acquires a secondhand perception of that which is best." Hard speaking, perhaps, but indisputably true. The constant association with what is best must be fruitful of good to every man, whatever his natural gifts may be, whatever the field in which he employs them. And high as must be our admiration for the work of Dickens's unaided genius, to deny that education would have removed from that work so much of what is not best, and which too often cramps and hinders what is, adds nothing to his praise; to allow it, takes nothing away.

I have said that in *David Copperfield* Dickens is freer from defect than in any other of his works. It is rarely that public opinion has ratified an author's judgment so completely as it has here. As we all know, this was Dickens's favourite, and the reason we all know. It may be noted in passing how characteristic of the two men is their choice. To Dickens *David Copperfield* was, to use his own words, his favourite child, because in its pages he saw the reflection of his own youth. Thackeray, though he never spoke out on such matters, is generally believed to have looked not a little into his own heart when he wrote *Pendennis*. Yet his favourite was *Esmond*, for *Esmond* he rightly felt to be the most complete and perfect of his works ; in that exquisite book his *art* touched its highest point. With *David Copperfield*, no doubt the secret of the writer's partiality is in some sense the secret of the reader's. Though none, perhaps, have been so outspoken as Hogg, every man takes pleasure in writing about himself, and we are always pleased to hear what he has to say ; egotism, as Macaulay says, so unpopular in conversation, is always popular in writing. But not in the charm of autobiography alone lies the fascination which this delightful book has exercised on every class of readers. It is not only Dickens's most attractive work, but it is his best work. And it is his best for this reason, that whereas in all his others he is continually striving to realise the conception of his fancy, in this alone his business is to idealise the reality ; in this alone, as it seems to me, his imagination prevails over his fancy. In this alone he is never grotesque, or for him so rarely that we hardly care to qualify the adverb. Nowhere else is his pathos so tender and so sure ; nowhere else is his humour, though often more boisterous and more abundant, so easy and so fine ; nowhere else is his observation so vivid and so deep ; nowhere else has he held with so sure a hand the balance between the classes. If in the character of Daniel Pegotty more eloquently and more reasonably than he has ever done elsewhere, even in honest Joe Gargery, he has enlarged on his favourite abiding-place for virtue, he has also nowhere else been so ready and so glad to welcome her in those more seemly places wherein for the most part he can find no resting-place for her feet. Weak-minded as Doctor Strong is, fatuous, if the reader pleases, we are never asked to laugh at the kindly, chivalrous old scholar, as we are at Sir Leicester Dedlock ; Clara Pegotty is no better woman than Agnes Wickfield. And even in smaller matters, and in the characters of second-rate importance, we may find the same sureness of touch. It has been made a reproach against him that his characters are too apt to be forgotten in the externals of their callings, that they never speak without some allusion to their occupations, and cannot be separated from them. In the extraordinary number and variety of characters that he has drawn, no doubt one can find instances of this. For so many of these characters, nearly all, indeed, of the comic ones, real as he has made them to us, are not, when we come to examine them, realities, but rather conceptions of his fancy, which he has to shape into realities by the use of certain traits and peculiarities of humanity with which his extraordinary observation has supplied him. Major Pendennis, and Costigan, and Becky Sharp *are* realities whom Thackeray idealises, makes characters of fiction out of. But Sam Weller and Mrs. Gamp are the children of fancy whom Dickens makes real, partly by the addition of sundry human attributes, but even more so by the marvellous skill and distinctness with which he brings them and keeps them before us. But in order to do this he is obliged never to lose sight, or to suffer us to lose sight, of those peculiarities, whether of speech, or manner, or condition, which make them for us the realities that they are. And in so doing it cannot but happen that he seems to thrust those peculiarities at times somewhat too persistently upon us. In *David Copperfield* this is not so, or much less so than anywhere else, except, of course, in *The Tale of Two Cities*, Dickens's only essay at the romance proper, where the characters are subordinate to the story. We may see this, for example, by comparing Omer, the undertaker, in *David Copperfield*, with Mould, the undertaker, in *Martin Chuzzlewit*. Mould and all his family live in a perpetual atmosphere of funerals; his children are represented as solacing their young existences by "playing at buryin's down in the shop, and follerin' the order-book to its long home in the iron safe; " and Mr. Mould's own idea of fellowship is of a person "one would almost feel disposed to bury for nothing, and do it neatly, too! " On his first introduction, after old Anthony's death, he sets the seal on his personality by the remark that Jonas's liberal orders for the funeral prove " what was so forcibly observed by the lamented theatrical poet—*buried at Stratford*—that there is good in everything." [1] That touch is very comical, but also very grotesque; it is a touch of fancy, not of nature. But when David Copperfield, as a man, recalls himself to the recollection of the good-hearted Omer, who had known him as a boy, the undertaker is revealed in a very different fashion. " To be sure," said Mr. Omer, touching my waistcoat with his forefinger; " and there was a little child too! *There was two parties. The little party was laid along with the other party.* Over at Blunderstone it was, of course. Dear me ! And how have you been since ? " [2] Every one must be conscious of the difference here.

"Coragio! and think of 2850," wrote Macaulay in his diary, to

(1) *Martin Chuzzlewit*, chap. xix.
(2) *David Copperfield*, chap. xxi.

console himself for some bitter pill of American criticism he had been forced to swallow. We need not cast our thoughts quite so far into the future to see that much of what gave Dickens his popularity, and still keeps it with so many of us, will avail him nothing then. Those qualities which so endeared his writings to the great mass of his contemporaries, and won the respect even of those who could not always admire the method and direction of their employment, will have for posterity no more attraction than will many of the subjects on which he so lavishly and dauntlessly expended them. Our descendants will have, we may be very sure, too frequent and too real claims upon their compassion to let them spare many tears for those rather theatrical personages which Dickens too often employed to point his moral. Harsh as it may seem to say, whatever his writings may actually have done to reduce the sum of human suffering will tell against rather than for them. It will always be so with those who employ fiction for the purpose of some particular social or political reformation ; for the wrongs they help to remove, and the evils they help to redress, will seem slight and unreal in the pages of fiction, because they have so long ceased to form a part of actual existence. A soul of good-nature and kindness is a quality we are right to recognise in contemporary work, and for that work it constitutes a special and a noble title to our praise; but posterity will judge the writings of one whom their forefathers called a great writer by the sheer value of the writing, and such praise, if it be found to rest on no more practical foundation, will seem to them, to use the words of one of Dickens's own characters, pious, but not to the purpose. It is inevitable that much of his serious and sentimental work will have for future generations neither the attraction nor the solidity that it had for his own. For the tears he sought to draw, the graver feelings he sought to move, he went too often, if I may use the word, to local sources, too often to artificial. What Lamb said of comedy is surely true to a certain extent of all fiction : our "fire-side concerns," attractive as they are to us, cannot in reason have the same attraction for those who have never warmed themselves at our hearth. Each age has its own fireside ; each age provides its own tears. The "familiar matter of to-day" will not be the familiar matter of to-morrow. It is the splendid sorrows of a Priam or a Lear that touch the heart of Time.

> "The cease of majesty
> Dies not alone; but like a gulf doth draw
> What's near it with it; it is a massy wheel,
> Fix'd on the summit of the highest mount
> To whose huge spokes ten thousand lesser things
> Are mortised and adjoin'd : which when it falls
> Each small annexment, petty consequence,
> Attends the boisterous ruin. Never alone
> Did the king sigh, but with a general groan."

But the quality of a humour founded in the roots of our common humanity can never wax old nor die, and it seems impossible to imagine a day when the world will refuse to laugh with Dickens. The careless glance of curiosity, or the student's all-ranging eye, may turn a century hence upon the little Nells and Pauls, the Joes and the Trotty Vecks; but the Wellers and the Pecksniffs, the Swivellers and the Micawbers must surely abide for ever, unchanging and immortal—immortals of lesser note, and with more of mortal mixture, but still of the same lineage with Falstaff. And then with the laughter that they stir will be remembered and confessed the real worth of the noble praise Dean Stanley gave to their creator's memory, praise whose significance our own age has in truth too ample means for judging :—"Remember, if there be any who think you cannot be witty without being wicked; who think that in order to amuse the world, and to awaken the interest of hearers or readers, you must descend to filthy jests, and unclean suggestions, and debasing scenes, so wrote not the genial loving humorist we now mourn. However deep his imagination led him to descend into the dregs of society, he still breathed an untainted atmosphere around him; he was still able to show by his own example that, even in dealing with the darkest scenes and most degraded characters, genius could be clean and mirth decent."

MOWBRAY MORRIS.

L.J. Jennings

"American Novels"

Quarterly Review 155 (January 1883), 201–29

ART. VII.—1. '*Arthur Mervyn*' and '*Edgar Huntly*.' By Charles Brockden Brown. New York, 1803–4.
2. '*The Partisan*,' '*Katharine Wilton*,' and '*Mellichampe*.' By W. Gilmore Simms. New York, 1835–37.
3. '*Margaret, a Tale of the Real and Ideal*.' By Sylvester Judd. New York, 1845.
4. '*Louisiana*.' By Frances Hodgson Burnett. London, 1880.
5. '*Democracy*.' New York, 1880.
6. '*The Grandissimes*,' '*Old Creole Days*,' '*Madame Delphine*.' By G. W. Cable. New York, 1880–81.
7. '*The Portrait of a Lady*,' and other works. By Henry James, Jun. London.
8. '*A Modern Instance*.' By W. Howells. Edinburgh, 1882.

WE regret to observe that some American writers still have much fault to find with us in England, especially with the language which is commonly in use here, and which to their gentle sense appears no better than a vulgar dialect. But there is one offence which they cannot fairly lay to our charge, no matter how much ingenuity they may apply to the task of lengthening the old indictment against us. It is impossible for them to allege that they have been denied the respectful attention to which they were justly entitled. It is, indeed, almost sufficient to make the success of a novel, to announce that it comes from the pen of an American. English readers appear, for a time at least, to have grown weary of most of their own novelists, who are perhaps not altogether guiltless of the sin of provoking weariness, by their persistency in reproducing the same set of puppets, and forcing upon our notice, year after year, the rusty springs and machinery which move them. Some of these writers had nothing to start with but the thinnest possible material, and the exigencies of their trade have compelled them to go on painfully and laboriously beating it out, until it is difficult to say which has grown most weary of watching the process—the author or the reader. Even Sir Walter Scott could not multiply works of fiction continually without betraying manifest signs of exhaustion, and it is not surprising that writers, who never possessed a tenth part of his wealth of imagination or his fertility of invention, should fail where he did not succeed. Some had one good novel in them, and no more ; some, perhaps, had half-a-dozen. But they have given us scores—each one, as a rule, more commonplace than its predecessor. The English public are slow to turn their backs upon an old favourite, but there is a limit to their great patience, and these too prolific writers have done their best to reach it.

It is partly owing to these circumstances that the American novelist has, of late years, received so effusive a welcome. Publishers have accepted blindfold anything he has chosen to offer them. The reason is, that he has either provided us with total change of scenery and of characters, or we take up his books in the expectation that he will do so. It must be his own fault if he does not succeed, for the opportunities before him are boundless. America is the land of romance, difficult as it sometimes is to remember it in the presence of the wonderful material development of one part of the continent. No one has yet done full justice to the story of New England, or given us more than a partial glimpse of the men and women who laid the foundations of the great Republic. The old Spanish settlements afford an inexhaustible field for the romancist, and it has scarcely been touched. The Southern States are full of unwritten novels, and even the west and south-west, as more than one writer has shown, are not without their poetry and charm. Another Gilmore Simms, or a Fenimore Cooper, might easily hold the attention of the civilized world enthralled with narra-

tives based upon actual occurrences in the war of Secession.
But most of the American novelists who are at present all the
rage in this country, if not in their own, do not appear to have
the time, the capacity, or the inclination, to grasp any of these
themes. With the exception of Mr. Bret Harte, whose admirable
sketches of wild life in the West are thoroughly and distinctively
American, owing very little to European ' culture' or influences,
the writers whose works are so much in vogue in England either
neglect their own country altogether, or introduce us to types
of Europeanized Americans with which we are already too
familiar, and which add nothing to our knowledge of American
character. One little book of Hawthorne's—the 'Scarlet Letter'
—is worth all the laboured and tedious writings of the novelists
who boast of having founded a new school of fiction, based upon
the principle that the best novelist is he who has no story to
tell. A more convenient theory could scarcely be provided for
those who have turned to novel-writing as a pleasant means of
acquiring profit and reputation, without any natural gifts for
the work, and without even a true insight into its nature. For
writers who are unable either to invent a plot, or to infuse a
spark of the fire of imagination into their ' analytical' studies, it
is extremely satisfactory to have it laid down as a law, that a
story is quite superfluous to a novel, and that wooden dummies
are much more interesting than men and women. Their scornful question, what is the use of a plot? reminds us of another
question of a similar kind, put to his companions by the celebrated fox who had lost his tail. La Fontaine has expressed it
in his own inimitable manner :—

> ' Que faisons-nous, dit-il, de ce poids inutile,
> Et qui va balayant tous les sentiers fangeux ?
> Que nous sert cette queue ? Il faut qu'on se la coupe.'

And we know the sequel :—

> ' Votre avis est fort bon, dit quelqu'un de la troupe ;
> Mais tournez vous, de grâce, et l'on vous répondra.'

Any one who will go back to the works of the originators of
American fiction will remark at once, how thoroughly imbued
were their minds with the traditions and national feeling of
their own country. For them, the awful forests and prairies
of America, and the heroic struggles of its early settlers against
innumerable difficulties, had infinitely more attractions than
the ' gilded saloons' of Paris or London, or even than the canals
and palaces of Venice. The men and women who passed

across their stage were peculiar to the land of their birth, and the land, as well as the people, was brought with marvellous distinctness before the mental vision of those whose eyes had never gazed upon either. It is true that these writers could not boast that they had made fiction a 'finer art' than it ever was before, and they did not enjoy the opportunity of publishing elaborate praises of each other's performances in the pages of illustrated magazines. The most successful of all 'fine arts' in the present day—the art of puffery—was then comparatively unknown. We do not find, for instance, that the business of literary log-rolling was at all understood by Charles Brockden Brown, the pioneer of Cooper, and indeed the earliest of American novelists. His books—of which one at least, 'Arthur Mervyn,' used to be read in England—were produced under all sorts of difficulties, and no one would cite them as finished examples of literary workmanship. But they were interesting. They opened up a totally new vein in literature, and they were what they pretended to be—pictures of American life. The sketch given in 'Arthur Mervyn' of Philadelphia under a visitation of yellow fever will not soon be forgotten by those who have once become acquainted with it. We should not be disposed to call Charles Brockden Brown a great novelist, for the range of his powers appears to have been as limited as were his opportunities of observing varieties of character. He was too much under the influence, as his biographers have admitted, of the Radcliffe and Godwin school, but at the same time he had great descriptive gifts, and his plots were always interesting. The theory that a professed story-teller gets on best without any story, and that all he need do is to stand up and preach about the objective and the subjective sides of a fanciful character, had not then been formally laid down. The world was still under the impression that a novel was intended, among other things, to amuse. Brown was not equal to some of his successors, but we do not hesitate to say that he was superior to many of the recent 'American novelists,' whose most careless work is now received with praise so unqualified, that we might almost be led to suppose another Wizard of the North had suddenly appeared upon the scene. He was a true American, for whom America was a country good enough to live in, and Americans the most interesting of all subjects of study. His method was a little antiquated, and his style was sometimes open to great improvement; but, in spite of these and other defects, his productions were what they pretended to be—true and picturesque sketches of his own country and of the people who inhabited it.

They will be read for the light they throw on the United States of the early part of this century, long after the great majority of more recent novels are dead and forgotten.

Another writer, whose works are far less known than they deserve to be in this country, but who produced numerous powerful sketches of genuine American incident, was William Gilmore Simms. No one, perhaps, in these days reads the series of stories which Simms linked with events in the Revolutionary War, but they are much better worth reading than many of the novels which have made fame and fortune for inferior writers. Apart from their interest as stories, they have a permanent value for the fidelity with which they describe the South, and especially South Carolina, in the Revolutionary epoch. There was a basis of historical fact in all the romances of Gilmore Simms, and he took for his heroes the gallant soldiers whose names are still venerated by the people—Marion and Sumpter, Pickers, Moultrie, and other men of whom the 'Palmetto State' has good reason to be proud. The three works, in which we find him at his best, are those which we have placed at the head of this article; and it is satisfactory to know that a complete edition of his novels has been called for during the last few years in the United States, and that the name of so meritorious a writer is not likely to be forgotten by his countrymen. His fame, we cannot but think, is likely to increase as time goes on. The United States have thus far produced few imaginative writers of greater desert than Simms, in his particular line; but we may anticipate that many a clever man, who has hitherto allowed his time and thoughts to be diverted into the field of journalism or some kindred pursuit, will be tempted to compete for the honours of the successful novelist, now that it is seen how slender are the qualifications which suffice to win them. The Americans are, contrary to general supposition, a highly imaginative—and we may even add, a sentimental—people. But it is only in our own day that novel writing has been found to answer well, from a pecuniary point of view. Hitherto, transatlantic publishers were satisfied to take all the works of fiction which they required from the literature of the mother-country. When a three volume English novel could be had for nothing, and reprinted and sold for a couple of shillings, there did not seem to be much temptation to pay a native writer a high price for his work. But all at once, a demand sprang up from Europe for novels of American growth. Cooper, no doubt, was always a favourite, abroad as well as at home, but the modern revival of the taste for American fiction dates back only to Irving and Hawthorne. Irving's fanciful sketches were quite as popular in this country as Hawthorne's more minutely studied stories. The cry for something new is sure to recur at intervals, and it was natural that we should look to the United States for the desired novelty in the world of fiction. But the men who might have been best fitted to satisfy the demand were all engaged in other pursuits. Edgar Allan Poe's example was not encouraging to the young author who dreamt of making his imaginative faculties provide him with the means of livelihood. It is true that Poe was incredibly reckless and indiscreet in the management of his affairs, and that he seemed to have a natural faculty for pursuing the path which led to poverty and ruin. He was perpetually in debt, and when any money came into his hands, he gave himself no rest till he had flung it all away. It must be admitted, too, that the social circles into which he fell were not calculated to induce him to set before himself a loftier ideal of life; and that the rewards which he obtained for his work did not encourage him to form a high estimate of his calling. His remarkable genius might have entitled him to take rank as the greatest of all American imaginative writers, but he exercised it in a desultory and capricious manner, too frequently at moments when he was not completely master of his powers. For some time after his death, the younger school of writers avoided fiction. The literary calling offered but one lucrative post— that of the journalist. No doubt there were many who failed to earn a tolerable living in that, but the prizes of journalism are greater in the United States than they are in this country. The consequence is, that most of the literary ability in the Republic has been drawn into that pursuit. And now it is seen that even journalism does not reward its successful followers so well as fiction. A few years ago, the very novels which are to-day to be found on every railway bookstall, were not known to the general public even in America. They have been praised in England with that unanimity which sometimes breaks out in so surprising a way among critics. Justice has not been done, but some good effect will be accomplished if the present *furore* should suffice to bring forward one or two American writers, who could be named, of real and unquestionable genius, who have hitherto allowed themselves to be swallowed up in the waste of journalism. When they see the kind of production which passes muster in England as the highest form of the American novel, they may perhaps be stimulated to do credit to themselves and to their country, by giving us something better than the feeble and dreary compositions, which are advertised as superior to the old-fashioned productions of the authors of 'Vanity Fair' and 'David Copperfield.'

One of the most original, and at the same time most eccentric, novelists of the past was Sylvester Judd, the author of a very curious book entitled 'Margaret, a Tale of the Real and Ideal,' published in 1845. Mr. Judd was a Unitarian minister, and his novel was partly designed as an exposition of his religious principles. It remains to-day one of the most thoroughly characteristic fruits extant of New England theological training —a book which could have been produced in no other country but America, full of a wild sweet woodland flavour, and lit up here and there by fantastic touches of genius. With all its faults, there is a charm in this work which we shall look for in vain in the productions of the later school of American novelists. Mr. Lowell has said that 'the story of Margaret is the most emphatically American book ever written,' and we doubt very much whether he would be disposed to retract this judgment, notwithstanding all that has been written since. It would be useless to give any account of the plot of this tale, but we may find space for a description of a New England home in the old days, when simplicity was still the rule of life :—

'It is snowing, and has been for a whole day and night, with a strong north-east wind. We cannot approach the place by any of the ordinary methods of travel ; the roads, lanes, and by-paths are blocked up : no horse or ox could make his way through those deep drifts, immense mounds, and broad plateaus of snow. If we are disposed to adopt the means of conveyance formerly so much in vogue, whether snow-shoes or magic, we may possibly get there. The house or hut is half sunk in a snow bank ; the waters of the pond are covered with a solid enamel as of ivory ; the oxen and the cow in the barn-yard look like great horned sheep in their fleeces of snow. . . . , Flourishing in the centre of these high-rising and broad-spreading snows, unmoved amid the fiercest onsets of the storm, comfortable in the extremity of winter, the family are all gathered in the kitchen, and occupied as may be. In the cavernous fire-place burns a great fire, composed of a huge green back-log, a large green fore-stick, and a high cob-work of crooked and knotty refuse wood, ivy, horn-beam, and beech. Through this the yellow flame leaps and forks, and the bluish-grey smoke flows up the ample sluice-way of the chimney. From the ends of the wood the sap fries and drips on the sizzling coals below, and flies off in an angry steam. To a stranger the room has a sombre aspect, rather heightened than relieved by the light of the fire burning so brightly at mid-day. The only connexion with the external air is by the south window-shutter being left entirely open, forming an aperture through the logs of about two feet square ;

yet when the outer light is so obscured by a storm, the bright fire within must anywhere be pleasant. . . . Over the fire-place, on the rough stones that compose the chimney, which day and night through all the long winter are ever warm, where Chilion has fixed some shelves, are Margaret's flowers; a blood-root in the marble pot Rufus Palmer gave her, and in wooden moss-covered boxes, pinks, violets, and buttercups, green and flowering. At one end of the crane in the vacant side of the fire-place hang rings of pumpkin rinds drying for beer. On the walls are suspended strings of dried apples, bunches of yarn, and the customary fixtures of coats, hats, knapsacks, &c. On the sleepers above is a chain-work of cobwebs, loaded and knapped with dust, quivering and gleaming in the wind that courses with little or no obstruction through all parts of the house. Through the yawns of the back door, and sundry rents in the logs of the house, filter in unweariedly fine particles of snow, and thus along the sides of the room rise little cone-shaped, marble-like pilasters. Between Hash and his father, elevated on blocks, is the cider-barrel. These are some of the appendages, inmates, and circumstances of the room. Within doors, is a mixed noise of lapstone, mallets, swifts, fiddle, fire; without is the rushing of the storm.'

This is a homely picture, we admit, and we fear that some of the fashionable novelists of the present day would pronounce it 'vulgar'; but it tells us more about life in America than we have been able to gather from the borrowed splendours of Venetian and Parisian 'interiors' which we find in the writings of Mr. Howells and Mr. James.

The fact is that, in our eager search for the American novel, we are in danger of overlooking the very writers who have the best claim to our attention. Instead of perpetually asking for something new, we shall do well to go back to the old, which for most of us will be new. How many English readers, for instance, have even heard of John P. Kennedy, the author of 'Swallow Barn,' a novel which contains vividly-drawn scenes of Virginian life, in the days when Virginia was still the proudest of the American States? We do not say that it is an exciting novel; but are the novels which we are now asked to read so thrilling in their interest, that poor Kennedy can no longer presume to hold up his head? Was ever any reader kept out of bed by his desire to finish the 'Portrait of a Lady' or 'A Modern Instance'? If we want to know what America and Americans are like, it is precisely such books as 'Swallow Barn' that we must make up our minds to read. Then there was Mr. James K. Paulding, whose descriptions of the old Dutch settlers of New York and Pennsylvania were considered good enough fifty years ago to be translated into French, and who deserves a better fate now than to be allowed to sink into oblivion. We admit that these lesser stars were to a great extent eclipsed by the brighter light of Fenimore Cooper, whose highly original romances are still read by most people at least once in their lives. Thousands of boys, it has often been said, have been sent to the sea by reading 'Robinson Crusoe,' and with equal truth it might be affirmed that hosts of emigrants have been attracted to America by Cooper's fascinating pictures of the pleasures of wild life in the wilderness. Most settlers found out sooner or later that across the Atlantic, as everywhere else, there is a very wide difference between romance and reality, and perhaps few of them have encountered Indians so noble as Chingachgook and his son Uncas, or hunters quite so unselfish as Leather-stocking. These characters, and many others which Cooper brought into existence, will outlast all the creations of the school of Cooper's countrymen who have since risen up to profess the great and solemn principles of 'æsthetic realism.'

The prime objection which must be made to most of the American novels which are now prepared for the English market is that they are not American and are not novels. Occasionally, indeed, a work of true merit reaches this country, without any adventitious aids of puffing, and it rarely fails to receive its due deserts. Such a work was 'Democracy.' No doubt, it presented a somewhat one-sided picture of American political and social life, but every one who has been behind the scenes at Washington must be aware that the picture, so far as it went, was not in the least degree overcharged. But the qualities which recommended it to English readers were its liveliness and general interest, the clever way in which the story was told, and the freshness and originality of the style. There were some remarkable resemblances between this work and another little story which had a great success in England two or three years ago, entitled 'A Fair Barbarian;' and the same hand seems to be visible in another story, still in course of publication, called 'Through One Administration.' Each of these books is thoroughly American, although the writer of the two which have been publicly acknowledged is not an American by birth. Mrs. Burnett assuredly has nothing to learn from the more pretentious novelists who advertise themselves and each other so energetically in this country. One of the most charming sketches which any imaginative writer has produced for years past is this lady's 'Louisiana'—a book which Nathaniel Hawthorne might have been proud to call his own. Although the story is merely that of a young girl who becomes ashamed of her poor uneducated father, and disowns him in the presence of strangers, of the father's grief when he realizes the truth, and of the girl's subsequent remorse, there is so much tenderness in it, so true and profound a pathos, that it cannot fail to stir the most sluggish sympathies. The poor old man rebuilds his house, and tries to make it look fine, to correspond with the fine friends whom his daughter has made, but he feels sorrowfully that he cannot alter himself.

'"Thar's things," he says to his daughter, "as kin be altered, an' thar's things as cayn't. Let's alter them as kin. If ye'd like a cupoly put on the house, or, say, a coat of yaller-buff paint—Sawyer's new house is yaller buff, an' it's mighty showy ; or a organ or a pianny, or more dressin', ye shall hev 'em. Them's things as it ain't too late to set right, an' ye shall hev 'em."

'But she only cried the more in a soft, hushed way.

'"Oh, don't be so good to me," she said. "Don't be so good and kind."

'He went on as quietly as before.

'"If—fur instants—it was me as was to be altered, Louisianny, I'm afeared—I'm afeared we couldn't do it. I'm afeared as I've ben let run too long—jest to put it that away. We mought hev done it if we'd hev begun airlier—say forty or fifty years back—but I'm afeared we couldn't do it now. Not as I wouldn't be willin'—I wouldn't hev a thing agin it, an' I try my best—but it's late. Thar's whar it is. If it was me asked to be altered—made more moderner, an' to know more, an' to hev more style—I'm afeared thar'd be a heap o' trouble. Style didn't never seem to come nat'ral to me, somehow. I'm one o' them things as cayn't be altered. Let's alter them as kin."'

The daughter repents sorely of her fault, and makes atonement; but the iron had entered deeply into the father's soul. The wounds of age do not easily close. One day he is taken ill, and his mind wanders to his dead wife, 'Ianthy,' who had often been in his thoughts in the midst of his great loneliness and sorrow.

'He turned his eyes slowly upon Louisiana as she entered, and for a second or two regarded her wonderingly. Then a change came upon him, his face lighted up—it seemed as if he was all at once aware who had come to him.

'"Ianthy!" he said. "I didn't sca'cely know ye ! Ye've bin gone so long! Whar hev ye bin ?"

'But even then she could not realise the truth. It was so short a time since he had bidden her good-night and kissed her at the door.

'"Father!" she cried. "It's Louisiana ! Father, look at me !"

'He was looking at her, and yet he only smiled again.

'"It's ben such a long time, Ianthy," he said. "Sometimes I've thought ye wouldn't never come back at all."

' And when she fell upon her knees at the bedside, with a desolate cry of terror and anguish, he did not seem to hear it at all, but lay fondling her bent head and smiling still, and saying happily :

' " Lord ! I *am* glad to see ye ! . . . I didn't know ye was so nigh, Ianthy," he whispered. " Lord ! jest to think yer allers nigh, an' thar cayn't nothin' separate us." '

But before the close he recognizes his daughter once more :—

' That afternoon, when the sun was setting, the sick man wakened from a long, deep sleep. The first thing he saw was the bright pale-yellow of a tree out in the yard, which had changed colour since he had seen it last. It was a golden tree now as it stood in the sun, its leaves rustling in a faint, chill wind. The next thing, he knew that there were people in the room who sat silent and looked at him with kindly, even reverent eyes. Then he turned a little and saw his child, who bent towards him with dilated eyes and trembling, parted lips. A strange, vague memory of weary pain and dragging, uncertain days and nights came to him, and he knew and yet felt no fear.

' " Louisianny ! " he said.

' He could only speak in a whisper and tremulously. Those who sat about him hushed their very breath.

' " Lay yer head—on the piller—nigh me," he said. She laid it down and put her hand in his. The great tears were streaming down her face, but she said not a word.

' " I hain't got long—honey," he faltered. " The Lord, He'll keer —for ye."

' Then for a few minutes he lay breathing faintly, but with his eyes open and smiling as they rested on the golden foliage of the tree.

' " How yaller—it is ! " he whispered. " Like gold. Ianthy was powerful—sot on it. It—kinder beckons."

' It seemed as if he could not move his eyes from it, and the pause that followed was so long that Louisiana could bear it no longer, and she lifted her head and kissed him.

' " Father ! " she cried. " Say something to *me !* Say something to *me !* "

' It drew him back, and he looked up into her eyes as she bent over him.

' " Ye'll be happy—" he said, " afore long. I kinder—know. Lord ! how I've—loved ye, honey—an' ye've desarved it—all. Don't ye—do no one—a onjestice."

' And then, as she dropped her white face upon the pillow again, he saw her no longer—nor the people, nor the room, but lay quite still with parted lips and eyes wide open, smiling still at the golden tree waving and beckoning in the wind.

' This he saw last of all, and seemed still to see even when some one came silently, though with tears, and laid a hand upon his eyes.'

We cannot hope, by two or three quotations, to give a fair

idea of the charm and beauty of this little story—and yet for one reader who has admired 'Louisiana,' a hundred have read 'Daisy Miller,' with its artificial mannerisms and its tawdry smartness, and have fancied that they were being initiated into the secrets of American life and character.

That there are American girls like Mr. James's Daisy Miller, we are not prepared to deny; but if we were to exhibit her as a fair representative of young women in the United States, or of any large section of them, every American would think that he had a fair right to complain. Mr. Henry James has done scant justice to his countrywomen; perhaps he has studied them less than he has studied the women of Europe. In the truly 'first-class notice' (with a pretty portrait attached) which Mr. Howells has liberally devoted to Mr. James—Mr. Howells having received a similar notice, also with a pretty portrait, a few months previously—we are told that Mr. James's 'race is Irish on his father's side, and Scotch on his mother's;' that much of his early life was spent in Europe; that he was at Harvard a few years, and then 'took up his residence in England and Italy which, with infrequent visits home, has continued ever since.' It would therefore appear that the studies of Americans which Mr. James presents to us are made chiefly from a distance, and there are not a few Americans, proud of their own descent from the old stock, who would be inclined to receive with much coldness the credentials of his 'race.' New England blood was in Hawthorne's veins, but Mr. James comes almost as a stranger to make his 'analyses' of Americans, many of whom, in New York, New England, Virginia, or the Carolinas, would have no difficulty in showing a family descent in their own country of two hundred and fifty years. This may have something to do with the singularity of the 'types' which supply Mr. James with his American portraits. The women are all flirts, so far as they are anything; the men are very like the conventional American of the stage. Daisy Miller goes about Rome at all hours with an enamoured Italian, and refuses to heed the remonstrance of her mother and her friends, and all the while—as we are led to suppose—she is really in love with some one else. The hero of 'The American'—which is perhaps the best of Mr. James's books—is a man who does all sorts of impossible things; indeed, every situation in the book is impossible. An American of the kind depicted in Christopher Newman never could have obtained admission into the proud and exclusive French circle where he goes to seek a wife, but if he *had* once been admitted, and if the family had undertaken not to oppose his addresses to the lady he had honoured with his admiration, assuredly they would not have ' backed out '—to use his own phrase—in the infamous way described by the novelist. His affianced bride would not have given him up at a moment's notice without rhyme or reason ; and when he came into possession of a secret which placed the whole family in his power, a man like Christopher Newman would not have hesitated to use it. The plot, in fact, is simply chaotic—a wild caricature of real life ; but Mr. James contrived to make his story interesting. Since the production of this work, he appears to have been guided by the principle which is expressed in Mr. Howells's panegyric : ‘ Will the reader be content to accept a novel which is an analytic study rather than a story ? ' The answer to this question, from nine readers out of ten, will be emphatically No : on that point neither Mr. Howells nor Mr. James need be in doubt for a single moment. When once the general reader is made to understand that he is not to go to these gentlemen for entertainment, even of the tamest kind, but only for philosophic instruction and dawdling sentimentality, their occupation will be gone. The one thing which the public exact of the dramatist or the novelist is, that they shall be amused. If the amusement is provided, they may perhaps be willing to take a little ‘ instruction ' with it ; but when it is all pill and no sugar, the dose will be rejected. Mr. Howells seems to be buoyed up with the hope of finding a much more accommodating frame of mind prevailing, at least in England. It is an act of kindness to warn him beforehand, that he is providing for himself an ample fund of future disappointment.

Mr. James, in his latest completed work—‘ The Portrait of a Lady '—carries out unflinchingly the theories of his school. There is no story. The book is one of the longest of recent times—767 closely-printed pages ; and there is not a single interesting incident in it from beginning to end. No one can possibly care, for a single moment, what becomes of any of the characters. If an earthquake swallowed them all up in the middle of the second volume, the reader would only be tempted to thank the fates for a good deliverance. Three volumes of ‘ analysis ' in small type is somewhat trying, even to the most sternly cultivated æstheticism. The characters are described at enormous length by Mr. James ; then they describe themselves ; then they are described by the other characters. Between them all, it would be strange if their ‘ points ' were not sufficiently brought out. But nothing can relieve their inborn tediousness. Mr. James's descriptive writing is not remarkable for either grace or power, and his conversations are not brilliant. True Mr. Howells assures us that Mr. James's style 'is, upon the whole, *better than that of any other novelist;*' but some of us may perhaps hope for pardon if we prefer Scott, Thackeray, or George Eliot. It is evident that the Transatlantic æsthetic reformers will not run the risk of placing too low an estimate upon the services which they are rendering to literature. And then the theory is laid down, that the silly old custom of finishing a novel should be discarded. There is to be no beginning, no middle, and no end. It is like a lucky-bag at a bazaar—you thrust your hand in anywhere and take out anything you can find. As Mr. Howells says, the reader must be left 'arbiter of the destiny of the author's creations.' The novelist provides the characters, and everybody is left free to dispose of them according to his own taste. Thus, in 'The Portrait of a Lady,' the fate of all the personages in the book is left unsettled. We are shown at the close a glimpse of the lady and her lover—one of her lovers. 'He glared at her a moment through the dusk, and the next instant she felt his arms about her, and his lips on her own lips. His kiss was like a flash of lightning.' That is about all, but let no one do Mr. James the injustice to suppose that his scenes are all so warm as this. The flashes of lightning are few and far apart. As Professor Nichols observes, 'his morality [is] always reliable.' And no doubt it is worth something to be sure, when we take up a novel, that we shall have good 'reliable' morality in every page. That merit is possessed in an equal degree by Mr. Howells and Mr. James. So much it is due to them to acknowledge. Dull unspeakably dull, they may be ; but they are never improper.

We have said that Mr. James's conversations, though long, are never brilliant. Open his pages where one may, and it will be found that the men and women are prosing on in the same hum-drum fashion, and with apparently only one definite object in view—that of providing as many pages as possible of 'printed matter.' In a serial story, running, say, for twelve or eighteen months, this is a very important consideration. Mr. James has made himself, by practice, proficient in what may be called the tea-pot style of conversation :—

'"I wonder if he will have some tea. The English are so fond of tea."
'"Never mind that ; I have something particular to say to you."
'"Don't speak so loud or everybody will hear us," said Pansy.
'"They won't hear us if you continue to look that way : as if your only thought in life was the wish that the kettle would boil."
'"It has just been filled ; the servants never know!" the young girl exclaimed with a little sigh.

' "Do you know what your father said to me just now ? That you didn't mean what you said a week ago."

' " I don't mean everything I say. How can a young girl do that ? But I mean what I say to you."

        *   *   *   *   *   *

'Pansy raised the lid of the teapot, gazing into this vessel for a moment; then she dropped six words into its aromatic depths. " I love you just as much." '—' The Portrait of a Lady,' ii. 235, 236.

What sort of a cup of tea these six words made after they were dropped into the pot the author does not explain; but then he does not explain anything. The *dramatis personæ* wander about like babes in a wood. So, at least, it must seem to the ordinary reader, but we now know, from the information vouchsafed by Mr. Howells, that all this barren wilderness of conversation is intended as a mental exercise—it is an 'analytic study.' That Mr. James himself has studied before propounding his analysis must be taken for granted. But it is sometimes rather difficult to conjecture *where* he has studied for his characters, whether American or English—unless, perhaps, in the theatre, at a comic performance. His Lord Lambeth, for instance, in ' An International Episode,' put before us as a rather favourable type of the English gentleman, bears a very suspicious resemblance to Lord Dundreary. Here is a fragment of his conversation :—

' " I thought you Americans were always dancing."

' " I suppose we dance a good deal; but I have never seen much of it. We don't do it much, at any rate, in summer. And I am sure," said Bessie Alden, " that we don't have so many balls as you have in England."

' " Really ! " exclaimed Lord Lambeth. " Ah, in England it all depends, you know."

        *   *   *   *   *   *

' " Certainly, from what I have read about English society, it is very different."

' " Ah, well, you know," said her companion, " those things are often described by fellows who know nothing about them. You musn't mind what you read."

' " Oh, I *shall* mind what I read," Bessie Alden rejoined. " When I read Thackeray and George Eliot, how can I help minding them ! "

' " Ah, well, Thackeray—and George Eliot," said the young nobleman ; " I haven't read much of them."

" 'Don't you suppose they know about society?" asked Bessie Alden.

' " Oh, I daresay they know ; they were so very clever. But these fashionable novels," said Lord Lambeth, " they are awful rot, you know." '

Sometimes, however, this agreeable 'young nobleman' has a little more to say for himself than 'well, you know':—

"Damn my eyes!" exclaimed Lord Lambeth. "If one is to be a dozen times a day at the house, it is a great deal more convenient to sleep there. I am sick of travelling up and down this beastly avenue."'

Now no one is disposed to deny either to Mr. James or to Mr. Howells any reasonable degree of credit which they may choose to demand for this kind of work ; the reception of their novels in this country is sufficient proof of that. But what we are not prepared to concede is the extraordinary claim which has recently been put forward by one of them, and not disavowed by the other, to be accounted superior to Dickens and Thackeray. 'The art of fiction,' Mr. Howells gravely tells us, 'has in fact become a finer art in our day than it was with Dickens and Thackeray. We could not suffer the confidential attitude of the latter now, nor the mannerism of the former. . . . These great men are of the past—they and their methods and interests.' The 'school which is so largely of the future as well as the present, finds its chief exemplar in Mr. James.' Mr. Howells has every reason to be satisfied, and perhaps astonished, at the progress which his 'school' is making in England, but surely it must grieve him to find that in his own country it has few adherents. Every day, in every part of the United States, one or other of the characters of Dickens or Thackeray is sure to make his or her appearance in scores of newspapers ; for there is no part of the world where Dickens, especially, is more read and quoted. The accuracy of the portrait of Mr. Jefferson Brick, for example, is continually attested—as Mr. Howells must be well aware—by American journalists applying it to each other ten times a day. It is in the United States, and not in England, that one hears most of Elijah Pogram. Have any of the 'creations' of Mr. Howells or Mr. James taken this hold upon the popular mind, or passed into the daily literature of their country? Does anybody remember the name of one of Mr. Howells's characters, male or female? Does any one ever see that name quoted? We do not say that it is the duty of a novelist to be modest in his pretensions, but surely it is well for him to be prudent. And when he tells us that he and his companions in art have superseded Thackeray and Dickens, the majority of people will be constrained to make the reply which Martin Chuzzlewit gave to Colonel Diver, when he was asked which of the original Mr. Jefferson Brick's productions had caused the greatest sensation at the Court of St. James's—namely, that he had never heard of any of them.

Mr. Henry James has occasionally been so far faithless to the principles of his school, as to produce something which may be taken for a fairly developed and intelligible plot. But Mr. Howells is true to his faith. He literally has no story to tell. The two volumes which he has published under the title of 'A Modern Instance' contain nothing, so far as pure narrative is concerned, which could not be told in ten lines. The fact is, as the novelist himself explains to us, 'in one manner or other, the stories were all told long ago; and now we want merely to know what the novelist thinks about persons and situations.' Such is Mr. Howells's candid opinion.

' Mais tournez vous, de grâce, et l'on vous répondra.'

When an author has written half-a-dozen novels and a few odd plays, without the vestige of a plot in one of them, and not enough in all of them combined to make the foundation of a child's story, then it is quite obvious that a theory to account for and justify his style of art is no more than we have a right to expect. In 'A Modern Instance,' Mr. Howells appears to have called forth all the powers of his imagination. The hero, whose name is Bartley Hubbard, marries a girl who has fallen in love with him, deserts her, and disappears. He is described as a man with a ' yellow moustache,' wearing a ' diagonal coat ' —not deficient, therefore, in originality of appearance. When he enters a room, he shows his superiority to ordinary mortals by ' dropping into one of the empty chairs, and hanging his leg over the arm '—the arm of the chair, as we may venture to presume. We should ourselves absolutely decline to accept Marcia, the heroine, as an accurate type of the American young lady of the present day ; but Mr. Howells must be presumed to know best, and if his countrywomen like his portraits of them, well and good—it is not for us to object. In that case, they have a quick way of arranging their love affairs, as appears from the following passages :—

' "Bartley ! you shall *never* go !" she cried, throwing herself in his way. "Do you think I don't care for you, too ? You may kiss me— you may *kill* me, now !" The passionate tears sprang to her eyes, without the sound of sobs or the contortion of weeping, and she did not wait for his embrace. She flung her arms around his neck, and held him fast, crying : "I wouldn't kiss you for your own sake, darling ; and if I had died for it—I thought I should die last night— I was never going to let you put your arm round me again until you said—till —till—now. Don't you see?" She caught him tighter, and hid her face in his neck," &c. &c.

    *   *   *   *   *   *

'Whether Bartley perfectly divined or not all the feeling at which her words hinted, it was delicious to be clung about by such a pretty girl as Marcia Gaylord, to have her now darting her face into his neck-scarf with intolerable consciousness, and now boldly confronting him with all-defying fondness, while she tightly pushed him and pulled him here and there in the vehemence of her appeal; and Bartley laughed as he caught her head between his hands, and covered her lips and eyes with kisses.'—I. 57–59.

The young lady's mother presently enters the room, and finds her seated on Bartley's knee. This interruption, however, does not disconcert any one, except the mother :—

'"Oh, mother, it's you! I forgot about you. Come in! Or I'll set the table, if that's what you want." As Mrs. Gaylord continued to look from her to Bartley in her daze, Marcia added, simply, "We're engaged, mother. You may as well know it first as last, and I guess you had better know it first."'

Now all this, we are asked to believe, is true to the life ; but suppose any English novelist had given it as a representation of American manners and customs. Would not the eagle have screamed? Should we not have heard something about British ignorance and British 'condescension'? Then take another passage, which we cannot but regard as an outrage upon the high sense of 'chivalry' which we are told—and believe—characterizes all American men in their treatment of women. It is scarcely necessary to explain that this relates to a scene *after* marriage :—

'"Bartley!" she besought him in her despair. "Do you drive me from you?"

'"Oh, no : certainly not. That isn't my way. You have driven me from you, and I might claim the right to retaliate, but I don't. I've no expectation that you'll go away, and I want to see what else you'll do. You would have me before we were married ; you were tolerably shameless in getting me ; when your jealous temper made you throw me away, you couldn't live till you got me back again ; you ran after me. Well, I suppose you've learnt wisdom now. At least you won't try *that* game again. But what *will* you do ? " He looked at her, smiling, while he dealt her these stabs one by one.'

All this is said to a young mother, with her child in her arms. We must repeat that it would have fared ill with an English author who had drawn such a picture of any American.

Some one went up to Sheridan once at a dinner party, and told him his handkerchief was hanging out of his pocket. ' Thank you, sir,' replied Sheridan, ' I suppose you know the company best.' On the same principle, we must be silent when Mr. Howells tells us about his own countrymen. But we are not surprised that the circle of his admirers is larger here than it is on the other side of the Atlantic. There he appears to have achieved a *succès d'estime*; it remained for the more generous critics in England to discover that Bartley Hubbard and Marcia Gaylord ' are worthy of a place beside some of the finest of George Eliot's creations.' After that, we really think the successors of Dickens and Thackeray might mercifully relax the severity of their judgments on this doomed and benighted country.

Whatever may be the differences of opinion as to the value of the new ' school,' it must be acknowledged on all sides that a novelist enjoys an immense advantage in being a contributor to an illustrated magazine, which is ready not only to publish his works, but to issue elaborate articles on their merits—accompanied, as we have said, by that most affecting of souvenirs, a ' portrait of the author,' duly softened and idealized. The art of puffery gets ' finer ' every day, whatever we may think about the art of novel-writing. Literary men are only just beginning to learn how to use it with effect. They have looked on for years at its successful application to various branches of commerce, and at length it has dawned upon their minds, that it may just as well be made serviceable to them as to the vendor of a new universal pain-killer or of a ' liver-pad.' In England we are still a little behind-hand in this field ; the latest improvements have been brought out in America for special use in England. Thus, the ' analysis ' of Mr. Howells appeared last March, and his biographer certainly threw some light on the frame of mind which produces the æsthetic novel. It appears that Mr. Howells has somewhere exclaimed, ' Ah, poor real life, which I love, can I make others share the delight I find in thy foolish and insipid face ?' ' This,' adds the panegyrist, ' is his attitude throughout.' It is at least a remarkable attitude. The great masters of the craft which Mr. Howells does not quite disdain to profess did not find real life insipid ; not thus did it appear to the ' effete ' Thackeray and Dickens, or even to Hawthorne, or to some of the American novelists of the present day whose names are still comparatively unknown to English readers. We need not be surprised at the stilted and unnatural air of most of the men and women who figure in Mr. Howells's pages, when we learn that he has discarded nature as unworthy of further attention, and regards actual life as foolish and insipid. He prefers to paint from imagination. If a man has vast insight into human nature, and great gifts of imagination besides, he may possibly be able to place reliance upon his own unaided efforts. But Mr. Howells may depend upon it that, when any one tells him he is thus furnished for the fight, he is being lured to his destruction.

There is, however, more than one writer now living who deserves that credit for raising the character of American fiction, which has been so freely distributed among the select circle of *puffistes littéraires*. We need not refer at any length to Mr. Bret Harte, whose best works are known throughout the length and breadth of the land. It is true that these works are all short, but in such prosy days as our own they are none the worse on that account. As an 'analyst,' Mr. Bret Harte, it must be admitted, is nowhere. The youngest disciple of the Howells and James school would dissect a whole township while he was making a rough sketch of a wandering group in the Sierras. We admit also that Mr. Bret Harte seems to break down when he applies himself to any long and continuous effort. A more preposterous novel than 'Gabriel Conroy' was never written ; it is wonderful how a very clever man could have gone on writing it without feeling, as it were, at his fingers' ends that he was producing a tissue of silly imitations of Bowery melodramas. But while Mr. Harte was working in the field where no one had preceded him, and which he had made his own—the mining districts of California—there was no one who could be compared with him ; and we may safely say, in the midst of all the absurd braying of trumpets and beating of drums now going on, that his equal has not appeared since. It was Mr. Bret Harte's fortune to see California in the days of the 'Argonauts,' when gold-seeking was the all-absorbing passion of every man's mind. Those who pronounce real life 'insipid' should have been in the Sierras any time between 1849 and 1854. It might, perhaps, enlarge their ideas to go even now and take up their residence for a while among the drifting population of miners, mountaineers, and 'pikes,' which is still to be found in Nevada and California. The oft-repeated advice, 'go west,' would sometimes be as useful to the American novelist as to the newly arrived immigrant who is seeking occupation. It would at least enlarge his stock-in-trade. We should see less of the plaster images brought back from Venice, Paris, or London, and more of the living men and women who inhabit the American continent. Mr. Bret Harte's experiences were very different from those of the *littérateur* who takes to novel-writing because it pays. When the thirst for gold, which sets in motion all the deepest springs of human nature, broke out in 1849, there was a great rush from all parts of the world for California. The news, that gold was to be had for the mere trouble of digging for it, sent tens of thousands of adventurers in hot haste to the Sierras, and led to a state of society which has never had a parallel in any country. Among the gold-seekers there were not a few who found it easier to murder than to dig, and they either held small communities in terror, or were occasionally driven out by vigilance committees. Some phases of this remarkable era in Californian life were caught by Mr. Bret Harte, and he has embalmed them in 'Poker Flat,' the 'Luck of Roaring Camp,' and other sketches which will never be forgotten, for they describe scenes which will occupy no small space hereafter in American history, and which disclose a new world to European eyes. We have always regretted that Mr. Bret Harte deserted this great and unknown tract for another in which there were no special opportunities for the exercise of his remarkable powers. All the romance was not gone out of California when the gold fever declined; the days of savage lawlessness, tempered only by vigilance committees, had passed away; but life on the Pacific Coast is full of picturesque elements, and it will be many a year yet before it flows in the monotonous channels which have been worn by time in the Eastern States. Unfortunately, as we must maintain, Mr. Bret Harte chose to desert his literary mine before it was half worked out, and he sought for inspiration in Boston, where none was to be had, and afterwards in Europe, where he will almost surely not find it. It is not Paris or London that needs further description, but Red Dog or Sandy Bar; the old Spanish population of the Pacific Coast, and the curious settlements which lie scattered along the Sacramento valley. We are not anxious to see any more American 'side-shows,' in which haughty French Counts and English Duchesses strut clumsily across the stage; but we cannot hear too much of the personages who, if not actually indigenous to American soil, are very rarely seen far away from it.

The influence of Charles Dickens is, no doubt, apparent in Mr. Bret Harte's manner, but he has too original a mind to be much indebted to any one. As with Dickens, every striking feature of a scene, every peculiarity which marked out a man or woman from the general throng, was photographed on his memory, and he reproduced it with marvellous fidelity. We are, of course, referring to the Californian period of his career, when he first made his mark, in the pages of a local magazine which at that time was seen by very few persons east of the Rocky Mountains. We shall probably never again have such pictures of the nomadic tribes of adventurers who infested California some thirty years ago—vicious, hardened, reckless of life, and yet not altogether without some redeeming points. The little story, 'Tennessee's Partner,' contains half the history of those times in a few pages. Thoroughly characteristic of the desperate fraternity is the brief account of the arrest of Tennessee himself, by a lynching party :—

'As the toils closed around him, he made a desperate dash through the Bar, emptying his revolver at the crowd before the Arcade Saloon, and so on up to Grizzly Cañon; but at its further extremity he was stopped by a small man on a gray horse. The men looked at each other a moment in silence. Both were fearless, both self-possessed and independent; and both types of a civilization that in the seventeenth century would have been called heroic, but in the nineteenth, simply "reckless." "What have you got there?—I call," said Tennessee quietly. "Two bowers and an ace," said the stranger as quietly, showing two revolvers and a bowie knife. "That takes me," returned Tennessee; and with this gambler's epigram he threw away his useless pistol, and rode back with his captor.'

Then it will be remembered that Tennessee's partner comes forward and offers to buy him off, but Judge Lynch is incorruptible. Once more the figures of speech are borrowed from the popular game of 'euchre :'—

'He hesitated a moment as he slowly returned the gold to the carpet bag, as if he had not yet entirely caught the elevated sense of justice which swayed the tribunal, and was perplexed with the belief that he had not offered enough. Then he turned to the Judge, and saying, "This yer is a lone hand, played alone, and without my pardner," he bowed to the jury and was about to withdraw, when the Judge called him back. "If you have anything to say to Tennessee, you had better say it now." For the first time that evening the eyes of the prisoner and his strange advocate met. Tennessee smiled, showed his white teeth, and saying, "Euchred, old man!" held out his hand. Tennessee's partner took it in his own, and saying, "I just dropped in as I was passin' to see how things was gettin' on," let the hand passively fall, and adding that "it was a warm night," again mopped his face with his handkerchief, and without another word withdrew.'

Mr. Bret Harte is one of the writers who do not find it necessary to prove that they are Americans by an ostentatious display of hatred of everything English. There is no occasion with him for laboured satires on the country where he has found a hospitable greeting. All that he writes has a whiff in it of American air. And if the English public have anything more

than a passing fancy for American novels, they cannot do better
than choose those which are American in something more than the
name—which depict Americans as they really are, and which
serve to illumine the lesser known phases of the national character. The author of 'Democracy' has done this; so has the
author of 'Through One Administration'—if, indeed, those
works have two authors. It is certain that in each of these
stories a comparatively new vein has been opened up. The
novels of society in the United States have, as a rule, been
little better than absurd travesties. We see the kind of
American lady, for instance, that Mr. Howells can offer to our
notice in Marcia Gaylord, Florida Vervain, and others of the
same kind; while Mr. James has not yet shown us any one more
attractive than Daisy Miller and Isabel Archer. In 'Democracy' we are also introduced to the American girl who is a
franche coquette, but she is a coquette of a highly-amusing kind;
and in the other story we have named, there are female characters of a higher type—notably, in the wife who plays so
important a part in the tale, and who cuts a figure in politics
which may be new to English readers, but which is by no
means without precedent in Washington. Mrs. Burnett has
adventured boldly upon very delicate ground, but if political
corruption is ever to be driven out by Congress and the State
Legislatures, the novelist will have to reinforce the preacher
and the avowed reformer. It has been denounced for years
past from the pulpit, and condemned in the press; but we see
no reason to believe that it is less prevalent than ever it was.
'Lobbying' is a trade—a profession, as some of its members
insist on our calling it—which still pays better than almost any
other, especially when a man (or a woman) has gained a reputation for exercising real skill, and for having the faculty of
keeping silence. The fate of many a measure has been decided
by the strategy of the female lobbyist, especially when she
possesses the social advantages of Mrs. Amory in 'Through
One Administration.' It is very likely that the process of
telling the truth will be attended with some disagreeable incidents, and we may be sure that no one in Washington will be
particularly anxious to be identified with Senator Planefield,
any more than with Senator Silas P. Radcliffe. Mrs. Burnett
has cast off all disguises in her latest work, and if she has to
encounter some severe criticisms in her adopted country, no one
will be able to refuse her the praise to which she is justly
entitled of having given the world the best American novels of
the present day.

Another writer who has gained a great and well-deserved

reputation in the United States, although he is comparatively little known in this country, is Mr. George W. Cable, who is doing for the State of Louisiana what Nathaniel Hawthorne did for New England—reproducing for us the people and customs of an age which, though not remote, has passed away. The French and the Spaniards of the last century, who held Louisiana, left the impress of their civilization upon its people, and it will be long before it entirely disappears. Until 1803, when Napoleon ceded the State to the American Government, partly in consideration of receiving fifteen millions of dollars, but chiefly to prevent the control of the Mississippi falling into the hands of the English—until then, the City of New Orleans was almost as French as any city in France itself. The population was then, as it largely is now, composed of people of French descent or of Creoles. It is this mixed and singular community which Mr. Cable has studied with so much care—not from a distance, but on the spot. He has revived, or imagined, many strange and touching stories of days when the French were doing great work on the Mississippi, and he has thrown the charm of romance round the old streets, whose very names still tell of the departed glories of the colonial epoch. The time is probably not far distant, when the only visible remains of the French and Spanish domination will have to be sought in the curious cemeteries, where the dead are put to rest in sealed tombs above ground; for New Orleans stands from two to four feet below the level of the Mississippi, and it would be impossible to dig a grave without coming to water. On the monuments which are preserved in the French and Spanish cemeteries, many a quaint inscription is to be seen, dating back to the period when Bienville was governor of the State. The people retain to this day some of their old peculiarities, but Mr. Cable has dealt chiefly with the Louisiana of from fifty to thirty years ago, and this was entirely unknown to the majority of Americans prior to his labours. In 'The Grandissimes' he has presented a vigorous series of pictures of a somewhat earlier date—the period when Louisiana had just been sold, and her people were indignant at the unceremonious way in which they had been turned over to the United States. The colonists were faithful to the mother country, although the mother country was not faithful to them. Mr. Cable has given many illustrations of the bitterness which was at first caused by their compulsory transfer to the United States, and in 'The Grandissimes' he makes one of his principal characters die with the declaration on his lips, that 'old Louisiana will rise again. She will get back her trampled rights.' And doubtless the Louisianians wished sincerely for the fulfilment of some such prediction as that in the days when General Butler ruled over them with a rod of iron, or in the still darker days when they were delivered over, bound hand and foot, to be governed by the negroes. Many, who had the means to go, fled into Texas; others remained, only to be ruined. There was no 'vindictiveness' on the part of the United States Government; but a generation was destroyed.

'The Grandissimes' is the most carefully wrought-out of Mr. Cable's stories, but the most finished is, we think, 'Madame Delphine,' and some of his shorter sketches in 'Old Creole Days' are scarcely inferior to it. Madame Delphine is supposed to be one of the quadroons whose beauty made New Orleans famous, and whose descendants still attract the admiration of every traveller who visits the Crescent City. 'Old travellers,' as Mr. Cable tells us, 'spare no terms to tell their praises, their faultlessness of feature, their perfection of form, their varied styles of beauty—for there were even pure Caucasian blondes among them—their fascinating manners, their sparkling vivacity, their chaste and pretty wit, their grace in the dance, their modest propriety, their taste and elegance in dress. In the gentlest and most poetic sense, they were indeed the sirens of this land, where it seemed "always afternoon."' To this class belongs Madame Delphine, she and her daughter Olive, a beautiful girl, but bitterly oppressed by the law of the State, which forbad the marriage of a white man with a woman of the coloured race, no matter how fair she might be. The daughter falls in love, and with a man whom she cannot marry. There is no way of escape for her but one—and that one her mother alone can open up. Madame Delphine does not hesitate. She goes before a magistrate and swears that Olive is not her daughter; that her parents were of the white race, and committed the child to her charge to be brought up as her own. There is no longer any impediment to the marriage, and Madame Delphine is present at the ceremony, and bears bravely up, but afterwards she desires to see the priest, and makes confession :—

' " Olive *is* my child. The picture I showed to Jean Thompson is the half sister of my daughter's father, dead before my child was born. She is the image of her and of him; but, O God! Thou knowest! Oh, Olive, my own daughter ! " '
' She ceased and was still. Père Jerome waited, but no sound came. He looked through the window. She was kneeling, with her forehead resting on her arms—motionless.
' He repeated the words of absolution. Still she did not stir.

' " My daughter," he said, " go to thy home in peace." But she did not move.

' He rose hastily, stepped from the box, raised her in his arms, and called her by name.

' "Madame Delphine!" Her head fell back in his elbow; for an instant there was life in the eyes—it glimmered—it vanished, and tears gushed from his own and fell upon the gentle face of the dead, as he looked up to Heaven and cried:

' " Lord, lay not this sin to her charge!" '

In all these stories of Mr. Cable's there is one disadvantage which may, we fear, tend to diminish the pleasure of the ordinary reader in them. It is the free use which he is obliged to make of the Creole *patois*. If this difficulty can be patiently endured for a few pages, it will afterwards be easily surmounted, and it is not greater, after all, than that which must be faced in any novel which sets before us in true colours the local life of various States in America. For although we are often told that ' dialect' is peculiar to England, and that identically the same language is spoken all over the United States, the fact is that the local peculiarities of speech are as mysterious as those which still remain in the different counties of England. The New England dialect itself—the only place, as we are assured, where we may draw from the 'well of English undefiled'—is not without the 'provincialisms' which some American writers dwell so much upon as characteristic of old England alone. A couple of passages from Mrs. Stowe's 'Oldtown Fireside Stories' will serve as examples of what we mean :—

' " Your gran'ther used to know old Cack, boys. He was a drefful drinkin' old crittur, that lived there all alone in the woods by himself, a-tendin' saw and grist mill. He wa'nt allers jest what he was then. Time was that Cack was a pretty consid'ably likely young man, and his wife was a very respectable woman—Deacon Amos Petengall's dater from Sherburn.

' " Wal, I wouldn't say he was railly wickeder than the run; but he was one o' these 'ere high-stepping, big-feeling fellers that seem to be a hevin' their portion in this life. Drefful proud he was; and he was pretty much sot on this world, and kep' a sort o' court goin' on round him. Wal, I don't jedge him nor nobody; folks that hes the world is apt to get sot on it. ... 'Ye see, Cack,' said Cap'n Eb, 'I'm off my road, and got snowed up down by your bars,' says he. 'Want ter know!' says Cack. 'Calculate you'll jest have to camp down here till mornin',' says he." '

In the south and south-west there are well-marked 'provincialisms,' as the native writers who have written novels descriptive of that region have not failed to show. A story used to be told after the War by the Union soldiers of a Georgia woman, who, seeing a party of Kentucky cavalry passing her house, came out and said, 'Be you-uns kim all the way from Kintuck, critter back, to fight for we-uns?' The Indiana local peculiarities 'are well brought out in a very amusing book, entitled 'The Hoosier Schoolmaster,' by Mr. Edward Eggleston —Indiana being known as the 'Hoosier State.' Mr. Eggleston's scene is laid in the country districts, where 'high art' is not yet thoroughly understood, but there can be no doubt that he has faithfully described his people. He introduces us to a young man from the East, who has gone to Indiana in the hope of obtaining employment as a schoolmaster, and this is the way in which the candidate is addressed by the principal school trustee :—

'"I 'low it takes a right smart man to be school-master in Flat Crick. They'd pitch you out of doors, sonny, neck and heels, afore Christmas. . . . It takes a *man* to boss this deestrick. Howsumdever, if you think you kin trust your hide in Flat Crick school-house, I ha'n't got no objection. But ef you git licked don't come on us. Flat Crick don't pay no insurance, you bet. Any other trustees? Wal, yes. But as I pay the most taxes t'others jist let me run the thing. You can begin right off a Monday. They a'n't been no other applications. You see it takes some grit to apply for this school. The last master had a black eye for a month. But, as I said, you can jist roll up and wade in. I 'low you've got pluck, and that goes for a heap sight more'n sinnoo with boys. Walk in, and stay over Sunday with me. You'll hev to board roun', and I guess you better begin here."'

This passage enables us to catch a passing glimpse of Indiana life as well as of Indiana speech. Any one who desires to understand something about the American people—as distinguished from dubious examples of New York dandies and Boston young ladies—will do well to make himself acquainted with works like that of Mr. Eggleston. An American book-collector has said that he has in his library over seven hundred native American novels; whether he has included in his collection the hybrid æsthetic novel we are not aware. But stories like Mr. Cable's or Mr. Eggleston's would certainly not be omitted. There is evidently more 'life' in the country districts of Indiana than is dreamt of in the Bostonian school of philosophy. 'Book larnin',' says one of Mr. Eggleston's characters, 'don't do no good to a woman. I never knowed but one gal in my life as had ciphered into fractions, and she was so dog-on stuck up that she turned up her nose one night at a apple-peelin, bekase I tuck a sheet off the bed to splice out the table-cloth, which was ruther short. And the sheet was mos' clean, too. Had'n ben slep on more'n wunst or twicet.' This kind of realism would, no doubt, be too much for the delicate sensibilities of Mr. Eggleston's more artistic competitors.

We have now endeavoured, as well as we could within these narrow limits, to make clear the distinction which should be drawn between the real and the spurious American novel. This was a task which urgently required to be performed in the interests of literature as well as of 'art.' If we can get the genuine product of the country, there is no necessity to be contented with bad imitations of it. Numbers of American writers have given us stories, not deficient in general interest, and yet which are purely American, containing much that is most instructive and suggestive concerning their own country and its inhabitants. They must be amazed—such of them as are still living—when they find that while half England is running eagerly after the great American Novel, their own work has been left out of sight, and that English critics in important journals are declaring that now, for the first time, a school of 'imaginative composition' is making itself visible across the Atlantic. There has been nothing of the kind, it appears, till just lately, either in prose or verse. The delightful poems in which Whittier has told his beautiful tales of Indian or colonial life—some of them written nearly fifty years ago—are not worthy of even a passing word. The whole series of distinctively American novels, from 'Arthur Mervyn' down to 'The Grandissimes,' is dismissed with contempt. We are, so we are informed, looking on at the 'modest and unpretending' beginnings of American fiction. Modest and unpretending are happy phrases to apply to the claims which have been put forward by writers who insist upon our acknowledging that they have compelled Thackeray and Dickens to 'take back seats,' and are masters of a style 'better than that of any other novelist.' Can we wonder that the very members of this 'school' should be tempted to tell us plainly that English criticism 'is only the result of ignorance—simply of inability to understand'? This may appear a very ungrateful return for all the flattery which in this country has been lavished on the Howells and James school; but we cannot say that it is undeserved. Undoubtedly a good deal of 'ignorance' has been shown, and the present obsequious attitude of English critics in the presence of anything which is called 'American' reveals a clear 'inability to understand' true American literature. So far, then, the assertion is well founded. And as for its incivility, we have provoked that also. The respect of the Americans is never to be won by indiscriminate adulation. Before very long, the good sense of the public will correct the follies of the critics. They must already begin to have their doubts, whether the water-gruel diet on which they have been placed can really be the strong American meat of which they have heard so much. Eventually the truth will become clear to them. They will see that imaginative literature in America had passed through a long and respectable life before the Boston Mutual Admiration Society was even heard of; and they will come to the conclusion that, if the American novel has reached its highest perfection in the works proceeding from this band of brothers, then that they have had quite enough of it, arfd they will turn with joy from the prophets of realism to the old-fashioned novelists who had no 'style' worth mentioning—to Georges Sand and Balzac, to Walter Scott and Jane Austen, and even in the last resort to Thackeray and Dickens.

Arthur Tilley

"The New School of Fiction"

National Review 1 (April 1883), 257–68

THE NEW SCHOOL OF FICTION.

Two of the most successful novels that have been published in this country within the last eighteen months are the work of Americans, I mean Mr. Henry James' *Portrait of a Lady* and Mr. Howells' *A Modern Instance.* They bear a strong family resemblance. In both there is a charming young woman who, at an early stage of the story, falls in love with and marries a plausible scoundrel ; in both there is a silent adorer, whose claims on our pity are heightened by physical weakness ; in both the ultimate fate of the heroine is veiled in enigmatic obscurity. These however are mere external and accidental points of resemblance. The real resemblance, that which justifies the reader in recognising the two novels as belonging to the same family, lies far deeper. It lies in the elaborate analysis of character, in the absence of plot, in the sparing use of incident, in the studied realism, in the conscientious subordination of the artist to his art, in the acute powers of observation, and in the humour, which, never forced or obtrusive, seems to exist, not because the writer's own gifts lie specially in that direction, but because, as a healthy and impartial observer of human life, he cannot fail to take note of its humorous side.

I have spoken of these novels as successful, but this does not imply that they enjoy a wide popularity. I should say rather that it is confined to a small and select circle of admirers. But within this circle the admiration is very considerable, and it includes the reviewers. They have been almost unanimous in their praise. To have the reviewers on your side, especially in the land of the stranger, is certainly a success of its kind. It may possibly be the very kind of success which the author most values.

But it is evident that there must be a numerous class of novel-readers with whom Mr. James' and Mr. Howells' novels find no favour. To a novel-reader of the old-fashioned type, who likes a thrilling story, with a complicated plot, and plenty of incident, who fidgets and finally skips if the story stands still, whose childhood has been fed on Walter Scott, who still in his manhood never wearies of him, who has felt the full charm of the improvisation of George Sand, who on the brightest of summer days has been unable to tear himself from old Dumas, or has sat shivering before a burnt-out fire, till he had turned the last page of Gaboriau—to a novel-reader, I say, of this type, these novels must seem poor reading.

Such a novel-reader doubtless is the writer on "American Novels" in the January number of the *Quarterly Review*, who in a very lively and amusing, if one-sided, article, has handled the new school somewhat roughly. His wrath seems to have been specially kindled by a recent article in the *Century Magazine*, in which Mr. Howells, writing about Mr. James, has incidentally set forth the programme and principles of his school.

The writer of these lines, while fully sympathising with the *Quarterly Reviewer's* feelings, and yielding to none in his admiration for novelists who before all things are story-tellers, at the same time professes himself an admirer both of Mr. James and Mr. Howells; a qualified admirer, it must be admitted, but still an admirer. He has read them with patience and with pleasure. It may therefore perhaps be possible for him to contribute to the subject, if a less vigorous, at any rate a more dispassionate criticism, than that of the *Quarterly Reviewer*. The time for such a criticism is a favourable one. Both *The Portrait of a Lady* and *A Modern Instance*, are not only the latest, but they are on the whole the strongest and most highly finished novels of their respective authors. They are eminently the productions of a matured art. Moreover, there is a passage in Mr. Howells' article, in which the whole creed of the new school is so concisely stated, that it will serve as a convenient text.

The art of fiction has, in fact, become a finer art in our day than it was with Dickens or Thackeray. We could not suffer the confidential attitude of the latter now, nor the mannerism of the former, any more than we could endure the prolixity of Richardson or the coarseness of Fielding. These great men are of the past—they and their methods and interests: even Trollope and Reade are not of the present. The new school derives from Hawthorne and George Eliot rather than any others; but it studies human nature much more in its wonted aspects, and finds its ethical and dramatic examples in the operation of lighter but not really less vital motives. The moving accident is certainly not its trade; and it prefers to avoid all manner of dire catastrophe. It is largely influenced by French fiction in form; but it is the realism of Daudet rather than the realism of Zola that prevails with it, and it has a soul of its own which is above the business of recording the rather brutal pursuit of a woman by a man, which seems to be the chief end of the French novelist. This school, which is so largely of the future as well as the present, finds its chief examplar in Mr. James; it is he who is shaping and directing American fiction at least It is the ambition of the younger contributors to write like him; he has his following more distinctly recognizable than that of any other English-writing novelist. Whether he will so far control this following as to decide the nature of the novel with us remains to be seen. Will the reader be content to accept a novel which is an analytic study rather than a story, which is apt to leave him arbiter of the destiny of the author's creations? Will he find his account in the unflagging interest of their development? Mr. James' growing popularity seems to suggest that this may be the case; but the work of Mr. James' imitators will have much to do with the final result.

Such is Mr. Howell's lucid and instructive statement of the

method and principles of the new school. It has all the charm of American frankness and outspokenness. The *Quarterly Reviewer* would, perhaps, add "and of American cheek." But Mr. Howells does not mean, I suppose, that Richardson and Fielding, Dickens and Thackeray, are absolutely out of date. He only means that their methods are antiquated, that a more critical age looks for a more artistic method. Let us see how far this is true.

It appears from Mr. Howells' statement that the new school of fiction has three leading characteristics :—1. It abjures plot and narrative interest ; 2. It substitutes for these an elaborate analysis of character ; 3. It studies human nature mainly in its wonted aspects. I will consider them in the above order.

1. "Will the reader," asks Mr. Howells, "be content to accept a novel which is an analytic study rather than a story, which is apt to leave him arbiter of the destiny of the author's creations ?" Speaking for the English reader, I answer boldly, "No." Already he has been heard to murmur on this score. He rebelled against *Washington Square* ; he felt at the end of *The Portrait of a Lady* that he had been either robbed or laughed at, and it is a question which form of injury an Englishman resents most. His verdict on *A Modern Instance* was that it had no ending ; he rose from the reading of it with the feeling of a man who has but half-dined. The new school in short wholly underrates the strength of plot interest or pursuit as a human emotion. For we all have what Mr. James calls "a weakness for a plot" ; which the wise novelist will humour if he can.* Moreover we also demand that the plot shall be "rounded." Whether justly or not, we look upon our author's creations as partly our own, for is not our imagination as well as his necessary for their existence ? We feel therefore that we have a right to know their ultimate fate, and we resent their being hung up like Mahomet's coffin, midway between happiness and misery. Look at Greek tragedy, than which on questions of artistic propriety there can be no surer guide. Is not the catastrophe, the "dire catastrophe," of which Mr. Howells speaks with contempt, part of its very essence ? The catastrophe in a modern novel need not be a bloody one, it need not be physically dire ; but that it should be morally dire, human nature and art alike demand. Shakespeare has often been sneered at for winding up his tragedies with a wholesale slaughter of the *dramatis personæ*. The method is perhaps crude, but it is far better than losing your characters in a fog of uncertainty, or stranding them on a sand-bank of despair. George Eliot, in spite of "her weakness for making a rounded plot," is by no means free from blame on this score, but she would never have

---

* "Even George Eliot has a weakness for making a rounded plot."—*French Poets and Novelists (Ivan Turgénieff)*.

ventured to leave Dorothea chained for the remainder of her days to Casaubon. And this craving for a rounded plot is only part of our natural craving for completion, a craving which no artist with any dramatic feeling will disregard. For just as in real life it is this craving which helps to convince so many of us that there is another world, in which the tangled threads of this life will be smoothed out; so in the fictitious life of novels the same craving demands that the smoothing out, or rounding off, call it what you will, shall not be absent. For the creatures of imagination have no future life. Visibly they must realise their heritage of weal or woe.

Professor Bain, in treating of the question of pursuit or plot-interest, has rightly pointed out that disappointment none the less ensues when the pursuit is too long, than when it ends in nothing. It follows therefore that we demand not only a rounded plot, but a narrative that goes forward. A check in novel-reading is as little relished as a check in hunting; one of the great charms of Scott—in this he is second only to Homer—is the swiftness of his narrative. " Our story has hitherto moved with very short steps," says Mr. James, at the beginning of one of the chapters of *Washington Square* ; but Mr. James and Mr. Howells always move with short steps. I do not know that they are ever guilty of actually retracing their steps, as George Eliot is in *Daniel Deronda*, but they dawdle quite unpardonably. The result is that their readers get wearied in the pursuit, and, in the words of Professor Bain, " a feeling of disappointment ensues." The profane would call it boredom. In this busy age perhaps it may be an advantage to be able to put down a novel at any given moment with equanimity, and take it up again a fortnight afterwards without any sense of cooled ardour; but one cannot help feeling that it is not the genuine thing. The genuine thing is the burnt-down candle, and the cold grate.

2. But as a substitute for plot and narrative interest, we have, says Mr. Howells, the " unflagging interest" of the development of character, that is to say, the development of character, not by action, but by elaborate analysis of motives, by a relentless moral dissection.

And here we come to the influence of George Eliot upon the new school. " The new school," says Mr. Howells, " derives from Hawthorne and George Eliot rather than any others." With regard to its relationship to Hawthorne, it is not perhaps for an Englishman to gainsay Mr. Howells; but it is " a wise child," we are told, " that knows its own father." I should have said however that " realism " and " analysis of character " were the very last qualities to derive from Hawthorne, that his chief interests were in the spiritual world, and that he only studied individual character in the hope of finding there a clue to the great mysteries of human nature, especially to those of sin and redemption. With George Eliot it is far different. The novel of analysis is in a great measure her child. It is important therefore to investigate her method, before we can judge how far that of the new school is a legitimate or wise development of it.

To most great novelists, as to all great dramatists, human character is of primary interest. In Scott indeed this interest was probably second to the antiquarian or historical interest; the interest of reconstructing the life and society of a bygone age. But in a man so full of geniality and kindness for his fellow-creatures, it could not be otherwise than strong. And so, by the help of his great creative imagination, he has enriched the world with a larger number of living men and women than any other novelist except Balzac. But development of character had no interest for him. His characters are the same when we take leave of them, as when we are first introduced to them. It will be remembered that Carlyle, in his singularly unappreciative criticism of Scott, complained that he fashioned his characters from the skin inwards, instead of from the heart outwards. The answer is that Scott did so, because this is the way in which our fellow-creatures appear to us. We know their faces and voices long before we know their moral qualities. The majority of novelists never get beyond the " skin." Homer and Shakespeare go straight to the heart; but if you portray both the outer and the inner man, it is surely more logical and more artistic to begin with the outer man. It is a method which Balzac, and, in our own day, Turgenef have followed not successfully.

Balzac, who had just made his mark when Scott died, took a far keener interest than his great predecessor in the analysis of human character. No one but Shakespeare has embraced so wide a field in his psychological explorations, and, like Shakespeare, he develops his characters chiefly by action. To trace the downward career of a human soul, consumed by a master passion, is his dearest delight, and he does it with pitiless precision; but, though in the process his characters are laid bare to their inmost recesses, we never lose the illusion that we are spectators of a natural self-revelation. We see the result of the dissection, but the dissector's knife is kept carefully hid.

Thackeray, who, if he was a more delicate observer of human nature than Balzac—if, to keep up the metaphor, he dissected with a finer instrument—yet, because he did not cut so deep, and because he confined his investigations to the limited field of good society, must be accounted Balzac's inferior, is still, like Balzac, before all things, a student of character; and, like Balzac, though in a less degree, he finds the study of evil more interesting than that of good.

It is a marked distinction between George Eliot and the two novelists I have last mentioned—nay, I may almost say that is the mark which distinguishes her from all other novelists of the realist type, for in this Turgenef and Alphonse Daudet are at one with Balzac and Thackeray—that she finds virtue a more interesting study than vice. It is not that the others never paint virtuous people, but they are far less subtly designed, far less dramatically evolved, than their villains. It is George Eliot alone who takes pleasure in tracing the development of a weak and erring human being, struggling with evil, and finally vanquishing it. Silas Marner, Maggie Tulliver, Esther Lyon, Gwendolen Harleth—these are the witnesses to her loving sympathy for her fellow-creatures, to her fervent hope for, if not her sure belief, in the ultimate triumph of good.*

And this characteristic of George Eliot may be accounted for partly by the fact that she regarded human nature less from an artistic point of view than from an ethical. Balzac and Thackeray both regarded it as so much artistic material. "Balzac," says Mr. James, "believed that human life was infinitely dramatic and picturesque," and, in a less degree, the same may be said of Thackeray ; and for this reason the work of neither can escape the charge—a charge which by no means applies to the men themselves apart from their work—of being somewhat hard and cynical, somewhat unsympathetic. Now, although George Eliot's sympathy is not quite so large as Shakespeare's, or Sterne's, or Molière's—there are some forms of stupidity that are beyond the range even of her sympathy—it is still very large indeed, and most especially in the direction of those quiet, commonplace lives, of which there are so many in real life, but which, at first sight, seem wholly unpicturesque and undramatic, and which Balzac and Thackeray would have rejected as worthless material. And as, after all, the great majority of us are quiet, commonplace people, whose hopes and fears and struggles, though infinitely interesting to ourselves, are by no means suggestive of what a playwright would call a strong situation, it follows that we are drawn to George Eliot by the feeling that her men and women are beings of like nature with ourselves, subject to the same temptations, following the same "trivial round," burdened by the same "common task." But we are apt to forget that we

---

* "I have a belief of my own, and it comforts me."
"What is that ?" said Will.
"That by desiring what is perfectly good, even when we don't quite know what it is and cannot do what we would, we are part of the divine power against evil—widening the skirts of light, and making the struggle with darkness narrower."
—MIDDLEMARCH.

read her novels, not solely for the artistic pleasure they give us, but partly for instruction—for instruction in practical ethics. How far a novel ought to be a pure work of art, I am not now concerned to consider, but of this we may be quite sure, not only that George Eliot's works, judged as purely artistic productions, have many defects, but that George Eliot herself never intended them to be so judged. Thus, whether purposely or involuntarily, she often sacrifices artistic considerations to moral, and in each successive novel the moral element becomes more predominant, till, in *Daniel Deronda*, she is thought, by not a few competent judges, to have fairly crossed that strip of debateable ground between imaginative and didactic literature which the novel may be said to occupy.

Every artist has a right to choose his own method, and, if the result be successful, criticism has nothing further to say. If then George Eliot's creations are real flesh and blood, and not merely automata—as for the most part they undoubtedly are—it is nothing to us if she creates by means of analysis instead of by action. But Daniel Deronda, at least, has perished from over-analysis, and there are others, Rosamond Vincy, for instance, that have certainly suffered from it, that have certainly lost something of their distinctness of outline. And, generally, it seems to me that the elaborate dissection of her characters' motives to which she treats us, is, from the point of view of creation, merely supplementary. She first creates her characters by action and speech, in her quality of artist, and then proceeds to discuss them in her quality of moral philosopher.

But Mr. James and Mr. Howells are, before all things, artists; their work is artistic and not ethical in its aim. It is their object to amuse, and not to instruct. Now, from an artistic point of view, to describe a character instead of creating it, is fatal. To describe a character tersely and epigrammatically, no doubt, requires considerable gifts, acute powers of observation and a mastery of language; the gifts, in short, of a La Bruyère or a Theophrastus. But description does not in the least help us to realise a fictitious character; for that, imagination and creative power are necessary. Creation and description of character, in short, are two very different things. Indeed so different are they, that it is quite possible that if either Homer, or Shakespeare, or Scott were asked to describe one of his own characters, he would do it extremely ill.

3. It is, I said, one of George Eliot's greatest distinctions, and one of her most abiding sources of popularity, that she finds material for her creations in the sphere of ordinary life; that, in her hands, characters and incidents, apparently commonplace, become invested with a halo of romance and interest. This is

true realism, the realism which shows scrupulous reverence for the truth of nature, and yet can poetise that truth even in its most homely aspects.

But the new school, it seems, has improved upon George Eliot. "It studies human nature much more in its wonted aspects, and finds its ethical and dramatic examples in the operation of lighter but not really less vital motives." Here I must differ from Mr. Howells. I grant that the motives are lighter, but are they not also less vital ? Is not the distinction between Mr. James and George Eliot this : that whereas George Eliot's characters and their surroundings are apparently commonplace, Mr. James' are essentially so ; and for this reason, that their motives are less vital ? Is not this the distinction, for instance, between Dorothea and Isabel Archer, whom Mr. Howells boldly classes together as the most nobly imagined women in modern fiction ? Is it not the defect in *A Modern Instance* that Bartley and Marcia are not only apparently but essentially commonplace ? May it not be said that while George Eliot elevates the commonplace, the new school vulgarises it ? And if so, is this true realism? Is it not rather the sin of Zola—the sin, to borrow Goethe's distinction, of being naturalistic instead of natural? In *A Modern Instance* especially one cannot help being struck by the unsparing use of trivial incident, the copious details of vulgar middle-class love-making, the careful analysis of Bartley's beer-drinking.

The *Quarterly Reviewer* has not inaptly spoken of the dialogue of the new school as the tea-pot style of conversation. To make the conversation natural without being trivial is, no doubt, one of the greatest difficulties of a novelist. Miss Austin and Anthony Trollope are masters of the art. And Mr. James and Mr. Howells, in their earlier works, used to excel in it; but in their latest efforts it must be admitted that they have passed the line between the natural and the trivial, and it is partly this which gives an air of commonplace to their characters. It comes no doubt from an excessive desire to be true to nature, to make their characters talk as they would in real life. But if there is one thing in which a slavish reproduction of nature is impossible for the purposes of art, it is the conversation of ordinary human beings. Even the cleverest of us are painfully bald and disjointed in our talk. We are told that Anthony Trollope was once asked by a lady how it was that he knew so exactly what ladies said to one another in the privacy of their bed-rooms. The reason was, not that he listened at the key-hole and gave a verbatim report, but that by the aid of his imagination he divined what ladies would say in these supreme moments, and gave artistic form to it. A verbatim report would not have seemed to the lady half so natural.

But the theory that a novelist should be merely a faithful transcriber of human nature—that, armed with manifold note-books, he should go about industriously collecting every scrap of fact bearing any relation to his subject, jotting down a conversation here, sketching a face there—this theory, which M. Zola calls *naturalisme* and M. Brunetière *reportage*, need not be seriously discussed here. Whatever may be the value of such a method, there can be no question that it is not art, and, to do M. Zola justice, he has never pretended that it is. According to him the novel has passed out of the region of art into that of physiology and pathology. But Mr. James and Mr. Howells, if I am not mistaken, are anxious to retain the novel within the region of art. With the method of Zola then they can have no sympathy.

I by no means wish to decry the commonplace, or to hint that the novel which confines itself to this sphere is a degraded type. There is room, let Mr. Ruskin say what he will, for Dutch art as well as Italian art. Miss Burney, Miss Austen, Mrs. Gaskell, Anthony Trollope, these and others have given abiding pleasure to too large a number of their fellow-creatures, for their exquisite, if low-soaring, art to be treated with contempt. But their method points this moral—that the novelist who is concerned with commonplace characters must treat them lightly. He must enter into their mood. They do not trouble themselves with a painful analysis of their motives, they take life more simply and unconsciously; the last epithet that you would apply to them is "elaborate." And not only is elaborate analysis out of keeping with commonplace characters, but it is wholly unsuitable in a novel that deals with them. The commonplace is amusing, if it be treated lightly, but take it *au grand sérieux*, and it will become intolerable. It is too slight a framework to support a weighty analytic study. Burden it with such a weight, and the result is, from the artistic point of view, a want of harmony; from that of the ordinary reader, dulness. And when you have said of a novel that it is dull, there is nothing more to be said for it. It is an existence *manqué*.

But example is worth any amount of precept, and in Miss Austen's novels we have a perfect example of how the commonplace should be treated. Whatever exception may be taken to the character of Miss Austen's art, there can be no question but that in that art she is a consummate master. She is the one English novelist of whom it may be said that, artistically, her work is almost flawless. Her art is too like nature to admit of its being analysed, but we may learn from it that the commonplace must be treated both lightly and cheerfully, that transcendentalism and tragedy are alike out of place. Her novels end, instead of beginning, with a wedding.

In the above endeavour to examine the principles of what Mr. Howells claims to be the new school of fiction, and to consider how far they are consistent with the legitimate aims of the novelist's art, I have confined myself to generalities, and I have entirely left out of sight the many obvious merits of the two leading writers of this school. Only a short space remains in which to attempt briefly to supply this omission.

Mr. James seems to Mr. Howells, "a metaphysical genius working to æsthetic results." I should say, putting it, I fear, more baldly, that Mr. James is an exceedingly acute observer of human nature under one aspect, that of society with a big S; and that by the help of a lively and ingenious style, considerable artistic skill in details, and a thorough artistic love of good workmanship, he gives us the result of his observations in a pleasing and amusing form. But he is more critical than creative; more observant than imaginative. The culture, the reading, the catholic tastes, the European travel, the sound discrimination, which make his volume on *French Poets and Novelists* one of the most delightful and stimulating collections of criticisms in the language, and which lend a considerable charm to his novels, are perhaps the very reason why these novels are wanting in imaginative force; why they fail to make an abiding impression. Mr. James, it seems to me, judging by his later and what may be called his English work, has not the stuff in him for a great imaginative work. His short stories—*Daisy Miller, An International Episode, A Bundle of Letters*—stories in which he does not take life too seriously, but skims over it with the delicate humour which distinguishes him; episodes of life, rather than complete lives; idylls rather than epics—these are the works in which he has hitherto succeeded best. I admit that *The Portrait of a Lady* is on the whole his highest flight, and that it is more noble to soar and fall than to avoid a fall by flying low; but the faults of *The Portrait of a Lady* are not, so to speak, the defects of its virtues. They may all be traced to those principles against which I have been contending in these pages: they are the faults of absence of plot, over-analysis, and laboured realism; faults which may easily be eradicated without any detriment to Mr. James' good qualities, his delicate observation, his fine humour, his graceful style. Rather, these qualities will flourish all the more abundantly when they are no longer choked by the strange growths which Mr. James, rather in obedience to a pedantic theory than to the promptings of his own genius, has been tempted to cultivate. In one of his earliest stories, *A Passionate Pilgrim*, I believe, published in England, he has shown us that he does possess, in no slight measure, that shaping power of imagination so necessary to all artistic production. It would be well if he were to return to his earlier methods, and cultivate that faculty which he has allowed too long to lie fallow.

Mr. Howells, though bitten by the same theory as Mr. James, is a genius of a somewhat different order. He has more of the qualities of a true story-teller. His *A Foregone Conclusion* is more artistically conceived and modelled than any work of Mr. James. There is a dramatic flavour about it which makes you rise from its perusal with a feeling of satisfaction. Mr. Howells too has a wider range than his compeer. His observations have been carried on as much among the genuine native American as among the hybrid European variety; he knows the Far West as well as Boston; he is more at home with middle-class society than with the highly-refined ladies and gentlemen of Mr. James' world. Moreover his sympathy with external nature, combined with his remarkable powers of depicting it, gives his stories an air of freshness and freedom which contrasts pleasantly with Mr. James' somewhat artificial atmosphere. Mr. Howells, in short, studies nature wherever he can find it; Mr. James studies it only in the drawing-room. The greatest effort of imagination will not enable us to picture to ourselves a heroine of Mr. James' in a moment of dishabille. One thinks of them, under all circumstances, as exquisitely dressed.

But Mr. Howells' stories have for the most part been exceedingly slight, little more than carefully finished sketches. *A Modern Instance* is his first attempt on a larger scale. The excellence of its opening, the masterly portraiture of some of the minor characters, such as Squire Gaylord and Kinney, the vigorous painting of various phases of American life, go far to make the book a complete success. But it misses this from the inadequateness of its central idea and central figures. The story, that of a young man and woman attracted to one another by charm of face and figure; each wholly ignorant of the other's character; marrying in haste and repenting at leisure; the man's selfishness hardening into crime; the woman's spiritual deadness drifting into despair; if not a new story—what is it but Tito and Romola with a variation?—had great dramatic capabilities; and that Mr. Howells has not availed himself of them is due in a great measure to the same defects which mar *The Portrait of a Lady*—to too much attention to details, too much commonplace, too much analysis. Had Mr. Howells condescended to use some of the time-honoured machinery which he despises, the "dire catastrophe," the "moving accident," he would have written a far stronger and more satisfactory work.

The curious thing is, that both Mr. Howells and Mr. James have openly expressed their preference for novels of the more imaginative type. Mr. Howells regrets the loss of the poetry of Mr. James' earliest work, and "he owns that he likes a finished story." Mr. James says that "his ideal story-teller possesses a rarer skill than the finest required for producing an artful *réchauffé* of the actual." Why then do both these gentlemen disregard their own preferences? Is it out of pure regard for their readers? If so, let me assure them that their considerate unselfishness is being wasted. Human nature, in spite of modern improvements, remains much the same; it still enjoys a "rounded plot"; it still pursues, not for the sake of the pursuit, but for the sake of the end; it still loves to be amused; and, above all, it still hates to be bored.

ARTHUR TILLEY.

Karl Hillebrand

"About Old and New Novels"

Contemporary Review 45 (March 1884), 388–402

ABOUT OLD AND NEW NOVELS.

THIS essay—the scanty fruit of a long leisure, shortened only by light reading and reflection on it—was originally to be entitled, "Why are old novels so entertaining and modern ones so tedious?" Fortunately for him, the author met in time a highly cultured, and, on the whole, unprejudiced English lady who confessed to him that she had never been able to read "Tom Jones" to the end, whilst a young diplomat of literary pretensions assured him that "The Nabob" was infinitely more entertaining than "Don Quixote." Then only the author began to understand how relative an idea is attached to the word "entertaining," and that perhaps the modern reader is quite as accountable as the modern novelist, if the novel of to-day is so—well, so different from the old. Let us then speak only of this difference. For why establish supervision, distribute praise and blame, by which nobody learns anything, when it is so much more instructive to investigate the what and the why of certain phenomena, and to leave every one to be judge of his pleasure and displeasure.

As, however, there has been a question of entertaining reading, be it understood from the beginning that the amusement novel, properly so called—i.e., that which has no other aim but amusement, and which the French have brought to perfection in our century, shall be at present excluded from consideration, although it often shows more talent and artistic instinct than more pretentious work of the *genre*. If we thus exclude such novels it is because we wish to limit ourselves to those productions of literature which give themselves out as works of art, and which realize as well as explain to us the mode of thinking of the different periods. Let us not forget either that in all such historical comparisons dates must not be taken too

269

literally, and that exceptions are not to be taken into consideration. The fact that Manzoni, Jeremiah Gottholf, Gottfried Keller have written between 1820 and 1860, and have even given a voice to certain currents of the century, does not make it the less true, that, considered as artists—*i.e.*, in their way of seeing and treating their subject, they do not belong to the time which has seen the *floraison* of George Sand and Dickens, still less to the time which has produced a Freytag, George Eliot, and Octave Feuillet.* For whatever one may think of the fact, it would be difficult to deny it ; the whole literature of fiction in Europe, from Homer to Goethe, is severed by a deep abyss from that of our century, whose productions bear always, in spite of all differences, a certain family likeness ; in other terms, men, authors as well as readers, for three thousand years saw the task of literature in another light from that in which we have seen it for the last hundred years.

Strangely enough, the novelists of the younger generation, who, like E. Zola, Spielhagen, Henry James, and W. D. Howells, are never weary of treating their own art in a theoretico-critical way, which would probably never have occurred to a Charles Dickens—seem to have no consciousness whatever of this difference of periods. No doubt all the theories of those practitioners rest upon the tacit, sometimes also the outspoken, supposition of the superiority of the novel of to-day over that of former times, or at least of a progress in the development of this *genre*. To this there would be little to object, if the writers in question were awake to the fact that such a progress can only concern what is technical, and consequently is of very little artistic value. The progress in technique from Benozzi Sozzoli to the Caracci is very considerable ; nobody would admit as a consequence that the artistic value of the Farnese gallery is, in spite of its cleverest *raccourcis*, greater than that of a fresco in the Campo Santo, with all its defects in drawing and perspective. Now, it is difficult not to feel in these disquisitions of the specialists a consciousness of having also realized a progress. The new novel is " finer" than the old one, says Mr. Howells quite candidly, while the others plainly imply the same ; and they mean not only a superiority in composition, dialogue, &c., but also a more careful study of feelings and passions, a more delicate delineation of characters, a deeper knowledge of society and its influence on the individual ; for that the older writers could have no other reason for their reticence than ignorance or want of power to show their knowledge of these things, is an undoubted fact to our modern novelists, who have never learned the art of " wise omission."

---

* Björnsen too might be numbered among those few artists whom chance has allowed to be born in this unartistic time, were it not that he has so often, particularly in later times, let himself be carried away by the example of his contemporaries.

It is characteristic that this ignoring of the past and forgetting of all proportion show themselves most crudely in the North Americans, for whom even Dickens and Thackeray belong already to the antique. Thus, even people of an entirely European culture like Mr. H. James speak of M. Alphonse Daudet with an admiration so unlimited that one might be tempted to believe that the readers beyond the Atlantic are unaware of the existence of a Fielding. Fortunately, Mr. J. R. Lowell's beautiful speech on the author of " Tom Jones" proves that there are still Americans who know where the real models of the art of narration are to be sought for. Besides, there are people enough in the Old World also, who, like Mr. John Bright, do not hesitate to place any middling novelist or historian of our time above Homer and Thucydides, whom they ought to have had more opportunity to read than their American co-religionists. It is not uncommon to hear such *naïveté* praised as an enviable freshness of impression and judgment ; but this rests on a thorough confusion of ideas. Such impressions are not received, such judgments are not given, by people who stand nearer to Nature than ourselves, but on the contrary by such as have no bridge behind them which might have brought them over from Nature to our civilization. I can with confidence place the " Vicar of Wakefield" and " Numa Roumestan" in the hands of a boy who was brought up in the country and has never seen a newspaper : he will not hesitate a moment between the two. The trial would already be more doubtful with a young man of classical culture ; but as to a lad who had learned to read in leading articles and had left the professional school only to enter on the wholly artificial relations and modes of thinking of our society, one could scarcely expect from him that he should prefer the pure wine of Goldsmith to M. Daudet's intoxicating beverage. The great majority of the younger generation has come into the world as it were grown-up, has been born into the modern civilization, whilst we older ones have at least slowly grown into it, and have consequently some inkling of the fact that under the clothes there is also something like a body. Now, the clothing of our century—*i.e.*, our civilization, is perhaps more complicated and artificial than any that went before it, and those who live in it like to imagine that what is more complicated is also more valuable. Hence the accumulation of details which characterizes our literature and corresponds at the same time to our scientific habits. A microscopic anatomy of human nature—now in its coarser manifestations, as with M. Zola or Guy de Maupassant, now in its nobler organs, as with George Eliot and Ivan Turgenief, would be vainly searched for in the older authors. The style has become more complicated ; all sciences, every technic, are forced into service, all archaisms and neologisms gathered together in the dictionaries, unusual and surprising juxtaposition of words are used to make the descriptions more effective, without however attaining the wished-for effect. It is particularly the native country of taste, the home of measure and "sobriety," which pleases itself with these exercises ; and on the one hand, persons with no other talent than that of corrupting language, taste and morals, weary themselves—*cauta Minerva*—with manufacturing so-called *tableaux de mœurs*, while, on the other hand, richly gifted writers trade upon their facility in order to bring all their superfluity on the market and to suffocate the readers under the weight of their adjectives. But " when the taste for simplicity is once destroyed," says Walter Scott, " it is long ere a nation recovers it." It is perhaps worth while to investigate more clearly than has been hitherto done, the essence of this new tendency of mind and taste.

I.

The whole intellectual life of our century, and especially of the second half of it, is permeated by the scientific habits and the new morals which came into prominence shortly before the French Revolution, and which since the definitive defeat of romanticism towards the middle of our century, have attained almost absolute power. Now, both the scientific and the moral view of the world are not only insusceptible of artistic treatment—they are incompatible with it, nay, are the negation of it. Also, the novel, as far as it is an artistic *genre*, has suffered from the reign of these modern principles as much as, and more than, all other artistic *genres*, because, thanks to its form, it lends itself more easily to scientific treatment and moral jurisdiction than any other. No doubt there lived before the Revolution individual men who carried the scientific and moral standard into regions where they have no right nor currency ; but they were isolated instances ; now-a-days, this double point of view dominates the whole of literature, and—as our culture has become exclusively book-culture—of culture also. No doubt mankind lives on even to-day as if those principles did not exist. It would be impossible otherwise to live ; but as soon as it is bent upon judging, knowing or reproducing life, it no longer uses any but those two methods.

Science aims at the knowledge of the world and its causal connection. It destroys individual life in order to find its laws—*i.e.*, what is common to individual phenomena. Art, on the contrary, seeks to know and interpret the world by seizing and reproducing the unity of individual life ; it eliminates the general in order better to seize the particular, and in the particular it eliminates what is accidental that it may better see and show the essential. Now, as the general is only an abstraction of our intellect, and real life manifests itself only in the particular, it follows that art, in one sense, is truer than science. This, however, does not touch our question; what I want to prove is, that the so-called scientific treatment of an object can only be harmful to art, in the same way as the artistic treatment of science on its side can give rise to the monstrosities about which scientists are fond of telling edifying stories. When however M. Zola, for instance, declines the honour of having constructed works of art, the men of science will not therefore be much disposed to ascribe to him merits in science. For his works, whatever else they may be, are productions of the imagination, and consequently utterly useless to science, which reckons only on realities and can found no laws on such phantasms. Besides, all scientific labour is collective and progressive; artistic work is individual and self-inclusive. Each new work of science supersedes its predecessor, at least in part, until it is entirely antiquated. The scientific achievement remains immortal, the scientific work must perish. Would M. Zola resign himself to that, and does he seriously imagine that " Nana" and " Potbouilli" are scientific achievements—*i.e.*, rings in the infinite chain of science? Certainly not. At bottom, however, these gentlemen of the scientific school make their scientific pretensions in no such strict sense. What they aspire to is to create works of art by the instrument of science, and to treat of objects, which are the results of science, while they have only the instrument of art, as well as the standard for judging the artistic value of objects; and here arises the question whether such an enterprise is not from the beginning sure to be a failure.

The instrument, if I may so phrase it, which science uses to attain its aim, is understanding; that of art intuition. Science knows only a conscious knowledge of things, art only an unconscious one; and as the artist renders only what he has acquired unconsciously and directly through intuition, the artistic spectator or reader seizes what is given to him only intuitively, not consciously. Both proceed as we proceed in ordinary life and for practical purposes; art, therefore, is much nearer life than science. We know a person as a whole: often we do not even know whether his eyes are blue or brown, whether he has a high or a low forehead; and we are nevertheless surer of this our unconscious knowledge than the most accurate physiognomical analysis could make us. Language has equally formed itself unconsciously, is learned unconsciously, and is for the most part used unconsciously, particularly in emotion; but it renders our feeling more faithfully than any elaborate choice of expressions would be able to do. For the scientist, it is true, language is what numbers are for the mathematician; it gives no image, but only the abstract expression of things. The physician—we Germans call him the " artist," *Arzt*—seizes first the total impression of his patient,

without rendering to himself an account, often without being
able to render to himself an account, of its components; and he
relies exclusively on the thermometer and determinate symptoms,
precisely because he has not the " coup d'œil." Now our whole
cultured society, readers as well as authors, have no longer the " coup
d'œil." The latter *see* only what they have consciously considered,
and consequently give only that; the former on their side have got
accustomed to be content with that, nay, to be proud of it, because
they thus can give themselves an account of everything, which is no
small satisfaction to the vanity of the understanding. But what is
the consequence of the whole proceeding ?

An author undertakes to paint the inner man and the outer world.
He is to fulfil the former aim by an accurate psychological analysis;
the latter by a careful description. Now, in reality those psychological
qualities have no existence whatever; they are an abstraction of our
intellect, and therefore even the completest enumeration can produce
no living image, even if our imagination were able to reconstruct a
unity out of such plurality; whereas one characteristic feature would
suffice to evoke the total impression of a personality. For it is not
the parts which make man, but the cohesion; as soon as this ceases,
life ceases. Now, conscious intellect never seizes the cohesion; unconscious intuition alone seizes it; and to render this with conviction
is art—*i.e.*, reproduction of life. As much may be said of the
description of the outer world; a whole-page of M. Daudet, in
which he describes all the articles to be sold in the shop of a southern
provision-dealer, not omitting each individual smell, and all the
furniture with all the lights falling on it, is not worth the two
verses in which Heine calls up to us the cavern of Uraka, as if we
saw it with our bodily eyes. The former, in fact, is a faithful
inventory, which we never make in life, and which consequently
touches our imagination as little as the list of an upholsterer; these
two verses awake in us a sensation, and so dispose our mood as to
set at once our imagination to work, because there is action in
them, and the action therein shown acts in turn on the reader.

Art is more economical than science; and the lavishness of
authors who believe they proceed scientifically when they omit
nothing of what a careful examination of an object or an action and its
motives has revealed to them, is nothing but the profitless expenditure
of the prodigal. Art shows us Philina, in the general confusion and
despair, sitting quietly and rattling with her keys on the saved trunk,
and the irresistible stands more vividly before our eyes than would
have been possible by a long enumeration of her charms, or a detailed
description of the means by which she has succeeded in getting off so
cheaply, and a modern writer would certainly not have let pass the
opportunity of both without taking advantage of it; for second to

description, explanation is his principal pleasure. It is not to be denied that in these modern novels there is a more minute observation of social and psychological facts, a closer exposition of all laws of feeling and thought, a more conscientious watching over their growth, and a more laborious analysis of the passions and their motives, than are to be found in the older novels of this, and apparently of the past, century. The whole development of a man is gone through; and if possible even that of his parents and grandparents—for this, too, passes for an application of scientific results—until finally we have forgotten the man himself, as he is. True art cares little about the genesis of character; it introduces man as a finished being, and lets him explain himself by his acts and words. Shakspeare leaves it to the German *savant* to explain how Hamlet has become what he is; he contents himself with showing him as he is. And not drama alone shows man as he is; the novel, as long as it is a work of art, is contented to do so.

> " Pourquoi Manon, dans le première scène,
> Est-elle si vivante et si vraiment humaine
> Qu'il semble qu'on l'a vue et que c'est un portrait?"

asks Musset. Is it not precisely because she is not described, analyzed and explained, but simply appears and acts? because the poet gives us in few words the impression which he has himself received, and by the rendering of his sensation our sensation is produced? We never see persons and actions in fiction; we feel the impression they exercise; this is convincing; an enumeration of qualities and circumstances, even if it were possible to make it complete, produces no disposition whatever; it produces knowledge.

Let nobody say that the older writers contented themselves with sketches and gave only the outlines. It is by no means so. What the narrator gives are the dramatic moments of an action, the characteristic features of a person. The truth and liveliness with which he gives the particulars that contain the whole *in nuce*, awake the image of that whole with its antecedents, its consequences, its secondary circumstances—*i.e.*, the cohesion. His process is similar to that of the sculptor, who renders only the plastic elements of his object; of the painter, who renders only the picturesque elements of it, and makes an abstraction of all the rest. He takes only those traits which are fitted to produce a literary effect. Now, as I just said, it is with actions as with men. A minute and methodical enumeration of all the movements of the different regiments, accurately ascertained, which have taken part in a battle, such as we have it in the history of the war by the great General Huff, may have a scientific value; from an artistic point of view, it is without any effect, for it leaves us no intuitive image of the total action; whilst the description of the battle of Zutphen from the pen of " the poor man of Tockenburg," or that of the battle of Waterloo in Stendhal's " Chartreuse de Parme," are works of art, because they render faithfully the impression of such mass movements on the individual. If, on the contrary, the novelist proceeds with that scientifico-historical conscience, we get something like the struggle of the two washerwomen in the " Assommoir," which fills I don't know how many pages, and which nevertheless one has not before one's eyes, whereas the Homeric battle of Molly Seagrim remains unforgotten by whosoever reads it once only. Here, indeed, the total impression dominates the detail, whilst there the number of particulars forbids the forming of a total impressiom. M. Zola takes up his object like the man of science, destroying it in order to recompose it; Fielding, as the artist, who seeks and reproduces unity, not to speak of the art with which he renders the repulsive object attractive by irony, which alone gives such objects the passport to literature, drawing them out of common reality. This observation, however, would lead us to a controversy with the verists, realists, naturalists, or whatever their name, and I should like to defer this disquisition to another opportunity.

II.

Equally with the scientific view, the moralizing view of the world has come into prominence; and it proves to be still more dangerous to art than the former. All modern morals aim at making men better —*i.e.*, other—than they are. Art takes them as they are; it is content to comprehend them and to make them comprehensible. And the more mankind have abandoned the fundamental ideas of Christian charity, election by grace and predestination, which are so repulsive to rationalism, the more decisively the tendency of morals to change men has come to the foreground in literature. It is so with society; all are to become equal in virtue, as all are to become equal in possessions. These of course are Utopian views, which have little or no influence on the course of life: no moral system changes the nature of men, as no socialism is able to change the inequality of property; but they have an influence on the way of judging things; and, as judgment plays so large a part with modern writers, so it does also on literature.

Until the middle of the past century, every class and every individual accepted the world as we accept Nature, as a given order, in which there is little to be changed. People lived and acted, wrote and enjoyed naïvely, without reflection, or at least without comparing the existing world and its laws with reasoning and its norms.

A man of the people thought as little of becoming a burgher, as any of us wishes to become a prince of the blood. If any one ventured to raise himself and knew how to penetrate through his circumstances, it was because he felt himself, his strength of mind and will—*i.e.*, his individuality—and not because he thought himself justified by his quality as " man." What he became, he became

"Et par droit de conquête et pas droit de naissance."

His legal title was founded on his personal gifts, not on a so-called justice, which nowadays every mediocrity thinks himself ·entitled to invoke, and the idea of which is suggested to him by all ·our speeches and institutions, inasmuch as they almost directly ·entice him to leave his station in order to feel himself unhappy in a higher one, for which he is not fit. This eternal comparing of the actual world with the postulates of reason has " sickled o'er" our life ·in more than one sense. For the whole of this so-called humane morality consists in nothing else than in exhorting us to try to put ourselves in other people's steads, not by a direct intuition, but according to an all-levelling abstraction, which from its very nature must also mean putting other people in our stead. Both are fictions, which take place in our head alone, and have no reality. Every man feels differently, and *grosso modo* one might say that every nation and every class feels differently. This ignoring of natural limits has led in political life to pretending to and granting rights which those whom they concern do not know how to use ; in social life, to a dislocating of fixed relations and wandering from the natural atmosphere, which must always be a painful sensation ; in literature, to lending to their *dramatis personæ* thoughts and feelings which they cannot have, but especially to requiring them to be something different from what they really are, since they must correspond to the abstract moral type which we have constructed. Completely isolated are the writers who know how to divine to the reader the sensations of uncultivated people—as *e.g.*, Jeremiah Gottholf ; the large majority of readers properly so-called, prefer ideal figures in George Sand's style, which have nothing of the present but the certain.

In political and social life such aspirations do mischief enough, without, however, being able to change the essence of either State or society. In literature, where we treat not with live people on actual ground but with the docile creations of our imagination on much-enduring paper, the new view of the world has worked as its consequence a much deeper revolution. It is true that the pretensions of rationalism to regulate legislation according to preconceived ideas of equality and justice have not remained without influence ; on the whole, however,

States have continued in our century, as in all former ones, to register and codify existing customs and to regulate newly formed interests. and relations. It is true that in most countries each citizen has been recognized as of equal right and equal-value, but in fact power has remained in the hands of the man of culture and property. It is, true that people have tried to bestow on Egypt and Turkey the blessing of Western constitutions; but not a year was required to show that one thing does not suit all. The same is the case in society. It never enters the heads of children to find social order, in so far as they know it, unjust or even unnatural. We have seen the mason join his bricks, the peasant mow his grass, the woodcutter saw our wood, without even asking ourselves why our father had nothing of that kind to do. In this sense, almost all men before the revolution remained children, as nine-tenths. of them remain children to this day. And it is good that it should be so; for the whole machine of humanity would stop if we wanted continually to put ourselves into the place of others and to endeavour to ensure for every one, according to the exigencies of an abstract equality, the same conditions of life. So in consequence we stop short at good wishes, sufficient to make men, who formerly were quite happy in this limited existence, and reflected but little upon it, discontented with their lot, but insufficient to change this lot. " For there is nothing either good or bad but thinking makes it so," says Hamlet. When man ceases thinking on what he has to do in order to think that he has to do it, good-by to all content. Now, this is the clearest result of principle which underlies modern philanthropy as opposed to Christian charity, although it has called into existence many things which have alleviated and improved the life of the working classes within their station, helping them in illness, old age and want of work, without spoiling their normal existence by illusive pictures of a better condition. Besides, the positive wrong is, I repeat, much less than one might suppose, precisely because the mass of mankind continues taking the world as it is and does not demand that the sun should henceforth rise in the west.

In fact, it is only with men of letters, who are in quite a different relation with the world from other people, that the new way of thinking has become predominant; but then their number has wonderfully increased in the last three hundred years. As the whole of our culture has become a literary one, a book culture, all we who call ourselves cultured (*Gebildete*) are at bottom men of letters. The cultivated man of former times, who had been formed by commerce with men, for whom a book had interest, not as a book but only in so far as it reflected life, becomes rarer and rarer. Our whole civilization is influenced by literature; readers and authors live in the same atmosphere of unreality, or, to speak more accurately, they divide life into two halves, that of practical activity—the bookmaking of the author is also a practical activity—and that of intellectual activity, two spheres which touch each other nowhere, not even where the intellectual one borrows its object from the practical one; for it divests them immediately of their reality and shapes them only after having falsified them.

Tocqueville has a chapter headed : "How the men of letters became, towards the middle of the eighteenth century, the principal politicians." This is now universally the case in one sense; for even in England political life has been infected with the spirit of the men of letters, through the advance of the Radical on the one hand, and the reform of Toryism by Disraeli on the other ; the fact remains, however, particularly true of France, where the whole polity suffers cruelly under it. Nevertheless, art and literature are always the two activities most affected by it, and it is with them that we are here concerned.

III.

The novels of our time in which the moral point of view does not absolutely predominate may be counted on the fingers. Even where unveiled immorality, or at least indecency, displays itself, there is from beginning to end, with or without the author's consciousness, a certain didactic tendency. In the apparently most objectionable of all modern works of fiction, in "Madame Bovary," one feels that the writer has an intention which is not purely artistic, the intention to warn us against certain modes of education and kinds of readings. In M. Zola it is clear that his workmen and workwomen who perish in the mud are to serve as deterrent instances. Neither do so. The German novelists conceal the moral standard which they use in their novels, the English and North-Americans even boast of it. Certainly morals, as well as any other human interest, have their right of citizenship in art. Only it is important to know what is understood by morals : the natural and sound ones which culminate in the worship of truth, or the artificial, made up, unhealthy ones, whose mother is human vanity, whose godmother is falsehood. It is sound morals when Prince Hal leaves his pet favourite in the lurch as soon as, with the responsibility of the crown, the earnest of life begins for him; it is unhealthy morals when Victor Hugo disturbs the ideas of right and wrong by glorifying a galley-slave who has become the victim of an error of justice. This is not the place to examine at length what were the instinctive morals of men before the victory of rationalism, nor to recall to mind how Kant has scientifically established these unconscious ethics by his doctrine of the intelligible character, and Schopenhauer by his theory of compassion ; suffice it to state that the morals of our authors have another origin and another aim, and that these are as incompatible with art as the older ones are fitted to accommodate themselves to it. Now, modern morals may apparently differ as much from one another as Zola's from Howells'; but they have the same family feature—discontent with this world as it is; and the direct consequence of it is the sombre tone of all this literature.

" Ernst ist das Leben, heiter ist die Kunst,"

thought Schiller; to-day, art is to be earnest, a species of worship for Richard Wagner, a moral or political lesson for Gustav Freytag. And how could it be otherwise? If one compares unceasingly this world and human nature with a high, arbitrary, self-created *ideal*, void of all reality, they must appear very insufficient, and may well lead to bitter judgments. How morose at bottom are all the novels of George Eliot, in what one might call their key-note; how bitter Charlotte Brontë's, how infinitely sad Miss Poynter's " Among the Hills,"—to instance a little-known masterpiece of this sombre moralo-psychological art. All great narrators of former times, from Homer to Cervantes, and from Chaucer to Walter Scott, unchain our hearts by their good humour; even the tragic muse has always known how to translate

" Das düstre Spiel
Der Wahrheit in das heitre Reich der Kunst."

Here, on the contrary, we always feel oppressed by the long face and the lugubrious tone which our authors take when they relate things our ancestors were prone to laugh over. Sensuality even, which formerly used to present itself with ingenuousness, healthy and naked, or forced its entrance into literature by a smile, is now grave, reflective, a product of corrupt intelligence rather than of overstreaming force and fulness. In deference to truth it must, however, be said that the modern novel has on the whole kept itself freer than poetry from this unwholesome and over-refined sensuality. On the other hand, it has become more sentimentally charitable towards all those phenomena and types which were formerly the object of mirth. Who would dare nowadays to treat comically poor stammering Bridoison? Compassion for his infirmity would get the better of us; full of human tenderness, we should " put ourselves in his stead," and forthwith make a tragical figure of him. The dry *savant* whom the world has laughed at for centuries as an awkward or vain bookworm, becomes in George Eliot's hands an unfortunate, who sighing for a false ideal, is on the other hand seen by the noblest of women herself as an ideal. For whatever is comical objectively becomes tragical when it is taken subjectively : our tender little self suffers, and no wonder it pities itself.

How rudely would all the serene figures which live in our imagination be destroyed, if we were to put them under the discipline of our conscientious authors! Only fancy poor Manon under the birch-rod of Jane Eyre, the schoolmistress! Imagine Squire Western in M. Zola's *clinique :* "If you continue getting drunk every night, whilst your daughter is playing the harpischord, a terrible end is awaiting you, Mr. Western. Shall I describe it to you? I have accurately studied several cases of *delirium tremens potatorum,* the punishment which is in store for all alcoholized persons as you are." And our old friend Falstaff, whom that losel Shakspeare treated so indulgently, what lessons George Eliot would have read to him; " for really, Sir John, you have no excuse whatever. If you were a poor devil who had never had any but bad examples before your eyes ; but you have had all the advantages which destiny can give to man on his way through life! Are you not born of a good family? have not you had, at Oxford, the best education England is able to give to her children? have you not had the highest connections? And, nevertheless, how low you are fallen! Do you know why? I have warned my Tito over and over against it : because you have always done that only which was agreeable to you, and have shunned everything that was - unpleasant." "And you, Miss Phillis," Mr. Howells would say, " if you go on being naughty I shall write a writ against you, as I did against my hero Bartley, who, too, won everybody's heart, but at bottom was a very frivolous fellow ; or I shall deliver you up to my friend James, who will analyze you until nobody knows you again. That will teach you, to enter into yourself and to become another." " Become another," is that not the first requirement of a novel hero of our days? Fielding would have rather expected that the adder should lose her venom, than that Blifil should cease to be a scoundrel.

I spoke of Howells taking part against his own hero in the most perfect of his works. You will find something similar in almost every novel of our time. It seems as if the authors could not refrain from persecuting in an odious type certain persons whom they have learned to know and to hate in life—a disposition of mind which is the most contrary to the artist's disposition which could be thought out ; for he neither hates nor loves his objects personally, and to him Richard III. is as interesting as Antonio, " one in whom the ancient Roman honour more appears than any that draws breath in Italy." Remember only George Eliot's character, Rosamond, and with what really feminine perfidy she tries to discredit her. How differently Abbé Prévost treats his Manon! Even if Richardson, and, in our time, Jer. Gottholf, do take a moralizing tone, and begin with ever so many preachments and good lessons, the artist runs away with them ; they forget that they wanted to teach and paint their objects with artistic indifference: *sine ira nec studio,* not to speak of their morals being of a kind which have nothing in them rebellious to art. With George Eliot and W. D. Howells it is the contrary : they want to be objective, but the moralist soon gets the better of the artist.

I hope the reader has observed that I choose only novels and novelists of first rank, in order to compare them with those of former times, such indeed as might, perhaps, come out victoriously from such a comparison, if they were not infected by the moral epidemic of our time. How deeply our generation is steeped in it we generally forget, because habit makes appear as nature what is only a moral convention. Other times have advocated more severe conventions, but they remained on the surface ; ours seem lighter, more accommodating, but they penetrate to our marrow. It is incredible how great a mass of artificial feelings, interests, and duties we carry about, how our language and our actions are dominated by them. Fine scenery, fine arts, philanthropy, &c., without any inner want, fill our intellectual life; we believe in the reality of sensations we never experienced ; or we drive out Nature by culture. Shakspeare would not be able nowadays to create an Othello who would listen to Iago's insinuations, because no gentleman nowadays would allow such calumnies, and the gentleman has driven out the man. Language has suffered so much under this rule of conventionalism, that to the cultivated it has become quite insufficient for the direct translation of sensation. Let a lady to-day speak like the Queen of Cortanza or Margaret of Anjou, and how the public would protest against the coarseness of her language and feeling. This, by the way, is also the real reason why all our dramas are and must be so lifeless, as well as of the striking fact that all the more important works of fiction of our time move, with few exceptions, among the lower spheres of the people, where alone there still survives a direct relation between language and sensation. Even in America, which is always lauded as the virgin soil of a society without an inheritance, convention rules unconditionally, particularly in moral views; for this society has not yet even known how to free itself from the absurdest and most tyrannical of religions—puritanism, on whose inheritance it has grown and developed. Only a remnant of puritanism can give the key to the stilted tune of Hawthorne's adumbration, or explain how a writer of the taste and talent of Mr. W. D. Howells, who besides does not lack a keen sense of humour, has been able to create a comical figure like that of Ben Hallack, without as much as an inkling of the comicality of it.

People are never weary of inveighing against the prosaicism of our time—the yelling whistle of the locomotive, which has superseded the musical post-horn, the ungraceful chimney-pot, &c. : nobody thinks of the unnaturalness of our sensations. Where, however, is the source of all poetry, in the truth of our sensations or in the decoration of the stage on which we move? In the cut of our coat or in the heart which beats beneath it? Let us only learn again how to feel naturally, to think naturally, above all, to see naturally, and art will not fail to reappear. But " the spirit of history" takes good care that *we* should no more learn it, carrying us off irresistibly, and for a long while, I am afraid, in totally different tracks. And, who would demur against it? Only we must not imagine that art, too, can meet us on these tracks. The novel of the future will remain what the novel of the present is: a work of edification, of instruction, of amusement—perhaps, also, of the contrary; it will be long before it becomes a work of art.

KARL HILLEBRAND.

Henry James

"The Art of Fiction"

Longman's Magazine 4 (September 1884), 502–21

The Art of Fiction.

I SHOULD not have affixed so comprehensive a title to these few remarks, necessarily wanting in any completeness, upon a subject the full consideration of which would carry us far, did I not seem to discover a pretext for my temerity in the interesting pamphlet lately published under this name by Mr. Walter Besant. Mr. Besant's lecture at the Royal Institution—the original form of his pamphlet—appears to indicate that many persons are interested in the art of fiction and are not indifferent to such remarks as those who practise it may attempt to make about it. I am therefore anxious not to lose the benefit of this favourable association, and to edge in a few words under cover of the attention which Mr. Besant is sure to have excited. There is something very encouraging in his having put into form certain of his ideas on the mystery of story-telling.

It is a proof of life and curiosity—curiosity on the part of the brotherhood of novelists, as well as on the part of their readers. Only a short time ago it might have been supposed that the English novel was not what the French call *discutable*. It had no air of having a theory, a conviction, a consciousness of itself behind it—of being the expression of an artistic faith, the result of choice and comparison. I do not say it was necessarily the worse for that; it would take much more courage than I possess to intimate that the form of the novel, as Dickens and Thackeray (for instance) saw it, had any taint of incompleteness. It was, however, *naïf* (if I may help myself out with another French word); and, evidently, if it is destined to suffer in any way for having lost its *naïveté*, it has now an idea of making sure of the corresponding advantages. During the period I have alluded to there was a comfortable, good-humoured feeling abroad that a novel is a novel, as a pudding is a pudding, and that this was the end of it. But within a year or two, for some reason or other, there have been signs of returning animation—the era of discussion would appear to have been to a certain extent opened. Art lives upon discussion, upon experiment, upon curiosity, upon variety of attempt, upon the exchange of views and the comparison of standpoints; and there

is a presumption that those times when no one has anything particular to say about it, and has no reason to give for practice or
preference, though they may be times of genius, are not times of
development, are times, possibly even, a little, of dulness. The
successful application of any art is a delightful spectacle, but the
theory, too, is interesting ; and though there is a great deal of the
latter without the former, I suspect there has never been a genuine
success that has not had a latent core of conviction. Discussion,
suggestion, formulation, these things are fertilizing when they are
frank and sincere. Mr. Besant has set an excellent example in
saying what he thinks, for his part, about the way in which fiction
should be written, as well as about the way in which it should be
published ; for his view of the 'art,' carried on into an appendix,
covers that too. Other labourers in the same field will doubtless
take up the argument, they will give it the light of their experience,
and the effect will surely be to make our interest in the novel a
little more what it had for some time threatened to fail to be—
a serious, active, inquiring interest, under protection of which
this delightful study may, in moments of confidence, venture to
say a little more what it thinks of itself.

It must take itself seriously for the public to take it so. The
old superstition about fiction being 'wicked' has doubtless died
out in England ; but the spirit of it lingers in a certain oblique
regard directed toward any story which does not more or less admit
that it is only a joke. Even the most jocular novel feels in some
degree the weight of the proscription that was formerly directed
against literary levity ; the jocularity does not always succeed in
passing for gravity. It is still expected, though perhaps people
are ashamed to say it, that a production which is after all only a
'make believe' (for what else is a 'story?') shall be in some
degree apologetic—shall renounce the pretension of attempting
really to compete with life. This, of course, any sensible wideawake story declines to do, for it quickly perceives that the
tolerance granted to it on such a condition is only an attempt to
stifle it, disguised in the form of generosity. The old Evangelical
hostility to the novel, which was as explicit as it was narrow, and
which regarded it as little less favourable to our immortal part
than a stage-play, was in reality far less insulting. The only
reason for the existence of a novel is that it *does* compete with
life. When it ceases to compete as the canvas of the painter
competes, it will have arrived at a very strange pass. It is not
expected of the picture that it will make itself humble in order to

be forgiven; and the analogy between the art of the painter and the art of the novelist is, so far as I am able to see, complete. Their inspiration is the same, their process (allowing for the different quality of the vehicle) is the same, their success is the same. They may learn from each other, they may explain and sustain each other. Their cause is the same, and the honour of one is the honour of another. Peculiarities of manner, of execution, that correspond on either side, exist in each of them and contribute to their development. The Mahometans think a picture an unholy thing, but it is a long time since any Christian did, and it is therefore the more odd that in the Christian mind the traces (dissimulated though they may be) of a suspicion of the sister art should linger to this day. The only effectual way to lay it to rest is to emphasize the analogy to which I just alluded—to insist on the fact that as the picture is reality, so the novel is history. That is the only general description (which does it justice) that we may give of the novel. But history also is allowed to compete with life, as I say; it is not, any more than painting, expected to apologize. The subject-matter of fiction is stored up likewise in documents and records, and if it will not give itself away, as they say in California, it must speak with assurance, with the tone of the historian. Certain accomplished novelists have a habit of giving themselves away which must often bring tears to the eyes of people who take their fiction seriously. I was lately struck, in reading over many pages of Anthony Trollope, with his want of discretion in this particular. In a digression, a parenthesis or an aside, he concedes to the reader that he and this trusting friend are only 'making believe.' He admits that the events he narrates have not really happened, and that he can give his narrative any turn the reader may like best. Such a betrayal of a sacred office seems to me, I confess, a terrible crime; it is what I mean by the attitude of apology, and it shocks me every whit as much in Trollope as it would have shocked me in Gibbon or Macaulay. It implies that the novelist is less occupied in looking for the truth than the historian, and in doing so it deprives him at a stroke of all his standing-room. To represent and illustrate the past, the actions of men, is the task of either writer, and the only difference that I can see is, in proportion as he succeeds, to the honour of the novelist, consisting as it does in his having more difficulty in collecting his evidence, which is so far from being purely literary. It seems to me to give him a great character, the fact that he has at once so much in common with the philosopher and the painter; this double analogy is a magnificent heritage.

It is of all this evidently that Mr. Besant is full when he insists upon the fact that fiction is one of the *fine* arts, deserving in its turn of all the honours and emoluments that have hitherto been reserved for the successful profession of music, poetry, painting, architecture. It is impossible to insist too much on so important a truth, and the place that Mr. Besant demands for the work of the novelist may be represented, a trifle less abstractly, by saying that he demands not only that it shall be reputed artistic, but that it shall be reputed very artistic indeed. It is excellent that he should have struck this note, for his doing so indicates that there was need of it, that his proposition may be to many people a novelty. One rubs one's eyes at the thought; but the rest of Mr. Besant's essay confirms the revelation. I suspect, in truth, that it would be possible to confirm it still further, and that one would not be far wrong in saying that in addition to the people to whom it has never occurred that a novel ought to be artistic, there are a great many others who, if this principle were urged upon them, would be filled with an indefinable mistrust. They would find it difficult to explain their repugnance, but it would operate strongly to put them on their guard. ' Art,' in our Protestant communities, where so many things have got so strangely twisted about, is supposed, in certain circles, to have some vaguely injurious effect upon those who make it an important consideration, who let it weigh in the balance. It is assumed to be opposed in some mysterious manner to morality, to amusement, to instruction. When it is embodied in the work of the painter (the sculptor is another affair!) you know what it is; it stands there before you, in the honesty of pink and green and a gilt frame; you can see the worst of it at a glance, and you can be on your guard. But when it is introduced into literature it becomes more insidious— there is danger of its hurting you before you know it. Literature should be either instructive or amusing, and there is in many minds an impression that these artistic preoccupations, the search for form, contribute to neither end, interfere indeed with both. They are too frivolous to be edifying, and too serious to be diverting; and they are, moreover, priggish and paradoxical and superfluous. That, I think, represents the manner in which the latent thought of many people who read novels as an exercise in skipping would explain itself if it were to become articulate. They would argue, of course, that a novel ought to be ' good,' but they would interpret this term in a fashion of their own, which, indeed, would vary considerably from one critic to another. One would say that being good means representing virtuous and aspiring characters, placed in prominent positions; another would say that it depends for a 'happy ending' on a distribution at the last of prizes, pensions, husbands, wives, babies, millions, appended paragraphs and cheerful remarks. Another still would say that it means being full of incident and movement, so that we shall wish to jump ahead, to see who was the mysterious stranger, and if the stolen will was ever found, and shall not be distracted from this pleasure by any tiresome analysis or 'description.' But they would all agree that the 'artistic' idea would spoil some of their fun. One would hold it accountable for all the description, another would see it revealed in the absence of sympathy. Its hostility to a happy ending would be evident, and it might even, in some cases, render any ending at all impossible. The 'ending' of a novel is, for many persons, like that of a good dinner, a course of dessert and ices, and the artist in fiction is regarded as a sort of meddlesome doctor who forbids agreeable aftertastes. It is therefore true that this conception of Mr. Besant's, of the novel as a superior form, encounters not only a negative but a positive indifference. It matters little that, as a work of art, it should really be as little or as much concerned to supply happy endings, sympathetic characters, and an objective tone, as if it were a work of mechanics; the association of ideas, however incongruous, might easily be too much for it if an eloquent voice were not sometimes raised to call attention to the fact that it is at once as free and as serious a branch of literature as any other.

Certainly, this might sometimes be doubted in presence of the enormous number of works of fiction that appeal to the credulity of our generation, for it might easily seem that there could be no great substance in a commodity so quickly and easily produced. It must be admitted that good novels are somewhat compromised by bad ones, and that the field, at large, suffers discredit from overcrowding. I think, however, that this injury is only superficial, and that the superabundance of written fiction proves nothing against the principle itself. It has been vulgarised, like all other kinds of literature, like everything else, to-day, and it has proved more than some kinds accessible to vulgarisation. But there is as much difference as there ever was between a good novel and a bad one: the bad is swept, with all the daubed canvases and spoiled marble, into some unvisited limbo or infinite rubbish-yard, beneath the back-windows of the world, and the good subsists and emits its light and stimulates our desire for perfection. As I shall take the liberty of making but a single criticism of Mr. Besant, whose tone is so full of the love of his art, I may as well have done with it at once. He seems to me to mistake in attempting to say so definitely beforehand what sort of an affair the good novel will be. To indicate the danger of such an error as that has been the purpose of these few pages; to suggest that certain traditions on the subject, applied *a priori*, have already had much to answer for, and that the good health of an art which undertakes so immediately to reproduce life must demand that it be perfectly free. It lives upon exercise, and the very meaning of exercise is freedom. The only obligation to which in advance we may hold a novel without incurring the accusation of being arbitrary, is that it be interesting. That general responsibility rests upon it, but it is the only one I can think of. The ways in which it is at liberty to accomplish this result (of interesting us) strike me as innumerable and such as can only suffer from being marked out, or fenced in, by prescription. They are as various as the temperament of man, and they are successful in proportion as they reveal a particular mind, different from others. A novel is in its broadest definition a personal impression of life; that, to begin with, constitutes its value, which is greater or less according to the intensity of the impression. But there will be no intensity at all, and therefore no value, unless there is freedom to feel and say. The tracing of a line to be followed, of a tone to be taken, of a form to be filled out, is a limitation of that freedom and a suppression of the very thing that we are most curious about. The form, it seems to me, is to be appreciated after the fact; then the author's choice has been made, his standard has been indicated; then we can follow lines and directions and compare tones. Then, in a word, we can enjoy one of the most charming of pleasures, we can estimate quality, we can apply the test of execution. The execution belongs to the author alone; it is what is most personal to him, and we measure him by that. The advantage, the luxury, as well as the torment and responsibility of the novelist, is that there is no limit to what he may attempt as an executant—no limit to his possible experiments, efforts, discoveries, successes. Here it is especially that he works, step by step, like his brother of the brush, of whom we may always say that he has painted his picture in a manner best known to himself. His manner is his secret, not necessarily a deliberate one. He cannot disclose it, as a general thing, if he would; he would be at a loss to teach it to others. I say this with a due recollection of having insisted on the community of method of the artist who paints a picture and the artist who writes a novel. The painter *is* able to teach the rudiments of his practice, and it is possible, from the study of good work (granted the aptitude), both to learn how to paint and to learn how to write. Yet it remains true, without injury to the *rapprochement*, that the literary artist would be obliged to say to his pupil much more than the other, 'Ah, well, you must do it as you can!' It is a question of degree, a matter of delicacy. If there are exact sciences there are also exact arts, and the grammar of painting is so much more definite that it makes the difference.

I ought to add, however, that if Mr. Besant says at the beginning of his essay that the ' laws of fiction may be laid down and taught with as much precision and exactness as the laws of harmony, perspective, and proportion,' he mitigates what might appear to be an over-statement by applying his remark to 'general' laws, and by expressing most of these rules in a manner with which it would certainly be unaccommodating to disagree. That the novelist must write from his experience, that his 'characters must be real and such as might be met with in actual life;' that ' a young lady brought up in a quiet country village should avoid descriptions of garrison life,' and 'a writer whose friends and personal experiences belong to the lower middle-class should care-fully avoid introducing his characters into Society;' that one should enter one's notes in a common-place book; that one's figures should be clear in outline; that making them clear by some trick of speech or of carriage is a bad method, and 'describ-ing them at length' is a worse one; that English Fiction should have a 'conscious moral purpose;' that 'it is almost impossible to estimate too highly the value of careful workmanship—that is, of style;' that 'the most important point of all is the story,' that 'the story is everything'—these are principles with most of which it is surely impossible not to sympathise. That remark about the lower middle-class writer and his knowing his place is perhaps rather chilling; but for the rest, I should find it difficult to dissent from any one of these recommendations. At the same time I should find it difficult positively to assent to them, with the exception, perhaps, of the injunction as to entering one's notes in a common-place book. They scarcely seem to me to have the quality that Mr. Besant attributes to the rules of the novelist— the 'precision and exactness' of 'the laws of harmony, perspective, and proportion.' They are suggestive, they are even inspiring, but they are not exact, though they are doubtless as much so as the case admits of; which is a proof of that liberty of interpretation for which I just contended. For the value of these different injunctions—so beautiful and so vague—is wholly in the meaning one attaches to them. The characters, the situation, which strike one as real will be those that touch and interest one most, but the measure of reality is very difficult to fix. The reality of Don Quixote or of Mr. Micawber is a very delicate shade; it is a reality so coloured by the author's vision that, vivid as it may be, one would hesitate to propose it as a model; one would expose one's self to some very embarrassing questions on the part of a pupil. It goes without saying that you will not write a good novel unless you possess the sense of reality; but it will be difficult to give you a recipe for calling that sense into being. Humanity is immense and reality has a myriad forms; the most one can affirm is that some of the flowers of fiction have the odour of it, and others have not; as for telling you in advance how your nosegay should be composed, that is another affair. It is equally excellent and inconclusive to say that one must write from experience; to our supposititious aspirant such a declaration might savour of mockery. What kind of experience is intended, and where does it begin and end? Experience is never limited and it is never complete; it is an immense sensibility, a kind of huge spider-web, of the finest silken threads, suspended in the chamber of consciousness and catching every air-borne particle in its tissue. It is the very atmosphere of the mind; and when the mind is imaginative—much more when it happens to be that of a man of genius—it takes to itself the faintest hints of life, it converts the very pulses of the air into revelations. The young lady living in a village has only to be a damsel upon whom nothing is lost to make it quite unfair (as it seems to me) to declare to her that she shall have nothing to say about the military. Greater miracles have been seen than that, imagination assisting, she should speak the truth about some of these gentlemen. I remember an English novelist, a woman of genius, telling me that she was much commended for the impression she had managed to give in one of her tales of the nature and way of life of the French Protestant youth. She had been asked where she learned so much about this recondite being, she had been congratulated on her peculiar opportunities. These opportunities consisted in her having once, in Paris, as she ascended a staircase, passed an open door where, in the household of a *pasteur*, some of the young Protestants were seated at table round a finished meal. The glimpse made a picture; it lasted only a moment, but that moment was experience. She had got her impression, and she evolved her type. She knew what youth was, and what Protestantism; she also had the advantage of having seen what it was to be French; so that she converted these ideas into a concrete image and produced a reality. Above all, however, she was blessed with the faculty which when you give it an inch takes an ell, and which for the artist is a much greater source of strength than any accident of residence or of place in the social scale. The power to guess the unseen from the seen, to trace the implication of things, to judge the whole piece by the pattern, the condition of feeling life, in general, so completely that you are well on your way to knowing any particular corner of it—this cluster of gifts may almost be said to constitute experience, and they occur in country and in town, and in the most differing stages of education. If experience consists of impressions, it may be said that impressions *are* experience, just as (have we not seen it?) they are the very air we breathe. Therefore, if I should certainly say to a novice, ' Write from experience, and experience only,' I should feel that this was a rather tantalising monition if I were not careful immediately to add, ' Try to be one of the people on whom nothing is lost ! '

I am far from intending by this to minimise the importance of exactness—of truth of detail. One can speak best from one's own taste, and I may therefore venture to say that the air of reality (solidity of specification) seems to me to be the supreme virtue of a novel—the merit in which all its other merits (including that conscious moral purpose of which Mr. Besant speaks) helplessly and submissively depend. If it be not there, they are all as nothing, and if these be there, they owe their effect to the success with which the author has produced the illusion of life. The cultivation of this success, the study of this exquisite process, form, to my taste, the beginning and the end of the art of the novelist. They are his inspiration, his despair, his reward, his torment, his delight. It is here, in very truth, that he competes with life; it is here that he competes with his brother the painter, in *his* attempt to render the look of things, the look that conveys their meaning, to catch the colour, the relief, the expression, the surface,

the substance of the human spectacle. It is in regard to this that
Mr. Besant is well inspired when he bids him take notes. He cannot
possibly take too many, he cannot possibly take enough. All life
solicits him, and to ' render ' the simplest surface, to produce the
most momentary illusion, is a very complicated business. His case
would be easier, and the rule would be more exact, if Mr. Besant
had been able to tell him what notes to take. But this I fear he
can never learn in any hand-book ; it is the business of his life.
He has to take a great many in order to select a few, he has to
work them up as he can, and even the guides and philosophers
who might have most to say to him must leave him alone when
it comes to the application of precepts, as we leave the painter
in communion with his palette. That his characters ' must be
clear in outline,' as Mr. Besant says—he feels that down to his
boots ; but how he shall make them so is a secret between his
good angel and himself. It would be absurdly simple if he could
be taught that a great deal of ' description ' would make them so,
or that, on the contrary, the absence of description and the
cultivation of dialogue, or the absence of dialogue and the multi-
plication of ' incident,' would rescue him from his difficulties.
Nothing, for instance, is more possible than that he be of a turn
of mind for which this odd, literal opposition of description and
dialogue, incident and description, has little meaning and light.
People often talk of these things as if they had a kind of inter-
necine distinctness, instead of melting into each other at every
breath and being intimately associated parts of one general effort
of expression. I cannot imagine composition existing in a series
of blocks, nor conceive, in any novel worth discussing at all, of
a passage of description that is not in its intention narrative,
a passage of dialogue that is not in its intention descriptive, a
touch of truth of any sort that does not partake of the nature of
incident, and an incident that derives its interest from any other
source than the general and only source of the success of a work
of art—that of being illustrative. A novel is a living thing, all
one and continuous, like every other organism, and in proportion
as it lives will it be found, I think, that in each of the parts
there is something of each of the other parts. The critic who
over the close texture of a finished work will pretend to trace a
geography of items will mark some frontiers as artificial, I fear,
as any that have been known to history. There is an old-fashioned
distinction between the novel of character and the novel of
incident, which must have cost many a smile to the intending

romancer who was keen about his work. It appears to me as little to the point as the equally celebrated distinction between the novel and the romance—to answer as little to any reality. There are bad novels and good novels, as there are bad pictures and good pictures; but that is the only distinction in which I see any meaning, and I can as little imagine speaking of a novel of character as I can imagine speaking of a picture of character. When one says picture, one says of character, when one says novel, one says of incident, and the terms may be transposed. What is character but the determination of incident? What is incident but the illustration of character? What is a picture or a novel that is *not* of character? What else do we seek in it and find in it? It is an incident for a woman to stand up with her hand resting on a table and look out at you in a certain way; or if it be not an incident, I think it will be hard to say what it is. At the same time it is an expression of character. If you say you don't see it (character in *that—allons donc!*) this is exactly what the artist who has reasons of his own for thinking he *does* see it undertakes to show you. When a young man makes up his mind that he has not faith enough, after all, to enter the Church, as he intended, that is an incident, though you may not hurry to the end of the chapter to see whether perhaps he doesn't change once more. I do not say that these are extraordinary or startling incidents. I do not pretend to estimate the degree of interest proceeding from them, for this will depend upon the skill of the painter. It sounds almost puerile to say that some incidents are intrinsically much more important than others, and I need not take this precaution after having professed my sympathy for the major ones in remarking that the only classification of the novel that I can understand is into the interesting and the uninteresting.

The novel and the romance, the novel of incident and that of character—these separations appear to me to have been made by critics and readers for their own convenience, and to help them out of some of their difficulties, but to have little reality or interest for the producer, from whose point of view it is, of course, that we are attempting to consider the art of fiction. The case is the same with another shadowy category, which Mr. Besant apparently is disposed to set up—that of the 'modern English novel;' unless, indeed, it be that in this matter he has fallen into an accidental confusion of standpoints. It is not quite clear whether he intends the remarks in which he alludes to it to be didactic or historical. It is as difficult to suppose a person intending to write a modern English, as to suppose him writing an ancient English, novel; that is a label which begs the question. One writes the novel, one paints the picture, of one's language and of one's time, and calling it modern English will not, alas! make the difficult task any easier. No more, unfortunately, will calling this or that work of one's fellow artist a romance—unless it be, of course, simply for the pleasantness of the thing, as, for instance, when Hawthorne gave this heading to his story of Blithedale. The French, who have brought the theory of fiction to remarkable completeness, have but one word for the novel, and have not attempted smaller things in it, that I can see, for that. I can think of no obligation to which the 'romancer' would not be held equally with the novelist; the standard of execution is equally high for each. Of course it is of execution that we are talking— that being the only point of a novel that is open to contention. This is perhaps too often lost sight of, only to produce interminable confusions and cross-purposes. We must grant the artist his subject, his idea, what the French call his *donnée*; our criticism is applied only to what he makes of it. Naturally I do not mean that we are bound to like it or find it interesting: in case we do not our course is perfectly simple—to let it alone. We may believe that of a certain idea even the most sincere novelist can make nothing at all, and the event may perfectly justify our belief; but the failure will have been a failure to execute, and it is in the execution that the fatal weakness is recorded. If we pretend to respect the artist at all we must allow him his freedom of choice, in the face, in particular cases, of innumerable presumptions that the choice will not fructify. Art derives a considerable part of its beneficial exercise from flying in the face of presumptions, and some of the most interesting experiments of which it is capable are hidden in the bosom of common things. Gustave Flaubert has written a story about the devotion of a servant-girl to a parrot, and the production, highly finished as it is, cannot on the whole be called a success. We are perfectly free to find it flat, but I think it might have been interesting; and I, for my part, am extremely glad he should have written it; it is a contribution to our knowledge of what can be done—or what cannot. Ivan Turgénieff has written a tale about a deaf and dumb serf and a lap-dog, and the thing is touching, loving, a little masterpiece. He struck the note of life where Gustave Flaubert missed it—he flew in the face of a presumption and achieved a victory.

Nothing, of course, will ever take the place of the good old fashion of 'liking' a work of art or not liking it; the more improved criticism will not abolish that primitive, that ultimate, .test. I mention this to guard myself from the accusation of intimating that the idea, the subject, of a novel or a picture, does not matter. It matters, to my sense, in the highest degree, and if I might put up a prayer it would be that artists should select none but the richest. Some, as I have already hastened to admit, are much more substantial than others, and it would be a happily arranged world in which persons intending to treat them should be exempt from confusions and mistakes. This fortunate condition will arrive only, I fear, on the same day that critics become purged from error. Meanwhile, I repeat, we do not judge the artist with fairness unless we say to him, ' Oh, I grant you your starting-point, because if I did not I should seem to prescribe to you, and heaven forbid I should take that responsibility. If I pretend to tell you what you must not take, you will call upon me to tell you then what you must take; in which case I shall be nicely caught! Moreover, it isn't till I have accepted your data that I can begin to measure you. I have the standard; I judge you by what you propose, and you must look out for me there. Of course I may not care for your idea at all; I may think it silly, or stale, or unclean ; in which case I wash my hands of you altogether. I may content myself with believing that you will not have succeeded in being interesting, but I shall of course not attempt to demonstrate it, and you will be as indifferent to me as I am to you. I needn't remind you that there are all sorts of tastes: who can know it better ? Some people, for excellent reasons, don't like to read about carpenters ; others, for reasons even better, don't like to read about courtesans. Many object to Americans. Others (I believe they are mainly editors and publishers) won't look at Italians. Some readers don't like quiet subjects ; others don't like bustling ones. Some enjoy a complete illusion ; others revel in a complete deception. They choose their novels accordingly, and if they don't care about your idea they won't, *a fortiori*, care about your treatment.'

So that it comes back very quickly, as I have said, to the liking ; in spite of M. Zola, who reasons less powerfully than he represents, and who will not reconcile himself to this absoluteness of taste, thinking that there are certain things that people ought to like, and that they can be made to like. I am quite at a loss to imagine anything (at any rate in this matter of fiction) that people *ought* to like or to dislike. Selection will be sure to take care of itself, for it has a constant motive behind it. That motive is simply experience. As people feel life, so they will feel the art that is most closely related to it. This closeness of relation is what we should never forget in talking of the effort of the novel. Many people speak of it as a factitious, artificial form, a product of ingenuity, the business of which is to alter and arrange the things that surround us, to translate them into conventional, traditional moulds. This, however, is a view of the matter which carries us but a very short way, condemns the art to an eternal repetition of a few familiar *clichés*, cuts short its development, and leads us straight up to a dead wall. Catching the very note and trick, the strange irregular rhythm of life, that is the attempt whose strenuous force keeps Fiction upon her feet. In proportion as in what she offers us we see life *without* rearrangement do we feel that we are touching the truth; in proportion as we see it *with* rearrangement do we feel that we are being put off with a substitute, a compromise and convention. It is not uncommon to hear an extraordinary assurance of remark in regard to this matter of rearranging, which is often spoken of as if it were the last word of art. Mr. Besant seems to me in danger of falling into this great error with his rather unguarded talk about 'selection.' Art is essentially selection, but it is a selection whose main care is to be typical, to be inclusive. For many people art means rose-coloured windows, and selection means picking a bouquet for Mrs. Grundy. They will tell you glibly that artistic considerations have nothing to do with the disagreeable, with the ugly; they will rattle off shallow commonplaces about the province of art and the limits of art, till you are moved to some wonder in return as to the province and the limits of ignorance. It appears to me that no one can ever have made a seriously artistic attempt without becoming conscious of an immense increase—a kind of revelation—of freedom. One perceives, in that case—by the light of a heavenly ray—that the province of art is all life, all feeling, all observation, all vision. As Mr. Besant so justly intimates, it is all experience. That is a sufficient answer to those who maintain that it must not touch the painful, who stick into its divine unconscious bosom little prohibitory inscriptions on the end of sticks, such as we see in public gardens—'It is forbidden to walk on the grass; it is forbidden to touch the flowers; it is not allowed to introduce dogs, or to remain after dark; it is requested to keep to the right.' The young aspirant in the line of fiction, whom we continue to imagine, will do nothing without taste, for in that case his freedom would be of little use to him; but the first advantage of his taste will be to reveal to him the absurdity of the little sticks and tickets. If he have taste, I must add, of course he will have ingenuity, and my disrespectful reference to that quality just now was not meant to imply that it is useless in fiction. But it is only a secondary aid; the first is a vivid sense of reality.

Mr. Besant has some remarks on the question of ‘the story,’ which I shall not attempt to criticise, though they seem to me to contain a singular ambiguity, because I do not think I understand them. I cannot see what is meant by talking as if there were a part of a novel which is the story and part of it which for mystical reasons is not—unless indeed the distinction be made in a sense in which it is difficult to suppose that anyone should attempt to convey anything. ‘The story,’ if it represents anything, represents the subject, the idea, the data of the novel; and there is surely no ‘school’—Mr. Besant speaks of a school—which urges that a novel should be all treatment and no subject. There must assuredly be something to treat; every school is intimately conscious of that. This sense of the story being the idea, the starting-point, of the novel is the only one that I see in which it can be spoken of as something different from its organic whole; and since, in proportion as the work is successful, the idea permeates and penetrates it, informs and animates it, so that every word and every punctuation-point contribute directly to the expression, in that proportion do we lose our sense of the story being a blade which may be drawn more or less out of its sheath. The story and the novel, the idea and the form, are the needle and thread, and I never heard of a guild of tailors who recommended the use of the thread without the needle or the needle without the thread. Mr. Besant is not the only critic who may be observed to have spoken as if there were certain things in life which constitute stories and certain others which do not. I find the same odd implication in an entertaining article in the *Pall Mall Gazette*, devoted, as it happens, to Mr. Besant's lecture. ‘The story is the thing!’ says this graceful writer, as if with a tone of opposition to another idea. I should think it was, as every painter who, as the time for ‘sending in’ his picture looms in the distance, finds himself still in quest of a subject—as every belated artist, not fixed about his *donnée*, will heartily agree. There are some subjects which speak to us and others which do not, but he would be a clever man who should undertake to give a rule by which the story and the no-story should be known apart. It is impossible (to me at least) to imagine any such rule which shall not be altogether arbitrary. The writer in the *Pall Mall* opposes the delightful (as I suppose) novel of ' Margot la Balafrée ' to certain tales in which ' Bostonian nymphs' appear to have ' rejected English dukes for psychological reasons.' I am not acquainted with the romance just designated, and can scarcely forgive the *Pall Mall* critic for not mentioning the name of the author, but the title appears to refer to a lady who may have received a scar in some heroic adventure. I am inconsolable at not being acquainted with this episode, but am utterly at a loss to see why it is a story when the rejection (or acceptance) of a duke is not, and why a reason, psychological or other, is not a subject when a cicatrix is. They are all particles of the multitudinous life with which the novel deals, and surely no dogma which pretends to make it lawful to touch the one and unlawful to touch the other will stand for a moment on its feet. It is the special picture that must stand or fall, according as it seems to possess truth or to lack it. Mr. Besant does not, to my sense, light up the subject by intimating that a story must, under penalty of not being a story, consist of ' adventures.' Why of adventures more than of green spectacles ? He mentions a category of impossible things, and among them he places 'fiction without adventure.' Why without adventure, more than without matrimony, or celibacy, or parturition, or cholera, or hydropathy, or Jansenism ? This seems to me to bring the novel back to the hapless little *rôle* of being an artificial, ingenious thing —bring it down from its large, free character of an immense and exquisite correspondence with life. And what *is* adventure, when it comes to that, and by what sign is the listening pupil to recognise it ? It is an adventure—an immense one—for me to write this little article ; and for a Bostonian nymph to reject an English duke is an adventure only less stirring, I should say, than for an English duke to be rejected by a Bostonian nymph. I see dramas within dramas in that, and innumerable points of view. A psychological reason is, to my imagination, an object adorably pictorial ; to catch the tint of its complexion—I feel as if that idea might inspire one to Titianesque efforts. There are few things more exciting to me, in short, than a psychological reason, and yet, I protest, the novel seems to me the most magnificent form of art. I have just been reading, at the same time, the delightful story of ' Treasure Island,' by Mr. Robert Louis Stevenson, and the last tale from M. Edmond de Goncourt, which is entitled 'Chérie.' One of these works treats of murders, mysteries, islands of dreadful renown, hairbreadth escapes, miraculous coincidences and buried doubloons. The other treats of a little French girl who lived in a fine house in Paris and died of wounded sensibility because no one would marry her. I call 'Treasure Island' delightful, because it appears to me to have succeeded wonderfully in what it attempts; and I venture to bestow no epithet upon 'Chérie,' which strikes me as having failed in what it attempts—that is, in tracing the development of the moral consciousness of a child. But one of these productions strikes me as exactly as much of a novel as the other, and as having a 'story' quite as much. The moral consciousness of a child is as much a part of life as the islands of the Spanish Main, and the one sort of geography seems to me to have those 'surprises' of which Mr. Besant speaks quite as much as the other. For myself (since it comes back in the last resort, as I say, to the preference of the individual), the picture of the child's experience has the advantage that I can at successive steps (an immense luxury, near to the 'sensual pleasure' of which Mr. Besant's critic in the *Pall Mall* speaks) say Yes or No, as it may be, to what the artist puts before me. I have been a child, but I have never been on a quest for a buried treasure, and it is a simple accident that with M. de Goncourt I should have for the most part to say No. With George Eliot, when she painted that country, I always said Yes.

The most interesting part of Mr. Besant's lecture is unfortunately the briefest passage—his very cursory allusion to the 'conscious moral purpose' of the novel. Here again it is not very clear whether he is recording a fact or laying down a principle; it is a great pity that in the latter case he should not have developed his idea. This branch of the subject is of immense importance, and Mr. Besant's few words point to considerations of the widest reach, not to be lightly disposed of. He will have treated the art of fiction but superficially who is not prepared to go every inch of the way that these considerations will carry him. It is for this reason that at the beginning of these remarks I was careful to notify the reader that my reflections on so large a theme have no pretension to be exhaustive. Like Mr. Besant, I have left the question of the morality of the novel till the last, and at the last I find I have used up my space. It is a question surrounded with difficulties, as witness the very first that meets us, in the form of a definite question, on the threshold. Vagueness, in such a discussion, is fatal, and what is the meaning of your morality and your conscious moral purpose? Will you not define your terms and explain how (a novel being a picture) a picture can be either moral or immoral? You wish to paint a moral picture or carve a moral statue; will you not tell us how you would set about it? We are discussing the Art of Fiction; questions of art are questions (in the widest sense) of execution; questions of morality are quite another affair, and will you not let us see how it is that you find it so easy to mix them up? These things are so clear to Mr. Besant that he has deduced from them a law which he sees embodied in English Fiction and which is 'a truly admirable thing and a great cause for congratulation.' It is a great cause for congratulation, indeed, when such thorny problems become as smooth as silk. I may add that, in so far as Mr. Besant perceives that in point of fact English Fiction has addressed itself preponderantly to these delicate questions, he will appear to many people to have made a vain discovery. They will have been positively struck, on the contrary, with the moral timidity of the usual English novelist; with his (or with her) aversion to face the difficulties with which, on every side, the treatment of reality bristles. He is apt to be extremely shy (whereas the picture that Mr. Besant draws is a picture of boldness), and the sign of his work, for the most part, is a cautious silence on certain subjects. In the English novel (by which I mean the American as well), more than in any other, there is a traditional difference between that which people know and that which they agree to admit that they know, that which they see and that which they speak of, that which they feel to be a part of life and that which they allow to enter into literature. There is the great difference, in short, between what they talk of in conversation and what they talk of in print. The essence of moral energy is to survey the whole field, and I should directly reverse Mr. Besant's remark, and say not that the English novel has a purpose, but that it has a diffidence. To what degree a purpose in a work of art is a source of corruption I shall not attempt to inquire; the one that seems to me least dangerous is the purpose of making a perfect work. As for our novel, I may say, lastly, on this score, that, as we find it in England to-day, it strikes me as addressed in a large degree to 'young people,' and that this in itself constitutes a presumption that it will be rather shy. There are certain things which it is generally agreed not to discuss, not even to mention, before young people. That is very well, but the absence of discussion is not a symptom of the moral passion. The purpose of the English novel—'a truly admirable thing, and a great cause for congratulation'—strikes me, therefore, as rather negative.

There is one point at which the moral sense and the artistic sense lie very near together; that is, in the light of the very obvious truth that the deepest quality of a work of art will always be the quality of the mind of the producer. In proportion as that mind is rich and noble will the novel, the picture, the statue, partake of the substance of beauty and truth. To be constituted of such elements is, to my vision, to have purpose enough. No good novel will ever proceed from a superficial mind; that seems to me an axiom which, for the artist in fiction, will cover all needful moral ground; if the youthful aspirant take it to heart it will illuminate for him many of the mysteries of 'purpose.' There are many other useful things that might be said to him, but I have come to the end of my article, and can only touch them as I pass. The critic in the *Pall Mall Gazette*, whom I have already quoted, draws attention to the danger, in speaking of the art of fiction, of generalizing. The danger that he has in mind is rather, I imagine, that of particularizing, for there are some comprehensive remarks which, in addition to those embodied in Mr. Besant's suggestive lecture, might, without fear of misleading him, be addressed to the ingenuous student. I should remind him first of the magnificence of the form that is open to him, which offers to sight so few restrictions and such innumerable opportunities. The other arts, in comparison, appear confined and hampered; the various conditions under which they are exercised are so rigid and definite. But the only condition that I can think of attaching to the composition of the novel is, as I have already said, that it be interesting. This freedom is a splendid privilege, and the first lesson of the young novelist is to learn to be worthy of it. 'Enjoy it as it deserves,' I should say to him; 'take possession of it, explore it to its utmost extent, reveal it, rejoice in it. All life belongs to you, and don't listen either to those who would shut you up into corners of it and tell you that it is only here and there that art inhabits, or to those who would persuade you that this heavenly messenger wings her way outside of life altogether, breathing a superfine air and turning away her head from the truth of things. There is no impression of life, no manner of seeing it and feeling it, to which the plan of the novelist may not offer a place; you have only to remember that talents so dissimilar as those of Alexandre Dumas and Jane

Austen, Charles Dickens`and Gustave Flaubert, have worked in this field with equal glory. Don't think too much about optimism and pessimism ; try and catch the colour of life itself. In France to-day we see a prodigious effort (that of Emile Zola, to whose solid and serious work no explorer of the capacity of the novel can allude without respect), we see an extraordinary effort vitiated by a spirit of pessimism on a narrow basis. M. Zola is magnificent, but he strikes an English reader as ignorant ; he has an air of working in the dark ; if he had as much light as energy his results would be of the highest value. As for the aberrations of a shallow optimism, the ground (of English fiction especially) is strewn with their brittle particles as with broken glass. If you must indulge in conclusions let them have the taste of a wide knowledge. Remember that your first duty is to be as complete as possible—to make as perfect a work. Be generous and delicate, and then, in the vulgar phrase, go in !'

HENRY JAMES.

John M. Robertson

"Mr. Howells' Novels"

Westminster Review 122 (October 1884), 347–75

ART. II.—MR. HOWELLS' NOVELS.

SO much has been made in the mother-country of the challenge to America to produce a distinctively American poet, that it is rather puzzling to find almost no record of a similar demand for a fictionist. The explanation which first offers itself is that for a generation back the unique genius of Hawthorne has forestalled any such requirement; but the method of Hawthorne, rare and exquisite as it is, and concerned as it is in large part with American subjects, does not at all obviously realize what British critics might be conceived to expect from an American; and if it did, there would still be the question why so much stress was laid on the demand for a poet if it were admitted that America had produced a great and national novelist. Did not the existence of the novelist prove all that the desiderated poet was to attest? Or could it be that the challenge about the poet was so essentially puerile that it might have been met by the appearance of one whose grade in the company of singers should be no higher than that of Fenimore Cooper among writers of fiction, provided he had an equal endowment of nationalism? The problem fosters uneasy speculation as to whether the critical British patriot has of recent years felt forced to silence by the product of Joaquin Miller rather than by that of Walt Whitman. However that may be, it is certain that no English journalist will in these days seek to humble Americans by discussing the novelists of the States. Whatever *genre* be conceived by Whitmanites or the *Times* as the ideally American, it must be allowed that two such writers as Mr. Henry James and Mr. W. D. Howells have an art, a method, and a material of their own. Mr. James, while not following British models—unless he be held to have imitated "Daniel Deronda" in his "Portrait of a Lady"—has perhaps a somewhat undue tendency to take his characters to Europe; and there is a certain suggestiveness in this style of announcing one of his recent magazine stories :—" It belongs to the 'International' series, the scene shifting from London to New York, and back to London. Lady Barberina is the daughter of an English nobleman, who engages the affections of a young American physician, who is the heir to millions." Mr. James has indeed a way of devoting himself to the society of aliens who neither toil nor spin. But there is no such reproach against Mr. Howells. That writer, though he has made use of his acquaintance with Venice in several stories, is not only above the weakness of adorning his books with the English aristocracy, but is at pains to indicate his distinctively American attitude by his treatment of the English personages in his narratives. If Mr. Howells wants to introduce a particularly vulgar figure, or to set off the refinement and intelligence of his leading characters, he does so by bringing forward one or more members of the English nation, or, at a pinch, a Canadian, who shall be adequately ill-bred or good-naturedly stupid; and when that plan is not altogether convenient, he is likely to succeed in his purpose by conveying the idea that a particular sample of American manners is a copy from the English. Englishmen will hardly think of charging such an artist with deficiency in nationalness.

Mr. Howells, however, is too likeable an author to be classified on the strength merely of such a small peculiarity as that. It is probable that a feeling of personal attraction to the writer is about as common a result of reading his books here as it appears to be in the States. If the sincerest compliment we can pay an author is that of reading his books in quick succession, there can be little doubt that Mr. Howells has had as friendly a reception from the British public within the past two or three years as he could well wish; the attractions of Mr. Douglas's pocket edition combining with those of the novelist's style, humour, and piquant narrative to lead even temperate novel-readers into prolonged dissipation. An English reader, in whatever school his taste may have been formed, unless it shall have been the sensational, is likely to find something refreshing and stimulating in Mr. Howells' stories, and even the amateur of deep-laid plots may learn from them to relish better things. Here there are no mysterious crimes; no studies in circumstantial evidence; no staggering surprises; few rescues, and these quite ordinary. The novelist has gone beyond George Eliot in his abandonment of plot and intrigue, and challenges us to try how a dexterously-handled love-story will do on its own basis. And for a while it undoubtedly does very well indeed. These stories of light and lightly-treated incident, with their accidental meetings of young people which are the beginnings of loves that run, in most cases, with a ripple which to an old-fashioned romancer would represent the merest smoothness, but is to the ordinary reader a sufficiently palpitating series of anxieties; loves which come to nothing and loves which end in marriage; loves under peculiar and loves under ordinary circumstances, always with some environment of cleverly observed and deftly drawn characters, and generally an interesting pictorial background—in all respects they are readable and appetizing. It is only after the charm of the humour and the artist's self-possession has become quite familiar, after interest in the love-stories and satisfaction in the minor character-drawing have passed into retrospection and suffusive musing, that a sense of anything being lacking supervenes. And the reader, even if his turn of mind be critical, will probably hesitate at first to decide that his vague impression of inadequacy can legitimately be formulated into an objection to the work he is thinking of. In two of Mr. Howells' stories the theme and the treatment are alike so simple—there is so little hint of the author's personality, so little suggestion that he conceives himself to have presented to us a finished artistic production—that it is impossible to arraign him on their basis. The narratives in question are "Their Wedding Journey" and "A Chance Acquaintance," two of Mr. Howells' earlier novels. In the first we have simply the experiences, observations, impressions, and conversations of a young couple in their honeymoon —which they devote to travelling from Boston to Canada and back—the whole not properly amounting to a story, as even the pre-matrimonial history of the pair is only hinted at; and here there is really nothing to be discontented about on a final critical consideration. The author has given us a daintily written sketch, in which the personal element agreeably relieves interesting description and historical talk ; and we cannot say that he is in the least respect dissatisfying. We feel, not that the slightness of the sketch is a shortcoming, but that he can do more, and when a few clues in "Their Wedding Journey" are taken up and worked on in "A Chance Acquaintance," the feeling is strengthened ; a conviction of the author's ability being left without any suspicion of inadequacy. Thus far Mr. Howells' performances are, as wholes as well as in detail, fresh and original, suggesting an independent method and even a high standpoint ; just because they so fully realize all they seem to aim at. "A Chance Acquaintance," which remains one of his most felicitous productions, is a study of an abortive love affair between an aristocratic Bostonian and a bright, unconventional New England girl, who become acquainted on a holiday journey. It will at once recall "Pride and Prejudice" to the lovers of Jane Austen, an artist whose method has perhaps more points of affinity with that of Mr. Howells than has that of any other English writer ; though he has of necessity passed under the influence of George Eliot. Of course George Eliot's achievement, and all else that has gone between Jane Austen's day and ours, produce a pervading difference between the stories of Darcy's *tendresse* for Elizabeth Bennet and Mr. Miles Arbuton's for Kitty Ellison. Above all, the quality of American humour marks off Mr. Howells' story as a perfectly independent study and work of art, though it should be noted that Jane Austen to some extent anticipates American humour as well as American method in fiction. In "A Chance Acquaintance" the separating tendency of the wooer's social prejudices and the girl's strength of character has the effect of breaking off their unlikely looking and precipitately formed engagement; and in this and in a dozen other respects the story, with all its slightness, is a further evolved production than any of Jane Austen's. We have here the mark of the modern critical development—the implication that a good fictionist is not simply to concoct for us a story with an agreeable ending, but is to impress us with a sense of his faithfulness to an actual life which is full of broken threads and pathetic failures. Jane Austen, writing in girlhood and applying her exquisite powers with hardly any critical data before her, was content to smilingly finish off her stories in a way that would leave her tender-hearted readers contented. Since her day have appeared the Brontës, Thackeray, George Eliot, Balzac, and Tourguénief; and these have cast on the aspirant who follows them a burden of serious consideration of life which did not trouble the wonderful little woman who wrote her early stories so spontaneously in the quiet old parsonage of Steventon. "Pride and Prejudice" might or might not end "happily;" but "A Chance Acquaintance" is only a good story in virtue of the final breach between the ill-assorted lovers. Had Mr. Arbuton married Kitty, the story, one feels, would have been immeasurably less worth the telling; with its actual conclusion it represents a work of intelligent, sympathetic, subtle observation, and deliberate, finished art. The interludes of historical and descriptive detail make up with the curious little love episode an artistic whole— a story which is not exactly a novel, but is none the less a perfectly justifiable and satisfying literary product. Summing up, one pronounces it a sound and promising sample of realistic fiction, presenting as it does a quite agreeable set of phenomena, because the shifting scene is naturally one of amenity, but indicating no incapacity for handling grimmer details. We have the truthfulness of Tourguénief, with an inspiriting humour and cheerfulness which Tourguénief lacks; and to a sanguine reader all things seem possible with such a writer and such a method. It is perhaps not too much to say, however, that "A Chance Acquaintance," taken as a whole, represents, if not Mr. Howells' high-water mark, at least an unfulfilled promise of achievement on his part.

This is apt to look like saying that the novelist has failed in that he has not continued to give us simply stories which end unfortunately—that a pessimistic treatment of human relations in fiction is alone sound; a principle which the most confirmed pessimist would hardly venture to lay down in matters of art. Of course, no such principle is here advanced; but in point of fact the arrest of development asserted of Mr. Howells may to a large extent be indicated in terms of his later leaning to rose-colour. For purposes of exposition, it may be said that a love-story which ends unfortunately is potentially the testimony of a deeper thought, and consequently of a stronger artistic grasp, than are testified by a love-story which ends fortunately; that is to say, the presumption is against the latter being all through the more deeply thought and superior performance, though there is, of course, no certainty that the sad story will be such. The presumption is that the mere pleasant love-story is the device of a facile workman who produces what he knows the majority of readers enjoy, and is little concerned about giving any thoughtfully acquired conclusions of his own as to what life is like. Or, alternatively, we may say that it is presumably the work of one who does not think deeply, and has his natural habitat among the sunny shallows. This may seem a hard saying; but let any one fully compare for himself the work of a writer of pleasant love-stories—say Mr. Black—with that of a novelist of a more sombre turn—as George Eliot or Tourguénief, or even Thackeray—and say whether the former is not by a long way the less important kind of artist, precisely in respect of his fashion of making things nice. His function is the inferior one of titillating people's nerves agreeably by lightly bringing together under varying conditions persons of the two sexes, and exciting in the reader pleasurable sensations in sympathy with those of the heroes and heroines. His books are what Carlyle would call lollipops; and the feeling of his thoughtful readers is apt in time to become that of the sage over the "Idylls of the King," one of some "impatience at being treated so very like infants, though the lollipops were so superlative." It will perhaps be objected that Mr. Black has attempted work above the lollipop order. To answer that is impossible within the limits of the present paper; but it may in passing be suggested that it was perhaps a consciousness of having produced too many lollipops that inspired the attempts to produce something different. Now, the gist of the critical finding against Mr. Howells is, firstly, that after promising to give us sound realistic work, embodying both observation and meditation on life, he has descended to the function of producing lollipops; and, secondly, that when he has sought since to present the desirable realistic and conscientious work he has exhibited a lack of the necessary width and depth of thought—in short, deficient philosophic capacity.

Such a judgment is not to be passed on such an accomplished writer without a careful estimate of his excellences. Apart entirely from any question of his moral personality, Mr. Howells establishes on the very first acquaintance a peculiar claim to his reader's goodwill in respect of his perfect mastery of the language he writes in. To read any one of his stories is to experience that acute pleasure expressed in Dickens's cry over one of the " Idylls of the King "—" What a blessed thing it is to read a man who really can write ! " Felicity of style, constituting as it does the main element of immortality in any literary product, is one of the best gifts a fictionist can have ; and it is so strongly suggestive of all-round capacity that probably every critical reader on a first contact with the work of Mr. Howells places him higher as a writer and thinker than fuller acquaintance will justify, while the chances are that many will never consent to forego their first estimate. There is no describing that sense of tingling yet soothing satisfaction in falling into the hands of a good stylist. The one sensation it can judiciously be compared to is that of a skater on ice that is at once strong and pure, when prolonged experiment has removed all apprehension of cracks, roughnesses, and snowdrifts ; and when the only approximation felt to a shock is the recurrent thrill of the ice's smooth elastic strength. George Eliot taught us how full and how precious this enjoyment might be, and she added to the artistic gratification an impression of adequate mentality such as we do not seem likely to have from any one else for a while ; but though Mr. Howells must have been influenced by that great model in his pursuit of his art, he is perfectly original in his success. A general facility in tolerable and even good writing is now by no means uncommon among fictionists, but perfectly assured and accomplished work is still so rare ! The strained adjective, the *banal* or reiterated term, the overladen description, the spasmodic effort at impressiveness, the meaningless metaphysicism, the bankrupt reflection—who has not stumbled over them all again and again in his conscientious examination of the more or less promising romancers of the day ? Mr. Howells' stylistic success is that of the artist who delights in his work. In his short paper on Mr. Henry James, jun. (*Century Magazine*, November 1882), he has commented with a craftsman's satisfaction on that writer's fortunate use of language ; and it is easy to see that he is a vigilant critic of his own work, which is the stylist's final credential. Reviewing the prose of the leading English novelists of the past hundred years, to whom the debt of English literature is so great, one can see how, one after another, they have perfected expression ; the self-possessed irony of Fielding happily developing into the copiously but choicely phrased humour of Scott—seen best in his prefaces ; the wit and refinement of Jane Austen introducing a subtler precision, to which Charlotte Brontë added colour and boldness ; Dickens making his mark with his luxuriant whimsicality, and Thackeray evolving a lighter and choicer sarcasm ; till George Eliot brought into the language a new and complex harmony, in which all elements of strength seemed combined. But it is apparent at a glance that Mr. Howells comes after all these in order of evolution. Scott's carelessness is at times nothing short of exasperating ; Jane Austen's marvellous precocity could not consist with true finish of style ; Charlotte Brontë could be as commonplace at one time as she was triumphantly successful at another ; and there are more small slips in George Eliot—the most accomplished of all these—than one cares to mention. Mr. Howells, granted that he works on a lower plane, is more nearly a faultless stylist than even the last. This scrupulous care is perceived by a negative process : his adroitness and accuracy of touch compel notice every little while, just often enough to keep up a special current of pleasurable sensation. If any set of samples can convey an idea of the charm of these skilled touches, it is likely that a few will go as far as a mass.

A sufficient number may be taken from one novel, "A Modern Instance." In chapter v. of that story there is a slight but noticeable sample of the author's deftness in a sentence on lawyer Gaylord : " A man is master in his own house, generally, through the exercise of a certain degree of brutality, but Squire Gaylord maintained his predominance by an enlightened absenteeism." A different kind of power is shown in this sentence on Mrs. Gaylord in chapter viii. : " It was not apathy that she showed when their children died one after another, but an obscure and formless exultation that Mr. Gaylord should suffer enough for both." Here the impression produced is partly due to the striking character of the idea ; but Mr. Howells constantly attains the true triumph of style, that of making an ordinary phenomenon freshly appreciable. Take his account of Kinney the cook, " starting as a gaunt and awkward boy from the Maine woods, and keeping until he came back to them the same gross and ridiculous optimism," all the while carrying or finding adversity, " but with a heart fed on the metaphysics of Horace Greeley, and buoyed up by a few wildly interpreted maxims of Emerson." For the eclectic reader there is no need to italicise the piquant features in these quotations, and for others the service would perhaps be unblessed. But everybody must catch the adroit touch in the following account of a mortified scamp's soliloquy : " It was not that he cared for Kinney ; that fool's sulking was only the climax of a long series of injuries of which he was the victim at the hands of a hypercritical omnipotence." A new collocation of terms, as in Charlotte Brontë's " colossal hum," descriptive of the note of St. Paul's clock, is the sign of the gift of writing, and one has it in Mr. Howells in all kinds of manifestations. He is apt, indeed, to presume on it. Thus he describes the possessor of a stylographic pen, "striking the fist that held it upon his other fist, in the fashion of the amateurs of that reluctant instrument." The situation under description has both a serious and a romantic interest, and only the effect of that adjective "reluctant," can at all excuse the detailed allusion to the pen, which one perceives to be introduced chiefly to fire off the *mot*. But at times, on the other hand, he conveys a telling humorous touch with the happiest concision, as in the reference to the old sea-farers of Corbitant, who "had now all retired from the sea, and having survived its manifold perils, were patiently waiting to be drowned in sail-boats on the bay." Sometimes Mr. Howells' wit is as weighty as it is poignant, as in this reference to Mrs. Atherton, *née* Kingsbury, who in her younger days had thought she had "great interests," but has become an ordinary happy woman: "In her moments of question as to the shape which her life had taken since, she tried to think whether the happiness which seemed so little dependent on these things was not beneath the demands of a spirit which was probably immortal, and was certainly cultivated." The spirit of the artist in words, too, comes out in such a description as that of an "accipitral profile," in which we have a better vocable than the canonical "accipitrine," and a more telling term than aquiline; and, again, somewhat questionably, in a reference to negro melodists as lifting their "black voices." But questionable effects are rare in Mr. Howells' work; so rare that the following could hardly be paired from his books: "the old man had to endure talk of Bartley, to which all her former praises were as refreshing shudders of defamation." That is, perhaps, the worst phrase Mr. Howells has produced, and it is only bad enough to prove that he is mortal.

Such a degree of artistic conscientiousness commands respect. Such a writer has to be reckoned with as a thinker to the extent at least of his calculation of expression; and Mr. Howells has besides given us a very distinct declaration of artistic principles in regard to choice and treatment of theme. In chapter xvi. of "A Modern Instance" (i. 257) is this remark on Bartley Hubbard's compilation, for newspaper purposes, of an account of the prices and aspects of Boston lodgings: "He had the true newspaper instinct, and went to work with an intention which was as different as possible from the literary intention. He wrote for the effect which he was to make, and not from any artistic pleasure in the treatment." Then he has a remark elsewhere to the effect that Anthony Trollope's novels are tiresome; but the most notable details he gives us as to his

critical attitude are to be found in his graceful little paper on
Mr. Henry James. In that short but evidently deliberate study
he had the courage to write as follows :—

> The art of fiction has, in fact, become a finer art in our day than
> it was with Dickens and Thackeray. We could not suffer the con-
> fidential attitude of the latter now, nor the mannerism of the former,
> any more than we could endure the prolixity of Richardson or the
> coarseness of Fielding. These great men are of the past—they and
> their methods and interests ; even Trollope and Reade are not of the
> present. The new school derives from Hawthorne and George Eliot
> rather than any others ; but it studies human nature much more in
> its wonted aspects, and finds its ethical and dramatic examples in the
> operation of lighter but not really less vital motives. The moving
> accident is certainly not its trade ; and it prefers to avoid all manner
> of dire catastrophes. It is largely influenced by French fiction in
> form ; but it is the realism of Daudet rather than the realism of Zola
> that prevails with it ; and it has a soul of its own which is above the
> business of recording the rather brutish pursuit of a woman by a man,
> which seems to be the chief end of the French novelist. . . . . It is,
> after all, what a writer has to say rather than what he has to tell that
> we care for nowadays. In one manner or other the stories were all
> told long ago ; and now we want merely to know what the novelist
> thinks about persons and situations.

There is some obscurity here, and a danger of misunderstanding Mr. Howells in the attempt to choose between the
meanings naturally to be drawn from his opinion, on the one
hand, that we could not now suffer the confidential attitude of
Thackeray; and his proposition, on the other, that what we care
for is what a writer has to say rather than what he has to tell.
What is meant by " what he has to say," and " what the novelist
thinks about persons and situations ?" Is it that Mr. Howells
finds Thackeray's perpetual introduction of his individuality a
superseded method, but that he still desires an explicit, though
less free and easy, announcement of the author's views on
characters and conduct ? He had said in a previous paragraph
that there was on the part of Mr. James's readers, in regard to
Daisy Miller, a " mistake as to his attitude," a " confusion of
his point of view with his private opinion;" and that " they
would have liked him better if he had been a worse artist—
if he had been a little more confidential." We are either
witnessing a confusion of thought or a very subtle piece of
metaphysicizing—one fears, the former.

> No other novelist [says Mr. Howells a little further on], except
> George Eliot, has dealt so largely in analysis of motive, has so fully
> explained and commented on the springs of action in the persons of
> the drama, both before and after the facts. These novelists are more

alike than any others in their processes, but with George Eliot an ethical purpose is dominant, and with Mr. James an artistic purpose.

This is clearer, but it does not clear up the other passages. Is it meant than an author becomes " confidential," and accordingly primitive, when he harbours an ethical purpose; and that the true artist takes up some " point of view " which does not give the clue to his ethics or his " private opinion ? " Is George Eliot, after all, classed with Thackeray as " confidential ? " She was indeed confidential enough. Mr. Howells must excuse us if we cannot follow the logic of his criticism. Though we give it up as a whole, however, the different propositions remain interesting for us, and may fitly be discussed in the course of further consideration of his books.

It is important to think out that distinction between artistic and ethical purpose in a novelist's analysis of, and comment on, the motives of his characters. We may range alongside of it the distinction between the newspaper intention and the literary intention; though one's inclination is to dismiss the latter at once as superficial. According to this definition, the newspaper intention is in its degree a form of ethical purpose ; the latter terms presumably meaning a desire to move the reader to an act of moral judgment and influence his conduct. It would follow that Mr. James writes, not with any wish to make a moral impression on his readers, but rather for the sake of the satisfaction he finds in his study and his art. Now, it is tolerably certain that artists of every description, whatever pleasure they may have in the practice of their art, require appreciation to make their contentment anything like complete ; and it may reasonably be assumed that neither Mr. Howells nor Mr. James can be quite satisfied without that advantage. Mr. James, in his paper on Alphonse Daudet (*Century Magazine*, August 1883), as it happens, gives us his own idea of the nature of a novelist's intention, demurring to the definition of Mr. Charles Dudley Warner, that the object of the novel is to entertain.

I should put the case differently [says Mr. James] ; I should say that the main object of the novel is to represent life. I cannot understand any other motive for combining imaginary incidents, and I do not perceive any other measure of the value of such combinations. The *effect* of a novel—the effect of any work of art—is to entertain ; but that is a very different thing. The success of a work of art, to my mind, may be measured by the degree to which it produces a certain illusion ; that illusion makes it appear for the time that we have lived another life—that we have had a miraculous enlargement of experience.

Here we are on much sounder ground. On this view, the literary artist works with his special instinct, certainly, but is conscientiously producing an effect—that is, he is challenging his reader to recognize in his production a certain meritorious fidelity, however artistically modified, to the actual; his satisfaction in his work culminating in his knowledge that his claim is conceded. The difference between a Bartley Hubbard and a literary man, then, is simply that the former is a lower species of artifex—artisan rather than artist—and is mainly concerned to know that his article meets a "felt want;" while the latter's instinct or faculty impels him to produce his article and makes him count on its being appreciated because of the instinct's existence. Both wish to produce an effect, only the literary man has a motive over and above this, which the Hubbard has not, save in the limited form of a bias in favour of that sort of industry.

What, then, as to artistic *versus* ethical purpose? It will be granted that every novelist who aims at more than narrative of adventure, works in ethical ideas, and that his effects depend on a general harmony between his views of life and conduct and those of his readers. A certain moral code is understood between them and him, and this code is really part of his material. This being so, it is scarcely possible that he should be without ethical purpose. He deals with the relations of men and women—relations which are the application of ethics, and it is essential to his success that he shall induce his readers to make a moral estimate of at least some of his characters and their actions. But it is equally essential that he shall all the while make an artistic effect—that he shall make the reader feel the story to represent life, and to be satisfactory as such representation. The fault of the "novel with a purpose"—which ought rather to be called the novel with a "moral," in the sense of the "moral" of a fable—is that it fails truly to represent life, by reason of its giving factitious prominence to a subsidiary ethical idea, and implicitly attributing the character of a central truth to, say, the proposition that private lunatic asylums need to be looked after, or that dram-drinking may lead to ruin. The statistical and other observation which leads to this class of inferences, is not legitimately to be termed observation of "life," and the stories of which they are the *raisons d'être* cannot amount to anything deserving of being termed representation of life; and even if they only receive emphasis in a story with other and essentially wider interests, they similarly create a sense of false perspective. We sum up that the good novelist must create an impression, at once of the soundness and the delicacy of his moral judgment, and of the combined width clearness, and minuteness of his view of life. Now, Mr. Howells presumably would not say that George Eliot seriously comes short in the latter endowment : his characterization of her work as dominated by an ethical purpose, is not likely to have been meant to imply that she tends to fail artistically by cause of presenting sets of subsidiary details to enforce subsidiary social propositions. It will probably not be disputed that George Eliot is a wide-seeing artist who delights in observation, drawing conclusions from what she sees rather than selecting narrowly related phenomena to illustrate restricted conclusions. What then is the significance or the justification of the distinction drawn between her and Mr. James ? It would seem to be this, that the reader of George Eliot, by a process which he still recognizes as artistic representation of life, is led to meditate on the bases of human relations ; while the reader of Mr. James, though also witnessing representation of life, finds himself left with a sense of having studied a skilful composition—and nothing in particular beyond. If this be a true account of the matter, are we not established in the position that, roughly speaking, George Eliot does for us what Mr. James does, and something more ?

It is not here asserted that what Mr. Howells says of Mr. James and George Eliot is thoroughly accurate ; what has been done is simply to assume a practical and superficial rightness in the distinction, and to find the precise relations of the phenomena Mr. Howells seeks to express. Our business at present is to criticize, not the novels of Mr. James, but those of Mr. Howells, and, with that view, to get at Mr. Howells' idea of an enlightened novelist's attitude and procedure. We are so far led to assume, despite what he has said about the stories being all told, and its being the novelist's business to say what he thinks of the people and the situations, that he believes in the policy of telling a story in considerable detail without giving the reader any decided notions as to what he, the novelist, thinks. The remark cited must just be held to mean that the novel-reader now wants to know, not simply that Jack and Jill fell in love and quarrelled, or were separated, or came together again, but what were the little peculiarities and accidental minor details in the affair, the manners in which the various characteristics of the persons particularized the familiar situation for them—the mere fact of people meeting one or another fate being regarded as a matter of no great moment. At least, if Mr. Howells does not mean that, his meaning is in a mist for us. And if that interpretation be correct, the observation under notice was hardly worth making, because in the first place the variations in character of personages, and the tracing of the consequences, constitute newness of story still, as they have done for many a long day ; and in the next place it has for generations, not to say centuries, been understood that the narrator of the most striking story did well to give his readers an idea of the temperament and character of, if possible, all the figures he introduced.

Mr. Howells' theory and practice, then, can hardly illuminate each other. It has been already submitted that, after exhibiting a capacity and disposition to represent life subtly and justly, he proceeded to produce work apparently inspired chiefly by the desire to tickle ordinary palates—an alternative inference being that his powers of observation and reflection were more limited than at first seemed the case. Now, either view must be qualified by the admissions that some of Mr. Howells' later work shows an inclination to return to the paths of high-minded art, and a deeper intelligence than is inferable from the works objected to ; and that he has done some work more deeply thought and more finely handled in parts than "A Chance Acquaintance." The novel entitled "A Foregone Conclusion" has a suggestion of a kind of strength not apparent in "A Chance Acquaintance." It indicated an instinct for searching the deeper places of the soul ; an insight that did not swerve from the study of primary passion. But the story, which is in conception a romance, but is treated in the manner of the novel, is at best only a half-success. It is interesting to note that while Mr. Howells has written three semi-dramatic sketches, "Out of the Question," "A Counterfeit Presentment," and "The Parlour Car"—none of which have been played—"A Foregone Conclusion" has lately been dramatized, and played in London. In point of fact, its *motif* is much more feasible for the stage than that of any of the sketches named, none of these being actable—that is, in the present stage of development of the actor's art—while this has a basis of effective incident. One cannot, of course, conceive a satisfactory dramatization of this any more than of any other tolerably written story ; but the theme suggests a play, our drama being further from realism than the novel ; and one can conceive that if it had only appeared in a dramatic form, some of the weak points in the story would not have been apparent. However that may be, the story is, on a thoughtful retrospect, fundamentally unsatisfactory. The variation and vagueness of the implied moral standards, for one thing, suggests weakness. At one time we have Mrs. Vervain undisturbedly counting on Don Ippolito's making a new life for himself in America ; and Florida eagerly contemplating the same prospect ; the natural inference being that they expect him to become a free American citizen. But Ferris, the consul and representative of the land of freedom, is unable to conceive such a future for the priest, apart even from the difficulty about the act of emigration. He is not merely secretly jealous; he regards the idea of a priest's abandonment of his priesthood just as a Catholic might; and when at length Ippolito declares his love for Florida she is horrified. One asks what it all means; whether we are to regard the horror as sheer feminine inconsequence; and whether an American consul would have treated Ippolito's case as Ferris did? The fact seems to be that the author saw a good *motif* in the case of an unbelieving and gifted Venetian priest who should love an American lady, and desire to work out his salvation by beginning a new life in America; but that he has been unable to control it. He wanted to rely on the priestly character as the bar to Ippolito's love; yet he has not made Florida believe that the priestly character is a bar to secular American citizenship; and even after she has expressed her horror she tacitly unsays it by her pitying embrace. Ferris, again, is never made quite palpable. Here, as in another story, Mr. Howells has sought to give us an impression of strength in a man by making him rather brutal, a device that can only be effective with very easily impressible people. In point of fact, Ferris's *brusqueries* and brutalities, his rages and misconceptions, are rather boring than otherwise; he does not fully get hold of our intelligence, much less our sympathies. On the whole, the critical reader's feeling is that the book is weakened by the element of plot and misunderstanding, the manipulation of incident savouring too much of the old sensational method of keeping up the interest. Here was a theme that would sustain attention as well as need be, without the attribution of an intermittent superstition to any of the Protestant personages; and, above all, without any need of the conventional expedients of the painter's misinterpretation of things, and the two years' interval which goes to produce the titillation of the regulation happy ending, when Ferris and Florida meet again.

With all its shortcomings, it must in fairness be allowed the story shows remarkable talent in its easy handling of realistic incident and its general newness and freshness. The talent is so great, to use Mr. James's remark on the art of Mr. Keene, that we wonder why it is not greater; and when we proceed to other works the wonder is deepened. The author of "A Foregone Conclusion" gives us "Out of the Question" and "A Counterfeit Presentment," two semi-dramatic sketches which, though they have a species of delicacy that raises them above contemporary drama, can only be classed as specimens of dainty confectionery, indicating no higher artistic purpose than a desire to secure the patronage of the amateur of the maudlin. There is no true observation of life here—only an ingenious production of amatory sensations for their own sake ; the leading characters having just the bare requisite flavour of reality given them by the author's partial use of his observation. The delicate humour and the delicate sense of style prevent the artistic unconscientiousness of the work from obtruding itself in detail ; it is all of a piece ; but when each is reviewed as a whole the sense of its essential inferiority is the more decisive. A kind of struggle against the corrupting influence of the love-story market is visible in "A Fearful Responsibility"—visible in a rather curious way. That novel deals with the perplexities of a semi-invalid American professor who, during the civil war, is working in Venice on the subject of Venetian history, and who finds himself burdened with the responsibility of superintending the love affairs of a beautiful girl, the sister of one of his wife's bosom friends. He takes the line of being desperately careful and conventional, snapping off in a spasmodic way the young Austrian officer who attempts, without an introduction, to press his suit on the professor's young guest. The story is satisfying in scarcely a single detail. After all that has been said of the independence, the self-respecting unconventionality, and the self-reliance of the American girl, there is something disillusioning in the attitude of the three Americans concerned in the affair—the heroine, the professor, and his wife. One questions whether any English girl with an ordinary amount of character, much less an American one, would have behaved with such forcible feebleness as is exhibited here by the two women and by the professor, who weakly treats the women as candid and straightforward persons, and acts accordingly. His and their conventionalism is overdone for any English-speaking community. Of course it may be argued that the story is a study of weak-minded and vacillating conventionalism ; but for it to succeed as such there would be necessary a more important heroine. We must be interested in a girl for her own sake if we are to take a philosophic interest in her mistakes. "A Fearful Responsibility" is to the extent of three-fourths just a thin, undeveloped love-story. It is a curious testimony to the calibre and the interests of the majority of American and English-speaking readers that they can be counted on to regard as the chief interest in such a story, not the character of the professor, his mission, and its upshot, but the problem of the ultimate engagement or otherwise of the heroine and the officer whom she meets in the train and at the masked ball. Now, there is evidence that Mr. Howells, after preparing for a "happy ending," was impressed by the thinness of the whole business, and sought to give the story a greater specific gravity by falling back on a "sad ending." As has been said, he may have originally projected a study of mistaken conventionalism, which would call for an unhappy conclusion; but he surely intended something different when he began the twelfth chapter. It is there told how the professor is notified that, the war being over, his old university is re-opened; that it is henceforth to be also a " military institute ;" and that he will require a "competent military assistant" for some time. The last detail is never again mentioned, and the inference is irresistible that it was a preparation for a " happy ending," in which the young Austrian officer should go to America as Lily's husband, perfect his English, and become Professor Elmore's military assistant at Patmos. If that was not intended, the detail is either an inartistic trick or an inartistic excrescence.: that it was left standing by an oversight is the more satisfactory explanation. But the deflection to a grave ending does not save the novel. Here lies the trouble in nearly all Mr. Howells' books, that their ethical significance is too small in proportion to their elaboration—short as most of them are. It was not worth our while to have all this detail and suspense as preparation for the final reflection that it was perhaps a pity the officer was not encouraged. And even that degree of significance cannot rightly be extracted from the story : Mr. Howells will not even insist on his grave conclusion. Lily after going home becomes somewhat more staid ; goes to parties as of old, but neither flirts nor marries ; after several years falls into weak health ; seems to brood on the old Venetian episode, and so makes Elmore uncomfortable for his share in it ; recovers, and starts at the age of thirty a Kindergarten school in the West " with another young lady;" and "in due course " marries, " from all they (the Elmores) could understand, very happily ; " her husband being a clergyman. The latter circumstance is perhaps meant to do duty as a touch of gloom, but it is not emphasized. We have an account of Elmore's self-reproaches, and then the author's statement that they were practically unfounded; and the upshot of "A Fearful Responsibility" is that there was nothing fearful in the matter, there being simply no reason for believing that a heaven-made match had been frustrated. We feel we have been fooled. And here asserts itself the canon Mr. Howells would fain repudiate, that the front rank is only for those novelists whose art is rounded and controlled by an adequate theory of life—a theory which makes itself felt behind all their work. It may be confidently claimed that a recognition of some such comprehensive view of life—some such working philosophy—is part of our appreciation of every novel we pronounce great. What, precisely, let it be asked, is the difference between our critical frames of mind after reading a story by

Tourguénief and after reading one by Mr. Howells ? This, that Tourguénief leaves us, as a rule, contemplating life in the light of his story, while Mr. Howells sets us considering his story in the light of life. The one work is a competently made and impressive transcript of what we feel to be the actual ; the other, a clever and charming but unsatisfying combination of some aspects and sections of the actual with the pleasant. The one writer has made up his mind about life ; the other has not.

Perhaps this last proposition requires separate substantiation. That can best be obtained from an examination of " A Modern Instance," pronounced by many people Mr. Howells' most important novel, and undeniably a work showing much talent and observation. It sets forth the courtship and married life of a young couple, of whom the husband is a non-moral rather than a bad creature—a scamp rather than a scoundrel ; while the woman has very little mind or intelligent interest in life generally, but is intensely devoted and given to insane jealousy. In many respects the study is clear and finished. The portraiture of the young people before their marriage ; the treatment of Marcia's love and wild jealousy ; above all, the account of her utter self-abandonment and her passionate appeal to her father when, after casting off her lover in a frenzy, she finds she cannot live without him—all that portion of the story is strong and true. The Bartley Hubbard of the beginning does not thoroughly consist with the man of the later story ; but up to the first quarrel with Marcia there is no serious difficulty in thinking him. One of the flaws of Mr. Howells' method, however, becomes apparent just here, in the detailed account of Bartley's attempts to sell his horse and sleigh. That episode refuses to compose with the general story ; so far from being part of the presentation of Bartley's career as determined by his character, it makes the first difficulty in our conception of him. If the young man is to be conceived as shrewd and resolute in such a matter, yet without forethought or presence of mind in his other relations, we must have as much explained to us. We feel as if the horse-selling story was told mainly for its own sake, and in the presence of the study of a personality such a matter is out of place. Even the pictures of newspaper life have the air of independent studies. The artist, we are led to suspect, has no distinct selective principle to guide him ; no clear view of his theme as a whole ; and turns aside wherever a tempting opportunity for *genre* work offers itself. Another aspect of this want of purpose is the lack of clear impression, almost up to the impingement of the catastrophe, as to how the fortunes of the couple are tending. Bartley is represented as both resourceful and hard-working ; he is shrewd, unscrupulous, and, in the main, clever. Why should not such a man succeed as a journalist? He is just the kind of man who does. The account of his life as an unattached reporter, living a Bohemian life with his beautiful and quick-witted if narrow-headed wife, might quite easily be the prelude to a happy ending. There are thousands of such men in the world—smart, non-moral, without deep feeling, but getting along quite prosperously by dint of their smartness. If one is to be wrecked there must be good reason for it; and the reasons for the wreckage of Bartley Hubbard are not good. He takes rather too much mild beer, but not enough. He is only once drunk, and the incident serves another purpose than that of bringing him down in the world. He is made to grow fat, in order, it would almost seem, to increase our dislike for him, but the effect is chiefly to make us wonder how Marcia's old passion will survive this development of corpulence in the beloved object, apart from other considerations. The mild beer and the fat, one reasons, have no causal connection with the fall of his fortunes; and yet, perhaps, we are to understand that they made him stupid. His first real piece of ill-luck in Boston is the result of a piece of knavery which he short-sightedly does not lie away, as he easily might; and which in any case ought not to ruin a knave. He ought to become a well-to-do, greasy citizen. At first he was suspiciously clever; now he is not nearly clever rogue enough. Marcia, again, is made to turn against him by virtue of a delicacy of moral sentiment which we did not expect to find in her; and the result is that her act of judgment does not seem sufficiently real, especially as it does not precipitate the catastrophe. Finally, after Bartley has begun to go to the bad through what seems to be simply a loss of his old cleverness—whether through beer-drinking or inevitable fat—the catastrophe of his leaving his wife is brought about virtually by her crazy jealousy and her own declaration that she leaves him for ever; and we are left listening to the virtuous people execrating him, scamp as he is, for an act which Marcia's provocation might almost have made excusable in a better man. Every way we turn we are in a haze. If Marcia's burst of frantic jealousy had been well-founded—as at first we expect it will prove to be—we should feel standing-ground, but that is not the case. Never was the verdict of "faults on both sides" more helplessly grasped at. We vaguely feel, somehow, that Bartley would have prospered, with his unscrupulous views about journalism, if he had not got fat, and that then he would not have left his wife; which is hardly an adequate ethical induction from such a story. The novel, perhaps, would after all be less unsatisfactory than it is if the final rupture of the wedded lives of Marcia and Bartley were allowed to give what definiteness it can to the story ; for the crowning episode of the divorce is undoubtedly effective, though the details of the railway journey, like the horse-selling passages, are felt to be irrelevant. But the sense of confusion about the Hubbards is aggravated by the perplexity surrounding the other characters—Halleck, Atherton, and Clara Kingsbury. We start with tolerably clear opinions about these people, and end by finding that they—or at least the men—have changed on our hands like people in a dream. Halleck and Atherton catch our ear at first as the moral and clear-headed men standing in judgment over Hubbard ; and the author distinctly causes us to feel that Atherton is an extremely superior personage who speaks his (the author's) opinions on the metaphysics of ethics, divorce, and other matters. But at the close we reflect that Atherton, the superior man, has married a fribble—unreal even at that—for no better apparent reason than that she is rich and clings to him, he being her lawyer ; and we wonder whether, after all, the author meant us to regard him as a rather fine specimen of humbug. Clara Kingsbury we at first regard as a serviceable grotesque ; but we find her happily married to the superior man. Then Halleck is a kind of elusive conundrum. At first he is a kind of model of intrinsic worth, who contrasts finely with Hubbard ; but as his infatuation for Marcia develops, he becomes more and more unintelligible, our interest in her being largely dissipated just when his passion begins to be fully apparent. The significance of his career would seem to be that your good, unselfish man may have his life wrecked through a blind attachment to a small-minded woman whom he once saw as a village beauty, and finds years afterwards the infatuated and jealous wife of a scamp ; and that such a passion as his may fairly account, as things go, for his abandoning Unitarianism and embracing the career of a Christian clergyman, though at the very last he is left half hoping to marry the widow. The book is summed up in the words of Atherton, with which it closes: " Ah, I don't know ! I don't know !" And yet Atherton is a man with a cut-and-dry—extremely cut and extremely dry—moral code ; which he is always exploding on us. Why, after all he has said, does he not know ? The author, we feel, does not know either ; and yet he has always made us understand that he is speaking through Atherton. We feel that his ethics is a compound of emphasized, sermonized conventionalism and vague tolerance. It is not that we are impartially left to reflect on an obscure and delicate moral problem ; we have been listening to the most emphatic deliverances on every step of the case ; and at the finish the author's confidence suddenly fails him, and he begs us not to take him at his word. The fact is, Mr. Howells cannot help

328 • *A Victorian Art of Fiction*

feeling that the fictionist's art is nothing without some kind of philosophic purpose, and he falls back on an assumption of philosophic doubt. He would fain be regarded in this case as the artist who reproduces what he sees, and disclaims responsibility as to the verdict; but he cannot escape the consciousness that by the very process of selecting certain details for us he implies that these particular details lead to certain conclusions; and he backs out with a protest that it is difficult to say what the conclusions are. We, in turn, decide that Mr. Howells has flashes of illuminating cynicism, flashes of pessimism, and periods of convinced conventionalism; that with a wide problem before him he gets confused; and that he is happiest when he is doing love-stories for the general market, though he is at times moved to aim at higher things. There are signs that he would like to make Halleck marry Mrs. Hubbard, but that he feels such a consummation would disastrously cheapen the book.

Compare these impressions with those we get from reading one of the novelists we accept as great; and the shortcoming of Mr. Howells will be manifest. We do not leave a novel of Hawthorne, of Balzac, of Tourguénief, of George Eliot, of Thackeray even, in a state of mere confusion and discontent. We feel that they are equal to their work; that they have their personages in hand; that they have a philosophy which sums matters up. Hawthorne deals with a world which he treats as a series of problems; but his treatment of each is a process of analysis which ends in clearness and contemplation. We may agree with Mr. James that Balzac's explicit, didactic philosophizing is often preposterous; but his practical philosophy, of which the title is "La Comédie Humaine," is on the whole adequate. Tourguénief's pessimism is perfectly definite and all-embracing: the note is always clear. Thackeray's man-of-the-world cynicism is equally comprehensive of his world, as, unlike Trollope, he rarely projects a personality that is not perfectly within his range; and what need is there to dwell on the substantial completeness of George Eliot's mastery of all her wide range of presentation of life? We may feel that she makes out a more regular and palpable moral sequence in things than really exists, and that she at first was a little too copiously and formally didactic; but if we set aside the question of the rightness of her judgment and the soundness of her art in the case represented by the personality of Daniel Deronda, her clearness of view over all the ground before her is undisputed. George Eliot has given a philosophy to thousands who but for her would have none. Her "ethical purpose" is the expression of her working philosophy of Meliorism—the aspect in which her sympathy differentiates her from a great pessimist like Tourguénief. Mr. Howells would perhaps say that Tourguénief, like Mr. James, differs from George Eliot in being dominated by an artistic purpose; but the true view is that Tourguénief's art expresses a philosophy of sadness, while George Eliot's sadness is modified by the impulse to teach. One essential matter is that both have a rounded conception of life, and deliberately body it forth. Now, it may well be that an artist shall arise who shall see more variety in life than Tourguénief does; who shall equal Balzac's observation and surpass him in depth and sanity; who shall transform pessimism into world humour; and who shall draw from life a wider ethic than George Eliot's; but he will still be an artist with a philosophy, not a mere humorous, catholic observer, who is satisfied to be entertained by his observations and to present them in an entertaining form. He will differ from such an observer as the painter of great pictures differs from the producer of " sketches from Nature." The power to project and arrange a picture is the painter's decisive qualification; only when he can do that is he effectively an artist.

The want of a philosophy in a novelist, unfortunately, means not merely a defect in his books as wholes; it means that his characters, when he is not copying real personages, are apt to lack intelligibility. The great novelists all possess in some degree Shakspeare's power of creating people who are not sketched from any model, but who are made of the material of human nature and have a distinct individuality; indeed, it is obvious that every novelist is making, or attempting to make, such people during half his time. Now, it is the special weakness of the novelist without a philosophy that even his best characters have his own defect; and as every novelist of necessity invites acceptance of some of his characters as effective, it results that with him we find ourselves challenged to respect a number of people who have an air of superiority, but whose superiority we have to take for granted, not being able to perceive wherein it consists. What is meant may perhaps be made clearer by taking up for a moment the heroes of Byron, and one of their modern descendants, Gautier's Fortunio. Long ago inquisitive people began to ask what there was, after all, in the Laras and Corsairs to command our admiration; whether they were deeper or clearer thinkers than ordinary humanity; and the result of the inquiry was a rather sweeping verdict as to the sawdusty character of their interior. So with Fortunio, who is held up to us as something quite above the ordinary run of his fellow-creatures: we find in him, on examination, nothing in the nature of a soul by which he relates to ours. We know that the really impressive man, in the actual world, is so because of a certain attitude towards the world, a certain kind of sagacity, certain powers and peculiarities of mind, and a certain measure of knowledge ; and we feel that if there were any real personage of whom Fortunio is a theatrical presentment we should find him, if we met him at dinner, to be a Byronic fool, an aristocratic brute, or a tedious Philistine. Gautier, of course, is not a novelist at all, and we may read him for his scene-painting without feeling it is any the worse for the entire unreality of his heroes ; and we might accept Byron's heroes, if only the poetry were better, with some of the satisfaction of our predecessors, whose taste in poetry was more primitive ; but nothing can make amends for want of thoroughness in the creations of a writer who aims at being a novelist proper. Now, not a few of Mr. Howells' men are, in their way—that is, in a different way—as dubious entities as Fortunio, and for the same ultimate reason, that we feel the author assumes their scope to be relatively large when it is relatively small, and means them to be taken as effective minds when in point of fact he has not made us aware of their minds at all. Take Staniford in " The Lady of the Aroostook," Libby in " Dr. Breen's Practice," Halleck in " A Modern Instance," Ray in "A Woman's Reason," and even Ford in "The Undiscovered Country." Ray and Libby, we feel, we are challenged to accept as effective and admirable personalities, both being credited with a fine combination of strength, refinement, sagacity, modesty, and resource ; but the moment we try to conceive ourselves as meeting them we feel there is something wrong ; that the kind of man who exists in the environment of Ray and Libby has very distinct limitations, which are an important part of his description ; and that the author has not only not indicated these limitations, but has not enough breadth of view to perceive and define them. The novelist must in some respect be above his creatures ; and Mr. Howells is really above the kind of man he handles in respect of psychological subtlety ; but it is his fate to give his own superior kind of psychology to the limited personalities ; and the result is the discontent above indicated. Libby and Ray will not relate to actual humanity ; they are the ideals of an author who is not high enough in his point of view to know how his ideals will compare with those of thoughtful people. In a similar way, we feel that too much has been implicitly claimed for Halleck and Staniford when we proceed to sit in judgment on their conduct, which is that of men to whom we credit a different calibre from that which Mr. Howells at first led us to assume in them. Ford, again, is a variation on Ferris ; a man whom we feel we are expected to regard as of forcible character because of his hardness of outline, which is indeed so pronounced that an impression of force is almost inevitable ;

but whom, on a retrospect, we do not at all feel to be strong by virtue of any inward quality. We do not find that we have been enabled to perceive the true inwardness of these persons; we do not feel sure that they have any inwardness at all; and, to put the matter rather brutally, we decide that, with all their fineness of touch and style, Mr. Howells' novels are finally adapted for a lower order of readers than those who are capable of fully appreciating a writer of the first order.

It is generally claimed for Mr. Howells that he knows and can draw women very well; and as much may be allowed—with the qualification, however, that such praise implies a rather un-flattering judgment as to the average woman. Those of us who confess we find Mr. Howells' women charming, go far to say that we like a woman to be a trifle silly; that we do not want to find in her an intellectual or even a quite rational companion. He has drawn four married women—Mrs. Elmore, Mrs. Ellison, Mrs. Vervain, and Mrs. March—of whom two, he gives us to under-stand, are likeable fools; but the difference between them and the others, of whom the same is not hinted, is only one of degree. A certain infusion of charming foolishness, or childishness, enters into most of his heroines; indeed, it is now and then a little dis-maying. In "Out of the Question," where we are professedly introduced to an American girl who is both charming and sensible, in the person of Leslie Bellingham, we find her in a tolerably serious situation—comedy though it all be—talking as a satirist might make a "girl of the period" talk. Is this an approved sample of the American girl? we ask; and does Mr. Howells feel about her as he makes us feel? He is presumably in a satirical mood, for in other books he gives us considerably different heroines to be charmed with. On the whole, it is to be suspected that critical women will not be very well satisfied with Mr. Howells' gallery of women portraits, few of which are respect-fully done. Florida Vervain is the most memorable; she has something of the "dynamic" personality of George Eliot's women. Dr. Breen has a certain factitious importance through her doctorship, her abandonment of which will probably be resented by enthusiastic women readers as no more a telling comment on the claims of women than is Helen Harkness's failure to succeed in avocations for which she has not been trained —a kind of failure which would certainly be about equally com-plete in the case of a young man similarly situated, as the author, indeed, indirectly admits. In "The Parlour Car: A Farce," again, the farce consists in the conduct of the young lady, who is a charming goose, while the man is drawn respectfully enough, and endowed with sense and delicacy, though Mr. Howells does make him tell a story of his own goodness and prowess, which, as it happens, is again made to do duty in "The Lady of the Aroostook"—a proceeding which makes us displeased with both the novelist and the young man. The main point, however, is that the superior kind of man is made to cherish the love of a charming goose while perceiving her quality. The summing-up of Mr. Howells' views about women is that their supreme business in life is to fall happily in love; and, though this is to a large extent true, there is the drawback, resulting from his intellectual incompleteness, that his young women are pretty girls falling in love with suitable young men, never adorable women whose moral natures love deepens and irradiates. We must go to other novelists if we want to think women worshipful. Even Florida Vervain is, to some extent, a flash in the pan. Many male readers will be inclined to protest that Mr. Howells' charming girls are from the life, and that the worshipful heroines are not; but surely there is a realistic mean between Romola and Leslie Bellingham, or even between Dorothea Brooke and Grace Breen?

It is clear that a novelist, whose opinion about women is that above-mentioned, will of necessity tend to produce love-stories of a restricted importance. In all fiction, indeed, the relations of the sexes figure largely, as needs must be, seeing that they rest on the fundamental fact of life; but it is in their treatment that the difference between the greater and the lesser novelist comes out; the first presenting to us certain personages who interest us as individualities, and proceeding to show how love affects them; while the other proceeds to interest us in personages by letting us know they are in love, and exciting our curiosity as to how the affair will end. The first sees love as a great factor in life; the second treats it as a delightful and conspicuous episode, thus making, after all, less account of love than the other, who seems to make it subsidiary. Thus in "The Lady of the Aroostook" we have a young man and a girl, who are psychologically blank to us, brought together on a ship; and we see an attraction arising between them by degrees. This is the gist of the story. We are expected, on the strength of the universal sympathy with a love affair, to find sufficient interest in contemplating the growth of the love of these two characterless young people, in consideration of their curious position on board ship; and such is the stamina of average humanity that most of us get led along, and along, weakly curious, to the sweet end. It would almost seem as if Mr. Howells had sardonically resolved to experiment on the popular appetite for the amatory with the most uninteresting heroine he could construct, taking only care to make her beautiful and to put her in a piquant situation without any rival. There must indeed be some planned relation between the profoundly commonplace character of the lovely Lydia and the circumstance that Staniford falls in love with her purely because she is alone among the men and he is idle ; but the story is only an extreme instance of Mr. Howells' later method. In " A Woman's Reason," finally, he has reached quite the lowest artistic and intellectual plane that an artist of his culture and delicacy can deliberately stand on. He told us that the moving accident was not the trade of the new school of fiction ; but immediately afterwards he proceeded to write a story of which a large section was sheer Charles Reade. The narrative of Fenton's mishaps and coral-island experiences reads like a calculated imitation of that great sensationalist ; which amounts to saying that it is merely superior melodrama ; and even the story of Helen's struggles to make a living, though not told in the Reade style, is only a superior kind of manipulation of the "moving accident ; " the troubles of the two lovers, who are separated through Helen's feminine finesse and Fenton's undue straightforwardness, being just so much variously exciting incident designed to make the final meeting the more thrilling. There is a closing suggestion that her experiences have had an effect on her character, but the pretence is rather thin. Fenton, again, is almost an entire failure—how nearly so can only be conceived after reading the story. So hard pressed is the author in the effort to make his hero live that he resorts to the following desperate predication concerning his state of mind on the coral-island :—

In the maze which had deepened upon Fenton, the whole situation had an unreality, as of something read long ago and half forgotten, and now slowly recalled, point by point ; and there were moments of the illusion in which it was not he who was imprisoned there on that unknown island, but the hero of adventures whom he had admired and envied in boyhood, or known in some romance of later life. . . . . All these things seemed the well-known properties and stock experiences of the castaway of fiction ; *he himself the figment of some romancer's brain, with which the author was toying for the purposes of his plot, to be duly rescued and restored to the world when it should serve the exigency of the tale.*

·It is difficult to fully express the nefariousness of the art of this passage, especially in the italicized clauses : there is a suggestion of artistic humiliation about it which tends to overlay our derision with pity for the author's straits. Enough to say that a novelist must be hard pressed indeed for something to say when he psychologizes in this fashion.

As has been said, Mr. Howells seems to oscillate between the desire to cater for the popular appetite and a leaning to higher things. "The Undiscovered Country" may be assumed to represent one of these strivings after a worthy subject, and as such it may be regarded with a favour not exactly proportioned to its final value. That, however, is comparatively high. Not only does the book give copious proof of the author's quickness of eye and discursiveness of observation, but—method apart— it is evidently the result of a good deal of thought. It is the strongest of all his stories that end cheerfully, though the eternal device of making the lover suspect a rival is employed to intensify the *dénoûment*. In none of his books, perhaps, is there less of irrelevant or dispensable detail; the closeness of the tissue giving an impression of exceptional creative certainty. In dealing with such a subject as the spiritualistic aberrations of a visionary mesmerist, however, Mr. Howells could hardly attain to a philosophic success which he has failed to reach in his treatment of more normal phenomena. To succeed in such a case would require something more even than the special pains Mr. Howells has evidently devoted to it. A rounded artistic exposition of it could only come from one who had made up his mind on the various aspects of the matter, and this Mr. Howells does not seem to have done. At all events his narrative, close as it is in texture, will not stand examination from the point of view of logical scepticism any more than from that of believers in spiritualism; his science, on analysis, leaving a residuum of rubbish, and the fashion of holding the balances between credulity and disbelief being far from arresting attention. As regards the Shakers, too, deft and easy as is the presentment of them and their environment, we do not arrive at confidence in the trustworthiness of the picture. There remains a suspicion that Mr. Howells does not fully see through and round the Shaker idiosyncrasy; that he does not clearly recognize the peculiar limitations and bias of the members of the sect; that his account of them is at bottom romantic. It is the old drawback; he is not sufficiently above the subject-matter to present it in its true relations to general social phenomena. The author who can remain at all hazy on the subject of spiritualism is hardly the person to analyze rigorously the intellectual and moral nature of the Shakers. And, to make an end of the fault-finding, there is something disappointing in the usual optimistic dismissal of the married lovers in the case of such a marriage as that of Ford and Egeria. As before remarked, Ford is not quite solid, but he has telling aspects, and marriage seems an insufficient final classification in his case. As Phillips is made to say in the closing pages: "Imagine a Pythoness with a prayer-book, who goes to the Episcopal church, and hopes to get her husband to go too!" What are we to make of it? The problem is such a grave and important one. George Eliot, one regretfully reflects, deliberately avoided it; but she did not raise it and then drop it as Mr. Howells has done here. It is sufficiently inconsistent, however, to regret the evasion of an important problem by an author of whom one complains that he is not equal to the treatment of problems calling for philosophic power; and we must just note this missing of a great consideration as one of the evidences of Mr. Howells' limitations. We may put beside it the attitude maintained towards the civil war in " A Foregone Conclusion," where Ferris's experience of the struggle is treated as just so much time spent before he wins the woman he loves—a way of dealing with that colossal fact in the recent history of mankind which seems common among Americans, whose indifference sometimes makes us forget how ghastly the memory really is. Their novelists seem to regard it as an occurrence which separated lovers, not as something which could colour men's whole thoughts on life.

But enough has been said to justify, or at least to illustrate, the charge of intellectual insufficiency against Mr. Howells; and when that is done the critic has no further ground for adverse criticism. What has been said, indeed, is perhaps apt to mislead by laying so much more stress on the artist's shortcomings than on his skill. If " The Undiscovered Country " is on the whole but a love-story with a new species of complication, it yet has value even as a psychological study. The personality of Dr. Boynton is an original and meritorious projection; and the whole episode of Egeria's unhappiness under her father's experimenting and her intense feeling for the charm of physical nature after her fever, is soundly and even finely conceived. She may be a little colourless, she may be indebted somewhat to her beauty for our interest; but she is perfectly real. And Mr. Howells has such a strong natural faculty of observation that he has put some brilliantly real people into almost every story he has written. To say nothing of the almost invariable vitality of his ladies, Dr. Mulbridge and his mother in " Dr. Breen's Practice " are vividly genuine; so is Squire Gaylord in "A Modern Instance ;" so—to take a vicious type—is poor little Hicks in " The Lady of the Aroostook ;" so, in his peculiar way, is Arbuton in "A Chance Acquaintance." Our author's technique, too, is so fine that even his least adequately thought work—if we except the adventures of Lieutenant Fenton—never exhausts the patience of a reader fully mindful of the contrast between skilled writing and the bulk of the writing he reads. Thus, for instance, while the journalist Evans, in "A Woman's Reason," never seems to come within our acquaintance, it is impossible not to relish his " form ; " and despite the confectionery quality of "A Counterfeit Presentment," it is impossible not to perceive the delicacy and ingenuity with which our palates are titillated. The touch is as light and as winning as that of Marivaux, and the effects are complex beyond any Marivaux attempted. The pathos about the death of Mr. Harkness, in "A Woman's Reason," again, has an effortless poignancy such as one rarely finds. And Mr. Howells is never obtuse; never vulgar; never fatuous : on the contrary, he is, within his intellectual and ethical limits, perhaps the most alertly, the most instinctively, artistic of American novelists.

It may be asked whether, with a writer of such eminent accomplishment, who interests and amuses us in spite of ourselves, we do well to be so rigorously critical as to condemn him for what he lacks, especially at a time when so much work that is altogether worse is popular and unblamed. When there is considered the appalling crudity of such a book as "The Gilded Age," concocted as it was by two such clever men as Mark Twain and Mr. Charles Dudley Warner, and tolerantly received as it was by the flock of servile newspaper reviewers, it may seem as if it were an ill-timed undertaking to insist on the deficiencies of Mr. Howells. But criticism can no more afford to be adjusted on such views than the high-aiming artist can afford to fashion his product with an eye to the weakness of the many producers rather than to the strength of the few. Work that claims to be worthy of the present day must be tried by the highest present-day standards. We can go back to and enjoy the plays of Marivaux without scruple ; but when a novelist of our own day works on the lines of Marivaux we cannot choose but demur. On any judicial estimate Mr. Howells must be credited with having brought something to the store of the resources of fiction ; and it may well be that he will influence the art for good. He has indicated an ideal even while swerving from it. "Ah ! poor real life, which I love," he exclaims in "Their Wedding Journey," "can I make others share the delight I find in thy foolish and insipid face ! " He is entitled, after all, to an encouraging answer. Remembering, too, how an artist is tempted, nay almost coerced, by his world ; remembering to what a large extent *l'homme moyen sensuel* and his wife make up the American as the British reading public, we may admit that Mr. Howells would have had great difficulty in resisting the seductions of the love-story market : remembering the contrast between Russian pessimism and American optimism, we must concede that he is very differently situated from Tourguénief; that he is in the stream of a tyrannous tendency to light-hearted super-ficiality. At times he faces round : he has done a capital magazine sketch (*Atlantic Monthly*, January, 1882) of a forenoon's proceedings at a Boston police-court, which blends a deep note of reverie with the light, happy strokes of description ; and we have seen that he has fits of gravity and intensity in more than one story. Reviewing them all, one arrives at a notion that this gifted, sympathetic, unphilosophic novelist, with his acutenesses and his blindnesses, his felicities and his inefficiencies, may be a link between a past school and a future school ; an intermediate type in the evolution of fictional art. But, remembering the fate of intermediate types, we cannot promise him immortality.

R.L. Stevenson

"A Humble Remonstrance"

Longman's Magazine 5 (December 1884), 139–47

A Humble Remonstrance.

W E have recently enjoyed a quite peculiar pleasure: hearing, in some detail, the opinions about the art they practise of Mr. Walter Besant and Mr. Henry James; two men certainly of very different calibre: Mr. James so precise of outline, so cunning of fence, so scrupulous of finish, and Mr. Besant so genial, so friendly, with so persuasive and humorous a vein of whim: Mr. James the very type of the deliberate artist, Mr. Besant the impersonation of good nature. That such doctors should differ will excite no great surprise; but one point in which they seem to agree fills me, I confess, with wonder. For they are both content to talk about the 'art of fiction;' and Mr. Besant, waxing exceedingly bold, goes on to oppose this so-called ' art of fiction ' to the 'art of poetry.' By the art of poetry he can mean nothing but the art of verse, an art of handicraft, and only comparable with the art of prose. For that heat and height of sane emotion which we agree to call by the name of poetry, is but a libertine and vagrant quality; present, at times, in any art, more often absent from them all; too seldom present in the prose novel, too frequently absent from the ode and epic. Fiction is in the same case; it is no substantive art, but an element which enters largely into all the arts but architecture. Homer, Wordsworth, Phidias, Hogarth, and Salvini, all deal in fiction; and yet I do not suppose that either Hogarth or Salvini, to mention but these two, entered in any degree into the scope of Mr. Besant's interesting lecture or Mr. James's charming essay. The art of fiction, then, regarded as a definition, is both too ample and too scanty. Let me suggest another; let me suggest that what both Mr. James and Mr. Besant had in view was neither more nor less than the art of narrative.

But Mr. Besant is anxious to speak solely of ' the modern English novel,' the stay and bread-winner of Mr. Mudie; and in the author of the most pleasing novel on that roll, ' All Sorts and Conditions of Men,' the desire is natural enough. I can conceive then, that he would hasten to propose two additions, and read thus: the art of *fictitious* narrative *in prose*.

Now the fact of the existence of the modern English novel is not to be denied; materially, with its three volumes, leaded type, and gilded lettering, it is easily distinguishable from other forms of literature; but to talk at all fruitfully of any branch of art, it is needful to build our definitions on some more fundamental ground than binding. Why, then, are we to add 'in prose'? The 'Odyssey' appears to me among the best of romances; the 'Lady of the Lake' to stand high in the second order; and Chaucer's tales and prologues to contain more of the matter and art of the modern English novel than the whole treasury of Mr. Mudie. Whether a narrative be written in blank verse or the Spenserian stanza, in the long period of Gibbon or the chipped phrase of Charles Reade, the principles of the art of narrative must be equally observed. The choice of a noble and swelling style in prose affects the problem of narration in the same way, if not to the same degree, as the choice of measured verse; for both imply a closer synthesis of events, a higher key of dialogue, and a more picked and stately strain of words. If you are to refuse 'Don Juan,' it is hard to see why you should include 'Zanoni' or (to bracket works of very different value) the 'Scarlet Letter'; and by what discrimination are you to open your doors to the 'Pilgrim's Progress' and close them on the 'Faery Queen'? To bring things closer home, I will here propound to Mr. Besant a conundrum. A narrative called 'Paradise Lost' was written in English verse by one John Milton; what was it then? It was next translated by Chateaubriand into French prose; and what was it then? Lastly, the French translation was, by some inspired compatriot of George Gilfillan (and of mine), turned bodily into an English novel; and, in the name of clearness, what was it then?

But, once more, why should we add 'fictitious'? The reason why is obvious. The reason why not, if something more recondite, does not want for weight. The art of narrative, in fact, is the same, whether it is applied to the selection and illustration of a real series of events or of an imaginary series. Boswell's 'Life of Johnson' (a work of cunning and inimitable art) owes its success to the same technical manœuvres as (let us say) 'Tom Jones': the clear conception of certain characters of man, the choice and presentation of certain incidents out of a great number that offered, and the invention (yes, invention) and preservation of a certain key in dialogue. In which these things are done with the more art—in which with the greater air of nature—readers will differently judge. Boswell's is, indeed, a very special case, and almost a generic; but it is not only in Boswell, it is in every biography with any salt of life, it is in every history where events and men, rather than ideas, are presented—in Tacitus, in Carlyle, in Michelet, in Macaulay—that the novelist will find many of his own methods most conspicuously and adroitly handled. He will find besides that he, who is free—who has the right to invent or steal a missing incident, who has the right, more precious still, of wholesale omission—is frequently defeated, and, with all his advantages, leaves a less strong impression of reality and passion. Mr. James utters his mind with a becoming fervour on the sanctity of truth to the novelist; on a more careful examination truth will seem a word of very debateable propriety, not only for the labours of the novelist, but for those of the historian. No art—to use the daring phrase of Mr. James—can successfully ' compete with life'; and the art that does so is condemned to perish *montibus aviis*. Life goes before us, infinite in complication; attended by the most various and surprising meteors; appealing at once to the eye, to the ear, to the mind—the seat of wonder, to the touch—so thrillingly delicate, and to the belly—so imperious when starved. It combines and employs in its manifestation the method and material, not of one art only, but of all the arts. Music is but an arbitrary trifling with a few of life's majestic chords; painting is but a shadow of its gorgeous pageantry of light and colour; literature does but drily indicate that wealth of incident, of moral obligation, of virtue, vice, action, rapture, and agony, with which it teems. To 'compete with life,' whose sun we cannot look upon, whose passions and diseases waste and slay us—to compete with the flavour of wine, the beauty of the dawn, the scorching of fire, the bitterness of death and separation—here is, indeed, a projected escalade of heaven; here are, indeed, labours for a Hercules in a dress coat, armed with a pen and a dictionary to depict the passions, armed with a tube of superior flake-white to paint the portrait of the insufferable sun. No art is true in this sense: none can ' compete with life': not even history, built indeed of indisputable facts, but these facts robbed of their vivacity and sting; so that even when we read of the sack of a city or the fall of an empire, we are surprised, and justly commend the author's talent, if our pulse be quickened. And mark, for a last differentia, that this quickening of the pulse is, in almost every case, purely agreeable ; that these phantom reproductions of experience, even at their most acute, convey decided pleasure ; while experience itself, in the cockpit of life, can torture and slay.

What, then, is the object, what the method, of an art, and what the source of its power ? The whole secret is that no art does 'compete with life.' Man's one method, whether he reasons or creates, is to half-shut his eyes against the dazzle and confusion of reality. The arts, like arithmetic and geometry, turn away their eyes from the gross, coloured, and mobile nature at our feet, and regard instead a certain figmentary abstraction. Geometry will tell us of a circle, a thing never seen in nature ; asked about a green circle or an iron circle, it lays its hand upon its mouth. So with the arts. Painting, ruefully comparing sunshine and flake-white, gives up truth of colour, as it had already given up relief and movement ; and instead of vying with nature, arranges a scheme of harmonious tints. Literature, above all in its most typical mood, the mood of narrative, similarly flees the direct challenge and pursues instead an independent and creative aim. So far as it imitates at all, it imitates not life but speech : not the facts of human destiny, but the emphasis and the suppressions with which the human actor tells of them. The real art that dealt with life directly was that of the first men who told their stories round the savage camp-fire. Our art is occupied, and bound to be occupied, not so much in making stories true as in making them typical ; not so much in capturing the lineaments of each fact, as in marshalling all of them towards a common end. For the welter of impressions, all forcible but all discrete, which life presents, it substitutes a certain artificial series of impressions, all indeed most feebly represented, but all aiming at the same effect, all eloquent of the same idea, all chiming together like consonant notes in music or like the graduated tints in a good picture. From all its chapters, from all its pages, from all its sentences, the well-written novel echoes and re-echoes its one creative and controlling thought ; to this must every incident and character contribute ; the style must have been pitched in unison with this ; and if there is anywhere a word that looks another way, the book would be stronger, clearer, and (I had almost said) fuller without it. Life is monstrous, infinite, illogical, abrupt, and poignant ; a work of art, in comparison, is neat, finite, self-contained, rational, flowing, and emasculate. Life imposes by brute energy, like inarticulate thunder ; art catches the ear, among the far louder noises of experience, like an air artificially made by a discrete musician. A proposition of geometry does not compete with life ; and a proposition of geometry is a fair and luminous parallel for a work of art. Both are reasonable, both untrue to the crude fact ; both inhere in nature, neither represents it. The novel which is a work of art exists, not by its resemblances to life, which are forced and material, as a shoe must still consist of leather, but by its immeasurable difference from life, which is designed and significant, and is both the method and the meaning of the work.

The life of man is not the subject of novels, but the inexhaustible magazine from which subjects are to be selected ; the name of these is legion ; and with each new subject—for here again I must differ by the whole width of heaven from Mr. James —the true artist will vary his method and change the point of attack. That which was in one case an excellence, will become a defect in another ; what was the making of one book, will in the next be impertinent or dull. First each novel, and then each class of novels, exists by and for itself. I will take, for instance, three main classes, which are fairly distinct: first, the novel of adventure, which appeals to certain almost sensual and quite illogical tendencies in man ; second, the novel of character, which appeals to our intellectual appreciation of man's foibles and mingled and inconstant motives ; and third, the dramatic novel, which deals with the same stuff as the serious theatre, and appeals to our emotional nature and moral judgment.

And first for the novel of adventure. Mr. James refers, with singular generosity of praise, to a little book about a quest for hidden treasure ; but he lets fall, by the way, some rather startling words. In this book he misses what he calls the 'immense luxury' of being able to quarrel with his author. The luxury, to most of us, is to lay by our judgment, to be submerged by the tale as by a billow, and only to awake, and begin to distinguish and find fault, when the piece is over and the volume laid aside. Still more remarkable is Mr. James's reason. He cannot criticise the author, as he goes, 'because,' says he, comparing it with another work, ' *I have been a child, but I have never been on a quest for buried treasure.*' Here is, indeed, a wilful paradox ; for if he has never been on a quest for buried treasure, it can be demonstrated that he has never been a child. There never was a child (unless Master James) but has hunted gold, and been a pirate, and a military commander, and a bandit of the mountains ;

but has fought, and suffered shipwreck and prison, and imbrued its little hands in gore, and gallantly retrieved the lost battle, and triumphantly protected innocence and beauty. Elsewhere in his essay Mr. James has protested with excellent reason against too narrow a conception of experience; for the born artist, he contends, the 'faintest hints of life' are converted into revelations; and it will be found true, I believe, in a majority of cases, that the artist writes with more gusto and effect of those things which he has only wished to do, than of those which he has done. Desire is a wonderful telescope, and Pisgah the best observatory. Now, while it is true that neither Mr. James nor the author of the work in question has ever, in the fleshly sense, gone questing after gold, it is probable that both have ardently desired and fondly imagined the details of such a life in youthful day-dreams; and the author, counting upon that, and well aware (cunning and low-minded man!) that this class of interest, having been frequently treated, finds a readily accessible and beaten road to the sympathies of the reader, addressed himself throughout to the building up and circumstantiation of this boyish dream. Character to the boy is a sealed book; for him, a pirate is a beard in wide trousers and literally bristling with pistols. The author, for the sake of circumstantiation and because he was himself more or less grown up, admitted character, within certain limits, into his design; but only within certain limits. Had the same puppets figured in a scheme of another sort, they had been drawn to very different purpose; for in this elementary novel of adventure, the characters need to be presented with but one class of qualities— the warlike and formidable. So as they appear insidious in deceit and fatal in the combat, they have served their end. Danger is the matter with which this class of novel deals; fear, the passion with which it idly trifles; and the characters are portrayed only so for as they realise the sense of danger and provoke the sympathy of fear. To add more traits, to be too clever, to start the hare of moral or intellectual interest while we are running the fox of material interest, is not to enrich but to stultify your tale. The stupid reader will only be offended, and the clever reader lose the scent.

The novel of character has this difference from all others: that it requires no coherency of plot, and for this reason, as in the case of 'Gil Blas,' it is sometimes called the novel of adventure. It turns on the humours of the persons represented; these are, to be sure, embodied in incidents, but the incidents themselves, being

tributary, need not march in a progression; and the characters
may be statically shown. As they enter, so they may go out;
they must be consistent, but they need not grow. Here Mr.
James will recognise the note of much of his own work: he treats,
for the most part, the statics of character, studying it at rest or
only gently moved; and, with his usual delicate and just artistic
instinct, he avoids those stronger passions which would deform
the attitudes he loves to study, and change his sitters from the
humourists of ordinary life to the brute forces and bare types of
more emotional moments. In his recent 'Author of " Beltraffio," ' so just in conception, so nimble and neat in workmanship, strong passion is indeed employed; but observe that it is
not displayed. Even in the heroine the working of the passion
is suppressed; and the great struggle, the true tragedy, the
scène-à-faire, passes unseen behind the panels of a locked door.
The delectable invention of the young visitor is introduced,
consciously or not, to this end: that Mr. James, true to his
method, might avoid the scene of passion. I trust no reader will
suppose me guilty of undervaluing this little masterpiece. I
mean merely that it belongs to one marked class of novel, and
that it would have been very differently conceived and treated
had it belonged to that other marked class, of which I now proceed
to speak.

I take pleasure in calling the dramatic novel by that name,
because it enables me to point out by the way a strange and
peculiarly English misconception. It is sometimes supposed that
the drama consists of incident. It consists of passion, which
gives the actor his opportunity; and that passion must progres-
sively increase, or the actor, as the piece proceeded, would be
unable to carry the audience from a lower to a higher pitch of
interest and emotion. A good serious play must therefore be
founded on one of the passionate *cruces* of life, where duty and
inclination come nobly to the grapple; and the same is true of
what I call, for that reason, the dramatic novel. I will instance
a few worthy specimens, all of our own day and language:
Meredith's 'Rhoda Fleming,' that wonderful and painful book,
long out of print and hunted for at bookstalls like an Aldine;
Hardy's 'Pair of Blue Eyes'; and two of Charles Reade's,
'Griffith Gaunt' and the 'Double Marriage,' originally called
'White Lies' and founded (by an accident quaintly favourable
to my nomenclature) on a play by Maquet, the partner of the
great Dumas. In this kind of novel the closed door of the

'Author of " Beltraffio "'must be broken open ; passion must appear upon the scene and utter its last word ; passion is the be-all and the end-all, the plot and the solution, the protagonist and the *deus ex machinâ* in one. The characters may come anyhow upon the stage : we do not care; the point is, that, before they leave it, they shall become transfigured and raised out of themselves by passion. It may be part of the design to draw them with detail ; to depict a full-length character, and then behold it melt and change in the furnace of emotion. But there is no obligation of the sort ; nice portraiture is not required ; and we are content to accept mere abstract types, so they be strongly and sincerely moved. A novel of this class may be even great, and yet contain no individual figure ; it may be great, because it displays the workings of the perturbed heart and the impersonal utterance of passion ; and with an artist of the second class it is, indeed, even more likely to be great, when the issue has thus been narrowed and the whole force of the writer's mind directed to passion alone. Cleverness again, which has its fair field in the novel of character, is debarred all entry upon this more solemn theatre. A far-fetched motive, an ingenious evasion of the issue, a witty instead of a passionate turn, offend us like an insincerity. All should be plain, all straightforward to the end. Hence it is that, in 'Rhoda Fleming,' Mrs. Lovel raises such resentment in the reader; her motives are too flimsy, her ways are too equivocal, for the weight and strength of her surroundings. Hence the hot indignation of the reader when Balzac, after having begun the 'Duchesse de Langeais' in terms of strong if somewhat swollen passion, cuts the knot by the derangement of the hero's clock. Such person-nages and incidents belong to the novel of character ; they are out of place in the high society of the passions ; when the passions are introduced in art at their full height, we look to see them, not baffled and impotently striving, as in life, but towering above circumstance and acting substitutes for fate.

And here I can imagine Mr. James, with his lucid sense, to intervene. To much of what I have said he would apparently demur ; in much he would, somewhat impatiently, acquiesce. It may be true; but it is not what he desired to say or to hear said. He spoke of the finished picture and its worth when done ; I, of the brushes, the palette, and the north light. He uttered his views in the tone and for the ear of good society ; I, with the emphasis and technicalities of the obtrusive student. But the point, I may reply, is not merely to amuse the public, but to offer helpful advice to the young writer. And the young writer will not so much be helped by genial pictures of what an art may aspire to at its highest, as by a true idea of what it must be on the lowest terms. The best that we can say to him is this: Let him choose a motive, whether of character or passion; carefully construct his plot so that every incident is an illustration of the motive and every property employed shall bear to it a near relation of congruity or contrast; avoid a sub-plot, unless, as sometimes in Shakespeare, the sub-plot be a reversion or complement of the main intrigue; suffer not his style to flag below the level of the argument; pitch the key of conversation, not with any thought of how men talk in parlours, but with a single eye to the degree of passion he may be called on to express; and allow neither himself in the narrative nor any character in the course of the dialogue, to utter one sentence that is not part and parcel of the business of the story or the discussion of the problem involved. Let him not regret if this shortens his book; it will be better so; for to add irrelevant matter is not to lengthen but to bury. Let him not mind if he miss a thousand qualities, so that he keeps unflaggingly in pursuit of the one he has chosen. Let him not care particularly if he miss the tone of conversation, the pungent material detail of the ·day's manners, the reproduction of the atmosphere and the environment. These elements are not essential: a novel may be excellent, and yet have none of them; a passion or a character is so much the better depicted as it rises clearer from material circumstance. In this age of the particular, let him remember the ages of the abstract, the great books of the past, the brave men that lived before Shakespeare and before Balzac. And as the root of the whole matter, let him bear in mind that his novel is not a transcript of life, to be judged by its exactitude; but a simplification of some side or point of life, to stand or fall by its significant simplicity. For although, in great men, working upon great motives, what we observe and admire is often their complexity, yet underneath appearances the truth remains unchanged: that simplification was their method, and that simplicity is their excellence.

ROBERT LOUIS STEVENSON.

"Vernon Lee"
(Violet Paget)

"A Dialogue on Novels"

Contemporary Review 48 (September 1885), 378–401

A DIALOGUE ON NOVELS.

"AFTER all," said Mrs. Blake, the eminent novelist, "with the exception of very few touches, there is nothing human in 'Wuthering Heights;' those people with their sullenness and coldness and frenzy are none of them real men and women, such as Charlotte Brontë would have given us had she written the book instead of her sister. You can't deny that, Monsieur Marcel."

They had clambered through the steep, bleak Yorkshire village, which trickles, a water-course of rough black masonry, down the green hillside; past the inn where Branwell Brontë drank and raved; through the churchyard, a grim, grassless garden of blackened tombstones; under the windows of the Brontës' parsonage; and still higher, up the slippery slope of coarse, sere grass, on to the undulating flatness of Haworth Moor.

André Marcel, the subtle young French critic and novelist, who had come to Yorkshire in order to study the Brontës, listened to Mrs. Blake with disappointed pensiveness. Knowing more of English things than most Frenchmen, and with a natural preference for the exotic of all kinds, it was part of his mission to make known to the world that England really was what, in the days of Goethe, Italy had falsely been supposed to be—a sort of exceptional and esoteric country, whence æsthetic and critical natures might get weird and exquisite moral impressions as they got orchids and porcelain and lacquer from Japan. Such being the case, this clever woman with her clever novels, both so narrow and so normal, so full at once of scepticism and of respect for precedent, gave him as much of a sense of annoyance and hostility almost as his placid, pessimistic, purely artistic and speculative nature could experience.

They walked on for some minutes in silence, Marcel and Mrs.

Blake behind, Baldwin and his cousin Dorothy in front, trampling the rough carpet of lilac and black heather matted with long withered grass and speckled with the bright scarlet of sere bilberry leaves; the valleys gradually closing up all around; the green pasture slopes, ribbed with black stone fences, gradually meeting one another, uniting, disappearing, absorbed in the undulating sea of moorland, spreading solitary, face to face with the low, purplish-grey sky. As Mrs. Blake spoke, Dorothy turned round eagerly.

" They are not real men and women, the people in ' Wuthering Heights,' " she said; " but they are real all the same. Don't you feel that they are real, Monsieur Marcel, when you look about you now? Don't you feel that they are these moors, and the sunshine, the clouds, the winds, the storms upon them? "

" All the moors and all the storms upon them put together haven't the importance for a human being that has one well-understood real character of Charlotte Brontë's or George Eliot's," answered Mrs. Blake, coldly.

" I quite understand your point of view," said Marcel; " but, for all my admiration for Charlotte Brontë and George Eliot, I can't agree that either of them, or any writer of their school, can give us anything of the value of ' Wuthering Heights.' After all, what do we gain by their immense powers of psychological analysis and reconstruction? Merely a partial insight into a certain number of characters—characters which, whatever the genius of the novelist, can be only approximations to reality, because they are the result of the study of something of which we can never completely understand the nature—because it is outside ourselves."

Mrs. Blake, who could understand of Marcel's theories only the fact they were extremely distasteful to herself, began to laugh.

" If we are never to understand anything except ourselves, I think we had better leave off novel-writing at once, Monsieur Marcel," she said.

" I don't think that would suit Marcel at all," put in Baldwin, " and he does not by any means condemn the ordinary novel for being what he considers a mere approximation to reality. All he says is, that he prefers books where there is no attempt at completely solving what he considers the inscrutable—namely, the character of every one not oneself. He perceives, more than most people, perhaps even too much, the complexity of human nature; and what to you or me is a complete moral portrait is to him a mere partial representation. I personally think that it is all the better for us if we are unable to see every little moral nerve and muscle in our neighbours: there are in all of us remains of machinery which belongs to something baser, and is little or not at all put in movement. If we could see all the incipient thoughts and incipient feelings of even the best people, we should probably form a much less really just estimate of them than we do at present. It is not morally correct, any more than it is artistically correct, to see the microscopic and the hidden."

" I don't know about that," said Marcel. " But I know that, by the fatality of heredity on one hand, a human being contains within himself a number of different tendencies, all moulded, it is true, into one character, but existing none the less each in its special nature, ready to respond to its special stimulus from without ; on the other hand, by the fatality of environment every human being is modified in many different ways : he is rammed into a place until he fits it, and absorbs fragments of all the other personalities with whom he is crushed together. So that there must be, in all of us, even in the most homogeneous, tendencies which, from not having met their appropriate stimulus, may be lying unsuspected at the very bottom of our nature, far below the level of consciousness ; but which, on the approach of the specific stimulus, or merely on the occasion of any violent shaking of the whole nature, will suddenly come to the surface. Now it seems to me that such complications of main and minor characteristics, such complications inherited or induced, of half-perceived or dormant qualities, can be disentangled, made intelligible, when the writer is speaking of himself, may be shown even unconsciously to himself; but they cannot be got at in a third person. Therefore I give infinitely less value to one of your writers with universal intuition and sympathy, writing of approximate realities neither himself nor yourself, than to one who like Emily Brontë simply shows us men, women, nature, passion, life, all seen through the medium of her own personality. It is this sense of coming really and absolutely in contact with a real soul which gives such a poignancy to a certain very small class of books—books, to my mind the most precious we have—such as the Memoirs of St. Augustine, the ' Vita Nuova,' the ' Confessions ' of Jean-Jacques Rousseau ; and ' Wuthering Heights,' although an infinitely non-imaginative book, seems to me worthy to be ranked with these."

Dorothy Orme had been walking silently in front, her hat slung on her arm, her light curly hair flying in the wind, filling her arms with pale lilac heather ; and seeming to the Frenchman a kind of outcome of the moor, an illustration of " Wuthering Heights;" something akin to Emily Brontë's heroine, nay, rather to Emily Brontë herself, as she existed for his imagination. She turned round as he spoke, and said, with a curious mixture of surprise, pain, and reproach :

" I am glad you put ' Wuthering Heights ' with the ' Vita Nuova ; ' but how can you mention in the same breath those disgusting, degraded ' Confessions ' of Rousseau ? I once tried to read them, and they made me feel sick."

Marcel looked at her with grave admiration. " Mademoiselle," he said, "the 'Confessions' are not a book for you ; a diseased soul like Jean-Jacques ought never to be obtruded upon your notice : you ought to read only things like 'Wuthering Heights' and the 'Vita Nuova,' just as you ought to walk on these moors, but not among the squalor and confusion of a big town ; you fit into the one, and not into the other. But I put the 'Confessions' by the side of these other books because they belong, in their deeply troubling way, as the 'Vita Nuova' is in its perfect serenity, to that very small class of scarcely self-conscious revelations of personality which may teach us what the novel should aim at."

Dorothy did not answer. This young man, with his keen appreciation, his delicate enthusiasm alike for purity and impurity, puzzled her and made her unhappy. She felt sure he was good himself, yet his notions were so very strange.

"At that rate," put in Mrs. Blake, "there is an end of the novel as a work of art, if we are to make it into a study of the mere psychology of a single individual. As it is, the perpetual preoccupation of psychology has pretty well got rid of all real interest of plot and incident, and is rapidly getting rid of all humour; a comic character like those of Dickens, and even those of Thackeray, will soon be out of the question. Did you read an extraordinarily suggestive article by Mr. Hillebrand, which appeared in THE CONTEMPORARY last year, contrasting the modern novel with the old one ? It was very one-sided, of course; but in many things wonderfully correct. I felt that he must condemn my novels along with the others, but I was pleased; it was as if Fielding's ghost had told us his opinion of modern novelists."

Dorothy Orme was not addicted to literary discussions ; but the recollection of this article seemed suddenly to transform her.

"I read it," she cried eagerly; "I hated it. He was very angry with George Eliot because she had made the story of Dorothea and Casaubon tragic, instead of making it farcical, as I suppose Fielding or some such creature would have done : he would have liked some disgusting, ridiculous comedy of an old pedant, a sort of Don Bartolo, and a girl whom he bored and who made fun of him. Did he never ask himself whether the reality of a situation such as that of Dorothea and Casaubon would be more comic or tragic, whether we should be seeing things more as they really are, whether we should be entering more into the feelings of the people themselves, whether we should be placing ourselves more in the position to help, to diminish unhappiness, by laughing at Dorothea and Casaubon, or by crying at their story ? I am sure we are far too apt to laugh at things already. I dare say that the sense of the ridiculous is a very useful thing; I dare say it helps to make the world more supportable ; but not when the sense of the ridiculous makes us see things as they are not, or as they are merely superficially; when it makes us feel pleased and passive where we ought to be pained and active. People have a way of talking about the tendency which the wish for nobility and beauty has to make us see things in the wrong light; but there is much more danger, surely, of that sort of falsification from our desire for the comic. There's Don Quixote—we have laughed at him quite long enough. I wish some one would write a book now about the reverse of Don Quixote, about a good and kind and helpful man who is made unjust, unkind, and useless by his habit of seeking for the ridiculous, by his habit of seeing windmills where there are real giants, and coarse peasants where there are really princesses. The history of that man, absurd though it may seem as a whole, would yet be, in its part, the history of some little bit of the life of all of us; a bit which might be amusing enough to novelists of the old school, but is sad enough, I think, in all conscience, when we look back upon it in ourselves."

Marcel looked up. To him the weirdest and most exotic flowers of this moral and intellectual Japan called England, were its young women, wonderful it seemed to him in delicacy, in brilliancy of colour, in *bizarre* outline, in imaginatively stimulating and yet reviving perfume; and ever since he had met her a few days ago, this cousin of his old friend Baldwin, this Dorothy Orme, painter, sculptor, philanthropist, and mystic, with the sea-blue eyes, and the light hair that seemed always caught up by the breeze, this creature at once so mature and so immature, so full of enthusiasm, so unconscious of passion, so boldly conversant with evil in the abstract, so pathetically ignorant of evil in the concrete, had appeared to him as almost the strangest of all these strange English girls who fascinated him as a poet and a critic.

Baldwin had affectionately taken his cousin's arm and passed it through his own.

"You are quite right, Dorothy," he said; "you have put into words what I myself felt while reading that paper; but then, you know, unfortunately, as one grows older—and I am a good bit older than you—one is apt to let oneself drift into looking at people only from the comic side; it is so much easier, and saves one such a deal of useless pain and rage. But you are quite right all the same. A substitution of psychological sympathetic interest for the comic interest of former days has certainly taken place in the novel; and is taking place more and more every day. But I don't think, with Mrs. Blake and Hillebrand, that this is at all a matter for lamentation. Few things strike me more in old fiction, especially if we go back a century, than the curious callousness which many of its incidents reveal; a callousness not merely to many impressions of disgust and shame, which to the modern mind would counterbalance the pleasure of mere droll contrast, as is so constantly the case in Rabelais (where we can't laugh because we have to hold our nose), but also to impressions of actual pain at the pain, moral or physical, endured by the person at whom we are laughing; of indignation at the baseness or cruelty of those through whose agency that comic person is made comic. After all, a great deal of what people are pleased to call the healthy sense of fun of former days is merely the sense of fun of the boy who pours a glass of water down his companion's back, of the young brutes who worry an honest woman in the street, of the ragamuffins who tie a saucepan to a cat's tail and hunt it along. Sometimes it is even more deliberately wanton and cruel; it is the spiritual equivalent of the cock-fighting and bull-baiting, of the amusement at what Michelet reckons among the three great jokes of the Middle Ages : ' La grimace du pendu.' It is possible that we may at some future period be in danger of becoming too serious, too sympathizing, of losing our animal spirits ; but I don't see any such danger in the present. And I do see that it is a gain, not only in our souls, but in the actual influence on the amount of good and bad in the world, that certain things which amused our ancestors, the grimace of the dupe, of the betrayed husband, of the kicked servant, should no longer amuse, but merely make us sorry or indignant. Let us laugh by all means, but not when others are crying."

" I perfectly agree with you," said Marcel. " What people call the comic is a lower form of art ; legitimate, but only in so far as it does not interfere with the higher. Complete beauty in sculpture, in painting, and in music has never been compatible with the laughable, and I think it will prove to be the same in fiction. To begin with, all great art carries with it a poignancy which is incompatible with the desire to laugh."

" The French have strangely changed," exclaimed Mrs. Blake. " It is difficult to imagine that you belong to the country which produced Rabelais, and Molière, and Voltaire, Monsieur Marcel."

Marcel sighed. " I know it is," he said ; " it is sad, perhaps, as it is always sad to see that one is no longer a child, but a man. Our childhood, at least as artists, is over ; we have lost our laughter, our pleasure in romping. But we can understand and feel; we are men."

Mrs. Blake looked shrewdly at the young man. " It seems to me that they were men also, those of the past," she answered. " They laughed ; but they also suffered, and hoped, and hated; and the laugh seemed to fit in with the rest. Your modern French literature seems to me no longer French : it all somehow comes out of Rousseau. Balzac, Flaubert, Zola, Baudelaire, all that comes out of those ' Confessions ' which you choose to place by the side of the

'Vita Nuova.' And as Rousseau, who certainly was not a true Frenchman, has never seemed to be a genuine man either, but a sickly, morbid piece of half-developed precocity, so I cannot admit that the present phase of French literature represents manhood as opposed to the French literature of the past. Had there remained in France more of the old power of laughter, we should not have had your Zolas and Baudelaires, or rather the genius of your Zolas and Baudelaires would have been healthy and useful. Don't wish to lose that laugh of yours, Monsieur Marcel; our moral health here, in England, where evil is brutish, depends upon seriousness; yours, in France, where evil immediately becomes intellectual, depends upon laughter. I am an old woman, so you must not be offended with me."

"There is a deal of truth in what you say," said Baldwin. "The time will come, I am sure, when Frenchmen will look back upon the literature of the last twenty-five years, not as a product of maturity, but rather as a symptom of a particular sort of humourless morbidness which is one of the unbeautiful phases of growth."

Marcel shook his head. "You are merely falling foul of a new form of art because it does not answer to the critical standards which you have deduced from an old one. The art which deals with human emotions real and really appreciated is a growth of our century, and mainly a growth of my country; and you are criticizing it from the standpoint of a quite different art, which made use of only an approximation to psychological reality, for the sake of a tragic or comic effect; it is as if you criticized a landscape by Corot, where beauty is extracted out of the quality of the light, of the soil, and the dampness or dryness of the air, without a thought of the human figure, because it is not like the little bits of conventional landscape which Titian used to complete the scheme of his groups of Saints or Nymphs. Shakespeare and Cervantes are legitimate; but we moderns are legitimate also: they sought for artistic effects new in their day; we seek for artistic effects new in ours."

Baldwin was twisting a long brown rush between his fingers meditatively, looking straight before him upon the endless, grey and purple, thundercloud-coloured undulations of heather.

"I think," he said, "that you imagine you are seeking new artistic effects; but I think, also, that you are mistaken, simply because I feel daily more persuaded that artistic aims are only partially compatible with psychological aims, and that the more the novel becomes psychological the less also will it become artistic. The aim of art, of painting, sculpture, music, and architecture, is, if we put aside the mere display of technical skill, which, as a rule, appears only to the technically initiated—the aim of art is the production of something which shall give us the particular kind of pleasure associated with the word *beautiful*, pleasure given to our æsthetic faculties, which have a mode of action and necessities as special and as impossible to translate into the mode of action and necessities of our logical and animal faculties as it is impossible to translate the impressions of sight into the impressions of hearing. All art addresses itself, however unconsciously and however much hampered by extraneous necessities, to a desire belonging to these æsthetic faculties, to a desire for the beautiful. Now, to postulate such a predominant desire for the beautiful in a literary work dealing exclusively with human emotion and action seems to me utterly absurd. First, because mere beauty, the thing which gives us the specific æsthetic impression, exists, I believe, in its absolute reality only in the domain of the senses and of the sensuous impressions recalled and reconstructed by the intellect; and because I believe that it is merely by analogy, and because we perceive that such a pleasure is neither unreasoning and animal nor intellectual and utilitarian, that we apply to pleasing moral impressions the adjective beautiful. The beautiful, therefore, according to my view, can exist in literature only inasmuch as literature reproduces and reconstructs certain sensuous impressions which we name beautiful, or as it deals with such moral effects as give us an unmixed, direct unutilitarian pleasure analogous to that produced by these sensuous impressions of beauty. Now, human character, emotion, and action not merely present us with a host of impressions which, applying an æsthetical word to moral phenomena, are more or less ugly; but, by the very fatality of things, nearly always require for the production of what we call moral beauty a certain proportion of moral ugliness to make it visible. It is not so in art. A dark background, necessary to throw a figure into full light, is as much part of the beautiful whole as the figure in the light; whereas moral beauty—namely, virtue—can scarcely be conceived as existing, except in a passive and almost invisible condition, unless it be brought out by struggle with vice; so that we can't get rid of ugliness in this department. On the other hand, while the desire for beauty can never be paramount in a work dealing with human character and emotion, at least in anything like the sense in which it is paramount in a work dealing with lines, colours, or sounds; there are connected with this work, dealing with human character and emotion, desires special to itself, independent of, and usually hostile to, the desire of beauty—such desires as those for psychological truth and for dramatic excitement. You may say that these are themselves, inasmuch as they are desires without any proximate practical object, artistic; and that, in this sense, every work that caters for them is subject to artistic necessities. So far you may call them artistic, if you like; but then we must call artistic also every other non-practical desire of our nature; the desire which is gratified by a piece of scientific information, divested of all practical value, will also be artistic, and the man who presents an abstract logical argument in the best order, so that the unimportant be always subordinate to the important, will have to be called an artist. The satisfaction we have in following the workings of a character, when these workings do not awaken sympathy or aversion, is as purely scientific as the satisfaction in following a mathematical demonstration or a physiological experiment; and when these workings of character do awaken sympathy or aversion, this sympathy or aversion is a moral emotion, to which we can apply the æsthetical terms 'beautiful' and 'ugly' only by a metaphor, only in the same way that we apply adjectives of temperature to character, or adjectives belonging to music to qualities of painting. The beautiful, as such, has a far smaller share in the poem, novel, or the drama than in painting, sculpture, or music; and, what is more, the ugly has an immeasurably larger one, both in the actual sense of physical ugliness and in the metaphorical sense of moral deformity. I wonder how much of the desire which makes a painter seek for a peculiar scheme of colour, or a peculiar arrangement of hands, enters into the production of such characters as Regan and Goneril and Cousine Bette and Emma Bovary; into the production of the Pension Vauquer dining-room and the Dissenting chapel in Browning's 'Christmas Eve and Easter Day'? To compare a man who works with such materials, who, every now and then at least, carefully elaborates descriptions of hideous places and odious people, with an artist like Corot, seeking for absolute loveliness in those less showy effects which previous painters have neglected, is simply an absurdity. The arts which deal with man and his passions, and especially the novel, which does so far more exclusively and completely than poetry or the drama, are, compared with painting, or sculpture, or architecture, or music, only half-arts. They can scarcely attain unmixed, absolute beauty; and they are perpetually obliged to deal with unmixed, absolute ugliness."

There was a moment's silence.

"I can't make out our friend Baldwin," said Mrs. Blake; "he is too strangely compounded of a scientific thinker, a moralist, and an æsthete; and each of the three component parts is always starting up when you expect one of the others. Yesterday he was descanting on the sublime superiority of literature over art; now he suddenly tells us that, compared with art, literature is an ugly hybrid."

Dorothy Orme had been listening attentively, and her face wore an expression of vague pain and perplexity.

"I can't understand," she said. "What you say seems dreadfully true; it is what I have often vaguely felt, and what has made me wretched. Human nature does not seem to give one that complete, perfect satisfaction which we get from physical beauty; it is always mixed up, or in conflict with, something that gives pain. And yet one feels, one knows, that it is something much higher and nobler than mere combinations of lines, or sounds, or colours. Oh, why should art that deals with these things be the only real, the only thoroughly perfect art? Why should art that deals with human beings be a mistake? Don't you feel that there is something very wrong and very humiliating in such an admission?—in the admission that an artist is less well employed in showing us real men and women than in showing us a certain amount of heather and cloud and rock like that?"

And Dorothy pointed to the moor which spread, with immediately beneath them a sudden dip, a deep pool of rough, spray-like, blackish-purple heather round half-buried fragments of black rock, for what might be yards or miles or scores of miles; not a house, not a tree, not a track, nothing but the tufts of black and lilac heather and wind-bent rushes being there by which to measure the chain of moors: a sort of second sky, folds and folds and rolls and rolls of grey and purple and black-splashed cloud, swelling out and going in, beneath the folds and folds and rolls and rolls of the real sky, black-splashed, purple and grey, into which the moorland melted, with scarcely a line of divison, on the low horizon.

"I make no such admission, my dear Dorothy," answered Baldwin. "Nay, I think that the artist who shows us real men and women in their emotion and action is a far more important person than the artist who shows us trees and skies, and clouds and rocks; although the one may always give us beauty, and the other may often give us ugliness. I was saying just now that the art dealing with human character and emotion is only half an art, that it cannot fulfil the complete æsthetic purpose of the other arts, and cannot be judged entirely by their standard; but while fiction—let us say at once, the novel—falls short of absolute achievement on one side, it is able to achieve much more, something quite unknown to the rest of the arts, on the other; and while it evades some of the laws of the merely æsthetical, it becomes liable to another set of necessities, the necessities of ethics. The novel has less value in art, but more importance in life. Let me explain my idea. We have seen that there enter into the novel a proportion of interests which are not artistic, interests which are emotional and scientific; desire for the excitement of sympathy and aversion, and desire for the comprehension of psychological problems. Now one of the main differences between these emotional and scientific interests and the merely æsthetic ones is, I think, that the experience accumulated, the sensitiveness increased, by æsthetic stimulation serves merely (except we go hunting for most remote consequences) to fit us for the reception of more æsthetic experiences, for the putting out of more æsthetic sensitiveness, familiarity with beauty training us only for further familiarity with beauty ; whereas, on the contrary, our emotional and scientific experiences obtained from art, however distant all practical object may have been while obtaining them, mingle with other emotional and scientific experiences obtained, with no desire of pleasure, in the course of events ; and thus become part of our *viaticum* for life. Emotional and scientific art, or rather emotional and scientific play (for I don't see why the word art should always be used when we do a thing merely to gratify our higher faculties without practical purposes), trains us to feel and comprehend—that is to say, to live. It trains us well or ill ; and, the thing done as mere play becoming thus connected with practical matters, it is evident that it must submit to the exigencies of practical matters. From this passive acquiescence in the interests of our lives to an active influence therein is but one step; for the mere play desires receive a strange additional strength from the half-conscious sense that the play has practical results : it is the difference, in point of excitement, between gambling with markers and gambling with money. There is a kind of literature, both in verse and in prose, in which the human figure is but a mere accessory—a doll on which to arrange beautiful brocades and ornaments. But wherever the human figure becomes the central interest, there literature begins to diverge from art ; other interests, foreign to those of art, conflicting with the desire for beauty, arise; and these interests, psychological and sympathetic, in mankind, create new powers and necessities. Hence, I say, that although the novel, for instance, is not as artistically valuable as painting, or sculpture, or music, it is practically more important and more noble."

" It is extraordinary," mused Marcel, " how æsthetical questions invariably end in ethical ones when treated by English people : and yet in practice you have given the world as great an artistic literature as any other nation, perhaps even greater."

" I think," answered Mrs. Blake, who was always sceptical even when she assented, and who represented that portion of reasoning mankind which carries a belief in spontaneous action to the length of disbelief in all action at all—" I think that, like most speculative thinkers, our friend Baldwin always exaggerates the practical result of everything."

They had turned, after a last look at the grey and purple and blackish undulations of the moors, and were slowly walking back over the matted sere grass and the stiff short heather in the direction of Haworth ; the apparently continuous table-land beginning to divide once more, the tops of the green pasture-slopes to reappear, the valleys separating hill from hill to become apparent ; and a greyness, different from the greyness of the sky, to tell, on one side, of the neighbourhood down below, of grimy, smoky manufacturing towns and villages, from which, in one's fancy, these wild, uncultivated, uninhabited hill-top solitudes seemed separated by hundreds of miles.

"I don't think I exaggerate the practical effects in this case," answered Baldwin. "When we think of the difference in what I must call secular, as distinguished from religious, inner life, between ourselves and our ancestors of two or three centuries, nay, of only one century, ago, the question must come to us : Whence this difference ? Social differences, due to political and economical ones, will explain a great deal ; but they will not explain all. Much is a question of mere development. Nothing external has altered, only time has passed. Now what has developed in us such a number and variety of moral notes which did not exist in the gamut of our fathers ? What has enabled us to follow consonances and dissonances for which their moral ear was still too coarse ? Development ? Doubtless ; just as development has enabled us to execute, nay, to hear, music which would have escaped the comprehension of the men of former days. But what is development ? A mere word, a mere shibboleth, unless we attach to it the conception of a succession of acts which have constituted or produced the change. Now, what, in a case such as this, is that succession of acts ? We have little by little become conscious of new harmonies and dissonances, have felt new feelings. But whence came those new harmonies and dissonances, those new feelings ? Out of their predecessors : the power of to-day's perception arising out of the fact of yesterday's. But what are such perceptions ; and would mere real life suffice to give them ? I doubt it. In real life there would be mere dumb, inarticulate, unconscious feeling, at least for the immense majority of humanity, if certain specially gifted individuals did not pick out, isolate, those feelings of real life, show them to us in an ideal condition where they have a merely intellectual value, where we could assimilate them into our conscious ideas. This is done by the moralist, by the preacher, by the poet, by the dramatist ; people who have taught mankind to see the broad channels along which its feelings move, who have dug those channels. But in all those things, those finer details of feeling which separate us from the people of the time of Elizabeth, nay, from the people of the time of Fielding, who have been those that have discovered, made familiar, placed within the reach of the immense majority, subtleties of feeling barely known to the minority some hundred years before ? The novelists, I think. They have, by playing upon our emotions, immensely increased the sensitiveness, the richness, of this living keyboard ; even as a singing-master, by playing on his pupil's throat, increases the number of the musical intervals which he can intone."

"I ask you," went on Baldwin, after a minute, "do you think that our great-grandfathers and great-grandmothers would have been able to understand such situations as those of Dorothea and Casaubon, of the husband and wife in Howells' ' Modern Instance,' as that of the young widow in a novel which I think we must all have read a couple of years ago, Lucas Malet's ' Mrs. Lorimer ' ? Such situations may have existed, but their very heroes and heroines must have been unconscious of them. I ask you again, Mrs. Blake—for you know the book—could you conceive a modern girl of eighteen, pure and charming and loving, as Fielding represents his Sophia Western, learning the connection between her lover and a creature like Molly Seagrim, without becoming quite morally ill at the discovery ? But in the eighteenth century a nice girl had not the feelings, the ideal of repugnances, of a nice girl of our day. In the face of such things it is absurd to pretend, as some people do, that the feelings of mankind and womankind are always the same. Well, to return to my argument. Believing, as I do, in the power of directing human feeling into certain channels rather than into certain others ; believing, especially, in the power of reiteration of emotion in constituting our emotional selves, in digging by a constant drop, drop, such moral channels as have already been traced ; I must necessarily also believe that the modern human being has been largely fashioned, in all his more delicate peculiarities, by those who have written about him ; and most of all, therefore, by the novelist. I believe that were the majority of us, educated and sensitive men and women, able to analyze what we consider our almost inborn, nay, automatic, views of life, character, and feeling ; that could we scientifically assign its origin to each and trace its modifications ; I believe that, were this possible, we should find that a good third of what we take to be instinctive knowledge, or knowledge vaguely acquired from personal experience, is really obtained from the novels which we or our friends have read."

II.

" I am sorry that Miss Dorothy should have been reading ' Une Vie,' " said Marcel, as he sat next morning after breakfast in the country house near the big black Yorkshire city; " the book is perhaps the finest novel that any of our younger Frenchmen have produced, and I wish I, instead of Maupassant, were its author. But I shrink from the thought of the impression which it must have made upon this young girl, so frank and fearless, but at the same time so pure and sensitive. I am very sorry it should have fallen into her hands."

" I have no doubt that my cousin felt very sick after reading it," said Baldwin coldly ; " but I think that if there is any one who might read such a book without worse result than mere temporary disgust, it is exactly Dorothy. What I feel sorry about is, not that an

English girl should read the book, but that a Frenchman, or rather the majority of the French people, could write it."

Marcel looked surprised. " The book is a painful one," he said; "there is something very horrible, more that merely tragic, in the discovery, by a pure and ideal-minded woman, brought up in happy ignorance, of the brutish realities of life. But I cannot understand how you, Baldwin, who are above the Pharisaism of your nation, and who lay so much—so far too great (I think)—weight upon the ethical importance of the novel, can say that ' Une Vie ' is a book that should not have been written. We have, I admit, a class of novel which panders to the worst instincts of the public; and we have also, and I think legitimately, a class of novel which, leaving all prac- tical and moral questions aside, treats life as merely so much artistic material. But ' Une Vie ' belongs to neither of these classes. There is, in this novel, a distinct moral purpose; the author feels a duty——"

" I deny it," cried Mrs. Blake, hotly; " the sense of duty in handling indecent things can never lead to their being handled like this; the surgeon washes his hands; and this Guy de Maupassant, nay, rather this French nation, goes through no similar ablution. The man thinks he is obeying his conscience; in reality he is merely obeying his appetite for nastiness and his desire to outdo some other man who has raised the curtain where people have hitherto drawn it."

" Pardon me," answered Marcel, " you seem to me guilty of inconsistency : Baldwin to his theories of the ethical importance of novels; you, Mrs. Blake, to the notions which all English people have about the enlightenment of unmarried women on subjects from which we French most rigorously exclude them. Looking at the question from your own standpoint, you ought to see that such a sickening and degrading revelation as that to which Maupassant's heroine is subjected, is due to that very ignorance of all the realities of married life in which our girls are brought up, and which you con- sider so immoral. This being the case, what right have you to object to a book which removes that sort of ignorance that turns a woman into a victim, and often into a morally degraded victim?"

" My dear Monsieur Marcel," said Mrs. Blake, " I quite see your argument. I do consider the system of education of your French girls as abominably immoral, since they are brought up in an ignorance which would never be tolerated in entering upon the most trifling contract, and which is downright sinful in entering upon the most terribly binding contract of all. But I say that a woman should get rid of such ignorance gradually, insensibly; in such a manner that she should possess the knowledge without, if I may say so, its ever possessing her, coming upon her in a rush, filling her imagination and emotion, dragging her down by its weight; she ought certainly not to learn it from a book like this, where the sudden, complete, loathsome revelation would be more degrading than the actual degradation in the reality, because addressed merely to the mind. Hence such a book is more than useless, it is absolutely harmful : a blow, a draught of filthy poison, to the ignorant woman who requires enlightenment; and as to the woman who is not ignorant, who understands such things from experience or from the vicarious experience gleaned throughout years from others and from books, she cannot profit by being presented, in a concentrated, imaginative, emotional form, these facts which she has already learned without any such disgusting concentration of effect. Believe me, respectable, Pharisaic mankind knows what it is about when it taboos such subjects from novels; it may not intellectually understand, but it instinctively guesses, the enervating effect of doubling by the imagination things which exist but too plentifully in reality."

"I perfectly agree with Mrs. Blake," said Baldwin. "We English are inclined to listen to no such ·pleas as might be presented for ' Une Vie,' and to kick the man who writes a book like this downstairs without more ado; but I regret that, while the instinct which should impel such summary treatment would be perfectly correct, it should with most of my country-people be a mere vague, confused instinct, so that they would be quite unable to answer (except by another kick) the arguments which moral men who write immoral books might urge in defence."

"But why should you wish to kick a man because he does not conceal the truth?" argued Marcel. "Why should that be a sin in an artist which is a virtue in a man of science? Why should you fall foul of a book on account of the baseness of the world which it truthfully reflects? Is not life largely compounded of filthiness and injustice? is it not hopelessly confused and aimless? Does life present us with a lesson, a moral tendency, a moral mood? And if life does not, why should fiction?"

"Because," answered Baldwin, "fiction *is* fiction. Because fiction can manipulate things as they are not manipulated by reality ; because fiction addresses faculties which expect, require, a final summing up, a moral, a lesson, a something which will be treasured up, however unconsciously, as a generalization. Life does not appeal to us in the same way, at the same moment, in the same moods, as does literature ; less so even than science appeals to us in the same way as art (and yet we should be shocked to hear from a poet what would not shock us from a doctor). We are conscious of life in the very act of living—that is to say, conscious of it in the somewhat confused way in which we are conscious of things going on outside us while other things are going on inside us ; conscious by fits and starts, with mind and feelings, not tense, but slack ; with attention constantly diverted elsewhere; conscious, as it were, on a full stomach. The things which are washed on to our consciousness, floating on the stream, by the one wave, are washed off again by another wave. It is quite otherwise with literature. We receive its impressions on what, in the intellectual order, corresponds to an empty stomach. We are thinking and feeling about nothing else; we are tense, prepared for receiving and retaining impressions; the faculties concerned therein, and which are continually going off to sleep in reality, are broad awake, on the alert. We are, however unconsciously, prepared to learn a lesson, to be put into a mood, and that lesson learnt will become, remember, a portion of the principles by which we steer our life, that induced mood will become a mood more easily induced among those in which we shall really have to act. Hence we have no right to present to the intellect, which by its nature expects essences, types, lessons, generalizations—we have no right to present to the intellect exceptional things which it graves into itself, a casual bit of unarranged, unstudied reality, which is not any of these things; which is only reality, and which ought to have reality's destructibility and fleetingness; a thing which the intellect, the imagination, the imaginative emotions, accept, as they must accept all things belonging to their domain, as the essential, the selected, the thing to be preserved and revived. Hence, also, the immorality, to me, of presenting a piece of mere beastly reality as so much fiction, without demonstrating the proposition which it goes to prove or suggesting the reprobation which it ought to provoke. Still greater, therefore, is the immorality of giving this special value, this durability, this property of haunting the imagination, of determining the judgment, this essentially intellectual (whether imaginative or emotional) weight to things which, in reality, take place below the sphere of the intellect and the intellectual emotions, as, for instance, a man like Rabelais gives an intellectual value, which means obscenity, to acts which in the reality do not tarnish the mind, simply because they don't come in contact with it. In fact, my views may be summed up in one sentence, which is this: Commit to the intellect, which is that which registers, re-arranges, and develops, only such things as we may profit by having registered, re-arranged, and developed."

Dorothy had entered the room, and presently she and Marcel were strolling out on the lawn, leaving Mrs. Blake and Baldwin to continue their discussion.

"What is the use of talking about such things with a Frenchman?" exclaimed Mrs. Blake. "I could scarcely refrain from laughing when I saw you gravely arguing about morality and immorality in novels with that young man, who would give one of his fingers to have written 'Une Vie'; and who, after talking pessimistic idealism with Dorothy, and going on by the hour about the exotic frankness, and purity, and mixture of knowledge and innocence of English girls, probably shuts himself up in his room to write a novel the effect of which upon just such a girl he positively shrinks from thinking of, as the morbid, puling creature said about 'Une Vie.' Do you remember the preface to the 'Nouvelle Héloïse'? Rousseau declaring that if any modest girl read the book he had just written, she would be lost? That is how all the French are: they can neither understand that their books are sickening, nor that a decently constituted human being can recover after five minutes from the feeling of sickness which they inspire. It is impossible to argue with them on the subject."

"It *is* very difficult to argue with them on the subject," answered Baldwin, "but not so much for the reasons you allege. The difficulty which I experience in attacking the French novel to a Frenchman is, that I cannot honestly attack it in the name of the English novel; the paralyzing difficulty of being between two hostile parties which are both in the wrong. The French novel, by its particular system of selection and treatment of subject, by choosing the nasty sides of things and investing them with an artificial intellectual and emotional value, falsifies our views of life and enervates our character; the English novel, on the other hand, falsifies our views of life and enervates our character in a different way, by deliberately refusing to admit that things can have certain nasty sides, and by making us draw conclusions and pass judgments upon the supposition that no such nasty factors really enter into the arrangement of things. A girl, for instance, who has read only English novels has not merely got a most ridiculously partial idea of life, an idea which can be only of the most partial practical utility, but she has, moreover, from the fact of the disproportion between the immense amount of talk on some subjects and the absolute silence on others, acquired an actually false idea of life, which may become actually practically mischievous. I have taken the example of a girl, because men get to know but too easily the ugly sides of things and of themselves; and it has always struck me that there is something absolutely piteous, and which should make an honest man feel quite guilty, in the fact of girls being fed exclusively upon a kind of literature which conduces to their taking the most important steps, nay, what is almost worse, which conduces to their forming the most important ideals and judgments and rules of conduct, in ignorance of the realities of life, or rather in a deluded condition about them."

Mrs. Blake looked at Baldwin with an air of whimsical compassion. "My dear friend," she said, "I am an old woman and an old novelist. When I was young I thought as you do, for, permit·

me to say, all that array of scientific argument seems to tend to prolonging people's youth most marvellously in some respects. You say that it is unjust that women should be permitted to form ideals and rules of conduct, that they should be allowed to make decisions, while labouring under partial and erroneous views of life. Is that not exactly what Marcel answered when you called 'Une Vie' a filthy book? What does that book do, if it does not enlighten the ignorance of which you complain?"

Baldwin shook his head. " You misunderstand me. I said to you just now that the English novel is pernicious because it permits people, or rather let us say women (for the ethics of novels are, after all, framed entirely for the benefit or detriment of women), to live on in the midst of a partial, and therefore falsified, notion of life. That has nothing to do with my strictures on ' Une Vie ' or upon any other French novel whatsoever. I objected, in answer to Marcel, that a book like Maupassant's gave a false impression of life, because it presented as a literary work—that is to say, as something which we instinctively accept as a generalization, as a lesson—what is in truth a mere accidental, exceptional heaping up of revolting facts, as little like a generalization of life as a humpbacked dwarf is like a figure in a book of artistic anatomy; and I objected to it still more because, like nine out of ten French novels, it dragged the imagination over physical details with which the imagination has no legitimate connection, which can only enervate, soil, and corrupt it ; because, as I said, it gave an intellectual value to facts with which the intellect cannot deal with the very smallest profit in the world. I said just now that, in attacking the French novel, I felt the disadvantage of not being able to do so in the name of the English novel; at present the case is exactly reversed : I feel the difficulty of attacking the restrictions of the English novel, because the excesses of the French novel are staring me in the face. I assure you that one pays a price for the satisfaction of remaining independent between two rival systems of novel-writing, as one does for remaining independent between two rival political or religious parties : the price of being continually isolated and continually in antagonism ; dragged, or rather pushed away, from side to side, sickened, insulted in one's own mind, told by oneself that one is narrow-minded and immoral by turns. I know that, if I wrote a novel, it would be laughed at as stuff for school-girls by my French and Italian friends, and howled down as unfit for family reading by my own country-people."

" Very likely," answered Mrs. Blake, " and it would serve you right for not having the courage to decide boldly between the timidity of the English and the shamelessness of the French."

" I do decide. I decide boldly that both are in the wrong. I cannot admit that a man should give his adherence to either party if he think each represents an excess. At that rate, it would be impossible ever to form a third party in whom justice should reside, and things would always go on swinging from one absurdity or one evil to the other. I see that you consider me already as a partisan of the French novel. Permit me to say that I would rather that the English novel were reduced to the condition of Sunday reading for girls of twelve than that such a novel as Maupassant's 'Une Vie' or Gautier's 'Mademoiselle de Maupin' should be written in this country. I tell you frankly that I can scarcely think of a dozen modern French novels in which I should not like to cut out whole passages, sometimes whole chapters, from Balzac to Daudet. Let me explain myself, and recapitulate what I consider the sins of the modern French novel. One of these, fortunately rare, but gaining ground every day, can be dismissed at once: I mean the allusion to particular kinds of evil which are so exceptional and abnormal that any practical advantage derivable from knowledge of them must inevitably be utterly outweighed by the disadvantage of introducing into the mind vague and diseased suspicions. The other principal sins of modern French novelists are, to my mind, first: the presentation of remarkable evil without any comment on the part of the author, or without any presentation of remarkable good to counterbalance, by its moral and æsthetical stimulus, the enervating effect of familiarity with evil. The sight of evil is not merely necessary, if evil is to diminish; it is wholesome, if it awakens indignation: it is good for us to maintain our power of taking exception, of protesting, of hating; it is good for us, in moral matters, to have the instinct of battle. But this becomes impossible if evil is represented as the sole occupant of this earth: in that case we no longer have any one to fight for, and we run the risk of forgetting how to fight for ourselves. So much for the demoralizing effect of the pessimistic misrepresentation, or at all events the representation of an unfairly selected specimen of life. It distinctly diminishes our energies for good. The other, and I decidedly think even worse, great sin of French novelists is their habit of describing the physical sides of love, or of what people call love, whether it be socially legitimate or socially illegitimate. Such descriptions are absolutely unnecessary for the psychological completeness of their work, since, as I said to Marcel, they drag the mind and the intellectual emotions into regions below their cognizance, and cram them with impressions which they can never digest, which remain as a mere foul nuisance; besides, by stimulating instincts which require not stimulation, but repression, they entirely betray the mission of all intellectual work, which is to develop the higher sides of our nature at the expense of the lower. There is not a single description of this kind which might not most advantageously be struck out, and I could have gone on my knees to

Flaubert to supplicate him to suppress whole passages and pages of
'Madame Bovary,' which I consider a most moral and useful novel.
I don't think you yourself would be more rigorous in dealing with
the French novel."

Mrs. Blake looked puzzled. "I confess I can't well conceive
'Madame Bovary' with those parts left out," she said, "nor do I
clearly understand, since you are so uncompromising with the
French novel, why in the world you cannot rest satisfied with the English one. You seem to me to be merely removing its limits in order
to fence the French novel round with them. What do you want?"

"I want absolute liberty of selection and treatment of subjects to
the exclusion of all abnormal suggestion, of all prurient description,
and of all pessimistic misrepresentation. I want the English novelist
to have the right of treating the social and moral sides of all relations in life, as distinguished from treating their physical sides. I
want him to deal with all the situations in which a normal human
soul, as distinguished from a human body, can find itself. I want,
in short, that the man or woman who purports to show us life in a
manner far more minute and far more realistic than the poet, should
receive the same degree of liberty of action as the poet."

"As Swinburne in the first series of 'Poems and Ballads'?" asked
Mrs. Blake, with a sneer.

Baldwin looked quite angry. "If people are irrational, is that my
fault?" he exclaimed. "You know perfectly well that if I condemn
Maupassant, and Daudet, and Zola, I condemn Swinburne, in the
poems you allude to, a hundred times worse, because he has no possible moral intention to plead, because his abominations are purely
artistic. The liberty which I ask for the English novelist is the
liberty which is given to a poet like Browning, or Browning's wife—
the liberty in the choice of subject which we would none of us deny
to Shakespeare. Does the English public disapprove of 'The Ring
and the Book,' of 'Aurora Leigh,' of the plot of 'Othello' or of
'Measure for Measure'? Well, ask yourself what the English
public would say of a novelist who should treat 'Othello' or
'Measure for Measure,' who should venture upon writing 'Aurora
Leigh' or 'The Ring and the Book,' in prose. Let us look
a moment at this last. You will not, I suppose, deny that it is
one of the most magnificent and noble works of our day; to my
mind, with the exception perhaps of the 'Misérables,' by far the
most magnificent and the most noble. Now the plot of 'The Ring
and the Book' is one which no English novelist would dare to
handle; Mudie would simply refuse to circulate a novel the immense
bulk of which consisted in the question, discussed and rediscussed by
half-a-dozen persons : Has there been adultery between Pompilia and
Caponsacchi? Has Guido Franceschini tried to push his wife into

dishonour, or has he been dishonoured by his wife? Ask yourself what would have been the fate of this book had it been written by an unknown man in prose. Every newspaper critic would have shrieked that the situation was intolerable, and that the mind of the reader had been dragged through an amount of evil suggestion which no height of sanctity in Pompilia or Caponsacchi could possibly compensate. I foresee your answer: you are going to rejoin that poetry addresses a select, a higher, more moral, more mature public than does the novel; that the poet, therefore, may say a great deal where the novelist must hold his tongue. Is it not so? Well, to this I can only answer (forgive me, for you are a novelist yourself) that I would rather never put pen to paper than be a novelist upon such terms. What, is a man or woman who feels and understands and represents, as strongly and keenly and clearly as any poet, to be thrust into an inferior category merely because he or she happens to write in prose instead of writing in verse? Is the novel, the one great literary form produced by our age, as the drama and the epic were produced by other ages, to appeal to a public of which we are to take for granted that it is so infinitely less mature, so infinitely less intelligent, and less clean-minded than the public of the poet? A public of half-grown boys or girls, too silly to understand the bearings of things; a public of depraved men and women, in whom every suggestion of evil will awake, not invigorating indignation, but a mere disgusting and dangerous response? Tell me: is the novelist to confess that he addresses a public too foolish and too base to be addressed plainly?"

Mrs. Blake did not answer for a minute. In her youth, while she had still believed in the nobility of mankind, she had written a novel which had been violently attacked as immoral; and ever since, in proportion as her opinion of men and women had become worse and worse, she had carefully avoided what she called "sailing too near the wind;" a woman, the morality, as people called it, of whose books was due to deep moral scepticism, in the same way that the decorum, the safety, of certain great cities is due to the State's acquiescence in the existence of shameful classes.

"That's all very fine," she answered, "in theory; but look at the practical result of letting novelists treat certain subjects in a pure-minded way; you have it in France. In order to prevent people getting to the thin ice, we must forbid their going on to the pond; we must fence it round and write up 'No trespassing allowed.' Believe me, were the English novelist permitted to write a 'Ring and the Book' or an 'Aurora Leigh' in prose, he would have written 'Une Vie' or 'Nana' before the year was out."

Baldwin shook his head. "You are entirely mistaken," he said; "these novels are, could not be, the result of greater liberty

being given to the English novel, for they are not the result of
the liberty given to the French novelist. They are the result
simply of the demoralization of France, and of all nations influenced by France, in certain matters: a demoralization due
partly, perhaps, to a habit engrained in the race; partly, most
certainly, to the abominable system of foreign female education
and of foreign marriage; due, in short, to the fact of French
civilization (and under the head of French I include Italian, Spanish,
and Russian) being to a much greater extent a masculine civilization,
made by men for men, and therefore without the element of chastity
which women have elaborated throughout the centuries, and which
only women can diffuse. The French may not be more licentious
than the English; but they are less ashamed of licentiousness, or,
rather, not ashamed of it at all; and when I say the French I mean
the Latin peoples and the Russians and Poles as well. If you had
lived abroad as much as I have, you would know that the incidents
which revolt us most in French novels are the incidents which
are taken as matter of course in French-speaking countries, that
the allusions and discussions which seem to us most intolerable
are made freely wherever, out of the presence of unmarried women,
French or Italian is spoken. No thoroughbred English person—at
least, no thoroughbred Englishwoman—can have a conception of the
perfect simplicity, the innocence of heart I might almost say, with
which French and Italian and Russian women, absolutely virtuous in
their conduct and even theoretically opposed to vice, bandy about
suggestions, suspicions, accusations, which would make an Englishman's hair stand on end. There is, in what I may call the French
world, a positive habit of putting nasty constructions upon things,
which is as striking in its way as our English habit of always pretending that such a thing as vice cannot exist among our respectable
neighbours, a perfect Philistinism—or even Pharisaism—of evil, as
conventional as our Philistinism of good. The immorality of the
French novel is simply the immorality of French society."

"And you think," asked Mrs. Blake, sceptically, "that English
society is not sufficiently immoral to produce, if allowed to do so, a
French novel? My poor Baldwin!"

"I think so, most certainly. And I think that if English society
were sufficiently immoral to produce a French novel, the sooner it
did so the better; for in that case our English novel would be
almost the worst sign of our weakness and depravity—a white leprosy
of hypocrisy and cowardice. If England were sufficiently immoral
to produce a French novel, and restrained from so doing merely by
conventional reasons, why the whole of our nation would simply
be no better than a convent-bred young French girl of whom I
heard lately, who was not permitted to go to a ball for fear of meet-

ing young men, and who slipped out every night her mother was at a party, and took a solitary walk on the boulevards."

"Speaking of girls, there is your cousin walking along the road with Marcel," interrupted Mrs. Blake. "I think, considering the sort of young ladies to whom, according to his novels, he is accustomed, it would be as well that we should accompany these representatives of a moral and an immoral civilization on their walk."

Baldwin laughed. "You are more French than Marcel himself!" he exclaimed.

Baldwin and Mrs. Blake had soon overtaken the two young people on the road which, leading to a patch of moor that had got enclosed among the pasture land, wound along the round hills, covered with grass and corn and park land, above the big manufacturing city, which lay, wrapped in grey fog, with its hundreds of chimneys smoking away, invisible in the valley. The morning was fine; one appeared to be walking in the sunshine, feeling it on one's back and accompanied by one's shadow; but this sunlit patch extended only a few paces around one, and moved on as one moved, leaving all the rest of the earth veiled in a dense and not at all luminous mist of blackish grey—of the grey in which there is no blue at all, but which seems like a mere dilution of black; the grey of coal-smoke, heavy all round, but perceptibly thickening and gaining blackness in one spot, where the hidden chimneys of the black city slowly poured their blackish-grey smoke-wreaths into the blackish-grey sky.

"Oh, how can you write about such women," Dorothy was saying to Marcel, "and write about them so quietly—look at them and paint them as if they were merely a curious effect of light, merely a strange sky like this one?"

"What else are they?" answered Marcel. "I mean, what else can they be to an artist or a psychologist? We cannot destroy such women because there are other women, like you, Miss Dorothy, who are all that they are not, any more than we can forbid this smoke, this fog, to exist because there are mornings full of light, and breeze, and freshness. We cannot prevent their existing, and cannot hide from ourselves that as this fog, this smoke, has beauties strange and eerie, which make it valuable to a painter; so also such women, weak, perverse, heartless, destructive, have a value, a strange unhealthy charm for the imagination."

There was a brief silence; then Baldwin and Mrs. Blake heard Dorothy's voice, earnest and agitated, answering the languid voice of Marcel, as they walked on enveloped in the mist.

"No, no," she said; "you think that, because you have never felt what those women are, because it has never come home to you."

Marcel sighed. "I fear it has come home to me but too much, Miss Dorothy," he answered.

"That is not what I mean. You may have known women like that—I dare say you have—and still not have known all that their wickedness means. If you had you could not talk like that about skies and light and mist. I have known such a woman, known the full meaning of such a woman. I can't very well explain; my ideas are rather confused, you know; but I understand that I understood that woman's real meaning. I had a friend once; she was beautiful, and young, and noble, and she was dying; and her husband, instead of caring for her, cared for a woman such as you describe in your novel; the two betrayed and outraged her, and made her last years bitterness and ignominy. She is dead now, I am thankful. Last year I went to the play in Paris. They were giving one of those horrible, vulgar vaudevilles, full of half-dressed people, and horrid, hideous songs and jokes; it was all about a burlesque actress, a sort of apotheosis of her. There were lots of people in the theatre; and some one pointed out to me, in one of the boxes, the woman who had made my friend so unhappy. She was what people call a lady, quite young, beautifully dressed, with a beautiful, delicate face, and she was laughing and blushing a great deal behind her fan, and looking very happy. It was the first time that I had ever seen her, and I never expected to see her there. I could not take my eyes off her. I can't tell you how I felt: as if a precipice had suddenly opened before me. I shall never forget it. She seemed somehow to be the concentration of what was going on on the stage; the play seemed to be about her, the songs about her. She seemed to be framed, as it were, beautiful and delicate though she was, in all that indecency and vulgarity, those hideous gestures, that frightful music, those disgusting jokes. And the play seemed to become terrible, tragic, as if some one were being killed somewhere. I don't know how to explain it. But ever since that evening I have understood what a bad woman is."

Dorothy's voice died away, hot and hoarse.

"Did you hear?" Baldwin whispered to Mrs. Blake. "Well; what my cousin has just been saying is a thing which an English novelist would not be allowed to say; he would not be allowed to show us the bad woman in her box; and he would not be allowed, therefore, to show us what was passing in that girl's heart, all the rebellion of outraged love and respect, all that great and holy indignation. And yet, to have seen the contents of Dorothy's heart at that moment, braces our soul, does us more moral good than the sight of all the bad women in Christendom could do us harm; for it means that we have stood for a moment in the presence of the Lord, of the true God, whose name is Love and Indignation."

VERNON LEE.

H. Rider Haggard

"About Fiction"

Contemporary Review 51 (February 1887), 172–80

ABOUT FICTION.

THE love of romance is probably coeval with the existence of humanity. So far as we can follow the history of the world we find traces of it and its effects among every people, and those who are acquainted with the habits and ways of thought of savage races will know that it flourishes as strongly in the barbarian as in the cultured breast. In short, it is like the passions, an innate quality of mankind. In modern England this love is not by any means dying out, as must be clear, even to that class of our fellow-countrymen who, we are told, are interested in nothing but politics and religion. A writer in the *Saturday Review* computed not long ago that the yearly output of novels in this country is about eight hundred; and probably he was within the mark. It is to be presumed that all this enormous mass of fiction finds a market of some sort, or it would not be produced. Of course a large quantity of it is brought into the world at the expense of the writer, who guarantees or deposits his thirty or sixty pounds, which in the former case he is certainly called upon to pay, and in the latter he never sees again. But this deducted, a large residue remains, out of which a profit must be made by the publisher, or he would not publish it. Now, most of this crude mass of fiction is worthless. If three-fourths of it were never put into print the world would scarcely lose a single valuable idea, aspiration, or amusement. Many people are of opinion in their secret hearts that they could, if they thought it worth while to try, write a novel that would be very good indeed, and a large number of people carry this opinion into practice without scruple or remorse. But as a matter of fact, with the exception of perfect sculpture, really good romance writing is perhaps the most difficult art practised by the sons of men. It might even be maintained that none but a great man or woman can produce a *really* great work of fiction. But great men are rare, and great works are rarer still, because all great men do not write. If, however, a person is intellectually a head and shoulders above his or her fellows, that person is *primâ facie* fit and able to write a good work. Even then he or she may not succeed, because in addition to intellectual pre-eminence, a certain literary quality is necessary to the perfect flowering of the brain in books. Perhaps, therefore, the argument would stand better conversely. The writer who can produce a noble and lasting work of art is of necessity a great man, and one who, had fortune opened to him any of the doors that lead to material grandeur and to the busy pomp of power, would have shown that the imagination, the quick sympathy, the insight, the depth of mind, and the sense of order and proportion which went to constitute the writer would have equally constituted the statesman or the general. It is not, of course, argued that only great writers should produce books, because if this was so publishing as a trade would come to an end, and Mudie would be obliged to put up his shutters. Also there exists a large class of people who like to read, and to whom great books would scarcely appeal. Let us imagine the consternation of the ladies of England if they were suddenly forced to an exclusive fare of George Eliot and Thackeray! But it *is* argued that a large proportion of the fictional matter poured from the press into the market is superfluous, and serves no good purpose. On the contrary, it serves several distinctly bad ones. It lowers and vitiates the public taste, and it obscures the true ends of fiction. Also it brings the high and honourable profession of authorship into contempt and disrepute, for the general public, owing perhaps to the comparative poverty of literary men, has never yet quite made up its mind as to the status of their profession. Lastly, this over-production stops the sale of better work without profiting those who are responsible for it.

The publication of inferior fiction can, in short, be of no advantage to any one, except perhaps the proprietors of circulating libraries. To the author himself it must indeed be a source of nothing but misery, bitterness, and disappointment, for only those who have written one can know the amount of labour involved in the production of even a bad book. Still, the very fact that people can be found to write and publishers to publish to such an unlimited extent, shows clearly enough the enormous appetite of readers, who are prepared, like a diseased ostrich, to swallow stones, and even carrion, rather than not get their fill of novelties. More and more, as what we call culture spreads, do men and women crave to be taken out of themselves. More and more do they long to be brought face to face with Beauty, and stretch out their arms towards that vision of the Perfect, which we only see in books and dreams.

The fact that we, in these latter days, have as it were macadamized all the roads of life does not make the world softer to the feet of those who travel through it. There are now royal roads to everything, lined with staring placards, whereon he who runs may learn the sweet uses of advertisement; but it is dusty work to follow them, and some may think that our ancestors on the whole found their voyaging a shadier and fresher business. However this may be, a weary public calls continually for books, new books to make them forget, to refresh them, to occupy minds jaded with the toil and emptiness and vexation of our competitive existence.

In some ways this demand is no doubt a healthy sign. The intellect of the world must be awakening when it thus cries aloud to be satisfied. Perhaps it is not a good thing to read nothing but three-volumed novels of an inferior order, but it, at any rate, shows the possession of a certain degree of intelligence. For there still exists among us a class of educated people, or rather of people who have had a certain sum of money spent upon their education, who are absolutely incapable of reading *anything,* and who never do read anything, except, perhaps, the reports of famous divorce cases and the spiciest paragraphs in Society papers. It is not their fault; they are very often good people enough in their way; and as they go to church on Sundays, and pay their rates and taxes, the world has no right to complain of them. They are born without intellects, and with undeveloped souls, that is all, and on the whole they find themselves very comfortable in that condition. But this class is getting smaller, and all writers have cause to congratulate themselves on the fact, for the dead wall of its crass stupidity is a dreadful thing to face. Those, too, who begin by reading novels may end by reading Milton and Shakespeare. Day by day the mental area open to the operations of the English-speaking writer grows larger. At home the Board schools pour out their thousands every year, many of whom have acquired a taste for reading, which, when once it has been born, will, we may be sure, grow apace. Abroad the colonies are filling up with English-speaking people, who, as they grow refined and find leisure to read, will make a considerable call upon the literature of their day. But by far the largest demand for books in the English tongue comes from America, with its reading population of some forty millions. Most of the books patronized by this enormous population are stolen from English authors, who, according to American law, are outcasts, unentitled to that protection to the work of their brains and the labour of their hands which is one of the foundations of common morality. Putting aside this copyright question, however (and, indeed, it is best left undiscussed), there may be noted in passing two curious results which are being brought about in America by this wholesale perusal of English books. The

first of these is that the Americans are destroying their own literature, that cannot live in the face of the unfair competition to which
it is subjected. It will be noticed that since piracy, to use the
politer word, set in with its present severity, America has scarcely
produced a writer of the first class—no one, for instance, who can be
compared to Poe, or Hawthorne, or Longfellow. It is not, perhaps,
too rash a prophecy to say that, if piracy continues, American literature proper will shortly be chiefly represented by the columns of a
very enterprising daily press. The second result of the present state
of affairs is that the whole of the American population, especially the
younger portion of it, must be in course of thorough impregnation
with English ideas and modes of thought as set forth by English
writers. We all know the extraordinary effect books read in youth
have upon the fresh and imaginative mind. It is not too much to
say that many a man's whole life is influenced by some book read in
his teens, the very title of which he may have forgotten. Consequently, it would be difficult to overrate the effect that must be from
year to year produced upon the national character of America by the
constant perusal of books born in England. For it must be remembered
that for every reader that a writer of merit finds in England, he will
find three in America.

In the face of this constant and ever-growing demand at home
and abroad writers of romance must often find themselves questioning
their inner consciousness as to what style of art it is best for them
to adopt, not only with the view of pleasing their readers, but in the
interests of art itself. There are several schools from which they
may choose. For instance, there is that followed by the American
novelists. These gentlemen, as we know, declare that there are no
stories left to be told, and certainly, if it may be said without dis-
respect to a clever and laborious body of writers, their works go far
towards supporting the statement. They have developed a new style
of romance. Their heroines are things of silk and cambric, who
soliloquize and dissect their petty feelings, and elaborately review the
feeble promptings which serve them for passions. Their men—well,
they are emasculated specimens of an overwrought age, and, with
culture on their lips, and emptiness in their hearts, they dangle round
the heroines till their three-volumed fate is accomplished. About their
work is an atmosphere like that of the boudoir of a luxurious woman,
faint and delicate, and suggesting the essence of white rose. How
different is all this to the swiftness, and strength, and directness of
the great English writers of the past. Why,

"The surge and thunder of the Odyssey"

is not more widely separated from the tinkling of modern society
verses, than the laboured nothingness of this new American school of
fiction from the giant life and vigour of Swift and Fielding, and

Thackeray and Hawthorne. Perhaps, however, it is the art of the future, in which case we may hazard a shrewd guess that the literature of past ages will be more largely studied in days to come than it is at present.

Then, to go from Pole to Pole, there is the Naturalistic school, of which Zola is the high priest. Here things are all the other way. Here the chosen function of the writer is to

" Paint the mortal shame of nature with the living hues of art."

Here are no silks and satins to impede our vision of the flesh and blood beneath, and here the scent is patchouli. Lewd, and bold, and bare, living for lust and lusting for this life and its good things, and naught beyond, the heroines of realism dance, with Bacchanalian revellings, across the astonished stage of literature. Whatever there is brutal in humanity—and God knows that there is plenty—whatever there is that is carnal and filthy, is here brought into prominence, and thrust before the reader's eyes. But what becomes of the things that are pure and high—of the great aspirations and the lofty hopes and longings, which *do*, after all, play their part in our human economy, and which it is surely the duty of a writer to call attention to and nourish according to his gifts?

Certainly it is to be hoped that this naturalistic school of writing will never take firm root in England, for it is an accursed thing. It is impossible to help wondering if its followers ever reflect upon the mischief that they must do, and, reflecting, do not shrink from the responsibility. To look at the matter from one point of view only, Society has made a rule that for the benefit of the whole community individuals must keep their passions within certain fixed limits, and our social system is so arranged that any transgression of this rule produces mischief of one sort or another, if not actual ruin, to the transgressor. Especially is this so if she be a woman. Now, as it is, human nature is continually fretting against these artificial bounds, and especially among young people it requires considerable fortitude and self-restraint to keep the feet from wandering. We all know, too, how much this sort of indulgence depends upon the imagination, and we all know how easy it is for a powerful writer to excite it in that direction. Indeed, there could be nothing *more* easy to a writer of any strength and vision, especially if he spoke with an air of evil knowledge and intimate authority. There are probably several men in England at this moment who, if they turned their talents to this bad end, could equal, if not outdo, Zola himself, with results that would shortly show themselves in various ways among the population. Sexual passion is the most powerful lever with which to stir the mind of man, for it lies at the root of all things human; and it is impossible to over-estimate the damage that could be worked by a single English or American writer of genius, if he grasped it with a will. " But," say these writers, " our aim is most moral; from Nana and her kith and kin may be gathered many a virtuous lesson and example." Possibly this is so, though as I write the words there rises in my mind a recollection of one or two French books where——but most people have seen such books. Besides, it is not so much a question of the object of the school as of the fact that it continually, and in full and luscious detail, calls attention to erotic matters. Once start the average mind upon this subject, and it will go down the slope of itself. It is useless afterwards to turn round and say that, although you cut loose the cords of decent reticence which bound the fancy, you intended that it should run *uphill* to the white heights of virtue. If the seed of eroticism is sown broadcast its fruit will be according to the nature of the soil it falls on, but fruit it must and will. And however virtuous may be the aims with which they are produced, the publications of the French Naturalistic school are such seed as was sown by that enemy who came in the night season.

In England, to come to the third great school of fiction, we have as yet little or nothing of all this. Here, on the other hand, we are at the mercy of the Young Person, and a dreadful nuisance most of us find her. The present writer is bound to admit that, speaking personally and with humility, he thinks it a little hard that all fiction should be judged by the test as to whether or no it is suitable reading for a girl of sixteen. There are plenty of people who write books for little girls in the schoolroom ; let the little girls read them, and 'leave the works written for men and women to their elders. It may strike the reader as inconsistent, after the remarks made above, that a plea should now be advanced for greater freedom in English literary art. But French naturalism is one thing, and the unreal, namby-pamby nonsense with which the market is flooded here is quite another. Surely there is a middle path ! Why do *men* hardly ever read a novel ? Because, in ninety-nine cases out of a hundred, it is utterly false as a picture of life ; and, failing in that, it certainly does not take ground as a work of high imagination. The ordinary popular English novel represents life as it is considered desirable that schoolgirls should suppose it to be. Consequently it is for the most part rubbish, without a spark of vitality about it, for no novel written on those false lines will live. Also, the system is futile as a means of protection, for the young lady, wearied with the account of how the good girl who jilted the man who loved her when she was told to, married the noble lord, and lived in idleness and luxury for ever after, has only to turn to the evening paper to see another picture of existence. Of course, no humble producer of fiction, meant to interest through the exercise of the intelligence rather than through the senses, can hope to compete with the enthralling details of such cases as that of Lord Colin Campbell and Sir

Charles Dilke. That is the naturalism of this country, and, like all filth, its popularity is enormous, as will be shown by the fact that the circulation of one evening paper alone was, I believe, increased during the hearing of a recent case by 60,000 copies nightly. Nor would any respectable author wish to compete with this. But he ought, subject to proper reservations and restraints, to be allowed to picture life as life is, and men and women as they are. At present, if he attempts to do this, he is denounced as immoral; and perchance the circulating library, which is curiously enough a great power in English literature, suppresses the book in its fear of losing subscriptions. The press, too —the same press that is so active in printing " full and special " reports—is very vigilant in this matter, having the Young Person continually before its eyes. Some time ago one of the London dailies reviewed a batch of eight or nine books. Of these reviews nearly every one was in the main an inquiry into the moral character of the work, judged from the standpoint of the unknown reviewer. Of their literary merits little or nothing was said. Now, the question that naturally arose in the mind of the reader of these notices was—Is the novelist bound to inculcate any particular set of doctrines that may at the moment be favoured by authority ? If that is the aim and end of his art, then why is he not paid by the State like any other official ? And why should not the principle be carried further ? Each religion and every sect of each religion might retain their novelist. So might the Blue Ribbonites, and the Positivists, and the Purity people, and the Social Democrats, and others without end. The results would be most enlivening to the general public. Then, at any rate, the writer would be sure of the approbation of his own masters ; as it is, he is at the mercy of every unknown reviewer, some of whom seem to have peculiar views—though, not to make too much of the matter, it must be remembered that the ultimate verdict is with the public.

Surely, what is wanted in English fiction is a higher ideal and more freedom to work it out. It is impossible, or, if not impossible, it requires the very highest genius, such as, perhaps, no writers possess to-day, to build up a really first-class work without the necessary materials in their due proportion. As it is, in this country, while crime may be used to any extent, passion in its fiercer and deeper forms is scarcely available, unless it is made to receive some conventional sanction. For instance, the right of dealing with bigamy is by custom conceded to the writer of romance, because in cases of bigamy vice has received the conventional sanction of marriage. True, the marriage is a mock one, but such as it is, it provides the necessary cloak. But let him beware how he deals with the same subject when the sinner of the piece has not added a sham or a bigamous marriage to his evil doings, for the book will in this case be certainly called immoral. English life is surrounded by conventionalism, and English fiction has come to reflect the conventionalism, not the life, and has in consequence, with some notable exceptions, got into a very poor way, both as regards art and interest.

If this moderate and proper freedom is denied to imaginative literature alone among the arts (for, though Mr. Horsley does not approve of it, sculptors may still model from the naked), it seems probable that the usual results will follow. There will be a great reaction, the Young Person will vanish into space and be no more seen, and Naturalism in all its horror will take its root among us. At present it is only in the French tongue that people read about the inner mysteries of life in brothels, or follow the interesting study of the passions of senile and worn-out debauchees. By-and-by, if liberty is denied, they will read them in the English. Art in the purity of its idealized truth should resemble some perfect Grecian statue. It should be cold but naked, and looking thereon men should be led to think of naught but beauty. Here, however, we attire Art in every sort of dress, some of them suggestive enough in their own way, but for the most part in a pinafore. The difference between literary Art, as the present writer submits it ought to be, and the Naturalistic Art of France is the difference between the Venus of Milo and an obscene photograph taken from the life. It seems probable that the English-speaking people will in course of time have to choose between the two.

But however this is—and the writer only submits an opinion—one thing remains clear, fiction à l'Anglaise becomes, from the author's point of view, day by day more difficult to deal with satisfactorily under its present conditions. This age is not a romantic age. Doubtless under the surface human nature is the same to-day as it was in the time of Rameses. Probably, too, the respective volumes of vice and virtue are, taking the altered circumstances into consideration, much as they were then or at any other time. But neither our good nor our evil doing is of an heroic nature, and it is things heroic and their kin and not petty things that best lend themselves to the purposes of the novelist, for by their aid he produces his strongest effects. Besides, if by chance there is a good thing on the market it is snapped up by a hundred eager newspapers, who tell the story, whatever it may be, and turn it inside out, and draw morals from it till the public loathes its sight and sound. Genius, of course, can always find materials wherewith to weave its glowing web. But these remarks, it is scarcely necessary to explain, are not made from that point of view, for only genius can talk of genius with authority, but rather from the humbler standing-ground of the ordinary conscientious labourer in the field of letters, who, loving his art for her own sake, yet earns a living by following her, and is anxious to continue to do so with credit to himself. Let genius, if genius there be, come forward and speak on its own behalf! But if the reader is inclined to doubt the proposition that novel writing is becoming every day more difficult and less interesting, let him consult his own mind, and see how many novels proper among the hundreds that have been published within the last five years, and which deal in any way with every day contemporary life, have excited his profound interest. The present writer can at the moment recall but two—one was called " My Trivial Life and Misfortunes," by an unknown author, and the other, " The Story of a South African Farm," by Ralph Iron. But then neither of these books if examined into would be found to be a novel such as the ordinary writer produces once or twice a year. Both of them are written from within, and not from without; both convey the impression of being the outward and visible result of inward personal suffering on the part of the writer, for in each the key-note is a note of pain. Differing widely from the ordinary run of manufactured books, they owe their chief interest to a certain atmosphere of spiritual intensity, which could not in all probability be even approximately reproduced. Another recent work of the same powerful class, though of more painful detail, is called " Mrs. Keith's Crime." It is, however, almost impossible to conceive their respective authors producing a second " Trivial Life and Misfortunes " or a further edition of the crimes of Mrs. Keith. These books were written from the heart. Next time their authors write it will probably be from the head and not from the heart, and they must then come down to the use of the dusty materials which are common to us all.

There is indeed a refuge for the less ambitious among us, and it lies in the paths and calm retreats of pure imagination. Here we may weave our humble tale, and point our harmless moral without being mercilessly bound down to the prose of a somewhat dreary age. Here we may even—if we feel that our wings are strong enough to bear us in that thin air—cross the bounds of the known, and, hanging between earth and heaven, gaze with curious eyes into the great profound beyond. There are still subjects that may be handled *there* if the man can be found bold enough to handle them. And, although some there be who consider this a lower walk in the realms of fiction, and who would probably scorn to become a "mere writer of romances," it may be urged in defence of the school that many of the most lasting triumphs of literary art belong to the producers of purely romantic fiction, witness the " Arabian Nights," " Gulliver's Travels," " The Pilgrim's Progress," " Robinson Crusoe," and other immortal works. If the present writer may be allowed to hazard an opinion, it is that, when Naturalism has had its day, when Mr. Howells ceases to charm, and the Society novel is utterly played out, the kindly race of men in their latter as in their earlier developments will still take pleasure in those works of fancy which appeal, not to a class, or a nation, or even to an age, but to all time and humanity at large.

H. RIDER HAGGARD.

George Saintsbury

"The Present State
of the Novel. I"

Fortnightly Review 48 (September 1887), 410–17

THE PRESENT STATE OF THE NOVEL.

I:

THREE or four years ago the Editor of a Florentine journal, the *Revue Internationale*, asked me to give him an article on the present state of the English novel, and the Editor of the Fortnightly Review has now asked me to survey fiction with a yet more extensive view, taking in Europe and the United States of America. The commission is a large one, and it behoves the commissioner to take it up modestly. The only excuse that I can give for taking it up at all is, that for a good many years I have had to give weekly, if not daily, dreadful lines for purposes of business to probably as many English, French, and American novels as anybody else has read for pleasure. He who reads French novels reads at the present day, it need hardly be said, Russian also, though he may not read them as he would like to do, at first-hand. German novels I have read in less numbers, but I think sufficiently. With the recent fiction of Italy and Spain I cannot claim much direct acquaintance; but those who can, tell me that it is in both cases little but a more or less varied echo of that of France and England. I have heard that there are some striking novels in Dutch, but I do not think that anyone asserts that they are very many. Scandinavia, again, like Russia, has its prominent novelists, but they too can be read "in translations, sir, in translations;" and, though I myself detest a translation, I think that one thing may be said for it, even by its greatest ill-wishers. It must be an extraordinarily bad translation which does not convey to a tolerably experienced reader some idea of what the original is like, and whether it is worth reading or not. Certainly this would not be the case if many translators went on the principles of those two French translators of Sterne, one of whom (rather a great man in his way) confessed that he knew next to nothing of English, but hoped that he had a "profound and respectuous sentiment for the graces of the French tongue," while the other vouchsafed the warning that as M. Sterne's jokes were often bad, he had "left them on one side," and substituted good ones of his own. This ghastly thin-faced time of ours is not up to such nobility of vice, and the result is that even the worst translation generally has something of its original.

Let me, then, with this honest confession of what I do and what I do not know at first-hand, attempt the prescribed task, taking the home department first, then crossing the Channel, and finally grouping the American and Russian novels (both of them very closely connected with the French) together, and making a sort of tail of the minor nations. The first part should be taken first, not merely as the most important to an Englishman (or if Dr. Clark prefers it, a Briton), but as the most difficult, for it is no joke to review and summarily judge a department of literature in which the chief practitioners are in some cases one's personal friends and acquaintances. Fortunately there is no need to go through, before an English audience, the particular performances of each of our principal novelists. During the last lustre the number has been sensibly diminished, and as sensibly increased. Mr. Charles Reade, and just lately Mrs. Wood, have joined the ranks of the majority, and there is now, with the exception of Mr. George Meredith and Mrs. Oliphant, hardly anyone writing who had made much name five-and-twenty years ago. On the other hand, Mr. Stevenson and Mr. Rider Haggard have not only made themselves great names, but—which is more interesting to *Criticus*, if not to *Amicus*—have done a great deal to further that return to the pure romance, as distinguished from the analytic novel, which was seen to be coming several years ago. It is very amusing for a looker-on to see the renaissance, round the names of these two agreeable writers, of the squabbles which have so often occurred in former ages—the squabbles of the devotees of the bookish writer and the less bookish, of the discoverer of plagiarisms and the pooh-pooher of discoveries of plagiarisms, and so forth. It is not unsatisfactory to some little private vanities to remember that when, ten years ago, some of Mr. Stevenson's critical friends scoffed at the idea of his reprinting his *New Arabian Nights* from one of those periodicals which have "one regular subscriber besides the contributors," and urged him to stick to gossipy essays, there were those who took the other view. But let us try to be as little personal, both in this and other matters, as possible, even (if it be possible) to avoid submitting to that rather tyrannical demand which an amiable writer in these very pages put forth not long ago to all and sundry, to confess that they thought *The Ordeal of Richard Feverel* the greatest novel of the century (or was it of all time?), or else acknowledge themselves recreant and craven. I will do neither, though there are few persons to whom I yield in respect for Mr. Meredith's genius. So also I shall not say whether I like *Treasure Island* better than *King Solomon's Mines*, or *King Solomon's Mines* better than *Treasure Island*. I only wish I had either drawn the personage of John Silver or written the fight between Twala and Sir Henry.

Moreover the question happens not to be one of liking at all, still less one of ranking novelists old and new in order of merit. The question is to set in order, as well as may be, the chief characteristics of the English novels of the day, and to indicate, with as little rash-

ness as possible, which of them are on the mounting hand and which
are on the sinking. And for my part, and in the first place, I do
not see any reason to think the reappearance of the romance of
adventure at all likely to be a mere passing phenomenon. For the
other kind, as I shall hope to show in the course of these papers, has
gone hopelessly sterile in all European countries, and is very unlikely
to be good for anything unless it is raised anew from seed, and
given a pretty long course of time. In more than one sense it had
not, or has not (for it still flourishes after a sort), got so bad with us
as in other countries. The habits and public opinion of the nation
have kept us from that curious scholasticism of dull uncleanness
on which too many French novelists spend their time. There is
still too much healthy beefiness and beeriness (much of both as it
has lost) in the English temperament to permit it to indulge in the
sterile pessimism which seems to dominate Russian fiction. When
we come to the comparison with America, we are getting on very
delicate ground. Perhaps the best way of putting the difference is
to recall a pleasant observation of Thackeray's, in his remarks on
Maginn's *Maxims of Sir Morgan O'Doherty*. The good Sir Morgan
had laid it down as a maxim of fashionable life, that you were to
drink champagne after white cheeses, water after red (or was it the
other way?); and Thackeray rejoined very truly that fashionable
society did not trouble itself whether you did both, or neither, or
either. Now America, a little young at "culture," is taking her
literary etiquette books very seriously and trying to obey their
minutest directions; while Englishmen, whose literary breeding is
of an older stamp and tolerably well established, do not trouble
themselves about it at all. For my part, I think some of my friends
are very hard on Mr. Howells when he makes those comic little
critical excursions of his. Your virtuous beginner always plays the
game with surpassing strictness, and is shocked at the lax conduct
of oldsters.

In England we have escaped the worst of all these things. We
have a few romances of the future in which inspired proletarians of
heroic virtue do suit and service to angelic prostitutes of queenly
manners, but they are not taken very seriously. The "cult of the
young person," which some innocent British writers deplore, has at
least kept us from the last depth of dirty dulness, and England is
still a very long way from being America. Half a score of writers
possessing gifts which range from very considerable talent to decided
genius, and perhaps not less than half a thousand possessing gifts
ranging from very considerable talent to none at all, have elaborated,
partly by their own efforts and partly by following the great models
of the last generation, a kind of mixed mode or half-incident, half-
character novel, which at its best is sometimes admirable, and at its

average is often quite tolerable pastime. We are still curiously behindhand in the short story, the *nouvelle* properly so called, which is not a märchen, or a burlesque, or a tale of terror (these three we can sometimes do very well). If there is any falling off, the determined optimist may remember the mercies which tempered the domination of the Campaigner to poor Mr. Binney. If we have cut off the cigars we have considerably improved the claret; or in other words, if we have lost some graces, some charms of the finest and rarest kind, we have greatly bettered the *average*—(I must be pardoned italics here)—the average structure and arrangement of the average novel. How weak a point this has always been with our great novelists, at any rate since the beginning of this century, everybody who has studied literary history knows. Scott never seems to have had the slightest idea what was going to happen, or how it was going to happen, though as a matter of fact it generally did happen delightfully if irregularly enough. Dickens is supposed to have been very careful about his schemes, though if any man can explain to me what the plot of *Little Dorrit* is; why Mr. Tulkinghorn chose in that entirely irrational and unprofitable manner to persecute Lady Dedlock; why anything, no matter what, as it actually does happen in *Hard Times*, happens; and what the sense or meaning of Estella's general conduct is in *Great Expectations*, he will do more than I have ever been able to do for myself, or than anyone else has yet been able to do for me. Thackeray's sins (if in novel-writing it be not blasphemy to say that Thackeray sinned at all) are gross, palpable, and, for the matter of that, confessed by the sinner. In particular, if anyone will try to arrange the chronology of the various Pendennis books, and if his hair does not turn white in the process, he may be guaranteed against any necessity for a peruke arising from similarly hopeless intellectual labour. Of course these things are usually very small faults, except in cases such as that where out of sheer good nature and deference to old friends Scott spoilt the finale of *St. Ronan's Well*—cases in which the carelessness or wilful indifference to keeping the house in order really hurts the story. But they are faults, and I think that, on the whole, the tendency in average novel-writing during the last twenty years has been to correct them. Again, the average writing of the said novel is decidedly better, and, generally speaking, a distinct advance has been made in the minor details of craftsmanship. There are one or two popular writers (I could mention one in particular, if the object here were not to be as little personal as may be) who still sin flagrantly in the old direction of taking fair pains over the first and the third volume and flinging to the public the slovenliest botch of a second that it is likely to tolerate. But this want of literary conscience and literary self-respect is much rarer than it used to be, and appears to be regarded, by younger hands especially, with proper disgust.

Nevertheless I do not think, much as I respect many of its individual practitioners, that the English novel of the day in its average form is a work of art which ranks very high. To begin with, though it has for many years almost wholly devoted itself to character, how many characters has it produced that will live, that will accompany in the memories of posterity the characters of the masters of the past? Very few, I think. We read its books often with pleasure, and sometimes with admiration, at the moment, but they add little to the abiding furniture of our minds and memories. And here let me guard against an objection which is obvious enough, that a man furnishes his mind pretty early, and by the time he comes to forty has no room left. I do not find it so. I have within the last few years, within the last few months, read books for the first time whose characters I am quite certain I shall not forget till I forget everything. Nor am I short of memory, for, as far as mere facts go, I could give plenty of details of many novels published in the last fifteen or twenty years. But very few indeed of their characters and their incidents and stories have taken rank with Partridge at the theatre, with the Baron in his Patmos, with Esmond breaking his sword before Beatrix's princely lover, with Lavengro teaching Armenian to Isobel Berners, with Amyas flinging his sword into the sea. I must confess also that I hold a creed which may seem to some people, perhaps to most, irrational and even childish. I do not think that there is exactly the same amount of genius and of talent always present on the earth, but I do think that in the blossoming times of the intellect the genius and the talent are pretty constant in their total amount. If you get the sum spread widely about you get the kind of work which is now abundant, and nowhere so abundant as in the novel. Of the immense numbers of novels which are now written, a very large proportion cannot be called in any true sense bad, and of the still considerable number which are written by our best men there are few which may not be called in a very real sense good. The great models which they have before them, the large rewards of successful writing, and (for why should not a man magnify his own office?) the constant exposure and reprobation of the grosser faults of novel-writing on the part of critics,[1] have brought about a much higher general level of excellence, a better turn-

---

(1) At the same time I must admit that I could not undertake to teach the complete art of novel-writing in so many lessons. I was obliged once to confess as much, to a very amiable person who, in consequence of a critique of mine, sent me a cheque with an agreeable apology for its not being larger, and a request for more of that excellent advice. It was not possible to keep his cheque; but I have always thought that he must have been a very nice man. As a general rule authors do not send such documents to their critics; you may go a long way "without a cheque" on that road.

out of average work, than was ever known before. But, either from the very fact of this imitating and schoolmastering, or from sheer haste, or what not, we do not seem to get the very best things.

Undoubtedly, therefore, the return to the earliest form of writing, to the pure romance of adventure, is a very interesting thing indeed, and if anything could be wanting to make it more interesting it would be the close coincidence of three examples of it in England, each of which recognised the principle, each of which obtained a great popularity by this recognition, but which, both in the one book which will not last and the two which will, showed many of the faults of new experiments. It is unnecessary, and would be ungracious, to say much here of the faults of *Called Back*. It is sufficient to say that, without being more than critically unfair to the public, it is impossible to account for its temporary popularity, except on the ground that, with all its faults, it was distinctly an attempt to tell an interesting story. As literature, of course both *Treasure Island* and *King Solomon's Mines* are miles above *Called Back*, and they also exceed it in interest; but they, too, set the same simple aim before them, and succeed in it. Both writers seem, either from fear or some other reason, to have exercised a rather unnecessary economy of means, Mr. Stevenson voluntarily depriving himself of the most fertile source—a source more fertile than all others joined together— of romance interest, while Mr. Haggard drew on it only sparingly in the episode of Foulata. But we do not want a detailed criticism of these books, or of any books here. The point is, that in both the writers have deliberately reverted to the simpler instead of the more complicated kind of novel, and have pitched away minute manners-painting and refined character-analysis. I hold that they have done rightly and wisely. For the fictitious (as distinguished from the poetic) portraiture of manners and the fictitious dissection of character deal for the most part with minute and superficial points, and when those points have been attacked over and over again, or when the manners and characters of a time have become very much levelled and mannerised, an inevitable monotony and want of freshness in the treatment comes about. This seems to have been the case in all European languages more or less for a long time past. Except in the minutest details, manners have altered very little for the last half-century—a stability which has not been a little increased by the very popularity of novels themselves. A boy or girl now learns manners less from life than from books, and reproduces those manners in his or her own fresh generation. The novel has thus " bred in and in," until the inevitable result of feebleness of strain has been reached. But the incidents, and the broad and poetic features of character on which the romance relies, are not matters which change at all. They are always the same, with a sameness of nature, not of convention. The zest with which we read novels of character and manners is derived, at least in the main, from the unlikeness of the characters and manners depicted. The relish with which we read the great romances in prose, drama, and verse is derived from the likeness of the passions and actions, which are always at bottom the same. There is no danger of repetition here; on the contrary, the more faithful the repetition the surer the success, because the artist is only drawing deeper on a perennial source. In the other case he is working over and over again in shallow ground, which yields a thinner and weedier return at every cropping.

But it will be said, Are we to have nothing new? Are we simply to hunt old trails? Whereto I reply with a *distinguo*. A time may possibly come, may be near at hand, when some considerable change of political or social life may bring about so new a state of manners, and raise into prominence as an ordinary phase so different a side of human character, that the analytic novelist may once more find ready to his hand new material which in its turn will grow stale, just as the ordinary middle-class person fairly educated and acquainted with the novelists from Scott downwards is now getting stale in all European countries, even in those which, like Russia and America, seem as if they ought to have plenty of virgin soil to cultivate. And then that generation, whether it is the next or the next after, will have to return as we are doing to the romance for something fresh. For the romance is of its nature eternal and preliminary to the novel. The novel is of its nature transitory and is parasitic on the romance. If some of the examples of novels themselves partake of eternity, it is only because the practitioners have been cunning enough to borrow much from the romance. Miss Austen is the only English novelist I know who attains the first rank with something like a defiance of interest of story, and we shall see another Homer before we see another Jane. As for what we often hear about the novel of science, the novel of new forms of religion, the novel of altruism, and heaven knows what, it is all stark naught. The novel has nothing to do with any beliefs, with any convictions, with any thoughts in the strict sense, except as mere garnishings. Its substance must always be life, not thought, conduct not belief, the passions not the intellect, manners and morals not creeds and theories. Its material, its bottom, must always be either the abiding qualities or the fleeting appearances of social existence, *quicquid agunt homines* not *quicquid cogitant*. In the first and most important division there has been no change within recorded history, and if esoteric Buddhism were to become the Church of England established by law, and a Great British Republic, with the eminent member for the Camborne division of Cornwall as President, were to take the place of the monarchy, there would be no change in these. There would probably be none if the whole human race were evicted from this earth and re-established in Mars. In the other class of materials there *is* a change, and the very fact of this change necessitates a certain intermission of dead seasons to let the new form germinate and ripen. There is perhaps no reason why a really great romance should not be written at any time, but it is almost impossible that a continuous supply of great character-novels or novels of manners should be kept up, and no one will deny that for these many years the novel of character and manners has been almost solely cultivated. Even those of our novelists who, like Mr. Besant and Mr. Blackmore, have tried the historical romance, have always to a great extent treated it in the fashion of the other style. And so in a manner *consummatum est*. The average man and woman in England of the middle and late nineteenth century, has been drawn and quartered, analysed and "introspected," till there is nothing new to be done with him or her either as an *écorché*, or with the skin on, or with clothes on the skin. Merely as a man or woman, he or she can be dealt with still profitably, but then you have a romance and not a novel. Unfortunately, most of our best proved writers continue to write the novel and not the romance, or to treat the romance as if it were the novel. Thus we do not, and for this and the other reasons given we cannot, get the best things. Nor shall we till the aspect of society is quite changed, and till we have bathed once more long and well in the romance of adventure and of passion.

GEORGE SAINTSBURY.

Matthew Arnold

"Count Leo Tolstoï"

Fortnightly Review 48 (December 1887), 783–99

COUNT LEO TOLSTOI.

IN reviewing at the time of its first publication, thirty years ago, Flaubert's remarkable novel of *Madame Bovary*, Sainte-Beuve observed that in Flaubert we come to another manner, another kind of inspiration, from those which had prevailed hitherto; we find ourselves dealing, he said, with a man of a new and different generation from novelists like George Sand. The ideal has ceased, the lyric vein is dried up; the new men are cured of lyricism and the ideal; "a severe and pitiless truth has made its entry, as the last word of experience, even into art itself." The characters of the new literature of fiction are "science, a spirit of observation, maturity, force, a touch of hardness." *L'idéal a cessé, le lyrique a tari.*

The spirit of observation and the touch of hardness (let us retain these mild and inoffensive terms) have since been carried in the French novel very far. So far have they been carried, indeed, that in spite of the advantage which the French language, familiar to the cultivated classes everywhere, confers on the French novel, this novel has lost much of its attraction for those classes; it no longer commands their attention as it did formerly. The famous English novelists have passed away, and have left no successors of like fame. It is not the English novel, therefore, which has inherited the vogue lost by the French novel. It is the novel of a country new to literature, or at any rate unregarded, till lately, by the general public of readers: it is the novel of Russia. The Russian novel has now the vogue, and deserves to have it. If fresh literary productions maintain this vogue and enhance it, we shall all be learning Russian.

The Slav nature, or at any rate the Russian nature, the Russian nature as it shows itself in the Russian novels, seems marked by an extreme sensitiveness, a consciousness most quick and acute both for what the man's self is experiencing, and also for what others in contact with him are thinking and feeling. In a nation full of life, but young, and newly in contact with an old and powerful civilisation, this sensitiveness and self-consciousness are prompt to appear. In the Americans, as well as in the Russians, we see them active in a high degree. They are somewhat agitating and disquieting agents to their possessor, but they have, if they get fair play, great powers for evoking and enriching a literature. But the Americans, as we know, are apt to set them at rest in the manner of my friend Colonel Higginson of Boston. "As I take it, Nature said, some years since: 'Thus far the English is my best race; but we have had Englishmen enough; we need something with a little more buoyancy than the Englishman; let us lighten the structure, even at some peril in the process. Put in one drop more of nervous fluid, and make the American.' With that drop, a new range of promise opened on the human race, and a lighter, finer, more highly organized type of mankind was born." People who by this sort of thing give rest to their sensitive and busy self-consciousness may very well, perhaps, be on their way to great material prosperity, to great political power; but they are scarcely on the right way to a great literature, a serious art.

The Russian does not assuage his sensitiveness in this fashion. The Russian man of letters does not make Nature say: "The Russian is my best race." He finds relief to his sensitiveness in letting his perceptions have perfectly free play and in recording their reports with perfect fidelity. The sincereness with which the reports are given has even something childlike and touching. In the novel of which I am going to speak there is not a line, not a trait, brought in for the glorification of Russia, or to feed vanity; things and characters go as nature takes them, and the author is absorbed in seeing how nature takes them and in relating it. But we have here a condition of things which is highly favourable to the production of good literature, of good art. We have great sensititiveness, subtlety, and finesse, addressing themselves with entire disinterestedness and simplicity to the representation of human life. The Russian novelist is thus master of a spell to which the secrets of human nature—both what is external and what is internal, gesture and manner no less than thought and feeling—willingly make themselves known. The crown of literature is poetry, and the Russians have not yet had a great poet. But in that form of imaginative literature which in our day is the most popular and the most possible, the Russians at the present moment seem to me to hold, as Mr. Gladstone would say, the field. They have great novelists, and of one of their great novelists I wish now to speak.

Count Leo Tolstoi is about sixty years old, and tells us that he shall write novels no more. He is now occupied with religion and with the Christian life. His writings concerning these great matters are not allowed, I believe, to obtain publication in Russia, but instalments of them in French and English reach us from time to time. I find them very interesting, but I find his novel of *Anna Karénine* more interesting still. I believe that many readers prefer to *Anna Karénine* Count Tolstoi's other great novel, *La Guerre et la Paix*. But in the novel one prefers, I think, to have the novelist dealing with the life which he knows from having lived it, rather than with the life which he knows from books or hearsay. If one has to choose a representative work of Thackeray, it is *Vanity Fair* which one would take rather than *The Virginians*. In like manner I take *Anna*

Karénine as the novel best representing Count Tolstoi. I use the French translation; in general, as I long ago said, work of this kind is better done in France than in England, and *Anna Karénine* is perhaps also a novel which goes better into French than into English, just as Frederika Bremer's *Home* goes into English better than into French. After I have done with *Anna Karénine* I must say something of Count Tolstoi's religious writings. Of these, too, I use the French translation, so far as it is available. The English translation, however, which came into my hands late, seems to be in general clear and good. Let me say in passing that it has neither the same arrangement, nor the same titles, nor altogether the same contents, with the French translation.

There are many characters in *Anna Karénine*—too many if we look in it for a work of art in which the action shall be vigorously one, and to that one action everything shall converge. There are even two main actions extending throughout the book, and we keep passing from one of them to the other—from the affairs of Anna and Wronsky to the affairs of Kitty and Levine. People appear in connection with these two main actions whose appearance and proceedings do not in the least contribute to develop them; incidents are multiplied which we expect are to lead to something important, but which do not. What, for instance, does the episode of Kitty's friend Warinka and Levine's brother Serge Ivanitch, their inclination for one another and its failure to come to anything, contribute to the development of either the character or the fortunes of Kitty and Levine? What does the incident of Levine's long delay in getting to church to be married, a delay which as we read of it seems to have significance, really import? It turns out to import absolutely nothing, and to be introduced solely to give the author the pleasure of telling us that all Levine's shirts had been packed up.

But the truth is we are not to take *Anna Karénine* as a work of art; we are to take it as a piece of life. A piece of life it is. The author has not invented and combined it, he has seen it; it has all happened before his inward eye, and it was in this wise that it happened. Levine's shirts were packed up, and he was late for his wedding in consequence; Warinka and Serge Ivanitch met at Levine's country house and went out walking together; Serge was very near proposing, but did not. The author saw it all happening so—saw it, and therefore relates it; and what his novel in this way loses in art it gains in reality.

For this is the result which by his extraordinary fineness of perception, and by his sincere fidelity to it, the author achieves; he works in us a sense of the absolute reality of his personages and their doings. Anna's shoulders, and masses of hair, and half-shut eyes; Alexis Karénine's updrawn eyebrows, and tired smile, and

cracking finger joints; Stiva's eyes suffused with facile moisture—
these are as real to us as any of those outward peculiarities which in
our own circle of acquaintance we are noticing daily, while the
inner man of our own circle of acquaintance, happily or unhappily,
lies a great deal less clearly revealed to us than that of Count
Tolstoi's creations.

I must speak of only a few of these creations, the chief personages
and no more. The book opens with " Stiva," and who that has once
made Stiva's acquaintance will ever forget him ? We are living, in
Count Tolstoi's novel, among the great people of Moscow and St.
Petersburg, the nobles and the high functionaries, the governing class
of Russia. Stépane Arcadiévitch—" Stiva "—is Prince Oblonsky,
and descended from Rurik, although to think of him as anything
except " Stiva " is difficult. His *air souriant,* his good looks, his
satisfaction; his " ray," which made the Tartar waiter at the club
joyful in contemplating it; his pleasure in oysters and champagne,
his pleasure in making people happy and in rendering services; his
need of money, his attachment to the French governess, his distress
at his wife's distress, his affection for her and the children; his emotion and suffused eyes, while he quite dismisses the care of providing
funds for household expenses and education; and the French attachment, contritely given up to-day only to be succeeded by some
other attachment to-morrow—no, never, certainly, shall we come to
forget Stiva. Anna, the heroine, is Stiva's sister. His wife Dolly
(these English diminutives are common among Count Tolstoi's ladies)
is daughter of the Prince and Princess Cherbatzky, grandees who
show us Russian high life by its most respectable side; the Prince,
in particular, is excellent—simple, sensible, right-feeling; a man of
dignity and honour. His daughters, Dolly and Kitty, are charming.
Dolly, Stiva's wife, is sorely tried by her husband, full of anxieties
for the children, with no money to spend on them or herself, poorly
dressed, worn and aged before her time. She has moments of
despairing doubt whether the gay people may not be after all in the
right, whether virtue and principle answer; whether happiness does
not dwell with adventuresses and profligates, brilliant and perfectly dressed adventuresses and profligates, in a land flowing with
roubles and champagne. But in a quarter of an hour she comes
right again and is herself—a nature straight, honest, faithful, loving, sound to the core; such she is and such she remains; she can
be no other. Her sister Kitty is at bottom of the same temper, but
she has her experience to get, while Dolly, when the book begins,
has already acquired hers. Kitty is adored by Levine, in whom we
are told that many traits are to be found of the character and history
of Count Tolstoi himself. Levine belongs to the world of great
people by his birth and property, but he is not at all a man of the
world. He has been a reader and thinker, he has a conscience, he

has public spirit and would ameliorate the condition of the people, he lives on his estate in the country, and occupies himself zealously with local business, schools, and agriculture. But he is shy, apt to suspect and to take offence, somewhat impracticable, out of his element in the gay world of Moscow. Kitty likes him, but her fancy has been taken by a brilliant guardsman, Count Wronsky, who has paid her attentions. Wronsky is described to us by Stiva ; he is "one of the finest specimens of the *jeunesse dorée* of St. Petersburgh ; immensely rich, handsome, aide-de-camp to the emperor, great interest at his back, and a good fellow notwithstanding ; more than a good fellow, intelligent besides and well read—a man who has a splendid career before him." Let us complete the picture by adding that Wronsky is a powerful man, over thirty, bald at the top of his head, with irreproachable manners, cool and calm, but a little haughty. A hero, one murmurs to oneself, too much of the Guy Livingstone type, though without the bravado and exaggeration. And such is, justly enough, perhaps, the first impression, an impression which continues all through the first volume ; but Wronsky, as we shall see, improves towards the end.

Kitty discourages Levine, who retires in misery and confusion. But Wronsky is attracted by Anna Karénine, and ceases his attentions to Kitty. The impression made on her heart by Wronsky was not deep ; but she is so keenly mortified with herself, so ashamed, and so upset that she falls ill, and is sent with her family to winter abroad. There she regains health and mental composure, and discovers at the same time that her liking for Levine was deeper than she knew, that it was a genuine feeling, a strong and lasting one. On her return they meet, their hearts come together, they are married ; and in spite of Levine's waywardness, irritability, and unsettlement of mind, of which I shall have more to say presently, they are profoundly happy. Well, and who could help being happy with Kitty ? So I find myself adding impatiently. Count Tolstoi's heroines are really so living and charming that one takes them, fiction though they are, too seriously.

But the interest of the book centres in Anna Karénine. She is Stiva's sister, married to a high official at St. Petersburg, Alexis Karénine. She has been married to him nine years, and has one child, a boy named Serge. The marriage had not brought happiness to her, she had found in it no satisfaction to her heart and soul, she had a sense of want and isolation ; but she is devoted to her boy, occupied, calm. The charm of her personality is felt even before she appears, from the moment when we hear of her being sent for as the good angel to reconcile Dolly with Stiva. Then she arrives at the Moscow station from St. Petersburg, and we see the grey eyes with their long eyelashes, the graceful carriage, the gentle and caressing smile on the fresh lips, the vivacity restrained but waiting to break through, the fulness of life, the softness and strength joined, the harmony, the bloom, the charm. She goes to Dolly, and achieves, with infinite tact and tenderness, the task of reconciliation. At a ball a few days later, we add to our first impression of Anna's beauty, dark hair, a quantity of little curls over her temples and at the back of her neck, sculptural shoulders, firm throat, and beautiful arms. She is in a plain dress of black velvet with a pearl necklace, a bunch of forget-me-nots in the front of her dress, another in her hair. This is Anna Karénine.

She had travelled from St. Petersburg with Wronsky's mother; had seen him at the Moscow station, where he came to meet his mother, had been struck with his looks and manner, and touched by his behaviour in an accident which happened while they were in the station to a poor workman crushed by a train. At the ball she meets him again; she is fascinated by him and he by her. She had been told of Kitty's fancy, and had gone to the ball meaning to help Kitty; but Kitty is forgotten or at any rate neglected; the spell which draws Wronsky and Anna is irresistible. Kitty finds herself opposite to them in a quadrille together:—

" She seemed to remark in Anna the symptoms of an over-excitement which she herself knew from experience—that of success. Anna appeared to her as if intoxicated with it. Kitty knew to what to attribute that brilliant and animated look, that happy and triumphant smile, those half-parted lips, those movements full of grace and harmony."

Anna returns to St. Petersburg, and Wronsky returns there at the same time; they meet on the journey, they keep meeting in society, and Anna begins to find her husband, who before had not been sympathetic, intolerable. Alexis Karénine is much older than herself, a bureaucrat, a formalist, a poor creature; he has conscience, there is a root of goodness in him, but on the surface and until deeply stirred he is tiresome, pedantic, vain, exasperating. The change in Anna is not in the slightest degree comprehended by him; he sees nothing which an intelligent man might in such a case see, and does nothing which an intelligent man would do. Anna abandons herself to her passion for Wronsky.

I remember M. Nisard saying to me many years ago at the École Normale in Paris, that he respected the English because they are *une nation qui sait se gêner*—people who can put constraint on themselves and go through what is disagreeable. Perhaps in the Slav nature this valuable faculty is somewhat wanting; a very strong impulse is too much regarded as irresistible, too little as what can be resisted and ought to be resisted, however difficult and disagreeable the resistance may be. In our high society with its pleasure and dissipation, laxer notions may to some extent prevail; but in general an English mind will be startled by Anna's suffering herself to be so overwhelmed and irretrievably carried away by her passion, by her almost at once regarding it, apparently, as something which it was hopeless to fight against. And this I say irrespectively of the worth of her lover. Wronsky's gifts and graces hardly qualify him, one might think, to be the object of so instantaneous and mighty a passion on the part of a woman like Anna. But that is not the question. Let us allow that these passions are incalculable; let us allow that one of the male sex scarcely does justice, perhaps, to the powerful and handsome guardsman and his attractions. But if Wronsky had been even such a lover as Alcibiades or the Master of Ravenswood, still that Anna, being what she is and her circumstances being what they are, should show not a hope, hardly a thought, of conquering her passion, of escaping from its fatal power, is to our notions strange and a little bewildering.

I state the objection; let me add that it is the triumph of Anna's charm that it remains paramount for us nevertheless; that throughout her course, with its failures, errors, and miseries, still the impression of her large, fresh, rich, generous, delightful nature, never leaves us —keeps our sympathy, keeps even, I had almost said, our respect.

To return to the story. Soon enough poor Anna begins to experience the truth of what the Wise Man told us long ago, that " the way of transgressors is hard." Her agitation at a steeplechase where Wronsky is in danger attracts her husband's notice and provokes his remonstrance. He is bitter and contemptuous. In a transport of passion Anna declares to him that she is his wife no longer; that she loves Wronsky, belongs to Wronsky. Hard at first, formal, cruel, thinking only of himself, Karénine, who, as I have said, has a conscience, is touched by grace at the moment when Anna's troubles reach their height. He returns to her to find her with a child just born to her and Wronsky, the lover in the house and Anna apparently dying. Karénine has words of kindness and forgiveness only. The noble and victorious effort transfigures him, and all that her husband gains in the eyes of Anna, her lover, Wronsky, loses. Wronsky comes to Anna's bedside, and standing there by Karénine, buries his face in his hands. Anna says to him, in the hurried voice of fever :—

"'Uncover your face; look at that man; he is a saint. Yes, uncover your face; uncover it,' she repeated with an angry air. ' Alexis, uncover his face; I want to see him.'

" Alexis took the hands of Wronsky and uncovered his face, disfigured by suffering and humiliation.

"'Give him your hand; pardon him.'

" Alexis stretched out his hand without even seeking to restrain his tears.

"'Thank God, thank God!' she said; 'all is ready now. How

ugly those flowers are,' she went on, pointing to the wall-paper; 'they are not a bit like violets. My God, my God! when will all this end? Give me morphine, doctor—I want morphine. Oh, my God, my God!'"

She seems dying, and Wronsky rushes out and shoots himself. And so, in a common novel, the story would end. Anna would die, Wronsky would commit suicide, Karénine would survive, in possession of our admiration and sympathy. But the story does not always end so in life; neither does it end so in Count Tolstoi's novel. Anna recovers from her fever, Wronsky from his wound. Anna's passion for Wronsky reawakens, her estrangement from Karénine returns. Nor does Karénine remain at the height at which in the forgiveness scene we saw him. He is formal, pedantic, irritating. Alas! even if he were not all these, perhaps even his *pince-nez*, and his rising eyebrows, and his cracking finger-joints, would have been provocation enough. Anna and Wronsky depart together. They stay for a time in Italy, then return to Russia. But her position is false, her disquietude incessant, and happiness is impossible for her. She takes opium every night, only to find that "not poppy nor mandragora shall ever medicine her to that sweet sleep which she owed yesterday." Jealousy and irritability grow upon her; she tortures Wronsky, she tortures herself. Under these trials Wronsky, it must be said, comes out well, and rises in our esteem. His love for Anna endures; he behaves as our English phrase is, "like a gentleman"; his patience is in general exemplary. But then Anna, let us remember, is to the last, through all the fret and misery, still Anna; always' with something which charms; nay, with something, even, something in her nature, which consoles and does good. Her life, however, was becoming impossible under its existing conditions. A trifling misunderstanding brought the inevitable end. After a quarrel with Anna, Wronsky had gone one morning into the country to see his mother; Anna summons him by telegraph to return at once, and receives an answer from him that he cannot return before ten at night. She follows him to his mother's place in the country, and at the station hears what leads her to believe that he is not coming back. Maddened with jealousy and misery, she descends the platform and throws herself under the wheels of a goods train passing through the station. It is over—the graceful head is untouched, but all the rest is a crushed, formless heap. Poor Anna!

We have been in a world which misconducts itself nearly as much as the world of a French novel all palpitating with "modernity." But there are two things in which the Russian novel—Count Tolstoi's novel at any rate—is very advantageously distinguished from the type of novel now so much in request in France. In the first place, there is no fine sentiment, at once tiresome and false. We are not told to believe, for example, that Anna is wonderfully exalted and ennobled by her passion for Wronsky. The English reader is thus saved from many a groan of impatience. The other thing is yet more important. Our Russian novelist deals abundantly with criminal passion and with adultery, but he does not seem to feel himself owing any service to the goddess Lubricity, or bound to put in touches at this goddess's dictation. Much in *Anna Karénine* is painful, much is unpleasant, but nothing is of a nature to trouble the senses, or to please those who wish their senses troubled. This taint is wholly absent. In the French novels where it is so abundantly present its baneful effects do not end with itself. Burns long ago remarked with deep truth that it *petrifies feeling*. Let us revert for a moment to the powerful novel of which I spoke at the outset, *Madame Bovary*. Undoubtedly the taint in question is present in *Madame Bovary*, although to a much less degree than in more recent French novels, which will be in every one's mind. But *Madame Bovary*, with this taint, is a work of *petrified feeling*; over it hangs an atmosphere of bitterness, irony, impotence; not a personage in the book to rejoice or console us; the springs of freshness and feeling are not there to create such personages. Emma Bovary follows a course in some respects like that of Anna, but where, in Emma Bovary, is Anna's charm? The treasures of compassion, tenderness, insight, which alone, amid such guilt and misery, can enable charm to subsist and to emerge, are wanting to Flaubert. He is cruel, with the cruelty of petrified feeling, to his poor heroine; he pursues her without pity or pause, as with malignity; he is harder upon her himself than any reader even, I think, will be inclined to be.

But where the springs of feeling have carried Count Tolstoi, since he created Anna ten or twelve years ago, we have now to see.

We must return to Constantine Dmitrich Levine. Levine, as I have already said, thinks. Between the age of twenty and that of thirty-five he had lost, he tells us, the Christian belief in which he had been brought up, a loss of which examples nowadays abound certainly everywhere, but which in Russia, as in France, is among all young men of the upper and cultivated classes more a matter of course, perhaps, more universal, more avowed, than it is with us. Levine had adopted the scientific notions current all round him; talked of cells, organisms, the indestructibility of matter, the conservation of force, and was of opinion, with his comrades of the university, that religion no longer existed. But he was of a serious nature, and the question what his life meant, whence it came, whither it tended, presented themselves to him in moments of crisis and affliction with irresistible importunity, and getting no answer, haunted him, tortured him, made him think of suicide.

Two things, meanwhile, he noticed. One was, that he and his

university friends had been mistaken in supposing that Christian belief no longer existed; they had lost it, but they were not all the world. Levine observed that the persons to whom he was most attached, his own wife Kitty amongst the number, retained it and drew comfort from it; that the women generally, and almost the whole of the Russian common people, retained it and drew comfort from it. The other was, that his scientific friends though not troubled, like himself, by questionings about the meaning of human life, were untroubled by such questionings not because they had got an answer to them, but because, entertaining themselves intellectually with the consideration of the cell theory, and evolution, and the indestructibility of matter, and the conservation of force, and the like, they were satisfied with this entertainment and did not perplex themselves with investigating the meaning and object of their own life at all.

But Levine noticed further that he himself did not actually proceed to commit suicide; on the contrary he lived on his lands as his father had done before him, busied himself with all the duties of his station, married Kitty, was delighted when a son was born to him. Nevertheless he was indubitably not happy at bottom, restless and disquieted, his disquietude sometimes amounting to agony.

Now on one of his bad days he was in the field with his peasants, and one of them happened to say to him, in answer to a question from Levine why one farmer should in a certain case act more humanely than another: " Men are not all alike; one man lives for his belly, like Mitiovuck, another for his soul, for God, like old Plato."[1] " What do you call," cried Levine, " living for his soul, for God ? " The peasant answered: " It's quite simple—living by the rule of God, of the truth. All men are not the same, that's certain. You yourself, for instance, Constantine Dmitrich, you wouldn't do wrong by a poor man." Levine gave no answer but turned away with the phrase, *living by the rule of God, of the truth*, sounding in his ears.

Then he reflected that he had been born of parents professing this rule, as their parents again had professed it before them; that he had sucked it in with his mother's milk; that some sense of it, some strength and nourishment from it had been ever with him although he knew it not; that if he had tried to do the duties of his station it was by help of the secret support ministered by this rule; that if in his moments of despairing restlessness and agony, when he was driven to think of suicide, he had yet not committed suicide, it was because this rule had silently enabled him to do his duty in some degree, and had given him some hold upon life and happiness in consequence.

The words came to him as a clue of which he could never again

(1) A common name among Russian peasants.

lose sight, and which with full consciousness and strenuous endeavour he must henceforth follow. He sees his nephews and nieces
throwing their milk at one another and scolded by Dolly for it.
He says to himself that these children are wasting their subsistence
because they have not to earn it for themselves and do not know its
value, and he exclaims inwardly: " I, a Christian, brought up in the
faith, my life filled with the benefits of Christianity, living on these
benefits without being conscious of it, I, like these children, I have
been trying to destroy what makes and builds up my life." But now
the feeling has been borne in upon him, clear and precious, that
what he has to do is to *be good;* he has "cried to *Him.*" What will
come of it ?

" I shall probably continue to get out of temper with my coachman, to go into useless arguments, to air my ideas unseasonably ; I
shall always feel a barrier between the sanctuary of my soul and the
soul of other people, even that of my wife ; I shall always be holding
her responsible for my annoyances and feeling sorry for it directly
afterwards. I shall continue to pray without being able to explain
to myself why I pray ; but my inner life has won its liberty ; it will
no longer be at the mercy of events, and every minute of my
existence will have a meaning sure and profound which it will be
in my power to impress on every single one of my actions, that of
being good."

With these words the novel of *Anna Karénine* ends. But in
Levine's religious experiences Count Tolstoi was relating his own, and
the history is continued in three autobiographical works translated
from him, which have within the last two or three years been published
in Paris: *Ma Confession, Ma Religion,* and *Que Faire.* Our author
announces further, "two great works," on which he has spent six
years : one a criticism of dogmatic theology, the other a new translation of the four Gospels, with a concordance of his own arranging.
The results which he claims to have established in these two works
are, however, indicated sufficiently in the three published volumes
which I have named above.

These autobiographical volumes show the same extraordinary penetration, the same perfect sincerity, which are exhibited in the author's
novel. As autobiography they are of profound interest, and they are
full, moreover, of acute and fruitful remarks. I have spoken of the
advantages which the Russian genius possesses for imaginative
literature. Perhaps for biblical exegesis, for the criticism of religion
and its documents, the advantage lies more with the older nations of
the West. They will have more of the experience, width of knowledge, patience, sobriety, requisite for these studies ; they may probably be less impulsive, less heady.

Count Tolstoi regards the change accomplished in himself during
the last half-dozen years, he regards his recent studies and the ideas

which he has acquired through them, as epoch-making in his life and of capital importance. " Five years ago faith came to me; I believed in the doctrine of Jesus, and all my life suddenly changed. I ceased to desire that which previously I´desired, and, on the other hand, I took to desiring what I had never desired before. That which formerly used to appear good in my eyes appeared evil, that which used to appear evil appeared good."

The novel of *Anna Karénine* belongs to that past which Count Tolstoi has left behind him; his new studies and the works founded on them are what is important; light and salvation are there. Yet I will venture to express my doubt whether these works contain, as their contribution to the cause of religion and to the establishment of the true mind and message of Jesus, much that had not already been given or indicated by Count Tolstoi in relating, in *Anna Karénine*, Levine's mental history. Points raised in that history are developed and enforced; there is an abundant and admirable exhibition of knowledge of human nature, penetrating insight, fearless sincerity, wit, sarcasm, eloquence, style. And we have too the direct autobiography of a man not only interesting to us from his soul and talent, but highly interesting also from his nationality, position, and course of proceeding. But to light and salvation in the Christian religion we are not, I think, brought very much nearer than in Levine's history. I ought to add that what was already present in that history seems to me of high importance and value. Let us see what it amounts to.

I must be general and I must be brief; neither my limits nor my purpose permit the introduction of what is abstract. But in Count Tolstoi's religious philosophy there is very little which is abstract, arid. The idea of *life* is his master idea in studying and establishing religion. He speaks impatiently of St. Paul as a source, in common with the Fathers and the Reformers, of that ecclesiastical theology which misses the essential and fails to present Christ's gospel aright. Yet Paul's " law of the spirit of life in Christ Jesus freeing me from the law of sin and death " is the pith and ground of all Count Tolstoi's theology. Moral life is the gift of God, is God, and this true life, this union with God to which we aspire, we reach through Jesus. We reach it through union with Jesus and by adopting his life. This doctrine is proved true for us by the life in God, to be acquired through Jesus, being what our nature feels after and moves to, by the warning of misery if we are severed from it, the sanction of happiness if we find it. Of the access for *us*, at any rate, to the spirit of life, us who are born in Christendom, are in touch, conscious or unconscious, with Christianity, this is the true account. Questions over which the churches spend so much labour and time— questions about the Trinity, about the godhead of Christ, about the procession of the Holy Ghost, are not vital; what is vital is the doctrine of access to the spirit of life through Jesus.

Sound and saving doctrine, in my opinion, this is. It may be gathered in a great degree from what Count Tolstoi had already given us in the novel of *Anna Karénine*. But of course it is greatly developed in the special works which have followed. Many of these developments are, I will repeat, of striking force, interest, and value. In *Anna Karénine* we had been told of the scepticism of the upper and educated classes in Russia. But what reality is added by such an anecdote as the following from *Ma Confession* :—

"I remember that when I was about eleven years old we had a visit one Sunday from a boy, since dead, who announced to my brother and me, as great news, a discovery just made at his public school. This discovery was to the effect that God had no existence, and that everything which we were taught about him was pure invention."

Count Tolstoi touched, in *Anna Karénine*, on the failure of science to tell a man what his life means. Many a sharp stroke does he add in his latter writings :—

"Development is going on, and there are laws which guide it. You yourself are a part of the whole. Having come to understand the whole so far as is possible, and having comprehended the law of development, you will comprehend also your place in that whole, you will understand yourself.

"In spite of all the shame the confession costs me, there was a time, I declare, when I tried to look as if I was satisfied with this sort of thing!"

But the men of science may take comfort from hearing that Count Tolstoi treats the men of letters no better than them, although he is a man of letters himself :—

"The judgment which my literary companions passed on life was to the effect that life in general is in a state of progress, and that in this development we, the men of letters, take the principal part. The vocation of us artists and poets is to instruct the world ; and to prevent my coming out with the natural question, 'What am I, and what am I to teach?' it was explained to me that it was useless to know that, and that the artist and the poet taught without perceiving how. I passed for a superb artist, a great poet, and consequently it was but natural I should appropriate this theory. I, the artist, the poet—I wrote, I taught, without myself knowing what. I was paid for what I did. I had everything : splendid fare and lodging, women, society ; I had *la gloire*. Consequently, what I taught was very good. This faith in the importance of poetry and of the development of life was a religion, and I was one of its priests—a very agreeable and advantageous office.

"And I lived ever so long in this belief, never doubting but that it was true!"

The adepts of this literary and scientific religion are not numerous, to be sure, in comparison with the mass of the people, and the mass of the people, as Levine had remarked, find comfort still in the old religion of Christendom; but of the mass of the people our literary and scientific instructors make no account.   Like Solomon and Schopenhauer, these gentlemen, and "society" along with them, are, moreover, apt to say that life is, after all, vanity : but then they all know of no life except their own.

"It used to appear to me that the small number of cultivated, rich, and idle men, of whom I was one, composed the whole of humanity, and that the millions and millions of other men who had lived and are still living were not in reality men at all. Incomprehensible as it now seems to me, that I should have gone on considering life without see-ing the life which was surrounding me on all sides, the life of huma-nity ; strange as it is to think that I should have been so mistaken, and have fancied my life, the life of the Solomons and the Schopen-hauers, to be the veritable and normal life, while the life of the masses was but a matter of no importance—strangely odd as this seems to me now, so it was, notwithstanding."

And this pretentious minority, who call themselves "society," "the world," and to whom their own life, the life of "the world," seems the only life worth naming, are all the while miserable! Our author found it so in his own experience :—

"In my life, an exceptionally happy one from a worldly point of view, I can number such a quantity of sufferings endured for the sake of 'the world,' that they would be enough to furnish a martyr for Jesus.   All the most painful passages in my life, beginning with the orgies and duels of my student days, the wars I have been in, the illnesses, and the abnormal and unbearable conditions in which I am living now—all this is but one martyrdom endured in the name of the doctrine of the world.   Yes, and I speak of my own life, exceptionally happy from the world's point of view.

"Let any sincere man pass his life in review, and he will perceive that never, not once, has he suffered through practising the doctrine of Jesus ; the chief part of the miseries of his life have proceeded solely from his following, contrary to his inclination, the spell of the doctrine of the world."

On the other hand, the simple, the multitudes, outside of this spell, are comparatively contented :—

"In opposition to what I saw in our circle, where life without faith is possible, and where I doubt whether one in a thousand would confess himself a believer, I conceive that among the people (in Russia) there is not one sceptic to many thousands of believers. Just contrary to what I saw in our circle, where life passes in idleness, amusements, and dis-content with life, I saw that of these men of the people the whole life was passed in severe labour, and yet they were contented with life. Instead of complaining like the persons in our world of the hardship of their lot, these poor people received sickness and disappointments without any revolt, without opposition, but with a firm and tranquil confidence that so it was to be, that it could not be otherwise, and that it was all right."

All this is but development, sometimes rather surprising, but always powerful and interesting, of what we have already had in the pages of *Anna Karénine*. And like Levine in that novel, Count Tolstoi was driven by his inward struggle and misery very near to suicide. What is new in the recent books is the solution and cure announced.- Levine had accepted a provisional solution of the diffi-culties oppressing him ; he had lived right on, so to speak, obeying his conscience, but not asking how far all his actions hung together and were consistent :—

" He advanced money to a peasant to get him out of the clutches of a money-lender, but did not give up the arrears due to himself ; he punished thefts of wood strictly, but would have scrupled to impound a peasant's cattle trespassing on his fields ; he did not pay the wages of a labourer whose father's death caused him to leave work in the middle of harvest, but he pensioned and maintained his old servants ; he let his peasants wait while he went to give his wife a kiss after he came home, but would not have made them wait while he went to visit his bees."

Count Tolstoi has since advanced to a far more definite and strin-gent rule of life—the positive doctrine, he thinks, of Jesus. It is the determination and promulgation of this rule which is the novelty in our author's recent works. He extracts this essential doctrine, or rule of Jesus, from the Sermon on the Mount, and presents it in a body of commandments—Christ's commandments ; the pith, he says, of the New Testament, as the Decalogue is the pith of the Old. These all-important commandments of Christ are " commandments of peace," and five in number. The first commandment is : " Live in peace with all men ; treat no one as contemptible and beneath you. Not only allow yourself no anger, but do not rest until you have dissi-pated even unreasonable anger in others against yourself." The second is : " No libertinage and no divorce ; let every man have one wife and every woman one husband." The third : " Never on any pretext take an oath of service of any kind ; all such oaths are imposed for a bad purpose." The fourth : " Never employ force against the evil-doer ; bear whatever wrong is done to you without opposing the wrong-doer or seeking to have him punished." The fifth and last : " Renounce all distinction of nationality ; do not admit that men of another nation may ever be treated by you as enemies ; love all men alike as alike near to you ; do good to all alike."

If these five commandments were generally observed, says Count Tolstoi, all men would become brothers. Certainly the actual society in which we live would be changed and dissolved. Armies and wars would be renounced; courts of justice, police, property, would be renounced also. And whatever the rest of us may do, Count Tolstoi at least will do his duty and follow Christ's commandments sincerely. He has given up 'rank, office, and property, and earns his bread by the labour of his own hands. " I believe in Christ's commandments," he says, "and this faith changes my whole former estimate of what is good and great, bad and low, in human life." At present, " Everything which I used to think bad and low—the rusticity of the peasant, the plainness of lodging, food, clothing, manners—all this has become good and great in my eyes. At present I can no longer contribute to anything which raises me externally above others, which separates me from them. I cannot, as formerly, recognise either in my own case or in that of others any title, rank, or quality beyond the title and quality of man. I cannot seek fame and praise; I cannot seek a culture which separates me from men. I cannot refrain from seeking in my whole existence —in my lodging, my food, my clothing, and my ways of going on with people—whatever, far from separating me from the mass of mankind, draws me nearer to them."

Whatever else we have or have not in Count Tolstoi, we have at least a great soul and a great writer. In his biblical exegesis, in the criticism by which he extracts and constructs his Five Command-ments of Christ which are to be the rule of our lives, I find much which is questionable along with much which is ingenious and powerful. But I have neither space, nor, indeed, inclination, to criticise his exegesis here. The right moment, besides, for criticising this will come when the " two great works," which are in preparation, shall have appeared.

For the present I limit myself to a single criticism only—a general one. Christianity cannot be packed into any set of commandments. As I have somewhere or other said, " Christianity is a *source;* no one supply of water and refreshment that comes from it can be called the sum of Christianity. It is a mistake, and may lead to much error, to exhibit any series of maxims, even those of the Ser-mon on the Mount, as the ultimate sum and formula into which Christianity may be run up."

And the reason mainly lies in the character of the founder of Christianity and in the nature of his utterances. Not less important than the teachings given by Jesus is the *temper* of their giver, his temper of sweetness and reasonableness, of *epieikeia.* Goethe calls him a *Schwärmer,* a fanatic; he may much more rightly be called an opportunist. But he is an opportunist of an opposite kind from those who in politics, that " wild and dreamlike trade" of insin-cerity, give themselves this name. They push or slacken, press their points hard or let them be, as may best suit the interests of their self-aggrandisement and of their party. Jesus has in view simply "the rule of God, of the truth." But this is served by waiting as well as by hasting forward, and sometimes served better.

Count Tolstoi sees rightly that whatever the propertied and satisfied classes may think, the world, ever since Jesus Christ came, is judged; " a new earth " is in prospect. It was ever in prospect with Jesus, and should be ever in prospect with his followers. And the ideal in prospect has to be realised. " If ye know these things, happy are ye if ye do them." But they are to be done through a great and widespread and long-continued change, and a change of the inner man to begin with. The most important and fruitful utterances of Jesus, therefore, are not things which can be drawn up as a table of stiff and stark external commands, but the things which have most soul in them; because these can best sink down into our soul, work there, set up an influence, form habits of conduct, and prepare the future. The Beatitudes are on this account more helpful than the utterances from which Count Tolstoi builds up his Five Commandments. The very *secret* of Jesus, " He that loveth his life shall lose it, he that will lose his life shall save it," does not give us a command to be taken and followed in the letter, but an idea to work in our mind and soul, and of inexhaustible value there.

Jesus paid tribute to the government and dined with the publicans, although neither the empire of Rome nor the high finance of Judea were compatible with his ideal and with the " new earth " which that ideal must in the end create. Perhaps Levine's provisional solution, in a society like ours, was nearer to " the rule of God, of the truth," than the more trenchant solution which Count Tolstoi has adopted for himself since. It seems calculated to be of more use. I do not know how it is in Russia, but in an English village the determination of " our circle " to earn their bread by the work of their hands would produce only dismay, not fraternal joy, amongst that "majority " who are so earning it already. " There are plenty of us to compete as things stand," the gardeners, carpenters, and smiths would say, "Pray stick to your articles, your poetry, and nonsense; in manual labour you will interfere with us, and be taking the bread out of our mouths."

So I arrive at the conclusion that Count Tolstoi has perhaps not done well in abandoning the work of the poet and artist, and that he might with advantage return to it. But whatever he may do in the future, the work which he has already done, and his work in religion as well as his work in imaginative literature, is more than sufficient to signalise him as one of the most marking, interesting, and sympathy-inspiring men of our time—an honour, I must add, to Russia, although he forbids us to heed nationality.

MATTHEW ARNOLD.

George Saintsbury

"The Present State
of the Novel. II"

Fortnightly Review 49 (January 1888), 112–23

THE PRESENT STATE OF THE NOVEL.

II.

In dealing with the French novel as it is, a little more detail may be necessary than in dealing with the present state of the English novel; for although French novels, "scrofulous" and other, are very much more in English hands than they were even ten years ago, one can hardly presuppose in English readers the same familiarity with them which may be presupposed in reference to Mr. Mudie's native wares. Since I had the honour of writing somewhat at length in the Fortnightly Review on the chief French novelists of the century, wide gaps have been made in the list of those who were even then living. Sandeau is gone, and Flaubert, and About; M. Droz has long given up the practice of those delicately indelicate stories of which *Monsieur, Madame, et Bébé,* and *Entre Nous* will always remain the model, has "made his soul," and has in *Tristesses et Sourires* become edifying though not dull. M. Cherbuliez has not abandoned the novel, but has, since his academicianate, given himself more and more to politics, and has certainly done nothing equal to *Meta Holdenis* or the *Roman d'une Honnête Femme.* Of all the veterans, M. Feuillet alone is now writing; and though *La Morte* showed no loss of delicacy and some gain in healthiness, he is past the age of masterpieces, and not much more, masterly or not masterly, can be expected from him.

It can hardly be said that the place of these masters, or at least of the best of them, has been taken; but substitutes of a kind have of course arisen, and not a few writers who at the former date were comparative novices have either gained a wider popularity or have at any rate increased their volume of work. M. Zola, M. Daudet, M. André Theuriet, M. Ohnet, Madame Henry Gréville, M. Paul Bourget, M. Guy de Maupassant, the group of followers in Drozian steps, of whom the chief are M. Armand Silvestre, "Gyp," and the Vicomte "Richard O'Monroy," together with a few others, deserve some individual mention, and we may then proceed to classify them a little, and, as in the English case, to indicate some general critical considerations.

We must begin with such a Jove as the subject affords, the naturalist Zeus, the dirt-compeller. The popularity of M. Zola does not indeed surprise me, for there has always been a very considerable demand for obscene books; and when customers can get them without let or hindrance, at a moderate price, and with no loss of reputation if they are seen carrying them away, it is not to be supposed that the demand will be greatly lessened, at any rate for a time. Of course I admit that M. Zola is not a caterer for Holywell Street, pure and simple. No competent critic of literature can refuse admiration to much of the *Contes à Ninon*, to such an admirable story as that "Attaque du Moulin" which opens the *Soirées de Médan*, a story yielding to hardly anything of its kind in French, and worthy in its different style to be ranked not far below the "Prise de la Redoute" of Mérimée, which is the *Wandering Willie's Tale* (only not supernatural) of French literature. Again, the first part—the first hundred pages or so—of *L'Œuvre* could not, in its style, be very much better than it is. But M. Zola obviously has not the faculty of writing a long story that shall be a story, and according to the wont of many other men of talent who are not men of genius, he is perpetually trying to do by wrong means what he cannot do by the right means. His wearisome nonsense of "documents," his working-in (with a delightful unconsciousness of the bitter satire which his master Flaubert had already poured on the practice in *Bouvard et Pécuchet*) of a kind of small encyclopædia of elaborate nastiness into each book, his photographs of the ugly and disgusting, his actual obscenity itself, are all (and all, I repeat, no doubt unconsciously) attempts to get at the secret of the interesting, attempts to secure customers, very much as the legendary barber offered a glass of pine-apple rum to everybody who would come and be shaved, or as some shopkeepers put packets of doubtful sweetmeats into parcels of more doubtful tea. His purely literary merits—intense realisation of the object, vivid if coarse phrasing, and sometimes, but much more rarely, a knack of seizing snatches and scraps of character—would secure him a very small audience without his illegitimate attractions; and though I admit of course that it does not follow that everyone who admires M. Zola admires him directly and consciously for his filth, it is undeniably his filth which makes him popular. I do not know any really competent literary critic of any European country who admires M. Zola, without such large restrictions and deductions as render his admiration almost worthless. And indeed it would be odd if it were otherwise, for M. Zola's process is the negation of the first rule of literature, which is that what is presented shall be presented not merely as it is, but transformed, and, if I may say so, "*dis*realised." He is a strong and a capable artist who has gone about to break the rules of art, and in that old contest we know which is the victor. Also, though he is much stronger than his other masters, *les deux Goncourt*, he does not possess that rather sickly but still curious refinement of style which may possibly preserve them long after he has passed away. For pass away he must, having neither of the two and the only two lasting qualities of literature.

One of these is style, the other is the artistic presentation of matter. The first he probably could not have attained, except in a few passages, if he would; the second he has deliberately rejected, and so the mother of dead dogs awaits him sooner or later.

M. 'Alphonse' Daudet is a very different person, though I have never myself been able to share the admiration with which some people regard him. The two *Tartarins* and some of his stories, notably the "Chèvre de M. Séguin" (an imperishable thing), can never be praised or read too much. Tartarin himself is one of the figures which will not die, and I really do not know that he has had an equal in this immortality since Jerome Paturot, while his creator considerably exceeds Reybaud in purely literary skill. But a professed Daudetist would think scorn of anyone who regarded his idol as the creator of *Tartarin*, and the charming, ill-fated, too symbolical nanny. They rest his fame on the "great works," on the series from *Le Petit Chose* (if indeed they would admit *Le Petit Chose*, which I think nearly the best of the whole) to *Sapho*. My own attitude to this Daudet cult is, I am sorry to say, the dissidence of dissent. *Jack*, and *Fromont Jeune et Risler Aîné*, are better that their followers, but the imitation of Dickens which is so frequently quoted as a merit in them does not seem so to me. The taste of *Les Rois en Exile* is simply abominable; that of *Le Nabab* as bad or worse; that of *Numa Roumestan* not much better. For all appeal principally to the low and vulgar interest of "books with keys," books in which living persons are supposed to be sketched and satirised. And then we come to that curious pair *L'Évangéliste* and *Sapho*, where the naturalist *griffe* seems to have impressed itself well on M. Daudet's shoulder. The faults of these are so much the fault of naturalism in general that what we shall have to say on naturalism generally will almost apply to them. Its dulness appears most in *L'Évangéliste*, its dirtiness most in *Sapho*, though both are redeemed, especially the second, in some measure by the fact that M. Daudet, unlike M. Zola, and to an extent not reached by any of the younger French novelists, can conceive a human being, and not merely a Frenchman first dwarfed to a Parisian and then dwarfed further to a Parisian according to certain fancies and fashions. It is undoubtedly his power over the human that has got him (and so far deservedly) his popularity. It is lamentable to think how little use he has made of it, how he has prostituted it to vulgar personal curiosity and other things nearly (nothing is quite) as bad. That *Tartarin* will save him I do not doubt, but it will be so as by fire.

That extraordinary, or at first sight extraordinary phenomenon, the popularity of M. Ohnet, first escaped and then puzzled Frenchmen much more than it did English critics—an incident merely illustrative of old proverbs about lookers-on. Of late, no doubt, M. Jules Lemaître and other lively and sprightly writers have taken up the pen of protest; but I should like to be quite sure that the enormous sale of the books—the batch of six or seven has reached, I believe, collectively something like a thousand editions—has not stirred up active jealousy to the help of sluggish criticism. But *Serge Panine* and *Le Maître de Forges* very early struck not acuter but less interested judges as possessing all the qualities which obtain and deserve a real and immediate popularity. What Mr. Lewis Morris is in England to a perfect poet in the abstract and to the best poets of the day in the concrete, that M. Georges Ohnet is, exactly, to a perfect novelist in the abstract and to the best or most prominent novelists of the day in the concrete. The remark that popularity of this sort depends on the writer being slightly, but not impressively or insolently, above his audience—above them at a height to which they can easily rise, while such little effort as the rising gives them excites a pleasurable sense of effort, intelligence, and virtue—is a commonplace of the more abstract criticism. It is excellently exemplified by M. Ohnet, who has the further gift of mixing his attractions with great skill and impartiality. He has a style on which *raffinés* look down, but which is a little above the ordinary *feuilleton* writer. His stories, not immoderately interesting, have a certain attraction of plot; his characters, not quite alive, are a long way above the mere mannikins of the average novelist. He does a little cautious but stimulating indecency, has a touch of "document," and blends it (a wondrous mixture!) with a touch of romance. And so he hits that many-winged bird the public on all its wings. To be crowned by the Academy, and yet write a scene describing in full the advantage which a French gentleman takes when a French lady is thrown on his hospitality, is indeed to score with both barrels. Such a success would, no doubt, be impossible either at a time when there were many good novelists, or when those who were good were very good; but M. Ohnet just attains the happy and contemptible mean between a number of extremes, and he has his reward. Naturally the extremes are all very angry, which need not disturb us.

No other novelist can touch the popularity, as evidenced by "editions," of these three writers and of M. Feuillet when he still writes. Of the rest, there is no one who seems to me welcomed so much below his desert as M. André Theuriet. He has more than once got into considerable circulation, but it has usually been, I will not say by pandering, but by descending to the popular taste for a certain sort of incident, as in *Sauvageonne* and *Au Paradis des Enfants*, though the latter, as it seems to me, is the weakest book he has written. But if he will not give them a seduction or an adultery, his French readers leave, in third or fifth or seventh editions (which is equivalent with us to a difficult sale of the first), stories which, in a certain pure and unaffected style, in straightforward and unhesitating but cleanly grasp of character, and, above all, in sympathetic but not too florid description of nature, are surpassed by no work of the day. Richard Jefferies himself could not have bettered M. Theuriet's treatment of the woods of his beloved Lorraine or the plains of the Loire ; while in conception of human life, not in the least squeamish but not limited to certain sides only, no living French novelist except M. Daudet is his superior. Scarcely so much can be said of Madame Henry Gréville, and the reason is very clear : no mortal can write novels as this clever lady has been writing them for the last ten years and write them good. But her Russian stories are not (as I believe is sometimes thought in England) her only good ones, and in such books as *Rose Rozier* and *Cité Ménard*, the capacity which has been unluckily frittered away is evident enough.

In coming to M. Paul Bourget and M. Guy de Maupassant I come to dangerous ground. Both are representative figures of the newest school of novel-writing in France, and both are exceedingly clever men. I think myself that M. de Maupassant is the most really gifted writer, both in prose and verse, that has appeared in France for more than twenty years ; and I am sure that the country has not in that time had a more careful, learned, and accomplished craftsman—in prose, at least—than M. Bourget. But one devil seems to me to have entered into M. de Maupassant, and two devils —two very bad devils indeed—into M. Bourget. Both seem to think it absolutely necessary to transgress into subjects popularly known as " forbidden "—a phrase which, in France at least, seems to mean that a popular writer is forbidden to take up any other. One seems to think it necessary to treat those subjects, and all subjects, with that dreary analysis, falsely so-called, which the New World has sent with the Colorado beetle, and the phylloxera, and a hundred other plagues, to punish the rashness of Columbus and the crimes of his followers of all nations. Now as for Devil No. 1 it is awkward speaking. I profess myself to be absolutely free from squeamishness. I still think the condemners of Baudelaire's condemned poems fools for their pains. I am still a faithful lover of Madeleine de Maupin, and I think, to come to close quarters, M. de Maupassant's own *Boule de Suif* one of the most finished and delightful pieces of tragic comedy that our age has produced. But if we are to be " pagan," let us in the first place for heaven's sake remember that the pagan Pantheon *was* a Pantheon ; that your Greek did not worship the god who rhymes to " bedrape us " all day long and every day in the year. And let us in the second place remember that both that disproportioned deity and his comelier mother were in their original functions and capacities "very merry, laughing, quaffing, and unthinking" divinities, quite good-natured, unless people blasphemed them (which I have not the least intention of doing), and busy in their rather irregular fashion with making people happy and comfortable. "Our Lady of Pain" is quite a modern invention; she never gave pain in the old times to any one who did not go out of his or her way to resist or slight her deity. Now these two things your modern pagan novelist, and especially "them two clever ones" of whom I am more particularly speaking, do constantly neglect. M. de Maupassant is quite independent of his favourite motive as a mere stimulus, but he seems to drag it in as if it bewitched him. He can write on nothing else; nor should I care if his writing on nothing else gave us always or often such true and strange tragedy as in *M. Parent*; such admirable satire and tragi-comic portraiture as in the little masterpiece already mentioned, even such Aristophanic comedy as *Les Sœurs Rondoli*. But it does not. In most of his longer works and many of his shorter pieces, though there is generally vigorous writing and constantly a creative or interpretative touch (for M. de Maupassant, as has been said, is a poet) the naturalist dullness and the naturalist dirtiness strive for the mastery in a monotonous wrestle. As for M. Bourget, he is never exactly dirty, but he appears to be under a complete obsession of erotic ideas—under a kind of *névrose*, to use his own words. In one of his stories (I think *L'Irréparable* was published before M. Ohnet, greatly daring, conceived the idea above referred to) a gentleman of fashion and family plays the complete part of Lovelace to a young girl who is guest in his own house. In another a French visitor to England relates, with a frankness which must certainly charm English girls who have extended their usual welcome to French visitors, the strange thoughts which came to him when a young lady played tennis with him, walked with him, talked to him, and in other respects behaved as any English girl would. And then M. Bourget is an "analyst,"—heaven help him!—a lowest depth from which it may be Aphrodite herself, recognising a good though erring servant, has saved the author of *Boule de Suif*. In the preface to one of his books M. Bourget describes how he and Mr. Henry James held stupendous and terrible converse in the "hospitable *Athenæum*" (hospitable that is to Frenchmen and Americans). A meeting of two clever and agreeable persons is, of course, not stupendous and terrible in itself, but the notion of the author of *L'Irréparable* talking to the author of the *Portrait of a Lady* is full of form and fear. If it had only been Mr. Howells the thing would have been completer still, and the poor old novel of the past could hardly have got over that duumvirate.

For analysis (to give it its own word) is perhaps even a worse spirit than naturalism. I make these remarks certainly in no hostile spirit to M. Bourget, for whose talents I have a great respect, and to whom I am indebted for exceedingly amiable notice of certain work of mine. But the analytic method seems to me to stand to the photographic method in the relationship of something that is almost always bad to something that is sometimes good. There are times and seasons, as I have admitted above, when M. Zola's system produces, for a brief space at any rate, work that could hardly be surpassed in merit by any other method.. It is rather in his indiscriminate (or, as some would say, his very discriminating) choice of subjects, and in his stinting himself of other and far better methods, that the naturalist goes wrong. The analyst, as he is understood by the American, French, and to some extent Russian schools, who derive at farther or nearer stages from Balzac and Stendhal, is in this worse off than the naturalist pure and simple, that instead of mistaking a partial for a universal method, he takes for a complete method what is not strictly a method at all. The painful copying of an actual scene or action sometimes results in something that is at least an integral part of a story. The elaborate dissection of motives and characters can only result in something that stops short of being even part of a story—that is only preliminary to part of a story. To illustrate the comparison forcibly if grotesquely, the naturalist is as one who is supposed to supply a complete meal and offers nothing but dry bread. The analyst offers mere dough—something which, valuable and indispensable as a stage in the process of manufacturing the eatable, is not yet eatable at all. It is fair to M. Bourget to say that he himself has never been guilty of the utter futility of some of his American contemporaries (*not* of Mr. Henry James). It is difficult for a Frenchman to rise to the modern conception that a tale ought to tell nothing.

Few words must suffice for the group of tale-tellers of whom I have mentioned the three chief. They are sometimes very naughty, but I own to a weakness for them. For Rabelaisian fun M. Armand Silvestre has scarcely had a superior since the master himself; though (without that master's excuse and apparently out of pure relish for the thing) he is often simply nasty. At these times he makes me ill. If he would only, now that he has laid down his Parnassian trumpet (and a very nice trumpet, too, it was), take in hand some other instrument than that which plays such an important part in the choruses of *M. de Pourceaugnac !* But Molière's infatuation for it, if sufficiently unintelligible to an Englishman, had excuses which are not open to M. Silvestre. The pleasant lady who calls herself "Gyp" is a little monotonous in her perpetual handling of the "triangle," but at any rate she is never unladylike, and nearly always amusing. Also she has one grand distinction—she has invented in her Eve a type, or rather an individuality, which is of the rarest in French novels—the young girl, who is neither a model of innocence on the way to become something not at all innocent, nor a Hoyden, nor a Lydia Languish. That she may have been imagined not least as a foil to the frail dames around her, is quite conceivable, but that hardly detracts from her excellence. The allegorically and poetically named viscount is, I think, on the whole inferior to M. Silvestre and Madame de Martel. His last book was certainly inferior both to them and to himself; but Le Capitaine Parabère and his brother plungers are excellent company for the most part, when the reader is not a serious person and does not want serious persons for his companions. They are a merry family, these children of the *Vie Parisienne* and of M. Droz, though they are, perhaps, never quite so good as their father was in the days of old.

In the great company of novels and novelists which is present to the memory, there are not a few books and not a few authors (independent of the minor naturalists, of whom presently) deserving of some mention. There is a whole group of Provençal novelists, of whom M. Noel Blache is one of the best, and who have given to the southern provinces something of the same prominence in recent French novel-writing that Brittany used to enjoy in the heyday of the Romantic movement. Indeed, most provincial districts have their groups of painters in words, one of the most remarkable of whom is the author of a singularly powerful series (*Le Forestier, Le Marinier, Le Berger*), dealing with the districts north and south, but especially south, of the seaward course of the Loire. The author, M. Jules de Glouvet, is, I believe, a lawyer of some eminence. The warmest admirers of M. Viard may exclaim at me for putting "Pierre Loti" only in this category. Certainly *Le Mariage de Loti* is a very charming though an extremely affected book of its kind; and there are passages in *Asiyadé, Le Spahi, Mon Frère Yves, Pêcheur d'Islande*, which display great cleverness. But I have myself far too little affection for "preciousness," either in French or English, to care very greatly for a style which, though very closely connected with some styles now popular with us, seems to me to fail in all the best qualities of prose —simplicity, sanity, proportion, and, in the proper sense, grace. Attention has been recently drawn in England (and I am very glad of it) to the charming work of M. Anatole France, the chief of which is *La Crime de Sylvestre Bonnard*. M. France, like a majority of the best writers of the day, is an old Parnassien (they were very nearly *Quatre-vingt Rimeurs*, as M. de Banville altered it, in the three brave galleys of '66, '69, and '76, but few there are that abide by the oar now), and his prose shows the old practice in its style, as well as a faculty quite independent of such practice in the matter. I at least also think that the best work of a much better-known poet, M. Coppée, is in prose fiction. M. Jean Ricard made his appearance not long ago with a lurid but very powerful little story entitled *Pitchoun!* (the southern for "little one)"': his later work has not quite fulfilled its promise. In France, as in England, considerable attempts have been made to resuscitate the Dumasian romance—a praiseworthy attempt which has not hitherto been crowned with any very great success. Perhaps M. Paul Mahalin (of whose cheerfully-named *Hôtellerie Sanglante* it cannot be said that the title, like the Honourable Mrs. Boldero, "*prommy pas payy*") is the chief of them. Of the eminent M. Fortuné du Boisgobey, in whom to a not inconsiderable English body of clients French novelists appear to be summed up, I desire to speak with all respect. Novels which devote themselves to the elaborate detection of crime appear to have a singular fascination for some people — me they remind unpleasantly of a newspaper; but that is a mere personal matter and has nothing to do with criticism, which has only to pronounce the now veteran author very good of his kind. But to go through the various novels and novelists of whom and which memory, direct or refreshed, reminds me would be a long and, I fear, to readers a tedious process. Let me only mention among books some years old M. Henry Cochin's singularly original and delicate story of a strange case of mental aberration (the belief of an old Professor that time is going backward) and (not for schoolgirls) M. Pierre Giffard's remarkably strong and, despite its resemblance to the *roman comique*, fresh *Tournée du Père Thomas*, a theatrical story of quite the other day. If I do not put on a level with these M. Leon de Tinseau's very charming *L'Attelage de la Marquise*, it is because M. de Tinseau has unluckily gone on writing things by no means equal to his first attempt. M. Hector Malot, M. Mario Uchard, M. Louis Ulbach, may be mentioned as the chief of a great multitude of what the private lingo of the critic, who very likely would do no better, but who has at least the resolution to do no worse, calls circulating library novelists, often commendable, often interesting, but seldom extraordinarily good.

"I don't call this very popular pie," said the disdainful, but even in its disdain democratic, voice of the little boy whom Mr. Grant White met in an obscure New York eating-house, and who thus expressed his disapproval of the sample of the national viand placed before him. To this scion of democracy "popular" meant "good." It does not mean the same to me; and I am bound to admit that in the literal sense M. Ohnet, M. Zola, M. Daudet, and others do furnish "popular pie" to the novel-readers of France. But I can by no means admit that it is pie as good as has been furnished by any generation (taking a literary generation at some twenty years) since about 1820, or a little later, when the example of Scott stirred up French novelists to try fiction on a somewhat larger scale and with a somewhat wider appeal than the tales and novelettes which had satisfied France from the disappearance of Le Sage. It is the peculiarity of novels more than of any other literature that they are usually produced where they are good in schools; and of no country is this so true as of France. We generally think of the romantic novel as exemplified only, and it would be quite a sufficient "only," by the great names of Dumas, Balzac, Bernard, Mérimée. But round these great ones many minor stars were grouped, and such books as—to take one style only—Feval's *Fée des Grèves* and Achard's *Belle-Rose* were as good as all but the best of Alexandre. To my taste at any rate both the hills and the plains have sunk in level notably since those days, and I can see at least part of the reason. A Frenchman, unlike an Englishman or a German, rarely does good work except in a school, and the only school of much strength nowadays is the school of M. Zola. I have said something of the chief, I may now say something of the followers. Except M. de Maupassant (who is a free lance, and whom I have sometimes suspected of playing tricks on his master) they are but a feeble folk. M. Zola was right, indeed, in protesting in a rather Johnsonian manner against the rebuke administered to him by some rebellious pupils the other day. They certainly did not carry much weight either for eminence in the school or for eminence in letters. But of the orthodox Zolaists who is there of whom any sane criticism can say, having read him, anything that is good? The same suspicion of farce indeed attaches to some of them which, as I have said, attaches in my mind to M. Guy de Maupassant. When they expatiate (with ample documents) on the immense relief which a person who is suffering from dysentery experiences in returning from casual quarters to his own chambers, when they parody the famous scene in *Pot-Bouille* by elaborately describing the lying-in of a cow (both these instances are textual and comparatively harmless), it is really difficult to think that they are not, in more senses than one, M. Zola's merry men. Sometimes (the greatest *farceur* of all of them, M. J. K. Huysmans, is the best instance) they have something of their master's vigour, but none of them have anything of his occasional grasp of actual character, and all exaggerate the absurd pessimism which is the characteristic of such philosophy as he possesses. Whether this world is the best of all possible worlds is a complicated religious and philosophical question. No doubt it has in it toothache, gout, bad wine, bad weather, bad poets, political charlatans, American cheese, popular preachers, "advanced thinkers," spelling reformers, and many other evil beasts and evil things. But it is

certainly not such a bad world as the Zolaists, with a monotonous and unimaginative unanimity, make out. I have hinted before
that the objection to the new French morality or immorality is not
so much that it is immoral as that it is so utterly unamusing and
unpleasant. "Loveless, joyless, unendeared," are three words
which Milton might have written after reading any novel of the
school, except one or two of M. de Maupassant's, when he forgets
that he is a naturalist and remembers that he is a man of genius.
I remember one book in particular (it is unnecessary to mention it
by name, especially as the unlucky author has, I believe, since been
shot in one of those most irrational and unheroic of all encounters,
even in the eyes of men who rather believe in duelling, modern
French press duels). It gave an account of the life of a French
schoolboy. He was a dirty, immoral, and dull little schoolboy ; but
the most dreadful thing about him was his entire failure to get any
pleasure out of his misbehaviour. The word for the book and the boy
both was *assommant*, which, if I recollect aright, was what the poor
little wretch found Scott to be. "Almost thou persuadest me to be
a Christian," said a famous character, whether ironically or not the
learned dispute. Those of us who do not require persuasion may,
on this point at least if we have some charity, recognise this one virtue
in the latest school of French novel. It must surely not almost but
altogether persuade any reasonable reader that whatever royal road
there may be to happiness, the rejection of conventional religion,
conventional morals, and conventional propriety is not that road.

To sum up, then, the French novel does not appear to be in any
more healthy condition than the English ; indeed it may be said to
be in a much less healthy condition. Taking it all round, the
superiority of workmanship of which it has so long been said
that they order these things better in France has for a long time
been gradually disappearing in all branches of literature, and in
none so much as novel-writing. As a literary cause of inferiority I
do not think that any deserves to be ranked higher than that opposite
of the cause which, according to some good people, has weakened our
own novel—the absence of consideration for the young person. Doubtless it is not good to write always in the fear of Mr. Podsnap, but it is
a great deal worse to live in a perennial state of saying, "Who's
afraid of Mr. Podsnap?" "Be virtuous, and have done with it," said
Mr. Carlyle, with not altogether unjustifiable temper, to the senti-
ment-praters of the eighteenth century. "Be vicious and have done
with it" is what I feel inclined to say to the praters of the other
thing in the nineteenth. It may perhaps appear to some people
that I harp too much on this string ; they would not think so if
they had read, say, a couple of hundred French novels every year for
the last septennate. A hunger and thirst after Mrs. Trimmer, an

unholy affection for Hannah More, are the natural results of a long course of reading about plain and fancy adultery, diversified only by a few far from, brilliant excursions in the manner of M. Belot and M. Bonnetain. The horrible conventionality of invariably falling in love with some one else than one's husband, the intolerable infringement of the rights of man, which says, "Thou shalt not love thy own wife," might surely have forced themselves on such devotees of liberty (in print) as the descendants of the men of '89.

I should not, however, be indisposed to see something of a political explanation in the matter, which, it need hardly be said, is only part of a larger matter, to wit, the steady descent of French genius ever since the final overthrow of the old monarchy in 1830. For sixty years, as nearly as may be, it has been more and more difficult for any Frenchman of genius and feeling to take an interest in the political institutions of his country, and much debated as the connection of politics and literature is, it is simply an historical fact that almost all periods of great literary development have been periods of great national prosperity or brilliant national struggle. The age of Pericles, the age of Elizabeth, the age of Augustus, the age of the great Spanish poets, the age of Louis Quatorze, the age of that great English fight against anarchy and tyranny combined which Mr. Gladstone regrets, have been the chief literary ages of the world. Since 1830 every Government and every form of government has been more inglorious in the beginning, and more unfortunate in the end than that before it. For a moment it seemed as if the great disaster of 1870 might bring about something better, but it notoriously has done nothing but plunge the nation deeper than ever in government by mediocrities and dishonesties. The movement of 1830 was notoriously an attempt to do without politics in literature altogether, and to this was probably due its short-lived character.

I never knew in history any example of a people who appear to have lost that art of enjoyment which is really the art of life so much as the French, judged by their literature and their politics both. At the present day the common French remark, "Have we laughed?" has been set down by some humourists as a proof that to be amused is a rare and strange thing among the people. That is a joke or an over-refinement; but certainly the nation, for all its cafés and its theatres, its boulevards and its popular fêtes, is in both itself and its current literature, for the most part, a profoundly dismal one. Of its old beliefs, the belief that it is being betrayed by everybody survives almost alone, coupled with a certain belief in money-making. It does not take its politics, or its pleasures, or its literature with the slightest relish; and there is no truer copybook maxim than that what you do not do with a relish you do not do well.   GEORGE SAINTSBURY.

Garnet Smith

"Gustave Flaubert"

Gentleman's Magazine 265 (August 1888), 120–31

GUSTAVE FLAUBERT.

LITERATURE is the confession of society, and La Bruyère's re-mark at the beginning of his " Caractères," that he gave back to his century what it had given him, applies to all other authors whose notoriety is due to the fact that they first spoke the word that was on everybody's lips, that they first gave form to what was mutely felt by their generation. There must be some reason for the long-continued prevalence of the so-called realistic doctrine in literature and art in France ; and its sources are not one but many, the concurrence of which has made it so all-absorbing. It is partly due, no doubt, to the mere desire of novelty ; as romanticism drove classicism from the field, so when romanticism died from exhaustion realism seized upon the vacant place. Democracy has something to do with it ; in a democratic age it was but natural that attention should be drawn to the study of the obscure lives of the nameless masses ; in short, there is a natural affinity between realism and democracy. But the greatest fact to be considered is the enormous growth of natural science in recent years, its popularisation and predominance. Liter-ature became jealous of a vigorous and aggressive rival ; it would meet its rival half-way, or even come over to its side ; it would strive to be as accurate in its methods as science itself. In criticism, Sainte-Beuve had already treated the masters of literature as products of their age and circumstances, and it was not long before the scientific doctrine of the *milieu*, the doctrine of the influence of the environ-ment, the evolutionary theory that imperfection, unhappiness, and suffering are due to the fact that as yet the equilibrium between man and his surroundings is not complete, was eagerly accepted as a new criterion and basis for literature. By Taine and his followers—for Zola may be regarded as the logical outcome of Taine's essay on Balzac—the doctrine is carried to excess ; virtue and vice are found to be but physical products, and the environment is dwelt on till the other half of life—the heart, the will—is either denied or at least utterly neglected. Previous poets and novelists had been content with study-ing the psychology of their heroes ; but Zola now admonishes us that in future physiology, and not psychology, must be our study—that henceforth we must concern ourselves not with the head but with the whole body, that is, with the animal part of us in its animality only. And this physiology is a study of sensations, chiefly degraded ones, to the exclusion of sentiments—is pathology rather than physiology. As the invisible and mystic part of man's life is shunned or denied, so Beauty is dethroned, and revolting Ugliness set up in its place. The spirit of revolt that injured the Romantic movement so much sought by a perverted idealism to discover its heroes among the criminal classes, and the new theory still does the same. To produce a novel of the prevalent type, it is but necessary to study the life of some poor creature under the ban of society or belonging to the degraded classes; banish all beauty; depict the surroundings with the most wearisome precision of ugly details ; regard all vice as due to such surroundings—to fatality of temperament and hereditary tendencies— all crime as unblamable as chemical products ; deny all free-agency or power of the spirit to battle with circumstances ; finally, view the whole with an eye of utter indifference. As life, for the majority, is dull and slow, and the events in it are few and far between, so the realist, true to nature, must make no choice or selection as an artist would do, but rather strive to make his book as uninteresting and slow as life itself, of which it has to be the copy. But, above all, no sympathy must be displayed by the author ; and it is this utter indifference, this lack of sympathy, which above all else renders the theory and its results so hateful and disgusting, and will prove its death-blow. It is this neglect of sympathy and charity which makes the French realists appear so poor in comparison with their English brethren, and even with the pessimistic Russian novelists. Finally, Caricature is the inevitable goal of such realism ; and even our English novelists, to whom all honour is due, have not entirely escaped this grievous fault.

What was the origin of the doctrine, and by whom it was first brought into prominence, have long been among the favourite questions of the French critics. The question at first seems very simple; all novelists since Fielding have declared more or less definitely their intention to represent nature as it is, the only point left to criticism being as to with what eyes and what temperament they have viewed nature. Diderot is praised as being the forerunner of realism (Diderot, who, by the way, is altogether English) ; but Stendhal is generally fixed upon by the critics as the father of realism, and the true genealogical tree is said to be from Stendhal through Balzac to Flaubert. But there is room for much dispute in this ; for Stendhal really belongs to the eighteenth century, and he has far more affinity with Voltaire than with Flaubert. Stendhal is " spiritual," full of Voltairean persiflage, and wit is altogether unknown to realism. On Balzac there is a better claim. The revolution he brought about in novel-writing was due to the stress he laid on the material preoccupations and economical questions of life, on the ways in which money or the want of it influences the character—a subject utterly neglected by previous novelists, whose heroes are unaffected by such questions. In fact, as has been well said, Balzac was the first to " dégager de l'argent tout le pathétique terrible qu'il contient." Realist he is also in his pitiless accumulation of detail, his endless descriptions, his pretence of accuracy in technical matters, his inventory of the environment and demonstration of its influence on character, and his recognition of the law of hereditary temperament. But Balzac is a true roman-ticist also ; his characters are but the mouthpieces of his opinions ; he has ideas—and the true realist scorns ideas ; he dwells on the illusions of life, and, above all, is a thorough dreamer, haunted by visions of bou. lless wealth, or love, and the like. It is curious that the realists are so shy of mentioning Prosper Merimée ; they would at least find in him that utter indifference to his heroes which they practise. But I suppose he is too much of an aristocrat in art and theory for them, and in the true romantic spirit he extends his geographical horizon beyond the outskirts of Paris, which they cannot be persuaded to do on any account.

With one consent, all the French critics agree that Flaubert is the head of the realistic school. The influence that Flaubert had on succeeding literature is, indeed, far greater than the actual merits of his work would lead us to expect ; for on reading his books we are disappointed, except perhaps in the case of " Madame Bovary." " Madame Bovary" is regarded as the *chef-d'œuvre* of the realistic school, the book which will represent in the future to the general mind the passing phase of literature which goes under the name of realism. Flaubert is a man of one book ; for it is fairly certain that the rest of his works will live in remembrance only because they were written by the author of " Madame Bovary." Most curious it is that it should be the first of the series. Indeed, if it had been published at the end of his career, the critics would infallibly have demonstrated how all the rest of the works gradually led up to and prepared the way for " Madame Bovary," which is the crown and consummation of the whole method of procedure. But if we wish to gain a due appreciation of Flaubert's character, we must espe-cially remember that he was irritated beyond endurance if he heard himself named as the "author of 'Madame Bovary.'" He used to read aloud to his friends those passages which had received undoubted praise, mercilessly dissect them, satirise them, criticise them savagely. He would write "Salammbô" to prove that he was more than the author of "Madame Bovary," that his famous work was not the true expression of his character and genius. "They accuse me of being a realist—that is to say, that I only copy what I see, and that I am incapable of invention." Consequently "Salammbô" was written, and by "Salammbô" he wished to be judged. And, in truth, it seems as if the writing of "Madame Bovary" was a mere accident, due to the suggestion of his friend Bouilhet that he should write out in detail the story of one of his father's medical pupils. Flaubert was essentially an artist, an artist of the school of Théophile Gautier, a zealous adherent of the "art for art's sake" school. He was sure that the most harmonious word was always the right word, and had even reached and accepted the theory that "what you say is of little consequence; the way in which you say it is everything." It was the form and not the matter that he cared for. In a letter to Georges Sand he writes: "I remember having felt my heart beat strongly, having experienced a violent pleasure, in contemplating a wall of the Acropolis—a wall quite bare—the one on the left as you look at the Propylæa. Well, cannot a book, independently of what it says, produce the same effect?" Mere words had the same effect on him as sounds have for a musician or colours for a painter. His manner was to get hold of some sonorous phrase and repeat it again and again, till he utterly wearied his friends, who could see nothing remarkable in it. If they did not share his enthusiasm, he used to call them "*bourgeois*," as we would say Philistines, which he considered the direst insult he could pay them. In accordance with his theory he was convinced that a work of art should be quite impersonal, and that no trace of the author should be discovered in the work. It is amusing to read the correspondence between him and Georges Sand on the subject. The pair were so utterly different in frame of mind that it was useless for them to argue with one another, though Georges Sand took some time to see the folly of a continuation of the debate. She attacked his theory again and again with powerful arguments, to which he only replied by re-stating his theory in other words. Take a sample: "I feel an unconquerable aversion to set down on paper any of my own feelings; I even consider a novelist has no right to express his opinions on any subject whatever." To which Georges Sand replies: "As far as I am concerned, it seems to me an author can do nothing else. Can he separate his intellect from his heart? Are his intellect and heart indeed two sepa-rate things? In short, to avoid expressing oneself completely in one's works seems to me to be as impossible as it would be to weep with anything but one's eyes or to write with anything but one's brains."

Flaubert was an artist, seeing all things with the eyes of a painter ; though not so warmly and imaginatively as Théophile Gautier, whom he acknowledged as his master. He declared that an artist was one who regarded the world as made for art, and not art for the world. His style was founded on Chateaubriand, another painter in feeling, though Quinet's "Ahasvérus" also had made a deep impression on him, as may be seen in the "Tentation de Saint Antoine." The history of this work is most characteristic of the author. The first idea of it came to him when looking at a picture on the subject in Genoa. He worked at it for three years, not showing it even to his constant adviser Bouilhet. Though longing to travel in the East with a friend who was going there, he would wait till it was finished. At length the great day came ; the book was completed. He would read it aloud to his friends, absolute silence being demanded till the end was reached. It took four days, and the last page was finished in a dead silence. " Well? If you don't utter howls [*sic*] of enthusiasm nothing is capable of moving you." They would give him the verdict next day, and it was—to burn it ! Judge of the feelings of Flaubert ; but he took the advice and laid the work aside. Still he loved it, and in 1848 introduced fragments of it into a paper which Gautier then edited. When Bouilhet died the check on Flaubert was removed, and the book reappeared in its third form. But there are still the same faults as in the old one : it is a mixture of lyrism and misplaced erudition—action is altogether absent, the philosophy of history and religion is not touched upon in the slightest, and the whole is nothing but a long series of dissolving views of the seven sins, chimeras, heresiarchs, Eastern potentates and dead deities, one of whom is the great god Crepitus ! The whole book seems but written with the purpose of expressing the author's utter scorn of wretched humanity and the miserable religious beliefs to which it clings in its despair.

Here, indeed, we touch the very kernel and centre of Flaubert's temperament. The artist in him is killed by the misanthropist. Despite his determination to let nothing of himself appear in his works, they are, after all, nothing but a long homily on the *bêtise*, the stupidity of mankind. His was an arrested development. At the age of twenty-two he was struck down by a nervous malady and rendered a life-long invalid. Years were spent indoors secluded from the world, and his mind seems to have remained stationary at the point reached before the attack. He declared himself that he was a victim of physiology; every effort and every action was a pain to him. At times he complained that the acts of dressing or eating were intolerable. He did, indeed, travel in the intervals of his malady, but his was one of those natures which cannot endure the real and desire nothing less than the impossible. He was never weary of talking of the mediocrity of life, and used to repeat again and again Michelet's words, "Il n'y a rien de tentant que l'impossible"; but as soon as ever the apparently impossible was realised he was disgusted with it and longed for something else. His travels in the East were a burden and a weariness to him; all was stale and poor and far below expectation till he had got home again, when, of course, he longed to be back in the East. One day the friend who accompanied him said to him, "At last we are sailing up the Nile!" to which Flaubert replied dreamily, "Yes, but we shall never lave ourselves in the waters of the Ganges, and shall not see that Ceylon whose name of old was Taprobana. O Taprobana! Taprobana! what a delicious word!" with his usual delight in a melodious word. With such a temperament, irritated by his malady and enforced solitude, his fellow-men were naturally hateful to him. He would willingly have exclaimed with Danton "L'humanité m'ennuie." In one of his letters he breaks out, "When quite young I had already a complete presentiment of life. It was like the sickening odour of a cook's shop." All, except the few friends whom he admitted to his solitude, were "*bourgeois*" and stupid. He would write for those only who were capable of understanding him, and for a long time his audience consisted of one friend only, the letters to whom were prefaced "*Solus ad solum.*" At length he found his *alter ego* in Bouilhet, a poet of the school of Leconte de Lisle, who had deserted medicine for letters, and supported himself by tuition. Till 1869, when Bouilhet died, the two were inseparable, Bouilhet acting as Flaubert's literary Mentor, checking him in his usually uncritical admirations, and restraining his lyric extravagances. But a companionship so close that they even copied each other's gestures and tricks of speech was not altogether without its drawbacks; it led to too much mutual admiration. Flaubert and Bouilhet were by turns the priest and the divinity. They were so content with each other's society that they forgot or scorned the outside world, which, indeed, they only regarded through the medium of art; and the artist, as Flaubert said, need recognise nothing around him which would not serve to further his own personal consummation.

This misanthropism proved too strong for Flaubert to be a true artist like Théophile Gautier ; every page of " L'Education Sentimentale," " Bouvard et Pécuchet," and "Un Simple Cœur" is instinct with it. He intended " L'Education Sentimentale" to be a *résumé* of the social and political science of the century; but it is really nothing but a series of portraits of people whose acquaintance in real life we should have the greatest objection to make. He could vent his spleen by depicting such people; but we cannot see in what way the study of these characters could " serve to further his personal consummation." The germ of his last and, happily, incomplete novel, " Bouvard et Pécuchet," may be seen in the fact that before his first nervous attack he had begun a collection of commonplace remarks, *prudhomismes*, and the ready-made stock of society conversation. He would have been delighted with Swift's " Polite Conversations," if he had known it. " Bouvard et Pécuchet" is the history of two clerks who, on retiring into the country, finding time hang heavily on their hands, in sheer despair returned to their former occupation of sitting at desk and copying; this time, however, from books of general information. The second volume of the novel was to be a collection of all the stupid remarks Flaubert had found in his reading, and, to increase the collection, he had purposely pushed his researches into such subjects as botany, agriculture, geology, political economy, and the like. The whole was to be an encyclopædia of the *bêtise* of mankind, and its aim was, in his own words, "to produce such an impression of weariness and ennui that the reader would be led to believe that it had been written by an idiot!" Might we not with justice object that Flaubert must have been a Philistine himself to take a pleasure in searching out and noting down such social and literary crudities ? But, indeed, after a remark like this, it is hardly worth while to make mention of the " Candidate," Flaubert's solitary attempt at the drama, withdrawn after the first performance ; of " Herodias," a study in the manner of " Salammbô," full of the bric-à-brac of which Sainte-Beuve complained ; or of " The Legend," an excursion into mediæval story. Flaubert should have remembered his own words, " Disillusion is the foible of the weak. Distrust men who are disgusted with the world; they are almost always useless and powerless."

This mutilated realism is at present the accepted doctrine of French novelists, and meets with little opposition. A young writer here and there is seeking his way out of the dreary labyrinth. There are a few idealists, with Octave Feuillet at their head; the rest are but fervent followers of the popular school, striving to outbid each other in exaggeration. In order to see the full consequences of any theory, we must turn away from the master, who made it acceptable by his genius, and see what are the results produced by the clever disciples who work out the theory to its limits. An original genius is not satisfied with the principles laid down by his predecessors, which principles have been formulated and fossilised by a continuous succession of disciples till all their value has disappeared ; he breaks with his predecessors, and returns to nature for his inspiration. After the first surprise and revolt which he excites by the new way in which he expresses the old facts, his principles are in their turn narrowed and reduced to academic formulæ. That unconsciously working faculty of his which really constituted his genius naturally escapes the disciples ; his defects, or, above all, the faults of his qualities, are as often as not copied instead of his merits; the master and not the master's inspirer, nature, is followed, and the system carried out to its extreme, and exaggerated, feebly drags on till a new genius appears who dares to look at nature with his own eyes, and the same cycle is gone through. In this way realism is carried to the extreme by the disciples of Flaubert, and, the system being the narrow one characterised above, namely, the unsympathetic portrayal of the stupidity and animality of man regarded as without free-will or religion, utterly dominated by his environment, all that is left for them is to rival each other as to who can shock us the most and represent a one-sided view of nature in the most hideous way. The sterility of the system is well shown by the fact that the imitators, if they have any ideas at all, forget their principles on the first opportunity. Thus Zola, the noisiest of them all, who regards Stendhal, Balzac, and Flaubert as but prototypes of himself, is really one of those romanticists against whom he rails so bitterly and uselessly, as if romanticism had not died out long ago ; a romanticist because he takes for his heroes some *monstre* out of those classes left untouched by the old classicism. His epical qualities do not belong to his theory, however much he strives to carry out the latter by dwelling on the animal side of man, to the exclusion or denial of any intellectual one, by his love of the nauseous detail of diseased life accumulated with photographic accuracy in all its hideousness. The only good purpose which the books can serve is to excite our horror at the surroundings of the poor, and to keep before our eyes the necessity of an amelioration of their hopeless condition.

The brothers Goncourt, whom Zola praises so loudly, are strange disciples of realism. They, indeed, have the same hatred and contempt for antiquity, and regard literature as in a state of chaos before

Diderot ; but they deny their principle in studying as they do the eighteenth century, finding in it material for bric-à-brac and anecdotage.
They are stylists and painters like Flaubert, though Zola declares that
the only style needed is the art of making oneself heard—are stylists
seeking the quintessence of things, and euphuists, followers of both
Théophile Gautier and Flaubert in their substitution of painting for
prose, in their absorption of the idea by the image. In their " Idées
et Sensations," the ideas are few and, at best, paradoxes : when present at all they always appear under the form of sensations. Zola
laughs at novels of adventure in which "princes go about incognito
with their pockets full of diamonds," at idealistic novels in which
"tempestuous love sweeps away the lovers into a wonderful world
of dreams," and at descriptive novels, " où l'on entasse tout ce
qu'on peut imaginer de plus fou et de plus riche, toute la fantaisie
d'or des poètes." But the brothers Goncourt commit every one of
these sins again and again; they revive the old notion of romanticism
that inspiration must be sought in libertinage and the debauchery of
the heart. But in their love of medical pathology and microscopical
detail they are true to their system, and Zola either does not realise their
violations of the true doctrine, or winks at them because they are the
work of fellow-disciples. Feydeau, thoroughly unhealthy in tone, is
also a painter or sculptor of words, calls himself *plastique,* adding
to this the usual philosophy of disgust, and a lyrical irritation against
the insufficiency of life. Hector Malot is altogether true to the
doctrine, but the consequence is that he shows perfectly how wearisome it is. With endless detail and utter lack of sympathy for his
puppet-like personages, who are destitute of all character, he wilfully
blinds himself and plunges headlong into caricature, the Nirvana of
realism.

This realism is so useless and so tiresome, this naturalism has really
so little to do with nature, this view of life is merely due to the temperament of the exponents, whether this temperament be inborn or
superinduced, in conformation to a false but fashionable theory.
Pascal somewhere finds fault with painting on the ground that it is a
vanity which attracts admiration by the cunning portrayal of things
the originals of which you do not admire. This sounds a little
puritanic and *saugrenu*; but it well applies to realism both in
literature and art, for it is certain that the closer the resemblance to
actual nature, the less interesting. Indeed, the French might take a
lesson, both in literature and art, from the results of realism in the
Italian and Flemish schools of painting. In Italy, the artists were
versatile men of aristocratic tendencies ; their realism was always

closely attached to the study of the antique—that is, to the study of ideal beauty. The consequence was, that crude realism is only to be seen in pioneers like Masaccio, Andrea del Castagno, Pisanello. But under the influence of tradition each school gradually built up its canon of the beautiful, till those works were produced which are the wonder of the world. Notice the contrast in Flanders (I am not speaking of the school of Rubens). Art there is narrow and democratic; the masters are specialists; and instead of a continued progress towards the ideal, it is the early masters, like Ian van Eyck, who are the best; no subsequent improvements are made; the later disciples either search deliberately for the ugly or, at most, for the trivial; they only escape exciting disgust by the splendour of their colouring. In fact, the Flemish realists depicted man as so uninteresting, so degraded, so fear-ridden, that, from very repulsion, the painters found their way into the open air: realism, as far as man was concerned, was flung aside, and the painting of nature, of landscape, sprang into existence.

A novel may be either ideal or real. If ideal, its purpose is to delight and console: to delight, by intricacy of plot, by wealth of wit and colour; to console, by giving an artistically concentrated picture of the life which we should like to live, but which we are debarred from living by the pressure of circumstances and the cares of material existence, the mechanical drudgery of everyday life. In such ideal novels the art is essentially aristocratic; for, democratic as we are compelled to be, we often feel that the idea of life is the Aristotelian one of the full development of all our faculties. And such full development can only be obtained when we are free from material cares, always surrounded by beautiful objects, able to enjoy the pleasures of travel, scenery, books, the society of cultured people. The lives of those whose lot it is to learn life's education amid such fair surroundings are interesting to study; there is wide room for the analysis of motive. Their trials, errors, and conflicts are the same in essence, indeed, as those of the poor, but finer, more complicated; their education leads them to consider longer the consequences of the wrong they meditate, and if they fall their remorse is all the greater. But there is another education, perhaps a truer one, wherein there is no scope for such free development, in which the development is one almost entirely of the heart and the emotions; and this is the true theme for a naturalism that is sympathetic. Here the heroes are the poor and the oppressed—are those who are prevented by their position from playing any great or noticeable part in the world—who can but guess at the deep problems of life and learn life's lessons by stern experience, dreaming of a fuller and a higher life not theirs, in the leisure moments snatched from toil. But there is the danger that the sadness and apparent hopelessness of such existences may produce a corresponding sadness in the writer who depicts them ; and it is no far step to despair. Thus the Russian realistic novelists, with their innate melancholy and dreaminess, and their openness to every wave of doctrine, seem to preach such a gospel of despair. But at least this despair of theirs is a compassionate one, not due to the self-complacent study of degraded life ; and the invisible and mystic elements of life are not denied as they are by the French.

Room, indeed, there is for a realism such as this—for the sympathetic representation of the lives of the poor and simple; and well has this been done by English novelists, by whom the due limits of realism have been observed. Indeed, if a true æsthetic of naturalism were wanted, such might be found by an examination of our best English novelists ; and the French critics acknowledge this, confessing at the same time the utter failure and mistake of their own unsympathetic realists, and finding the key to the mystery of our success in the fact of the deep latent religious feeling which is always to be found at the bottom of the English mind, which colours the whole tone of the mind, and is ineradicable even if no definite religious belief is expressed, or any ground for such religion is sorrowfully denied. Realism need not depend on a materialistic view of life, on the disregard or denial of a heart which can struggle with, and even overcome, the cruel pressure of outward necessity. If there is no free-will there is at least the illusion of free-will; the drama of life is the representation of erring man struggling against a self-invoked fate, or the good man fighting against circumstances. If religion even be but the category of the ideal, a *résumé* of our supersensible needs, yet such stretching out of hands towards the invisible, such mysticism, would still be well worth depicting by a true artist. Art is ever a selection—selection of the beautiful ; the ugly and depraved but seem to enhance the contrast and to point out that the beautiful is the true. If our persons and lives are not beautiful, yet we would that that they were so ; and plainness of person at least we can redeem by beauty of character, which is founded on self-sacrifice. If the beautiful is rare and an exception, still the exception points to a higher law, but too often traversed. Nature is no longer viewed with optimistic eyes as in the days of Leibnitz and Pope ; nay, to Renan, Nature is absolutely insensible, transcendently immoral. Our will is free, our character is beautiful, in proportion as they rise above nature. Nature is the material which must pass through the alembic of man's mind ; a series of symbols whereby to express the workings of the human soul; the brute matter which owes all its form to art. Yet art, Antæus-like, is ever re-invigorated by touching mother-earth; and both elements are truly requisite. If art wanders too far from nature, it loses itself in mysticism ; if art embraces nature too closely, it becomes degraded. Realism, naturalism, is indeed necessary—is the unavoidable basis of art and life ; but let us recognise that it is but the means and not the end, an essential part, not the whole, of art and life.

GARNET SMITH.

William Watson

"The Fall of Fiction"

Fortnightly Review 50 (September 1888), 324–36

THE FALL OF FICTION.

It seems to be in the nature of most fashions, good or bad, at last to beget their contraries, and it is to the principle or law underlying this curious but familiar fact that we are disposed to refer what would otherwise be a somewhat perplexing phenomenon in the fiction of the passing hour. For some time past the fashionable tendency has been largely in the direction of a certain conscious, not to say wilful, thinness of narrative material. The old merits of fulness and " body "—virtues apparently hereditary in that lineage of robust minds which can be traced backwards without a break from George Eliot to Fielding—have been growing rarer and rarer. In their place the art of making a very little go a very long way has been carefully cultivated by undoubtedly dexterous hands. It has almost reached the point of sheer bravado in some developments of the "society" novel, notably a species grown in American soil, or rather in New York conservatories and forcing-beds, and distinguished by an elaborate triviality which no amount of clever-ness can render other than vapid. Such a fashion can never in the nature of things be long-lived. Those miracles of inexhaustible nothingness, in which the tiniest rivulet of incident just trickles across a continent of dialogue, cannot long be interesting, even as miracles, in an age to which the miraculous does not make a permanently successful appeal. Moreover, along with this slight-ness and attenuation, so unimpressive by contrast with the traditional weight and bulk of English intellectual bullion, there has been the inevitable concomitant of languor and *ennui* and enervation, and it is these which have produced at last that recurrent phenomenon in the natural history of fashions to which allusion was made in our opening sentence. For, if the immense popularity of Mr. Rider Haggard's stories has any symptomatic significance, the stage of languor has at last reached its term and is being succeeded by a frantic rebound to the opposite extreme of spasm. From elegant listlessness fiction has suddenly leapt into paroxysmal life. From coma it has passed into convulsions.

Mr. Haggard, in dedicating his novel of *Allan Quatermain* to his son, expresses the hope that he and other boys may find in it something that will help them to "attain to the state and dignity of English gentlemen." That there is anything in the temper and tendency of Mr. Haggard's books positively inimical to the pursuit of such an ideal we do not go so far as roundly to assert. It may really be that those productions are, as their author evidently believes, a school of great sentiments and noble manners. We would merely observe that this is not exactly the light in which we have hitherto been accustomed to regard them. No doubt we have been misled by an erroneous conception of the nature of true gentility. We had always supposed that a certain modesty and temperance of statement, a certain sobriety of intellectual tone, were among an English gentleman's typical traits. We had thought, too, that among the features notably absent from an English gentleman might be reckoned a gloating delight in details of carnage and horror and ferocity for their own ghastly sake. But with a sigh we resign these cherished delusions, upon becoming aware that Mr. Haggard's novels are the pabulum that is to go to the making of our future Sidneys and Falklands.

Speaking broadly, there are three means by which this writer produces his characteristic effects; and as these means are one and all eminently devoid of any such subtlety and complexity as might make the definition of them difficult, they can be specified and described with no less adequacy than ease. Firstly, there is the element of the physically revolting, as in circumstantial narratives of massacre, cruelty, and bloody death. Secondly, there is the element of the fantastic, preternatural, and generally marvellous. Thirdly, there is that old and simple but infinitely variable expedient which may be described, metaphorically, as digging a hole in order that somebody may be helped out of it : in other words, placing a character in some predicament of frightful peril, prolonging the agony by various more or less transparent artifices, and finally, with an inevitableness which we foresee from the first, and which therefore considerably lessens our interest in the problem of rescue, extricating the sufferer in the crowning moment of crisis and supreme suspense.

Before passing to a critical consideration of the measure of success attending Mr. Haggard's employment of these three artistic methods, we may as well illustrate the methods themselves by one or two direct examples. The following is a characteristic quotation from *She*.

"A great fellow bounded upon the platform, and Leo struck him dead with one blow of his powerful arm, sending the knife right through him. I did the same by another, but Job missed his stroke, and I saw a brawny Amahagger [name of an imaginary African race] grip him by the middle and whirl him off the rock. The knife not being secured by a thong, fell from Job's hands as he did so, and, by a most happy accident for him, lit upon its handle on the rock, just as the body of the Amahagger, being undermost, hit upon its point and was transfixed by it. . . . I had hacked at the head of one man with my hunting-knife . . . with such vigour that the sharp steel had split his skull down to the eyes, and was held so fast by it that as he suddenly fell sideways the knife was twisted right out of my hand. Then it was that the two others sprang upon me. . . . I hugged them until I heard their ribs crack and crunch up beneath my grip. They twisted and writhed like snakes. . . . I slowly crushed the life out of them," &c., &c.

Readers will perhaps censure us for tainting these pages with the reek of blood that rises like an exhalation from the gratuitously detestable details of the foregoing passage. Our excuse must be that we are discussing Mr. Haggard's novels, in which passages like the foregoing play too large and typical a part to be ignored. But we promise the justly-offended reader that we will not repeat the outrage. We have cited one passage to show Mr. Haggard's mastery of the horrible, and we shall need to make other extracts in order to illustrate his other gifts and charms. Some of these extracts, we admit, are sure to include similar ferocious touches, since ferocity and atrocity are seldom far off in the writings which are to exercise a formative influence upon the gentleman of the future. But we undertake that this, our first, shall also be our last extract made for the deliberate purpose of revealing to what depths of degradation a sensational novelist can coolly descend.

We may also plead a further excuse. Having lately been through a "course" of Mr. Haggard's novels, we have necessarily read some hundreds of paragraphs resembling, in essential features, the one quoted above, and possibly we have acquired, by often repeated experience, a comparative insensibility to their gruesomeness, and are unable to gauge its effect upon other minds. Indeed, we think Mr. Haggard makes a mistake, even from his own presumable point of view, in the superabundance of horrible detail which he accumulates. His excess defeats his intention. The same rule which applies to redundancy of literary ornament—the rule which Cowley embodies in those fine lines—

"Men doubt, because they stand so thick i' th' sky,
If those be stars that paint the galaxy,"

applies equally to matters not at all suggestive of the Milky Way. A single graphically described horror may interest us by virtue of that curious attraction in repulsion which, though a morbid and questionable, is not the less a real element of power; but the cannibal in us is soon appeased, and when our mental palate has been regaled with slaughtered humanity served up in every variety of appetising ways—speared, brained, caught in lion-traps, torn in twain by elephants, and so forth—we presently become, not so much revolted and nauseated by this sort of fare, as simply *blasé* and apathetic in the presence of further culinary blandishments. Some husbandry of horrors, some frugality of affrightments, is necessary, or we soon learn to look upon them without a thrill. The lavishly disgusting at last ceases even to disgust and is met with mere indifference.

Before dismissing this unattractive subject, we may observe that the repugnance inspired by the details of Mr. Haggard's murdering and massacring passages is sometimes still further aggravated by a tone of levity and even facetiousness accompanying the ghastly recital. One of his characters, a great amateur in homicide, with a hundred murders on his hands, deprecates some modes of killing a man as being not sufficiently "sportsmanlike." This person's favourite method is then circumstantially described, with a certain gusto suggestive of admiration—the admirer being Allan Quatermain, the autobiographic hero of two of the novels. For our own part, we are not so sensitive to the humorous side of carnage as Mr. Haggard appears to be, and we confess we find in it little to amuse. Nevertheless, it puts us in mind of an amusing story told of Dr. Johnson. One of his friends—if we are not mistaken, Bennet Langton—had been reading to him some acts of an unusually sanguinary play, and had then stopped to breathe himself. "Come," said Johnson, "let's have some more of it. Let's go into the slaughter-house again, Lanky. But I fear there is more blood than brains." Remembering our promise, however, we will not ask the reader to "go into the slaughter-house again" with us, though we cannot altogether insure him against hearing the sound of the slaughter, for, in the world of Mr. Haggard's imagination, the human *abattoir* is seldom far distant.

A more legitimate source of interest in these stories is the use made of the marvellous and the preternatural; but before coming to that, we would offer a few words upon another and inferior element of sensationalism—the employment of incidents which, though perhaps not outside the pale of nature, are yet gratuitously improbable. In works of fiction, to borrow words which Dryden applies to the drama, "we know we are to be deceived, and we desire to be so; but no man ever was deceived but with a probability of truth, for who will suffer a gross lie to be fastened on him?" However true Dryden's words may have been in his own day, they seem less so in ours, when the ability to imbibe unlimited quantities of literature making enormous demands upon credulity is no uncommon gift. It might be thought that the capacities of credulity would soon be glutted by heavy aliment; but, on the contrary, they appear susceptible of infinite dilatation by what they absorb. The intellect, in allowing what Dryden calls "a gross lie" to be "fastened" on it, forfeits its self-respect; but having once done so it has nothing further to lose, and may go on permitting similar liberties to be taken with it, without much additional sense of lost dignity. The vastness of the indigestible mass which it can take in may be illustrated by a kind of theorem in moral geometry, thus: two equal improbabilities, meeting, are conjointly thrice as great as either singly, because their meeting is itself a third equal improbability. If, therefore, we go on superadding coincident improbabilities, the resultant sum of improbableness, increasing by a compound ratio at every addition, reaches at length an unstateably vast magnitude; and yet the capacities of credulity, once proved by a single experiment, do not seem to be overtasked by a hundred. It is only by the help of this theory that we can understand an ordinary reader's acceptance of an episode in Mr. Haggard's novel *Jess*, which we epitomise as follows :—

The hero, Captain John Niel, described as a "decidedly intellectual" and altogether a singularly shrewd and wideawake person, is making a journey in South Africa accompanied by Jess and escorted by one Muller, who has previously tried to murder him, who has a violent and scarcely disguised grudge against him, and whom he knows to be an unmitigated villain. Circumstances tending to engender grave suspicion of Muller's designs accumulate very largely on the way. Yet this shrewd man, Niel, allows himself and Jess to be guided into a snare of the most palpable sort. By Muller's directions, who pretends to be guiding him to a ford, he drives into the river at a point where "the water rang with an angry music and there was a great swirl of eddies." Presently, but not until the horses are off their feet, Niel becomes really aware of the treachery. He manages to get the horses turned round, only to find Muller and two hired assassins with him pointing their rifles at himself and his fair charge. The three murderers, who are only some ten or fifteen feet distant, fire at John and Jess, but miss them providentially. The wind gets under the cart, and, notwithstanding its considerable freight, lifts it clean off the wheels, so that it floats. The murderers, evidently still very near, shoot again and again, but, so far as John and Jess are concerned, only succeed in riddling their clothes. One of the two hired bravos has upon him a document, a certain warrant which Muller wants to get. Mr. Haggard, however, does not want him to get it, and therefore at the very moment when Muller is wondering how he can gain possession of it the lightning most opportunely kills both bravos, and Muller, "forgetting about the warrant, and everything else in the horror of what he took to be a visible judgment, rushed to his horse and galloped wildly away, pursued by all the terrors of hell." A little farther on, the wheel of the cart that bears John and Jess bumps against something— Mr. Haggard apparently forgetting that he has already made the cart and the wheels part company—and the cart itself gets fast upon a rock, there swaying to and fro in the water. Horrors thicken, and at last, when the pair have come to the conclusion that they must infallibly die before dawn, Jess takes this favourable opportunity of declaring her passion for John. In these circumstances a love scene ensues, "perhaps as wild and pathetic," Mr. Haggard remarks, "as ever the old moon above us looked upon." He further observes that "between the one and the other was spanned a bridge of passion made perfect and sanctified by the approaching end." The perfecting and sanctifying of this bridge takes some time, until at last it happily occurs to Jess that John can swim though she cannot, and she insists upon his saving his own life by swimming to the shore. But just then the traces broke, and the cart began to spin round and heave over. "John realized that it was all up," so he seized Jess round the waist and sprang off into the water, of course, just in the nick of time before the cart filled and foundered. They arrive safe upon land to find that their two leaders, which had broken loose from the cart whilst struggling in the water, and which had had no visible prospect of anything but drowning, are safely grazing on shore. Here it occurs to Mr. Haggard that John and Jess, exhausted by their terrific and prolonged struggles and sufferings, cannot live through many more pages without something to eat, and accordingly "they had not gone twenty yards before John gave an exclamation of joy, and rushed at something white that had stuck in the reeds. It was the basket of food."

We will only remark that the foregoing episode, composed of a series of incidents each in itself unlikely enough to happen, but not utterly inconceivable, acquires in its totality an aggregate of incredibleness which we shrink from attempting to gauge, but which a certain all-gulping class of novel-readers make no mouths at. We now proceed to some consideration of Mr. Haggard's claims to rank as an artist in the marvellous and the fantastic.

The mental mood to which an artist in the fantastic makes appeal is what may be called the mood of æsthetical credence—an assent of the imagination overruling a denial from the intellect. In order that this mood be appealed to with success, there is needed one of two conditions. Either the element of fantasy must be an atmosphere that wraps and subtly interpenetrates the whole fiction, obscuring all everyday relations, and practically allowing us no standard of probability to which the improbable can be referred; or it must have some distinct basis of legend, some starting-point in localized superstitions. Hawthorne, who in his New England witch-stories made successful use of supernatural motives conformably to the second of these conditions, made also a notable incursion upon a realm of fantasy unsupported by either the one or the other, with the result that all his inimitable grace and power could not save the novel of *Transformation* from being, on its fantastic side, a splendid failure. Now Mr. Haggard is a writer from whom the qualities of noble style, delicate humour, and subtle pathos are as conspicuously absent as they are eminently present in Hawthorne; but his preternatural conceptions, though infinitely wilder and more crude, are generically of the same type as Hawthorne's Donatello, inasmuch as they are examples of the marvellous brought into arbitrary contact with the familiar, over against which it stands without hope of fusion. Our own mental posture, as his readers, is in consequence one of grotesque ambiguity; we are kept standing with one foot on the dry land of realism, and the other in the deep sea of preternaturalism, with the result that we can neither swim nor walk. To say the truth, the secret of how to win æsthetical credence is one which Mr. Haggard has not discovered. He appears to think that a natural tendency to scepticism in the presence of monstrously impossible fictions is to be conciliated by frequent asseveration. He is always making affidavit, *This is strictly matter of fact, incredible as it may appear.* "As I am a living and honourable man" is, we recollect, the precise formula of affirmation used in one instance.

These observations apply with the most directness to the story called *She.* Some feminine readers of good judgment find in this story not a little to condemn upon moral grounds. Certainly there is something rather revolting in the effect which *She* herself produces by the mere display of her physical charms; but on the whole, we should say the story was non-moral rather than immoral. We fancy it is the most popular of this author's books, and we think it is the worst, its horrors being the coarsest, its artistic machinery the most lumbering and creaky, and, altogether, its monstrosities the most crudely monstrous that Mr. Haggard's writings can show. "He who forsakes the probable," says Dr. Johnson, "may easily find the marvellous." Now the delicately and airily marvellous is not found so easily, but the clumsily and violently marvellous is at the command of any daubing scene-painter who chooses to lay on his colours with a trowel. Mr. Haggard takes Central Africa as his province—certainly a province wide enough for imagination to deploy in—and from the mystery and poetry of "antres vast and deserts idle," a true artist might win finely fantastic material. But is there anything finely fantastic in all this grotesque upholstery of charnel-caves and anthropophagous banquets, pyramids of human skeletons, and revels in which the dancers carry corpses for flambeaux? Is there anything delicately marvellous in the central conception of a woman two thousand years old, whose conduct and carriage are least objectionable when they happen to be merely those of a common-place coquette? Is there anything imaginative in the conception of the elixir itself, to which *She* owes her abnormal longevity? The prolonged life of Bulwer's Zanoni was the result of a sublimated physical and psychical condition induced by the elimination from his nature of all human passion, and sustained by the occult knowledge which had come as the reward of such self-repression and abnegation. This is at least a noble and splendid fancy. In *She,* the protoplasmic principle from which the vital forces of the world are replenished is something very hot, that rolls up and down a cave and makes a noise.

She has, however, some redeeming features. The character of Ustane is a graceful creation, and her death is perhaps the most moving and effective incident in Mr. Haggard's writings. But the scene that follows—in which, five minutes after her death, her lover Leo is clasped in the arms of her murderess, is inexpressibly revolting. The famous scene between Richard III. and the Lady Anne pales its ineffectual fires before this. Mr. Haggard's fires glow with a more truly infernal candescence.

Ustane, we may observe in passing, is a more idealized version of Foulata in *King Solomon's Mines*. Each is a savage woman enamoured of a civilized man; each is actuated by the same half-animal-like fidelity of love; and each is murdered by a witch. With Ustane's death the sole human interest of the story expires. Thenceforward we are given up, bound hand and foot, to the mercies of the genius of nightmare—of nightmare that is an insane law unto itself, and mad with a methodless madness. The desert has, however, an oasis or two. In an account of the memorials of an imaginary prehistoric people there occurs, for example, a really fine passage describing an allegorical statue of Truth bestriding the earth. Mr. Haggard concludes the description by saying, that "it is at any rate suggestive of some scientific knowledge that these long-dead worshippers of Truth recognised the fact that the globe is round." This certainly does inspire us with an increased respect for the wisdom of the ancients Here was a people who had discovered that a sphere is spherical.

In *King Solomon's Mines* we have of course to wade through much minutely circumstantial slaughter of men, women, and elephants before we are rewarded with a vision of the fabulous Ophir. Probably that part of the story which Mr. Haggard's admirers find most enthralling is where the three heroes of the adventure reach the actual treasure-chamber of the sapient king, and as that part includes some of Mr. Haggard's characteristic "effects" it will repay our attention for a few moments. Allan Quatermain, Sir Henry Curtis, and Captain Good, accompanied by the girl Foulata, have compelled the malignant hag Gagool to act as their conductress to the place. Before reaching the secret treasure-chamber where Solomon's diamonds are stored, they pass through the Place of Death, where the corpses of the defunct kings of Kukuanaland sit with water slowly dripping upon them from the rock ceiling, until by its agency they are converted into stalactites—a charming conception. The latest of these royalties had been very ably decapitated only the other day by Curtis in single combat, but already sat there, "the head perched upon the knees, the vertebræ projecting a full inch above the level of the shrunken flesh of the neck," in short, the nucleus of a very pretty stalactite. From this hall there appears at first no sign of any entrance to the treasure-chamber, but presently the witch Gagool leans against the wall of the cave, and "we perceived that a mass of stone was slowly rising from the floor and vanishing into the rock above, where doubtless there was a cavity prepared to receive it." The narrator, Allan Quatermain, has little doubt that this was accomplished by means of "some very simple lever, which was moved ever so little by pressure on a secret spot." Through the opening caused by this ingenious arrangement our friends enter a passage leading to the secret chamber, the hag going with them. They find three chests of diamonds, formerly the property of King Solomon. The third chest "was only about a fourth full, but the stones were all picked ones. . . . some of them as large as pigeons' eggs. Some of these biggest ones, however, we could see by holding them up to the light, were a little yellow. . . . What we did *not* see, however, was the look of fearful malevolence that old Gagool favoured us with as she crept, crept like a snake, out of the treasure-chamber and down the passage towards the massive door of solid rock." As nobody saw Gagool's look, it seems reasonable to inquire upon what testimony it is recorded ; but the reader whose stomach has already been the receptacle of so many camels, can make room for a gnat or two. To resume : a series of cries "came ringing up the vaulted path. It is Foulata's voice." The three men run to her assistance, to find old Gagool characteristically murdering the girl, and, worse still, the rock-door closing down. Foulata falls and "Gagool throws herself on the ground to twist herself like a snake through the crack of the closing stone. She is under—Ah, God ! too late ! too late ! The stone nips her and she yells in agony. Down, down it comes, all the thirty tons of it, slowly pressing her old body against the rock below. Shriek upon shriek, such as we never heard, *then a long sickening crunch*, and the door was shut, just as we, rushing down the passage, hurled ourselves against it. It was all done in four seconds." The three men thus find themselves entombed alive. Now, considering that Gagool was an old lady quite as astute as she was unprincipled, and that she knew all about how to manage that door, of which she alone preserved the secret, she bungled this business in a way which is certainly very remarkable, and which lessens the respect we had previously felt for her undoubted though misapplied abilities. She had gone outside to work that door—to get it closed upon the three men and Foulata— and while it was in the act of descending she re-entered beneath it. This was running it very fine, and we cannot even see that she had a motive for such rashness, for she made no attack upon the girl until the latter seized and held her to prevent her second egress, a matter which the murdered girl herself there and then voluntarily explains, in a dying deposition characterized by a zealous concern for historical accuracy which no doubt reflects great credit upon any girl in those circumstances, but which, nevertheless, appears somewhat gratuitous except upon the assumption that her statement was delivered with one eye upon a curious public. On the whole, we should recommend Mr. Haggard to re-write this scene and let Gagool kill Foulata before going outside to see about the door, that is, if he can bring himself to sacrifice something for the sake of a counterbalancing gain; for of course, however reluctantly, the *crunch* will have to be given up.

This story exhibits some of Mr. Haggard's choicest flowers of humour. Captain Good is caught by a party of savages at a time when he happens to be divested of his nether garment, and to keep up the first impression thus produced upon their untutored minds, he goes for several days without that article of clothing. This incident, amplified by various detail, is quite the strong feature and pivot of interest throughout several chapters, Mr. Haggard being evidently delighted with such fair fruit of his humorous invention. We are sure it is meant for humour; not, indeed, because we ourselves find anything very amusing in it, but because we know of nothing else that it can be meant for. Though it affects us rather sadly, we think it can hardly be intended as an experiment in pathos.

Another sort of "humour" not uncommon in Mr. Haggard's pages is more objectionable. To do him justice, we must say it is mostly put into the mouths of some of his characters, not spoken in his own person. Two examples of it will suffice :—

"My plan was . . . to shoot myself, trusting that the Almighty would take the peculiar circumstances of the case into consideration and pardon the act."

"Good day, cousin, good day. Forget not to thank the Almighty God for our glorious victories. He will expect it from an elder of the Church."

We will not incur the charge of priggishness by affecting to find anything very shocking in this. But it is very cheap, foolish, and vulgar, and were best left to the professional literary buffoon in another country, which counts this sort of "humour" among its natural products.

In *Allan Quatermain*, a kind of sequel to *King Solomon's Mines*, the same trio of adventurers, having again penetrated the heart of Africa, at last find themselves by a wonderful accident embarked upon a subterranean river. A writer of genuine Arabesque romance might conduct you for thousands of miles through the earth's entrails by this mode of travel, and neither pilot nor passenger would ever be troubled with anything so prosaic as the necessity of ventilation. But it is one of the ignominies of this hybrid species of invention—jolting you at every step from the naturalistic to the fantastic and back again—that its practitioner is perpetually reduced to the humiliating necessity of seeking at least some show of support for his imagination in physical fact or hypothesis. Here, for instance, the need of fresh air occurs to him, and he meets the difficulty by going out of his way to suggest that the water of the lake from which the river flowed "had sufficient air in it to keep the atmosphere of the tunnel from absolute stagnation, this air being given out as it proceeded on its headlong way." Not pretending to science, we hazard no opinion as to the sufficiency of this bold theory, being content humbly to admire its daring. Of course, its drawback is that it supposes a fearfully impetuous rush on the part of a stream which could throw off in its course enough of air-charged vapour to enable human lungs to perform their functions without inconvenience ; and this enormously enhances the original improbability—already sufficiently vast—of a canoe with four occupants being borne safely an immense distance through the viscera of the earth. This, however, is duly accomplished, and our voyagers at last emerge into daylight, the river debouching into a lake upon whose shore is built a beautiful city. And now we confess that on reaching this point of the story our interest and curiosity were at last really roused. Here, we thought, is undoubtedly a fine opening for fantastic invention : what will he make of it? For once we were prepared to accept unlimited impossibilities as appropriate to the situation, and even demanded by it. For, after a so marvellous and terrible journey, to land us at a comparatively dull destination were an anti-climax in romance, and therefore bad art. Judge of our disappointment on finding that at this juncture, when a new reign of wonder might legitimately be inaugurated, the intrinsically commonplace sets in with a severity that does not relax throughout many chapters. The people of this city that is throned upon mythic mountains in the bosom of the mysterious continent are simply a handsome and capable white race, with a mixture of civilized and barbaric traits, and with manners and customs and politics that have neither the satiric interest to be found in such creations as Swift's Laputans, the philosophic interest which might be embodied in the conception of a truly ideal community and state, nor the romantic interest attaching to unique imaginative beings. Where they resemble familiar human types they are uninteresting ; and where they depart from familiar human types, the departure, being capricious and arbitrary, brings little accession of interest.

An essentially commonplace love affair between Sir Henry Curtis and the queen of this people involves the nation in civil war, and a great and bloody battle is described. The description, however, is surprisingly free from Mr. Haggard's usual favourite aids to effect, which are, it is almost unnecessary to say, ghastly incidents of mortality, narrated with a disgusting insistence upon such particulars as are the most hideous and repulsive. The result of this unusual

forbearance is to exemplify the tameness and triteness of his
descriptive powers when their principal mainstay is withdrawn.
The battle occupies a considerable area of paper, but seems a mere
academic battle or diagram of a battle, without life, or force, or fire ;
as it were, a military thesis—

> "Wherein the toga'd consuls can propose
> As masterly,"

to say the least, as Mr. Rider Haggard.

We have dwelt at greater length upon Mr. Haggard's best-known
stories than we had intended, and can only devote a few words to
his later and minor efforts to raise alternately the eyebrows and the
gorge of his readers. *Maiwa's Revenge* shows no advance in any
commendable direction ; and as a writer on sport, Mr. Haggard must
be either profoundly ignorant or serenely confident in the ignorance
of his admirers : witness the ridiculous elephant-hunt that covers so
large a space in this story.

Against *Mr. Meeson's Will* a charge of gross plagiarism has elsewhere been preferred, and, though we have not heard Mr. Haggard's
answer, the accusation seems one that can hardly be rebutted. In
other quarters similar allegations have already been made with
reference to Mr. Haggard's other stories. We ourselves do not feel
disposed to press such charges, our conviction of the inherent worth-
lessness of these novels being dissociated from any inclination to
trace their ancestry. At the same time, any one who feels disposed to
collate *She* with Moore's *Epicurean*, *Allan Quatermain* with Dr. Mayo's
Kaloolah, and *Jess* with Miss Olive Schreiner's *The Story of an African
Farm*, will find himself repaid. Bulwer's Margrave seems to be a
literary progenitor of Ayesha ; and from Bulwer in his feebler moods
Mr. Haggard appears to catch his trick of spurious philosophizing.
This is for the most part merely tiresome, but sometimes rises to the
ridiculous by being put into ludicrously incongruous mouths. An
African savage thus moralizes : "Out of the dark we come, into the
dark we go. Like a storm-driven bird at night we fly out of the
No-where. For a moment our wings are seen in the light of the
fire, and lo ! we are gone again into the No-where." Our dusky
brother seems to have been studying Carlyle and Mr. Bailey's
Festus.

If it suited us to condescend to such humble particularities, we could
produce from Mr. Haggard's writings an array of sentences betoken-
ing an ignorance of the principles of syntax which might discredit
any schoolboy. We care not to pursue such small game. For after
all, individual solecisms sink into insignificance beside the collective
folly and futility of these books. As the world is said to be wiser
than its wisest man, so Mr. Haggard's writings in their totality are
worse than the worst things which they contain.

We have spoken with a degree of severity which will perhaps be attributed to private animus. We not only disclaim any such motive, we go farther, and do not hesitate to say that it is to the very fact of the utter absence of all personal considerations that our severity itself is due. The intrusion of such considerations would have brought human compunctions and relentings—would have begotten an unwillingness to deliver the maximum sentence which we believe such eminent offences against good taste and good sense demand. It is only by rigidly shutting our eyes to everything but the general and public aspect of the case that we are enabled to go through the performance of such an unpleasant judicial duty. It is not that we grudge Mr. Haggard his undeserved success, but that we grudge the comparative neglect of meritorious fiction which the rage for meretricious fiction implies. We believe Mr. Haggard's own inmost literary conscience will ratify our pronouncement. He is a clever man, well able to take the measure of his own charlatanry—very likely the last person in the world to mistake his own charlatanry for genius. He is a clever man, for to gauge public taste is not done by a sort of fluke, but argues very considerable if not always scrupulous talents; and he has accurately gauged the taste of a section of the reading public, which the triumph of his experiment proves to be a large section. But that taste—the taste for such an ill-compounded *mélange* of the sham-real and the sham-romantic—is a deplorable symptom. There is among the very poor in our large cities a class of persons who nightly resort to the gin-shop to purchase a mixture of every known liquor, the heterogeneous rinsings of a hundred glasses. The flavour of this unnameable beverage defies imagination, but the liquor has for its lovers one transcendent virtue—it distances all rivalry in the work of procuring swift and thorough inebriation. Its devotees would not thank you for a bottle of the finest Château Yquem, when the great end and aim of drinking—the being made drunk—can be reached by such an infinitely readier agency. The taste for novels like Mr. Rider Haggard's is quite as truly the craving for coarse and violent intoxicants because they coarsely and violently intoxicate. But the victims of this thirst are without the excuse which the indigent topers to whom we liken them may plead. The poor tippler might say that he bought his unutterable beverage because he could not afford a better. But the noblest vintages of literature may be purchased as cheaply as their vilest substitutes. When we have abundance of exquisite grapes in our vineyards, is it not almost incredible that persons who pretend to some connoisseurship should be content to besot themselves with a thick, raw concoction, destitute of fragrance, destitute of sparkle, destitute of everything but the power to induce a crude inebriety of mind and a morbid state of the intellectual peptics? It is indeed almost incredible, but the pity of it is, it is true.

from

William Sharp

"New Novels"

Academy 37 (January 18, 1890), 41–43

A Hazard of New Fortunes. In 2 vols. By W. D. Howells. (Edinburgh: David Douglas.)

Olga Zanelli. In 3 vols. By F. L. Cartwright. (Sonnenschein.)

A Hurricane in Petticoats. In 3 vols. By Leslie Keith. (Bentley.)

Brownie's Plot. In 2 vols. By Thos. Cobb. (Ward & Downey.)

Lord Allanroe; or, Marriage not a Failure. By B. E. T. A. (Digby & Long.)

Rogues. By R. H. Sherard. (Chatto & Windus.)

My Wonderful Wife. By Marie Corelli. (White.)

Basil Morton's Transgression. By the Marquise Lanza. (New York: Minerva Publishing Co.)

Miss Meredith. By Amy Levy. (Hodder & Stoughton.)

MR. HOWELLS's new novel will be accepted by many as his ablest production. It is unquestionably inferior only to *The Rise of Silas Lapham*, if to that. Mr. Howells has now taken an assured place among those novelists who are read because they are the vogue. That his writings will withstand the veering of the popular breeze remains to be proved. It is by no means the certainty his ardent admirers so vehemently assert. There has been ample occasion for this novelist to show his range, to display his profundity of insight, to fulfil convincingly his "mission." To assert that he has adequately acted up to his pronunciamento, that he has won victory all along the line, that his standard has allured the worthiest adherents, would be to be as uncritical as to state that his method is no more his own than that of a dozen scribes of the day, that his successes have been side-issues of little significance, that he has no following because he has no leadership. It seems not unlikely that in the healthy reaction which is setting in against the pseudo-realism of which Mr. Howells is one of the most eminent exponents, much injustice may be done to an author who has so often, and for so prolonged a period, charmed us by his graces of style, delicacy of humour, and winsome sentiment. Possibly it is inevitable; and, after all, the rude justice of the public taste is no such barbaric tyrant as it is often represented. But the critic who studies the drift of the newer fiction, who looks to the causes of "mutations infinite," as well as merely to their advent, who, in particular, has carefully studied the writings of Mr. Howells, will recognise that in him we have the genuine connecting link between the crude realists in method like Tolstoi, and the crude realists in thought like Zola. He is a realist, by his own account and by that of his friends and enemies alike; and, though in no one of his books, nor in them all collectively, do I find warrant for the application, yet it may be allowed to pass for the present, as this is not the occasion for an examination into the absurdity of the claim of realism by a school of writers who are, one and all, hopelessly blind, or indifferent, to the most imperative requirements of the true realistic method. Perhaps realism in literary art may be approximately defined as the science of exact presentment of many complexities, abstract and concrete, in one truthful, because absolutely reasonable and apparently inevitable, synthesis; this, *plus* the creative energy which in high development involves what is misleadingly called the romantic spirit, and *minus* that weakness of the selective faculty which is the dominant factor in the work of the so-called realists of the Zolaesque school. Thus regarded, realism and romance are found to be as indissoluble as soul and body in a living human being. The true artist, no doubt, is he who is neither a realist nor a romanticist, but in whose work is observable the shaping power of the higher qualities of the methods of genuine realism and the higher qualities of the methods of genuine romance. It is no slight tribute to Mr. Howells that he so often has, as it were, steered his bark within sight of the haven of the ideal novelist. Unfortunately, against his helm is the opposing weight of a theory which, inadequately apprehended or stubbornly adhered to, has ever influenced him to a less happy course. Not only has he written much, and liberally changed his characters and scenery, he has also guided us himself to the proper standpoint whence to regard his collective achievement. The result, on the whole, from the promise of *The Undiscovered Country* to his maturest productions, *Silas Lapham* and *A Hazard of New Fortunes*, is one of disappointment. He has, very inaptly it seems to me, been termed the American Tolstoi, the counterpart of the cele-

brated Russian novelist whom he so enthusiastically admires, and one of whose books he
ranks as among the very foremost, if not (as
I seem to remember) *the* foremost, novel of
the world. While Tolstoi, however, is a
fascinating painter of human life and human
events, despite of certain radical artistic
shortcomings, Mr. Howells is an agreeable
depicter of types and situations, not by virtue
of rare insight or sympathy, but through
sheer faculty of artistic presentment. The
one is primarily a thinker, a philosopher, a
historian perhaps, and only an artist inter-
mittently and transiently; the other, so it
seems to me at least, is primarily and almost
invariably the artist, but seldom the adequate
historian of any complex episode, rarely a
philosopher in any deep sense, never, almost,
a profound thinker. He is not shallow; but
it would be rash to go beyond the courteous
reticence of negatives Still, I am tempted
to repeat of him what I have in effect recently
written elsewhere upon Tolstoi's collective
work, namely, to indicate his radical inability to focus essential and unessential
details into one quintessential picture as the
real cause of his failure to fascinate us in any
very high degree. This fatal lack of discrimination, this too impartial regard of all
the dross and *débris* of every-day life, this
equality of emphasis upon the important and
the trivial, the vital and the altogether
irrelevant, means just so much loss in art.
One of the acutest of Mr. Howells's critics
(Mr. John M. Robertson) has observed
that the ethical significance of his books is
too small in proportion to their elaboration.
What was true then is still truer now.
It was the same critic who, when appreciating certain differences between Mr.
Howells and Tourguénieff, remarked that
the latter as a rule leaves us contemplating
life in the light of his story, while the former
sets us considering his story in the light of
life. The distinction is admirable. To this
day (and shall it be so always?) Mr. Howells
is to be judged with the scrupulously suspicious heed we should pay to the record of
observance on the part of a very short-sighted
man. But lest there should seem anything
churlish in this acknowledgment of such a
book as Mr. Howells's latest, let me hasten to
add that it is written with the wonted charm
and grace, the familiar delicate humour, and
with the happy, epigrammatic concision of,
say, its most serious rival, *The Rise of Silas
Lapham*. It is, however, only fair to add

that the author is guilty of several annoying lapses in style, as, for instance, the atrocious barbarism, "he fed it into himself."

Hall Caine

"The New Watchwords
of Fiction"

Contemporary Review 57 (April 1890), 479–88

THE NEW WATCHWORDS OF FICTION.

A LITTLE circle of influential writers for the Press are doing their best to persuade the public that " the critical orthodoxies " of the day are opposed to all forms of idealism in literature, that " romanticism " is a " backwater," and that the " stream of tendency " is towards a newer and purer " realism." Now, I feel very strongly that this is utterly untrue, and that somebody should say so with all the emphasis he can command, and thereby warn the public against an error that must be fatal to the making of good literature, the appreciation of good literature, and the moral effects of good literature wherever it gains credence and support. But first let me say what I take these two words " realism " and " idealism " to mean when applied to the literature that we call imaginative. I take realism to mean the doctrine of the importance of the real facts of life, and idealism the doctrine of the superiority of ideal existence over the facts of life. I am not a logician, and may lack skill in stating my definitions, but I think plain people will grasp my plain meaning.

Long ago M. Zola put forth a sort of manifesto in support of the writings of the brothers De Goncourt, and, as nearly as I can remember it, he therein told the world that the school to which they belonged had set out with one clear aim, and one only, that of reproducing actual life. No romance, no poetry, no uncommon incidents, no effects, no situations were to be touched by them. These things had been the machinery of an earlier school of writers, of Dumas and Hugo and Sue. Only the plain, unvarnished, naked, stark fact was to be employed, and with such materials they were going to produce results that should be beyond comparison more potent than any results of romanticism in their influence on man and the world. Well, we know what the end of it has been; but I am not going to discuss

Zolaism in its effects. Clean-minded people are weary of the talk of it, and I grieve to see that a writer of pure and noble instincts, Thomas Hardy, in his recent protest against the painful narrowness of English fiction, has been betrayed into prescribing a remedy for the evil that is a thousand times worse than the disease. One frequent reply to the plea of the French realist is that in his determination to paint the world as it is he has only painted the world's cesspools. And indeed it is a sufficient answer to say that, though there may be many Madame Bovarys in the world, the Madame Bovarys are not the women whom right-minded people want to know more about, and that though the world holds many harlots, we do not wish to look down into the deep pit that is a harlot's heart. But there is a better rejoinder to the demand of the realist that he should be allowed to paint the world as it is, and that is that he never can—no, not if he were a thousand times a Balzac. And in attempting to do so he is not only missing the real aim of true literature, but running a fearful risk of following a false literature that can never do the world any good.

What I mean is this: the largest view that any one man can take of life " as it is " usually shows him more that is evil than good. The physical eye sees, must see, and always has seen, an enormous preponderance of evil in the world. It is only the eye of imagination, the eye of faith, that sees the balance of good and evil struck somewhere and in some way. And if the physical eye in its pride goes abroad to believe only what it can see, it comes home either blurred with tears, as Carlyle's was when he asked himself what God could be doing in the world he had made for man, or shining with ridicule, as Voltaire's was when he protested that there was no God in the rascally world at all. For the former of these there is the salvation of faith always hovering near, but the latter is by much the more likely chance, and for that there is no salvation whatever. It brings cynicism with it, and cynicism is the deadliest enemy that good literature ever had or can have.

Now this is the real pitfall of realism—cynicism. It never has, and never will, lay hold of an imaginative mind, for imagination and cynicism cannot live together, and no man of imagination ever was or will be a cynic. But it possesses, like a passion, another type of mind that none can dare to undervalue, a type of mind that is often stronger than the imaginative mind and always more trustworthy on the lesser issues of life. And it is an evil thing in literature, because it leads to nothing. It prompts no man to noble deeds, it restrains no woman from impurity, it degrades the virtues by taking all the unselfishness out of them that is their spiritual part. So when we hear the realist boast that he is painting " life as it is," it will be a sufficient answer to say that he is talking nonsense ; but we can add with truth that, if it were possible for him to paint the world as he sees it, the chances are that he would thereby be doing the world much harm.

The true consort of imagination is enthusiasm, the man of imagination has never lived who was not also an enthusiast, and enthusiasm is the only force that has ever done any good in the world since the world began. It is the salt of the earth, the salt without which the earth would rot, and when things rot they stink. We see how surely it has been so with French fiction, which, for twenty years past, has been the least imaginative fiction produced in Europe. It has no salt of enthusiasm in it, and so it rots and stinks. It is cynical, and so it does the world no good. But enthusiasm, living with imagination in the hearts of great men, has again and again set the world aflame, and purified as well as ennobled every nature it has touched, save only the natures that were touched already with fanaticism.

And this enthusiasm, which cannot live at peace with realism, lives and flourishes with idealism. It seems to say, " If we cannot paint the world as it is, we can paint it as it should be," and that is idealism. Don't say the idealist, by my own showing, starts from nowhere. He starts from exactly the same scene as the realist, the scene of daily life, and with the same touch of mother earth, only he realizes that the little bit of life that has come under his physical eye is only a disproportionate fragment of the whole, and the eye of imagination tells him of the rest. If he sees the wicked prosper in this life, he does not content himself with a mere picture of the wicked man's material prosperity, leaving his reader to cry " If this is true, what is God doing ? " No ; but he shows side by side with the material prosperity a moral degradation so abject and so pitiful, that the reader must rather cry, " Not that, not that at any price ! " Thus he shows the man who has failed, as the world goes, that to have succeeded might have been a worse fate, and he reminds the man who has won in life's battle that the man who has lost may yet be his master. Lifting up the down-trodden, encouraging the heavy-laden, " helping, when he meets them, lame dogs over stiles," he does the world some good in his way, and he does it, not by painting life as he sees it, but by virtue of the inward eye that we call Idealism.

Now this idealism has nearly always taken the turn of romanticism when applied to literature. It was so when Schiller, in his youth and wild inexperience, struggled to express himself in " The Robbers," when Goethe wrote " Faust," when Coleridge wrote " The Ancient Mariner," when Scott wrote " Old Mortality " and " The Bride of Lammermoor." Romance seemed to these writers the natural vehicle for great conceptions. Not that they wanted big situations, startling effects, picturesque accessories, for their own sakes only. These were all good in their way, and no writer of true instincts could have undervalued them. But they were not the prizes for which the authors set out. They had no life of their own apart from the central fire that brought them into existence. It was not the Slough of Despond that produced Christian, but Christian that called for the Slough of Despond. Then, again, Idealism claims Romance as her handmaiden, but she does not require that the handmaiden shall be of surpassing beauty; she may be a very plain-featured body. Romanticism does not live only in the loveliest spots in this world of God, and it does not belong exclusively to the past, as some writers imply. It exists within the four-mile radius at the present hour, and could be found there if only we had a second great idealist like Dickens to go in search of it.

To condemn all forms of romance, as the Zola manifesto tried to do, to banish from fiction all incidents that are out of the common, all effects that are startling and "sensational," all light and colour that are not found in every-day life, is to confound the function of the novelist with that of the historian. To the historian fact is a thing for itself, it is sacred, it dominates all else. To the novelist fact is only of value as a help towards the display of passion; he does not deliberately falsify fact, but fact—mere fact—has no sanctity for him, and he would a thousand times rather outrage all the incidents of history than belie one impulse of the human heart.

The idea at the bottom of the Zola manifesto is a sophism, and a shallow sophism. It seems to say that the novelist, like the historian, has for his chief function that of painting the life of his time, and leaving behind him a record as faithful and yet more intimate. To accept this is to narrow the range of imaginative art, which should have no limits whatever, certainly none of time or healthy human interest. The real function of the novelist has been too frequently propounded, and ought to be too obvious to stand in need of definition. It is that of proposing for solution by means of incident and story a problem of human life. Passion therefore, not fact, lies at the root of the novelist's art. Passion is the central fire from which his fact radiates, and fact is nothing to him except as it comes from that central fire of passion. He looks about him, not for startling situations (though these he would be a fool to despise), but for the great mysteries of life, and then he tries to find light through them. These mysteries are many, and do not belong to an age, but to all time. Two good men love one woman, and one of them goes up to Paradise while the other goes down to Hell. There is a problem of life, a human tragedy occurring constantly. How is it to be solved? What will or should the rejected man do? That is the question the novelist sets himself, and to answer such a question is the novelist's highest and all but his only natural function. But, in answering it, must he limit himself to life as he has seen it? If so, the chances are a thousand to one that he will make the rejected man kill his favoured rival, or else the woman, or both. That is realism, that is painting "life as it is." And is the world likely to be much the better of it ?

The idealist goes differently to work. Instead of asking himself what solution to this problem life and the world have shown him, he asks his own heart of what solution human nature at its highest is capable. This leads him to the heroisms which it is so easy for the cynic to deride. And the heroisms, for their better effects, often tempt him to a more inspiring scene and picturesque age than he lives in. He wants all that the human heart can do, and he gets heroism ; he wants heroism to look natural, and he gives it a certain aloofness, and that is Romanticism.

It is easy to foresee the kind of objection that may be urged to Idealism as an aim in fiction, and no writer could put it more forcibly than Mr. Russell Lowell did in one of his early letters to the author of "Uncle Tom's Cabin."

"A moral aim is a fine thing; but, in making a story, an artist is a traitor who does not sacrifice everything to art. Remember the lesson that Christ gave us twice over. First, he preferred the useless Mary to the dishwashing Martha; and next, when that exemplary moralist and friend of humanity, Judas, objected to the sinful waste of the Magdalen's ointment, the great Teacher would rather it should be wasted in an act of simple beauty than utilised for the benefit of the poor. Cleopatra was an artist when she dissolved her biggest pearl to captivate her Antony-public. May I, a critic by profession, say the whole truth to a woman of genius? Yes? And never be forgiven? I shall try, and try to be forgiven, too. In the first place, pay no regard to the advice of anybody. In the second place, pay a great deal to mine! A Kilkenny-cattish sort of advice? Not at all. My advice is to follow your own instincts, to stick to nature, and to avoid what people commonly call the 'Ideal'; for that, and beauty and pathos and success, all lie in the simply natural. . . . . There are ten thousand people who can write 'ideal' things for one who can see and feel and reproduce nature and character. Ten thousand, did I say? Nay, ten million. What made Shakspere so great? Nothing but eyes and—faith.in them. The same is true of Thackeray. I see nowhere more often than in authors the truth that men love their opposites. Dickens insists on being tragic, and makes shipwreck."

Now, forcible and effective, sound and true as this seems at first sight to be, it is, I make bold to say, one of the most misleading bits of criticism ever put forth by a great critic. Surely it would not be hard to dispute every clause of it, but only one of its clauses concerns us at present, and that is the broad statement that "ten million" can write "ideal" things for "one who can see and feel and reproduce nature and character." Exactly the reverse of this is the manifest truth. Indeed, to outstrip Mr. Lowell in his flight of numbers, I will say that there is hardly a living human being who cannot in some measure "see and feel and reproduce nature and character." The merest child can do it, and often does it (such is the strength of the talent for mimicry in man), with amazing swiftness and fidelity. The veriest

stable-boy, the simplest village natural, will startle you with his reproductions of the oddities of character, and the novelist who has rendered,
however faithfully, however humorously or pathetically, the scene on
which his bodily eyes have rested, has achieved no more than the come-
dian on the stage. But lest this statement of mine should seem to be too
daring a negative to the word of so high an authority, let me set Mr.
Lowell in contrast with one who can do him no dishonour by a contradiction. "As the actual world," says Bacon, "is inferior to the rational soul,
so Fiction gives to Mankind what History denies, and in some measure
satisfies the mind with shadows when it cannot enjoy the substance.
And as real History gives us not the success of things according to the
deserts of vice and virtue, Fiction corrects it, and presents us with the
fates and fortunes of persons rewarded and punished according to
merit." Obviously Bacon, with all his strong common-sense, was not
one of those " who avoid what people commonly call the ' Ideal.' " And
Burton, quoting this passage in the Terminal Essay to his monumental
" Thousand Nights and a Night," adds, in his virile way : " But I would
say still more. History paints, or attempts to paint, life as it is, a
mighty maze, with or without a plan : Fiction shows or would
show us life as it should be, wisely ordered and laid down on fixed
lines. Thus Fiction is not the mere handmaid of History ; she has a
household of her own and she claims to be the triumph of Art, which,
as Goethe remarked, is ' Art because it is not Nature.' " Goethe
hits the nail on the head. Merely to " reproduce nature and character " is not Art at all ; it is Photography. And for one man capable of
that moulding and smelting of nature and character which is rightly
called Art, there are whole worlds of men capable of using the " eyes,"
of which Mr. Lowell makes too much, as a sort of human camera. Of
course one cannot be blind to the real force that lies somewhere at
the back of this demand for the real to the neglect of the ideal. A bad
ideal, an imperfect ideal, a wild and mad ideal, is a trivial and commonplace thing, and rather than have such vague imaginative varnishes
one asks for the solid facts of life. We know the fascination of fact—
any sort of fact, no matter what, any life, however remote or mean—
and if it is only real enough we feel it. " Tell us what you know,"
is our cry again and again when writers seem to be busied with telling
us only what they fancy. This craving for the *real* is good and
healthy, but it ought by no means to be set (as Mr. Lowell sets it) in
opposition to the craving for the ideal. A novelist should know his
facts, he should know the life he depicts ; yet this knowledge should
not be the end of his art, but only its beginning. That should be
his equipment to start with, and his art should be adjudged by the
good use he puts it to, not by the display he makes of it. Burton
could not have expressed more clearly the difference between fiction
as Mrs. Beecher Stowe had unconsciously practised it, and as her genial

critic would have had her follow it, than by that contrast, drawn from Bacon, of fiction and history : " Fiction is not the mere handmaid of History ; she has a household of her own." And I would add for myself as the essence of my creed as a novelist : *Fiction is not nature, it is not character, it is not imagined history ; it is fallacy, poetic fallacy, pathetic fallacy, a lie if you like, a beautiful lie, a lie that is at once false and true—false to fact, true to faith.*

Towards such healthy Romanticism as Bacon describes English fiction has long been leaning, and never more so than during the last five-and-twenty years. We may see this in the homeliest fact, namely, that craving for what is called poetic justice which makes ninety-nine hundredths of English readers impatient of any close to a story but a happy'one. The craving is right and natural, though it may be puerile to expect that the threads of all stories should be gathered up to a happy ending. I know that it is usual to attribute to such arbitrary love of what is agreeable the inferiority in which the fiction of this country is said to stand towards the fiction of the rest of Europe. We are asked to say how fiction can live against such conditions of the circulating libraries as degrade a serious art to the level of the nursery tale. The answer is very simple : English fiction has lived against them, and produced meantime the finest examples of its art that the literature of the world has yet seen. Unlike the writers who pronounce so positively on the inferiority of fiction in England, I cannot claim to know from " back to end " the great literatures of Europe ; but I will not hesitate to say that not only would the whole body of English fiction bear the palm in a comparison with the whole body of the fiction of any other country, but the fiction of England during the past thirty years (when its degeneracy, according to its critics, has been most marked) has been more than a match for the fiction of the rest of the world. Indeed, I will be so bold as to name six English novels of that period, and ask if any other such bulk of work, great in all the qualities that make fiction eminent—imagination, knowledge of life, passion and power of thought—can be found among the literatures of France, Russia, or America. The six novels are " Daniel Deronda," " The Cloister and the Hearth," " Lorna Doone," " The Woman in White," " The Ordeal of Richard Feverel," and " Far from the Madding Crowd." All these novels are products of romanticism, and the circumstance that they were written amid the hampering difficulties that are said to beset the feet of fiction is proof enough that where power is not lacking in the artist there is no crying need for licence in the art.

But if liberty is the one thing needful for English fiction, it is not the liberty of the realism of the Third Empire in France, but the liberty of the romanticism of the age of Elizabeth in England ; the liberty of all great and healthy passions to go what lengths they will. For many years past the cynicism that has been only too vocal in English criticism has been telling us that it is a poor thing to give way to strong feeling, that strong feeling is the mark of an untaught nature, and that education should help us to control our emotions and conceal them. I am told that this type of superfine cynicism comes from Oxford, but on that point I can offer no opinion. Whatever its source its effects are baneful, for it cuts at the root of the finest quality that imaginative writing can have, the quality of passion. No such plea ever had a hearing in the days when English literature was at its best. It was not a childish weakness to give way to powerful emotions when " Lear " was written. Powerful emotions were sought for their own sakes, and no man was shocked when Cordelia perished in a just cause. Sentiment is different now, and with great passions of the purest kind lying everywhere about us, we who write to please must never touch them, or, touching them, we must never probe them deeply. And this is one of the ways in which the thing called realism is compelled to play its own game backwards.

A doctrine may fairly be judged by the example of its best exponents, and of all the champions of realism the healthiest, I think, is Turgenieff. I do not place Flaubert in that position, because his work seems always to be clouded by the moral shadows that over-hung his own life. Neither do I place M. Daudet there, for the reason that the ethical character of his best work is disfigured by what I cannot but consider a wilful determination to find the balance of justice on the wrong side of the world's account. But I place Turgenieff at the head of the realists, because he seems to me to have been an entirely healthy man, who came to an honest conclusion, that poetic justice is false to human life, and that human life is the only model for imaginative art. Well, what of Tourgenieff? We shall never know how much we have lost in him by that accident of exile which brought him under the influence of Flaubert. He does not of set purpose make " the wicked prosper and the virtuous miscarry," still less does he paint the world's cesspools under pretence of painting the world ; but he leaves you without hope, without expectation, and in an atmosphere of despair more chilling than the atmosphere of a vault. His novels may be just representations of actual life, but they begin nowhere and end nowhere ; and, like the little bits of nature that come under a photographic camera, they are transcripts, not pictures of life. It is not because they end sadly that they outrage poetic justice. It is because they do not in any true sense end at all. " Macbeth " ends sadly, but it ends absolutely, because it ends with justice. " Cato " also ends sadly, but it ends only as the broken column ends, merely because there is no capital to crown it. And, rightly followed, justice is the only end for a work of imaginative art, whatever may be the frequent end of life. Without it what is a work of art ? A fragment, a scrap, a passing impression. The incidents of life are only valuable to art in degree as they are subservient to an idea, and an idea is only valuable to man in the degree to which it helps him to see that come what will the world is founded on justice. Torn by the wind a bird's nest falls to the ground, and all the young birds perish. That is a faithful representation of a common incident of life, but a thousand such incidents massed together would not make a work of art. Justice is the one thing that seems to give art a right to exist, and justice—poetic justice, as we call it—is the essence of Romanticism.

And is this Romanticism a " backwater " ? Has the stream of literary orthodoxies ceased to flow with it ? A little band among the writers of the time are answering, " Yes," but we answer " No ;" Romanticism is not a " backwater," can never be a " backwater," and the stream of literary orthodoxies in England is at this moment flowing more strongly with Romanticism than at any time since the death of Scott. It is true that realism has lately had its day in England as well as in France. In France it has been nasty, and in England it has been merely trivial. But the innings of realism is over ; it has scored badly or not at all, and is going out disgraced. The reign of mere fact in imaginative literature was very short, it is done, and it is making its exit rapidly, with a sorry retinue of either teacup-and-saucer nonentities or of harlots at its heels. And the old Romanticism that was before it is coming into its own again.

Surely it is impossible to mistake the signs of the times in the affairs of literature. What is going on in Europe ? I never meet a Frenchman of real insight but he tells me that Zolaism as a literary force is as nearly as possible dead in France. Its dirty shroud keeps a wraith of it flitting before men's eyes. And what is France going back to ? The Idealism of George Sand ? The Romanticism of Hugo ? Perhaps not, though Hugo is not as far gone in France as some people would have us believe. France is at this moment waiting for a new man, and depend upon it, when he comes, he will be a romanticist. If such are the signs of the literary horizon in France, what are they in the rest of Europe ? What in Russia, where Tolstoi has taken all that is good in the Realism of France and engrafted it on to the brave and noble and surpassing idealism of English poetry at the beginning of this century ? What in the Scandinavian countries (the stronghold of the purer and higher Realism), where Björnsen, as I can attest from some personal knowledge of Norway, is a stronger force than Ibsen, himself more than half an idealist ? What in America, where the sturdy romance of the soil is pushing from its stool the teacup Realism of the last twenty years, and even the first champions of such Realism, who have said that there is sufficient incident in " the lifting up of a chair," and that " all the stories are told," are themselves turning their backs on their own manifesto, and coming as near to Romanticism as their genius will let them ?

On every side, in every art, music, the drama, painting, and even sculpture, the tendency is towards Romance. Not the bare actualities of life " as it is," but the glories of life as it might be; not the domination of fact, but of feeling. I think one might show this yet more plainly by illustrations drawn from the stage of the time. The cry of the stage of to-day is Romance, the cry of fiction is Romance, the cry of music is Romance, and I do not think I belie the facts when I say that the cry of the Science of this hour is also for Romance.

Romance is the cry of the time, and the few cynics of the Press may deride it as much as they like, but Romance is going to be once more the tendency of literature, and the sum and substance of its critical orthodoxy. The world now feels exactly the same want as it has always felt. It wants to be lifted up, to be inspired, to be thrilled, to be shown what brave things human nature is capable of at its best. This must be the task of the new Romanticism, and the new Romanticism can only work through Idealism. It can never be the task of the old realism. The Realists are all unbelievers; unbelievers in God, or unbelievers in man, or both. The Idealist must be a believer; a believer in God, a believer in man, and a believer in the divine justice whereon the world is founded.

So I say that these two are going to be the watchwords of fiction for the next twenty years at least—ROMANTICISM AND IDEALISM.

HALL CAINE.

J.M. Barrie

"Brought Back from Elysium"

Contemporary Review 57 (June 1890), 846–54

BROUGHT BACK FROM ELYSIUM.

SCENE.—*The Library of a Piccadilly club for high thinking and bad dinners; Time, midnight. Four eminent novelists of the day regarding each other self-consciously. They are (1) a Realist, (2) a Romancist, (3) an Elsmerian, (4) a Stylist. The clock strikes thirteen, and they all start.*

REALIST (*staring at the door and drawing back from it*).—I thought I heard—something?

STYLIST.—I—the——(*pauses to reflect on the best way of saying it was only the clock*).

(*A step is heard on the stair.*)

ELSMERIAN.—Hark! It must be him and them. (*Stylist shudders*). I knew he would not fail us.

ROMANCIST (*nervously*).—It may only be some member of the club.

ELSMERIAN.—The hall-porter said we would be safe from intrusion in the library.

REALIST.—I hear nothing now. (*His hand comes in contact with a bookcase*). How cold and clammy to the touch these books are. A strange place, gentlemen, for an eerie interview. (*To Elsmerian*). You really think they will come? You have no religious doubts about the existence of Elysian Fields?

ELSMERIAN.—I do not believe in Elysium, but I believe in him.

REALIST.—Still if——

(*The door is shaken and the handle falls off.*)

ROMANCIST.—Ah! Even I have never imagined anything so weird as this. See, the door opens!

(*Enter an American novelist.*)

OMNES.—Only you!

·AMERICAN (*looking around him self-consciously*).—I had always suspected that there was a library, though I have only been a member for a few months. Why do you look at me so strangely?

ELSMERIAN (*after whispering with the others*).—We are agreed that since you have found your way here you should be permitted to stay; on the understanding, of course, that we still disapprove of your methods as profoundly as we despise each other.

AMERICAN.—But what are you doing here, when you might be asleep downstairs?

ELSMERIAN (*impressively*).—Have you never wished to hold converse with the mighty dead?

AMERICAN.—I don't know them.

ELSMERIAN.—I admit that the adjective was ill-chosen, but listen: the ghosts of Scott and some other novelists will join us presently. We are to talk with them about their work.

REALIST.—And ours.

ELSMERIAN.—And ours. They are being brought from the Grove of Bay-trees in the Elysian Fields.

AMERICAN.—But they are antiquated, played out; and, besides, they will not come.

ROMANCIST.—You don't understand. Stanley has gone for them.

AMERICAN.—Stanley!

ELSMERIAN.—It was a chance not to be missed. (*Looks at his watch*). They should have been here by this time; but on these occasions he is sometimes a little late.

(*Their mouths open as a voice rings through the club crying, "I cannot stop to argue with you; I'll find the way myself."*)

REALIST.—It is he, but he may be alone. Perhaps they declined to accompany him?

ELSMERIAN (*with conviction*).—He would bring them whether they wanted to come or not.

(*Enter Mr. Stanley with five Ghosts.*)

Mr. STANLEY.—Here they are. I hope the row below did not alarm you. The hall-porter wanted to know if I was a member, so I shot him. Waken me when you are ready to send them back.

(*Sits down and sleeps immediately.*)

FIRST GHOST.—I am Walter Scott.

SECOND GHOST.—I am Henry Fielding.

THIRD GHOST.—My name is Smollett.

FOURTH GHOST.—Mine is Dickens.

FIFTH GHOST.—They used to call me Thack.

ALL THE GHOSTS (*looking at the sleeper*).—And we are a little out of breath.

AMERICAN (*to himself*).—There is too much plot in this for me.

ELSMERIAN (*to the visitors*).—Quite so. Now will you be so good as to stand in a row against that bookcase. (*They do so.*) Perhaps you have been wondering why we troubled to send for you ?

Sir WALTER.—We——

ELSMERIAN.—You need not answer me, for it really doesn't matter. Since your days a great change has come over fiction—a kind of literature at which you all tried your hands—and it struck us that you might care to know how we moderns regard you.

REALIST.—And ourselves.

ELSMERIAN.—And ourselves. We had better begin with ourselves, as the night is already far advanced. You will be surprised to hear that fiction has become an art.

FIELDING.—I am glad we came, though the gentleman (*looking at the sleeper*) was perhaps a little peremptory. You are all novelists ?

ROMANCIST.—No, I am a Romancist, this gentleman is a Realist, that one is a Stylist, and——

ELSMERIAN.—We had better explain to you that the word novelist has gone out of fashion in our circles. We have left it behind us——

Sir WALTER.—I was always content with story-teller myself.

AMERICAN.—Story-teller ! All the stories have been told.

Sir WALTER (*wistfully*).—How busy you must have been since my day.

ROMANCIST.—We have, indeed, and not merely in writing stories— to use the language of the nursery. Now that fiction is an art, the work of its followers consists less in writing mere stories (to repeat a word that you will understand more readily than we) than in classify- ing ourselves and (when we have time for it) classifying you.

THACKERAY.—But the term novelist satisfied us.

ELSMERIAN.—There is a difference, I hope, between then and now. I cannot avoid speaking plainly, though I allow that you are the seed from which the tree has grown. May I ask what was your first step toward becoming novelists.

SMOLLETT (*with foolish promptitude*).—We wrote a novel.

THACKERAY (*humbly*).—I am afraid I began by wanting to write a good story, and then wrote it to the best of my ability. Is there any other way ?

STYLIST.—But how did you laboriously acquire your style ?

THACKERAY.—I thought little about style. I suppose, such as it was, it came naturally.

STYLIST.—Pooh ! Then there is no art in it.

ELSMERIAN.—And what was your aim ?

THACKERAY.—Well, I had reason to believe that I would get some- thing for it.

ELSMERIAN.—Alas ! to you the world was not a sea of drowning souls, nor the novel a stone to fling to them, that they might float on it to a quiet haven. You had no aims, no methods, no religious doubts, and you neither analysed your characters nor classified yourselves.

AMERICAN.—And you reflected so little about your art that you wrote story after story without realising that all the stories had been told.

Sir WALTER.—But if all the stories are told, how can you write novels?

AMERICAN.—The story in a novel is of as little importance as the stone in a cherry. I have written three volumes about a lady and a gentleman who met on a car.

Sir WALTER.—Yes, what happened to them?

AMERICAN.—Nothing happened. That is the point of the story.

STYLIST.—Style is everything. The true novelist does nothing but think, think, think about his style, and then write, write, write about it. I daresay I am one of the most perfect stylists living. Oh, but the hours, the days, the years of introspection I have spent in acquiring my style!

THACKERAY (*sadly*).—If I had only thought more of style! May I ask how many books you have written?

STYLIST.—Only one—and that I have withdrawn from circulation. Ah, sir, I am such a stylist that I dare not write anything. Yet I meditate a work.

Sir WALTER.—A story?

STYLIST.—No, an essay on style. I shall devote four years to it

Sir WALTER.—And I wrote two novels in four months!

STYLIST.—Yes, that is still remembered against you. Well, you paid the penalty, for your books are still popular.

DICKENS.—But is not popularity nowadays a sign of merit?

STYLIST.—To be popular is to be damned.

Sir WALTER.—I can see from what you tell me that I was only a child. I thought little about how novels should be written. I only tried to write them, and as for style, I am afraid I merely used the words that came most readily. (*Stylist groans.*) I had such an interest in my characters (*American groans*), such a love for them (*Realist groans*), that they were like living beings to me. Action seemed to come naturally to them, and all I had to do was to run after them with my pen.

ROMANCIST.—In the dark days you had not a cheap press, nor scores of magazines and reviews. Ah, we have many opportunities that were denied to you.

FIELDING.—We printed our stories in books.

ROMANCIST.—I was not thinking of the mere stories. It is not our stories that we spend much time over, but the essays, and discussions and interviews about our art. Why, there is not a living man in this room, except the sleeper, who has not written as many articles and essays about how novels should be written as would stock a library.

SMOLLETT.—But we thought that the best way of showing how they should be written was to write them.

REALIST (*bitingly*).—And as a result, you cannot say at this moment whether you are a Realist, a Romancist, an American Analyst, a Stylist, or an Elsmerian ! Your labours have been fruitless.

SMOLLETT.—What am I?

ROMANCIST.—I refuse to include you among novelists at all, for your artistic views (which we have discovered for you) are different from mine. You are a Realist. Therefore I blot you out.

Sir WALTER (*anxiously*).—I suppose I am a Romancist?

REALIST.—Yes, and therefore I cannot acknowledge you. Your work has to go.

AMERICAN.—It has gone. I never read it. Indeed, I can't stand any of you. In short, I am an American Analyst.

DICKENS (*dreamily*).—One of the most remarkable men in that country.

AMERICAN.—Yes, sir, I am one of its leading writers of fiction without a story—along with Silas K. Weekes, Thomas John Hillocks, William P. Crinkle, and many others whose fame must have reached the Grove of Bay-trees. We write even more essays about ourselves than they do in this old country.

ELSMERIAN.—Nevertheless, Romanticism, Realism, and Analysis are mere words, as empty as a drum. Religious doubt is the only subject for the novelist nowadays; and if he is such a poor creature as to have no religious doubts, he should leave fiction alone.

STYLIST.—Style is everything. I can scarcely sleep at nights for thinking of my style.

FIELDING.—This, of course, is very interesting to us who know so little, yet, except that it enables you to label yourselves, it does not seem to tell you much. After all, does it make a man a better novelist to know that other novelists pursue the wrong methods? You seem to despise each other cordially, while Smollett and I, for instance, can enjoy Sir Walter. We are content to judge him by results, and to consider him a great novelist because he wrote great novels.

ELSMERIAN.—You will never be able to reach our standpoint if you cannot put the mere novels themselves out of the question. The novelist should be considered quite apart from his stories.

REALIST.—It is nothing to me that I am a novelist, but I am proud of being a Realist. That is the great thing.

ROMANCIST.—Consider, Mr. Smollett, if you had thought and written about yourself as much as I have done about myself you might never have produced one of the works by which you are now known. That would be something to be proud of. You might have written romances, like mine and Sir Walter's.

ELSMERIAN.—Or have had religious doubts.

STYLIST.—Or have become a Stylist, and written nothing at all.

REALIST.—And you, Sir Walter, might have become one of us.

THACKERAY.—But why should we not have written simply in the manner that suited us best? If the result is good, who cares for the label?

ROMANCIST (*eyeing Sir Walter severely*).—No one has any right to be a Romancist unconsciously. Romance should be written with an effort —as I write it. I question, sir, if you ever defined romance?

Sir WALTER (*weakly*).—I had a general idea of it, and I thought that perhaps my books might be allowed to speak for me.

ROMANCIST.—We have got beyond that stage. Romance (that is to say, fiction) has been defined by one of its followers as "not nature, it is not character, it is not imagined history; it is fallacy, poetic fallacy; a lie, if you like, a beautiful lie, a lie that is at once false and true—false to fact, true to faith."

(*The Ghosts look at each other apprehensively*).

Sir WALTER.—Would you mind repeating that? (*Romancist repeats it*). And are my novels all that? To think of their being that, and I never knew! I give you my word, sir, that when I wrote "Ivanhoe," for example, I merely wanted to—to tell a story.

REALIST.—Still, in your treatment of the Templar, you boldly cast off the chains of Romanticism and rise to Realism.

ELSMERIAN.—To do you justice, the Templar seems to have religious doubts.

STYLIST.—I once wrote a little paper on your probable reasons for using the word "wand" in circumstances that would perhaps have justified the use of "reed." I have not published it.

Sir WALTER.—This would be more gratifying to me if I thought that I deserved it.

AMERICAN.—I remember reading "Ivanhoe" before I knew any better; but even then I thought it poor stuff. There is no analysis in it worthy of the name. Why did Rowena drop her handkerchief? Instead of telling us that, you prance off after a band of archers. Do you really believe that intellectual men and women are interested in tournaments?

Sir WALTER.—You have grown so old since my day. Besides, I have admitted that the Waverley novels were written simply to entertain the public.

ELSMERIAN.—No one, I hope, reads my stories for entertainment. We have become serious now.

AMERICAN.—I have thought at times that I could have made something of "Ivanhoe." Yes, sir, if the theme had been left to me I would have worked it out in a manner quite different from yours. In my mind's eye I can see myself developing the character of the hero. I would have made him more like ourselves. The Rebecca, too, I would have reduced in size. Of course the plot would have had to go overboard, with Robin Hood and Richard, and we would have had no fighting. Yes, it might be done. I would call it, let me see, I would call it, " Wilfrid : a Study."

THACKERAY (*timidly*).—Have you found out what I am ?

AMERICAN.—You are intolerably prosy.

STYLIST.—Some people called Philistines maintain that you are a Stylist ; but evidently you forgot yourself too frequently for that.

ROMANCIST.—You were a cynic, which kills romanticism.

REALIST.—And men allow their wives to read you, so you don't belong to us.

AMERICAN (*testily*).—No, sir, you need not turn to me. You and I have nothing in common.

DICKENS.—I am a——— ?

REALIST.—It is true that you wrote about the poor ; but how did you treat them ? Are they all women of the street and brawling ruffians ? Instead of dwelling for ever on their sodden misery, and gloating over their immorality, you positively regard them from a genial standpoint. I regret to have to say it, but you are a Romancist.

ROMANCIST.—No, no, Mr. Dickens, do not cross to me. You wrote with a purpose, sir. Remember Dotheboys Hall.

ELSMERIAN.—A novel without a purpose is as a helmless ship.

DICKENS (*aghast*).—Then I am an Elsmerian ?

ELSMERIAN.—Alas! you had no other purpose than to add to the material comforts of the people. Not one of your characters was troubled with religious doubts. Where does Mr. Pickwick pause to ask himself why he should not be an atheist ? You cannot answer. In these days of earnest self-communion we find Mr. Pickwick painfully wanting. How can readers rise from his pages in distress of mind ? You never give them a chance.

THACKERAY.—No, there is nothing sickly about Pickwick.

ELSMERIAN.—Absolutely nothing. He is of a different world (I am forced to say this) from that in which my heroes move. Not, indeed, that they do move much. Give me a chair and a man with doubts, and I will give you a novel. He has only to sit on that chair———

STYLIST.—As I sit on mine, thinking, thinking, thinking about my style.

DICKENS.—Young people in love are out of fashion in novels nowadays, I suppose ?

ELSMERIAN.—Two souls in doubt may meet and pule as one.

THACKERAY.—As a novelist I had no loftier belief than this—that high art is high morality, and that the better the literature the more ennobling it must be.

REALIST.—And this man claimed to be one of us !

DICKENS.—I wrote for a wide public (*Stylist sighs*), whom I loved (*Realist sighs*). I loved my characters, too (*American sighs*), they seemed so real to me (*Romancist sighs*), and so I liked to leave them happy. I believe I wanted to see the whole world happy (*Elsmerian sighs*).

Sir WALTER.—I also had that ambition.

THACKERAY.—Do you even find Mr. Pickwick's humour offensive nowadays ?

ROMANCIST.—To treat a character with humour is to lift him from his pedestal to the earth.

ELSMERIAN.—We have no patience with humour. In these days of anxious thought humour seems a trivial thing. The world has grown sadder since your time, and we novelists of to-day begin where you left off. Were I to write a continuation of " The Pickwick Papers," I could not treat the subject as Mr. Dickens did ; I really could not.

STYLIST.—Humour is vulgar.

AMERICAN.—Humour, sir, has been refined and chastened since the infancy of fiction, and I am certain that were my humorous characters to meet yours mine would be made quite uncomfortable. Mr. Pickwick could not possibly be received in the drawing-room of Sara H. Finney, and Sam Weller would be turned out of her kitchen. I believe I am not overstating the case when I say that one can positively laugh at your humour.

DICKENS.—They used to laugh.

AMERICAN.—Ah, they never laugh at mine.

DICKENS.—But if I am not a Realist, nor a Romancist, nor an Elsmerian, nor a St——

AMERICAN.—Oh, we have placed you. In Boston we could not live without placing everybody, and you are ticketed a caricaturist.

DICKENS (*sighing*).—I liked the old way best, of being simply a novelist.

AMERICAN.—That was too barbarous for Boston. We have analysed your methods, and found them puerile. You have no subtle insight into character. You could not have written a novel about a lady's reasons for passing the cruet. Nay, more, we find that you never drew either a lady or a gentleman. Your subsidiary characters alone would rule you out of court. To us it is hard work to put all we have to say about a lady and gentleman who agree not to become engaged into three volumes. But you never send your hero twelve miles in a coach without adding another half-dozen characters to your list. There is no such lack of artistic barrenness in our school.

SMOLLETT (*enthusiastically*).—What novels you who think so much about the art must write nowadays! You will let us take away a few samples? (*The live novelists cough.*)

REALIST (*huskily*).—You—you have heard of our work in the Grove of Bay-trees?

Sir WALTER (*apologetically*).—-You see we are not in the way of hearing—(*politely*). But we look forward to meeting you there some day.

THACKERAY.—And resuming this conversation. None of you happens to be the gentleman who is rewriting Shakespeare and Homer, I suppose? It is of no consequence; I—I only thought that if he had been here I would have liked to look at him. That is all.

FIELDING (*looking at the sleeper*).—He said he would take us back.

(*The novelists shake Mr. Stanley timidly, but he sleeps on.*)

STYLIST (*with a happy inspiration*).—Emin——

Mr. STANLEY (*starting to his feet*).—You are ready? Fall in behind me. Quick mar——

Sir WALTER.—You won't mind carrying these books for us? (*Gives Stanley samples of Realism, Elsmerism, &c.*)

Mr. STANLEY.—Right. I shall give them to the first man we meet in Piccadilly to carry.

ROMANCIST (*foolishly*).—He may refuse.

Mr. STANLEY (*grimly*).—I think not. Now then——

ELSMERIAN (*good-naturedly*).—A moment, sir. We have shown these gentlemen how the art of fiction has developed since their day, and now if they care to offer us a last word of advice——

Sir WALTER.—We could not presume.

THACKERAY.—As old-fashioned novelists of some repute at one time, we might say this: that perhaps if you thought and wrote less about your styles and methods and the aim of fiction, and, in short, forgot yourselves now and again in your stories, you might get on better with your work. Think it over.

Mr. STANLEY.—Quick march.

(*The novelists are left looking at each other self-consciously.*)

J. M. BARRIE.

J.A. Symonds

"*La Bête Humaine.*
A Study in Zola's Idealism"

Fortnightly Review 56 (October 1891), 453–62

LA BÉTE HUMAINE.

A STUDY IN ZOLA'S IDEALISM.

It is one of the *mauvaises plaisanteries* of the epoch to call M. Zola a realist. Actually, he is an idealist of the purest water; and if idealists are Philistines, then Gath can claim him for her own. The ponderousness of his method, the tedium of his descriptions, and the indecencies in which he revels, do not justify his claim to stand outside the ranks of those who treat reality from an ideal point of view. Walt Whitman, one of the staunchest idealists who ever uttered prophecy, might be made to pass for a realist on the same grounds of heaviness, minuteness, and indecency. The fact is that Zola, like Whitman, approaches his art-work in the spirit of a poet.

These assertions have an odour of paradox, and require demonstration. That may be supplied by an analysis of *La Bête Humaine*. I will call this book the poem of the railway. It is, indeed, a great deal more than that. But the unity of subject, movement, composition, interest; which constitutes a creation of idealizing art, and distinguishes that from the haphazard incompleteness of reality, is found by Zola in the biography of an engine on the line between Paris and Havre. "La Lison," as the locomotive is named, might be termed the heroine of the romance.

This unity, which constitutes an ideal creation of the brain, separating that from fact or from any literal transcripts of reality, is sustained with extraordinary ability and constructive genius throughout *La Bête Humaine*. All the personages of the drama are in one way or another connected with the company of the Ouest line : as directors, station-masters, guards, engine-drivers, stokers, pointsmen, with their wives and mistresses. The unity of place is equally preserved. Of the many tragic episodes to which the action gives rise, all are prepared at Paris or Havre in buildings attached to the railway stations, and all are consummated at a certain fatal point between the stopping-places of Malaunay and Barentin. There is a tunnel which plays an important part in each catastrophe, and a wayside house of doom at Croix-de-Maufras. This house, in truth, has a right to claim equality with the palace of Atreus at Mycenæ. It is just as mysterious, and no less haunted by the Furies of an ancient crime. Guilty and innocent alike are drawn within its neighbourhood to be involved in the mesh of destiny, which eventually involves all the *dramatis personæ*. The scheme by which Zola has worked out this unity of subject, place and retribution is so mathematically perfect, so mechanically exact, as to set all the probabilities of actual events at defiance. Only the extreme vivacity and photographic accuracy of each incident in detail blind us to the immense demand continually made upon our credulity by the poet's ideality.

What is the meaning of the title. We find it in this sentence: "Posséder, tuer, cela s'équivalait-il, dans le fond sombre de la bête humaine?" (p. 196). Murder and sexual desire, co-existent, confounding their qualities, emergent one out of the other, in the nature of the irredeemable wild beast, man: that is the double subject of the book. These two brutal factors persist in humanity. The machinery of modern life, the train which goes hurling and howling down the grooves of progress, remains an idle instrument beside the passions of the human beast. "Ah! c'est une belle invention, il n'y a pas à dire," says one of the persons in the story: "on va vite, on est plus savant. . . Mais les bêtes sauvages restent des bêtes sauvages, et on aura beau inventer des mécaniques meilleures encore, il y aura quand même des bêtes sauvages dessous" (p. 45.) That other great invention of the civilised brain, legal justice, fails to solve the problems of social life, cannot penetrate the passions which impel the wild beast, man, to improbable or inconceivable actions. The ineptitude of the judge, M. Denizet, acute and industrious in the search after truth as he may be, forms a moral pendant to the blind brute force of the locomotive which whirls human beings to destruction. Justice does not fathom the profundities of the beast's heart any better than the railway engine is capable of sympathizing with its emotions.

The poetic unity which marks *La Bête Humaine* out as a masterpiece of the constructive imagination, cannot be fully appreciated without passing the main actors of its drama in review. The first to whom we are introduced is a man called Roubaud, "sous-chef de gare," or second station-master, at Havre. He had risen from the ranks, passing through several grades in the company's service, until his vigour and good conduct prepared him for a higher post. That, however, might have still been long in coming had he not married a young woman called Séverine, who was the protégée of the President Grandmorin, one of the acting directors in the company. Séverine, a daughter of Grandmorin's gardener, had been taken into the great man's family upon the death of her father, and grew up in humble companionship with his only daughter Berthe. Roubaud, now on the verge of forty, wooed and won this girl, his junior by fifteen years. Grandmorin gave her a marriage portion of £400, advanced her husband to his post of station-master, and promised to leave her by his will a house at Croix-de-Maufras, on the line between Rouen and Havre. The property was valued at about £1,600.

Séverine is described as one of those graceful, fascinating women who charm men without possessing any peculiar beauty. Her great attraction for the rough railway-servant was the distinction she derived from her education in Grandmorin's family. Rather tall and slender, she had a wealth of undulating dark hair, framing her pale face, and eyes of clear grey blue—"yeux de pervenche." Roubaud suspected nothing wrong in the protection extended to her by the president; for though there were disquieting rumours afloat about his conduct, he had reached an advanced if vigorous old age, stood well at the Imperial Court, and owned a property of some three millions of francs.

During the opening scene between husband and wife, which takes place in a little room overlooking the station of the Ouest at Paris, an accident leads Roubaud to the discovery that M. Grandmorin had foully abused his quasi-guardianship of the young woman when she was a girl of sixteen. The wild beast in the man awakes. His first impulse is to murder his wife, and he very nearly does so with fists and feet. On second thoughts, he determines to murder Grand-morin. Opportunity enables him to do so that very evening in a railway carriage between Malaunay and Barentin. The weapon used is a knife which Séverine had just given him. The place selected is the tunnel which has been already mentioned. But the deed had not been completed before the train emerged from the tunnel, and swept on along a hedgerow. There lay a young man, who had just time to catch the vision of Roubaud stabbing his victim in the throat, while a mass of something black weighed on the murdered person's legs. He could not, however, remember with any distinctness the features of the two men, and was not certain whether the black mass was a woman or a railway-rug.

It is not necessary to describe how Roubaud's professional fami-liarity with railway trains enabled him and Séverine to escape detection by shifting from one carriage to another, and back again, at well-chosen moments. Enough that they reached Havre appa-rently as usual, and though suspected of the crime (their alleged motive being a wish to anticipate Grandmorin's bequest of the house at Croix-de-Maufras), they were finally dismissed without a stain upon their reputations.

The young man who obtained that fleeting vision of the murder is Jacques Lantier, a son of Gervaise (the heroine of Zola's *L'Assom-moir*), and brother of a suicidal painter (the hero of Zola's *L'Œuvre*). There is also one of the Lantiers in Zola's *Germinal*. His peculiarity of temperament has to be noticed. Coming of what would now be called a neuropathical stock, he was the victim of an inborn homicidal instinct. It took the special form, that, from the age of dawning manhood, he never desired a woman without at the same time being irresistibly impelled to kill her. "Tuer une femme, tuer une femme! cela sonnait à ses oreilles, du fond de sa jeunesse, avec la fièvre grandissante, affolante du désir. Comme les autres, sous l'éveil de la puberté, rêvent d'en posséder une, lui s'était enragé à l'idée d'en tuer une" (p. 57). A vague impression haunts his brain that this terrible perversion of the sexual instinct derives from a remote ancestry. Sitting by women in the theatre, passing them in the streets, suddenly the insane abominable impulse comes upon him, like a force superior to his will and reason. "Puisqu'il ne les connaissait pas, quelle fureur pouvait-il avoir contre elles? car, chaque fois, c'était comme une soudaine crise de rage aveugle, une soif toujours renaissante de venger des offenses très anciennes, dont il aurait perdu l'exacte mémoire. Cela venait-il donc de si loin, du mal que les femmes avaient fait à sa race, de la rancune amassée de mâle en mâle, depuis la première tromperie au fond des cavernes?" For the rest, Jacques Lantier is a young man of more than ordinary refinement; physically attractive, with well-formed hands and a face that would have been eminently sympathetic but for the restlessness of the brown eyes, shot at times with flakes of red. His position in the railway company, which connects all these people in one sphere of work, is that of engine-driver. Debarred from the society of women by the fearful malady which preys upon his brain, Lantier has made a mistress of his engine, the strong, beautiful, responsive creature, Lison, who twice daily performs the journey between Havre and Paris with express trains.

Lantier found himself in the evening of Grandmorin's murder on the bank above the tunnel's mouth, owing to a series of incidents which must be related. A group of persons highly important to the plot of *La Bête Humaine* appear now upon the stage. Jacques had gone to visit a female cousin of his father, who brought him up at Plassans when his mother Gervaise deserted him at the age of six. This woman, "tante Phasie," as she is called, was left a widow with two daughters, Flore and Louisette. For her second husband she married a miserable, lifeless creature named Misard, who is employed upon the line of the Ouest as signalman, at Croix-de-Maufras. The house inhabited by the Misards stands close to the railway, so that it is shaken by the thunder of all the trains that pass; and at night the glare of their illuminated carriages startles the sleepers in the bedrooms, and leaves upon wakeful brains the silhouettes of countless travellers going and coming upon the iron highway of the world. Close by lies the deserted garden and the empty house which Séverine is destined to inherit from the President Grandmorin. We are, therefore, at the local centre of the tragedy. Misard, the signalman, is actuated by only one motive in life, a slow, persistent avarice. It works in his dull brain like a spreading disease; and just at this moment it has brought him to the commission of a crime. He is poisoning Phasie by little doses introduced into her food, in order to gain possession of some thousand francs which she has recently inherited. The woman knows what her husband has in view. But she fancies herself strong and keen-witted enough to defeat him, and persists in this illusion till she dies of poison on the night which determines one of the great crises of the tragedy.

The two girls, Flore and Louisette, both of them play parts in this closely-woven drama. Louisette went out to service in the country house of Grandmorin. One day she left her situation in a miserable plight, telling a dark story of her master's violence, signs of which were only too visible upon her body. Instead of going home to Phasie, she took refuge in the woods with a sort of gentle savage, a veritable Orson, whom she called her " bon ami," and whom in the natural course of events she would probably have married. The name of this man is Cabuche. Endowed with herculean strength, he had killed a man by accident in a tavern brawl, and had been sentenced to five years' penal servitude. Leaving the prison at the end of four years with a good character for discipline and industry, Cabuche found himself avoided by his neighbours, and went off to live in a hut close to some deserted quarries. Here he employed himself in excavating huge blocks of stone and carting them down to the nearest railway station. The pure and intimate relation which sprang up between him and the innocent child Louisette, forms one of those romantic episodes that bloom like flowers upon the arid rock of Zola's human wilderness. Louisette died of fever in the forest hut; and Cabuche, knowing well the real cause of her death, vowed to take the life of Grandmorin. Suspicion naturally fell on him when the president was murdered; and it was only due to political reasons for quashing the whole investigation that the good-hearted giant did not fall a victim to M. Denizet's (the magistrate's) well-reasoned system of analysis. Eventually, by another train of circumstances which illustrates Zola's plot-weaving and dexterous manipulation of his characters, Cabuche is condemned for a murder of which he is equally guiltless. He and Louisette are the victims of fatality, crime in others, the mistakes of justice.

Flore has her own place on the railway. At Croix-de-Maufras, close by Misard's signal-box, there is a level crossing. It is her duty to attend to the opening and shutting of the barriers at this point. Zola has drawn in Flore the portrait of an Amazon, a primeval virgin, a nymph of Dian's train. " Une grande fille de dix-huit ans, blonde, forte, à la bouche épaisse, aux grands yeux verdâtres, au front bas sous de lourds cheveux. Elle n'était point jolie, elle

avait les hanches solides et les bras durs. d'un garçon " (p. 37).
Possessed of enormous physical force, she kept importunate suitors
at a distance by the weight of her arms and fists. " Elle était vierge
et guerrière, dédaigneuse du mâle, ce qui finissait par convaincre les
gens qu'elle avait pour sûr la tête dérangée " (p. 53). The fact is that
she had early set her affections upon Jacques Lantier, and was open
to no other influence of the passions. On the evening of his visit to
"la tante Phasie," chance brought them alone together in the
president's deserted garden. The emotional trouble of the girl
roused Lantier's latent malady. He was seized with the irresistible
impulse to kill instead of possessing this woman on the point of
yielding. Rushing from her arms to avoid the horrible suggestion,
he roamed in the dark over field and hedge until he sank exhausted
at the spot where the vision of Grandmorin's murder flashed across
his eyes. The ending of Flore's history may here be related. Seeing
Jacques devote himself to another woman, and growing in course of
time to hate them both, she determined to wreck an express train
which she knew would carry the lovers to Paris on a certain day.
Flore attained her object by contriving to arrest Cabuche's waggon
with its load of blocks upon the level crossing just before the train
came by. The smash, of course, was awful. But Flore had the
disappointment of finding that neither Jacques nor his mistress had
been killed. He was carried, bruised and wounded, into Grandmorin's house at Croix-de-Maufras. There Séverine, for she was the
woman, nursed him, and there he eventually murdered her with the
same knife Roubaud had used to stab the president. But this is
anticipating the order of events. When Flore saw that she had
failed in the main part of her design, and reflected on the number
of human lives she had sacrificed—lives hitherto unreckoned by
her, for daily cargoes of passengers, unknown, unheeded, had been
always going and coming on the wings of steam before her eyes—
she walked straight into the tunnel, and standing upright before an
approaching train, was shattered to bits by the iron cuirass of the
engine. They laid what was left of her mangled form by the side of
her mother Phasie, who was lying dead of Misard's poison in the
signalman's house.

Up to the present point of the analysis we have had several types
of murderers presented to us. There is Roubaud, who kills from
motives of revenge and retrospective jealousy; Misard, who poisons
his wife to get her money; Cabuche, who commits an accidental
homicide through heat of blood and strength of muscle; Lantier,
who is the subject of a perverted instinct, changing the natural
impulse of sex into blood-lust; Flore, whose jealousy prompts her to
sacrifice a hecatomb of human victims in the hope of killing her
lover and her rival; Grandmorin, whose abnormal vices in old age

lead to the death of innocent Louisette. There remains one other personage necessary to the unity of this remarkable plot. He is Lantier's stoker, a debauched drunkard, called Pecqueux, who works in good relations with the engine-driver on their common pet, la Lison. Poor Lison, by the way, ends her own locomotive life in the wreck of the train at Croix-de-Maufras. Lantier and Pecqueux have to drive another, and do so with their usual harmony until Pecqueux obtains ocular evidence that Lantier has been tampering with his mistress Philomène. Of Philomène, one of Zola's disagreeable characters, it is only necessary to say that she lives in the station at Havre, keeping house for her brother, the "chef de dépôt," and pursuing a course of reckless immorality. Lantier was never in any true sense her lover. But the stoker's jealousy once roused he determines to revenge himself. It happens, accordingly, that being more drunk than usual one day he refuses to obey the engine-driver's orders and insults him. They are alone together on their locomotive, carrying a trainful of soldiers, packed in cattle-pens, to Paris; for the Franco-Prussian War has broken out, troops are being concentrated, and these men will be drafted from Paris to the frontier. The quarrel begun by Pecqueux ends in a struggle for supremacy between the two men, in the course of which both fall from the engine and are killed upon the spot. *La Bête Humaine* winds up with a description of the train and its freight of soldiers hurling along the rails, dashing through stations, driverless, uncontrollable. In what I have called the idealism of Zola, this termination of the story with its prospect of carnage and the vision of man's mechanical instrument let loose upon the pathway of destruction is highly dramatic. He closes *Nana* with the shouts of the Parisians yelling, "À Berlin!" The whole series of the Rougon-Macquart volumes lead up to the fall of the Empire. Again, with special reference to this particular romance, the crowding together of a mass of human animals, soldiers, food for powder, who are launched into eternity through the jealous fury of a drunken homicide—nothing, I assert, could be better arranged to sustain the central idea, or less probable as a piece of fortuitous reality. It also has to be remarked that Pecqueux's fatal quarrel begins at Croix-de-Maufras, which I have called the local centre of the tragic drama. Dante himself could not have designed the machinery of a poem with more mathematical precision than Zola has displayed in the construction of this plot. Nature and the course of events, it need hardly be said, do not act in this way.

Before proceeding to draw final critical conclusions, I have to resume what, after all, is the most interesting matter in the book— Lantier's love-affair with Séverine. We have seen how the engine-driver had a vision of the murder of Grandmorin in the railway-carriage. Called as a witness, he made a clean breast of all he knew, but positively declared his inability to identify any of the accused persons. Still he became naturally an object of great anxiety to the Roubauds; and their strange behaviour toward him, displayed in petty acts of courtesy and signs of curiosity, convinced him that Roubaud was the murderer, and that the black mass he had discerned so dimly was the body of Séverine. The three persons came thus to be drawn together in a complicity of knowledge, though they never discussed the details of the crime. Roubaud almost pushed Lantier into his wife's arms; and Lantier found, to his great astonishment, that he could love her without awakening the homicidal demon in his breast. The very fact that she was a murderess seemed to render her inviolable. Séverine, yielding by slow degrees to the young man's passion, discerned for the first time what it was to love with the heart. Her previous relations with Grandmorin and Roubaud had not aroused the woman in her. Lantier's delicate attentions, the difficulties of the situation, and finally the rapture of possession, made her his slave. She grew to hate her husband, who, since the epoch of the murder, abandoned himself wholly to the vice of gaming. Then she prompted her lover to kill the man who stood in the way of their union. But Lantier, in spite of his peculiar homicidal insanity, could not murder in cold blood. At last they agreed to decoy Roubaud alone one evening to the empty house at Croix-de-Maufras, and there Lantier promised he would do the deed. The knife which had stabbed Grandmorin was ready on the table. However, just at the fatal moment, certain imprudences of Séverine brought a paroxysm of his malady upon her lover. Lantier thrust the knife of destiny into her throat, at the very point on the railway where Grandmorin received his death-blow, and in the room where Grandmorin's crime with her had been committed so many years ago. He escaped unseen, leaving the house-door open; and when Roubaud arrived with Misard, they found the unfortunate Cabuche there covered with Séverine's blood. The presence of Cabuche is well *motivirt* (as Goethe would say); and accessory circumstances lead M. Denizet to the conclusion that he was the murderer of both Grandmorin and Séverine, instigated in each case by Roubaud. During the course of the judicial proceedings Roubaud confesses the murder of the president, and is condemned. Cabuche has to bear the guilt of Séverine's assassination.

This analysis of *La Bête Humaine* shows in how true a sense it may be called a poem. It has all those qualities of the constructive reason by which an ideal is distinguished from the bare reality. Not only does it violate our sense of probability in life that ten persons should be either murderers or murdered, or both together, when all of them exist in close relations through their common connection with one line of railway, but the short space of time required for the evolution of this intricate drama of blood and appetite is also unnatural. Eighteen months suffice for the unfolding and termination of the whole series of homicidal tragedies. At the end, the stage is swept literally bare by the violent deaths of all the principal persons who played their parts upon it, with the exception of Misard, who marries a woman of bad character, Roubaud, who goes to life-imprisonment, and the unfortunate Cabuche, who receives a similar doom. Even la Lison is destroyed, and her successor is consigned to probable perdition by the insane fury of Pecqueux. Nor is this all. The conditions of place are manipulated with equal idealistic ingenuity. I have already pointed out how all the threads of the drama are tied together in one knot at Croix-de-Maufras, that place upon the line between Malaunay and Barentin at the entrance to the fatal tunnel. When Lantier comes to the president's deserted house, at the commencement of the story, he regards it with a superstitious dread. "Cette maison, il la connaissait bien, il la regardait à chacun de ses voyages, dans le branle grondant de la machine. Elle le hantait sans qu'il sût pourquoi, avec la sensation confuse qu'elle importait à son existence" (p. 51). It was here that he fled from Flore under one access of his homicidal mania, and it was here that he murdered Sévérine under the pressure of another. Here Grandmorin had previously corrupted the girlhood of Madame Roubaud. In its close vicinity stood the house where Madame Misard died of poison, hard by the level crossing where Flore wrecked the train, not far from the tunnel where Grandmorin was stabbed, Flore committed suicide, and Pecqueux made his slaughterous attack on Lantier. Nor must we forget the fatal knife, that present which Sévérine gave her husband in the opening scene, which he used to assassinate the president, which Sévérine meant should be the instrument of Roubaud's death, and which Lantier finally plunged into her own throat. It is impossible to contend that this interweaving of a numerous *dramatis personœ* in one mesh of homicidal crime, this concentration of so many murderous incidents upon one spot, this crowding of them into less than two years, and this part played by the fatal knife, are realistic—if realism means a faithful correspondence to facts as we observe them, and a reproduction of the events of life as they are known to us.

It may be urged that not a single character, or motive, or circumstance in the whole prose-poem (a long poem of four hundred and fifteen closely-printed pages) has been idealised. That is quite true. The people are studied from life. They act and talk naturally. They say and do a large number of things which are usually concealed in literature, but which are none the less veracious. The mechanism and management of a great main line in France have been reproduced with carefully accumulated details which we may assume to be exact. Few of M. Zola's critics know as much about such things as he does. Also, the conduct of a train, its composition, the relations of guards, station-masters, engine-drivers, stokers, pointsmen, to one another, to the machine they set in motion and control, and to the passengers they carry, are presented with Zola's usual detail, and with more than his usual feeling for the poetry inherent in this phase of modern life. The only point for criticism is at the end of the romance, when the train, with its freight of military cattle, starts forth driverless upon that terrific course. Here we might, indeed, pause to wonder how long the engine would speed on alone with no one to stoke up its furnace. Here, and here perhaps for once, M. Zola yields consciously to the incorrigible idealism of an artist. The romance closes with the prospect of a tragedy which fitly winds the poem up, but which might very probably have failed for want of coals.

Zola's realism consists, then, in his careful attention to details, in the naturalness of his connecting motives, and his frank acceptance of all things human which present themselves to his observing brain. The idealism which I have been insisting on, which justifies us in calling *La Bête Humaine* a poem, has to be sought in the method whereby these separate parcels of the plot are woven together, and also in the dominating conception contained in the title which gives unity to the whole work. We are not in the real region of reality, but in the region of the constructive imagination from the first to the last line of the novel. If that be not the essence of idealism— this working of the artist's brain not in but on the subject-matter of the external world and human nature—I do not know what meaning to give to the term.

JOHN ADDINGTON SYMONDS.

Janetta Newton-Robinson

"A Study of
Mr. Thomas Hardy"

Westminster Review 137 (February 1892), 153–64

A STUDY OF MR. THOMAS HARDY.

ALMOST the highest praise awarded by modern criticism is to say that a writer has distinction and originality. These are, nevertheless, qualities which the admirers of Mr. Thomas Hardy find him to possess in an unusual degree. He occupies himself almost exclusively with scenes that he knows and loves, and his mind is so saturated with the local sentiment of his native district that vivid and caressing phrases run naturally from his pen, inspired by a life-long familiarity. He has been called the "Historian of Wessex," but it is, in fact, Old England which he reproduces for us, surviving in a remote western county, the names of towns, hills, and heaths being veiled under a thin disguise. It must, however, be understood to be an idealised Old England, peopled by an idyllic race of joyous peasants, pagan for the most part, or with the imaginative pantheistic mind of the savage. For these rustics pass their lives in close communion with Nature, and freedom from the cramping pressure of the complex social conventionalities of more thickly populated regions; they are childlike in their ignorance and circumscribed experience, though their language is racy and expressive, and they can be shrewd, humorous, and even poetical. Mr. Hardy has had a marked success in his attempt to invest local types with wide human interest, for he not only possesses the power, so all-important to a novelist, of bringing his men and women into the world alive, but he has the gift of humour, and can throw around them an imaginative glamour, a poetical atmosphere, strangely precious in these days of realism. To these rare endowments he adds the merits of artistic perception and presentation, and a singular freshness and subtlety of observation, which give precision and force to his rendering of Nature. So marked and peculiar is his idiosyncracy that he is only at his best and truly himself among the heaths, cider orchards, and dairy farms of Wessex, but he there finds material which he manipulates with the most varied artistic skill, rich in poetic charm. Beneath the repose of his rural scenes throbs a strong pulse of passion, a dramatic intensity of vision, which give significance to the most homely detail. The descriptions are those of a poet and an artist in words, the pictures being none the less faithful for the essentially imaginative manner in which they are conveyed, while the language used is picturesque, yet precise, avoiding stale conventional formulæ of expression, and at its best terse and even epigrammatic, without loss of lucidity and fulness of suggestion.

Mr. Hardy's heroines are no less successful than his humorous bucolic portraits. His latest novel, *Tess of the d'Urbervilles*, develops a conception of woman as simple yet general in type as that of Venus or Diana, for though Mr. Hardy's genius is eminently modern, there is, nevertheless, something of the Greek spirit in the large and typical handling of many of his characters. The chorus of love-lorn dairymaids in this book is, however, rather of the operatic than the Hellenic stage. But the nature of the heroine, of Tess herself, is charged with inarticulate poetry, and she fulfils the humblest duties with unconscious dignity. To make use of one of Mr. Hardy's own favourite adjectives, she is elemental, and superior to all accidents of station or errors of inexperience. With her muteness, her docility, her passionate eyes, and proud endurance, she pervades the book and attracts irresistibly. Her mind is so preoccupied by the essentials of the life of the emotions, that the incidental does not affect her. She exists in a state of dreamy exaltation, and though she may be driven to an act of desperation, there is no scheming in her; she shows rather an impassioned receptivity, a not unheroic submission to fate as interpreted by her husband's will.

Much of the special charm of this novel lies in the pictures of the life at Talbothay's Dairy, and at the upland farm of Flintcombe Ash. A delicate discrimination of the sentiment which clings to inanimate things is one of Mr. Hardy's most delightful qualities, and gives poetical value to his treatment of Nature. His glowing words vitalise the mists, meads, and streams of the valley of the Froom with an etherealised latter-day Pantheism. Such a chapter as that in which Tess and Angel Clare walk together at dawn, through the morning mists of the meadows near Dairyman Crick's, is a splendid achievement of prose poetry; and the book has many other passages little inferior in grace and graphic energy.

The intensity of Mr. Hardy's mind, however, sometimes leads him astray, and tempts him to throw an unpleasant phosphorescent glow upon his pages, or to introduce some melodramatic incident or distasteful detail. The scene in which Angel Clare, the somnambulist, carries his bride out into the stormy night, and lies down to rest by her side on the tomb of an ancient monk, is fantastic and almost absurd. Mr. Hardy's love of the bizarre breaks forth repeatedly, and he is liable to fall into a vein of morbid fancifulness. A note of almost barbaric crudeness and harshness is struck from time to time, induced perhaps by an excessive strain after effect. The impression thus produced resembles that of some weird mediæval grotesque, which fascinates by the force of the distorted imagination which gave it birth; for though this quality is not pleasing, it has nevertheless artistic value, as it helps to complete the picture of the bucolic mind, so prone to want of reticence and morbid imaginings. The chapter entitled the "Gargoyle" in *Far from the Madding Crowd*, was written by Mr. Hardy in his sardonic mood; and the frenzy of Boldwood, or the opening of Fanny's coffin, in the same book, the death of Mrs. Yeobright in *The Return of the Native*, and other most impressive scenes, leave the reader disturbed and uncomfortable. The strength of the metaphors also is frequently quite startling, as, for example, when we are told that "the sun was resting on the hill like a drop of blood on an eyelid."

Mr. Hardy has no direct descent from any other novelist. His method is poetical rather than psychological, yet there is a sound basis of thought and analysis in all his work, and his perception of fine shades of feeling and evanescent moods is of the quickest. He has not the wit and intellectual grasp of George Meredith, the moral force and earnestness of George Eliot, nor Thackeray's knowledge of the world; he works on a different plane from these masters of his art. Despite his verve and spontaneity he is always restrained and master of himself; but he is a nervous writer, and his sentences glow with inner fire, for he strangely unites the freshness of an Elizabethan author with a gloomy pessimistic impressiveness which belongs solely to the present century.

Far from the Madding Crowd is the work which first assured Mr. Hardy's fame, for it shows great and various power. The action takes place wholly in Wessex, and there are none of those attempts to draw the more sophisticated classes of society in which this author is never entirely successful. The book opens with a humorous description of Farmer Oak, and a lightly touched yet vivid portrait of the dark-haired Bathsheba Everdene in her red jacket, seated on a pile of furniture in a spring waggon. These sketches are given with hardly a superfluous word. Mr. Hardy can make a few bold lines do the duty of multitudes of patient strokes laid on by less skilful hands. His method of description is not one of amplitude of phrase, or of minute reproduction of elaborate detail. First grasping a scene under some strongly imaginative aspect, he swiftly and firmly outlines its suggestive features, bringing them before his reader by a few apt similes, or compendious and exact words—words sometimes figurative, but more often simply precise, and having a picturesque accent, mainly on account of their unfamiliarity in the given connection.

The fine picture of the Great Barn, with the sheep-shearers, the skin of the timid ewes blushing pink under Gabriel's denuding shears, and in fact most of the chapters describing the life on Bathsheba's farm, are masterpieces of humour and character-drawing. Every sentence adds some delicate touch of observation, while the action of the story is never allowed to stand still, and the interest is sustained throughout. The rustics are quaint and genial figures, simple yet sententious, credulous yet canny, revealing subtle traits of character, and grotesque or pathetic at will. They are the results of conscientious psychological study. The astonishing shrewdness of the old-fashioned countryman, the racy humour of his talk, his surprising use of words and similes, inconceivable ignorance, and occasional sharpness of comprehension, are all given, together with sub-humorous indications of unexpected delicacy of feeling, misplaced vanity, or odd self-complacencies. No talk in village parliament was ever quite so racy and epigrammatic as that we hear at the Maltster's, for it has been emphasised and freed from the superfluous and commonplace; but the humour and spirit of the assembly are correctly given. The lumps of native ore have been separated and polished, till, instead of a few dim sparkles, we have detached and glittering crystals. It is in thus seizing the genius of rustic methods of expression that Mr. Hardy excels, and we appreciate his power all the more because he does not attempt the phonetic spelling of dialect, but merely reproduces those characteristic words and idioms which best illustrate the working of the countryman's brain, his manner of arriving at a conclusion, or of sustaining his part in conversation with what passes in his circle for tact, politeness, and distinction.

Gabriel Oak is a delightful mixture of sterling moral quality and simplicity with sagacity and humour. He is, perhaps, the best finished of a series of similar figures to be found in divers of Mr. Hardy's novels, though the noble and pathetic John Loveday, the Trumpet Major, even more entirely wins our hearts; and Dick Dewy is irresistibly sweet-natured and engaging. Bathsheba Everdene, with her " impulsive nature under a deliberate aspect," must also take a high place in the author's list of heroines, for she has a charm which renders Gabriel's devotion completely intelligible. The fascination exercised over her by the dashing Sergeant Tray is in keeping with Mr. Hardy's general conception of feminine nature. His women are nearly all, on occasion, weakly impulsive. Their fancy is caught by externals, and solid worth is unappreciated till its value is learnt by sad experience. Love with them is blind and impulsive, though in their lovers it is often clear-sighted and tenderly protective. Such characters as Gabriel Oak, John Loveday, Dick Dewy, and even the unrelenting Clym Yeobright, are handled with lingering affection, as much from the charm of their sweet, simple natures as from a sense that Gabriel's submissive devotion is required to give effect to Bathsheba's peremptory ways; while the disdainful discontent of the magnificent Eustacia is contrasted with Clym's earnest purpose and self-renunciation.

Mr. Hardy's books, though suggestive and stimulating from their thoughtfulness and freshness of observation, have, nevertheless, a curiously oppressive atmosphere. The author makes no profession of pessimism; his characters are not unusually unfortunate, nor his plots needlessly tragical, while the narrative is always relieved by a vein of penetrating and delightful humour. But a heavy sense of the mystery of life pervades his mind. He never attempts to give optimistic interpretations of the rulings of Providence; he never gives us to understand that all is ordered for the best. He does not glow with active benevolence towards his fellow-men, but gazes at them with a saddened, compassionate wonder, a tender irony. He makes few comments, but we know that he has felt the pity and the mystery. At the same time, his work is morally sound. Good and unselfish conduct is pointed out with admiration, and meanness and self-seeking are shown to be unlovely and disastrous. But the characters are delicately shaded, and the author's non-committal tone and absence of partisanship may possibly bewilder those accustomed to draw a sharp line between the sheep and the goats.

Mr. Hardy's love and understanding of the Dorsetshire heath country find expression in *The Return of the Native*, perhaps the most fascinating of all his works. The book abounds in passages of rare quality, such as no other author could have written, conveying with precision and poetry the most elusive and intangible, but very real suggestions of wild moorland scenery. Here is an illustration :

" When other things sank brooding to sleep the heath appeared slowly to awake and listen. Every night the Titanic form seemed to await something, but it had waited thus unmoved during so many centuries, through the crises of so many things, that it could only be supposed to await one last crisis—the final overthrow."

Sounds are often much neglected in description, but this writer is no less observant through the ear than through the eye, and eagerly notes the " linguistic peculiarity of the heath ":

" A worn whisper, dry and papery, brushing so distinctly across the ear, that by the accustomed the material minutiæ in which it originated could be realised as by touch. It was the united products of infinitesimal vegetable causes, and these were neither stems nor twigs, neither leaves nor fruit, neither blades nor prickles, neither lichen nor moss.

" They were the mummied heath-bells of the last summer, originally tender and purple, now washed colourless by Michaelmas rains, and dried to dead skins by October suns. So low was an individual sound from these, that a combination of hundreds only just emerged from silence, and the myriads of the whole declivity reached the ear but as a shrivelled and intermittent recitative. Yet scarcely a single accent among the many afloat that night could have such power to impress a listener with thoughts of its origin. One outwardly saw the infinity of these combined multitudes—one perceived that each of the tiny trumpets was seized on, entered, scoured, and emerged from by the wind as thoroughly as if it were as vast as a crater.

"The spirit moved them. . . . . It was not, after all, that the left-hand expanse of old blooms spoke, or the right hand, or those of the slope in front. It was the single person of something else speaking through each in turn."

Here is a fanciful simile: "The pause was filled in by the intonation of a pollard thorn a little way to windward, the breezes filtering through its unyielding twigs as through a strainer. *It was as if the night sang dirges with clenched teeth.*"

Mr. Hardy's mind works in a "Dichter's Land" of his own creation, and to fully understand him we must allow ourselves to be carried over the border. Thus in the *Return of the Native* we are transported into a new world, the microcosm of Egdon Heath, and are made to feel that no one of the characters would be appropriate or even possible elsewhere. The poetical atmosphere of the book is due to this intimate relation of animate to inanimate existence. Each personage seems, as it were, to typify some mood of the great rugged heath. The rebellious, undisciplined Eustacia might stand for its stormy grandeur, Clym for its steadfastness, Mrs. Yeobright for its forbidding sternness or grim tenderness, while Thomasin represents its more smiling and genial aspects, and Grandfer and Christian Cantle, with the chorus of "natives," afford relief and local colour. In any case, between these figures and their setting there is a subtle harmony. The sentiment of the wild heathland around them permeates and colours their every word and action. These people are its products as much as its mummied heath-bells and black-eyed adders. We may even go further and add that the author, in allowing us to enter this heath world, has unconsciously given the key to much that was obscure in his own personality. Direct self-revelation forms no part of Mr. Hardy's method, but in learning to understand the speech of Egdon, we learn to comprehend its exponent, for the tongue that has accustomed itself to interpret the mystic voices of the heath, must ever after retain a fuller and a richer accent than clings around the speech of other men.

"Elaborate landscape backgrounds in novels should fulfil two purposes," says a writer in the *Saturday Review.* "They should indicate to the reader subtle inferences and thin shades of emotion too delicate and evanescent to admit of direct expression; and, further, they should play a part similar to that of the chorus in a drama, emphasising its central idea, rounding into unity the impression conveyed by the whole work, and suggesting, it may be, the presence of those vast mysterious forces by which human life is encompassed and directed." These purposes are well fulfilled by Mr. Hardy's descriptive passages, which are never mere excrescences, but integral parts of the work.

Eustacia, wandering nocturnally in her "tiger-beetle beauty," is the capricious and magnificent goddess of the heath, and the most impressive, though not the most charming, of Mr. Hardy's wayward heroines. Here are some of the sentences which describe her :

" She was the raw material of a divinity. She had the passions and instincts which make a model goddess—that is, those that make not quite a model woman."

" One had fancied that such lip-curves were mostly lurking underground in the South, as fragments of forgotten marbles. So fine were the lines of her lips that, though full, each corner of her mouth was as keenly cut as the point of a spear."

" She had Pagan eyes full of nocturnal mysteries."

Paired with this brilliant creature is Clym Yeobright, the "real perusing man," with his " lonely face, suggesting tragical possibilities," and his plan for "instilling high knowledge into empty minds," his " mission to preach to the bucolic world the possibility of culture before luxury." " But," Mr. Hardy continues, naïvely, " Yeobright's mind was not well proportioned."

" A man who advocates æsthetic effort and depreciates social effort is only likely to be understood by a class to whom social effort has become a stale matter. The Egdon eremites could not rise to a serene comprehensiveness without going through the process of enriching themselves."

Much of what is pathetic and tender in Mr. Hardy's books springs from his clear perception of the fact that every human being has been more or less dwarfed and thwarted by circumstance, that " our natural pride of life has been hindered in its blooming by our necessities." Even Eustacia, the undisciplined, excites compassion in her forlorn disappointment, rather than the disapproval she merits through her lack of wifely sympathy with Clym's misfortune. We excuse her because we are made to understand that she, even more than Clym himself, is feeling " the grimness of the general human situation." She has been called a " soulless instinct-led Undine of the earth," and we must pity rather than condemn her.

Word-pictures such as that of Thomasin kneeling in the loft under a dusty ray of sunshine, rolling aside a brown heap of dried fern with her bared arms, and picking out the warmly-tinted store russets and ribstones, impress the mind as forcibly as if seen on canvas. In other moments, writing in a less chastened mood, the author gives rein to the exuberance of his fancy, as in the weird scene of the game of dice for Thomasin's spade guineas, where the " red sandstone automaton," encircled by the dusky forms of the

" heath-croppers," throws his single cracked die, lighted only by the glimmer of his thirteen glow-worms.

The Trumpet Major is not written under such stress of emotional insight as the *Return of the Native*, nor has it the force of *Far from the Madding Crowd*. It is quieter and more restrained, though equally fresh and vivacious, and very perfect in an artistic sense. Like all Mr. Hardy's novels, it is a love-story. Anne Garland and her lovers, the " swash-buckling " Festus Derriman, the " weather-cock " Bob, and honest, pathetic John Loveday, compose a charming idyll, with the Weymouth of George III., the village mill, and the quiet country neighbourhood convulsed by rumours of " Boney's " threatened descent as an appropriate environment. The familiarity with the minute details of rural domestic economy that is shown, even in such a supreme moment as the cleaning of the miller's house and the preparation of Bob and Matilda's wedding-feast, is so amazing that we are tempted to believe Mr. Hardy himself must have masqueraded in the uniform of one of those gallant dragoons who came to Mrs. Loveday's assistance with the meat-chopper.

Under the Greenwood Tree is described on its title-page as a " rural painting of the Dutch school." It is informed with a spirit of innocent gaiety, and is written throughout in a tenderly playful strain. The members of Mellstock parish choir form a genial group of quaint, simple figures, living amidst the echoes of fiddle-strings and Christmas carols, even-tempered, sociable, and cheery, loving their sweet old hymn-tunes and brown cider mugs, and showing a kindly tolerance, not unmixed with complacency, in their treatment of Thomas Leaf, a creature simpler and feebler even than themselves. A humorous yet touching procession runs through the book. Grand-father William, with his bass viol, a " perfect figure of wonder in the way of being fond of music "; Reuben Dewy, the Tranter, awkward but generous, clumsily tapping a barrel of his best cider; Thomas Leaf, the simpleton, warmed by a mug of mead and the excitement of a wedding, rashly involving himself in a pointless story; Robert Penny, the shoemaker, flashing the round glasses of his spectacles, and exhibiting the mould of Fancy Day's little foot, left in her well-worn boot, to the assembled choir, while honest, simple-hearted Dick Dewy regards it " with a delicate feeling that he had no right to do so without having asked the owner of the foot's permission." Geoffrey Day, the keeper, honey-taking, is a good portrait; but better still is the second Mrs. Day, spreading her new damask table-cloth " by instalments " as the meal proceeds, and her husband philosophically explains to sympathising Dick Dewy that her "quare-ness " is so " growed into her that it would kill her to take it out."

" She do belong to that class of womenkind that becomes second wives—a rum class, rather."

" 'Indeed,' said Dick Dewy, with sympathy for an indefinite something.

" ' Yes ; 'tis very trying for a female, especially if you've been a first wife, as she hev.'

" ' Very trying it must be.'

" ' Yes ; you see her first husband was a young man who let her go too far ; in fact, she used to kick up Bob's a-dying at the least thing in the world. And when I married her and found it out, I thought, thinks I, " It's too late now to begin to cure ye," so I let her bide. But she's quare, very quare, at times.'

" ' I'm sorry to hear that.'

" ' Yes—there ; wives be such a provoking class of society, because though they be never right, they be never more than half wrong.' "

At the Tranter's party we are admitted into the very atmosphere of the assembly, and allowed to watch the workings of the speakers' minds, as well as their changes of facial expression. Mr. Hardy has caught the turns of phrase, the habits of thought, the tone and spirit of the rustic gathering. He has always in mind the surroundings amidst which it is held, and the narrow daily round of its members' lives, from which they only escape by the enjoyment of such gossip or discussion as that we are privileged to overhear. The lovemaking of two unsophisticated natures has seldom been more gracefully treated than in the courtship of Dick Dewy and Fancy Day, though the love passages between Anne Garland and Bob Loveday, and Elfride Swancourt's first kiss, have the same lightness and delicacy of touch.

Mr. Hardy's first published novel, *Desperate Remedies*, though crude in many respects, gave much promise of what he should become. Cytherea has already a share of the fascination of Eustacia, Bathsheba, or Elfride, though the firmness and fulness of outline with which they are drawn has not yet been attained. The style of the book is comparatively faulty, though redeemed by sentences like these—" Sudden hopes that were rainbows to the sight, proved but mists to the touch ; " or, when Springrove dreams of an ideal wife who shall be " a child among pleasures, and a woman among pains." In the description of the " Three Tranters' Inn," with Farmer Springrove and his men making cider, there is a foreshadowing of much of the best work in *Far from the Madding Crowd* and elsewhere ; while Cytherea's piteous answer to Owen when he reminds her of her duty to society, and she pleads that " what to society is but a thought is a whole life to her," is pregnant with deep meaning and pathos.

Mr. Hardy's mind has not required the stimulus and friction of city life to quicken its perceptions, but through its inherent vitality and energy has obtained the power of giving the familiar events of the homely life of a rural district their proper value as tragic arbiters of human fate. He has apparently led a somewhat retired life, and his training and experience must have been in many respects other than those of the majority of writers. He comes before the world, therefore, with the freshness which is gained by a new point of view, and his conclusions have something of the interest which the report of an astronomer, observing celestial phenomena from some remote station, has for his brother-workers in another quarter of the globe.

Elfride Swancourt, the central figure of *A Pair of Blue Eyes*, is a most winsome creation. She charms by her plasticity and ready sympathies, her eyes " blue as autumn distance," her impulsive mistakes and tender self-abandonment. Mr. Hardy has much understanding of the position of women. He shows them, like Paula Power, the " Laodicean," hesitating and weighing their lovers ; realising all that depends on their choice of a husband, yet often led astray by passion against their better judgment ; reluctantly submitting to the sway of sex, half-rebellious and half-eager. " The charm of woman," he asserts, " lies partly in her subtlety in matters of love." Perhaps Mr. Hardy is too ready to sacrifice the uprightness of his feminine characters to that most exquisite elusive thing, the " charm of woman," to which, indeed, his own work in fiction is one long tribute, but he wishes men to remember that what they blame is often only the defect of the quality. Thus, when Knight is impatient with Elfride for her weak passivity and prevarication, it is pointed out that these faults are correlated with the confiding tenderness and plasticity which were her chief attractions in her lover's eyes.

The Hand of Ethelberta is described as a " comedy in chapters." It is written in a somewhat extravagant key, and though following *Far from the Madding Crowd* in date of publication, falls far below the same standard of excellence. Ethelberta, despite her " squirrel-coloured hair," vigorous personality, and persistent devotion to the interests of her family, is not a sympathetic character. Mr. Hardy has somewhere suggested an appalling doubt as to whether " honesty be a virtue in itself," but even if this be held an open question, Ethelberta must needs be condemned for her absolute lack of the quality. However, it is unnecessary to take the situations which occur in this story too seriously, but it is difficult to determine how to regard a book so anomalous in tone. Much of the descriptive part is singularly fine. The passage conveying what Ethelberta saw as she rode her donkey along the top of the ridge of hills above Knollsea, on her way to Combe Castle, when " two climates were wrestling for mastery immediately in her pathway," is perhaps the most magnificent page that even Mr. Hardy has ever written, though such warm praise may be inspired by a loving familiarity with the striking prospect there so poetically described.

A Laodicean and *Two on a Tower* are termed " romances " by their author, and claim, therefore, to be criticised from a special standpoint. In the first-named the suspense as to Paula's choice between her two suitors, on which the interest depends, is so long drawn out that in less capable hands it might be tedious. The whole is, however, conceived with masterly completeness, the *dénouement* finely led up to, and the conclusion impressive and satisfactory. Every incident is well considered, and enhances the unity of the effect. The book has, however, hardly the feeling of its author's best work. It is colder and less spontaneous ; fanciful and original as ever, but with a less happy inspiration. The element of romantic melodrama gives a sense of unreality. Paula's position as an "interloper encased in the feudal lumber of the De Stancy family," invests her with a piquant interest ; but when we are told that she is an impersonation of the modern spirit of imaginative reason, in contrast with the picturesque fabric of mediævalism, we regard her with an awe akin to terror. She is a mysterious and metaphysical young woman, and we hesitate whether to ascribe her slowness in action to the praiseworthy prudence of a lonely heiress, or to the lukewarmness of mere indecision. On the whole, we are inclined to like her for her serene and self-possessed attitude of suspended judgment, but she is a more abstract study than any other of Mr. Hardy's heroines, and for that reason less interesting. The importance of environment is remembered here, as elsewhere, but Stancy Castle is a dreamlike structure. It does not take hold of the imagination by its poetry and genuine feeling, like Egdon Heath or the apple orchards among which the "Woodlanders" play their parts ; the effect is rather that of an enchanted palace in a fairy tale. *Two on a Tower*, like *A Laodicean*, is a "romance," and appeared in the following year.

Wessex Tales must not be passed over without a tribute to the thrilling interest of *The Three Strangers*. Mr. Hardy has the care in workmanship and the artistic finish necessary for the short story ; yet he is not at his best in this form. He has not room to develop himself, and his finer touches are crowded out. His recent volume of short stories, *A Group of Noble Dames*, shows singularly little of his distinctive excellence.

In *The Woodlanders* Mr. Hardy is on his own ground. This is a story from "one of those spots outside the gates of the world where . . . . from time to time dramas of a grandeur and unity truly Sophoclean are enacted in the real by virtue of the concentrated passions and closely-knit interdependence of the lives there." It is a study of rural life in a cider district, and is deeply tinged with poetic feeling. For example, Marty South and Giles Winterbourne are planting trees :

" 'How they sigh directly they are put upright, though while they are lying down they don't sigh at all,' said Marty.

" 'Do they ?' said Giles. 'I've never noticed it.'

" She erected one of the young pine trees into its hole, and held up her finger; the soft musical breathing instantly set in, which was not to cease night or day till the grown tree was felled—probably long after the two planters should have been felled themselves."

Thus, through a delicate and sympathetic suggestion, we are allowed to watch and listen, while a young pine tree draws its first breath, and takes up the burden of its life, beginning its ceaseless conflict with the forces, which are first to nourish and strengthen it, but ultimately to lay it low.

Michael Henchard, in *The Mayor of Casterbridge*, is a powerful study of a strong and concentrated nature. His will, containing the last wishes of an illiterate broken-hearted man, has a true ring of bitter desolation. A note of pathos is also struck in Mother Cuxsom's lament for Mrs. Henchard.

" ' Well, poor soul, she is helpless to hinder anythin now," answered Mother Cuxsom. ' And all her shining keys will be took from her, and her cupboards opened, and things a' didn't wish seen, anybody will see, and her little wishes and ways will all be as nothing.' "

It is easy to give telling specimens of Mr. Hardy's quality, but a mind so peculiar and original cannot be appreciated through quotations. Indeed, to use his own words, we feel that we might as well attempt to " carry an odour in a net " as to convey the intangibilities of his inspiration in the coarse meshes of criticism. Mr. Hardy's charm emanates from his personality. His mingling of poetry and realism, of imagination and precision, of wayward *bizarrerie* and winning grace is strangely fascinating, conditioned as it is by a thoughtfulness which is that of a philosopher, if not of a scholar or man of the world. Though there is a certain reserve and a marked idiosyncrasy in Mr. Hardy's manner, which may render him to some extent *caviare* for the general, his firm and humorous treatment of the broad truths of human nature must needs ensure the steady growth of his literary fame.

JANETTA NEWTON-ROBINSON.

Edmund Gosse

"The Tyranny of the Novel"

National Review 19 (April 1892), 163–75

THE TYRANNY OF THE NOVEL.

A Parisian Hebraist has been attracting a moment's attention to his paradoxical and learned self by announcing that strong-hearted and strong-brained nations do not produce novels. This gentleman's soul goes back, no doubt, in longing and despair to the heart of Babylon and the brain of Gath. But if he looks for a modern nation that does not cultivate the novel, he must, I am afraid, go far afield. Finland and Roumania are certainly tainted; Bohemia lies in the bond of naturalism. Probably Montenegro is the one European nation which this criterion would leave strong in heart and brain. The amusing absurdity of this whim of a pedant may serve to remind us how universal is now the reign of prose fiction. In Scandinavia the drama may claim an equal prominence, but no more. In all other countries the novel takes the largest place, claims and obtains the widest popular attention, is the admitted tyrant of the whole family of literature.

This is so universally acknowledged now-a-days that we scarcely stop to ask ourselves whether it is a heaven-appointed condition of things, existing from the earliest times, or whether it is an innovation. As a matter of fact, the predominance of the novel is a very recent event. Most other classes of literature are as old as the art of verbal expression: lyrical and narrative poetry, drama, history, philosophy,—all these have flourished since the sunrise of the world's intelligence. But the novel is a creation of the late afternoon of civilization. In the true sense, though not the pedantic one, the novel began in France with *La Princesse de Clèves*, and in England with *Pamela*—that is to say, in 1677 and in 1740 respectively. Compared with the dates of the beginning of philosophy and of poetry, these are as yesterday and the day before yesterday. Once started, however, the sapling of prose fiction grew and spread mightily. It took but a few generations to overshadow all the ancient oaks and cedars around it, and with its monstrous foliage to dominate the forest.

It would not be uninteresting, if we had space to do so here, to mark in detail the progress of this astonishing growth. It would be found that, in England at least, it has not been by any means regularly sustained. The original magnificent outburst of the

English novel lasted for exactly a quarter of a century, and closed with the publication of *Humphrey Clinker*. During this period of excessive fertility in a hitherto unworked field, the novel produced one masterpiece after another, positively pushing itself to the front and securing the best attention of the public at a moment when such men as Gray, Butler, Hume, and Warburton were putting forth contributions to the old and long-established sections of literature. Nay: such was the force of the new kind of writing that the gravity of Johnson and the grace of Goldsmith were seduced into participating in its facile triumphs.

But, at the very moment when the novel seemed about to sweep everything before it, the wave subsided and almost disappeared. For nearly forty years, only one novel of the very highest class was produced in England; and it might well seem as though prose fiction, after its brief victory, had exhausted its resources, and had sunken for ever into obscurity. During the close of the eighteenth century and the first decade of the nineteenth, no novel, except *Evelina*, could pretend to disturb the laurels of Burke, of Gibbon, of Cowper, of Crabbe. The publication of *Caleb Williams* is a poor event to set against that of the *Lyrical Ballads;* even *Thalaba the Destroyer* seemed a more impressive phenomenon than the *Monk*. But the second great burgeoning of the novel was at hand. Like the tender ash, it delayed to clothe itself when all the woods of romanticism were green. But in 1811 came *Sense and Sensibility,* in 1814 *Waverley;* and the novel was once more at the head of the literary movement of the time.

It cannot be said to have stayed there very long. Miss Austen's brief and brilliant career closed in 1817. Sir Walter Scott continued to be not far below his best until about ten years later. But a period of two decades included not only the work of these two great novelists, but the best books also of Galt, of Mary Ferrier, of Maturin, of Lockhart, of Banim. It saw the publication of *Hajji Baba*, of *Frankenstein*, of *Anastatius*. Then, for the second time, prose fiction ceased for a while to hold a position of high predominance. But Bulwer Lytton was already at hand; and five or six years of comparative obscurity prepared the way for Dickens, Lever, and Lover. Since the memorable year 1837 the novel has reigned in English literature; and its tyranny was never more irresistible than it is to-day. The Victorian has been peculiarly the age of the triumph of fiction.

In the history of France something of the same fluctuation might be perceived, although the production of novels of a certain literary pretension has been a feature of French much longer and more steadily than of English life. As Mr. Saintsbury has pointed out, " it is particularly noteworthy that every one of the eight names

which have been set at the head " of the nineteenth-century literature of France " is the name of a novelist." Since the days of
Flaubert—for the last thirty years, that is to say—the novel has
assumed a still higher literary function than it held even in the
hands of George Sand and Balzac. It has cast aside the pretence
of merely amusing, and has affected the airs of guide, philosopher,
and friend. M. Zola, justified to some extent by the amazing
vogue of his own writings, and the vast area covered by their
prestige, has said that the various classes of literary production
are being merged in the novel, and are ultimately to disappear
within it :

> " Apollo, Pan, and Love,
>   And even Olympia Jove
> Grow faint, for killing Truth hath glared on them ;
>   Our hills, and seas, and streams,
>   Dispeopled of their dreams,"

become the mere primary material for an endless series of
naturalistic stories. And even to-day, when the young David of
symbolism rises to smite the Goliath Zola, the smooth stones he
takes out of his scrip are works of fiction by Maurice Barrès and
Edouard Rod. Schools pass and nicknames alter ; but the novel
rules in France as it does elsewhere.

We have but to look around us at this very moment to see how
complete the tyranny of the novel is. If one hundred educated
and grown men—not, of course, themselves the authors of other
books—were to be asked which are the three most notable works
published in London during the present season, would not ninety-
and-nine be constrained to answer, with a parrot uniformity, *Tess
of the D'Urbervilles, David Grieve, The Little Minister* ? These are
the books which have been most widely discussed, most largely
bought, most vehemently praised, most venomously attacked.
These are the books in which the " trade " has taken most interest,
the vitality of which is most obvious and indubitable. It may be
said that the conditions of the winter of 1892 were exceptional—
that no books of the first class in other branches were produced.
This may be true ; and yet Mr. Jebb has issued a volume of his
Sophocles, Mr. William Morris a collection of the lyric poems of
years, Mr. Froude his *Divorce of Catherine of Aragon*, and Mr.
Tyndall his *New Fragments*. If the poets in chorus had blown
their silver trumpets and the philosophers their bold bassoons, the
result would have been the same : they would have won some
respect and a little notice for their performances ; but the novelists
would have carried away the money and the real human curiosity.
Who shall say that Mr. Freeman was not a better historian than
Robertson was ? yet did he make £4,500 by his *History of Sicily ?*

I wish I could believe it. To-day Mr. Swinburne may publish a new epic, Mr. Gardiner discover to us the head of Charles I. on the scaffold, Mr. Herbert Spencer explore a fresh province of sociology, or Mr. Pater analyze devils in the accents of an angel,—none of these important occurrences will successfully compete, for more than a few moments, among educated people, with the publication of what is called, in publishers' advertisements, "the new popular and original novel of the hour." We are accustomed to this state of things, and we bow to it. But we may, perhaps, remind ourselves that it is a comparatively recent condition. It was not so in 1730, nor in 1800, nor even in 1835.

Momentary aberrations of fashion must not deceive us as to the general tendency of taste. Mr. Hall Caine would have us believe that the public has suddenly gone crazy for stage-plays. "Novels of great strength and originality," says the author of *The Scapegoat*, "occasionally appear without creating more than a flutter of interest, and, meanwhile, plays of one-tenth their power and novelty are making something like a profound impression." What plays are these? Not the Ollendorfian attitudinizings of M. Maeterlinck, surely! The fact is that two years ago it would have been impossible for any one to pen that sentence of Mr. Caine's, and it is now possible merely because a passion for the literary drama has been flogged into existence by certain able critics. With a limited class, the same class which appreciates poetry, the literary drama may find a welcome; but to suppose that it competes, or can, in this country, even pretend to compete, with the novel is a delusion, and Mr. Caine may safely abandon his locusts and wild honey.

That we see around us a great interest in the drama is, of course, a commonplace. But how much of that is literary? When the delights of the eye are removed from the sum of pleasure, what is left? Our public is interested in the actors and their art, in the scenery and the furniture, in the notion of large sums of money expended, lost or won. When all these incidental interests are extracted from the curiosity excited by a play, not very much is left for the purely literary portion of it,—not nearly so much, at all events, as is awakened by a great novel. After all that has been said about the publication of plays, I suspect that the sale of dramatic contemporary literature remains small and uncertain. Mr. Pinero is read; but one swallow does not make a summer. Where are the dramatic works of Mr. Sydney Grundy, which ought —if Mr. Caine be correct—to be seen on every book-shelf beside the stories of Mr. Hawley Smart?

If, however, I venture to emphasize the fact of the tyranny of the novel in our current literature, it is without a murmur that I do so. Like the harmless bard in *Lady Geraldine's Courtship*, I " write no satire," and, what is more, I mean none. It appears to me natural and rational that this particular form of writing should attract more readers than any other. It is so broad and flexible, includes so vast a variety of appeals to the emotions, makes so few painful demands upon an overstrained attention, that it obviously lays itself out to please the greatest number. For the appreciation of a fine poem, of a learned critical treatise, of a contribution to exact knowledge, peculiar aptitudes are required : the novel appeals to all. Experience, moreover, proves that the gentle stimulus of reading about the cares, passions, and adventures of imaginary personages, and their relations to one another, a mild and irresponsible mirroring of real life on a surface undisturbed by responsibility, or memory, or personal feeling of any kind, is the most restful, the most refreshing, of all excitements which literature produces.

It is commonly said, in all countries, that women are the chief readers of novels. It may well be that they are the most numerous, and that they read more exhaustively than men, and with less selection. They have, as a rule, more time. The general notion seems to be that girls of from sixteen to twenty form the main audience of the novelist. But I am inclined to think that the real audience consists of young married women, sitting at home in the first year of their marriage. They find themselves without any constraint upon their reading : they choose what they will, and they read incessantly. The advent of the first-born baby is awaited in silent drawing-rooms, where through long hours the novelists supply the sole distraction. These young matrons form a much better audience than those timorous circles of flaxen-haired girls, watched by an Argus-eyed mamma, which the English novelist seems to consider himself doomed to cater for. I cannot believe that it is anything but a fallacy that young girls do read. They are far too busy with parties and shopping, chatting and walking, the eternal music and the eternal tennis. Middle-aged people in the country, who are cut off from much society, and elderly ladies, whose activities are past, and who like to resume the illusions of youth, are far more assiduous novel-readers than girls. But, if we take these and all other married and unmarried women into consideration, there is still apparently an exaggeration in saying that it is they who make the novelist's reputation. Men read novels a great deal more than is supposed, and it is probably from men that the first-class novel receives its *imprimatur*. Men have made Mr. Thomas Hardy, who owes nothing to the fair sex ; if women read him now, it is because the men have told them that they must. Occasionally we see a very original writer who decidedly owes his fame to the plaudits of the ladies. M. Paul Bourget is the most eminent example that occurs to the' memory. But such instances are rare, and it is probably to the approval of male readers that most eminent novelists owe that prestige which ultimately makes them the favourites of the women. Not all men are pressed by the excessive agitations of business life which are habitually attributed to their sex. Even those who are most busy find time to read, and we have been lately informed that among the most constant and assiduous students of new novels are Lord Tennyson and Mr. Gladstone. Every story-teller, I think, ought to write as though he believed himself addressing these illustrious veterans.

As I say, I do not revolt against the supremacy of the novel. I acknowledge too heavy a debt of gratitude to my great contemporaries to assume any but a thankful attitude towards them. In my dull and weary hours each has come like the angel Israfel, and let me listen to the beating of his heart, be it lyre or guitar, a solemn instrument or a gay one. I should be bankrupt instantly if I sought to repay to Mr. Meredith or Mr. Besant, Mr. Hardy or Mr. Norris, Mr. Stevenson or Mr. Kipling—to name no others— one-tenth part of the pleasure which, in varied quantity and quality, the stories of each have given me. I admit (for which I shall be torn in pieces) that the ladies please me less, with some exceptions; but that is because, since the days of the divine Mrs. Gaskell, they have been so apt to be either too serious or not serious enough. I suppose that the composition of *The Wages of Sin* and of *Donovan* serves some excellent purpose. Doubtless these books are useful to great growing girls. But it is not to such stories as these that I owe any gratitude, and it is not to their authors that I address the presumptuous remarks which follow.

A question which constantly recurs to my mind is this : Having secured the practical monopoly of literature, having concentrated public attention on their wares, what are the novelists going to do next ? To what use will they put the unprecedented opportunity thrown in their way ? It is quite plain that to a certain extent the material out of which the English novel has been constructed is in danger of becoming exhausted. Why do the American novelists inveigh against plots ? Not, we may be sure, through any inherent tenderness of conscience, as they would have us believe; but because their eminently sane and somewhat timid natures revolt against the effort of inventing what is extravagant. But all the obvious plots, all the stories which are not in some degree extravagant, seem to have been told already, and for a writer with the temperament of Mr. Howells there is nothing left but the careful portraiture of a small portion of the limitless field of ordinary humdrum existence. So long as this is fresh, this also may amuse and please; to the practitioners of this kind of work it seems as though the infinite prairie of life might be surveyed thus for centuries, acre by acre. But that is not possible. A very little while suffices to show that in this direction also the material is promptly exhausted. Novelty, freshness, and excitement are to be sought for at all hazards, and where can they be found?

The novelists hope many things from the happy system of nature, that supplies them, year by year, with fresh generations of the ingenuous young. The procession of adolescence moves on and on, and the front rank of it, for a month or a year, is duped by the novelist's report of that astonishing phenomenon, the passion of love. In a certain sense, we might expect to be tired of love-stories as soon as, and not before, we grow tired of the ever-recurring March mystery of primroses and daffodils. Each generation takes its tale of love under the hawthorn-tree as something quite new, peculiar to itself, not to be comprehended by its elders; and the novelist pipes as he will to this idyllic audience, sure of pleasing, if he adapt himself never so little to their habits and the idiosyncracies of their time. That theory would work well enough if the novelist held the chair of Erotics at the University of life, and might blame-lessly repeat the same (or very slightly modified) lectures to none but the students of each successive year. But, unfortunately, we who long ago took our degree, who took it, perhaps, when the Professor was himself in pinafores, also continue to attend his classes. We are hardly to be put off with the old, old commonplaces about hearts and darts. Yet our adult acquiescence is necessary for the support of the Professor. How is he to freshen up his oft-repeated course of lectures to suit our jaded appetites?

It would be curious to calculate how many tales of love must have been told since the vogue of the modern story began. Three hundred novels a year is, I believe, the average product of the English press. In each of these there has been at least one pair of lovers, and generally there have been several pairs. It would be a good question to set in a mathematical examination: What is the probable number of young persons who have conducted one another to the altar in English fiction during the last hundred years? It is almost terrible to think of this multitude of fictitious love-makings,—

> " For the lovers of years meet and gather;
>   The sound of them all grows like thunder;
>   O into what bosom, I wonder,
>   Is poured the whole passion of years? "

One would be very sorry to have the three hundred of one year poured into one's own mature bosom. But how curious is the absolute unanimity of it all! Thousands and thousands of books, every one of them, without exception, turning upon the attraction of Edwin to Angelina, exactly as though no other subject on earth interested a single human being! The novels in which love has not formed a central feature are so few that I suspect that they could be counted on the fingers of one hand. At this moment, I can but recall a single famous novel in which love has no place. This is, of course, *L'Abbé Tigrane*, that delightful story in which all the interest revolves around the intrigues of two priestly factions in a provincial cathedral. But, although M. Ferdinand Fabre achieved so great a success in this book, and produced an acknowledged masterpiece, he never ventured to repeat the experiment. Eros revels in the pages of all his other stories.

This would be the opportunity to fight the battle of the novelists against Mrs. Grundy. But I am not inclined to waste ink on that conceded cause. After the reception of books like *Tess of the D'Urbervilles* and even *David Grieve*, it is plain that the English novelist, who cares and dares, may say almost anything he or she likes without calling flame out of heaven upon his head. There has been a great reform in this respect, since the days when our family friend Mr. Punch hazarded his very existence by referring, in grimmest irony, to the sufferings of "the gay." We do not want to claim the right which the French have so recklessly abused of describing at will, and secure against all censure, the brutal, the abnormal and the horrible. No doubt a silly prudishness yet exists. There are still clergymen's wives who write up indignantly from The Vicarage, Little Pedlington. I have just received an epistle from such an one, telling me that certain poor productions I am editing "make young hearts acquainted with vice, and put hell-fire in their hearts." "Woe unto you in your evil work," says this lady, doubtless a most sincere and conscientious creature, but a little behind the times. Of her and her race individually I wish to say nothing but what is kind; but I confess I am glad to know that the unreflecting spirit they represent is passing away. It is passing away so rapidly that there is really no need to hearten the novelists against it. If they are so poor-spirited as to be afraid to say what they feel they ought to say because of this kind of criticism, their exposition of the verities is not likely to be of very high value.

But I should like to ask our friends the leading novelists whether they do not see their way to enlarging a little the sphere of their labours. What is the use of this tyranny which they wield, if it does not enable them to treat life broadly and to treat it whole? The varieties of amatory intrigue form a fascinating subject, which is not even yet exhausted. But, surely, all life is not love-making.

Even the youngest have to deal with other interests, although this may be the dominant one ; while, as we advance in years, Venus ceases to be even the ruling divinity. Why should there not be novels written for middle-aged persons ? Has the struggle for existence a charm only in its reproductive aspects ? If every one of us regards his or her life seriously, with an absolute and unflinching frankness, it will be admitted that love, extended so as to include all its forms—its sympathetic, its imaginative, its repressed, as well as its fulfilled and acknowledged, forms—takes a place far more restricted than the formulæ of the novelist would lead the inhabitant of some other planet to conjecture.

Unless the novelists do contrive to enlarge their borders, and take in more of life, that misfortune awaits them which befell their ancestors just before the death of Scott. About the year 1830 there was a sudden crash of the novel. The public found itself abandoned to Lady Blessington and Mr. Plumer Ward, and it abruptly closed its account with the novelists. The large prices which had been, for twenty years past, paid for novels were no longer offered. The book-clubs, throughout the kingdom, collapsed, or else excluded novels. When fiction reappeared, after this singular epoch of eclipse, it had learned its lesson, and the new writers were men who put into their work their best observation and ripest experience. It does not appear in the thirties that any one understood what was happening. The stuff produced by the novelists was so ridiculous and ignoble that " the nonsinse of that divil of a Bullwig " seemed positively unrivalled in its comparative sublimity, although these were the days of *Ernest Maltravers*. It never occurred to the authors when the public suddenly declined to read their books (it read " Bullwig's," in the lack of anything else) that the fault was theirs. The same excuses were made that are made now,—" necessary to write down to a wide audience ; " " obliged to supply the kind of article demanded ; " " women the only readers to be catered for ; " " mammas so solicit- ous for the purity of what is laid before their daughters." And the crash came.

The crash will come again, if the novelists do not take care. The same silly piping of the loves of the drawing-room, the same obsequious attitude towards a supposititious public clamouring for the commonplace, inspire the majority of the novel writers of to-day. Happily, we have, what our fathers in 1835 had not, half a dozen careful and vigorous men of letters who write, not what the foolish publishers ask for, but what they themselves choose to give. The future rests with these few recognized masters of fiction, and with their successors, the vigorous younger men who are preparing to take their place. What are these novelists going to do ? They were set down to farm the one hundred acres of an estate called Life, and because one corner of it—the two or three acres hedged about, and called the kitchen-garden of Love—offered peculiar attractions, and was very easy to cultivate, they have neglected the other ninety-seven acres. The result is that by over-pressing their garden, and forcing crop after crop out of it, it is well-nigh exhausted, and will soon refuse to respond to the incessant hoe and spade ; while, all the time, the rest of the estate, rich and almost virgin soil, is left to cover itself with the weeds of newspaper police-reports.

It is supposed that to describe one of the positive employments of life,—a business or a profession, for example,—would alienate the tender reader, and check that circulation about which novelists talk as nervously as if they were delicate invalids. But what evidence is there to show that an attention to real things does frighten away the novel reader ? The experiments which have been made in this country to widen the field of fiction in one direction, that of religious and moral speculation, have not proved unfortunate. What was the source of the great popular success of *John Inglesant* and then of *Robert Elsmere*, if not the intense delight of readers in being admitted, in a story, to a wider analysis of the interior workings of the mind than is compatible with the mere record of the billing and cooing of the callow young ? We are afraid of words and titles. We are afraid of the word " psychology," and, indeed, we have seen follies committed in its name. But the success of the books I have just mentioned was due to their psychology, to their analysis of the effect of associations and sentiments on a growing mind. To make such studies of the soul even partially interesting, a great deal of knowledge, intuition, and workmanlike care must be expended. The novelist must himself be acquainted with something of the general life of man.

But the interior life of the soul is, after all, a very much less interesting study to an ordinarily healthy person than the exterior. It is surprising how little our recent novelists have taken this into consideration. One reason, I cannot doubt, is that they write too early and they write too fast. Fielding began with *Joseph Andrews*, when he was thirty-five ; seven years later he published *Tom Jones* ; during the remainder of his life, which closed when he was forty-seven, he composed one more novel. The consequence is that into these three books he was able to pour the ripe knowledge of an all-accomplished student of human nature. But our successful novelist of to-day begins when he is two- or three-and-twenty. He " catches on," as they say, and he becomes a laborious professional writer. He toils at his novels as if he were the manager of a bank or the captain of an ocean steamer. In one narrow groove he slides up and down, up and down, growing infinitely skilful at his task of making bricks out of straw. He finishes the last page of "The Writhing Victim" in the morning, lunches at his club, has a nap ; and, after dinner, writes the first page of "The Swart Sombrero." He cannot describe a trade or a profession, for he knows none but his own. He has no time to look at life, and he goes on weaving fancies out of the ever-dwindling stores of his childish and boyish memories. As these grow exhausted, his works get more and more shadowy, till at last even the long-suffering public that once loved his merits, and then grew tolerant of his tricks, can endure him no longer.

The one living novelist who has striven to give a large, competent, and profound view of the movement of life, is M. Zola. When we have said the worst of the *Rougon-Macquart* series, when we have admitted the obvious faults of these books,—their romantic fallacies on the one hand, their cold•brutalities on the other,—it must be admitted that they present the results of a most laudable attempt to cultivate the estate outside the kitchen-garden. Hardly one of the main interests of the modern man has been neglected by M. Zola, and there is no doubt at all that to the future student of nineteenth-century manners his books will have an interest outweighing that of all other contemporary novels. An astonishing series of panoramas he has unrolled before us. Here is *Le Ventre de Paris*, describing the whole system by which a vast modern city is daily supplied with food ; here is *Au Bonheur des Dames*, the romance of a shop, which is pushed upwards·and outwards by the energy of a single ambitious tradesman, until it swamps all its neighbours, and governs the trade of a district ; here is *L'Argent*, in which, with infinite pains and on a colossal scale, the passions which move in *la haute finance* are analyzed, and a great battle of the money-world chronicled ; here, above all, is *Germinal*, that unapproachable picture of the agony and stress of life in a great mining community, with a description of the processes so minute and so technical that this novel is accepted by experts as the best existing record of conditions which are already obsolete.

In these books of M. Zola's, as every one knows, successive members of a certain family stand out against a background of human masses in incessant movement. The peculiar characteristic of this novelist is that he enables us to see why these masses are moved, and in what direction. Other writers vaguely tell us that the hero "proceeded to his daily occupation," if, indeed, they deign to allow that he had an occupation. M. Zola tells us what that occupation was, and describes the character of it carefully and minutely. More than this : he shows us how it affected the hero's character, how it brought him into contact with others, in what way it represented his share of the universal struggle for existence. So far from the employment being a thing to be slurred over or dimly alluded to, M. Zola loves to make that the very hero of his piece, a blind and vast commercial monster, a huge all-embracing machine, in whose progress the human persons are hurried helplessly along, in whose iron wheels their passions and their hopes are crushed. He is enabled to do this by the exceptional character of his genius, which is realistic to excess in its power of retaining and repeating details, and romantic, also to an extreme, in its power of massing these details on a huge scale, in vast and harmoniously-balanced compositions.

I would not be misunderstood, even by the most hasty reader, to recommend an imitation of M. Zola. What suits his peculiarly-constituted genius might ill accord with the characteristics of another. Nor do I mean to say that we are entirely without something analogous in the writings of the more intelligent of our later novelists. The study of the Dorsetshire dairy-farms in Mr. Hardy's superb *Tess of the D'Urbervilles* is of the highest value, and more thorough and intelligible than what we enjoyed in *The Woodlanders*, the details of the apple-culture in the same county. To turn to a totally different school : Mr. Hall Caine's *Scapegoat* is a very interesting experiment in fresh fields of thought and experience, more happily conceived, if I may be permitted to say so, than fortunately executed, though even in execution far above the ruck of popular novels. A new Cornish story, called *Inconsequent Lives*, by that very promising young story-teller, Mr. Pearce, seemed, when it opened, to be about to give us just the vivid information we want about the Newlyn pilchard-fishery ; but the novelist grew timid, and forebore to fill in his sketch. These are instances in which, occasionally, or fantastically, or imperfectly, the real facts of life have been dwelt upon in recent fiction. But when we have mentioned or thought of a few exceptions, to what inanities do we not presently descend !

If we could suddenly arrive from another planet, and read a cluster of novels from Mudie's, without any previous knowledge of the. class, we should be astonished at the conventionality, the narrowness, the monotony. All I ask for is a larger study of life. Have the stress and turmoil of a successful political career no charm ? Why, if novels of the shop and the counting-house be considered sordid, can our novelists not describe the life of a sailor, of a game-keeper, of a railway-porter, of a civil engineer ? What capital central figures for a story would be the whip of a leading hunt, the foreman of a colliery, the master of a fishing smack, or a speculator on the Stock Exchange ! It will be suggested that persons engaged in one or other of these professions are commonly introduced into current fiction, and that I am proposing as a novelty what is amply done already. My reply is that our novelists may indeed present to us a personage who is called a stoker or a groom, a secretary of state or a pin-maker, but that, practically, they merely write these denominations clearly on the breasts of lay-figures. For all the enlightenment we get into the habits of action and habits of thought entailed by the occupation of each, the fisherman might be the groom and the pin-maker the stock-broker. It is more than this that I ask for. I want to see the man in his life. I am tired of the novelist's portrait of a gentle-man, with gloves and hat, leaning against a pillar, upon a vague landscape background. I want the gentleman as he appears in a snap-shot photograph, with his every-day expression on his face, and the localities in which he spends his days accurately visible around him. I cannot think that the commercial and professional aspects of life are unworthy of the careful attention of the novelist, or that he would fail to be rewarded by a larger and more interested audience for his courage in dealing closely with them. At all events, if it is too late to ask our accepted tyrants of the novel to enlarge their borders, may we not, at all events, entreat their heirs-apparent to do so?

EDMUND GOSSE.

Hubert Crackanthorpe

"Reticence in Literature.
Some Roundabout Remarks"

Yellow Book 2 (July 1894), 259–69

Reticence in Literature
Some Roundabout Remarks

By Hubert Crackanthorpe

DURING the past fifty years, as every one knows, the art of fiction has been expanding in a manner exceedingly remarkable, till it has grown to be the predominant branch of imaginative literature. But the other day we were assured that poetry only thrives in limited and exquisite editions ; that the drama, here in England at least, has practically ceased to be literature at all. Each epoch instinctively chooses that literary vehicle which is best adapted for the expression of its particular temper : just as the drama flourished in the robust age of Shakespeare and Ben Jonson ; just as that outburst of lyrical poetry, at the beginning of the century in France, coincided with a period of extreme emotional exaltation ; so the novel, facile and flexible in its conventions, with its endless opportunities for accurate delineation of reality, becomes supreme in a time of democracy and of science— to note but these two salient characteristics.

And, if we pursue this line of thought, we find that, on all sides, the novel is being approached in one especial spirit, that it would seem to be striving, for the moment at any rate, to perfect itself within certain definite limitations. To employ a hackneyed, and often quite unintelligent, catchword—the novel is becoming realistic.

Throughout the history of literature, the jealous worship of beauty—which we term idealism—and the jealous worship of truth —which we term realism—have alternately prevailed. Indeed, it is within the compass of these alternations that lies the whole fundamental diversity of literary temper.

Still, the classification is a clumsy one, for no hard and fast line can be drawn between the one spirit and the other. The so-called idealist must take as his point of departure the facts of Nature ; the so-called realist must be sensitive to some one or other of the forms of beauty, if each would achieve the fineness of great art. And the pendulum of production is continually swinging, from degenerate idealism to degenerate realism, from effete vapidity to slavish sordidity.

Either term, then, can only be employed in a purely limited

and relative sense. Completely idealistic art—art that has no point of contact with the facts of the universe, as we know them—is, of course, an impossible absurdity; similarly, a complete reproduction of Nature by means of words is an absurd impossibility. Neither emphasization nor abstraction can be dispensed with: the one, eliminating the details of no import; the other, exaggerating those which the artist has selected. And, even were such a thing possible, it would not be Art. The invention of a highly perfected system of coloured photography, for instance, or a skilful recording by means of the phonograph of scenes in real life, would not subtract one whit from the value of the painter's or the playwright's interpretation. Art is not invested with the futile function of perpetually striving after imitation or reproduction of Nature; she endeavours to produce, through the adaptation of a restricted number of natural facts, an harmonious and satisfactory whole. Indeed, in this very process of adaptation and blending together, lies the main and greater task of the artist. And the novel, the short story, even the impression of a mere incident, convey each of them, the imprint of the temper in which their creator has achieved this process of adaptation and blending together of his material. They are inevitably stamped with the hall-mark of his personality. A work of art can never be more than a corner of Nature, seen through the temperament of a single man. Thus, all literature is, must be, essentially subjective; for style is but the power of individual expression. The disparity which separates literature from the reporter's transcript is ineradicable. There is a quality of ultimate suggestiveness to be achieved; for the business of art is, not to explain or to describe, but to suggest. That attitude of objectivity, or of impersonality towards his subject, consciously or unconsciously, assumed by the artist, and which nowadays provokes so considerable an admiration, can be attained only in a limited degree. Every piece of imaginative work must be a kind of autobiography of its creator—significant, if not of the actual facts of his existence, at least of the inner working of his soul. We are each of us conscious, not of the whole world, but of our own world; not of naked reality, but of that aspect of reality which our peculiar temperament enables us to appropriate. Thus, every narrative of an external circumstance is never anything else than the transcript of the impression produced upon ourselves by that circumstance, and, invariably, a degree of individual interpretation is insinuated into every picture, real or imaginary, however objective it may be. So then, the disparity between the so-called

idealist and the so-called realist is a matter, not of æsthetic philosophy, but of individual temperament. Each is at work, according
to the especial bent of his genius, within precisely the same limits.
Realism, as a creed, is as ridiculous as any other literary creed.

Now, it would have been exceedingly curious if this recent
specialisation of the art of fiction, this passion for draining from the
life, as it were, born, in due season, of the general spirit of the
latter half of the nineteenth century, had not provoked a considerable
amount of opposition—opposition of just that kind which every
new evolution in art inevitably encounters. Between the vanguard
and the main body there is perpetual friction.

But time flits quickly in this hurried age of ours, and the
opposition to the renascence of fiction as a conscientious interpretation of life is not what it was ; its opponents are not the men
they were. It is not so long since a publisher was sent to prison
for issuing English translations of celebrated specimens of French
realism ; yet, only the other day, we vied with each other in doing
honour to the chief figure-head of that tendency across the Channel,
and there was heard but the belated protest of a few worthy individuals, inadequately equipped with the jaunty courage of ignorance,
or the insufferable confidence of second-hand knowledge.

And during the past year things have been moving very rapidly.
The position of the literary artist towards Nature, his great
inspirer, has become more definite, more secure. A sound, organ-
ised opinion of men of letters is being acquired ; and in the little
bouts with the *bourgeois*—if I may be pardoned the use of that
wearisome word—no one has to fight single-handed. Heroism is
at a discount ; Mrs. Grundy is becoming mythological ; a crowd
of unsuspected supporters collect from all sides, and the deadly
conflict of which we had been warned becomes but an interesting
skirmish. Books are published, stories are printed, in old-established
reviews, which would never have been tolerated a few years ago.
On all sides, deference to the tendency of the time is spreading.
The truth must be admitted : the roar of unthinking prejudice is
dying away.

All this is exceedingly comforting : and yet, perhaps, it is not a
matter for absolute congratulation. For, if the enemy are not
dying as gamely as we had expected, if they are, as I am afraid,
losing heart, and in danger of sinking into a condition of passive
indifference, it should be to us a matter of not inconsiderable
apprehension. If this new evolution in the art of fiction—this
general return of the literary artist towards Nature, on the brink

of which we are to-day hesitating—is to achieve any definite, ultimate fineness of expression, it will benefit enormously by the continued presence of a healthy, vigorous, if not wholly intelligent, body of opponents. Directly or indirectly, they will knock a lot of nonsense out of us, will these opponents ;—why should we be ashamed to admit it ? They will enable us to find our level, they will spur us on to bring out the best—and only the best—that is within us.

Take, for instance, the gentleman who objects to realistic fiction on moral grounds. If he does not stand the most conspicuous to-day, at least he was pre-eminent the day before yesterday. He is a hard case, and it is on his especial behalf that I would appeal. For he has been dislodged from the hill top, he has become a target for all manner of unkind chaff, from the ribald youth of Fleet Street and Chelsea. He has been labelled a Philistine : he has been twitted with his middle-age ; he has been reported to have compromised himself with that indecent old person Mrs. Grundy. It is confidently asserted that he comes from Putney, or from Sheffield, and that, when he is not busy abolishing the art of English literature, he is employed in safeguarding the interests of the grocery or tallow-chandler's trade. Strange and cruel tales of him have been printed in the monthly reviews ; how, but for him, certain well-known popular writers would have written masterpieces ; how, like the ogre in the fairy tale, he consumes every morning at breakfast a hundred pot-boiled young geniuses. For the most part they have been excellently well told, these tales of this moral ogre of ours ; but why start to shatter brutally their dainty charm by a soulless process of investigation ? No, let us be shamed rather into a more charitable spirit, into making generous amends, into rehabilitating the greatness of our moral ogre.

He is the backbone of our nation ; the guardian of our mediocrity ; the very foil of our intelligence. Once, you fancied that you could argue with him, that you could dispute his dictum. Ah ! how we cherished that day-dream of our extreme youth. But it was not to be. He is still immense ; for he is unassailable ; he is flawless, for he is complete within himself ; his lucidity is yet unimpaired ; his impartiality is yet supreme. Who amongst us could judge with a like impartiality the productions of Scandinavia and Charpentier, Walt Whitman and the Independent Theatre ? Let us remember that he has never professed to understand Art, and the deep debt of gratitude that every artist in the land should consequently owe to him ; let us remember that he is above us, for he belongs to the great middle classes ; let us remember that he commands votes, that he is candidate for the County Council; let us remember that he is delightful, because he is intelligible.

Yes, he is intelligible ; and of how many of us can that be said ? His is no complex programme, no subtly exacting demand. A plain moral lesson is all that he asks, and his voice is as of one crying in the ever fertile wilderness of Smith and of Mudie.

And he is right, after all—if he only knew it. The business of art is to create for us fine interests, to make of our human nature a more complete thing : and thus, all great art is moral in the wider and the truer sense of the word. It is precisely on this point of the meaning of the word " moral " that we and our ogre part company. To him, morality is concerned only with the established relations between the sexes and with fair dealing between man and man : to him the subtle, indirect morality of Art is incomprehensible.

Theoretically, Art is non-moral. She is not interested in any ethical code of any age or any nation, except in so far as the breach or observance of that code may furnish her with material on which to work. But unfortunately, in this complex world of ours, we cannot satisfactorily pursue one interest—no, not even the interest of Art, at the expense of all others—let us look that fact in the face, doggedly, whatever pangs it may cost us—pleading magnanimously for the survival of our moral ogre, for there will be danger to our cause when his voice is no more heard.

If imitation be the sincerest form of flattery, then our moral ogre must indeed have experienced a proud moment, when a follower came to him from the camp of the lovers of Art, and the artistic objector to realistic fiction started on his timid career. I use the word timid in no disparaging sense, but because our artistic objector, had he ventured a little farther from the vicinity of the coat-tails of his powerful protector, might have secured a more adequate recognition of his performances. For he is by no means devoid of adroitness. He can patter to us glibly of the " gospel of ugliness " ; of the " cheerlessness of modern literature " ; he can even juggle with that honourable property-piece, the maxim of Art for Art's sake. But there have been moments when even this feat has proved ineffective, and some one has started scoffing at his pretended " delight in pure rhythm or music of the phrase," and flippantly assured him that he is talking nonsense, and that style is a mere matter of psychological suggestion. You fancy our performer nonplussed, or at least boldly bracing himself to brazen the matter out. No, he passes dexterously to his curtain effect—a fervid denunciation of express trains, evening newspapers, Parisian novels, or the first number of THE YELLOW BOOK. Verily, he is a versatile person.

Sometimes, to listen to him you would imagine that pessimism and regular meals were incompatible ; that the world is only ameliorated by those whom it completely satisfies, that good predominates over evil, that the problem of our destiny had been solved long ago. You begin to doubt whether any good thing can come out of this miserable, inadequate age of ours, unless it be a doctored survival of the vocabulary of a past century. The language of the coster and cadger resound in our midst, and, though Velasquez tried to paint like Whistler, Rudyard Kipling cannot write like Pope. And a weird word has been invented to explain the whole business. Decadence, decadence : you are all decadent nowadays. Ibsen, Degas, and the New English Art Club ; Zola, Oscar Wilde, and the Second Mrs. Tanqueray. Mr. Richard Le Gallienne is hoist with his own petard ; even the British playwright has not escaped the taint. Ah, what a hideous spectacle. All whirling along towards one common end. And the elegant voice of the artistic objector floating behind : " *Après vous le déluge.*" A wholesale abusing of the tendencies of the age has ever proved, for the superior mind, an inexhaustible source of relief. Few things breed such inward comfort as the contemplation of one's own pessimism—few things produce such discomfort as the remembrance of our neighbour's optimism.

And yet, pessimists, though we may be dubbed, some of us, on this point at least, how can we compete with the hopelessness enjoyed by our artistic objector, when the spectacle of his despondency makes us insufferably replete with hope and confidence, so that while he is loftily bewailing or prettily denouncing the completeness of our degradation, we continue to delight in the evil of our ways ? Oh, if we could only be sure that he would persevere in reprimanding this persistent study of the pitiable aspects of life, how our hearts would go out towards him ! For the man who said that joy is essentially, regrettably inartistic, admitted in the same breath that misery lends itself to artistic treatment twice as easily as joy, and resumed the whole question in a single phrase. Let our artistic objector but weary the world sufficiently with his despair concerning the permanence of the cheerlessness of modern realism, and some day a man will arise who will give us a study of human happiness, as fine, as vital as anything we owe to Guy de Maupassant or to Ibsen. That man will have accomplished the infinitely difficult, and in admiration and in awe shall we bow down our heads before him.

In one radical respect, the art of fiction is not in the same position as the other arts. They—music, poetry, painting, sculpture, and the drama—possess a magnificent fabric of accumulated tradition. The great traditions of the art of fiction have yet to be made. Ours is a young art, struggling desperately to reach expression, with no great past to guide it. Thus, it should be a matter for wonder, not that we stumble into certain pitfalls, but that we do not fall headlong into a hundred more.

But, if we have no great past, we have the present and the future—the one abundant in facilities, the other abundant in possibilities. Young men of to-day have enormous chances : we are working under exceedingly favourable conditions. Possibly we stand on the threshold of a very great period. I know, of course, that the literary artist is shamefully ill-paid, and that the man who merely caters for the public taste, amasses a rapid and respectable fortune. But how is it that such an arrangement seems other than entirely equitable ? The essential conditions of the two cases are entirely distinct. The one man is free to give untrammelled expression to his own soul, free to fan to the full the flame that burns in his heart : the other is a seller of wares, a unit in national commerce. To the one is allotted liberty and a living wage ; to the other, captivity and a consolation in Consols. Let us whine, then, no more concerning the prejudice and the persecution of the Philistine, when even that misanthrope, Mr. Robert Buchanan, admits that there is no power in England to prevent a man writing exactly as he pleases. Before long the battle for literary freedom will be won. A new public has been created—appreciative, eager and determined ; a public which, as Mr. Gosse puts it, in one of those admirable essays of his, " has eaten of the apple of knowledge, and will not be satisfied with mere marionnettes. Whatever comes next," Mr. Gosse continues, " we cannot return, in serious novels, to the inanities and impossibilities of the old well-made plot, to the children changed at nurse, to the madonna-heroine and the god-like hero, to the impossible virtues and melodramatic vices. In future, even those who sneer at realism and misrepresent it most wilfully, will be obliged to put their productions more in accordance with veritable experience. There will still be novel-writers who address the gallery, and who will keep up the gaudy old convention, and the clumsy *Family Herald* evolution, but they will no longer be distinguished men of genius. They will no longer sign themselves George Sand or Charles Dickens."

Fiction has taken her place amongst the arts. The theory that writing resembles the blacking of boots, the more boots you black, the better you do it, is busy evaporating. The excessive admiration for the mere idea of a book or a story is dwindling ; so is the comparative indifference to slovenly treatment. True is it that the society lady, dazzled by the brilliancy of her own conversation, and the serious-minded spinster, bitten by some sociological theory, still decide in the old jaunty spirit, that fiction is the obvious medium through which to astonish or improve the world. Let us beware of the despotism of the intelligent amateur, and cease our toying with that quaint and winsome bogey of ours, the British Philistine, whilst the intelligent amateur, the deadliest of Art's enemies, is creeping up in our midst.

For the familiarity of the man in the street with the material employed by the artist in fiction, will ever militate against the acquisition of a sound, fine, and genuine standard of workmanship. Unlike the musician, the painter, the sculptor, the architect, the artist in fiction enjoys no monopoly in his medium. The word and the phrase are, of necessity, the common property of everybody ; the ordinary use of them demands no special training. Hence the popular mind, while willingly acknowledging that there are technical difficulties to be surmounted in the creation of the sonata, the landscape, the statue, the building, in the case of the short story, or of the longer novel, declines to believe even in their existence, persuaded that in order to produce good fiction, an ingenious idea, or " plot," as it is termed, is the one thing needed. The rest is a mere matter of handwriting.

The truth is, and, despite Mr. Waugh, we are near recognition of it, that nowadays there is but scanty merit in the mere selection of any particular subject, however ingenious or daring it may appear at first sight ; that a man is not an artist, simply because he writes about heredity or the *demi-monde*, that to call a spade a spade requires no extraordinary literary gift, and that the essential is contained in the frank, fearless acceptance by every man of his entire artistic temperament, with its qualities and its flaws.

Thomas Bradfield

"The Romances of
Nathaniel Hawthorne"

Westminster Review 142 (August 1894), 203–14

THE ROMANCES OF NATHANIEL HAWTHORNE.

THE principal source of fascination in the stories of Nathaniel Hawthorne proceeds from an exquisite sympathy with the spiritually mysterious and appalling in our nature. His delineation of the peculiar phases of mental experience upon which he loves to dwell is usually accompanied by a vivid romanticism of situation and incident singularly original; and his descriptive pencil is never more at home than when it lingers over what is weird, unreal, or ghostly. In addition, Hawthorne's romances belong to a region of fancy which allows of them being informed by a unique power of subtle introspection. This power, in union with his fine insight, suggests that the novelist's imagination was of the phase which, according to Mr. Ruskin's classification, is in part analytical penetration and in part contemplative.[1] His genius, in its peculiar treatment of the idiosyncracies of his characters, may be said to resemble the whirlpool in its power of drawing all within its influence to one centre, although his artistic skill and sympathy enable him to dignify his conceptions with distinct if somewhat exclusive individualities. Our first experience of his works is one of mingled surprise and delight, to be succeeded by awe, not to say terror, as we grow more and more impressed with what is haunting and gruesome in his pages. Then it is we recognise how much of Hawthorne's power lies in the profound interest he evinces towards individuals in exceptionally ideal situations—situations which he is able to present to the reader, by the magic of his rare genius, with unique and thrilling intensity.

The contemplative element in his imagination may have led the romancer, for the selection of his subjects, to those set types of humanity to be found not so long ago among the ancestral descendants of the early village folk of New England; just as for his incidents he loved to explore the traditions of these earliest settlers of America. But, beyond suggestive touches of local and historical interest—fresh and attractive of themselves—there is always an original charm proceeding from the author's simple, direct, penetrating insight into enduring phases of thought and feeling in connection with his personages. Into the fanciful semblance of his favourite types of humanity he breathes the warm spirit of an existence

---

[1] *Modern Painters.* Vol. i.: "Imagination."

which, to borrow the romancer's own language, renders his conceptions, if not actually human, yet so like humanity that they must be preternatural. The subtle and cultured art of Hawthorne's genius in no way shows its fine quality more distinctly than in the manner in which these delineations, although not of this world, are invested with a verisimilitude so natural, and in some instances so winning, as to draw us towards them in spite of their imaginative exclusiveness. Their affinity to humanity is unmistakable, sicklied o'er, though they be, with the pale cast of unreality. Another drawback to our sympathising to the full with Hawthorne's characters arises from the peculiarity of these not evolving the scenes of pathos and power which are the mainstays of his stories; on the contrary, the scenes are presented so as to illustrate by the force of their accumulated impressions the leading emotion or interest of the conception.

This brings us to another peculiarity of Hawthorne's artistic treatment. The special feature of his subject which he wishes to bring prominently out is illustrated by his powerful and painstaking fancy in so marked a manner as to make the spiritual lineaments of the character appear exaggeration if not deformity. No inapt illustration of this exceptional treatment may be found in that description of perspective drawing known as anamorphosis, where a portrait or figure is in one special point of view a distorted representation. Hawthorne's characters, in the point of view of the absorbing idea he is desirous of emphasising, loses that harmony and consistency essential to an exact representation of human nature. It is characteristic that the eccentricity is generally most strikingly displayed in connection with some profoundly significant ethical position. In *The Scarlet Letter*, for instance, the great and absorbing point of interest springs from the inevitable result of the sin of adultery as it affects two otherwise beautiful and noble characters. In *Transformation* it may be said that Hawthorne lavishes all the riches of his cultured imaginative subtlety upon foreshadowing the after-effect of a murder, committed under an impulse, in which the two chief characters of the romance are concerned in as exquisitely delicate a manner as their guilty deed will allow. To take two dissimilar but very suggestive instances from the shorter pieces : in *Roger Malvin's Burial* we have the picture of a sensitive-minded man, who had been induced to leave a companion to die while he himself escaped, passing through all the terrible experiences of one who had been guilty of some dastardly iniquity, and who finds no respite from the avenging recollection until by accident he has killed his son—has " shed blood dearer to him than his own "; in *Mr. Higginbotham's Catastrophe* we have a happier but equally fatalistic accumulation of incidents, only in this instance the event is allowed to cast its shadow before, and in the end the tragic result is averted. But perhaps the most striking and intense illustration of the strange distorted manner in which Hawthorne's characters appear under the effect of a fixed or absorbing idea is to be found in *Egotism, or the Bosom Serpent*, an allegory which, when viewed in any other light than the fantastic one in which the story-teller presents it, loses its powerful meaning. Again, the character of the man who goes in search of the unpardonable sin, Etham Brand, a powerful and grotesque study, is only saved from becoming repulsive by that element of intense gloom and solitariness in his life which inevitably draws the victim to his doom, and finally leads him to plunge into the burning furnace. The vivid intensity of Hawthorne's genius when concentrated upon any particular feature of his conception, whether of incident or character, may be likened to the glare of fierce light which smote upon the face and figure of Etham Brand in this story, when the iron door of the lime-kiln was thrown open before him. As Turner in his pictures, by " distinctness of shadow expresses vividness of light," so in the representations of the American novelist, amid the gloomy fatalistic consequences of their actions, hovers a shining tenderness, ever ready, like a sanctifying peace, to descend when the destinies are satisfied.

Among the loveliest features of Hawthorne's works is the subtle and consummate manner in which he diffuses an etherealised atmosphere over his descriptions of natural scenery and imparts an idealised effect to the various situations in which his characters are placed. As Roger Malvin's burial—the novelist himself tells us—was " one of the few incidents of Indian warfare susceptible of the moonlight of romance," so most of the subjects Hawthorne's fancy delighted to elaborate, if we may judge of them as they appear now, were susceptible of an influence with a similar enchantment. Hawthorne's power in this respect sprang from the subtle informing charm of his genius, by which he was able to infuse something new and strange and wonderful into his work. Sensitive critic of himself as he was, Hawthorne, however, slighted the rare magic of his own powers when he dwelt so repeatedly upon the necessity of having an atmosphere as of " clear, brown twilight " in which to read his stories. There may be, as he says in the Preface to *Transformation*, great difficulty in writing a romance " about a country where there is no shadow, no antiquity, no mystery, no picturesque and gloomy wrong "; but the essential fascination of his genius transcended considerations of surroundings and created for itself the atmosphere best suited for its appreciation. That the beautiful tendrils of his fancy instinctively entwined themselves around what was congenial and vitalising, and gained strength from these accessories to the romantic and imaginative, is true enough. But it is pressing their assistance too far to regard them as indispensable. It would be easy, as it were, to confront the novelist from his own pages with instances which show how his genius itself creates the atmosphere of romance without need of antiquity or far-off lands. Hawthorne seems in this respect to resemble Ralph Cranfield, in his beautiful story *The Threefold Destiny*, who went a weary world-search for mysterious treasures which he found after all lay at his own door.

To illustrate briefly what we have stated, we will glance for a moment at some of the more remarkable of Hawthorne's short stories to be found in *Twice-told Tales* (First Series, 1837 ; Second Series, 1842) ; *Mosses from an Old Manse* (1846) ; and *The Snow Image and Other Tales* (1851). The subtlety, variety, and originality of the author's conceptions are what impress the mind most when we first become acquainted with these fascinating volumes. When, as in numerous instances, the novelist's characters are exhibited in connection with fears and forebodings which assail the human mind, as the result of some inherited tendency or of sin committed, the weird and gruesome element of Hawthorne's genius is predominant. This striking feature, and others referred to in Edgar Poe's succinct estimate of the romancer's powers—his possession of the "purest style, the finest taste, the most available scholarship, the most delicate humour, the most touching pathos,"—indicate some of the exceptional attractions which are to be found in the early stories. Special mention may be made of three graceful fantasies, worked out with peculiar happiness and vigour—*David Swan, The Great Carbuncle*, and *The Great Stone Face*. In a different manner, we have realistic sketches marked by careful finish and pathetic interest, such as *The Old Apple Dealer, The Toll Gatherer's Day,* and *The Village Pump ;* elaborate allegorical fancies with profound meaning underlying the quaint, even grim humour with which they are accompanied, as *The Christmas Banquet, The Devil in Manuscript,* and *Chippings with a Chisel*—this last having about it a flavour of Addison's famous paper on Westminster Abbey ; studies full of delicate insight and a vein of original thought, pursued with graceful exuberance through a succession of delightful pictures, as in *Sights from a Steeple, The Maypole of Merry Mount,* or *The Vision of the Fountain ;* tender or fantastic apologues, through which runs a vein of refined irony, as in *The Celestial Railroad, A Select Party,* and *Earth's Holocaust ;* and fairy legends of beauty — quaint, pathetic, or sentimental—like *The Threefold Destiny, Edward Fane's Rosebud,* or *The Lily's Quest*. To give one or two instances of the higher and more radiant flight of the romancer's imaginative conceptions, as well as of his finished and fascinating descriptive powers, we may mention *The Prophetic Pictures, The Birth-Mark, Dr. Heidegger's Experiments, Roger Malvin's Burial,* and *Rappacini's Daughter*, all of which are elaborated with rare psychological insight and invested with that weird glamour, that haunting fascination, which, if we dare coin a word, we might term Hawthornesque. In many of the short stories the gaily-dressed fantasies turn to ghostly and sepulchral images of themselves—the intensely thrilling, even harrowing effect, however, generally issues in a clear, artistically ordered work, which at its close is irradiated with some lovely thought, which seems to spring out of it as naturally as fragrance from the leaves of a flower. The short stories of these volumes also instance the ease, variety, and finish of Hawthorne's admirable style—a style graceful, vigorous, and flowing, into which the freshness of morning no less than the repose and beauty of summer woodlands seems at times to steal; a style giving life and buoyancy and fascination to whatever it describes, changing like a prism with metaphor and trope; easy, natural, varied, as it grows warm with feeling, vivid with landscape, or eloquent with human misery and wrong.

The rare attraction and subtle spiritual insight of Hawthorne's short stories are seen with elaborated distinctness in the four extended romances to which he owes his more solid reputation. *The Blithedale Romance*, as the outcome of experiences earlier than the production of *The Scarlet Letter*, or *The House of the Seven Gables*, although written after these, may be referred to first of all as the most realistic of his works. The story deals with actual circumstances in the light of an enthusiasm which sought to carry out an impracticable experiment in Socialism. This "transcendental picnic," as the scheme of the Brook Farm Community was called, cost Hawthorne his last thousand dollars, and gave the world a fresh and delightful book. The place and incidents of the Socialist settlement were chosen by Hawthorne for the background of his story, ostensibly, as he tells us, because he required "a theatre a little removed from the highways of ordinary travel, where the creatures of his brain may play their phantasmagorical antics without exposing them to too close a comparison with the actual events of real life." Yet, with all the interest it may derive from its exceptional setting, the story disappoints on account of the vagueness of its purpose and incompleteness of design. The aspiration stirring the enamoured Socialists is the enduring charm of the romance, which required no imaginative touches or beauty of surrounding to make lovelier than when it sprang radiant from the hearts of the little band of colonists. Hawthorne's genius could do for their noble ideal what the members of the community themselves failed to accomplish. It could give reality to a vision, and by associating vivid personalities with the futile attempt bestow upon posterity a living memorial of a lofty but ineffectual enthusiasm.

We now pass to *The Scarlet Letter*, a work of far grander aim and profounder intensity of genius than any other of Hawthorne's romances—a work, indeed, which, if not the most artistic outcome of

his powers, is supremely beautiful, daring, and original in conception, and finished in workmanship. The little group of figures—
a group worthy to have been portrayed by the powerful and discerning art of Rembrandt—in whom the interest of the story centres,
are conceived with consummate vigour, delicacy, and imaginative
suggestiveness. Hester Prynne, Arthur Dimmesdale, and the child
Pearl, are wrought into the recollection, not only by the artist's
minute and repeated touches, but by intense interest, sympathy,
and regret. The restrained tenderness and pathos throughout—like
springs of living water held in by stern granite rock—are all the
more impressive on account of the forlorn nature of the position of
Hester and the minister. The burning consciousness of her guilt,
typified by the scarlet letter worn upon the fallen woman's breast,
so that it is seen of all, is less hard to bear than the consciousness of
the same wrong hidden in an otherwise pure and unsullied mind.
Hester Prynne living a life of iron-minded resignation in her lonely
cottage, until the symbol of her shame becomes idealised with
another meaning, even to those who had imposed it upon her ; and
the Rev. Arthur Dimmesdale, preaching the Word of God with the
sublimest fervour and eloquence to his all-confiding people, yet with
the secret consciousness of his own unworthiness shrivelling away
his life, until driven to brand himself with the same stigma as that
so long borne publicly by his fellow-sinner—are conceptions which
reveal the human spirit in two transcendentally remarkable phases
of its convulsions with the result of sin. Idealistically more daring
and marvellous is the inspiration of the elf-child Pearl, with her
Protæan variety of moods and diversions, and the fanciful manner
in which she, as it were, plays with the secret of her mother's
shame, and unwittingly performs the part of a Nemesis towards both
parents. There is no need to dwell upon the scenes of masterly
power and refinement of insight by which the work is characterised,
but one most exquisite feature of rare poetic subtlety lies in the
manner with which the natural world around is portrayed in harmony with the peculiar feelings and positions of the two principal
characters, as if a spiritual pencil had felt the influence of the guilt
between them, and had passed with etherealised touch over the
scenes amid which they move. If the agonising chapter descriptive
of the minister's vigil is the most dramatic in the book, assuredly
the meeting between Hester and Arthur in the forest is the loveliest
and most touching. Hawthorne's vision in presenting vividly and
sympathetically the influence of the overshadowing guilt at the heart
of the story, so that it is never allowed to escape, raises the work to
a very high level, inspiring it at times with something of the daring,
although its execution is deficient in the restraint and unity of
Greek tragedy ; a work, however, worthy of the new world, with a
strength and freshness as of the pine forest, and a vitality and

intensity belonging to youthful blood—its depths of moral purpose imparting splendour to the desolation which, as the inevitable consequence of sin, pervades the story throughout.

Although *The House of the Seven Gables* may not possess the intensity and interest of *The Scarlet Letter*, it is to us a lovelier and more fascinating story, and belongs to a higher region of imaginative art. From the first we seem spirited into another world—the characters and their surroundings possessing that indefinable charm which belongs to ideal scenes and personages. These are of the simplest and most attractive description. A sister, the elaborately delineated, delightfully aristocratic old maiden, Hepzibah Pyncheon, who is tenderly attached to her brother Clifford—the most exquisitely inspired and finely delineated of all Hawthorne's characters—but from whom she has long been separated by the falsity of a relative, the Judge Pyncheon of the story; a bright, nimble-minded, joyous-hearted maiden, Phœbe, brought by stress of circumstances into the circle; and an intelligent, interesting, if somewhat moody artist, Holgrave. These are the suggestive characters to which the ancient and picturesque domicile of the Pyncheon family, the House of the Seven Gables, forms an artistic and appropriate background. Slowly, leisurely, but always beautifully, the story unfolds itself, like one of the legendary flowers in the quaint old garden behind the memorable house—with, too, a fragrance all its own. Everything in connection with the little group of characters is old-world, lovely, attractive, with an awe and interest owing to a mysterious shadow hovering round the inmates of the grotesque mansion. After the most startling event in the story—the sudden death of Judge Pyncheon—the shadow vanishes, and the romance closes in light and joyance. The feature of Hawthorne's genius which here stands out with more than usual refinement and charm is the art by which the exquisite group of characters, brought together by the simplest device of interest, are portrayed as forming parts of a harmonious whole. Among the pictures left upon the memory when we have closed the story, that of the dreamy, idealistic Clifford, with his refined, fanciful sensibilities, and tender, lovable admiration of what is beautiful and pleasing, so that his very existence seems to depend upon sunshine, is the most original and striking. One leading trait of this æsthetic dreamer is nowhere more finely illustrated than in his intercourse with Phœbe, who to his sensitive epicurean nature is as the light and fragrance of a spiritual bloom. Further, in no other of his stories does Hawthorne's humour play with such genuine and spontaneous effect. Its bright and glancing flashes usually linger on the surface, as if they had no power to penetrate deeply or warm through and through. His humour, as a rule, does not spring from the heart, or call forth irresistible mirth. Like his pathos, it is generally reserved, almost steeled, as if shy of showing itself. But through this story ever and again there are indications of a freer and heartier impulse, as in the inimitable description of Hepzibah's experience on the first morning of her opening her little shop, with the references to the boy who devoured a whole caravan of ginger-bread animals; and in such touches as those describing Holgrave's friends, who " ate no solid food, but lived on the scents of other people's cookery, and turned up their noses at that." But it is as a whole that the work impresses one with its irresistible beauty. It is not often that the flower of romance blossoms so luxuriantly, or, when it does, bears such refreshing as well as ennobling fruit.

Transformation is the most unsatisfactory although in some parts the most richly descriptive of the longer stories. The author's method of elaborating his conception is so transparently revealed as to create impatience, and in the end disappointment, notwithstanding the fascination of individual parts. This conflicting experience arises from the contradiction between the chief incident of the story—one peculiarly suitable to Hawthorne's genius—and the surroundings he introduces of no special affinity to its essential interest. This essential interest culminates in a crime of an extra-ordinarily subtle and impulsive nature. The peculiar power of Hawthorne's imagination is here finely illustrated, and his delinea-tion of the result of the crime upon the two personages concerned in it one of curious psychological discrimination. The story has no conventional ending, and perhaps fails to please some on that account; but from the peculiar nature of the leading incident such an ending is impossible; and, so far as the Hawthornesque element is concerned, *Transformation* might suitably have formed another twice-told tale with a haunting interest running through it, like Roger Malvin. On other grounds—those, for instance, which made the book such a favourite with Dean Stanley, who had read it, he tells us himself, seven times—*Transformation* is a most enthralling work. Its descriptive powers are of the highest order; its art appreciation delicate and original; its autobiographical touches of supreme and engrossing interest; its literary charm of style and thought in every way worthy of the author's lofty and cultured powers. With regard to one point of autobiographical interest, the touching and beautiful impression which lingers in the memory of one of the characters, Hilda—as pure and ethereal a conception as ever floated before a poet's mind—becomes transfigured, when we remember that Hilda is an idealised picture of the novelist's daughter Una, whom those who knew have enshrined by their references as a woman of the tenderest sensibility and grace. Una's great trial from early years was physical delicacy, and as a sequel to this we may add that, after having at thirty-three sustained the irreparable loss of her betrothed, her golden hair turned grey, and while devoting herself to religious duties she died in an English convent in 1877.

These admirable romances, with the short tales already referred to, constitute Hawthorne's noblest contribution to the imaginative literature of his country. The incomplete stories published after his death hardly increase our " rich surprise " at his fertile ingenuity. It is doubtful, had he been able, as he longed to do in the closing months of his life, " to write a sunshiny book," whether this would have materially added to the lustre of his reputation. For other and fresh illustrations of his original mind, we may turn to his various Note-books, and from these derive more intellectual wealth, as well as a closer fellowship with his richly-endowed faculties. Vivid flashes of mental and spiritual insight, imaginative suggestions of exquisite subtlety, incisive criticism upon natural and artistic subjects, incidental references to his own tastes and pursuits, make up the charm of writings which afford more and more delight on each re-perusal, and bring us face to face with the man in a most delightful and natural manner.

But it is as a writer of romance that Hawthorne principally concerns us now, with regard to whose special if limited imaginative powers, whose beautiful though peculiar inspiration of weird and ghostly rather than flesh-and-blood interest, we may add a few general considerations. Hawthorne's conceptions, for the most part, are deficient in human sympathy ; his stories, long as well as short, are constructed without scaffolding of incidents or motives to sustain them ; and beyond some absorbing idea as the central influence through the whole, independent of the usual accessories of the novel. If we turn in thought to one or two of our finest works of fiction—*Tom Jones* or *Waverley, Vanity Fair* or *Pickwick, Shirley* or *Adam Bede*—and compare these with *The Scarlet Letter* or *The House of the Seven Gables*, we are at once conscious of the vast difference both in design and effect, although there is a similar spirit at work throughout all, conducing to artistic harmony. But in the works we have mentioned in contrast to those of Hawthorne, the human interest is predominant and illustrated by rare delineation of character, in connection with stirring and varying incidents which go to make up life ; and these, moreover, are presented with a distinct aim, as regards essential points in the narrative and to the final artistic result. But with Hawthorne, human interest, the impulse and diversion of action, the conflicts of feeling, the ambitions, fascinations, meannesses and vices of the world are not the keys upon which his skilled fingers loved to play. His harmonies are drawn from other sources, and although the ideas to which his fancy is most attracted are to its touch as strings of an Æolian harp, owing to the peculiar nature of these, the music which he calls forth is at times strange, unearthly, even harrowing. Hawthorne painted souls more than bodies, moods and impressions at those significant moments which affect the current of the afterlife, rather than the ambitions and energies called forth by action and stimulated by contact with the world. Referring again to the morbidly intricate and repellent in his works, we must not forget that accompanying these there is generally a touch of light which leads the mind to some higher consideration beyond the tangled and gloomy web. Masked under the modest reserve of a story-teller the noblest spirit is at work, and a beautiful and impressive lesson is found enclosed within the fancy. If Ruskin's assertion is sound, that the "perfect function of the imagination is the intuitive perception of ultimate truth," we have here one source of that noble feature of Hawthorne's stories by which through the contemplation of things lovely he rose to the appreciation of what is true. In his search for the beautiful, he too found more truth than philosophers in seeking the true, and through his divinations we are able to share in lofty and radiant secrets.

Hawthorne's method as a novelist—the process by which he arrived at the material for his stories—was very different from that of most gifted writers who have attained eminence in the same field. The American romancer's times of deepest inspiration were in those self-withdrawing moments when "the visible scene would enter unaware into his mind," and be carried "far into his heart." It was then that natural objects with which his spirit had affinity found recognition, to be presented to the world again in the light of his exquisite genius. But this affinity was essential before these could arrest his attention and become fused with his transcendental witchery. He himself felt the want of something substantial for his fancy to unite with. If he has a realistic background, such as that of *The Blithedale Romance*, we perceive how this enables him to present his scenes and characters more firmly and impressively; but if he abandons himself entirely to his own mental conjuring, as in *Transformation*, we have as the result a story hanging together as loosely as gossamer threads—hazy, beautiful, incomplete—and notwithstanding the light streaming over it from its vivid pictures of fascinating scenery, a confusing failure. The true cohesion of Hawthorne's stories lies in the subtle interest he is able to evoke by means of that penetrative imagination which is the rarest feature of his genius.

From his various Note-books we are able to form a very clear picture of the novelist's singularly pure, noble, and disinterested character. To the sterling qualities of the man, to his singleness of heart and mind, to his profound tenderness in his family circle, to the loyalty of his attachment to his friends as well as relatives, the testimony from all sides is exceptionally cordial and harmonious. A quiet, retiring, vision-loving, beauty-haunted spirit, Hawthorne recalls Joubert's assertion that "poets are great-souled, heavenly-minded children." The American romancer was a great-souled, heavenly-minded child in many respects. The world never lost for him its robe of wonder ; to the last, as in his earliest years, it was to him a dream of mystic beauty—perhaps the more so as he grew old. This visionary gift revealed much to his inward eye unperceived by others, and was the source whence he derived many of his indefinable mental treasures. When we picture a congenially-suitable home for his unique spirit, we recall the Old Manse, where he lived in 1843, and which is associated with the collection of stories that may be said to have first diffused a new fragrance of genius beyond his own country. Hawthorne, living in this beautiful and secluded place, might well feel that those early writings were " attempts to open an intercourse with the world." " Like his own Hilda in *Transformation*," to quote the sympathetic words of an admirer, " he was spiritually compelled to descend from his aërial hermitage, and unburden his heart in the world's confessional." One characteristic feature of the man, no less than the writer, is here indicated—his imaginative solitariness. The natural tendency of Hawthorne's mind turned towards the companionship of his own thoughts, and, as with others of the world's visionaries, he found a welcome asylum in dreams and experiences beyond the visible things around him. Something of the same spirit in the instance of Keats led that poet to entwine his fancies round the mythic images of Greece, and banished into regions of unsatisfied splendour the longings and aspirations of Shelley ; it craved for some new sensation or experience with Byron, and made its home in a world of sensuous refinement with De Musset ; while it developed an accompaniment of cynical melancholy to the wild mysticism of Heine. With Hawthorne the exquisitely-wrought sensitiveness of his being took an even rarer, more ethereal direction, and he lived in the actual, so that no dream of his mind seems more imaginary than parts of his own life. It was not so much from his genius as from his temperament—if we may distinguish the two—that this proceeded—from that habit in his early life to which he alluded when he wrote : " I lived in Maine like a bird of the air, so perfect was the freedom I enjoyed. But it was there I got my cursed habit of solitude." But the natural tendency of his mind was towards solitude, and scenes and times most congenial to inward communing. Mr. Conway suggests that Hawthorne might have been a fit emblem of twilight for Buonarotti to have carved over the gates of the New World ; but Hawthorne's nature, like the subjects which were most suitable to the play of his genius, required the " moonlight of romance " for its profoundest moments. The quiet, almost shy, manner of Miles Coverdale in *The Blithedale Romance*, his delicate observation, his open and natural tastes, his love for some lonely spot where he may meditate unobserved, and indulge his fancies without check, are also exquisitely true of Hawthorne, who has sometimes been identified with the character.

Hawthorne was a romancer, and the cycle of troubadour minstrelsy had long closed. Belonging to the region of true vision as his conceptions do, some of them, however, suggest that their author had not altogether escaped the intense quivering of his day. In some of his works ideas and experiences are reflected which indicate that his rapt gaze was not always fixed upon the azure. But, regarding Hawthorne's life as that of a singularly high-minded, disinterested man, gifted with a profound spiritual insight as the source of his sympathy with the beautiful and good, we may not inappropriately imagine gathering round his massive forehead a shining light, similar to that which his own fancy has pictured flowing over the sweet, thoughtful countenance of him who resembled the Great Stone Face. With this impression in our mind, as we leave the " high pavilion of his thoughts," comes also the recollection of many hours of delightful intercourse with his fresh and original pages—with his idealisation of innumerable scenes and characters full of weird, grotesque, fascinating interest—with his visions of tender, lofty, and ennobling beauty, as well as of ineffable charm and witchery.

THOMAS BRADFIELD.

"Vernon Lee"
(Violet Paget)

"On Literary Construction"

Contemporary Review 68 (September 1895), 404–19

ON LITERARY CONSTRUCTION.

THE craft of the writer consists, I am convinced, in manipulating the contents of his reader's mind, that is to say, taken from the technical side as distinguished from the psychologic, in construction. Construction is not only a matter of single words or sentences, but of whole large passages and divisions; and the material which the writer manipulates is not only the single impressions, single ideas and emotions, stored up in the reader's mind and deposited there by no act of his own, but those very moods and trains of thought into which the writer, by his skilful selection of words and sentences, has grouped those single impressions, those very moods and trains of thought which were determined by the writer himself.

We have all read Mr. Stevenson's "Catriona." Early in that book there is a passage by which I can illustrate my meaning. It is David Balfour's walk to Pilrig :

" My way led over Mouter's Hill, and through an end of a clachan on the braeside among fields. There was a whirr of looms in it went from house to house ; bees hummed in the gardens ; the neighbours that I saw at the doorsteps talked in a strange tongue ; and I found out later that this was Picardy, a village where the French weavers wrought for the Linen Company. Here I got a fresh direction for Pilrig, my destination ; and a little beyond, on the wayside, came by a gibbet and two men hanged in chains. They were dipped in tar, as the manner is ; the wind span them, the chains clattered, and the birds hung about the uncanny jumping jacks and cried."

This half-page sounds as if it were an integral part of the story, one of the things which happened to the gallant but judicious David Balfour. But in my opinion it is not such a portion of the story, not an episode told for its own sake, but a qualifier of something else; in fact, nothing but an adjective on a large scale.

Let us see. The facts of the case are these : David Balfour, having at last, after the terrible adventures recorded in " Kidnapped," been saved from his enemies and come into his lawful property, with a comfortable life before him and no reason for disquietude, determines to come forward as a witness in favour of certain Highlanders, whom it is the highest interest of the Government to put to death, altogether irrespective of whether or not they happen to be guilty in the matter about which they are accused. In order to offer his testimony in what he imagines to be the most efficacious manner, David Balfour determines to seek an interview with the Lord Advocate of Scotland ; and he is now on his way to his cousin of Pilrig to obtain a letter from him for the terrible head of the law. Now if David Balfour actually has to be sent to Pilrig for the letter of introduction to the Lord Advocate, then his walk to Pilrig is an intrinsic portion of the story, and what happened to him on his walk cannot be considered save as an intrinsic portion also. This would be true enough if we were considering what actually could or must happen to a real David Balfour in a real reality, not what Stevenson wants us to think did happen to an imaginary David Balfour. If a real David Balfour was destined, through the concatenation of circumstances, to walk from Edinburgh to Pilrig by that particular road on that particular day ; why, he was destined also—and could not escape his destiny—to come to the gibbet where, on that particular day, along that particular road, those two malefactors were hanging in chains.

But even supposing that Stevenson had been bound, for some reason, to make David Balfour take that particular day the particular walk which must have brought him past that gibbet ; Stevenson would still have been perfectly free to omit all mention of his seeing that gibbet, as he evidently omitted mentioning a thousand other things which David Balfour must have seen and done in the course of his adventures, because the sight of that gibbet in no way affected the course of the events which Stevenson had decided to relate, any more than the quality of the porridge which David had eaten that morning. And as it happens, moreover, the very fact of David Balfour having walked that day along that road, and of the gibbet having been there, is, as we know, nothing but a make-believe on Stevenson's part, and so there can have been no destiny at all about it. Therefore, I say that this episode, which leads to no other episode, is not an integral part of the story, but a qualifier, an adjective. It acts, not upon what happens to the hero, but on what is felt by the reader. Again, let us look into the matter. This beginning of the story is, from the nature of the facts, rather empty of tragic events ; yet tragic events are what Stevenson wishes us to live through. There is something humdrum in those first proceedings of David Balfour's, which are to lead to such hairbreadth escapes. There is something not heroic enough in a young man, however heroic his intentions, going to ask for a letter of introduction to a Lord Advocate. But what can be done ? If adventures are invented to fill up these first chapters, these adventures will either actually lead to something which will complicate a plot already quite as complicated as Stevenson requires, or—which is even worse—they will come to nothing, and leave the reader disappointed, incredulous, unwilling to attend further after having wasted expectations and sympathies. Here comes in the admirable invention of the gibbet. The gibbet is, so to speak, the shadow of coming events cast over the smooth earlier chapters of the book. With its grotesque and ghastly vision, it puts the reader in the state of mind desired : it means tragedy. " I was pleased," goes on David Balfour, " to be so far in the still countryside ; but the shackles of the gibbet clattered in my head. . . . . There might David Balfour hang, and other lads pass on their errands, and think light of him." Here the reader is not only forcibly reminded that the seemingly trumpery errand of this boy will lead to terrible dangers; but he is made to feel, by being told that David felt (which perhaps at that moment David, accustomed to the eighteenth-century habit of hanging petty thieves along the roadside might not) the ghastliness of that encounter.

And then note how this qualifier, this adjectival episode, is itself qualified. It is embedded in impressions of peacefulness : the hillside, the whirr of looms and hum of bees, and talk of neighbours on doorsteps ; nay, Stevenson has added a note which increases the sense of peacefulness by adding an element of unconcern, of foreignness, such as we all find adds so much to the peaceful effect of travel, in the fact that the village was inhabited by strangers—Frenchmen— to whom David Balfour and the Lord Advocate and the Appin murder would never mean anything. Had the gibbet been on the Edinburgh Grassmarket, and surrounded by people commenting on Highland disturbances, we should have expected some actual adventure for David Balfour ; but the gibbet there, in the fields, by this peaceful foreign settlement, merely puts our mind in the right frame to be moved by the adventures which will come slowly in their due time.

This is a masterpiece of constructive craft : the desired effect is obtained without becoming involved in other effects not desired, without any debts being made with the reader ; even as in the case of the properly chosen single adjective, which defines the meaning of the noun in just the desired way, without suggesting any further definition in the wrong way.

Construction—that is to say, co-ordination. It means finding out what is important and unimportant, what you can afford and cannot afford to do. It means thinking out the results of every movement you set up in the reader's mind, how that movement will work into, help, or mar the other movements which you have set up there already, or which you will require to set up there in the future. For, remember, such a movement does not die out at once. It continues and unites well or ill with its successors, as it has united well or ill with its predecessors. You must remember that in every kind of literary composition, from the smallest essay to the largest novel, you are perpetually, as in a piece of music, introducing new *themes*, and working all the themes into one another. A theme may be a description, a line of argument, a whole personage ; but it always represents, on the part of the reader, a particular kind of intellectual acting and being, a particular kind of mood. Now, these moods, being concatenated in their progression, must be constantly altered by the other moods they meet ; they can never be quite the same the second time they appear as the first, nor the third as the second ; they must have been varied, and they ought to have been strengthened or made more subtle by the company they have kept, by the things they have elbowed, and been—however unconsciously—compared and contrasted with ; they ought to have become more satisfactory to the writer as a result of their stay in the reader's mind.

A few very simple rules might be made, so simple as to sound utterly childish ; yet how many writers observe them ?

Do not, if you want Tom to seem a villain, put a bigger villain, Dick, by his side ; but if, for instance, like Tolstoi, you want Anatole to be the trumpery wicked Don Juan, put a grand, brilliant, intrepid Don Juan—Dologhow—to reduce him to vulgar proportions. Do not, again, break off in the midst of some event, unless you wish that event to become important in the reader's mind and to react on future events ; if, for some reason, you have brought a mysterious stranger forward, but do not wish anything to come of his mysteriousness, be sure you strip off his mystery as prosaically as you can, before leaving him. And, of course, *vice versa*.

I have compared literary themes to musical ones. The novel may be considered as a gigantic symphony, opera, or oratorio, with a whole orchestra. The essay is a little sonata, trio, sometimes a mere little song. But even in a song, how many melodic themes, harmonic arrangements, accents, and so forth ! I could wish young writers, if they have any ear, to unravel the parts of a fugue, the themes of a Beethoven sonata. By analogy, they would learn a great many things.

Leaving such learning by musical analogy alone, I have sometimes recommended to young writers that they should draw diagrams, or rather *maps*, of their essays or stories. This is, I think, a very useful practice, not only for diminishing faults of construction in the individual story or essay, but, what is more important, for showing the young writer what amount of progress he is making, and to what extent he is becoming a craftsman. Every one will probably find his own kind of map or diagram. The one I have made use of to explain the meaning to some of my friends is as follows : Make a stroke with your pen which represents the first train of thought or mood, or the first group of facts you deal with. Then make another pen-stroke to represent the second, which shall be proportionately long or short according to the number of words or pages occupied, and which, connected with the first pen-stroke, as one articulation of a reed is with another, will deflect to the right or the left according as it contains more or less new matter ; so that, if it grow insensibly from stroke number one, it will have to be almost straight, and if it contain something utterly disconnected, will be at right angles. Go on adding pen-strokes for every new train of thought, or mood, or group of facts, and writing the name along each, and being careful to indicate not merely the angle of divergence, but the respective length in lines. And then look at the whole map. If the reader's mind is to run easily along the whole story or essay, and to perceive all through the necessary connection between the parts, the pattern you will have traced will approximate most likely to a perfect circle or ellipse, the conclusion re-uniting with the beginning as in a perfect logical exposition ; and the various pen-strokes, taking you gradually round this circle or ellipse, will correspond in length very exactly to the comparative importance or complexity of the matter to dispose of. But in proportion as the things have been made a mess of, the pattern will tend to the shapeless ; the lines, after infinite tortuosities, deflections to the right and to the left, immense bends, sharp angles and bags of all sorts, will probably end in a pen-stroke at the other end of the paper, as far off as possible from the beginning. All this will mean that you have lacked general conception of the subject, that the connection between what you began and what you ended with is arbitrary or accidental, instead of being logical and organic. It will mean that your mind has been rambling, and that you have been making the reader's mind ramble hopelessly, in all sorts of places you never intended ; that you have wasted his time and strength and attention, like a person pretending to know his way in an intricate maze of streets, but not really knowing which turning to take. Every one of those sharp angles has meant a lack of connection, every stroke returning back upon itself a useless digression, every loop an unnecessary reiteration ; and the entire shapelessness of your diagram has represented the atrocious fact that the reader, while knowing what you have been talking about, has not known why you have been talking about it—and is, but for a number of random pieces of information which he must himself re-arrange, no wiser than when you began.

What will this lead to? What will it make the reader expect? What will it actually bring the reader's mind to? This is the meaning of the diagrams. For, remember, in literature all depends on what you can set the reader to do; if you confuse his ideas or waste his energy, you can no longer do anything.

I mentioned just now that in a case of bad construction the single items might be valuable, but that the reader was obliged to re-arrange them. Such re-arrangement is equivalent to re-writing the book; and, if any one is to do that, it had better not be the reader, surely, but rather a more competent writer. When the badly arranged items are themselves good, one sometimes feels a mad desire to hand them over thus to some one else. It is like good food badly cooked. I think I have scarcely ever been so tormented with the desire to get a story re-written by some competent person, or even to re-write it myself, as in the case of one of the little volumes of the Pseudonym Series, a story called "A Mystery of the Campagna." I should like every young writer to read it, as a perfect model of splendid material, imaginative and emotional, of notions and descriptions worthy of Merimée (who would have worked them into a companion piece to the wonderful "Venus d'Ille"), presented in such a way as to give the minimum of interest with the maximum of fatigue. It is a thing to make one cry merely to think of; such a splendid invention, such deep contagious feeling for the uncanny solemnity, the deathly fascination of the country about Rome, worked up in a way which leaves no clear impression at all, or, if any, an impression of trivial student restaurant life.

One of the chief defects of this unlucky little book of genius is that a story of about a hundred pages is narrated by four or five different persons, none of whom has any particular individuality, or any particular reason to be telling the story at all. The result is much as if you were to be made to hear a song in fragments, fragments helter-skelter, the middle first and beginning last, played on different instruments. A similar fault of construction, you will remember, makes the beginning of one of our greatest masterpieces of passion and romance, "Wuthering Heights," exceedingly difficult to read. As if the step-relations and adopted relations in the story were not sufficiently puzzling, Emily Brontë gave the narrative to several different people, at several different periods, people alternating what they had been told with what they actually witnessed. This kind of construction was a fault, if not of Emily Brontë's own time, at least of the time in which many of the books which had impressed her most had been written, notably Hoffman's, from whose "Majorat" she borrowed much for "Wuthering Heights." It is historically an old fault for the same reason which makes it a fault with beginners, namely, that it is undoubtedly easier to narrate in the first person, or as an eye-witness, and that it is easier to co-ordinate three or four sides of an event by boxing them mechanically as so many stories one in the other, than to arrange the various groups of persons and acts as in real life, and to change the point of view of the reader from one to the other. These mechanical divisions also seem to give the writer courage : it is like the series of ropes which take away the fear of swimming : one thinks one might always catch hold of one of them, but, meanwhile, one usually goes under water all the same. I have no doubt that most of the stories which we have all written between the ages of fifteen and twenty were either in the autobiographical or the epistolary form, that they had introduction set in introduction like those of Scott, that they shifted narrator as in " Wuthering Heights," and altogether reproduced, in their immaturity, the forms of an immature period of novel-writing, just as Darwinians tell us that the feet and legs of babies reproduce the feet and legs of monkeys. For, difficult as it is to realise, the apparently simplest form of construction is by far the most difficult ; and the straightforward narrative of men and women's feelings and passions, of anything save their merest outward acts ; the narrative which makes the thing pass naturally before the reader's mind, is by far the most difficult, as it is the most perfect. You will remember that " Julie " and " Clarissa " are written in letters, " Werther " and " Adolphe " as confessions with postscripts ; nay, that even Homer and the " Arabian Nights " cannot get along save on a system of narrative within narrative ; so long does it take to get to the straightforward narrative of Thackeray, let alone that of Tolstoi. For a narrative may be in the third person, and may leave out all mention of eye-witness narration, and yet be far from what I call straightforward. Take, for instance, the form of novel adopted by George Eliot in " Adam Bede," " Middlemarch," " Deronda "—in all save her masterpiece, which has the directness of an autobiography—" The Mill on the Floss." This form I should characterise as that of *the novel built up in scenes*, and it is well worth your notice because it is more or less the typical form of the English three-volume novel. It represents a compromise with that difficult thing, straightforward narrative ; and the autobiographical, the epistolary, the narration-within-narration dodges have merely been replaced by another dodge for making things easier for the writer and less efficacious for the reader, the dodge of arranging the matter as much as possible as in a play, with narrative or analytic connecting links. By this means a portion of the story is given with considerable efficacy ; the dialogue and gesture, so to speak, are made as striking as possible ; in fact, we get all the apparent lifelikeness of a play. I say the *apparent* lifelikeness, because a play is in reality excessively unlifelike, owing to the necessity of things, which could not have happened together, being united in time and place; to quantities of things being said which never could have been said nor even thought; to scenes being protracted, rendered explicit and decisive far beyond possibility, merely because of other scenes (if we may call them scenes), the hundred other fragments of speech and fragments of action which really made the particular thing happen, having to be left out. This is a necessity on the stage because the scene cannot be changed sufficiently often, and because you cannot let people remain for an instant without talking either to some one else or to themselves. But this necessity, when applied to a novel, actually mars the action, and, what is worse, alters the conception of the action, for the form in which any story is told inevitably reacts on the matter.

Take "Adam Bede." The hero is supposed to be exceedingly reserved, more than reserved, one of those strenuous natures which cannot express their feelings even to themselves, and run away and hide in a hole whenever they do know themselves to be feeling. But, owing to the division of the book into scenes, and connecting links between the scenes, one has the impression of Adam Bede perpetually *en scène*, with appropriate background of carpenter's shop or wood, and a chorus of village rustics; Adam Bede always saying something or doing something, talking to his dog, shouldering his tools, eating his breakfast, in such a way that the dullest spectators may recognise what he is feeling and thinking. Now, to make an inexplicit personage always explain himself is only equalled by making an un-analytical person perpetually analyse himself; and, by the system of scenes, by having to represent the personage walking immersed in thoughts, hurrying along full of conflicting feelings, this is the very impression which we get, on the contrary, about Arthur and Hetty, whose misfortunes were certainly not due to overmuch introspection.

Now you will mark that this division into scenes and connecting links occurs very much less in modern French novels: in them, indeed, when a scene is given, it is because a scene actually took place, not because a scene was a convenient way of showing what was going on; and I think you will all remember that in Tolstoi's great novels one scarcely has the sense of there being any scenes at all, not more so than in real life. Pierre's fate is not sealed in a given number of interviews with Helène; nor is the rupture between Anna and Wronsky—although its catastrophe is brought about, as it must be, by a special incident—the result of anything save imperceptible disagreements every now and then, varied with an outbreak of jealousy. Similarly, in Tolstoi you never know how many times Levine went to the house of Kitty's parents, nor whether Pierre had twenty or two thousand interviews with Natacha; you only know that it all happens as it inevitably must, and happens, as most things in this world do, by the force of accumulated action.

There are some questions of construction in novels connected with this main question of the really narrative or partially dramatic form of construction, of the directness or complication of arrangement. One of these is the question of what I would call the *passive* description, by which I mean the setting up, as it were, of an elaborate landscape, or other background, before the characters are brought on the stage. The expression I have just used, " brought on the stage," shows you that I connect this particular mode of proceeding with the novel in scenes. And it is easy to understand that, once the writer allows himself to think of any event happening as it would on the stage, he will also wish to prepare a suitable background, and, moreover, most often a chorus and set of supernumeraries ; a background which, in the reality, the principal characters would perhaps not be conscious of, and a chorus which, also in the reality, would very probably not contribute in the least to the action. Another drawback, by the way, of the construction in scenes and connecting links is, that persons have to be invented to elicit the manifestation of the principal personage's qualities : you have to invent episodes to show the good heart of the heroine, the valour of the hero, the pedantry of the guardian, &c., and meanwhile the real action stops ; or, what is much worse, the real action is most unnaturally complicated by such side business, which is merely intended to give the reader information that he either need not have at all, or ought to get in some more direct way. Note that there is all the difference in the world between an episode like that of the gallows on the road to Pilrig, which is intended to qualify the whole story by inducing a particular frame of mind in the reader, and an episode like that of Dorothea (in "Middlemarch") sharing her jewels with her sister on the very afternoon of Mr. Casaubon's first appearance, and which is merely intended to give the reader necessary information about Dorothea ; information that might have been quite simply conveyed by saying, whenever it was necessary, " Now Dorothea happened to be a very ascetic person, with a childishly deliberate aversion to the vanities." This second plan would have connected Dorothea's asceticism with whatever feelings and acts really sprang from it ; while the first plan merely gives you a feeling of too many things happening in one day, and of Mr. Casaubon appearing, not simply as a mere new visitor, but as the destined husband of Dorothea. For, remember that the reader tends to attribute to the personages of a book whatever feelings you set up in him, so that, if you make the reader feel that Casaubon is going to be the bridegroom, you also, in a degree, make Dorothea feel that Casaubon is to be the bridegroom. And that, even for Dorothea, is rather precipitate.

Another question of construction is the one I should call the question of *retrospects*. The retrospect is a frequent device for dashing into the action at once, and putting off the evil day of explaining why people are doing and feeling in the particular way in which we find them, on the rising of the curtain. This, again, is a dramatic device, being indeed nothing but the narrative to or by the confidants which inevitably takes place in the third or fourth scene of the first act of a French tragedy, with the author in his own costume taking the place of the nurse, bosom friend, captain of the guard, &c. The use of this retrospect, of this sort of folding back of the narrative, and the use of a number of smaller artifices of foreshortening the narrative, seems to me not disagreeable at all in the case of the short story. The short story is necessarily much more artificial than the big novel, owing to its very shortness, owing to the initial unnaturalness of having isolated one single action or episode from the hundred others influencing it, and to the unnaturalness of having, so to speak, reduced everybody to be an orphan, or a childless widow or widower, for the sake of greater brevity. And the short story, being most often thus artificially pruned and isolated, being in a measure the artificially selected expression of a given situation, something more like a poem or little play, sometimes actually gains by the discreet display of well-carried-out artifices. While, so far as I can see, the big novel never does.

There is yet another constructive question about the novel—the most important question of all—whose existence the lay mind probably does not even suspect, but which, I am sure, exercises more than any other the mind of any one who has attempted to write a novel ; even as the layman, contemplating a picture, is apt never to guess how much thought has been given to determining the place where the spectator is supposed to see from, whether from above, below, from the right or the left, and in what perspective, consequently, the various painted figures are to appear. This supreme constructive question in the novel is exactly analogous to that question in painting ; and in describing the choice by the painter of the point of view, I have described also that most subtle choice of the literary craftsman: choice of the point of view whence the personages and action of a novel are to be seen. For you can see a person, or an act, in one of several ways, and connected with several other persons or acts. You can see the person from nobody's point of view, or from the point of view of one of the other persons, or from the point of view of the analytical, judicious author. Thus, Casaubon may be seen from Dorothea's point of view, from his own point of view, from Ladislaw's point of view, or from the point of view of George Eliot ; or he may be merely made to talk and act without any explanation of why he is so talking and acting, and that is what I call nobody's point of view.

Stories of adventure, in which the mere incident is what interests, without reference to the psychological changes producing or produced by that incident, are usually written from nobody's point of view. Much of Wilkie Collins and Miss Braddon is virtually written from nobody's point of view ; and so are the whole of the old Norse sagas, the greater part of Homer and the " Decameron," and the whole of " Cinderella" and " Jack the Giant Killer." We moderns, who are weary of psychology—for poor psychology is indeed a weariness—often find the lack of point of view as refreshing as plain water compared with wine, or tea, or syrup. But once you get a psychological interest, once you want to know, not merely what the people did or said, but what they thought or felt, the point of view becomes inevitable, for acts and words come to exist only with reference to thoughts and feelings, and the question comes, Whose thoughts or feelings ?

This is a case of construction, of craft. But it is a case where construction is most often determined by intuition, and where craft comes to be merged in feeling. For, after having separated the teachable part of writing from the unteachable, we have come at last to one of the thousand places—for there are similar places in every question, whether of choice of single words or of construction of whole books—where the teachable and the unteachable unite, where craft itself becomes but the expression of genius. So, instead of trying to settle what points of view are best, and how they can best be alternated or united, I will now state a few thoughts of mine about that which settles all questions of points of view, and alone can settle them satisfactorily—the different kinds of genius of the novelist.

I believe that the characters in a novel which seem to us particularly vital are those that to all appearance have never been previously analysed or rationally understood by the author, but are, on the contrary, those which, connected always by a sort of similar emotional atmosphere, have come to him as realities—realities emotionally borne in upon his innermost sense.

Mental science may perhaps some day, by the operation of stored-up impressions, of obscure hereditary potentialities, of all the mysteries of the subconsciousness, explain the extraordinary phenomenon of a creature being apparently invaded from within by the personality of another creature, of another creature to all, intents and purposes imaginary. The mystery is evidently connected, if not identical, with the mysterious conception—not reasoned out, but merely felt, by a great actor of another man's movements, tones of voice, states of feeling. In this case, as in all other matters of artistic activity, we have all of us, if we are susceptible in that particular branch of art (otherwise we should not be thus susceptible) a rudiment of the faculty whose exceptional development constitutes the artist. And thus, from our own very trifling experience, we can perhaps, certainly not explain what happens to the great novelist in the act of creation of his great characters, but guess, without any explanation, at what does happen to him. For, in the same way that we all of us, however rudimentally, possess a scrap in ourselves of the faculty which makes the actor; so also we possess in ourselves, I think, a scrap of what makes the novelist; if we did not, neither the actor nor the novelist would find any response in us. Let me pursue this. We all possess, to a certain small degree, the very mysterious faculty of imitating, without any act of analysis, the gestures, facial expression, and tone of voice of other people; nay, more, of other people in situations in which we have never seen them. We feel that they move, look, sound like that; we feel that, under given conditions, they would necessarily move, look, and sound like that. Why they should do so, or why we should feel that they do so, we have no notion whatever. Apparently because for that moment and to that extent we *are* those people: they have impressed us somehow, so forcibly, at some time or other, they or those like them, that a piece of them, a pattern of them, a word (one might think) of this particular vital spell, the spell which sums up their mode of being, has remained sticking in us, and is there become operative. I have to talk in allegories, in formulæ which savour of cabalistic mysticism; but I am not trying to explain, but merely to recall your own experiences; and I am sure you will recognise that these very mysterious things do happen constantly to all of us.

Now, in the same way that we all feel, every now and then, that the gestures and expression and tones of voice which we assume are those of other people and of other people in other circumstances; so likewise do we all of us occasionally feel that certain ways of facing life, certain reactions to life's various contingencies—certain acts, answers, feelings, passions—are the acts, answers, feelings, passions, the reactions to life's contingencies of persons not ourselves. We say, under the circumstances *I* should do or say so and so, but Tom, or Dick, or Harry would do or say such another thing. The matter would be quite simple if we had seen Tom, Dick, or Harry in exactly similar circumstances; we should be merely repeating what had already happened, and our forecast would be no real forecast, but a recollection. But the point is, that we have *not* seen Tom, Dick, or Harry doing or saying in the past what we thus attribute to him in the future. The matter would also be very simple if we attained to this certainty about Tom, Dick, or Harry's sayings and doings by a process of conscious reasoning. But we have not gone through any conscious reasoning; indeed, if some incredulous person challenges us to account by analysis for our conviction, we are most often unable to answer; we are occasionally even absolutely worsted in argument. We have to admit that we do not know why we think so, nay, that there is every reason to think the contrary; and yet there, down in our heart of hearts, remains a very strong consciousness, a consciousness like that of our own existence, that Tom, Dick, or Harry would, or rather will, or rather—for it comes to that—*does* say or do that particular thing. If subsequently Tom, Dick, or Harry is so perverse as not to say or do it, that, oddly enough, does not in the least obliterate the impression of our having experienced that he did say or do it, an impression intimate, warm, unanalytical, like our impressions of having done or said certain things ourselves. The discrepancy between what we felt sure must happen and what actually did happen is, I think, due to the fact that there are two persons existing under the same name, but both existing equally—Tom, Dick, or Harry as felt by himself, and Tom, Dick, or Harry as felt by us; and although the conduct of these two persons may not have happened to coincide, the conduct of each has been perfectly organic, inevitable with reference to his nature. I suppose it is because we add to our experience, fragmentary as it needs must be, of other folk, the vitality, the unity of life, which is in ourselves. I suppose that, every now and then, whenever this particular thing I am speaking of happens, we have been tremendously impressed by something in another person— emotionally impressed, not intellectually, mind; and that the emotion, whether of delight or annoyance, which the person has caused in us, in some way grafts a portion of that person into our own life, into the emotions which constitute our life; and that thus our experience of the person, and our own increasing experience of ourselves, are united, and the person who is not ourselves comes to live, somehow, for our consciousness, with the same reality, the same intimate warmth, that we do.

I hazard this explanation, at best an altogether superficial one, not because I want it accepted as a necessary premise to an argument of mine, but because it may bring home what I require to make very clear—namely, the absolutely sympathetic, unanalytic, subjective creation of characters by some novelists, as distinguished from the rational, analytic, objective creation of characters by other novelists; because I require to distinguish between the personage who has been borne in upon the novelist's intimate sense, and the personage who has been built up out of fragments of fact by the novelist's intelligent calculation. Vasari, talking of the Farnesina Palace, said that it was not " built, but really born "—*non murato ma veramente nato.* Well, some personages in novels are built up, and very well built up; and some—some personages, but how few!—are really born.

Such personages as are thus not built up, but born, seem always to have been born (and my theory of their coming into existence is founded on this) of some strong feeling on the part of their author. Sometimes it is a violent repulsion—the strongest kind of repulsion, the organic repulsion of incompatible temperaments, which makes it impossible, for all his virtues, to love our particular Dr. Fell; the reason why, we cannot tell. Our whole nature tingles with the discomfort which the creature causes in us. Such characters —I take them at random—are Tolstoi's Monsieur Karénine and Henry James's Olive Chancellor. But the greater number, as we might expect, of these really born creatures of unreality are born of love—of the deep, unreasoning, permeating satisfaction, the unceasing ramifying delight in strength and audacity; the unceasing, ramifying comfort in kindliness; the unceasing, ramifying pity towards weakness—born of the emotion which distinguishes the presence of all such as are, by the necessity of our individual nature and theirs, inevitably, deeply, undyingly beloved. These personages may not be lovable, or even tolerable, to the individual reader— he may thoroughly detest them. But he cannot be indifferent to them; for, born of real feeling, of the strongest of real feelings, the love of suitable temperaments, they are real, and awaken only real feeling. Such personages—we all know them!—such personages are, for instance, Colonel Newcome, Ethel Newcome; Tolstoi's Natacha, Levine, Anna, Pierre; Stendhal's immortal Duchess; and those two imperfect creatures, pardoned because so greatly beloved, Tom Jones and Manon Lescaut. Their power—the power of these creatures born of emotion, of affinity, or repulsion—is marvellous and transcendent. It is such that even a lapse into impossibility—though that rarely comes, of course—is overlooked. The life in the creatures is such that when we are told of their doing perfectly incredible things—things we cannot believe that, being what they were, they could have done—they yet remain alive, even as real people remain alive for our feelings when we are assured that they have done things which utterly upset our conception of them. Look, for instance, at Mr. James's Olive Chancellor. It is inconceivable that she should have ever done the very thing on which the whole book rests—taken up with such a being as Verena; yet she lives. Why? Because the author has realised in her the kind of temperament—the mode of feeling and being most organically detestable to him in all womankind. Look again at Meredith's adorable Diana. She could not have sold the secret, being what she was. Well, does she fall to the ground? Not a bit. She remains and triumphs, because she triumphed over the heart of her author. There is the other class of personage—among whom are most of the personages of every novel, most of the companions of those not built up, but born; and among whom, I think, are all the characters of some of those whom the world accounts as the greatest philosophers of the human heart—all the characters, save Maggie and Tom, of George Eliot; all, I suspect, of the characters of Balzac.

Such are tho two great categories into which all novelists may, I think, be divided, the synthetic and the analytic, those who feel and those who reason. According as he belongs to one category or the other, the novelist will make that difficult choice about points of view. The synthetic novelist, the one who does not study his personages, but *lives* them, is able to shift the point of view with incredible frequency and rapidity, like Tolstoi, who in his two great novels really *is* each of the principal persons turn about; so much so, that at first one might almost think there was no point of view at all. The analytic novelist, on the contrary, the novelist who does not live his personages, but studies them, will be able to see his personages only from his own point of view, telling one what they are (or what he imagines they are), not what they feel inside themselves, and, at most, putting himself at the point of view of one personage or two, all the rest being given from the novelist's point of view; as in the case of George Eliot, Balzac, Flaubert, and Zola, whose characters are not so much living and suffering and changing creatures, as illustrations of theories of life in general, or of the life of certain classes and temperaments.

It is often said that there are many more wrong ways of doing a thing than right ones. I do not think this applies to the novel, or perhaps to any work of art. There are a great number of possible sorts of excellent novels, all very different from one another, and appealing to different classes of minds. There is the purely human novel of Thackeray, and particularly of Tolstoi—human and absolutely living; and the analytic and autobiographical novel of George Eliot, born, as regards its construction, of the memoir. There is the analytic, sociological novel of Balzac, studying the modes of life of whole classes of people. There is the novel of Zola, apparently aiming at the same thing as that of Balzac, but in reality, and for all its realistic programme, using the human crowd, the great social and commercial mechanisms invented by mankind—the shop, the mine, the bourgeois house, the Stock Exchange—as so much matter for passionate lyrism, just as Victor Hugo had used the sea and the cathedral. There is the decorative novel—the fantastic idyl of rural life or of distant lands—of Hardy and Loti; and many more sorts. There is an immense variety in good work; it appeals to so many sides of the many-sided human creature, since it always, inasmuch as it is good, appeals successfully. In bad work there is no such variety. In fact, the more one looks at it, the more one is struck at its family resemblance, and the small number of headings under which it can be catalogued. In examining it, one finds, however superficially veiled, everlastingly the same old, old faults—inefficacious use of words, scattered, illogical composition, lack of adaptation of form or thought; in other words, bad construction, waste, wear and tear of the reader's attention, incapacity of manipulating his mind, the craft of writing absent or insufficient. But that is not all. In this exceedingly monotonous thing, poor work (as monotonous as good work is rich and many-sided), we find another fatal element of sameness : lack of the particular emotional sensitiveness which, as visual sensitiveness makes the painter, makes the writer.

For writing—I return to my original theory, one-sided, perhaps, but certainly also true in great part—is the art which gives us the emotional essence of the world and of life ; which gives us the moods awakened by all that is and can happen, material and spiritual, human and natural—distilled to the highest and most exquisite potency in the peculiar organism called the writer. As the painter says : "Look, here is all that is most interesting and delightful and vital, all that concerns you most in the visible aspect of things, whence I have extracted it for your benefit ; " so the writer on his side says : " Read ; here is all that is most interesting and delightful and vital in the moods and thoughts awakened by all things ; here is the quintessence of vision and emotion ; I have extracted it from the world and can transfer it to your mind." Hence the teachable portion of the art of writing is totally useless without that which can neither be taught nor learned—the possession of something valuable, something vital, essential, to say.

We all of us possess, as I have remarked before, a tiny sample of the quality whose abundance constitutes the special artist ; we have some of the quality of the philosopher, the painter, the musician, as we have some of the quality of the hero ; otherwise, philosophy, painting, music, and heroism would never appeal to us. Similarly and by the same proof, we have all in us a little of the sensitiveness of the writer. There is no one so dull or so inarticulate as never in his or her life—say, under the stress of some terrible calamity—to have said or written some word which was memorable, never to be forgotten by him who read or heard it : in such moments we have all had the power of saying, because apparently we have had something to say ; in that tremendous momentary heightening of all our perceptions we have attained to the writer's faculty of feeling and express- ing the essence of things. But such moments are rare ; and the small fragments of literary or artistic faculty which we all are born with, or those are born with to whom literature and art are not mere dust and ashes, can be increased and made more efficient only to a limited degree. What we really have in our power is either to waste them in cumbering the world with work which will give no one any pleasure, or to put them to the utmost profit in giving us the highest degree of delight from the work of those who are specially endowed. Let us learn what good writing is in order to become the best possible readers.   VERNON LEE.

Havelock Ellis

"Concerning
Jude the Obscure"

Savoy No. 6 (October 1896), 35–49

CONCERNING JUDE THE OBSCURE

HE eighteenth century is the great period of the English novel. Defoe, Richardson, Fielding, Goldsmith, Sterne, and Jane Austen initiated or carried towards perfection nearly every variety of fiction ; they had few or no rivals throughout Europe. Scott, with his incomparable genius for romance, was left to complete the evolutionary process.

Yet it was Scott, as we too often forget, who marred everything and threw the English novel into disorganization from which it has not even to-day recovered. Those jerry-built, pseudo-mediæval structures which he raised so rapidly and so easily, still retain, I hope, some of the fascination which they possessed for us when we were children ; they certainly retain it for a few of those children of a larger growth whom we call men of genius. But Scott's prodigious facility and the conventional unreality of his view of life ruined the English novel. By means of his enormous reputation he was enabled to debase the intellectual and moral currency in this department of literature to the lowest possible limit. It is a curious illustration of our attitude towards these things that Scott's method of paying off his debts by feverish literary production seems only to arouse our unqualified admiration. The commercial instinct in our British breasts is so highly developed that we glory in the sight of a great man prostituting his fame to make money, especially in a good cause. If he had paid off his debts at the gaming table, or even at the stock exchange, perhaps we should have been shocked. As he only flung his own genius and art on to the table to play against a credulous public his virtue remains immaculate. But a fate works through these things, however opaque the veil of insular self-satisfaction over our eyes. Scott, the earlier Scott, was a European influence, manifested in Manzoni, down through Hendrik Conscience to the drivel of Paul Féval. Since Scott no English novelist has been a force in European literature.

This may seem too stringent a judgment of so copious a branch of literature. But it is because the literature of fiction is so copious that we need a stringent clue to guide us through its mazes. A man cannot be too keen in grasping at the things that concern himself, too relentless in flinging aside those things that for him at least have no concern. For myself, at all events, I find now little in nineteenth-century English fiction that concerns me, least of all in popular fiction. I am well content to read and ponder the novels that seem to me assuredly great. In the next century, perhaps, I shall have time to consider whether it were well to read " Robert Elsmere " or " The Heavenly Twins," but as yet the question is scarcely pressing.

If that is the case, I may be asked, why read Thomas Hardy? And I must confess that that question occurred to me—long a devout admirer of Mr. Hardy's work—some fourteen years ago, and I found it unanswerable.[1] For while he still seemed to me a fine artist, I scarcely regarded him as a great artist in the sense in which I so regarded some English novelists of the last century, and some French and Russian novelists of this century. Moreover, Mr. Hardy was becoming a popular novelist. For it may be a foolish fancy, but I do not like drinking at those pools which are turbid from the hoofs of my fellow creatures ; when I cannot get there before the others I like to wait until a considerable time after they have left. I could not read my Catullus in peace if I had an uneasy sense that thousands of my fellow creatures were writing to the newspapers to say what a nice girl Lesbia was, and how horrid a person Gellius, condescending to approve the poet's fraternal sentiments, lamenting the unwholesome tone of his Atys. It is my felicity that the railroad that skirts the Lago di Garda still sets but few persons down for Sermione. Nor am I alone in this. The unequalled rapture of Lamb's joy in the Elizabethan dramatists was due to the immensity of the solitude in which at that moment they lay enfolded. Indeed this attitude of mind is ancient and well-rooted. The saviours of mankind, with what at first sight seems an unkindly delight, have emphasized the fact that salvation belongs to the few. Yet not only is religion a sacred mystery, but love also, and art. When the profane are no longer warned away from the threshold it is a reasonable suspicion that no mystery is there.—So it was that I ceased to read Mr. Hardy's novels.

But since then things have somewhat changed. The crowd thickened, indeed, especially when " Tess " appeared, for that book chanced to illustrate a fashionable sentimental moral. But last year, suddenly, on the appearance of Mr. Hardy's latest book, a great stampede was heard in the land. Noisy bands of the novelist's readers were fleeing in every direction. Although it

[1] I may here mention that, in 1883, I published in the "Westminster Review" a somewhat detailed study of the whole of Mr. Hardy's work up to that date.

was still clearly premature to say that peace reigned in the Warsaw of " Tess's " admirers, I detected at least an interesting matter for investigation. —Thus I returned to Mr. Hardy's work.

That work is now very considerable, remembering the brief space of twenty-five years over which it is spread. The *damnosa hæreditas* of Scott still afflicts nearly all our novelists with a fatal productiveness. The bigger the burden you lay on the back of Posterity the sooner he is certain to throw it off. And the creature's instinct is right ; no man, not even a Goethe, is immortally wise in fifty volumes. There are few novelists who can afford to write much. Even Balzac, the type of prolific imagination in fiction, is no exception. Content to give the merest external impression of reality, he toiled terribly in moulding the clay of his own inner consciousness to produce a vast world of half-baked images, which are immensely impressive in the mass but crumble to pieces in your fingers when you take them up. Mr. George Meredith is, perhaps, our nearest modern English counterpart to Balzac. There is a pro- digious expenditure of intellectual energy in the crowd of Meredith's huge novels. To turn from, let us say, " The Hand of Ethelberta " to " Evan Harrington," is to feel that, intellectually, Hardy is a mere child compared to Meredith. There never was a novelist so superhumanly and obstreperously clever as Mr. Meredith. One suspects that much of the admiration expended on Meredith, as on Browning, is really the reader's admiration of his own cleverness in being able to toddle along at the coat-tails of such a giant. Crude intellect is as much outside art as crude emotion or crude morals. One admires the splendid profusion of power, but the perfected achievement which alone holds our attention permanently is not to be found among these exuberantly brilliant marionettes. It is all very splendid, but I find no good reason for reading it, since already it scarcely belongs to our time, since it never possessed the virtues which are independent of time. Like Balzac, George Meredith has built to his own memory a great cairn in literature. No doubt it will be an inspiring spectacle for our race to gaze back at.

There are really only two kinds of novels which are permanently interest- ing to men. The first contains those few which impress us by the immortal power with which they present a great story or a great human type. Such are the " Satyricon," " Petit Jehan de Saintré," " Don Quixote," " Gil Blas," " Tom Jones." These books are always modern, always invigorating. They stand foursquare, each on its own basis, against every assault of time. The other class of novels—holding us not less closely, though it may be less masterfully —appeal by their intimate insight into the mysteries of the heart. They are the books that whisper to us secrets we half-knew yet never quite understood. They throw open doors into the soul that were only ajar. The men who write them are not always great masters of style or of literary architectonics, but by some happy inspiration they have revealed themselves as great masters of the human heart. Such books are full of the intimate charm of something that we remember, of things that chanced to us " a great while since, a long, long time ago," and yet they have the startling audacity of the modernest things. Among them are " Manon Lescaut," " Adolphe," " Le Rouge et le Noir," some of Dostoieffsky's novels. If any of Mr. Hardy's novels may claim to be compared with the immortals it is the books of this class which we should bear in mind.

The real and permanent interest in Mr. Hardy's books is not his claim to be the exponent of Wessex—a claim which has been more than abundantly recognized—but his intense preoccupation with the mysteries of women's hearts. He is less a story-teller than an artist who has intently studied certain phases of passion, and brings us a simple and faithful report of what he has found. A certain hesitancy in the report, an occasional failure of narrative or style, only adds piquancy and a sense of veracity to the record. A mischievous troll, from time to time—more rarely in Mr. Hardy's later work—is allowed to insert all sorts of fantastic conceits and incidents. Such interpolations merely furnish additional evidence in favour of the genuine inspiration of the whole document. We realize that we are in the presence of an artist who is wholly absorbed in the effort to catch the fleeting caprices of the external world, unsuspected and incalculable, the unexpected fluctuations of the human heart.

The great novelists of the present century who have chiefly occupied themselves with the problems of passion and the movements of women's hearts —I mean Paul Heyse and George Meredith, together with Goethe, who may be called their master—have all shown a reverent faith in what we call Nature as opposed to Society ; they have all regarded the impulses and the duties of love in women as independent of social regulation, which may or may not impede the free play of passion and natural morality. Mr. Hardy fully shares this characteristic. It was less obvious in his earlier novels, no doubt, although Cytherea of his first book, "Desperate Remedies," discovered the moral problems which have puzzled her youngest sisters, and Eustacia in " The Return of the Native " sank in what she called " the mire of marriage " long before Sue experienced her complicated matrimonial disasters. For Hardy, as for Goethe and Heyse, and usually for Meredith the problems of women's hearts are mostly independent of the routine codes of men.

The whole course of Mr. Hardy's development, from 1871 to the present, has been natural and inevitable, with lapses and irregularities it may be, but with no real break and no new departure. He seems to have been led along the path of his art by his instincts ; he was never a novelist with a programme, planning his line of march at the outset, and boldly affronting public reprobation ; he has moved slowly and tentatively. In his earlier books he eluded any situation involving marked collision between Nature and Society, and thus these books failed to shock the susceptibilities of readers who had been brought up in familiarity with the unreal conventionalities which rule in the novels of Hugo, Dickens, Thackeray, and the rest. " Far from the Madding Crowd " first appeared in the " Cornhill," from which a few years earlier Thackeray had excluded Mrs. Browning's poem, " Lord Walter's Wife," as presenting an immoral situation. It was not until " Two on a Tower " appeared, in 1882, that the general public—led, if I remember rightly, by the " Spectator "— began to suspect that in reading Mr. Hardy's books it was not treading on the firm rock of convention. The reason was, not that any fundamental change was taking place in the novelist's work, but that there really is a large field in which the instincts of human love and human caprice can have free play without too obviously conflicting with established 'moral codes. Both in life and in art it is this large field which we first reach. It is thus in the most perfect and perhaps the most delightful of Mr. Hardy's early books, " Under the Greenwood Tree." The free play of Fancy's vagrant heart may be followed in all its little bounds and rebounds, its fanciful ardours and repressions, because she is too young a thing to drink deep of life—and because she is not yet married. It is all very immoral, as Nature is, but it succeeds in avoiding any collision with the rigid constitution of Society. The victim finally takes the white veil and is led to the altar ; then a door is closed, and the convent gate of marriage is not again opened to the intrusive novel-reader's eye. Not by any means because it is considered that the horrors beyond are too terrible to be depicted. The matter does not appear to the novelist under this metaphor. Your wholesome-minded novelist knows that the life of a pure-natured English-woman after marriage is, as Taine said, mainly that of a very broody hen, a series of merely physiological processes with which he, as a novelist, has no further concern.

But in novels, as in life, one comes at length to realize that marriage is not necessarily either a grave, or a convent gate, or a hen's nest, that though the conditions are changed the forces at work remain largely the same. It is still quite possible to watch the passions at play, though there may now be more tragedy or more pathos in the outcome of that play. This Mr. Hardy proceeded to do, first on a small scale in short stories, and then on a larger scale. " Tess " is typical of this later unconventional way of depicting the real issues of passion. Remarkable as that book no doubt is, I confess that on the whole it has made no very strong appeal to me. I was repelled at the outset by the sub-title. It so happens that I have always regarded the conception of " purity," when used in moral discussions, as a conception sadly in need of analysis, and almost the first time I ever saw myself in print was as the author of a discussion, carried on with the usual ethical fervour of youth, of the question : " What is Purity ? " I have often seen occasion to ask the question since. It seems to me doubtful whether anyone is entitled to use the word " pure " without first defining precisely what he means, and still more doubtful whether an artist is called upon to define it at all, even in several hundred pages. I can quite conceive that the artist should take pleasure in the fact that his own creative revelation of life poured contempt on many old prejudices. But such an effect is neither powerful nor legitimate unless it is engrained in the texture of the narrative ; it cannot be stuck on by a label. To me that glaring sub-title meant nothing, and I could not see what it should mean to Mr. Hardy. It seemed an indication that he was inclined to follow after George Eliot, who —for a large " consideration "—condescended to teach morality to the British public, selling her great abilities for a position of fame which has since proved somewhat insecure ; because although English men and women are never so happy as when absorbing unorthodox sermons under the guise of art, the permanent vitality of sermons is considerably less than that of art.

Thus I was not without suspicion in approaching " Jude the Obscure." Had Mr. Hardy discovered the pernicious truth that whereas children can only take their powders in jam, the strenuous British public cannot be induced to devour their jam unless convinced that it contains some strange and nauseous powder ? Was " Jude the Obscure " a sermon on marriage from the text on the title-page : " The letter killeth " ? Putting aside the small failures always liable to occur in Mr. Hardy's work, I found little to justify the suspicion. The sermon may, possibly, be there, but the spirit of art has, at all events, not been killed. In all the great qualities of literature " Jude the Obscure " seems to me the greatest novel written in England for many years.

It is interesting to compare " Jude " with a characteristic novel of Mr. Hardy's earlier period, with " A Pair of Blue Eyes," or " The Return of the Native." On going back to these, after reading " Jude," one notes the graver and deeper tones in the later book, the more austere and restrained roads of art which Mr. Hardy has sought to follow, and the more organic and radical way in which he now grips the individuality of his creatures. The individuals themselves have not fundamentally changed. The type of womankind that Mr. Hardy chiefly loves to study, from Cytherea to Sue, has always been the same, very human, also very feminine, rarely with any marked element of virility, and so contrasting curiously with the androgynous heroines loved of Mr. Meredith. The latter, with their resolute daring and energy, are of finer calibre and more imposing ; they are also very much rarer in the actual world than Mr. Hardy's women, who represent, it seems to me, a type not un-common in the south of England, where the heavier Teutonic and Scandinavian elements are, more than elsewhere, modified by the alert and volatile elements furnished by earlier races. But if the type remains the same the grasp of it is now much more thorough. At first Mr. Hardy took these women chiefly at their more obviously charming or pathetic moments, and sought to make the most of those moments, a little careless as to the organic connection of such moments to the underlying personality. One can well understand that many readers should prefer the romantic charm of the earlier passages, but—should it be necessary to affirm ?—to grapple with complexly realized persons and to dare to face them in the tragic or sordid crises of real life is to rise to a higher plane of art. In " Jude the Obscure " there is a fine self-restraint, a complete mastery of all the elements of an exceedingly human story. There is nothing here of the distressing melodrama into which Mr. Hardy was wont to fall in his early novels. Yet in plot " Jude " might be a farce. One could imagine that Mr. Hardy had purposed to himself to take a conventional farce, in which a man and a woman leave their respective partners to make love to one another and then finally rejoin their original partners, in order to see what could be made of such a story by an artist whose sensitive vision penetrated to the tragic irony of things ; just as the great novelists of old, De la Sale, Cervantes, Fielding, took the worn-out conventional stories of their time, and filled them with the immortal blood of life. Thus " Jude " has a certain symmetry of plan such as is rare in the actual world—where we do not so readily respond to our cues—but to use such a plot to produce such an effect is an achievement of the first order.

Only at one point, it seems to me, is there a serious lapse in the art of the book, and that is when the door of the bedroom closet is sprung open on us to reveal the row of childish corpses. Up to that one admires the strength and sobriety of the narrative, its complete reliance on the interests that lie in common humanity. We feel that here are real human beings of the sort we all know, engaged in obscure struggles that are latent in the life we all know. But with the opening of that cupboard we are thrust out of the large field of common life into the small field of the police court or the lunatic asylum, among the things which for most of us are comparatively unreal. It seems an unnecessary clash in the story. Whatever failure of nervous energy may be present in the Fawley family, it is clear that Mr. Hardy was not proposing to himself a study of gross pathological degenerescence, a study of the hereditary evolution of criminality. If that were so, the story would lose the wide human significance which is not merely stated explicitly in the preface, but implicitly throughout. Nor can it be said that so wholesale a murder was required for the constructive development of the history ; a much less serious catastrophe would surely have sufficed to influence the impressionable Sue. However skilful Mr. Hardy may be in the fine art of murder, it is as a master of the more tender and human passions that he is at his best. The element of bloodshed in " Tess " seems of dubious value. One is inclined to question altogether the fitness of bloodshed for the novelist's purpose at the present period of history. As a factor in human fate bloodshed to-day is both too near and too remote for the purposes of art. It is too rare to be real and poignant to every heart, and in the days of well-equipped burglars and a " spirited " foreign policy it is too vulgar to bring with it any romance of " old unhappy far-off things." Our great sixteenth-century dramatists could use it securely as their commonest resource because it was then a deeply-rooted fact both of artistic convention and of real life. In this century bloodshed can only be made humanly interesting by a great psychologist, living on the barbarous outskirts of civilization, a Dostoieffsky to whom the secret of every abnormal impulse has been revealed. In Mr. Hardy's books bloodshed is one of the forms put on by the capricious troll whose business it is to lure him from his own work. But that cupboard contains the only skeleton in the house of " Jude the Obscure." On the whole, it may be said that Mr. Hardy here leads us to a summit in art, where the air is perhaps too rare and austere for the more short-winded among his habitual readers, but, so far as can yet be seen, surely a summit.—So at least it seems to one who no longer cares to strain his vision in detecting mole-hills on the lower slopes of Parnassus, yet still finds pleasure in gazing back at the peaks.

But I understand that the charge brought against " Jude the Obscure " is not so much that it is bad art as that it is a book with a purpose, a moral or an immoral purpose, according to the standpoint of the critic. It would not be pleasant to admit that a book you thought bad morality is good art, but the bad morality is the main point, and this book, it is said, is immoral, and indecent as well.

So are most of our great novels. " Jane Eyre," we know on the authority of a " Quarterly " reviewer, could not have been written by a respectable woman, while another "Quarterly " (or maybe " Edinburgh") reviewer declared that certain scenes in " Adam Bede " are indecently suggestive. " Tom Jones " is even yet regarded as unfit to be read in an unabridged form. The echo of the horror which " Les Liaisons Dangereuses" produced more than a century ago in the cheerfully immoral society of the *ancien régime* has scarcely even to-day died down sufficiently to permit an impartial judgment of that powerful and saturnine book. " Madame Bovary," which Taine regarded in later days as fit for use in Sunday schools, was thought so shocking in the austere court of Napoleon III. that there was no alternative to prosecution. Zola's chief novels, which to-day are good enough to please Mr. Stead, the champion of British Puritanism, were yesterday bad enough to send his English publisher to prison. It seems, indeed, on a review of all the facts, that the surer a novel is of a certain immortality, the surer it is also to be regarded at first as indecent, as subversive of public morality. So that when, as in the present case, such charges are recklessly flung about in all the most influential quarters, we are simply called upon to accept them placidly as necessary incidents in the career of a great novel.

It is no fortuitous circumstance that the greatest achievements of the novelist's art seem to outrage morality. " Jude the Obscure " is a sufficiently great book to serve to illustrate a first principle. I have remarked that I cannot find any undue intrusion of morality in the art of this book. But I was careful to express myself cautiously, for without doubt the greatest issues of social morality are throughout at stake. So that the question arises : What is the function of the novelist as regards morals ? The answer is simple, though it has sometimes been muddled. A few persons have incautiously asserted that the novel has nothing to do with morals. That we cannot assert ; the utmost that can be asserted is that the novelist should never allow himself to be made the tool of a merely moral or immoral purpose. For the fact is that, so far as the moralist deals with life at all, morals is part of the very stuff of his art. That is to say, that his art lies in drawing the sinuous woof of human nature between the rigid warp of morals. Take away morals, and the novelist is *in vacuo*, in the region of fairy land. The more subtly and firmly he can weave these elements together the more impressive becomes the stuff of his art. The great poet may be in love with passion, but it is by heightening and strengthening the dignity of traditional moral law that he gives passion fullest play. When Wagner desired to create a typically complete picture of passion he chose the story of Tristram ; no story of Paul and Virginia can ever bring out the deepest cries of human passion. Shakespeare found it impossible to picture even the pure young love of Romeo and Juliet without the aid of the violated laws of family and tradition. " The crash of broken commandments," Mr. Hardy once wrote in a magazine article, " is as necessary an accompaniment to the catastrophe of a tragedy as the noise of drum and cymbals to a triumphal march ;" and that picturesque image fails to express how essential to the dramatist is this clash of law against passion. It is the same in life as in art, and if you think of the most pathetic stories of human passion, the profoundest utterances of human love, you probably think most readily of such things as the letters of Abélard and Héloise, or of Mlle. de Lespinasse, or of the Portuguese nun, and only with difficulty of the tamer speech of happier and more legitimate emotions. Life finds her game in playing off the irresistible energy of the individual against the equally irresistible energy of the race, and the stronger each is the finer the game. So the great artist whose brain is afire with the love of passion yet magnifies the terror and force of moral law, in his heart probably hates it.

Mr. Hardy has always been in love with Nature, with the instinctive, spontaneous, unregarded aspects of Nature, from the music of the dead heather-bells to the flutter of tremulous human hearts, all the things that are beautiful because they are uncontrolled by artificial constraint. The progress of his art has consisted in bringing this element of nature into ever closer contact with the rigid routine of life, making it more human, making it more moral or more immoral. It is an inevitable progression. That love of the spontaneous, the primitive, the unbound—which we call the love of " Nature "—must as it becomes more searching take more and more into account those things, also natural, which bind and constrain " Nature." So that on the one side, as Mr. Hardy has himself expressed it, we have Nature and her unconsciousness of all but essential law, on the other the laws framed merely as social expedients without a basis in the heart of things, and merely expressing the triumph of the majority over the individual ; which shows, as is indeed evident from Mr. Hardy's work, that he is not much in sympathy with Society, and also shows that, like Heyse, he recognizes a moral order in Nature. This conflict reaches its highest point around women. Truly or falsely, for good or for evil, woman has always been for man the supreme priestess, or the supreme devil, of Nature. " A woman," said Proudhon—himself the incarnation of the revolt of

Nature in the heart of man—"even the most charming and virtuous woman, always contains an element of cunning, the wild beast element. She is a tamed animal that sometimes returns to her natural instinct. This cannot be said in the same degree of man." The loving student of the elemental in Nature so becomes the loving student of women, the sensitive historian of her conflicts with "sin" and with "repentance," the creations of man. Not, indeed, that any woman who has "sinned," if her sin was indeed love, ever really "repents." It is probable that a true experience of the one emotional state as of the other remains a little foreign to her, "sin" having probably been the invention of men who never really knew what love is. She may catch the phrases of the people around her when her spirit is broken, but that is all. I have never known or heard of any woman, having for one moment in her life loved and been loved, who did not count that moment as worth all other moments in life. The consciousness of the world's professed esteem can never give to unloved virtue and respectability the pride which belongs to the woman who has once "sinned" with all her heart. One supposes that the slaves of old who never once failed in abject obedience to their master's will mostly subdued their souls to the level of their starved virtues. But the woman who has loved is like the slave who once at least in his life has risen in rebellion with the cry : "And I, too, am a man !" Nothing that comes after can undo the fine satisfaction of that moment. It was so that a great seventeenth-century predecessor of Mr. Hardy in the knowledge of the heart, painted Annabella exultant in her sin even at the moment of discovery, for "Nature" knows no sin.

If these things are so, it is clear how the artist who has trained himself to the finest observation of Nature cannot fail, as his art becomes more vital and profound, to paint morals. The fresher and more intimate his vision of Nature, the more startling his picture of morals. To such an extent is this the case in "Jude the Obscure," that some people have preferred to regard the book as a study of monstrosity, of disease. Sue is neurotic, some critics say; it is fashionable to play cheerfully with terrible words you know nothing about. "Neurotic" these good people say by way of dismissing her, innocently unaware that many a charming "urban miss" of their own acquaintance would deserve the name at least as well. In representing Jude and Sue as belonging to a failing family stock, I take it that Mr. Hardy by no means wished to bring before us a mere monstrosity, a pathological "case," but that rather, with an artist's true instinct—the same instinct that moved so great an artist as Shakespeare when he conceived "Hamlet"—he indicates the channels of least resistance along which the forces of life most impetuously rush. Jude and Sue are represented as crushed by a civilization to which they were not born, and though civilization may in some respects be regarded as a disease and as unnatural, in others it may be said to bring out those finer vibrations of Nature which are overlaid by rough and bucolic conditions of life. The refinement of sexual sensibility with which this book largely deals is precisely such a vibration. To treat Jude, who wavers between two women, and Sue, who finds the laws of marriage too mighty for her lightly-poised organism, as shocking monstrosities, reveals a curious attitude in the critics who have committed themselves to that view. Clearly they consider human sexual relationships to be as simple as those of the farmyard. They are as shocked as a farmer would be to find that a hen had views of her own concerning the lord of the harem. If, let us say, you decide that Indian Game and Plymouth Rock make a good cross, you put your cock and hens together, and the matter is settled ; and if you decide that a man and a woman are in love with each other, you marry them and the matter is likewise settled for the whole term of their natural lives. I suppose that the farmyard view really is the view of the ordinary wholescme-minded novelist —I mean of course in England—and of his ordinary critic. Indeed in Europe generally, a distinguished German anthropologist has lately declared, sensible and experienced men still often exhibit a knowledge of sexual matters such as we might expect from a milkmaid. But assuredly the farmyard view corresponds imperfectly to the facts of human life in our time. Such things as " Jude " is made of are, in our time at all events, life, and life is still worthy of her muse.

" Yes, yes, no doubt that is so," some critics have said in effect, " but consider how dangerous such a book is. It may be read by the young. Consider how sad it would be if the young should come to suspect, before they are themselves married, that marriage after all may not always be a box of bonbons. Remember the Young Person." Mr. Hardy has himself seemingly, though it may only be in seeming, admitted the justice of this objection when in the preface to his book he states that it is " addressed by a man to men and women of full age." Of course there is really only one thing that the true artist can or will remember, and that is his art. He is only writing for one person—himself. But it remains true that a picture of the moral facts of the world must arouse moral emotions in the beholder, and while it may not be legitimate to discuss what the artist ought to have done, it is perfectly legitimate to discuss the effect of what he has done.

I must confess that to me it seems the merest cant to say that a book has been written only to be read by elderly persons. In France, where a different tradition has been established, the statement may pass, but not in England nor in America, where the Young Person has a firm grip of the novel, which sne is not likely to lose. Twenty years ago one observed that one's girl friends— the daughters of clergymen and other pillars of society—found no difficulty, when so minded, in reading *en cachette* the works of Ouida, then the standard-bearer of the Forbidden, and subsequent observation makes it probable that they are transmitting a similar aptitude to their daughters, the Young Persons of to-day. We may take it that a novel, especially if written in English, is open to all readers. If you wish to write exclusively for adult readers, it is difficult to say what form of literature you should adopt ; even metaphysics is scarcely safe, but the novel is out of the question. Every attempt to restrict literature is open to a *reductio ad absurdum*. I well remember the tender-hearted remonstrance of an eminent physician concerning a proposal to publish in a medical journal a paper on some delicate point in morbid psychology : " There are always the compositors." Who knows but that some weak-kneed suggestible compositor may by Jude Fawley's example be thrust on the downward road to adultery and drink ? With this high-strung anxiety lest we cause our brother to offend, no forward step could ever be taken in the world ; for " there are always the compositors." There would be nothing better than to sit still before the book of Ecclesiastes, leaving the compositors to starve in the odour of sanctity.

But why should the Young Person not read " Jude the Obscure " ? To me at least such a question admits of no answer when the book is the work of a genuine artist. One can understand that a work of art as art may not be altogether intelligible to the youthful mind, but if we are to regard it as an ensample or a warning, surely it is only for youth that it can have any sort of saving grace. " Jude " is an artistic picture of a dilemma such as the Young Person, in some form or another, may one day have to face. Surely, on moral grounds, she should understand and realize this beforehand. A book which pictures such things with fine perception and sympathy should be singularly fit reading. There is probably, however, much more foxiness than morality in the attitude of the Elderly Person in this matter. " Don't trouble about traps, my little dears," the Elderly Person seems to say ; " at your age you ought not to know there are such things. And really they are too painful to talk about ; no well-bred Young Person does." When the Young Person has been duly caught, and emerges perhaps without any tail, then the Elderly Person will be willing to discuss the matter on a footing of comfortable equality. But what good will it be to the Young Person then ? The Elderly Person's solicitude in this matter springs, one fears, from no moral source, but has its origin in mists of barbarous iniquity which, to avoid bringing the blush of shame to his cheek, need not here be investigated. " Move on, Auntie ! " as little Sue said to the indignant relation who had caught her wading in the pond, " this is no sight for modest eyes ! "

So that if the Young Person should care to read " Jude " we ought for her own sake, at all events, to be thankful. But our thankfulness may not be needed. The Young Person has her own tastes, which are at least as organically rooted as anyone else's ; if they are strong she will succeed in gratifying them ; if they are not, they scarcely matter much. She ranks " A Pair of Blue Eyes " above " Jude the Obscure," likes Dickens more than either, and infinitely prefers Marie Corelli to them all. Thus she puts her foot down on the whole discussion. In any case it ought to be unnecessary to labour this point ; there is really little to add to Ruskin's eloquent vindication for young girls of a wholesome freedom to follow their own instincts in the choice of books.

To sum up, " Jude the Obscure " seems to me—in such a matter one can only give one's own impressions for what they are worth—a singularly fine piece of art, when we remember the present position of the English novel. It is the natural outcome of Mr. Hardy's development, along lines that are genuinely and completely English. It deals very subtly and sensitively with new and modern aspects of life, and if, in so doing, it may be said to represent Nature as often cruel to our social laws, we must remark that the strife of Nature and Society, the individual and the community, has ever been the artist's opportunity. " Matrimony have growed to be that serious in these days," Widow Edlin remarks, " that one really do feel afeard to move in it at all." It is an affectation to pretend that the farmyard theory of life still rules unquestioned, and that there are no facts to justify Mrs. Edlin. If anyone will not hear her, let him turn to the Registrar-General. Such facts are in our civilisation to-day. We have no right to resent the grave and serious spirit with which Mr. Hardy, in the maturity of his genius, has devoted his best art to picture some of these facts. In " Jude the Obscure " we find for the first time in our literature the reality of marriage clearly recognized as something wholly apart from the mere ceremony with which our novelists have usually identified it. Others among our novelists may have tried to deal with the reality rather than with its shadow, but assuredly not with the audacity, purity and sincerity of an artist who is akin in spirit to the great artists of our best dramatic age, to Fletcher and Heywood and Ford, rather than to the powerful though often clumsy novelists of the eighteenth century.

There is one other complaint often brought against this book, I understand, by critics usually regarded as intelligent, and with the mention of it I have done. "Mr. Hardy finds that marriage often leads to tragedy," they say, "but he shows us no way out of these difficulties ; he does not tell us his own plans for the improvement of marriage and the promotion of morality." Let us try to consider this complaint with due solemnity. It is true that the artist is god in his own world ; but being so he has too fine a sense of the etiquette of creation to presume to offer suggestions to the creator of the actual world, suggestions which might be resented, and would almost certainly not be adopted. An artist's private opinions concerning the things that are good and bad in the larger world are sufficiently implicit in the structure of his own smaller world ; the counsel that he should make them explicit in a code of rules and regulations for humanity at large is a counsel which, as every artist knows, can only come from the Evil One. This complaint against " Jude the Obscure " could not have arisen save among a generation which has battened on moral and immoral tracts thrown into the form of fiction by ingenious novices. The only cure for it one can suggest is a course of great European novels from " Petit Jehan de Saintré " downwards. One suggestion indeed occurs for such consolation as it may yield. Has it not been left to our century to discover that the same hand which wrote the disordered philosophy of " Hamlet " put the times into joint again in " The New Atlantis," and may not posterity find Thomas Hardy's hand in " Looking Backward " and " The Strike of a Sex ? " Thus for these critics of " Jude " there may yet be balm in Utopia.

HAVELOCK ELLIS.

George Moore

"A Tragic Novel"

Cosmopolis 7 (July 1897), 38–59

A TRAGIC NOVEL.

I MUST begin this article by referring to the article which I published in this review last October : for what I have now to say is, in the main, a continuation of what I then said. In the October article I pointed out that England has not produced tragic novelists as have France and Russia ; that, unlike English poetry, English fiction had concerned itself only with secondary ideas. The discovery is so simple a one that I blush for having made it ; but someone had to make it, and its importance is vital, for it must change our view of the value of at least a third of our imaginative literature.

The object of the English novel has ever been to divert young people rather than to help men and women to understand life. The achievements of English novelists may be compared with those of Rossini, Donizetti, and Bellini : the later works of Verdi offer a striking comparison with some modern developments of the English novel. Of contemporary writers I do not desire to speak ; but of the dead it is my right to speak as plainly as I please. Now, I suppose it is quite clear that Balzac, Flaubert, Tourguéneff, and Tolstoi compare better with Beethoven, Wagner, Mozart, and Berlioz than Scott, Dickens, Thackeray, and Eliot. It will be admitted, too, that Shelley and Wordsworth increase our knowledge, or, shall I say, our perception of life much more than Dickens and Thackeray ; that a wider hiatus would be created by the destruction of the poems than by that of the novels, that after the suppression of Shakespeare, the next widest hiatus would be made by the suppression of Balzac.

He who has read Balzac is a creature apart ; his mind is, as it were, inoculated with a new perception of life. He who has come under the influence of Shelley feels, sees, and thinks Shelley till he dies. Wordsworth never enslaved me to the same extent, but I feel Wordsworth sufficiently to divine the unalterable influence he must possess over many minds. These are supreme, but there may be minor influences. Poe does not contribute to the same extent as Shelley and Balzac, but he does contribute a little ; but in what do Scott's tales of chivalry contribute to our perception of life ? They were once, and perhaps are still, considered entertaining, but were they ever any more ? Would our perception of life be much more increased by reading Dickens than by hanging a set of Rowlandson's or Gillray's caricatures on our dining-room walls ? The difference in the aim of English poetry and English fiction might be analysed more searchingly. I hope some critic may undertake the task, but my intention is here no more than to lead the reader to separate the books that have increased his perception of life from those which have merely enabled him to pass the time.

In Balzac there is everything : in other writers we find one, two, or three things ; in Balzac we find everything—everything except "L'Education Sentimentale." We find "Madame Bovary," although no one but Flaubert could have written it ; neither in the plan nor in the characters is there much to distinguish it from a novel by Balzac. True, that none could have thrown into the composition such strange concision of thought, such unexpected beauty of phrase as its author ; but if Balzac had written it, it would have been essentially better written. Balzac would have endowed it with larger lungs and a livelier heart, and the characters would have unfolded as steam unfolds, and less like indiarubber piping. For there is an admixture of indiarubber in the characters in "Madame Bovary" ; they are not all flame, like the characters in the "Comédie Humaine" ; nor do they live with the same intense and volatile, unanalysable life as the men and women in Tourguéneff or Tolstoi. The temper of Flaubert's mind did not admit that they should. Balzac and the Russians loved life, Flaubert was ever anxious to express his contempt of life ; and it was his extraordinary literary genius that enabled him to refrain from direct expression of his personal feeling in the presentation of his characters; but they had been conceived in the gall and wormwood of his heart, and their destiny was to exhibit the baseness and futility of the human race. The wonder, therefore, is not that his men and women are not quite so intense as Balzac's, or Tourguéneff's, or Tolstoi's, but that they are perhaps the next in intensity, and certainly the next in power of presentation. I would remind those who are inclined to doubt the truth of this analysis that never after "Madame Bovary" did Flaubert attempt to describe the evolution of a soul; once the master qualities of his mind were fully developed it was impossible for him even to try. When he discovered, as he did in "Madame Bovary," that he was the greatest descriptive writer the world had ever seen, it was not unnatural that the idea should have occurred to him that he might write the descriptive novel of all time, whereas on Balzac's own ground he must remain inferior. So he abandoned the psychological novel, and invented a new form, one admirably calculated to receive his entire genius, his unique powers of description, and all his philosophical mind. In such a book human character could only appear in vigorous silhouette; but marvellously drawn edges of character are surely what a great philosopher, a perfect artist, and a profound thinker would do best.

"L'Education Sentimentale" was considered the most tedious of books when it first appeared; but so was Wagner's music. Now the music of the Ring is the music that interests, and the music of Sémiramide is the music that bores. The way Rossini went Scott is going; and, unless an exception be made in favour of some mechanical critics, no one now thinks "L'Education Sentimentale" as tedious as "Ivanhoe." But when it appeared very few had any inkling of Flaubert's meaning, and how very faint that inkling was we can judge from Tourguéneff's letters. Even he seems to have considered the book as the gigantic and unhappy failure of a man of genius, rather than as the most wonderful novel ever written. But when we consider Tourguéneff's special talent, it is not surprising that he did not understand. Since then it has been read by novelists in search of material, and they held their tongues, partly because it was easier to steal than to appreciate, partly because they did not wish to draw attention to their thefts. The most luminous and far-seeing of critics seem to have had nothing more interesting to say than that the book is extraordinary. Other critics thought it heavy, dull, overweighted with matter, a sad falling off from "Madame Bovary." No one has thrown down the glove in cold print and claimed for the book its due. Something wholly new in literature ; a novel? (have it so, if you will) ; a book, at all events, the like of which did not exist in the past, the like of which the future will not reproduce, a new thing come into human life ; a new force, a new influence that was not there before, and will be there for ever—the time when it shall be forgotten is unthinkable—a book which is more than a mere pastime, like Dickens or Scott ; a book from which each reader shall acquire a new manner of feeling, seeing, thinking ; a book that shall mould the reader's mind, as Balzac, Shelley, and Wordsworth. The mechanical critics have not perceived that the impact of this book is like that of a religion ; that it forms the souls of at least thirty or forty readers in every generation. But what is the evocation of thirty souls to them ? The million readers whom Maupassant and George du Maurier have interested represent the tumult of a generation. That is their point of view; mine is that the smallest sect is more worthy of attention than the largest carnival.

If my readers have acceded to my request to read the October article before reading this one, it will probably seem to them that an æstheticism the very opposite to that of the earlier article is now being advocated. The October article laid stress on the fact that the subconscious, the principal guiding factor in human life, had never found expression in English novels, and at first sight " L'Education Sentimentale " will seem the most striking example that could be selected of the objective method. It will seem to the reader like a series of pictures of the external world painted for no purpose but the display of the writer's descriptive power. The reader may not perceive (for thirty years readers have failed to perceive) that in all these pictures the idea is to the front, that it is the idea, and always the idea.

According to Hindu mythology, Brahma created the passing spectacle of life to relieve his eternal ennui. He sits watching the generations rising out of the void and falling into the void ; their aspirations and tribulations as little one as the other, and this for ever and ever, through endless time. Inspired by this sublime conception Flaubert must have said to himself, " I will be Brahma, and with the impartiality of a God I will paint everything that may happen in the life of a young man, the friends he knows, the things he sees, the places he visits ; and to no one thing will I give importance or relief, an immense bas-relief it shall be ; for nothing matters, philosophically all things are equal. My impartiality shall end by terrifying the reader. Scene after scene shall rise up before him and fall into the echoless void. My unheroic hero shall inherit a fortune, he shall lose a fortune, he shall inherit another ; everything shall happen, and it shall be the same as if nothing had happened. To-day we shall see a man living with his wife, to-morrow he shall be living with his mistress ; a little later he shall follow a different occupation, he shall return to his wife and shall be about to break with her again. There shall be restaurants, studios, houses of ill-fame, racecourses ; there shall be gardens and a forest ; there shall be revolutions ; a king shall be over-thrown, and a Republic established, and the Republic shall shoot down the people in the name of law and order just as the king did. The entire phantasmagoria of life shall pass before the reader, scene after scene all equally trivial, all equally meaningless—the eternal spectacle of human misery and the eternal spectre of ennui watching over it ; that shall be my book."

Magic lantern shades evoke an idea of thinness and crudity : an endless gallery of Dutch pictures gives an idea of permanency. Shall I say judgment day at the Royal Academy ? Ten thousand pictures passed in review ! But all good ! Long river lands, battle pieces, interiors, a lady in her carriage, a lady in her drawing-room. We will take the two last :—

Un coupé bleu, attelé d'un cheval noir stationnait devant le perron. La portière s'ouvrit, une dame y monta, et la voiture avec un bruit sourd

se mit à rouler sur le sable. Frédéric, en même temps qu'elle, arriva de
l'autre côté, sous la porte cochère. L'espace n'était pas assez large, il fut
contraint d'attendre. La jeune femme, penchée en dehors du vasistas,
parlait tout bas au concierge. Il n'apercevait que son dos, couvert d'une
mante violette. Cependant, il plongeait dans l'intérieur de la voiture, tendue
de reps bleu, avec des passementeries et des effilés de soie. Les vêtements
de la dame l'emplissaient ; il s'échappait de cette petite boîte capitonnée
un parfum d'iris et comme une vague senteur d'élégance féminine. Le
cocher lâcha les rênes, le cheval frôla la borne brusquement, et tout
disparut.

Frédéric s'en revint à -pieds en suivant les boulevards.

Il regrettait de n'avoir pu distinguer Madame Dambreuse.

It is possible that it will occur to someone to say that the
passage quoted is mere reporting, and that all that is required
to write like it is a notebook and the advantage of an experience. Well, let him who thinks so go forth with a notebook
and put the matter to a practical test. When he compares
his recorded facts with Flaubert's text, he will find what
he has written is a jumble ; should he strive to reduce his
facts to order, they will shrivel up like cigarette papers. He
will in the end confine himself to the statement : " As
Madame Dambreuse got into her carriage, she leaned forward
to speak to the concierge, and so Frédéric failed to catch
sight of her face." For him who cannot write like
Flaubert this is the best way out of the difficulty. But
sound, colour, space, form, perfume are in Flaubert ;
nothing has been omitted that could be included, nothing
has been included that could be omitted ; every detail
contributes to enforce the unity of the picture. The very
movement of the lady, her head and back, as she leans to
speak to the concierge, is indicated, and this without an adjective, by a mere statement. Then the exquisite little coda,
"Frédéric returned on foot, following the boulevards. He
regretted he had not seen Madame Dambreuse." For beauty
of selection, for beauty of drawing, for beauty of colour, the
Dutchmen have not done better. It is as fine as the finest
work by Peter de Hooch or Van der Meer.

The next picture, a lady sitting in her drawing-room, is one
which every novelist from Fielding down to the last brand-new
genius fresh from the Bodley Head has tried to paint, and
all French novelists since Balzac. We will take one of the

most talented, Maupassant, for example. His novel " Fort
comme la Mort" abounds in descriptions of ladies in drawing-
rooms. But if the reader compares any one with the one I
am about to quote, he will be struck by the emptiness of the
drawing, the thinness of the colour, the absence of solidity
in structure. The Maupassant is merely charming, the
Flaubert is profound, yet the subject is the most trivial and
the most ordinary :—

> Il distingua des habits noirs, puis une table ronde éclairée par un grand
> abat-jour, sept ou huit femmes en toilettes d'été, et, un peu plus loin,
> Madame Dambreuse dans un fauteuil à bascule. Sa robe de taffetas lilas
> avait des manches à crevés, d'où s'échappaient des bouillons de mousseline,
> le ton doux de l'étoffe se mariant à la nuance de ses cheveux ; et
> elle se tenait quelque peu renversée en arrière, avec le bout de son pied sur
> un coussin, tranquille comme une œuvre d'art pleine de délicatesse, une
> fleur de haute culture.

There are in " L'Education Sentimentale" hundreds of
similar pictures. That all are equally perfect is not the most
important criticism. What is important to remember is that
they are all symbols of the idea, and that by their very
number they express it. But such admirable objectivity does
not represent the whole of Flaubert's method. He can be,
when he wishes, as purely subjective as Racine, and his art
lies in the dexterity with which he passes from the objective
to the subjective, as occasion requires, either abruptly or by a
series of delicate transitions. Sometimes the introduction of a
word will enable him to get back to the key. So subtle are his
modulations that in the very same passage he is by turns
subjective and objective. It is marvellous writing when
Frédéric goes to see La Maréchale for the first time.

> La porte de l'antichambre était ouverte. Deux bichons havanais
> accoururent. Une voix cria :
> " Delphine ! Delphine ! est-ce vous, Jeba ? " Il se tenait sans avancer,
> les deux petits chiens happaient toujours. Enfin Rosannette parut,
> enveloppée dans une sorte de peignoir en mousseline blanche garnie de
> dentelles, pieds nus dans les babouches. " Ah, pardon, monsieur ! Je vous
> prenais pour le coiffeur. Une minute, je reviens."
> Et il restait seul dans la salle à manger.
> Les persiennes en étaient closes. Frédéric la parcourait des yeux, en se
> rappelant le tapage de l'autre nuit, lorsqu'il remarqua au milieu, sur la
> table, un chapeau d'homme, un vieux feutre bossué, gras, immonde. " A
> qui donc ce chapeau ? " Montrant impudemment la coiffe décousue, il
> semblait dire : " Je m'en moque. Après tout, je suis le maître."

La Maréchale survient. Elle le prit, ouvrit la serre, l'y jeta, referma la porte (d'autres portes, en même temps, s'ouvraient et se fermaient), et, ayant fait passer Frédéric par la cuisine, elle l'introduisit dans son cabinet de toilette.

On voyait tout de suite que c'est l'endroit de la maison le plus hanté et comme son vrai centre moral. Une perse à grand feuillage tapissait les murs, les fauteuils et un vaste divan élastique. Sur une table de marbre blanc s'espaçaient de larges cuvettes en faïence bleue...

Ending with

et les senteurs de pâtes d'amandes et de benjoin s'exhalaient.

"Vous excuserez le désordre ! Ce soir, je dîne en ville."

Et comme elle tournait sur ses talons, elle faillit écraser un des petits chiens. Frédéric les déclara charmants. Elle les souleva tous les deux, et, haussant jusqu'à lui leur museau noir :

"Voyons, faites une risette, baisez le monsieur."

Un homme habillé d'une sale redingote à collet en fourrure entra brusquement. "Félix, mon brave," dit-elle, "vous aurez votre affaire dimanche, sans faute."

L'homme se mit à la coiffer. Il lui apprenait des nouvelles de ses amies. Mme de Rochegune, Mme de St-Florentin, Mmè Lombard, toutes étant nobles comme à l'hôtel Dambreuse. Puis de causer théâtres ; on donnait le soir, à l'Ambigu, une représentation extraordinaire.

"Irez-vous ?"

"Ma foi, non ! Je reste chez moi."

A little later Mlle. Vatnaz comes in, and after some conversation she asks the Maréchale what she is going to do that night. The Maréchale says she is going to Alphonsine's, which is the third version of the way she intends to spend the evening. It would be difficult to say which method prevails in this passage. To continue my musical phraseology, Flaubert is always in modulation.

Of the many hundreds, maybe thousands, of courtesans who figure in the pages of fiction, La Maréchale is certainly the truest, perhaps the most sympathetic. True that the author has not thought it necessary to endow her with those "redeeming traits of character" with which the vulgar conscience of the hour is caught like a noisy foolish bluebottle in a pot of treacle. She neither gives up her numerous lovers for one great passion, nor is she converted by a priest, nor is her lack of conscience exaggerated till she becomes the symbol of the evil under which the world groans. She does not accomplish Frédéric's ruin ; she is even less responsible for it than the beautiful and good Madame Arnoux.

Balzac has shown how the virtuous woman may ruin her husband, and the unvirtuous woman may prove his consolation and safeguard ; but this question hardly arises. No one, not even those who borrow and do not pay back, are responsible for Frédéric's ruin ; in no circumstances could he escape ruin, and it would be difficult to imagine circumstances in which La Maréchale would have lived virtuously, not even if she had not had a mother, which in the experience of the Maréchale is the worst luck that can befall a girl. There are good and bad courtesans as there are good and bad virtuous women. By no adventitious aids does Flaubert strive to engage our sympathy. He merely helps us to understand. When we do not understand we do not sympathise ; pity is the corollary of knowledge, and all living things are pitiful : the saint as well as the courtesan. See truly and all differences disappear. Assassin, thief, lecher, madman, are all equally worthy of pity. " Judge not, and ye shall not be judged." We see her living as she was born to live ; there have always been courtesans, and presumably there always will be, and she works out her destiny instinctively, as you and I do. Pity the poor little Maréchale and poor Mlle. Vatnaz, her friend, pity them all, even Arnoux, the ever unfaithful husband ; everything that lives is to be pitied.

Mlle. Vatnaz is a vague person, who passes through the book as mysteriously and sometimes incomprehensibly as a shadow. She and the Maréchale quarrel over Delmar, that superb mummer who speaks at public meetings, and when he has no more to say turns his profile to the audience. It would be difficult to say who gets Delmar in the end. I fancy that Flaubert leaves it in obscurity. But Mlle. Vatnaz is

Une de ces célibataires parisiennes qui, chaque soir, quand elles ont donné leurs leçons, ou tâché de vendre de petits dessins, de placer de pauvres manuscrits, rentrent chez elles avec la crotte à leurs jupes, font leur dîner, le mangent toutes seules, puis, les pieds sur une chaufferette, à la lueur d'une lampe malpropre, rêvent un amour, une famille, un foyer, la fortune, —tout ce qui leur manque.

Hussonnet, journalist and dramatist, is very slightly sketched, and does not compare with his prototype, the illustrious Brixou (I know I have spelt that last name wrong, and shall be told that I have not read Balzac) ; still, there are moments when he presents a keen edge of character, when he says : "la charpente on me l'accorde, pour les caractères j'ai assez roulé ma bosse, pour les traits d'esprit, c'est mon métier.". I quote from memory, and cannot vouch for the accuracy of this last quotation. But Regimbart is admirable ; we know him in every moment of his public life, not a word is wasted, and each appearance adds something to the portrait. We know the café he goes to first, when he leaves home in the morning, about eight o'clock. In that café he takes his vin blanc ; in the next café he takes his vermout, in the next his absinthe ; he breakfasts in a little café near the Place de la Bourse ; in another café he takes his coffee after breakfast, in another he takes his absinthe before dinner ; I have forgotten the café in which he dines, and there are two or three more where he plays billiards till midnight. Regimbart speaks little ; he is dissatisfied with everything, and passes for an *esprit fort.* He is considered an authority on politics ; he wears an enormous felt hat, and is recognised far away in the crowd. It is to him Frédéric goes when he returns to Paris and finds that Madame Arnoux has left the house in the Rue Montmartre. Frédéric misses him in the first café, "Monsieur Regimbart vient de sortir," and that morning he does not go to the next or the next café. In the café where he breakfasts, the garçon answers "Monsieur Regimbart, il déjeune en haut." But he is not there ! "Well, then, he must have just gone out !" The pursuit of Regimbart is continued all day. In the evening it rains; and, soaked through, Frédéric finds him, I think, about midnight playing billiards.

On the occasion of his ridiculous duel with M. de Cisy, Frédéric at once thought of Regimbart, and directed his steps towards an estaminet in the Rue St. Denis. The shop was shut, but a light was burning above the door, which was ajar ; he pushed it open, and entered. The empty room was lit by a tallow dip placed on the edge of the counter ; the chairs, their legs uppermost, were piled on the tables. The master and mistress, with their waiter, were supping in the corner next the kitchen. Regimbart, his hat on his head, was sharing their repast, inconveniencing the waiter, who, if

I remember rightly, was obliged to turn aside at every mouthful.

> Le citoyen commença par ne rien répondre ; il roulait des yeux, avait l'air de réfléchir, fit plusieurs tours dans la salle et dit enfin : "Oui volontiers !"
>
> Et un sourire homicide le dérida, en apprenant que l'adversaire était un noble.
>
> "Nous le ferons marcher tambour battant, soyez tranquille ! D'abord... avec l'épée." "Mais peut-être," objecta Frédéric, "que je n'ai pas le droit..."
>
> "Je vous dit qu'il faut prendre l'épée," répliqua brutalement le citoyen. "Savez-vous tirer ?"
>
> "Un peu !"
>
> "Ah ! un peu ! voilà comme ils sont tous ! et ils ont la rage de faire l'assaut ! qu'est-ce que ça prouve, la salle d'armes ! Ecoutez-moi : tenez-vous bien à distance en vous refermant toujours dans des cercles, et rompez ! Rompez ! c'est permis. Fatiguez-le ! Puis fendez-vous dessus franchement ! Et surtout pas de malice, pas de coups à la Fougère ! non ! de simples une-deux, des dégagements. Tenez, voyez-vous ? en tournant le poignet comme pour ouvrir une serrure. Père Vauthier, donnez-moi votre canne. Ah ! cela suffit."
>
> Il empoigna la baguette qui servait à allumer le gaz, arrondit le bras gauche, plia le bras droit, et se mit à pousser des bottes contre la cloison. Il frappait du pied, s'animait, feignant même de rencontrer des difficultés, tout en criant : "Y es-tu là ? y es-tu ?" et sa silhouette énorme se projetait sur la muraille, avec son chapeau qui semblait toucher au plafond. Le limonadier disait de temps en temps : "Bravo ! très bien !" Son épouse également admirait, quoique émue ; et Théodore, un ancien soldat, en restait cloué d'ébahissement, étant du reste fanatique de M. Regimbart.

Compared with this, how thin Thackeray's humour seems, and how trivial and noisy Dickens'. Here we have fiction raised to the level of an art. It is surely as wonderful to write like this as it is to paint like Velasquez or Rembrandt. The illusion exceeds that of painting. It is like a perfectly acted scene. The dialogue has been chosen with such rare insight that every accent is audible and every gesture visible. It is impossible to read it without supplying the entire pantomime and every intonation.

Pellerin is a slightly more prominent character in the book than Regimbart. He is a painter who reads *tous les ouvrages esthétiques* in the hopes of discovering the veritable theory of Beauty. He wastes his days in discussions ; he believes in the necessity of a rule or in a reformation in artistic questions.

He overflows at the slightest provocation with admiration for the past centuries, and is full of contempt for the sterility of his own, of which he is the most sterile fruit of all. When Frédéric commissions him to paint the Maréchale's portrait, his mind passes in review all the great portraits of the world. He is tempted by reminiscences of Rubens, he is haunted by recollections of Titian ; he thinks of Reynolds, Gainsborough ; he meditates a Natter or a Boucher. At last, in a sudden burst of inspiration, he cries, "Eh bien ! Non. Je reviens à mon idée ! Je vous flanque en Vénitienne." On Madame Arnoux's birthday all bring her something. One man brings "une écharpe syrienne," another "une boîte de bonbons," Pellerin "un fusain, une espèce de danse macabre; une fantaisie hideuse d'une exécution médiocre."

I am tortured with desire of quotation, I am as a man in a treasure-house : to choose implies rejection and any omission seems a loss. But space, space, that everlasting cry of the journalist, forbids ! I must leave Pellerin for Frédéric, about whom the narrative of the four women who loved him hangs, and all the interminable episodes. What weaving and interweaving, what crossing and intercrossing ! "L'Education Sentimentale" is more intricate than an anthill, its network is more perplexing than the lines of rails at a great junction. By what foresight is the arrival of all the trains settled ? we ask ourselves ; and when thinking of this book we ask ourselves similar questions. The texture is woven as closely as the music of "Tristan"—echoes, transformations, modulations, never a full close, always a suspended cadence. A devilish ingenuity united to a sublime conception ; profusion of detail and an extraordinary oneness ; and the analysis of the characters constantly interrupted by a description of the surroundings. Would not these last few lines apply equally well to Wagner as to Flaubert ? Apart from the context, might they not easily pass as an extract from an article on "Tristan"? Notwithstanding his legends and his Gods, Wagner was a naturalistic writer, and the literary equivalent of his music is "L'Education Sentimentale." But "L'Education Sentimentale" is more voluminous than "Tristan." The book seems to me more wonderful than any single opera ; for an adequate comparison I want the whole " Ring "—or, well, very nearly the whole.

It is impossible to remember " L'Education Sentimentale " as we remember any other novel. We remember the motives, but the harmonies which accompany them are even more unrememberable in the fiction than in the music. At every moment our attention is drawn to some casual phenomenon, but always the conception dominates the particular, and draws it into the universal scheme, and every one of these passing details serves to thicken the weft ; in places the mind misses the threads which link the pattern, and suspects an omission. But on a second or third reading we perceive the foreshortening. To weave so closely that division would be impossible was Flaubert's aim, and to this end he not only piled detail upon detail, but invented what in literature is the equivalent of the suspended cadence in music. He avoided the full close as systematically as Wagner ; he never ends a chapter at the place indicated by the ordinary rules of composition. The opening chapter offers an excellent example of what I mean, and it will enable me to get back to Frédéric Moreau, about whom my paper tells me it is necessary I should begin to speak at once.

It was on the 15th of September, 1840, on board the steam boat that left the Quay Bernard about six o'clock in the morning, that Frédéric met Madame Arnoux. The departure of the steamboat is described, the river's banks, and the people on board. He speaks to her husband, learns that his name is Jacques Arnoux, and that he owns a newspaper called *L'Art Industriel*, and deals in pictures ; but he does not succeed in getting into conversation with Madame : an opportunity occurs, but he lets it pass. Here is Flaubert's first portrait of her :—

Elle avait un large chapeau de paille avec des rubans roses qui palpitaient au vent derrière elle. Ses bandeaux noirs, contournant la pointe de ses grands sourcils, descendaient très bas et semblaient presser amoureusement l'ovale de sa figure. Sa robe de mousseline claire, tachetée de petits pois, se répandait en plis nombreux. Elle était en train de broder quelque chose ; et son nez droit, son menton, toute sa personne se découpait sur le fond de l'air bleu.

Frédéric is returning to Nogent, the boat stops at Surville, and there he gets out. When he turned, she was standing by the rudder. He sent forth a look into which he strove to put his soul; but it was as if he had done nothing, she did not stir. Now in the course of ordinary literary composition, a writer would seize on this point to conclude a chapter. The picture is complete. The departure of the boat, the river banks, the acquaintanceship begun with Arnoux, the lady standing by the rudder, her straw hat, its rose-coloured ribbons floating behind her, a young man looking after her from the quay, paying no heed to his servant's salutations: all is there. But Flaubert does not choose to end on a full close, and the narrative is carried on in some words addressed to his servant. His drive home is described, his meeting with his mother, and after dinner the neighbours come in to welcome him; and later still, just as he is going to bed, the servant brings in a card. It is from Deslauriers, a school friend. The next chapter begins with an account of Deslauriers' father, then it passes into an account of the schooldays of the two young men, and then, by an almost imperceptible transition, returns to the moment when Frédéric is walking with Deslauriers. Madame Moreau sends the servant to beg her Frédéric to return. Deslauriers asks him not to, they continue walking to and fro; they meet the Père Roque, the father of Louise, one of the four women who loved Frédéric. Suddenly a light shines in the window of a low-built house on the left bank of the river, Deslauriers takes off his hat.

"Vénus, reine des cieux, serviteur ! Mais la pénurie est la mère de la sagesse. Nous a-t-on assez calomniés pour cela, miséricorde." Cette allusion à une aventure commune les mit en joie. Ils riaient très haut dans les rues.

But though it is permissible, even meritorious, to avoid known rhythms, it becomes obligatory, if such a course be adopted, to discover new rhythms in nature; art may not be unrhythmical. And the rhythm of Flaubert's composition in "L'Education Sentimentale," though irregular, is never unrhythmical, as is sometimes the case in "Madame Bovary," for there I think I detect attempts to discover the elliptical metres which he used with such effect in the later work. By avoiding all well-known *points de repères* he obtains a density of composition which at first fatigues, but which delights the reader when he is able to follow the evanescent metre in its thousand sinuosities.

But I, too, though I can lay claim to neither malice, nor foresight, am adopting a very irregular form of composition in this article. Once again I have wandered from the pressing question of Frédéric's character, and this is a matter I am anxious to make clear, for it has afforded a base for all the arguments that have hitherto been urged against the book. It has not been understood that the scheme of composition demanded a sort of Egyptian oneness in the characters themselves ; they are part of the passing spectacle that Brahma is for ever watching. True that they grow older, that their faults become inveterate, but their characters are not developed in sets of scenes devised for that purpose ; the Orientalism of the conception forbids that they should, and until this is understood there can be no advance in the comprehension of this extraordinary book ; it will seem wooden, inchoate, laborious, abnormal. Nor should it be objected that Flaubert was wrong to impose such limitations on himself. By indefinitely extending his range in one direction he contracted it in the other.

Frédéric and Arnoux are described on page 5, and like Egyptian sculptures they stand in their symbolic attitudes for five hundred pages. But I swear to you they are even as grand in their monumental simplicities. Frédéric ! the very name is a discovery ; is it not typical of the false romantism of which he is the incarnation ? or is the character so well described that we read it into the very syllables of the name ?

Frédéric pensait à la chambre qu'il occuperait là-bas, au plan d'un drame, à des sujets de tableau, à des passions futures. Il trouvait que le bonheur mérité par l'excellence de son âme tardait à venir. Il se déclama des vers mélancoliques ; il marchait sur le pont à pas rapides ; il s'avança jusqu'au bout, du côté de la cloche ;—et dans un cercle de passagers et de matelots il vit un monsieur qui contait des galanteries à une paysanne, tout en lui maniant la croix d'or qu'elle portait sur la poitrine.

A few moments later Frédéric gets into conversation with Arnoux, and very soon they are talking about women.

> Le Monsieur en bottes rouges donna des conseils au jeune homme ; il
> exposait des théories, narrait des anecdotes, se citait lui-même en exemple,
> débitant tout cela d'un ton paterne, avec une ingénuité de corruption
> divertissante.

We must not pause to admire the writing ; the point here is
that the characters of both men are always restrained within
these narrow limits, and that what would be a weakness in any
other scheme of composition is an essential part of Flaubert's.
Arnoux is always the type of the unfaithful husband and the
spendthrift ; Frédéric is always the type of the young man
whose natural timidity prevents him from ever taking advantage of an opportunity. He is not stupid ; foolish, yes ;
above all things incapable of action, and for the purpose of
Flaubert's scheme of composition a more convenient type
could not have been selected. No other type of character
would allow his descriptive method such free play.
All the same difficulties arose. Notwithstanding the fact that
on board the steamboat he was dreaming of future passions
and that a little later in the book he leaves Madame Dambreuse's drawing-room reflecting that it would be " crânement
beau d'avoir une pareille maîtresse," he remains a prudent man,
if I may be permitted a vulgar Latinism, until he goes away with
La Maréchale in the last quarter of the book. No reason is
assigned for his prudence ; to assign one would enlarge the
limits of the psychology within which Flaubert deemed it
necessary to remain. And for no psychological reasons does
Frédéric remain virtuous. His virtue cannot be explained
either by his natural timidity or his love of Madame Arnoux,
the scheme of composition alone is answerable. But in every
work of art there is a corner into which we may not look ;
and if I look into this corner it is not to discover a weakness
but to indicate a strength. Flaubert was strong enough to
accept the necessary imperfection, and to do this is the sign
of strength in the artist who has passed middle age ; in youth
we accept imperfections because we are not aware of them.
There are other discrepancies, and they are accepted as
frankly. It was impossible that Frédéric should take part in the
Revolution, whether as Royalist or Republican. From the first
he is set forth as a man incapable of action, and to describe

the Revolution without him would split the book up, would be, in a word, a violation of artistic principle intolerable to Flaubert. The complacent spectator falls well in with the artistic scheme, and Flaubert adopted it. But, though Frédéric's physical courage is never called into question, it was even established by his conduct in the duel with Cisy (was that the reason for the duel?), it is doubtful if he would walk about the streets when bullets are flying like hail, merely to see the spectacle. But the Revolution exhibited in extraordinary light the futility of human effort; it could not be abandoned, so Frédéric walked about the streets regardless of the danger he was incurring. On second thought, I incline to the supposition that in a besieged town the folk soon become careless of danger of the bullets. If this is so, a few lines have been omitted. But of the validity of my first objection I am sure. Later in the book I discern certain efforts of composition. Was it necessary that Madame Arnoux should be invited to dine at Madame Dambreuse's? And after ten years of meditations these are the specks which I find on what I believe to be the most extraordinary work of art produced since the Greeks and Michelangelo.

For this article to be complete I should have to quote the four beautiful pages descriptive of the days that Frédéric spends with Madame Arnoux when she goes to live at Passy (330-333), and I should have to quote also the four perhaps still more wonderful pages when the poor little Maréchale tells Frédéric in the forest of Fontainebleau the story of her life (400-404). But such extended quotation is not possible, and I pass on to the time when Frédéric, through vanity, becomes the lover of Madame Dambreuse.

Il n'éprouvait pas à ses côtés ce ravissement de tout son être qui l'emportait vers Madame Arnoux, ni le désordre gai où l'avait mis d'abord Rosannette, mais il la convoitait comme une chose anormale et difficile parce qu'elle était noble, parce qu'elle était riche, parce qu'elle était dévote se figurant qu'elle avait des délicatesses de sentiment rare comme des dentelles, avec des amulettes sur la peau et des pudeurs dans la dépravation.

Is not such writing like an engraved and jewelled Damascus blade, and of edge so fine that a silk handkerchief can be cut through with it in mid air. The funeral of M. Dambreuse is celebrated. The thirty superior persons I spoke of in the beginning of this article recite it to each other in the moonlight in the Champs-Elysées under the chestnut trees.

La fosse de M. Dambreuse était dans le voisinage de Manuel et de Benjamin Constant. Le terrain dévale, en cet endroit, par une pente abrupte. On a sous les pieds des sommets d'arbres verts ; plus loin, des cheminées de pompes à feu, puis toute la grande ville.

Frédéric put admirer le paysage pendant qu'on prononçait les discours. Le premier fut au nom de la Chambre des députés, le deuxième, au nom du conseil général de l'Aube, le troisième, au nom de la Société houillière de Saône-et-Loire, le quatrième, au nom de la Société d'agriculture de l'Yonne ; et il y en eut un autre, au nom d'une Société philanthropique. Enfin on s'en allait, lorsqu'un inconnu se mit à lire un sixième discours, au nom de la Société des antiquaires d'Amiens.

Et tous profitèrent de l'occasion pour tonner contre le socialisme dont M. Dambreuse était mort victime. C'était le spectacle de l'anarchie et son dévouement à l'ordre qui avait abrégé ses jours. On exalta ses lumières, sa probité, sa générosité, et même son mutisme comme représentant du peuple, car s'il n'était pas orateur, il possédait en revanche ces qualités solides mille fois préférables, etc... Avec les mots qu'il faut dire : " Fin prématurée,—regrets éternels,--l'autre patrie,—adieu, ou plutôt non, au revoir." La terre mêlée de cailloux retomba ; et il ne devait plus en être question dans le monde.

But the chapter does not end on this terrible last phrase, the story goes on. There is the return home, and, very tired, Frédéric enters his rooms. Again occurs a natural close for the chapter ; but, for reasons already given, Flaubert prefers to carry it on, and without any transitional description, by the mere phrase " quand il se présenta le lendemain à l'hôtel Dambreuse," etc.

The philosophic tide of incident flows on, and Rosannette, *bourgeoise déclassée*, begins to long for a settled life ; she even begins to dream of an at-home day. In this book everything is in a state of change, yet nothing really changes ; the book is as changeful and as immovable as life itself. It is sometimes hard to remember what happens next. Frédéric does not marry Madame Dambreuse, in consequence of some disparaging observation she made about Madame Arnoux. He bade her good-bye, and so the terror of the book draws upon one like a nightmare ; and for ever coming to the grapple something new surges out of the deep. On every page there is an extraordinary foreshortening : the end of the liaison, for instance, with Rosannette, or the discovery made, of course, in some obscure café to which he goes in search of Regimbart, that Arnoux is now a dealer in church ornaments, "Sculpture polychrome, encens de rois mages," &c. Frédéric starts off at once, and then occurs the inevitable description of the shop window. Later still Pellerin is called in to paint the portrait of Rosannette's dead baby, and the last appearance of this sublime failure is as good as any.

"Pourvu que ce soit ressemblant," objecta Rosannette.

"Eh bien ! je me moque de la ressemblance. A bas le Réalisme ! C'est l'esprit qu'on peint. Laissez-moi ! Je vais tâcher de me figurer ce que ça devrait être."

Il réfléchit, le front dans la main gauche, le coude dans la droite ; puis, tout à coup :

"Ah ! une idée, un pastel ! avec des demi-teintes colorées, passé presque à plat, on peut obtenir un modèle, sur les bords seulement."

While the portrait is being done (was it ever begun ?) something else must happen … Arnoux is about to be put into prison in consequence of some money transaction ; £400, the exact sum, is given. Frédéric goes off to the rescue, and the stream of anecdote flows on and on. With the imperturbable tranquillity of a God, Flaubert continues to narrate ; never any faintest trace of impatience or weariness. At last we come to the celebrated scene when Madame Arnoux calls to see Frédéric, in what intention is not stated, possibly she hardly knows herself. But Frédéric feels it is too late, and lets her go. Her hair, which throughout the novel has been beautiful, and as black as a swallow's wings, is now white ; she cuts off a lock which she throws on the table as she goes away, never to be seen again by Frédéric. The sadness of this last interview is one of the saddest things in literature, divinely sad, divinely beautiful. It is the end of all things, the end of the world. They go for a walk in the streets, they tell of the old days—all the sentimental sadness of existence is in this scene. When I read this book, above all when I read this scene, it seems to me that all novels waxed into one novel ; that I stand, as I stand with Shelley, on the highest height, where the sound of journalistic babbling about Thackeray, Dickens, Eliot, and the Brontës only reaches my ear sufficiently to remind me that I am still on earth.

But you want to know how the book ends ? You think. it ends on this chapter; no, but the chapter ends with the departure of Madame Arnoux, so much Flaubert does concede. In the beginning of the next chapter, we find Frédéric and Deslauriers once again reconciled, "brought together again by the fatality of their nature." I forgot to say that Deslauriers married the heiress whom Frédéric thought of marrying. He tells how his wife one day eloped with a singer ; since then he has been, needless to say, in various employments. Pellerin also, having tried Gothic and humanitarian art, has become a photographer ; I forgot to say that Frédéric, having spent two-thirds of his fortune, is living in the country *en petit bourgeois*. They ask each other, and each informs the other, regarding his friends. Madame Arnoux is in Rome with her son ; Arnoux is dead. Sénécal has disappeared. Deslauriers met La Maréchale coming out of a shop—she has grown enormously fat, she who was so very slender ; she now is the widow of a certain M. Oudry. Regimbart "se traîne devant les cafés, affaibli, courbé en deux, vidé, un spectre." Then comes the explanation regarding the political signification of "la tête de veau" which has always perplexed Frédéric throughout the book. "'Tu me parais bien calmé sur la politique ?'--'Effet de l'âge,' dit l'avocat, et ils résumèrent leur vie." One thinks he failed because he was too logical, the other because he was too sentimental. And disinterring the days of their youth, they said at every phrase, "Do you remember ?" At last the end is reached. It was in 1837 that they visited La Turque, and the allusion which Deslauriers made in the second chapter to this adventure is at length explained : " C'est là ce que nous avons eu de meilleur."

"Oui, peut-être bien. C'est là ce que nous avons eu de meilleur," dit Deslauriers, and so ends their Sentimental Education.

This end will be considered sad by those who seek in art what they seek in life ; but it will exalt and refresh those who are capable of the joy of art.

The long tragedy culminating in these last pages is more profound than that of sudden death ; for it is life and not death that is tragic, and Frédéric's tragedy is the tragedy of everyone who inherits five hundred a year and upwards. We may say it begins even a little lower down in the economic scale, it is the tragedy of everyone who lives upon unearned increment, as the Socialists would put it, though it is far from my thoughts to draw any social morality from this sublime book, which exhibits not the misery of a class, but the eternal misery of life itself. The tragedy of Frédéric's life is the tragedy of leisure; the tragedy of work is a different tragedy. Every man of leisure is Frédéric. He may write the books Frédéric did not write, he may represent the constituencies Frédéric did not represent. At the bottom of his success he will find Frédéric ... For it will not be contended that success redeems the immedicable platitude of human life.

In these concluding pages, we feel that not one man has fallen, but that all have fallen; life has been ravished of all the enchanting illusion through which she works out her sublime deception for an end which we may never fathom, which lies perchance behind the stars. I do not stop to argue with those who ask of what use is the demonstration of such unpalatable truths ? My concern is not with those who look upon literature as another form of bicycling, or with those who believe in the progress or the reformation of mankind. I write in the hope of attracting the attention of those few who understand that the sadness of life is the joy of art. Those few will lay the book down, when they have read the last pages, happy and exalted. Their thought will collect in the happy cloudland of contemplation, and they will see that this book is as wonderful as Michaelangelo's sculpture, Velasquez's portraits, or Wagner's operas. They will recognise that this is a tragic novel.

As Flaubert waited till the last page to explain an allusion made on the first, I have waited till now before giving a needed definition. Tragedy does not depend on the death of the chief character at the end of the piece, nor on the number of syllables contained in each line. Tragedy is the continuous development of a primary idea, comedy is the exhibition of manners; one is the kernel, the other the shell of life. But as the book itself, this article dribbles out in a series of reflections.

" L'Education Sentimentale" is most representative of our modern literary ideal, and stands graphically opposed to the ancient. The ancient writers collected and arranged ; and as " Homer" is the type of the impersonal narratives which generations may combine, " L'Education Sentimentale " is the type of the personal vision that a man sitting alone in his study may bring into focus.

While remaining itself obscure, this novel has given birth to a numerous literature. The " Rougon-Macquart" series is nothing but "L'Education Sentimentale" re-written into twenty volumes by a prodigious journalist—twenty huge balloons which bob about the streets, sometimes getting clear of the house-tops. Maupassant cut it up into numberless walking sticks ; Goncourt took the descriptive passages, and turned them into Passy rhapsodies. The book has been a treasure cavern known to forty thieves, whence all have found riches and fame. The original spirit has proved too strong for general consumption ; but, watered and prepared, it has had the largest sale ever known.

GEORGE MOORE.

Arthur Symons

"Balzac"

Fortnightly Review 71 (May 1899), 745–57

BALZAC.

I.

THE first man who has completely understood Balzac is Rodin, and it has taken Rodin ten years to realise his own conception. France has refused the statue in which a novelist is represented as a dreamer, to whom Paris is not so much Paris as Patmos; "the most Parisian of our novelists," Frenchmen assure you. It is a hundred years this month since Balzac was born : a hundred years is a long time in which to be misunderstood with admiration.

In choosing the name of the *Human Comedy* for a series of novels in which, as he says, there is at once "the history and the criticism of society, the analysis of its evils, and the discussion of its principles," Balzac proposed to do for the modern world what Dante, in his *Divine Comedy*, had done for the world of the Middle Ages. Condemned to write in prose, and finding his opportunity in that restriction, he created for himself a form which is perhaps the nearest equivalent for the epic or the poetic drama, and the only form in which, at all events, the epic is now possible. The world of Dante was materially simple compared with the world of the nineteenth century ; the " visible world " had not yet begun to " exist," in its tyrannical modern sense ; the complications of the soul interested only the schoolmen, and were a part of theology ; poetry could still represent an age and yet be poetry. But to-day poetry can no longer represent more than the soul of things ; it has taken refuge from the terrible improvements of civilisation in a divine seclusion, where it sings, disregarding the many voices of the street. Prose comes offering its infinite capacity for detail ; and it is by the infinity of its detail that the novel, as Balzac created it, has become the modern epic.

There had been great novels, indeed, before Balzac, but no great novelist ; and the novels themselves are scarcely what we should to-day call by that name. The interminable *Astrée* and its companions form a link between the *fabliaux* and the novel, and from them developed the characteristic eighteenth-century *conte*, in narrative, letters, or dialogue, as we see it in Marivaux, Laclos, Crebillon *fils*. Crebillon's longer works, including *Le Sopha*, with their conventional paraphernalia of Eastern fable, are extremely tedious ; but in two short pieces, " La Nuit et le Moment " and " Le Hasard du Coin du Feu," he created a model of witty, naughty, deplorably natural comedy, which to this day is one of the most characteristic French forms of fiction.

Properly, however, it is a form of the drama rather than of the novel. Laclos, in *Les Liaisons Dangereuses*, a masterpiece which scandalised the society that adored Crebillon, because its naked human truth left no room for sentimental excuses, comes much nearer to prefiguring the novel (as Stendhal, for instance, is afterward to conceive it), but still preserves the awkward, traditional form of letters. Marivaux had indeed already seemed to suggest the novel of analysis, but in a style which has christened a whole manner of writing, that precisely which is least suited to the writing of fiction. Voltaire's *contes*, *La Religieuse* of Diderot, are tracts or satires in which the story is only an excuse for the purpose. Rousseau, too, has his purpose, even in *La Nouvelle Héloïse*, but it is a humanising purpose; and with that book the novel of passion comes into existence, and along with it the descriptive novel. Yet with Rousseau this result is an accident of genius; we cannot call him a novelist; and we find him abandoning the form he has found, for another, more closely personal, which suits him better. Restif de la Bretonne, who followed Rousseau at a distance, not altogether wisely, developed the form of half-imaginary autobiography in *Monsieur Nicolas*, a book of which the most significant part may be compared with Hazlitt's *Liber Amoris*. Morbid and even mawkish as it is, it has a certain uneasy, unwholesome humanity in its confessions, which may seem to have set a fashion only too scrupulously followed by modern French novelists. Meanwhile, the Abbé Prevost's one great story, *Manon Lescaut*, had brought for once a purely objective study, of an incomparable simplicity, into the midst of these analyses of difficult souls; and then we return to the confession, in the works of others not novelists: Benjamin Constant, Mme. de Staël, Chateaubriand, in *Adolphe*, *Corinne*, *René*. At once we are in the Romantic movement, a movement which begins lyrically, among poets, and at first with a curious disregard of the more human part of humanity.

Balzac worked contemporaneously with the Romantic movement, but he worked outside it, and its influence upon him is felt only in an occasional pseudo-romanticism, like the episode of the pirate in *La Femme de Trente Ans*. His vision of humanity was essentially a poetic vision, but he was a poet whose dreams were facts. Knowing that, as Mme. Necker has said, " the novel should be the better world," he knew also that " the novel would be nothing if, in that august lie, it were not true in details." And in the *Human Comedy* he proposed to himself to do for society more than Buffon had done for the animal world.

" There is but one animal," he declares, in his *Avant-Propos*, with a confidence which Darwin has not yet come to justify. But " there exists, there will always exist, social species, as there are zoological species." " Thus the work to be done will have a triple form : men, women, and things; that is to say, human beings and the material representation which they give to their thought; in short, man and life." And, studying after nature, "French society will be the historian, I shall need to be no more than the secretary." Thus will be written "the history forgotten by so many historians, the history of manners." But that is not all, for "passion is the whole of humanity." "In realising clearly the drift of the composition, it will be seen that I assign to facts, constant, daily, open or secret, to the acts of individual life, to their causes and principles, as much importance as historians had formerly attached to the events of the public life of nations." " Facts gathered together and painted as they are, with passion for element," is one of his definitions of the task he has undertaken. And in a letter to Mme. de Hanska he summarises every detail of his scheme.

"The *Études des Mœurs* will represent social effects, without a single situation of life, or a physiognomy, or a character of man or woman, or a manner of life, or a profession, or a social zone, or a district of France, or anything pertaining to childhood, old age, or maturity, politics, justice, or war, having been forgotten.

"That laid down, the history of the human heart traced link by link, the history of society made in all its details, we have the base. : . .

" Then, the second stage is the *Études philosophiques*, for after the *effects* come the *causes*. In the *Études des Mœurs* I shall have painted the sentiments and their action, life and the fashion of life. In the *Études philosophiques* I shall say *why the sentiments, on what the life*. . . .

" Then, after the *effects* and the *causes*, come the *Études analytiques*, to which the *Physiologie du mariage* belongs, for, after the *effects* and the *causes*, one should seek the *principles*. . . .

" After having done the poetry, the demonstration, of a whole system, I shall do the science in the *Essai sur les forces humaines*. And, on the bases of this palace I shall have traced the immense arabesque of the *Cent Contes drolatiques !* "

Quite all that, as we know, was not carried out; but there, in its intention, is the plan; and after twenty years' work the main part of it, certainly, was carried out. Stated with this precise detail, it has something of a scientific air, as of a too deliberate attempt upon the sources of life by one of those systematic French minds which are so much more logical than facts. But there is one little phrase to be noted : " La passion est toute l'humanité." All Balzac is in that phrase.

Another French novelist, following, as he thinks, the example of the *Human Comedy*, has endeavoured to build up a history of his own time with even greater minuteness. But *Les Rougon-Macquart* is no more than system; Zola has never understood that detail

without life is the wardrobe without the man. Trying to outdo
Balzac on his own ground, he has made the fatal mistake of taking
him only on his systematic side, which in Balzac is subordinate to a
great creative intellect, an incessant, burning thought about men and
women, a passionate human curiosity for which even his own system
has no limits. "The misfortunes of the *Birotteaus*, the priest and
the perfumer," he says, in his *Avant-Propos*, taking an example at
random, "are, for me, those of humanity." To Balzac manners are
but the vestment of life; it is life that he seeks; and life, to him, is
but the vestment of thought. Thought is at the root of all his work;
a whole system of thought, in which philosophy is but another form
of poetry; and it is from this root of idea that the *Human Comedy*
springs.

II.

The two books into which Balzac has put his deepest thought, the
two books which he himself cared for the most, are *Séraphita* and
Louis Lambert. Of *Louis Lambert* he said: "I write it for myself
and a few others"; of *Séraphita*: "J'y mets ma vie!" "One could
write *Goriot* any day," he adds; "*Séraphita* only once in a lifetime."
I have never been able to feel that *Séraphita* is altogether a success.
It lacks the breadth of life; it is glacial. True, he aimed at producing very much such an effect; and it is, indeed, full of a strange,
glittering beauty, the beauty of its own snows. But I find in it
at the same time something a little factitious, a sort of romanesque,
not altogether unlike the sentimental romanesque of Novalis; it has
not done the impossible, in humanising the most abstract speculation,
in fusing mysticism and the novel. But for the student of Balzac it
has extraordinary interest; for it is at once the base and the summit
of the *Human Comedy*. In a letter to Mme. de Hanska, written in
1837, four years after *Séraphita* had been begun, he writes: "I am
not orthodox, and I do not believe in the Roman Church. Sweden-
borgianism, which is but a repetition, in the Christian sense, of
ancient ideas, is my religion, with this addition: that I believe in the
incomprehensibility of God." *Séraphita* is a prose poem in which
the most abstract part of that mystical system, which Swedenborg
perhaps materialised too crudely, is presented in a white light, under
a single, superhuman image. In *Louis Lambert* the same fundamental conceptions are worked out in the study of a perfectly human
intellect, "an intellectual gulf," as he truly calls it; a sober and
concise history of ideas in their devouring action upon a too feeble
physical nature. In these two books we see directly, and not
through the coloured veil of human life, the mind in the abstract of a
thinker whose power over humanity was the power of abstract

thought. They show this novelist, who has invented the description of society, by whom the visible world has been more powerfully felt than by any other novelist, striving to penetrate the correspondences which exist between the human and the celestial existence. He would pursue the soul to its last resting-place before it takes flight from the body; further, on its disembodied flight; he would find out. God, as he comes nearer and nearer to finding out the secret of life. And realising, as he does so profoundly, that there is but one substance, but one ever-changing principle of life, "une seule plante, un seul animal, mais des rapports continus," the whole world is alive with meaning for him, a more intimate meaning than it has for others. "The least flower is a thought, a life which corresponds to some lineaments of the great whole, of which he has the constant intuition." And so, in his concerns with the world, he will find spirit everywhere; nothing for him will be inert matter, everything will have its particle of the universal life. One of those divine spies, for whom the world has no secrets, he will be neither pessimist nor optimist; he will accept the world as a man accepts the woman whom he loves, as much for her defects as for her virtues. Loving the world for its own sake, he will find it always beautiful, equally beautiful in all its parts. Now let us look at the programme which he traced for the *Human Comedy*, let us realise it in the light of this philosophy, and we are at the beginning of a conception of what the *Human Comedy* really is.

III.

This visionary, then, who had apprehended for himself an idea of God, set himself to interpret human life more elaborately than anyone else. He has been praised for his patient observation; people have thought they praised him in calling him a realist; it has been discussed how far his imitation of life has the literal truth of the photograph. But to Balzac the word realism was an insult. Writing his novels at the rate of eighteen hours a day, in a feverish solitude, he never had the time to observe patiently. It is humanity seen in a mirror, the humanity which comes to the great dreamers, the great poets, humanity as Shakespeare saw it. And so in him, as in all the great artists, there is something more than nature, a divine excess. This something more than nature should be the aim of the artist, not merely the accident which happens to him against his will. We require of him a world like our own, but a world infinitely more vigorous, interesting, profound; more beautiful with that kind of beauty which nature finds of itself for art. It is the quality of great creative art to give us so much life that we are almost overpowered by it, as by an air almost too vigorous to breathe: the exuberance of creation which makes the Moses of Michel Angelo something more than human, which makes Lear something more than human, in one kind or another of divinity.

Balzac's novels are full of strange problems and great passions. He turned aside from nothing which presented itself in nature; and his mind was always turbulent with the magnificent contrasts and caprices of fate. A devouring passion of thought burned on all the situations by which humanity expresses itself, in its flight from the horror of immobility. To say that the situations which he chose are often romantic is but to say that he followed the soul and the senses faithfully on their strangest errands. Our probable novelists of to-day are afraid of whatever emotion might be misinterpreted in a gentleman. Believing, as we do now, in nerves and a fatalistic heredity, we have left but little room for the dignity and disturbance of violent emotion. To Balzac, humanity had not changed since the days when Œdipus was blind and Philoctetes cried in the cave; and equally great miseries were still possible to mortals, though they were French and of the nineteenth century.

And thus he creates, like the poets, a humanity more logical than the average life; more typical, more sub-divided among the passions, and having in its veins an energy almost more than human. He realised, as the Greeks did, that human life is made up of elemental passions and necessity; but he was the first to realise that in the modern world the pseudonym of necessity is money. Money and the passions rule the world of his *Human Comedy*.

And, at the root of the passions, determining their action, he saw "those nervous fluids, or that unknown substance which, in default of another term, we must call the will." No word returns oftener to his pen. For him the problem is invariable. Man has a given quantity of energy; each man a different quantity: how will he spend it? A novel is the determination in action of that problem. And he is equally interested in every form of energy, in every egoism, so long as it is fiercely itself. This pre-occupation with the force, rather than with any of its manifestations, gives him his singular impartiality, his absolute lack of prejudice; for it gives him the advantage of an abstract point of view, the unchanging fulcrum for a lever which turns in every direction; and as nothing once set vividly in motion by any form of human activity is without interest for him, he makes every point of his vast chronicle of human affairs equally interesting to his readers.

Baudelaire has observed profoundly that every character in the *Human Comedy* has something of Balzac, has genius. To himself, his own genius was entirely expressed in that word "will." It recurs constantly in his letters. "Men of will are rare!" he cries. And, at a time when he had turned night into day for his labour: "I rise every night with a keener will than that of yesterday." "Nothing wearies me," he says, "neither waiting nor happiness." He exhausts the printers, whose fingers can hardly keep pace with his brain ; they call him, he reports proudly, "a man-slayer." And he tries to express himself : "I have always had in me something, I know not what, which made me do differently from others ; and, with me, fidelity is perhaps no more than pride. Having only myself to rely upon, I have had to strengthen, to build up that self." There is a scene in *La Cousine Bette* which gives precisely Balzac's own sentiment of the supreme value of energy. The Baron Hulot, ruined on every side, and by his own fault, goes to Josépha, a mistress who had cast him off in the days of his prosperity, and asks her to lodge him for a few days in a garret. She laughs, pities, and then questions him.

" ' Est-ce vrai, vieux,' reprit-elle, ' que tu as tué ton frère et ton oncle, ruiné ta famille, surhypothéqué la maison de tes enfants et mangé la grenouille du gouvernement en Afrique avec la princesse ? '

" Le Baron inclina tristement la tête.

" ' Eh bien, j'aime cela ! ' s'écria Josépha, qui se leva pleine d'enthousiasme. ' C'est un *brûlage* général ! c'est sardanapale ! c'est grand ! c'est complet ! On est une canaille, mais on a du cœur.' "

The cry is Balzac's, and it is a characteristic part of his genius to have given it that ironical force by uttering it through the mouth of a Josépha. The joy of the human organism at its highest point of activity : that is what interests him supremely. How passionate, how moving he becomes whenever he has to speak of a real passion, a mania, whether of a lover for his mistress, of a philosopher for his idea, of a miser for his gold, of a Jew dealer for masterpieces ! His style clarifies, his words become flesh and blood ; he is the lyric poet. And for him every idealism is equal : the gourmandise of Pons is not less serious, not less sympathetic, not less perfectly realised, than the search of Claës after the Absolute. "The great and terrible clamour of egoism" is the voice to which he is always attentive ; "those eloquent faces, proclaiming a soul abandoned to an idea as to a remorse," are the faces with whose history he concerns himself. He drags to light the hidden joys of the *amateur*, and with especial delight those that are hidden deepest, under the most deceptive coverings. He deifies them for their energy, he fashions the world of his *Human Comedy* in their service, as the real world exists, all but passive, to be the pasture of these supreme egoists.

IV.

In all that he writes of life, Balzac seeks the soul, but it is the soul as nervous fluid, the executive soul, not the contemplative soul, that, with rare exceptions, he seeks. He would surprise the motive force of life : that is his *recherche de l'Absolu* ; he figures it to himself as almost a substance, and he is the alchemist on its track. " Can man by thinking find out God ? " Or life, he would have added ; and he would have answered the question with at least a Perhaps.

And of this visionary, this abstract thinker, it must be said that his thought translates itself always into terms of life. Pose before him a purely mental problem, and he will resolve it by a scene in which the problem literally works itself out. It is the quality proper to the novelist, but no novelist ever employed this quality with such persistent activity, and at the same time subordinated action so constantly to the idea. With him action has always a mental basis, is never suffered to intrude for its own sake. He prefers that an episode should seem in itself tedious rather than it should have an illogical interest.

It may be, for he is a Frenchman, that his episodes are sometimes too logical. There are moments when he becomes unreal because he wishes to be too systematic, that is, to be real by measure. He would never have understood the method of Tolstoi, a very stealthy method of surprising life. To Tolstoi life is always the cunning enemy whom one must lull asleep, or noose by an unexpected lasso. He brings in little detail after little detail, seeming to insist on the insignificance of each, in order that it may pass almost unobserved, and be realised only after it has passed. It is his way of disarming the suspiciousness of life.

But Balzac will make no detour, aims at an open and an unconditional triumph over nature. Thus, when he triumphs, he triumphs signally ; and action, in his books, is perpetually crystallising into some phrase, like the single lines of Dante, or some brief scene, in which a whole entanglement comes sharply and suddenly to a luminous point. I will give no instance, for I should have to quote from every volume. I wish rather to remind myself that there are times when the last fine shade of a situation seems to have escaped. Even then, the failure is often more apparent than real, a slight bungling in the machinery of illusion. Look through the phrase, and you will find the truth there, perfectly explicit on the other side of it.

For, it cannot be denied, Balzac's style, as style, is imperfect. It has life, and it has idea, and it has variety ; there are moments when it attains a rare and perfectly individual beauty ; as when, in *Le Cousin Pons*, we read of " cette prédisposition aux recherches qui fait faire à un savant germanique cent lieues dans ses guêtres pour trouver une vérité qui le regard en riant, assise à la marge du puits, sous le jasmin de la cour." But I am far less sure that a student of Balzac would recognise him in this sentence than that he would recognise the writer of this other : " Des larmes de pudeur, qui roulèrent entre les beaux cils de Madame Hulot, arrêtèrent net le garde national." It is in such passages that the failure in style is equivalent to a failure in psychology. That his style should lack symmetry, subordination, the formal virtues of form, is, in my eyes, a less serious fault. I have often considered whether, in the novel, perfect form is a good, or even a possible thing, if the novel is to be what Balzac made it, history added to poetry. A novelist with style will not look at life with an entirely naked vision. He sees through coloured glasses. Human life and human manners are too various, too moving, to be brought into the fixity of a quite formal order. There will come a moment, constantly, when style must suffer, or the closeness and clearness of narration must be sacrificed, some minute exception of action or psychology must lose its natural place, or its full emphasis. Balzac, with his rapid and accumulating mind, without the patience of selection, and without the desire to select where selection means leaving out something good in itself, if not good in its place, never hesitates, and his parenthesis comes in. And often it is into these parentheses that he puts the profoundest part of his thought.

Yet, ready as Balzac is to neglect the story for the philosophy, whenever it seems to him necessary to do so, he would never have admitted that a form of the novel is possible in which the story shall be no more than an excuse for the philosophy. That was because he was a great creator, and not merely a philosophical thinker; because he dealt in flesh and blood, and knew that the passions in action can teach more to the philosopher, and can justify the artist more fully, than all the unacting intellect in the world. He knew that though life without thought was no more than the portion of a dog, yet thoughtful life was more than lifeless thought, and the dramatist more than the commentator. And I cannot help feeling assured that the latest novelists without a story, whatever other merits they certainly have, are lacking in the power to create characters, to express a philosophy in action; and that the form which they have found, however valuable it may be, is the result of this failure, and not either a great refusal or a new vision.

V.

The novel as Balzac conceived it has created the modern novel, but no modern novelist has followed, for none has been able to follow, Balzac on his own lines. Even those who have tried to follow him most closely have, sooner or later, branched off in one direction or another, most in the direction indicated by Stendhal. Stendhal has written one book which is a masterpiece, unique in its kind, *Le Rouge et le Noir;* a second, which is full of admirable things, *La Chartreuse de Parme;* a book of profound criticism, *Racine et Shakspeare;* and a cold and penetrating study of the physiology of love, *De l'Amour,* by the side of which Balzac's *Physiologie du Mariage* is a mere *jeu d'esprit.* He discovered for himself, and for others after him, a method of unemotional, minute, slightly ironical analysis, which has fascinated modern minds, partly because it has seemed to dispense with those difficulties of creation, of creation in the block, which the triumphs of Balzac have only accentuated. Goriot, Valérie Marneffe, Pons, Grandet, Madame de Mortsauf even, are called up before us after the same manner as Othello or Don Quixote ; their actions express them so significantly that they seem to be independent of their creator ; Balzac stakes all upon each creation, and leaves us no choice but to accept or reject each as a whole, precisely as we should a human being. We do not know all the secrets of their consciousness, any more than we know all the secrets of the consciousness of our friends. But we have only to say "Valérie !" and the woman is before us. Stendhal, on the contrary, undresses Julien's soul in public with a deliberate and fascinating effrontery. There is not a vein of which he does not trace the course, not a wrinkle to which he does not point, not a nerve which he does not touch to the quick. We know everything that passed through his mind, to result probably in some significant inaction. And at the end of the book we know as much about that particular intelligence as the anatomist knows about the body which he has dissected. But meanwhile the life has gone out of the body ; and have we, after all, captured a living soul ?

I should be the last to say that Julien Sorel is not a creation, but· he is not a creation after the order of Balzac ; it is a difference of kind ; and if we look carefully at Frédéric Moreau, and Madame Gervaisais, and the Abbé Mouret, we shall see that these also, profoundly different as Flaubert and Goncourt and Zola are from Stendhal, are yet more profoundly, more radically, different from the creations of Balzac. Balzac takes a primary passion, puts it into a human body, and sets it to work itself out in visible action.. But since Stendhal, novelists have persuaded themselves that the primary passions are a little common, or noisy, or a little heavy to handle, and they have concerned themselves with passions tempered by reflection, and the sensations of elaborate brains. It was Stendhal who substituted the brain for the heart, as the battle-place of the novel ; not the brain as Balzac conceived it, a motive-force of action, the main-spring of passion, the force by which a nature directs its accumulated energy ; but a sterile sort of brain, set at a great distance from the heart, whose rhythm is too faint to disturb it. We have been intellectualising upon Stendhal ever since, until the persons of the modern novel have come to resemble those diaphanous jelly-fish, with balloon-like heads and the merest tufts of bodies, which float up and down in the Aquarium at Naples.

Thus, coming closer, as it seems, to what is called reality, in this banishment of great emotions, and this attention upon the sensations, modern analytic novelists are really getting further and further from that life which is the one certain thing in the world. Balzac employs all his detail to call up a tangible world about his men and women, not, perhaps, understanding the full power of detail as psychology, as Flaubert is to understand it; but, after all, his detail is only the background of the picture; and there, stepping out of the canvas, as the sombre people of Velazquez step out of their canvases at the Prado, is the living figure, looking into your eyes with eyes that respond to you like a mirror.

The novels of Balzac are full of electric fluid. To take up one of them is to feel the shock of life, as one feels it on touching certain magnetic hands. To turn over volume after volume is like wandering through the streets of a great city, at that hour of the night when human activity is at its full. There is a particular kind of excitement inherent in the very aspect of a modern city, of London or Paris; in the mere sensation of being in its midst, in the sight of all those active and fatigued faces which pass so rapidly; of those long and endless streets, full of houses, each of which is like the body of a multiform soul, looking out through the eyes of many windows. There is something intoxicating in the lights, the movement of shadows under the lights, the vast and billowy sound of that shadowy movement. And there is something more than this mere unconscious action upon the nerves. Every step in a great city is a step into an unknown world. A new future is possible at every street corner. I never know, when I go out into one of those crowded streets, but that the whole course of my life may be changed before I return to the house I have quitted.

I am writing these lines in Madrid, to which I have come suddenly, after a long quiet in Andalusia; and I feel already a new pulse in my blood, a keener consciousness of life, and a sharper human curiosity. Even in Seville I knew that I should see to-morrow, in the same streets, hardly changed since the Middle Ages, the same people that I had seen to-day. But here there are new possibilities, all the exciting accidents of the modern world, of a population always changing, of a city into which civilisation has brought all its unrest. And as I walk in these broad, windy streets and see these people, whom I hardly recognise for Spaniards, so awake and so hybrid are they, I have felt the sense of Balzac coming back into my veins. At Cordova he was unthinkable; at Cadiz I could realise only his large, universal outlines, vague as the murmur of the sea; here I feel him, he speaks the language I am talking, he sums up the life in whose midst I find myself.

For Balzac is the equivalent of great cities. He is bad reading for solitude, for he fills the mind with the nostalgia of cities. When a man speaks to me familiarly of Balzac I know already something of the man with whom I have to do. "The physiognomy of women does not begin before the age of thirty," he has said ; and perhaps before that age no one can really understand Balzac. Few young people care for him, for there is nothing in him that appeals to the senses except through the intellect. Not many women care for him supremely, for it is part of his method to express sentiments through facts, and not facts through sentiments. But it is natural that he should be the favourite reading of men of the world, of those men of the world who have the distinction of their kind ; for he supplies the key of the enigma which they are studying.

VI.

The life of Balzac was one long labour, in which time, money, and circumstances were all against him. In 1835 he writes : " I have lately spent twenty-six days in my study without leaving it. I took the air only at that window which dominates Paris, which I mean to dominate." And he exults in the labour : " If there is any glory in that, I alone could accomplish such a feat." He symbolises the course of his life in comparing it to the sea beating against a rock : " To-day one flood, to-morrow another, bears me along with it. I am dashed against a rock, I recover myself and go on to another reef." "Sometimes it seems to me that my brain is on fire. I shall die in the trenches of the intellect."

Balzac, like Scott, died under the weight of his debts ; and it would seem, if one took him at his word, that the whole of the *Human Comedy* was written for money. In the modern world, as he himself realised, more clearly than anyone, money is more often a symbol than an entity, and it can be the symbol of every desire. For Balzac money was the key of his only earthly paradise. It meant leisure to visit the woman whom he loved, and at the end it meant the possibility of marrying her.

There were only two women in Balzac's life : one, a woman much older than himself, of whom he wrote, on her death, to the other : " She was a mother, a friend, a family, a companion, a counsel, she made the writer, she consoled the young man, she formed his taste, she wept like a sister, she laughed, she came every day, like a healing slumber, to put sorrow to sleep." The other was Mme. de Hanska, whom he married in 1850, three months before his death. He had loved her for twenty years ; she was married, and lived in Poland : it was only at rare intervals that he was able to see her, and then very briefly ; but his letters to her, lately published in the *Revue de Paris*, are a simple, perfectly individual, daily record of a great passion. For twenty years he existed on a divine certainty without a future, and almost without a present. But we see the force of that sentiment passing into his work; *Séraphita* is its ecstasy, everywhere is its human shadow; it refines his strength, it gives him surprising intuitions, it gives him all that was wanting to his genius. Mme. de Hanska is the heroine of the *Human Comedy*, as Beatrice is the heroine of the *Divine Comedy*.

A great lover, to whom love, as well as every other passion and the whole visible world, was an idea, a flaming spiritual perception, Balzac enjoyed the vast happiness of the idealist. Contentedly, joyously, he sacrificed every petty enjoyment to the idea of love, the idea of fame, and to that need of the organism to exercise its forces, which is the only definition of genius. I do not know, among the lives óf men of letters, a life better filled, or more appropriate. A young man who, for a short time, was his secretary, declared: " I would not live your life for the fame of Napoleon and of Byron combined ! " The Comte de Gramont did not realise, as the world in general does not realise, that, to the man of creative energy, creation is at once a necessity and a joy, and, to the lover, hope in absence is the elixir of life. Balzac tasted more than all earthly pleasures as he sat there in his attic, creating the world over again, that he might lay it at the feet of a woman. Certainly to him there was no tedium in life, for there was no hour without its vivid employment, and no moment in which to perceive the most desolate of all certainties, that hope is in the past. His death was as fortunate as his life ; he died at the height of his powers, at the height of his fame, at the moment of the fulfilment of his happiness, and perhaps of the too sudden relief of that delicate burden.

ARTHUR SYMONS.

"Vernon Lee"
(Violet Paget)

"The Aesthetics
of the Novel"

Literature 5 (July 29, 1899), 98–100

Among my Books.

THE ÆSTHETICS OF THE NOVEL.

There seems a general notion that wherever literature is cultivated for its own sake it must become a fine art like painting and music; and that the novel, more especially, since it gives pleasure, must give the special pleasure due to beauty, and, as a result, we call many things in a book beautiful, and imagine them to be analogous to a fine picture or a lovely song, which, honestly considered, are simply and utterly ugly.

It has taken me years to get rid of this prejudice; and cost me several pangs to admit to myself that it is otherwise. Yet it ought merely to prove the richness of human nature thus to find that the novel, for instance, has ample resources for fascinating our attention without the help of the very special quality called beauty. In the first place, *we like words*, and, above all, *we like a statement*; the forms made by logical thought are full of the special attractions of logic, and the material in which all that concerns our ego is expressed, is shaped, it would seem, in a sort of interesting egoistic solution. Certain it is that there must be a real pleasure in such things, since it is sufficient to overcome the effort of gathering up thoughts and interpreting words. Think of the quite unnecessary statement and argument in which mankind indulges, and the eager, often delighted manner in which people will talk and listen about anything, particularly about nothing at all. The attraction of all kinds of literature is primarily based upon this double pleasure: the pleasure of using words and the pleasure of realizing a statement or demonstration; neither of which pleasures are more æsthetic than are those of moving our limbs or of indiscriminately using our eyes. For this reason we often take up a book or newspaper, absolutely irrespective of its contents, and if a book, why not a novel? After this elementary attractiveness of the spoken or written word come the satisfactions (rather than definite pleasures) of expectation and fulfilment, of watching movement and of sympathetic participation therein; of emotional excitement (there is an undoubted pleasure, for instance, even in being annoyed and certainly in being angry); the immense and altogether superior satisfaction of leaving one's own concerns behind and forcing oneself from the routine of life by identification with other folk; a kind of play, masquerade, eminently a holiday satisfaction, to which is closely allied the agreeable sense of irresponsibility which seems to grow with the perception of the responsibility of the characters we are watching, a feeling, by the way, in no way connected with fiction as such, since we have it equally in reading the newspaper, histories, and memoirs. Or are we always ready to consider other folks' affairs as mere inventions, delighted, as we are, to rid ourselves of the perpetual consequences and complications which prevent our life from being the more amusing play of perception and volition which it might be? Add to this, in greater or lesser degree, the perception, which is pleasant, of skill and tact on the part of the author, sometimes (what to some critical natures is equally pleasing) the lack of skill and tact of the author. When we have summed up these various items of literary satisfaction, we can pass on to a new kind of factor of pleasure, which is immensely attractive to certain minds, and which is especially present in the novel—I mean the gaining (or thinking we gain) a knowledge of mankind and of life. For when we are young, particularly, we are troubled by a delusive longing for such knowledge, and hoodwinked by a false sense of capability whenever we think we have got it.

These are what I should call the non-æsthetic attractions of the novel, attractions frequently sufficient to compensate for the most rough and ready disregard for all our instincts of beauty and harmony. The æsthetic attractions are wholly different. The novelist can show us beautiful places, make us live in company with delightful personalities—from Stendhal's Duchess to Tolstoi's Natacha, from Robinson Crusoe to Diana Warwick. I do not mean merely *ethically laudable* persons (no one, I am sure, would care to live with Romola or Daniel Deronda), but creatures whose vigorous, harmonious personalities, sometimes mainly physical, the author has felt as he would feel a melody or a sunset, and, in consequence, conveyed to us not by mere reproduction of their characteristics, but by the far more efficacious means of direct emotional contagion, his admiration, love, delight, inevitably kindling ours. Besides this, there is the specific æsthetic quality of literature. What it is, I do not, and I suppose

nobody nowadays does, know: a charm due to the complex patterns into which (quite apart from sound) the
parts of speech, verbs and nouns and adjectives, actives
and passives, variously combined tenses, can be woven
even like lines and colours, producing patterns of action
and reaction in our mind, our nerve tracks (who knows?),
our muscles and heart-throes and breathing, more
mysterious, even, than those which we can dimly perceive,
darkly guess, through the senses of sight and hearing. In so
far as any of these effects are produced by the novel,
the novel participates in the nature of other æsthetic
productions ; I do not say of other works of art, for we are
continually reverting to the old use of *art* as mere craft,
and confusing with beauty what is mere *logic*, dexterity,
technical knowledge, or tact.

But the novel can get along perfectly without any
such æsthetic qualities, as I hope to have shown by my
enumerations of the many other factors of pleasure, or,
at least, of interest, which the novelist has at disposal.
And such non-æsthetic interest is sufficient, not merely
for the readers who are more scientific, cr more dramatic,
or more practical, or more technically ingenious than
æsthetic, but sufficient even for æsthetic readers in their
scientific, or dramatic, or practical, or technical moments
and capacities ; for even the most æsthetically sensitive
persons must have other sides .to their characters, else
they would be dunces, criminals, paupers, bores, and
general incapables. The difference between the people
who are æsthetically sensitive and those who are not (and
here we have the key to the varying power of reading
novels like, let us say, " *A Vau l'eau* ") is not merely that
the æsthetic people ask for beauty as the scientific do for
knowledge and the dramatic for human emotion, but that
the æsthetic people suffer very acutely whenever the
novel contains downright ugliness ; suffer in a much more
positive manner than the scientific or dramatic reader
suffers from glaring absurdity or hopeless tameness of
situation ; for in the one case there is irritation or boredom,
in the other something verging on physical disgust. So that,
regarding the novel, the question becomes simply : which,
in the individual case, happens to be the stronger, the
satisfaction of the many non-æsthetic capacities for pleasure, or the displeasure inflected on the æsthetic instinct
by subject or treatment which do not in the least offend

any other craving of human nature ? It is a question, in fact, between the individual writer and the individual reader ; and I doubt whether it can ever be made a question of right and wrong. Some persons *can* read " *A Vau l'eau* " without any misery and with much satisfaction, even getting up from their reading decidedly the richer in knowledge and sympathy. Others are so harrowed that any possibilities of pleasure or profit are absolutely paralysed, and there is no sort of use in going on with the book. A third class can get through the novel in a middle condition of balanced, neutralized satisfaction and dissatisfaction, occasionally varied by a momentary predominance of pleasure or loathing.

I have ventured to say that in such questions there is no absolute right or wrong, and that a book like this (I have purposely chosen the most excessive instance) may increase the spiritual health of some readers and momentarily jeopardize that of others, all equally estimable persons. But what, I hear a class of readers (and that class is represented, as well as the others, in my own person), what is the use of being utterly depressed and sickened by a hundred and fifty pages of trivial hideousness ? The sickening and the depression do no good, quite the contrary ; and, as I said, where there is nothing else, the book had best be thrown into the fire. But the stimulation which the book can give to sympathetic understanding is a good, a very good thing, since we can never have enough of it in life. A novel like " A Vau l'eau " can give the right kind of reader an increased insight into the commonest, but also the most powerful, needs and passions of mankind, and in so far it can tend to make his attitude and action in life more useful, or at least less mischievous. It can teach, moreover, pity for people who may, perhaps, be helped ; teach also resolute idealism in our own persons by disclosing the very unideal sloughs above which our common human nature has so insecurely and so partially raised itself. But in the question of novels, as in all others, the most useful thing, perhaps, is to be at the same time very æsthetic and very capable of momentarily shelving our æstheticism, or rather of being able to see and understand dispassionately, while keeping the most passionate aversions and preferences.

VERNON LEE.

R2